PSYCHOLOGY of READING

John Downing

University of Victoria

Che Kan Leong

University of Saskatchewan

PSYCHOLOGY of READING

Macmillan Publishing Co., Inc.
New York

Collier Macmillan Publishers
London

Acknowledgments

We wish to extend our sincere gratitude to those authors and publishers who have granted us permission to use these illustrations.

Figures 4–1 and 4–2, p. 53, are from Han's Jensen, *Sign, Symbol and Script* (Berlin, Federal Republic of Germany: VED Deutscher Verlag der Wissenschaften), Figures 22 and 33.

Figure 7–3, p. 117, and Figure 7–6, p. 126, respectively, are adapted from J. D. French, illustration of "The Recticular Formation," *Scientific American*, May 1957, p. 54, and Georg von Békésy, illustration of "The Ear," *Scientific American*, August 1957, pp. 66–67. Copyright © 1957 by Scientific American, Inc. All rights reserved.

Figure 7–7, p. 129, is from A. M. Liberman, "The Grammars of Speech and Language," *Cognitive Psychology*, 1 (1970), Figure 4, p. 307.

Figure 9–2, p. 171, is from Glenn M. Kleinman, "Speech Recoding in Reading," *Journal of Verbal Learning and Verbal Behavior*, 14 (1975), pp. 323–329, Figure 2.

Figure 9–3, p. 186, is from J. Morton and K. Patterson, "A New Attempt at an Interpretation or an Attempt at a New Interpretation," in M. Coltheart, K. E. Patterson, and J. C. Marshal (eds.), *Deep Dyslexia* (London: Routledge and Kegan Paul, Ltd., 1980), Figure 2a.

Figure 10–2, p. 206, is from David La Berge and S. Jay Samuels, "Towards a Theory of Automatic Information Processing in Reading," *Cognitive Psychology*, 6 (1974), pp. 293–323, Figure 7.

Figure 10–3, p. 207, is from S. Jay Samuels, "Introduction to Theoretical Models of Reading," in W. Otto, C. W. Peters, and N. Peters (eds.), *Reading Problems: A Multidisciplinary Perspective* (Reading, Mass.: Addison Wesley Publishing Co. © 1977), Figure 2–7, p. 30. Reprinted with permission.

Figure 10–4, p. 212, is from David E. Rumelhart, "Towards an Interaction Model of Reading," in S. Dorniv (ed.), *Attention and Performance VI* (Hillsdale, N.J.: Lawrence Erlbaum Associates, Inc., 1977), Figure II, p. 596. Reprinted with permission of the author and the publisher.

Printed in the United States of America

Macmillan Publishing Co., Inc.
866 Third Avenue, New York, New York 10022

Collier Macmillan Canada, Inc.

Library of Congress Cataloging in Publication Data

Downing, John A.
Psychology of reading.

Bibliography: p. 343
Includes index.
1. Reading, Psychology of. I. Leong, Che Kan.
II. Title.
BF456.R2D68 372.4'1'019 81-8457
ISBN 0-02-330020-5 AACR2

Printing: 1 2 3 4 5 6 7 8 Year: 2 3 4 5 6 7 8 9

Preface

The need for a book on psychological aspects of reading first became clear to one of us, John Downing, when he was the instructor of a graduate course on psychology of reading at the University of California at Berkeley in 1967–1968. At that time, graduate-level texts on reading psychology were rare. Those that existed tended to have a narrow focus in the content and treatment of various topics pertaining to psychology applied to reading. In the years that followed, the need for such a work became more evident, but the writing of such a book remained a daunting task. It was not until the mid-1970s that a book of significance on the subject appeared in print. In the meantime and especially in the last five or six years, there have been significant developments in the scientific study of reading, as proven by many articles on related disciplines published in both journals and anthologies. The time seems ripe for a work which attempts an integration of the research and theory of the science of reading, and to some extent the art of its pedagogy, under one cover.

It was in the mid-1970s that John Downing initiated this important and challenging project. He mapped out the overall scheme of the work, wrote some of the draft chapters, and ensured progress of the writing. It was in 1977 that Che Kan Leong was invited to join in this undertaking, the scope of which also increased in magnitude and complexity. The two authors had first met in 1973, when Che Kan Leong contributed a chapter on reading behavior of Chinese children to John Downing's book *Comparative Reading*. Thereafter, we collaborated on several other projects with equally satisfying results. Our latest partnership culminated in the writing of this book, from which we have both learned a considerable amount.

We have not modelled this book on any existing text on the subject, the closest being Edmund Huey's *The Psychology and Pedagogy of Reading*, first published in 1908. We have taken the position that reading is the interpretation of symbols within the broad framework of literacy acquisition and development. Our emphasis is on the understanding of symbol systems, on knowledge acquisition over and above the mere teaching and learning of reading as a skill. We have followed a cognitive and psycholinguistic approach in our attempt to understand the processes of reading.

Very briefly, the 15 chapters in this book are organized into six fairly distinct but related areas. One area considers reading as a complex, interrelated skill (Chapters 2 and 3). A second relates to aspects of orthography and language (Chapters 4, 5 and 6). The third area deals with physiological and neurological aspects pertaining to reading (Chapters 7 and 8). The fourth area discusses theoretical and empirical studies of lexical access and learning to comprehend (Chapters 9 and 10). The fifth group of chapters centers round the affective and social bases of reading (Chapters 11, 12, and 13). The sixth area covers research, theory, and relevant practice in reading difficulties (Chapters 14 and 15). In treating these six vast and important areas, we have attempted to be comprehensive in drawing on current as well as significant studies of earlier years from psychology, language, and education. As is inevitable in a volume of this nature and magnitude, we are obliged to be selective at times. Any commission or inadvertent omission of specific views should be seen within the total context of the work.

For John Downing, the University of Victoria, British Columbia was the academic base for writing his various chapters. His work was greatly assisted by the many discussions that he had with his colleagues on the Faculty of Education and in the Departments of Psychology and Linguistics there. Some of his writing was done in England during visits to the Psychology Departments at the Universities of Bristol, Leicester, London, and Reading, and he owes much to the debates that took place there on the chapters that he was drafting at that period in his 1975–1976 study leave from the University of Victoria. Later in the same year of leave, John Downing continued his first drafts for this book during his visit to the Institute of Psychology, Academy of Education Sciences, Moscow, U.S.S.R. and his stay at the Flinders University of South Australia. He is grateful to colleagues in those places also for their thoughtful comments and suggestions on the ideas for this book as they developed. In the years that followed, seminars in many other places have shaped John Downing's chapters into their present published form, and he is very appreciative of the many constructive suggestions made by colleagues and students on those occasions.

For Che Kan Leong, the University of Saskatchewan in Saskatoon, Saskatchewan was the center where much of the writing was done. He is indebted to the university's administration and to the many colleagues and friends both within and outside the university for their direct and indirect assistance. The 1977–1978 sabbatical year at the two universities in Hong Kong, at the Paedologisch Instituut of the Free University of Amsterdam, and in several states in Australia, especially Queensland, provided opportunities for reflection, discussion, and gathering of materials. The subsequent years with conferences in North America and Europe also yielded concrete results. Colleagues of assistance included, among others, Felix Oteruelo and Stephen Wong, who read and critiqued portions of the chapters on physiological aspects; John McLeod, on concepts of reading difficulties; J. P. Das on cognitive processing; Merrill Hiscock and Dirk Bakker of Amsterdam, on laterality and developmental dyslexia. Helpful comments on language awareness, lexical access, and learning to comprehend came from Rumjahn Hoosain of the University of Hong Kong, Jay Samuels of the University of Minnesota, Donald Doehring of McGill University, and John Morton of the MRC Applied Psychology Unit, Cambridge, England. There are other individuals who helped to lighten the onerous task and who deserved mention, unfortunately made impossible because of space limitations.

In particular, we are indebted to Lloyd C. Chilton, Executive Editor of the Macmillan Publishing Company, for his patience and encouragement in the writing and publication of this book and Hurd Hutchins for his supervision of its production. We thank Helmar Heimann for the cover design. We owe our greatest debt, however, to our respective families for their strong support in our undertaking. Their understanding and the assistance given us by our colleagues and friends have sustained us throughout these several years. Any shortcoming in the volume is necessarily our own.

There is an additional thought we would like to share with our readers. We debated many times on an appropriate title. It could have been *The Psychology of Reading.* But this seems to be a large claim, for there are many psychological theories of reading. Hence we eschewed the *the.* We might have called the work *Psychology Applied to Reading.* This probably reflects the content, though it seems clumsy. Even the present title, *Psychology of Reading,* can be all-encompassing, implying the coming together of several related disciplines. This is what we have attempted to do.

With a sense of humility towards those who have gone before us and to those whose current work also benefits us, we sincerely hope that our present volume will stimulate our readers to "read, mark, learn, and inwardly digest" the many facets of reading and will continue in their quest for more.

JOHN DOWNING
Victoria, British Columbia
CHE KAN LEONG
Saskatoon, Saskatchewan

Contents

PSYCHOLOGY of READING

CHAPTER 1

Reading—In Perspective

It was some three hundred and fifty years ago that Francis Bacon wrote: "Reading maketh a full man, conference a ready man, and writing an exact man." The force of this aphorism is not diminished in the 1980s, even though our technological advances have resulted in new media, in addition to print, to which the aphorism must apply. The emphasis on reading within the context of literacy acquisition generally operates at different levels: in the school, at home, and in society at large. Tangible examples of concern for and action to promote literacy by governments include the Right to Read Program, the Education of the Handicapped Act (Public Law 94–142) in the U.S.A. and the official British Government report on reading and language (The Bullock Report, 1975), among others.

Reading as Literacy Acquisition

It is within the broader context of literacy acquisition that we have attempted this present work on the psychology of reading. The concept of *literacy* varies and includes "ability to read and write" (Saksena, 1970, p. 11) as well as "adult literacy." In this book, we will emphasize processes of reading, although writing and spelling must also be seen as integral literacy activities. We use the term *writing* to refer to the physical activity of penmanship as well as creative writing. *Writing system* refers to orthography, while *spelling* is restricted to the recall or reproduction of words in the writing system. In speaking of *literacy*, we include the development and functioning of young children as well as older individuals. We are conscious of the lack of agreement in measuring literacy, as standards and conditions vary (see Gray, 1956; Kirsch and Guthrie, 1977–1978; Hunter and Harman, 1979). UNESCO (1965), for example, defines a literate person as one who has acquired the knowledge and skills to engage in activities for effective functioning in the community and suggests a number of years of schooling as a yardstick for measuring literacy. This grade-completion equivalency (usually fourth or fifth grade) to identify functional literacy or illiteracy suffers from lack of clear definitions and objective evidence. It is likely that this practice underestimates the rate of illiteracy among different age groups (Harman, 1970). Even if grade equivalencies are accepted, there are wide individual and national differences in actual performance levels as suggested by Samuels (1969) and shown in Downing's (1973) international study of reading behavior in fourteen countries.

There is the further problem that, as societal demands change, the level required for functional literacy also changes (Jenkinson, 1967; Resnick and Resnick, 1977). For example, the earlier estimate by Gray (1955) of completion of grade four as the minimum attainment of functional literacy would be upgraded by Curry (1967) to grade eight and by Jenkinson (1967, p. 280) to "a minimum of grade seven reading but . . . rapidly moving upwards to grade nine." In studies outside of North America, Simmons (1970) suggested that completion of sixth grade in Tunisia is necessary, while Malmquist (1965) of Sweden stated a minimum of ninth grade (rising to twelfth grade) is essential for literacy. More recently, the Report of the Committee on Reading of the National Academy of Education (Carroll and Chall, 1975) takes the position that the goal in literacy should be to ensure that every adult can read and understand the whole spectrum of reading materials he or she is likely to encounter in daily life. This goal would mean the eventual attainment of twelfth grade literacy by all adults.

Thus the continual shifting of estimated grade level necessary for functional literacy indicates the need for the identification of knowledge and skills needed for "participation in the processes for balanced development of self as a member of collectivity" (Saksena, 1970, p. 13). Saksena suggests more specific goals related to a particular culture as knowledge and skill requirements are relative to time and place. This broader view steers us clear of the narrow prescription of literacy as activities or mere subject areas of "reading," "writing" and "spelling" in schooling. Bhola (1970, p. 33) is emphatic that "a functional literacy programme is not merely an instructional programme. . . . A functional literacy programme is . . . also at the same time a social change programme." This change must be linked with the "literate environment in the community and nation" and, where no such environment exists, it must be created (Bhola, 1970, p. 41). In their book, *Adult Illiteracy in the United States*, Hunter and Harman (1979) show that the concept of literacy is subject to historical change and relative to social goals and needs. The attainment and maintenance of a fully literate society relies heavily on adequate performance in functional reading tasks related to real-world experiences (Carroll and Chall, 1975). The continuous process of applying knowledge and specific skills to the tasks of reading, writing and spelling determines functional literacy (Kirsch and Guthrie, 1977–1978). Bormuth's (1975, p. 72) concept is appropriate: "Literacy is the ability to exhibit all of the behaviors a person needs in order to respond appropriately to all possible reading tasks." This reference to all possible reading tasks reminds us of the oft-quoted declaration from Edmund Huey (1908, p. 6): "And so to completely analyse what we do when we read would almost be the acme of a psychologist's achievements, for it would be to describe very many of the most intricate workings of the human mind." It is the aim of this book to attempt to unravel some of the intricacies of the mind in the act of reading. We will discuss the state-of-the-science of reading by drawing on findings from research and theory and with reference to sound practice in teaching and learning reading.

Toward a Definition of Reading

It is customary to begin a text on the psychology of reading by defining the term *reading*. This is a formidable task. There are divergent viewpoints: some emphasizing the "code cracking" approach and others the "meaning" approach. In contemporary language, reading can be approached "bottom-up" or "top-down" with the interactive mode, sometimes via data (bottom-up), sometimes via schemata (top-down), as the most likely behavior. It is difficult to define reading in an all-encompassing manner. There is not one kind of reading, but many kinds. Reading is performed for many purposes, and calls for different acquisition and processing strategies. It is therefore not surprising that there are different emphases. Take, for example, the classical linguistic viewpoint of Fries (1963) that reading consists of the transfer from auditory signs to visible signals, or Elkonin's (1973b) definition of reading as "the re-creation of the sound form of a word according to its graphic model [representation]." These definitions are usually regarded as emphasizing speech sounds. Similarly, Venezky (1967, p. 102) suggests that learning to read "requires primarily the translation from written symbols to sound, a procedure which is the basis of the reading process and is probably the only language skill unique to reading (comprehension, for example, while a necessary criterion for reading, is a function of both speech and writing)." Thus initial reading includes the ability to decode but is not confined to that subskill. As well, the reader comes to the reading task with existing language and comprehension subskills so that the process is not the same as translating from writing to meaning. On the emphasis on meaning, the view of Tinker and McCullough (1962, p. 13) that reading is "the construction of new meanings through manipulation of concepts already possessed by the reader," with the resulting meanings "organized into thought processes according to the purposes adopted by the reader," is fairly typical. Smith (1978) suggests that, with fluent readers, comprehension may precede word identification and that a reader may disambiguate meaning "without making any prior decisions about words" (p. 213). Any decoding a reader performs, according to Smith, is not to transform visual symbols into sound, but to transform the visual representation of language into meaning.

The above sampling of views on reading as decoding or as meaning derivation should not be taken to mean a strict dichotomy between the two. Even with the apparently heavy code-emphasis of Elkonin in reading the more "phonetic" Cyrillic language, his "re-creation of the sound form" does not mean neglecting comprehension. Such re-creation refers to the complex phonemic representation and not just a simple association between print and speech. In fact, Elkonin is emphatic that the child must *understand* the features of speech encoded in the writing system. Hence, "the Great Debate" (Chall, 1967) on learning to read is not an "either–or" of code-emphasis versus meaning-emphasis, but one of a continuum or different levels of processing. Thus, notwithstanding Chall's (1979) recent reaffirmation of the benefits of code-emphasis in the absence of "any viable data to disconfirm it" (p. 33), the interactive approach may be equally facilitating to beginning readers.

It seems to us that the definition of Gibson and Levin (1975, p. 5) is as concise and yet as comprehensive as any: "Reading is extracting meaning from text." For readers to do this, they will need to: (1) decode written symbols to sound, (2) have recourse to the lexicon or mental dictionary to extract meaning for the printed word from semantic memory and (3) incorporate this meaning into their language acquisition process. The more recent view of Venezky (1976, p. 6) states that: "Reading is the translation from writing to a form of language from which the reader already is able to derive meaning." This presupposes processes involving language and the existing language abilities on which the reader must draw. To some extent it relates to language awareness which we will discuss in Chapter 6 specifically. We may of course debate the meaning of "meaning," just as philosophers, linguists, psychologists and educators have done before us to explicate "meaning." This is not our immediate concern in Chapter 1; we will leave to subsequent chapters the question of how children come to comprehend. Gibson and Levin make it clear that the word *text* in their definition quoted at the beginning of this paragraph refers not only to print but also to combinations of text and pictures, diagrams, graphs, illustrated instructions and other reading material. We wish to enlarge on the implications of this broader definition.

As a starting point, we will refer to two linguists who seem to provide some clues to this issue of reading as symbol interpretation. First, Chao (1968) draws a distinction between writing and other visual symbols. He asserts that "visual symbols do not begin to be writing until they have a close correspondence to language. . . . If a sign represents a specific part of language, it is writing; if it represents things directly, it is not" (p. 101). Chao's definition of *writing* seems to fit well the everyday usage of that term. It is a limited type of visual sign. What is even more interesting is Chao's choice of words when he goes on to give us an example: "The same road sign [↙] will be read by an English-speaking person as *no left turn*, by a German as *links abbiegen verboten*" (p. 101). He concludes that such visual signs are not *writing*, but it is notable that he describes the English and German responses to this sign as *reading*.

The second clue for solving the problem of the conflicting types of definitions of reading is provided by Hall (1961):

> Any grapheme or sequence of graphemes used in spelling a word always symbolizes ("means") some fact of language, be it a phoneme (as in alphabetic writing) or a morpheme (as in Chinese characters). In any utterance, meaning is conveyed by morphemes and their combinations into phrases and clauses; by the term *meaning*, we here refer to the way in which these linguistic features symbolize the facts of the universe in which we live. Note especially that the SPELLING of any word has no "meaning" i.e., symbolizes nothing, directly, except the linguistic characteristics of the morpheme it represents (in an alphabetic orthography, its phonemic structure); this kind of meaning may be termed *linguistic* meaning, as opposed to *real-life* meaning. This latter is conveyed, not by written (graphemic) shapes, but by spoken morphemes and only by spoken morphemes (pp. 4–5).

Chao's definition of writing shows that reading covers a broader area than writing. We can read road signs which contain no writing. Similarly we read charts, graphs and maps. Palmists read the lines in our hands. The old farmer reads the sky to forecast the weather. The deaf read lips. Hunters read the spoor of game. A phonetician reads the symbols of the International Phonetic Alphabet and hears the sounds of an unknown language. All these forms of reading have the common characteristic of interpretation of visual signs. Sometimes reading (e.g. as in Braille) can be the interpretation of other than visual signs, but *reading is always the interpretation of signs.* If we relate Hall's distinction between "linguistic meaning" and "real-life meaning" to Chao's discussion it becomes clear that both types of definition of reading can be correct. The group of letters *rugate* constitutes a visual stimulus which can be interpreted as a sign for certain English speech sounds, or it can be interpreted as a sign that something is wrinkled, or it can be interpreted as a sign for both.

The discussion thus far suggests that a narrow concept of reading limited to either pronouncing speech sounds or understanding "real-life meaning" will be incomplete because it excludes an important segment of what most people include in their concept of reading (see Gibson and Levin, 1975; Venezky, 1976). For research purposes, it may be important to define quite narrowly the particular aspect of reading being investigated; but, for more general purposes, a broader definition of reading seems called for. Reading should be defined to include various kinds of behavior that people engage in when they say they are reading. These various kinds of behavior all involve the interpretation of signs. Thus a brief definition of our objectives for this book might be:

Reading is the interpretation of signs.

One immediate delimitation must be made because the kind of reading that is of chief concern to teachers and parents is narrower than the general interpretation of signs. We must distinguish between two distinct categories of signs among those mentioned above. The signs read by palmists, hunters and farmers are natural phenomena that have not been deliberately created with any communicational intent. In contrast, signs such as those used in maps, Braille, and written or printed text are arbitrary *symbols* deliberately created for the purpose of communication. It is this latter type of reading that is the concern of this book, although it is valuable to remember its affiliation with the other behavior of interpreting natural phenomena as signs when we consider the evolutionary basis of the processes employed in reading text, maps, and so on. Hence, for the particular purposes of this book we shall revise our definition of reading as follows:

Reading is the interpretation of symbols.

We will elaborate on this definition.

Reading as Interpreting Symbols

The term *interpretation* refers to both a product and a process. The product or the outcome of reading arises with the successful completion of the reading act or when readers comprehend what they read. This is in itself a large statement, as there are different levels of comprehending: memorization, paraphrase or translation, inferences and application. Readers comprehend to the extent that they bring their previous knowledge to bear on the text which should be organized so as to facilitate understanding. The process aspect explains how to get to the product; or as one cognitive psychologist has put it: "Ask not what is inside your head but what your head is inside of." We emphasize the process aspect because it is flexible and adaptable, with manifold resources.

The term *symbols* is used in the semiotic sense of Charles Morris (1955) rather than as symbolic forms or the relation of language to myth, religion, art, science and other kinds of human endeavours and experiences (Gardner, Howard and Perkins, 1974). The semiotic approach focuses on the relationship between linguistic, gestural, pictorial, musical and other kinds of *symbol systems*. Chao (1968, p. 195) explains the term symbols well: "a symbol is something which can be conveniently produced and has a conventionalized, visually arbitrary, relation to what is symbolized." Fodor, Bever and Garrett (1974, p. 152) offer a similar explanation: "the defining property of a symbol is that it *is* an arbitrarily selected object which, nevertheless, succeeds in referring." Thus signs closely resemble referents or objects referred to, while symbols are a representation only. Signs have fixed characteristics, symbols are arbitrary. This arbitrariness, however, probably follows some tacit conventions. An example will illustrate this. The wet, icy roads in the Canadian prairies in winter are signs that the roads are slippery and motorists should take care. There is some fixed characteristic, some causal law why icy roads are slippery and dangerous to drive on. Hence the term *sign* or *signs* is applicable. The road sign which says, "Slow Down" or "Stop/Arrêt" on the same highway is both a sign and a symbol. Symbols can extend in space (e.g. maps, drawings) and in time (e.g. spoken discourse). These are things and events. As signs and symbols mediate between an object and an interpretant, the interpretation of symbols in the semiotic sense attempts to study the triadic relation between signs/symbols, things signified and cognition itself.

In agreement with Gibson and Levin, we suggest that letters of the alphabet, lines in a diagram, patterns in a picture, notes of a musical score, gestures of a ballet dancer, are all parts of symbol systems with their own internal rules of organization. As symbol systems these different instances can be read, albeit in different ways. We know, for example, perceiving print is not the same as perceiving in general, as the literature has shown. Further, the same symbol systems (e.g. language) may occur in different modes (listening, visual, print), just as the same modes (the electronic mode of television or the radio) may be a vehicle for different symbol systems. One particular aspect of different modes—listening and reading print—is of relevance to our inquiry into literacy acquisition. The question here is whether listening as part of *auding* draws on the same internal representation or requires the same basic mental operations as reading print. We will return to this later.

It is thus with some trepidation that we define reading in terms of interpreting symbols. We do so for at least two reasons. One is the more general reason of broadening the scope of reading from reading text materials to reading other symbol systems as part of the quest "toward the literate society." The other is the more specific reason of emphasizing the commonality in reading different writing systems among nations. On this second question, our earlier comparative reading project (Downing, 1973) has attempted to uncover reading behavior across linguistic boundaries with different symbol systems. On the first question of defining reading with focus on reading text materials but also including other conventionalized symbol systems such as pictures, maps and music, our intent is to underscore the importance of *knowing*. Reading should be learning through reading. Teaching reading should be teaching how to learn through reading. Knowing is not just knowing *what* but knowing *how* and knowing *with* (Broudy, 1977).

Bruner (1963) suggested that the generation of hypotheses and inspirations is at first of a nonverbal, cognitive nature, best apprehended as visual imagery. It is only later that true logical, propositional thinking develops. There are thus different processes and strategies in knowing. There are also different neurological substrates serving "verbal" and "nonverbal" activities and analytic and synthetic modes of information processing. Later, we will discuss some of the differential and reciprocal functions of the cerebral hemispheres and will emphasize processing strategies (see Chapters 7, 8 and 15). We will not, however, go so far as to identify hemispheric preferences in the exploration of literacy as some authors have done (e.g. Rico, 1978). Rico has suggested a configuration or primary graphic strategy as a means of expanding nonliteral comprehension, which is taken to be the right-hemisphere function, and which in turn is thought to transfer to verbal communication, supposedly a left-hemisphere function. There is some attraction in this kind of reasoning, but the neurologizing can be misleading. We wish to emphasize that attention can be drawn to reading spatial symbol systems without necessarily implicating the brain. This balanced view is needed as there are even commercialized teaching materials purporting to teach "right-brained kids in left-brained schools!" This neurologizing is unwarranted.

Nearly fifty years ago El Koussy (1935) stressed the importance of the *K* factor or the spatial factor. More recently, Macfarlane Smith (1964) wrote an informative book on spatial ability and its educational and social significance. He did so without any reference to hemispheric functions. These works remind us that we should remember not only the brain, but also other factors as well. Even those who argue that school systems stress *left-hemisphere skills* recognize the need for a balanced view. Nebes (1977, p. 105), for example, sees the verbal and nonverbal dichotomy this way: "Many problems can be solved either by analysis or synthesis; but if people are taught to habitually examine only one approach, their ability to choose the most effective and efficient answer is diminished." Increased understanding of the neurological substrates of language will hopefully lead to better training in how to choose between and how to use the skills of both hemispheres of the human brain. This seems to be an argument for a well-proportioned curriculum which includes reading text materials, reading pictures, reading music and other symbol systems. The reference to analysis-by-synthesis reminds us of that central theme in Neisser's (1967) book *Cognitive Psychology*. He says this of reading:

> Reading for meaning seems to be a kind of analysis-by-synthesis, a construction which builds a non-sensory structure just as "lower levels" of cognition synthesize visual figures or spoken words. Reading is externally guided thinking. Perhaps we should not be surprised that it is so poorly understood; we may not understand it until we understand thought itself (p. 136).

Recently, Wolf (1977) has drawn on relevant research to show that reading defined as reading text materials is too narrow. He examines the relations between the reading process and artistic styles and argues for the broader interpretation of reading that Gibson and Levin and we also have attempted. Wolf emphasizes the need to go beyond the child's ability to recognize or read print and believes that we should "analyze the child's capacity for processing information of various kinds" (p. 428) as a means to advance human knowledge and understanding.

Reading and "Auding"

Part of human understanding can be through "looking at script in order to language" and part through listening. The relationship between reading and auding (listening to speech in order to comprehend) is not a direct, one-to-one correspondence. The ability to understand a stretch of discourse is multidimensional in nature. Whether understanding is through spoken or printed language, the individual has to deal with different aspects of language: vocabulary, grammatical features of syntax and semantics (see Chapters 5, 6, 9 and 10 in this volume; and Carroll, 1972). In listening comprehension, prosodic elements of language are also involved. In reading print, the succession of rapid fixations will merge together to build up a meaningful message, at least in skilled reading.

Kleiman and Schallert (1978) have written of "some things the reader needs to know that the listener doesn't." They explain that spoken and written discourse differs in: (1) prosodic information such as intonation, stress and constituent boundaries inherent in speaking but not marked in texts, (2) varying situations in which both or either modes are used, (3) different functions for spoken and written communication, (4) different characteristics of the two modes and (5) the permanence of writing as compared with the transient, temporal nature of speech. Some or many of these devices are exploited to advantage by writers. For example, poems and plays are meant to be read orally, listened to, and played out or enacted. Only in this way will the gentle, gossamerlike quality of Portia's plea for mercy which "droppeth as the gentle rain from heaven" in Shakespeare's *The Merchant of Venice* be properly appreciated. So also can one savour the sensuous quality of the passage in *Antony and Cleopatra* describing Cleopatra gliding down the Nile in a barge. We are *told* that "age does not wither her, nor custom stale, her infinite variety." Again, the cut-and-thrust dialogue in *The Taming of the Shrew* must be spoken to be enjoyed in the way that the audience in the Bard's days must have done. Shakespeare explains the power of "poetic meaning" thus:

> The poet's eye, in a fine frenzy rolling,
> Doth glance from heaven to earth, from earth
> to heaven,
> And, as imagination bodies forth
> The forms of things unknown, the poet's pen
> Turns them to shapes, and gives to airy nothing
> A local habitation and a name.
>
> *Midsummer Night's Dream,* ACT V, SCENE 1

Much of Shakespeare's poetry will pale in its beauty without the power of his dramatic diction. The same argument applies to other forms of dramatic and poetic work. The content of poetry is intimately bound up with its form—the verse, the melody, the rhythm. These prosodic and poetic elements are an integral part of reading works of poetry. It is also likely that poetry, as a form of art, follows a set of rules characteristic of presentational symbolism as compared with the discursive symbolism of language in prose, through which historical, philosophical and scientific materials are expressed (Langer, 1960). Langer (1953) speaks of poetry and literature generally as an "illusory experience" and this artlike and childlike quality in language perception and usage is one that teachers should sensitize children to through storytelling, games and play activities. It is "doing things with words" and the use of language and how it affects its user (pragmatics) that we should encourage (Bruner, 1975, 1978).

This prosodic mode of meaning is well discussed by Firth (1958). He points out that poets do not have the monopoly on this form of meaning. "Whenever a man speaks, he speaks in some sense as poet. Poets have often emphasised that a great deal of the beauty and meaning of the language is in the sound of it" (p. 193). This beauty is achieved through the use of alliterations, assonance, onomatopoeic words and other prosodic devices. Firth drew attention to the effect of putting together words not usually associated with each other as at a high level of meaning. This he calls collocative meaning, which is a creative expression of the writer. We can call to mind Dr. Samuel Johnson's comment on the metaphysical poets that they "yoked heterogeneous ideas by violence together." John Donne, for example, compared the constancy of lovers to a pair of compasses, in which one point of the compasses is at the center while the other always revolves round it within a constant locus. The heterogeneous idea is an act of creation in which the poet sees the familiar element in the strange, and the strange element in the familiar. Thus, the speaker/writer and listener/reader need to enter into the spirit of the context of the discourse.

The shared linguistic context is less evident in reading written text. Readers must rely on the framework (content and style) set by the author. In interpreting words, sentences and paragraphs, they must bring their previous knowledge to bear on new knowledge and to the task of integrating both. Some examples may be cited. In reading Thomas Gray's "Elegy Written in a Country Churchyard" for the first time, students may well appreciate the line "the curfew tolls the knell of parting day. . . ." They may just as well read the line as "the curlew tolls the knell of parting day" if they know only the words. Thus the shared linguistic context is both *referential* and *metalingual.* It is referential in that the context tells us something. It is metalingual in that we need to enter into the code, the register the poet is using. Other examples of knowing the code are reflected in bringing to focal awareness what we think we know. Thus Carroll (1972, 1977) has emphasized that reading and reading comprehension be considered in the light of general language comprehension and the student's general cognitive maturity. The three levels of reading skills, language competence and cognitive ability are all related and represent the "developmental parameters" of reading comprehension (see Chapters 6 and 10). The empirical aspects of the reading-auding relationship will be developed in Chapter 10 when comprehension is discussed.

A Wider Range of Reading Tasks

When we use the broader definition of reading as interpreting symbols, we should be alert to other modes of representing meaning. We will attempt only a sketch of some of these other modes of communication that may fall within literacy acquisition. Of relevance to this section is our discussion of the analysis of the child's task of learning how to read and its relation to the development of the English writing system in general (Chapters 4 and 5 in this volume).

Some of the graphic systems of communication are outlined by Clark and Woodcock (1976). The Blissymbolics, for example, are suggested as useful for severely handicapped children learning to read. The originator Charles Bliss (1965) proposed his semantography as a system of representing meaning graphically. Vanderheiden and Harris-Vanderheiden (1976) educed some evidence for the use of this system with severely handicapped individuals. Sign language with its system of a sequence of signs in English grammatical order provides a further venue for research into the relationship between structure and function of one form of language and the extent to which this form relates to or differs from spoken language. A variant form, American Sign Language (ASL or Ameslan) has been the subject of intensive studies (e.g. Bellugi and Klima, 1975; Stokoe, 1972). Bellugi and Klima did not find support for the popular notion that signs are processed more in terms of meaning; they found that signs are highly encoded units. Of the more than two thousand signs in the first dictionary of Ameslan (Stokoe, Casterline, and Croneberg, 1965), many are arbitrary rather than iconic or, if once iconic, have lost much of their iconicity. Tweney and Heiman (1977) found from their experiments that grammatical structure plays the same functional role in sign language as in spoken language and that it is possible that the same general cognitive capabilities underlie representations in visual or auditory modes (see also Klima and Bellugi, 1979).

In turning to the reading of pictures, we may ask if picture literacy is analogous to reading comprehension. There is a vast body of research on the perception of pictures (see N. Goodman, 1968; Hagen, 1974 for different views). Sigel (1978) defines a picture as any two-dimensional representation, which can vary in: (1) the details presented (e.g. portrait or sketch), (2) the levels of representation; and (3) the spatial perspectives (e.g. flat or three-dimensional) presented. He suggests that comparable cognitive processes are involved at the deep level in both picture comprehension and literacy, although different rule systems are involved. In children, the awareness that a picture is not a replica of a referent but a representation, and that pictorial representations are similar to but different from objects represented, is a cognitive achievement that evolves gradually. "This achievement necessitates mental coordination on the part of a child of two apparently unrelated events" (Sigel, 1978, p. 103). This achievement is a function of development and reflects cultural and subcultural influences. This achievement is brought about by acquiring knowledge through various developmental epochs in visual, motor or haptic modes. These different modes may alter the form, but not the underlying meaning.

Wolf (1977) actually compares the perception

of aesthetic work to a kind of skilled reading. As fluent readers use different cues—grapho-phonological, syntactic and semantic—to interpret the printed page, so aesthetic perceivers use different *notational* systems like rhythm, harmonic sequences, tone contrasts, perspectives and other structural devices. Some symbol systems are more notational than others and are syntactically more discrete and better articulated (e.g. writing systems). Drawing on eye-tracking studies during picture reading, Kolers (1973c) explains some of the different rules in interpreting pictures. In general, pictures are semantically interpretable but are syntactically amorphous. Sentences abide by certain grammatical rules and the relational aspects of words are important. Pictures are not just read holistically or immediately as a Gestalt, but also read over time, much as written words are read. Kolers (1973c, p. 38) suggests that an important difference between reading pictures and reading words is based not on the supposedly simultaneous processing of the one and the supposedly serial processing of the other, but on "the presence and absence of rules governing construction of the item and complementary rules governing interpretation." He goes on to say: "Pictures are freely open to many interpretations because they are rich in semantic information, but deficient in syntactic regularities; any part can be seen as 'modifying' any other. Sentences are more constrained by the rules of syntax, and notations are even more constrained" (pp. 38–39). Kolers also makes the important point that, in relating the reading of written words, children should be taught something about the idea of representation itself and the role of symbols in that process. What Kolers has stated as an experimental psychologist, psycholinguists and other psychologists including the present authors have emphasized variously as language awareness, cognitive clarity and reading as reasoning (see Chapter 6). Researchers and practitioners need to help children to *discover* what reading is, what it is for, and the joy it can bring to them.

What about the reading of maps, graphs and other forms of visual symbols that children encounter in schools? This is part of the much larger philosophical issue of symbolic or abstract space and spatial experience that theorists like Cassirer (1944), Werner and Kaplan (1963), Piaget and Inhelder (1956); Piaget, Inhelder, and Szeminska (1960) have grappled with. Cassirer (1944) has sought to understand the fundamental form of human culture and has discussed the abstract knowledge of space and spatial relations at different levels: organic space, perceptual space and symbolic space. Werner and Kaplan (1963) discussed development in terms of differentiation and subordination of parts to the whole. They made an important point (from the developmental-educational perspective) that the child should be helped to move from reacting-to to knowing-about. Knowing-about progresses from the sensorimotor through the perceptual to the contemplative levels of development or from concrete to abstract knowledge of the world. Piaget and Inhelder (1956); Piaget, Inhelder, and Szeminska (1960) deal with perceptual-scale space. Their main concern is the development of the child's knowledge of space as a geometric entity culminating in a Euclidean image of the world.

Against this background of philosophical investigation of abstract, representational space, Hart and Moore (1973), a geographer and a psychologist, and Downs and Stea (1973, 1977), a psychologist and a town planner respectively, have made conceptual and empirical contributions to *knowing* our everyday spatial environment. Hart and Moore show how children develop their frame of reference of spatial environment (e.g., homes, schools, shops and so on). The researchers emphasize five domains of development: (1) *levels* of organization of spatial cognition (sensorimotor, preoperational, concrete, and formal operations); (2) *types* of spatial relations (topological, projective and Euclidean); (3) *modes* of representation (enactive, iconic and symbolic), (4) *systems* of reference (egocentric, fixed and coordinated) and (5) *types* of topographical representations (route and survey). Thus, knowing one's spatial environment and solving spatial problems involve some basic problems of cognition itself. Starting from their own actions and explorations, children move through the egocentric system to a coordinated system akin to a spatial map and organize their spatial world in an integrated representation. Downs and Stea (1977, p. 6) conceive of this development in terms of cognitive mapping, which is "an abstraction covering those cognitive or mental abilities that enable us to collect, organize, store, recall, and manipulate information about the spatial environment." Cognitive mapping is both a product and a process and it is also a cross section representing the world at one instant in time. Cognitive mapping enables us to organize and manipulate our knowledge of the world and to get from here to there. This question of spatial problem solving was recently investigated by Hardwick, McIntyre and Pick (1976) in first-graders, fifth-graders and college students. The qualitative differences in mental manipulation of cognitive mapping is interpreted as a two-stage operation. There is a stage of transformation applied to ordinal spatial relationships and a stage applied to specific relationships between self and spatial layout. Both stages of the manipulation sequence are required for successful cognitive mapping. Also, such accurate mental manipulation is found to increase with age.

Skill and Knowledge

In the preceding sections we have discussed reading via the listening mode, reading maps and presentation forms such as poetry and pictures. The question may be raised about the relevance to reading in the conventional sense. Our central concern in these sections is less with the practice of the alternative modes of reading. We are more interested in other forms of print media representing knowledge. Knowledge here is interpreted as an activity, a process of knowing. There are many forms of media which are variant modes of symbolic representations that we have not discussed. The wide-ranging work *Media and Symbols: The Forms of Expression, Communication, and Education* (Olson, 1974) bears testimony to the diverse ways in which different media, both print and nonprint, may be utilized in literacy acquisition. The contributors to that volume have critically examined the potentials of prose, pictorial, electronic and other media and also direct experience in improving children's learning and in relation to different intellectual purposes. Take, for example, popular television programs dealing specifically with teaching children the patterns and values of "the literate society"—"Sesame Street" and "The Electric Company." These programs are an example of the "desanctification of print" and attempt to promote literacy through the electronic medium. "The Electric Company" is more specialized than "Sesame Street" and deals specifically with reading or the systematic relationship between print and speech. But, by their very forms and contents, these alternative modes of literacy acquisition are generally thought to deal only with one level (generally a low level) of literacy. The higher integrative levels are achieved through reading print (prose) itself.

If reading is accepted as reading for meaning, and if the highest level of comprehension involves logical propositional thinking and general reasoning, then reading also goes beyond simply interpreting the printed page. In their *Psychology of the Child*, Piaget and Inhelder (1969, p. 90) reiterate that "language does not constitute the source of logic but is, on the contrary, structured by it. The roots of logic are to be sought in the general coordination of actions (including verbal behavior), beginning with the sensorimotor level, whose schemes are of fundamental importance. The schematism continues thereafter to develop and to structure thought, even verbal thought, in terms of the progress of actions, until the formation of the logico-mathematical operations." They emphasize the unity of diverse manifestations of "semiotic functions" of imitation, symbolic play, drawing, mental images, and language in the developing child. Although Piaget and associates have not discussed reading in their developmental theory, other developmental psychologists of the Genevan persuasion have emphasized that reading, language, and symbolic representations have a common source rooted in cognitive structures (e.g. Furth, 1978; Murray, 1978). The School for Thinking of Furth and Wachs (1974) for children aged between five and seven years treats reading within an overall thinking atmosphere. The recent position of Piaget (1976) seems to indicate that perception is not the basis of understanding and that children move from a perceptually dominated world to one of conceptual understanding through a process of construction. Insofar as we can relate this to reading, our emphasis on the interactive model of reading (Chapters 6, 9 and 10) seems to come close to this active, integrative process. Our elaboration in Chapters 2 and 3 on reading as *a* skill and on principles of skill acquisition has consistently emphasized *understanding* the *integration* of a complex set of processes—cognitive, attitudinal and manipulative. The attainment of this complex skill is facilitated by positive affective factors (Chapter 11), supportive home background (Chapter 12) and stimulating school environment (Chapter 13).

Reference to skill acquisition brings us to the slightly different views of learning through experience and learning through media of Olson and Bruner (1974). They explained knowledge and skill in this way:

> The set of features that are more or less invariant across different activities may be considered as the structural or invariant features of objects and events that constitute our *knowledge* about those objects and events. Similarly,

> the set of operations or constituent acts that are invariant when performed across different objects and events may be considered as the structural basis of the activities themselves—that we call *skills and abilities.* It is our hypothesis that "knowledge" reflects the invariants in the natural and social environment while "skills or abilities" reflect the structure of the medium of performatory domain in which various activities are carried out (p. 129, original italics).

Following Piaget, Olson and Bruner emphasize that objects and events are not just passively recorded but actively acted upon. Knowing is mediated through some form of human activity and knowing-how is not the same as knowing-that. While there may be a difference between perceptual knowledge and representational knowlege, Olson (1970) suggests that perceptual knowledge is substantially altered by performatory acts in different media. This reminds us of the philosopher Polanyi's assertion (in Grene, 1969, p. 131) that "To see a problem is to see something hidden that may yet be accessible. The knowledge of a problem is . . . a knowing of more than you can tell." It is likely that we know much more that we can tell in other symbolic forms. We acquire knowledge through performance in a mode and by that mode becoming practiced and automatic. To Olson (1970, p. 187) "it is the performatory attempts in various media which provide the occasion for apprehending further information from the perceptual world." He states that "What is called intelligence is developed through mastering a cultural medium" and thus "intelligence is skill in a medium, or, more precisely, skill in a cultural medium" (p. 193). In industrial and developing countries the linguistic and literate medium constrains intelligence. Much of what goes on in schools is concerned with the acquisition of literate skills and hence certain forms of intellectual achievement. Olson (1970, 1976, 1977a, 1977b) points out some consequences of the textually biased schooling. He makes the provocative statement that "the prose text is not *the* structure of language and the knowledge represented by that text is not *the* structure of knowledge, but the form of knowledge appropriate to one specialized technology. To master that form . . . it is necessary to master that technology" (Olson, 1977b, p. 77, original italics). One consequence of this, according to Olson, is that knowledge may be inaccessible to people with fewer literacy skills and that the translation of knowledge into a literate form may lose some of the special properties of the original form of expression.

Olson's forceful argument draws attention to literacy acquisition in other media. Rather than de-emphasizing the prose/literate medium, we should be aware of the different roles that the various media play and the different levels at which they contribute to knowledge. Where direct experience is the most valuable, the enactive mode is preferred. But this is sometimes not possible or desirable. We must be content with vicarious experience most of the time. Iconic symbols are best for organizing and communicating information about simultaneous, topographical features of objects, and about relational aspects of objects. In *Visual Thinking,* Arnheim (1969) stresses the role of visual imagery in creative thinking. He suggests that metaphoric, holistic and transformational operations are initially mediated through visual imagery, and that logical mathematical thinking is valuable for systematic reasoning but not adequate for the initial stages of creative thinking. For learning that involves information already well analyzed and that involves complex concepts and relationships, the print mode is often superior to other modes (Carroll, 1974). Furthermore, print itself carries very little information; what it conveys in meaning also depends on the world knowledge we bring to bear in interpretation. The fervent hope for schooling is that it should bring about important changes in cognitive functioning (Anderson, Spiro, and Montague, 1977). This in turn may help learners to modify their world view and also assist in instruction (Lesgold, Pellegrino, Fokkema, and Glaser, 1978). Wittrock (1978b) points to the "cognitive movement" in instruction which should encourage a synthesis of research into cognition, affect, and brain function for better instruction and learning.

The Scope of This Book

In the preceding sections we have discussed some of the broader issues pertaining to reading in the larger definition which goes beyond simply reading script. We have cast reading within the framework of literacy acquisition. We have taken the position that reading is the interpretation of symbols, to underscore the broader aspect of reading different kinds of print and nonprint materials. The emphasis is on the understanding of symbol systems, and on knowledge acquisition over and above the mere teaching and learning of reading as a skill. We have taken a cognitive and psycholinguistic approach in our attempt to understand processes of reading acquisition and reading in general.

Having established our general frame of reference, we will now focus our attention on reading behavior in the more conventional sense and on those factors that facilitate or impede reading. The ensuing chapters set forth our review, discussion, critique and integration of research and theory pertaining to reading. The chapters fall into six fairly distinct but related areas and may be read as such in terms of these groups. One area comprises reading as *a* complex, interrelated skill (Chapters 2 and 3). A second area relates to aspects of language: the historical and crossnational aspect of orthography (Chapter 4), psycholinguistic analyses of the English writing system (Chapter 5) and language awareness (Chapter 6). The third area deals with physiological aspects pertaining to reading, with Chapter 7 centering on neurological substrates of language and Chapter 8 on seeing and reading. The fourth area discusses theoretical and empirical studies of lexical access and coding processes (Chapter 9) and coming to comprehend (Chapter 10). The fifth group of chapters centers on the affective bases of reading (Chapter 11), with two related chapters on home background (Chapter 12) and school environment (Chapter 13). The sixth area covers research, theory, and relevant practice into the almost perennial problem of "why Johnny can't read," with Chapter 14 devoted to reading disabilities and difficulties and Chapter 15 to developmental dyslexia or reading retardation.

In treating these six vast and important areas, we have attempted to be comprehensive by including relevant contemporary literature without neglecting significant studies of earlier years. We have drawn on works from related disciplines: experimental and child psychology, neuropsychology, psycholinguistics, and education to provide a broader-based perspective. As is unavoidable with a volume of this nature and magnitude we are forced to be selective at times, and this selection probably reflects our background and bias. We hope to make amends by our extensive and intensive discussion.

To be more specific, a resumé of the contents of each chapter will help our readers in determining the way they may prefer to read this volume. Chapter 2, "Reading as a Skill," emphasizes the complex, holistic nature of reading, subsuming various subskills. General skill characteristics including timing, automaticity, internal and external cues and feedback are discussed in relation to reading. The hierarchy of subskills is modular in organization and is well accounted for by the "substrata-factor theory of reading" of Holmes (1970). Chapter 3, "Principles of Skill Acquisition in Reading," discusses the various phases of mastering a complex skill—cognitive, mastery, automaticity and overlearning—and generally elaborates on the earlier chapter. Heuristics in instruction are outlined.

Chapter 4, "Orthography and Reading," examines in depth the historical development of orthography and how different writing systems affect reading. This leads to Chapter 5, "Psycholinguistic Analyses," which focuses on the nature of English orthography as a system of codes. The chapter traces the classical phonemic description through the lexical representation of Chomsky and Halle (1968) to Venezky's (1970a, 1970b) morphophonemics. From these and other descriptions, it is suggested that the English orthography is a complex multi-code with phonemic signals as clues to morphemic units. From the phonological representation of the writing system, we move to Chapter 6 on "Language Awareness." This consists of one part on language structure and one part on language function. The structural portion discusses transformational generative grammar and case grammar as relevant for language studies. The function portion explicates "learning how to mean" and how children reflect on and objectify language. Early readers probably progress from "cognitive confusion" to "cognitive clarity" in coming to understand and use print. The internalized mentalistic view of language in the tradition of Chomsky can be reconciled with the communicative competence of language.

From reading as a complex, language-based skill, we move to Chapter 7, "Neurological Substrates of Language and Reading." This provides some basic understanding of how cerebral structure and functions relate to language and reading. The intertwined hearing and speaking functions are discussed in relation to the perception of the complex speech code and to reading and its difficulties. Chapter 8, "Seeing and Reading," follows Chapter 7 logically to explain how the visual system affects the psychological processes of reading. The relevant physiological mechanism of eye movements in reading is discussed in relation to cognitive and linguistic variables. Reading behind the eyes refers to some visual defects with bearings on the reading act.

The next two chapters study in-depth empirical evidence on accessing word meaning and textual comprehension. From an information-processing perspective, Chapter 9, "Perceptual and Cognitive Processes," brings together a body of current research literature to focus on the nature of the lexical access code and the access procedure. Different lines of laboratory and in situ studies related to short-term memory, lexical decision of homophonic and heterophonic words, the Stroop effect, and paralexic errors in deep dyslexia are discussed in some detail to show the complex pros and cons of phonological and visual access to word meaning. The more likely procedure in processing words is the dual coding, multiple paths model. This leads in Chapter 10, "Other Cognitive Aspects," to discussions on "bottom-up" (data-driven), "top-down" (concept-driven) and interactive models of reading. The last-named paradigm is more in tune with current levels-of-processing framework of memory research with a continuum of different levels from visual pattern recognition to semantic elaboration. The cognitive approach to comprehension deals with the role of listening and reading comprehension and visual imagery. Sentential and intrasentential linguistic devices, textual organization, and cognitive contribution from readers are basic to processes of comprehension.

In the affective domain, Chapter 11, "Affective Bases," focuses attention on readers' attitudes, emotions and motives. Such factors as arousal, attention, stress, intrinsic and extrinsic motivation, curiosity and interests, and purposes of reading all affect reading performance. The next two chapters are on cultural and environmental factors. Chapter 12, "The Home Background," emphasizes culture and the family as influential factors in the development of reading skill. The esteem for literacy, sex-role expectations, social class differences and language of the culture all have their effects on the child. Chapter 13, "The School Environment," brings out such complex dimensions as physical features of the school, characteristics of the school system, knowledge and skills of the teacher, as both relevant and important in understanding reading.

The last two chapters examine critically the concept of reading disabilities. A differentiation is made on theoretical, empirical and clinical grounds between poor readers (Chapter 14 "Reading Disabilities and Difficulties") and "retarded" readers or those with developmental dyslexia (Chapter 15 "Specific Reading Disability"). Chapter 14 draws attention to varying terms and concepts. The chapter focuses attention on empirical studies aimed at analyzing the independence or interdependence of decoding and comprehension in skilled and less skilled readers. Evidence tends toward lexical access speed and vocalization latencies as important verbal sources of reading difficulties. These sources of individual differences in reading are part of the continuum of general language comprehension and the ability to organize language units into meaningful relationships. Chapter 15 conceives of children with specific reading disability as inefficient processors in one or several higher cortical functions. Empirical and clinical evidence shows that these children exhibit different cognitive patterns, and that they are inefficient in temporal order perception and verbal processing. They also lag behind in their functional cerebral development. The relationship of laterality and reading proficiency is discussed in the light of current neuropsychological knowledge. Reading strategies based on reciprocal brain functions are outlined, with a plea for interdisciplinary research into reading dysfunction.

Thus it is that in the following chapters we have grappled with the intricacies of how children and other readers "read, mark, learn, and inwardly digest." This is no small feat, as Huey (1908) reminded us so many years ago. E. L. Thorndike's (1917) comparison of children's oral reading of paragraphs to the solving of a mathematical problem is also appropriate. He suggested that: "The mind is assailed, as it were, by every word in the paragraph. It must select, repress, soften, emphasize, correlate, and organize, all under the influence of the right mental set or purpose or demand" (p. 329). We can only hope that we have in a small way contributed to the solution of the puzzlement in reading.

CHAPTER 2

Reading as a Skill

Andreas (1972, p. 4) states: "Psychology seeks to find and formulate the laws of behavior." The behavior need not be external observable acts. It may be internal and not directly observable. Woodworth and Marquis (1949, p. 3) wrote that, "Psychology studies the individual's activities. . . ." They pointed out that, "The word 'activity' . . . includes not only motor activities like walking and speaking, but also cognitive (knowledge-getting) activities like seeing, hearing, remembering, and thinking, and emotional activities like laughing and crying and feeling happy or sad." Which of these kinds of activities studied by psychologists are related to the problem of this book—how do people learn to interpret symbols in reading?

To commence this task and to plan a comprehensive attack on this problem we need to know where reading behavior fits into the psychologist's general overall map of human behavior. Is reading unique or does it belong to a more general type or category of behavior? Clay (1972, p. 8) provides a starting point. She states:

> Reading is a process by which the child can, on the run, extract a sequence of cues from printed texts and relate these, one to another, so that he understands the precise message of the text. The child continues to *gain in this skill* throughout his entire education, interpreting statements of ever-increasing complexity (italics added).

Clay's reference to reading in the singular as "a skill" is perfectly appropriate within the science of psychology. Most psychologists would agree that reading is a type of behavior that belongs in the category of "a skill."

This description of reading as "*a* skill" may seem surprising to students of education who are accustomed to frequent reference to "reading skills" (in the plural) in their curriculum and instruction courses. It is important to note this difference in the language usage of these different disciplines. The term *skills* in curriculum and instruction courses usually refers to mental or motor activities that should be taught as part of the curriculum. In psychology, in contrast, the term *skill* is a label for a specific category of behavior—"particular, more or less complex, activities which require a period of deliberate training and practice to be performed adequately and which often have some recognized useful function," say Borger and Seaborne (1966, pp. 127–128), indicating that their concern, as psychologists, is with "the individual, with competence, with proficiency. It may manifest itself in the exercise of recognized skills like driving, in the playing of games like tennis, or marbles, also in more widespread accomplishments such as riding a bicycle, the tying of shoe laces or just walking." Psychologists have also investigated, Borger and Seaborne continue, "the conditions under which skill develops, the factors making for more or less rapid achievement of a given criterion, and to do this *in a way which is only incidentally concerned with the particular type of activity involved*" (italics added). For psychologists, therefore, reading is just another example of the category of behavior called "skill." They are searching for a scientific understanding of skilled behavior—*of all kinds.*

On first consideration this abstraction of skill from the particular kind of activity may seem to the educator to be somewhat abstruse. However, it is a fundamental principle of science that theories should explain a wide spectrum of phenomena. Also, from the point of view of the practical educator, the wide range of scientific research on skill development in general, should provide valuable insights into the acquisition of the skill of special interest to the reader of this book—reading. Indeed, research on skill learning is one of the oldest interests of scientific psychology. Well-designed experiments on the acquisition of skill were begun toward the end of the nineteenth century, and continuous progress in this aspect of research has been made since then to the present day. A valuable source of knowledge is thus available to the educator who wants to understand how children acquire the skill of reading. Therefore, next in this chapter, we will, first of all, summarize what psychological research says about skill learning in general and then, secondly, go on to relate it to the specific skill of reading. We are deliberately keeping these two steps quite separate for a very good reason. First, we want to establish as starkly as possible the conclusions that psychological research has reached on skill learning in general. Then we can compare these conclusions about skill in general with descriptions of reading behavior in particular to see if reading fits well into the psychologists' category of skill. If it does, then all psychological findings on skill learning can be applied to the acquisition of reading. Many general findings may have been overlooked by reading teachers.

The Goal of Skill Acquisition

For the scientific study of skill we need objective criteria. What is the ideal of skill performers? What kind of behavior are they trying to achieve? These questions lead to the more basic question—what are the psychological qualities of a skilled performance that can be recognized objectively?

Definition of "Skill"

Cronbach (1963, p. 309) states: "By *skill* we refer to a performance in which a complete sequence of actions is carried out in a more or less fixed way. There are some skills in which control of movement makes a great difference in the result, and others where judgment and reasoning are more important. . . . The expert performs more smoothly and more automatically than others. Skilled performance is a series of actions, each regulated by cues; the expert senses relevant ones quickly, interprets them promptly and correctly, and runs off the sequence without pause." McDonald (1965, p. 387) refers to this type of behavior as "skill performances." He writes that: "From a psychological point of view, playing football or chess or using a typewriter or the English language correctly demands complex sets of responses—some of them cognitive, some attitudinal, and some manipulative." He takes as an example "skill" in playing baseball, and points to the player's need "to perform sets of responses with ease, quickness and economy of motion." But McDonald emphasizes that it is not merely a matter of motor behavior. The player "must also *understand*" the game and must like playing the game and have appropriate attitudes about winning and sportsmanship. "The total performance . . . is a complex set of processes—cognitive, attitudinal, and manipulative. This complex integration of processes is what we usually mean when we refer to 'skill'. . . ." Cronbach's and McDonald's definitions are cited because they are good examples of the generally acceptable textbook descriptions of the behavior categorized as "skill." A concise definition of skill that covers these descriptions is provided by Whiting (1975):

> Complex, intentional actions involving a whole chain of sensory central and motor mechanisms which through the process of learning have come to be organized and co-ordinated in such a way as to achieve predetermined objectives with maximum certainty (p. 6).

Characteristics of Skill Performance

As students study our list of characteristics of skills in general they should be thinking about this question—*what aspect of reading behavior is a reflection of this general skill characteristic?* These insights should be noted or kept in mind until later when they can be compared with the authors' conclusions on that question.

Our list of characteristics of the performance of a skill is a consensus of a wide range of psychological research reports and reviews. Space does not permit an historical survey of how all of these conclusions were reached. For a full account of the psychological study of skill features, the student may consult Borger and Seaborne (1966), Cronbach (1977), De Cecco and Crawford (1974), McDonald (1965), and Whiting (1975) from whose work the following list was compiled. It should be noted that some of the features in this list are overlapping. This is because we did not want to stray too far from the original statements of the authors cited.

1. The performance of any skill involves a *highly complex* pattern of behavior. For example, Whiting writes that "the student of skill acquisition is concerned with the study of the development of highly organized, complex human behavior involving the whole person functioning as a coordinated unit" (p. 7).

2. A skilled performer executes this complex pattern *smoothly,* without faltering. Whiting makes a penetrating point on this characteristic:

> One of the anomalies in the acquisition of skill, is that on the one hand, the *complexity* of the procedure is being stressed while on the other, the highly skilled person's behavior is often described as effortless, polished, smooth, beautifully-timed, etc., giving the impression of *simplicity.* It is only when an awareness of the difficulties involved in passing from the "unskilled" to the "skilled" category are appreciated that the immense complexity of the problem is realised. One of the reasons why many highly skilled people are poor teachers of such skills is a lack of such awareness (p. 7).

3. This unhesitating smoothness is the product of *integration* (or coordination) of the many different aspects of behavior involved in the complex pattern. Some authors describe this feature of a skill as *organization.* This term emphasizes the dynamic nature of the integration process. It is the central psychological characteristic of skill.

4. *Timing* is a very important aspect of this integration or organization of the behavior pattern of a skill. This timing process is complex. Not only does an activity take time to perform but time is also needed to make decisions on how to react to information received. In addition, a variety of activities with different time characteristics are being integrated. When *speed* is a criterion of a high level of skill, the timing aspect is directed toward quicker execution. However, in many skills *flexibility* in timing is more important than rapidity because timing must vary according to the changing needs of the situation in which the skill is performed.

5. The smooth performance of a skill is derived from the performer's being *ready for a wide range of events* that may or may not occur from moment to moment. Borger and Seaborne conclude that this "constant state of readiness for action . . . is one of the main features of skilled performance" (p. 136). This readiness is complicated by the need to be ready both for events set in motion by others and events that are the consequence of performing the skilled activity itself.

6. This readiness for action depends to a great extent on the performer's *anticipation* of future events. Cronbach (1977, p. 408) notes how the skilled performer "makes use of signals well in advance of the action." Again this anticipation process applies both to predicting events being controlled by others and the outcomes of one's own acts. Cronbach states that "In a well-coordinated movement, each subordinate act occurs at just the right time." This is because "The expert develops an individualized program." But also, "Pacing is controlled in part by external events. From time to time, unexpected cues call forth an adaptive action that lasts for several seconds. The performer plans as he goes."

7. The skilled performer can run through the behavior pattern *automatically.* Samuels (1976a) notes that this automaticity in the developed skill "enables a behavior which formerly required attention to occur without the services of attention. This is tantamount to putting a plane on automatic pilot, thus freeing the pilot to direct attention to other things" (pp. 323–324). This does not mean, of course, that the ability to attend to the skill atrophies. What develops, rather, is the power to switch between automatic and conscious control as needed. Thus, Borger and Seaborne note: "One interesting feature of skilled activity is the possibility of change from 'automatic' to a more flexible and conscious control. Many routine and highly practiced activities can proceed quite smoothly with the minimum of attention being given to them. Yet, if an unusual situation arises—an odd noise in a machine, for example—the smooth flow of the operation is interrupted, and control passes to a 'higher level': we start thinking about what to do next" (p. 149).

8. Several writers have pointed to the analogy between the program in a computer and the automaticity of skilled behavior. The function of this automatic neural program appears to be to *free the performer's attention for other activities.* Samuels (1976a) states: "A quarter of a century of research on attention has led to the conclusion that the brain acts as a single channel processor. This means that, at any given moment, attention can

be at only one place at a time" (p. 323). The internal program allows the performer to carry out a behavior pattern automatically while paying attention to something else.

9. There is some debate about the extent to which skilled performers are conscious of their own activities and as to whether they need understand why they perform the skill in the way that they do. But the truth is that *consciousness of one's own activities and their functions is a characteristic of skill performance at some times but not at others.* Thus, Borger and Seaborne are quite accurate in stating that "proficiency does not necessarily involve the explicit recognition of the contributing factors" (p. 131). It may or may not involve such recognition.

10. Psychological descriptions of skill performance generally employ the term *cue.* Cronbach (1977, p. 400) gives this definition: "A relevant cue is any stimulus from outside or from within the body that can help a person to recognize a situation or to direct an action." A skill performance involves a continuous stream of reactions to such external or internal cues.

11. These reactions depend on the performer's attention to relevant cues and a process of *translating* them into appropriate action. The cues are often quite obscure and the translation process is usually so rapid that it is not apparent to an observer.

12. The two principal sources of cues are: (a) *changes in the outside environment,* and (b) *changes within the performer.* These changes may be produced by external forces or by the actions of the skill performer. For example, in tennis the players react to the movement of the ball that is produced by their own actions as well as their opponents'. They also react to sensations within their own bodies that are caused by their own movements.

13. Cues from such changes produced by the activity are used in the *feedback* process. Feedback, according to Cronbach (1977, p. 402), "consists of repeated sensing and correcting." For example, the car driver's "action has certain consequences. Knowledge of these consequences is fed back to the driver in visual and other cues. If he is dissatisfied, he takes a further action; soon *its* consequences in turn are fed back" (p. 402). Many experiments have been conducted by psychologists in which feedback has been withheld or delayed. For example, Fairbanks and Guttman (1958) delayed the auditory feedback that individuals receive from hearing their own speech. The result was a disorganized, stumbling manner of speaking similar to stuttering. The evidence from research is so clear that Bilodeau and Bilodeau (1961) considered that studies of feedback show that it is the strongest and most important variable controlling performance of motor skills. Even earlier, Ammons (1954) had concluded that feedback is one of the most reliable and exhaustively tested principles in psychology. Its great importance is as a constant regulator of the pattern of behavior all the time homing in on the goal of greater accuracy in skill performance.

14. The skill performer's utilization of cues depends on *selective attention.* In any situation requiring skill performance one is bombarded with available information. Successful skill response requires one to ignore the irrelevant stimuli and attend only to the relevant cues. In acquiring a skill one learns what to ignore as well as what to pay attention to. Also, as skill develops, the performer's sensitivity to cues changes in several ways. Whiting (1975) states:

> The skill performer cannot utilize *all* the potential information available in a display and . . . much of this information will be of little value in controlling the skill. For these reasons, and because in many skills there is only a limited time available in which to take in information, he needs to be selective (p. 13).

15. One type of change in sensitivity that occurs as a skill is learned is the *shift from external cues to internal cues.* Cronbach (1977, p. 400) gives this example: "The boy starting to play a horn can judge whether or not his action is right only by the tone that comes out. Soon he finds that the right action *feels* different from the wrong. . . . Lip muscle cues are now as significant as the sound cues." De Cecco and Crawford state that "this gradual change from reliance on external cues to reliance on internal cues characterizes most skill learning" (p. 248). These internal cues are a part of feedback. Fitts (1951) concluded that successful skill development depends on this increasing reliance on internal feedback. It should be noted that "internal" refers to kinesthetic sensation—the information directed to higher levels of the central nervous system from receptors in joints, muscles and tendons.

16. Another change that occurs as skill develops is that the performer utilizes *perceptual units of increasing size.* The evidence for this came from one of the earliest investigations of skill development. Bryan and Harter (1899) found that

learners of the Morse code heard patterns of dots and dashes for letters. Later they developed still larger perceptual units for whole words and some short phrases. Another classic study in psychology explains this phenomenon. Miller (1956) in his famous article on "The Magical Number Seven, Plus or Minus Two" showed that the span of immediate memory is limited to about seven "bits" of information. But these bits can vary in an important quality. They may be in simple elements or they may consist in larger chunks of the simpler parts. Thus, one can retain more information by employing larger chunks. For example, Dcese (1958) gives the problem of memorizing the number 010110100110101011011100111100111100 from reading it only once. The normal solution is to reorganize it into sequences of three: 010—110—100—110, and so on. These units could also be given new code names. Many studies confirm that skill development depends on building these larger units of perceptual organization.

17. *Larger units of action* are also developed as skill grows. Cronbach (1977, p. 408) states that the expert's "movements are tied into long sequences" or "programs." Borger and Seaborne give this descriptive example of touch typing: "At the start, each letter is typed individually, as a separate act. A skilled typist on the other hand will type whole words and even phrases as a *unit*—i.e. the pattern which comprises the whole sequence of movements making up the word or phrase appears to be ready at the outset, the programme simply *runs itself off.* With the arrival of this stage, a copy typist can type *behind* the material that she is reading, building up one programme while executing the last one" (p. 135).

18. Yet another change that is observed as skill develops is *cue reduction and addition.* Cronbach (1977, p. 400) notes: "As a person acquires experience, more and more cues become useful in selecting the right response. A beginner depends upon the most obvious cues. Later many additional cues guide him." But Cronbach notes also that the experienced person can select the most appropriate response on the basis of fewer cues than can the inexperienced person. McDonald points out that, "The skilled performer also responds to subtler cues than does the beginner," as well as learning "to respond to fewer cues" (pp. 395–396).

19. The ability to cope with stress increases as skill develops. Bartlett (1948) found that highly skilled Air Force pilots maintained their performance under stress, whereas less experienced flyers lost some of their skill when subjected to stressful conditions such as fatigue, sickness, emotional pressures, or confusing cues. Indeed, Cronbach (1977, p. 412) notes that, "Whereas stress upsets the nonexpert performer, it often brings the expert to his peak." Loss of skill in less skilled performers when they are subjected to stress usually takes the form of regression to an earlier, more primitive level of performance.

20. Skills may be analyzed into smaller units of behavior called "subskills" or "subroutines." Skill has often been described as a *hierarchy of subskills,* but the use of the word "hierarchy" is ambiguous and has led to some confusion and controversy about this aspect of skill. Some behavioristic descriptions give an appearance of rigidity of ordering in the sequence of subskills that make up a skill. This rigidity is reflected in many articles and books by curriculum and instruction specialists in reading. Since this rigidity of ordering of the sequence of subskills is a matter of doubt in psychology but rather widely accepted among educators, it is important to examine this question closely.

Many educators may feel comforted by the assertion by De Cecco and Crawford that "we must learn all the subordinate chains before we can perform a particular skill" (p. 249). It appears to give a scientific respectability to pedagogical notions about there being some essential sequence of instruction. But, if we reflect on the many fine variations of response to subtle changes in cues that occur in most instances of skill performance, the conception of skill as a chain of subskills seems oversimplified.

The concept of hierarchy used by Borger and Seaborne, however, is less controversial in psychology. They note: "It seems likely that the structure of organisms is hierarchical in character, with control shifting between levels according to the demands of the situation" (p. 149). These authors thus shift the emphasis from hierarchical units of behavior to hierarchical units of control. Bruner's (1971) description of skill performance is consistent with their position, and takes account of the great variability of behavior and cues:

> In broad outline, skilled action requires recognizing the features of a task, its goal, and means appropriate to its attainment; a means of converting this information into appropriate action, and a means of getting feedback that compares the objective sought with present state attained. . . . When we learn something like a skill, it is in the very nature of the case

> that we master a wide variety of possible ways for attaining an objective—many ways to skin the cat. For we learn ways of constructing many responses that fit our grasp of what is appropriate to an objective (p. 112).

Elliott and Connolly (1974) have concerned themselves directly with this issue of the hierarchical structure of skill that is not simply a rigid sequence of subskills. They note that, "The concept of control has been particularly useful, since it relates to the problem of determining a sequence of operations which are not intrinsically determinate. If an operation is not determined by the one before it, in . . . a chain, then it is a problem to decide how it is determined" (p. 136). Elliott and Connolly go on to suggest that, through "feedback control . . . what determines a sequence might be whether or not successive operations reduce the discrepancy between the state of affairs external to the operator, and some model or envisioned representation of what the state of affairs ought to be." Then subskills or "subroutines may thus be thought of as hierarchically organized in the pursuit of activities that are voluntary with respect to their guiding plan. Practiced sequences of acts would be definable as subroutines, comprised in turn of lower order behavioral elements available to more than one higher order sequence" (p. 137).

This explanation by Elliott and Connolly fits well with Bruner's (1970) view that skill is *modular* in organization. Subskills or subroutines, once mastered, become modules that are available for use in a variety of known and new contexts. This modular organization may be hierarchical in terms of control without there being any necessary sequence of either learning or performance.

21. One final minor point needs to be mentioned. Some authors such as De Cecco and Crawford try to draw a distinction between "verbal learning" and "psychomotor skills" but we go along with Cronbach's (1977, p. 395) position that, "Many principles of psychomotor learning apply also to performance where the motor element is of only minor importance." Indeed, Cronbach goes on to assert strongly that "the learning of a skill *is* largely intellectual. In learning a skill one relies on attention, memory, interpretation, and even deliberate problem solving. Only after the intellectual work has set the pattern for the task does excellence of execution come into its own. Even then, novel conditions can call for additional intellectual analysis." Welford (1968) also suggests that the commonly drawn distinction between sensorimotor and mental skills is difficult to maintain. Whiting (1975) remarks that although "verbal, mental, perceptual, social and motor are common adjectives in relation to skills" it would "be wrong . . . to assume that the processes involved in learning any of these skill categories is essentially different from the learning of another" (Whiting, 1975, p. 6). More recently, Whiting and Brinker (1980) have expressed this position more forcefully: "The long standing tendency to polarise the practical, doing, making side of man's action systems and the so-called logical, conceptual, thinking side is unfortunate. . . . While . . . 'intelligent' does not entail 'intellectual,' since the latter involves a considerable degree of thinking involvement, it also cannot be denied that movements, in subserving overt actions, have a cognitive involvement, i.e. they are intelligently carried out" (p. 2).

At this point, students will find it helpful to go back to characteristic number 1 in our list and then review the *italicized* words in each item and relate them to (1) any skill (such as tennis or chess) that they are very familiar with, and then (2) do the same review again, but this time related to the skill of reading.

Reading and Its Skill Characteristics

Now the authors will attempt the second of these suggested tasks for the student of the psychology of reading. How do observations of reading behavior fit the psychologist's generalized description of skill performance? This consideration of the features of skill as found in reading behavior may help us to judge what characteristics of skilled reading the novice must aim to acquire.

Everyone who has been involved in psychological research about reading is in agreement about its great *complexity* (skill characteristic number 1). For example, Kolers (1968) describes reading as "one of the most complex . . . operations" of "the workings of mind" (p. xiii).

There is no doubt either that the second item in our list of skill characteristics applies equally well to reading. The skilled reader executes the complex pattern of behavior *smoothly*—in the sense that we defined this feature—without faltering. However, smoothness in any skill does not imply a fixed steady tempo. The outcome appears smooth but this is achieved by many variations in activities and timing. Reading is no exception to this rule. Studies of eye movements in reading provide the evidence for this. They show that the eyes do not move in a continuous smooth flow along the line of print. Anderson and Dearborn (1952) provide a vivid description of this behavior that is very well established by many studies of eye movements in reading:

> As is well known, in reading the eyes do not move across the line in a continuous sweep. They move rather in a rapid series of stop-and-go movements. The eyes start out at the beginning of the first line, stay there an instant, jump to the next place, stop there briefly, jump again, and so on until the end of the line is reached. The eyes then make the return sweep to the beginning of the next line, at which point a new series of leaps and pauses is initiated (p. 101).

These authors also describe the well-known phenomenon of *regressions* in reading. These are movements of the eyes backward to an earlier point already passed. Kolers (1968) links together our first two general characteristics of skill in a very important observation:

> These two facts, that the eyes do not move continuously and that they sometimes regress, are by themselves sufficient to indicate that reading is a complex process. They imply that the message the reader obtains from printed text is not put together in his mind as a faithful but passive uptake of words in the order in which they appear on the page, because, as a result of eye movements, the order in which they are perceived is different from their order on the page (p. xvi).

The third item in our list of skill characteristics was that the unhesitating behavior of the skilled performer is the product of *integration* or *organization* of many different aspects of behavior. Reid (1973) considers that it is essential to study how the reader "fuses" his or her subskills in "action." She notes that "even the early learning of reading is a process in which the learner has to do a great many things at the same time" (p. 31). Merritt (1970) states that "the essential basis" of skilled reading is "the ability to respond simultaneously to a variety of kinds of sequence. Just as we can respond simultaneously to a variety of attributes of a single object, so we can respond to a variety of attributes of a speech sequence. Thus we can respond to a speech sequence at the level of sound, syntax and meaning simultaneously just as we can respond to a ball in terms of its roundness, speed and hardness simultaneously at the time of catching it in flight, making whatever adjustments are called for by each attribute" (p. 53). (Incidentally, Merritt's analogy with ball games confirms point number 21 in our list of skill characteristics—that is, that there is no fundamental difference between verbal and motor skills in their psychological features—and we need not refer to this again). Goodman, Goodman and Burke (1978) sum up the central importance of integration: "What distinguishes more and less proficient reading is how well integrated it is; how efficiently and effectively cues of all sorts are used, strategies applied, and meaning created" (p. 14).

Timing (characteristic number 4) is widely recognized as an important feature of skilled reading. For example, Bond and Tinker (1973) state: "The proficient reader will have several speeds, each of which can be used as the occasion demands" (p. 451). The research evidence justifies the conclusion by Strang, McCullough and Traxler (1967) that, "The efficient reader varies his speed according to the purpose, according to the difficulty of the content, and according to his familiarity with the type of material" (p. 270). *Speed* is important on some occasions when the purpose of reading demands rapid extraction of information, but *flexibility* of timing is the more noteworthy feature of skill performance in reading.

Being *ready for a wide range of events* was next in our list of features of skills in general. We noted that this means readiness for both the action of others and the consequences of one's own activities. In reading, these two aspects are the actions of the author and the activities of the reader. Many descriptions of reading point out this characteristic interaction between reader and author. For example, Goodman, Goodman and Burke (1978) state: "Reading is language. Language has two aspects—productive and receptive. It is always an interaction between the producer and the receiver. Both are interactive participants in communication. . . . So reading is a receptive written language process, one in which the reader constructs meaning, actively, from a printed display authored by a writer" (p. 10). Goodman (1967) very aptly calls this process a "psycholinguistic guessing game." Clearly, as in any other complex game of skill, the player must be ready for the outcomes of his or her own plays as well as the plays of the other participants in the game. Reading, again, is not different from other skills in this respect. Authors and readers cope with each other's moves several steps ahead, just as in such games as chess or tennis. Some authors are particularly devious in their traps for readers. The skilled reader must be ready for anything.

As in any other skill, this readiness largely depends on the reader's *anticipation* of future events (characteristic number 6)—events produced by the author or outcomes of the reader's own acts. Merritt (1968) conducted experiments that showed that anticipation is an essential feature of skilled reading. When words are presented in random order instead of in their regular sequence, reading speed is significantly reduced. He showed that this is because the reader is prevented from anticipating what words will probably occur next. Merritt's (1970) conclusions from his studies of anticipation subskills in reading are summarized in the following quotation:

> What we have found so far is that one of the responses to a word is the anticipation of the next word. Similarly, one of the responses to a letter or a phoneme is the anticipation of the next letter, or the next phoneme. One of the responses of a group of words, syntactically structured, is the anticipation of the form and class of the next word. Word meanings, too, determine the kinds of word we may anticipate (p. 53).

Merritt's work shows that this anticipation is based to a large extent on transitional probability—the frequency with which these items or classes of items have followed each other in one's previous experience. Thus the interaction of all the different cues produces a substantial curtailment of possibilities. Merritt notes that such anticipations reduce the reader's area of search.

Chapman and Hoffman (1977) illustrate the effects of anticipation in reading skill performance by the following examples:

Text One

a is saying individual the is our aloud ability our in rarely purposes respond reader the silently only skill upon our is word of called conducted reading reading It Most by is private fluent that for element of to to use course one each to

Text Two

The element to use in each individual ability for reading it silently is, of course, only our word of saying. It is a reader that the private skill is aloud called upon to respond. Most to one reading is conducted rarely by our own fluent purposes.

Text Three

The ability to respond to each individual word by saying it aloud is, of course, only one element in reading. It is a skill that the fluent reader is rarely called upon to use. Most of our reading is conducted silently for our own private purposes (p. 67).

All three texts contain exactly the same set of words, but Chapman and Hoffman point out that Text One takes the longest time to read because the word order is random. Text Three takes the shortest time because the word order is normal—what we would anticipate from past experience. But Text Two is not as difficult as Text One because in Text Two the sentence structures are normal even though nouns have been randomized with each other, adjectives have been similarly exchanged with one another and so on. Thus, some anticipation was possible in Text Two. Chapman and Hoffman emphasize the importance of these two types of cues in anticipation in reading—syntactic cues and semantic cues.

Our characteristic number 7 of skills in general was that the skilled performer acts *automatically*. Chapman and Hoffman also stress the automaticity of the anticipation subskills they describe. They write that "fluent readers react quite automatically" to syntactic and semantic cues. They add: "We cannot emphasize too strongly that it is the automatic aspect with which we are concerned" (p. 67). Samuels (1976a) also stresses the importance of automaticity. He writes: "In order to have both fluent reading and good comprehension, the student must be brought beyond accuracy to automaticity in decoding" (p. 323).

The function of automaticity in skill performance is to free one's attention for some other activity. This was our general characteristic number 8. Huey in 1908 stated that, "to perceive an entirely new word . . . requires considerable time and close attention," but "repetition progressively frees the mind from attention to details, makes facile the total act, shortens the time and reduces the extent to which consciousness must concern itself with the process" (p. 104). Oliver (1976), writing nearly three-quarters of a century later, calls this the "principle of automaticity." That is: "The skilled reader must identify words automatically in order to be able to attend to the meaning-getting process" (p. 2).

Skill characteristic number 9 was less clear-cut. We had to say that skill performers are sometimes conscious of their own activities, but at other times they appear to perform without being consciously aware of what they are doing. The latter is true, of course, when the behavior is running off automatically. An important observation here is that the skill performer appears to be able to switch from automatic to conscious attentive control as circumstances require.

Certainly, skilled readers *can be* consciously aware of their own activities. For example, Olshavsky (1976–1977) required tenth grade students to "think aloud" after silently reading each clause of a short story. These verbal protocols were analyzed and ten problem solving strategies were identified. Furthermore, there is evidence that, under more natural reading conditions, awareness of certain aspects of one's own activities is associated with superior skill in reading. Thus, Samuels, Begy and Chen (1975–1976) found that good readers (college students and fourth grade pupils) were significantly more aware of having made false word identifications. Smith (1967) interviewed twelfth grade students after they had read a passage of text. She reported that, "Good readers were more certain of the procedures they used than poor readers were when they read for details." Also, the inferior quality of their answers to questions about the content of the text read arose from "the poor readers' lack of insight into the procedures they used" (p. 81). Flavell (1970), more generally, has found that people's awareness of cognitive processes enables them to modify their processing activities to fit their goals. In summary, skilled readers can become consciously aware of at least some of their reading processes and this consciousness can be used to improve their level of skill.

The term *cue* is as frequently used in describing reading skill as it is in other skills (characteristic number 10). Cronbach's definition of *cue* as any external or internal stimulus that can help recognition or action fits the concept of reading cues. For example, Wheat and Edmond (1975) write that "comprehension is reached through the use of three major cueing systems: (1) graphophonic; (2) syntactic; and (3) semantic" (p. 524). The complexity of the relationships between internal cues and external cues is indicated in the description of these three systems given by Goodman, Goodman and Burke (1978):

1. In an alphabetic writing system, the *graphophonic system* includes the distinctive features of letters and spelling patterns which make up the orthography of the written language, the sound system or phonology, and the phonic system which we define as the relationships between orthography and phonology of the language.
2. The *syntactic system* includes the surface structures, grammatical rules and deep structures of the language itself. In reading and listening as receptive processes, the language user is responding to the surface representation and supplying the rest of the grammar.
3. The *semantic system* of cues is the meaning itself. It depends directly on the experiences and conceptual development of the reader; that is, meaning is input by the reader as well as output from reading. Readers make use of linguistic and conceptual schema as they read (p. 11).

Goodman et al. note that these "three cue systems . . . are always in integral relationship to each other in actual language use."

The use of the concept of *cue* is not restricted to the type of theory represented by the above quotations. *Cue* is widely used by authors with quite divergent views. For example, Samuels, Begy and Chen (1975–1976) write that "a skilled or fluent reader is one who is able to use context and a minimal visual cue as a word recognition strategy. Recognition here is seen as a constructive act, in that having seen but a minimal visual cue, the reader is able to construct the entire word from the partial percept" (p. 75).

Skill characteristic number 11 in our list is also reflected in descriptions of reading. Reading skill like other skills is a process of *translating* cues into appropriate action. Also it is just as true in reading that the translation process is usually so rapid that it is not apparent to an observer. Indeed, because most of the process goes on inside one's head in reading, it is particularly obscure. This has led to much controversy about the nature of this translation process. Unfortunately, the fact that this translation process is not directly observable has also led some authors to ignore it altogether. Therefore, Kolers (1968) comments that "what the reader understands from what he has read is the result of a construction he makes and not the result of a simple transmission of the graphic symbols to his mind. Failure to appreciate this obvious fact invalidates most contemporary theories of reading" (pp. xvi–xvii). One modern theory that does take account of the process of translating cues into action is that stated by Goodman et al. (1978). They believe that "readers are active contributors to the reading process. . . . Reading is an exchange of meanings with an author. While the print is only a code used in the process, reader experience and understanding are the grid through which the author's message is screened" (p. 22).

In reading also *cues come both from within the reader and from the outside environment* (our skill characteristic number 12). Here also the internal aspect is often overlooked in reading because it is less obvious. Many current methods of teaching reading ignore the internal cues and assume that the only relevant cues are those in the external environment—the printed letters of the text. The quotation from Goodman et al. in the preceding paragraph indicates also that an equally important source of cues is within the reader. The passage quoted is concerned with comprehension. The "author's message" produces internal responses that become cues for other activities. For example, the reader may fail to make sense of the author's message and this is the cue for additional information-seeking activities. But internal cues of many other kinds also are recognized by research on the psychology of reading. At this point let us just note one of many possible examples—the electrical activity of nerve cells in speech muscles that accompany silent reading.

Although no movements of the lips or speech organs can be detected by an unaided observer, the firing of nerve cells in the muscles during silent reading can be picked up by the electromyographic (EMG) technique. Electrodes are placed on the surface adjacent to the speech muscles. These detect the electrical activity in the nerves and record it. Such activity occurs even when there is no actual movement of the muscles and no speech sounds are produced. Conrad (1972), reviewing the numerous studies of this phenomenon, concludes that, "the case that appears to be proved is that silent reading is accompanied by articulation" (p. 209). The presence of these internal responses of speech motor nerves raises the possibility that they may become cues for further reactions. Then they would be *cues from within the reader.* Thus Egorov (1953) writes: "The child has only to place his speech organs in a position close to the one in which they are found when they pronounce this word orally for the existing connections to be totally effected. . . . This is how these brain mechanisms operate that are at the basis of the inferential process that takes place when children solve the problems of combining letters and syllables into words" (p. 74).

These two examples from Goodman et al. and Egorov show that cues from within the reader as well as from the printed page in the external environment may be very important in a variety of ways in reading and in the acquisition of reading skill.

Item number 13 in our list was *feedback.* In the teaching of reading the importance of giving students feedback about the quality of responses is generally recognized as a principle of good instruction, but this aspect is to be dealt with in Chapter 3 when we turn to skill acquisition. What is less generally recognized in the field of reading education is that feedback is an essential part of the reading process itself. In all skills from playing golf to flying a jet plane performers are homing in on some target, some outcome, some good result. Feedback gives performers the information they need to adjust their actions to home in on the target. Reading is no exception. Goodman (1976b) considers that the essence of reading is a "constructive . . . search for meaning" (p. 58). Just as tennis players search for the best way to hit the ball in their exchanges with opposing players, so readers search for the best way to interpret the meaningful written signals produced by authors. In this search, just as tennis players predict future moves in the game as far ahead as possible, so readers predict the words that are coming as far ahead as possible. Both in tennis playing and in reading, skill performers constantly adjust and revise their predictions as they receive feedback on their accuracy. Thus Goodman (1976b) writes: "In reading, as in listening, the language user must continuously predict underlying grammatical patterns because it is from these that meaning may be decoded" (p. 60). Goodman asserts that "the search for meaning is itself what makes it possible for the reader to predict the grammatical structures" (p. 64). He suggests: "Readers' language competence enables them to create a grammatical and semantic prediction in which they need only sample from the print to reach meaning" (p. 59). The essential element of feedback is recognized by Goodman, Goodman and Burke (1978), for example, when they write that "readers monitor to make sure that further sampling confirms their predictions. Disconfirmation brings regressing, reprocessing and correction" (p. 13). The most skilled readers are those who make the best use of feedback. Goodman's (1976b) research on miscues led him to conclude that "more proficient readers have an ability to recognize when their miscues need correction" (p. 70).

Reading skill requires *selective attention* no less than does any other skill (characteristic number 14). As early as 1908, Huey observed that "far more is quietly ignored" than is read "intensely" (p. 404). In recent years, more detailed studies of selective attention in reading have shown it to be an essential subskill. Serafica and Sigel (1970) point out that the reader "must scan for relevant information and distinguish them [relevant cues] from irrelevant cues" (p. 107). They compared a group of boys who were retarded in reading with a matched control group of boys who were normal readers. It was found that on a cognitive styles test the retarded readers were more analytic in their responses than the normal readers. Serafica and Sigel state: "The boys with reading disability in this study do not seem lacking in an analytic ability. If the initial phase of learning to read requires differentiation of graphic symbols from one another, the nonreaders were better equipped for that task than were the boys who showed no reading problems" (p. 111). This is reminiscent of an earlier finding by Solomon cited by Robinson (1953a). The only predictive result of a Rorschach Test was the undue concern with unimportant details shown by some of her eight-year-old subjects. These children were more prone to reading disability. Skill development is closely related to learning what to ignore as well as what is important to attend to. As Clay (1972) has put it: "the child must learn where and how to attend to print" (p. 162). Reading skill, like other skills, is more efficient as the performer's sensitivity to cues changes in various ways.

In our general list of skill characteristics the first type of change in sensitivity that we noted was the *shift from external cues to internal cues* (item number 15). We noted earlier that internal cues are an important feature of reading skill. Several writers also have described how the importance of internal cues increases as skill develops. For example, Harris and Sipay (1975) note that "the beginner has to read aloud to obtain meaning. Gradually he reduces the response to mumbling, to silent lip movement, to subvocal reading with tiny movements that cannot easily be detected, to a 'hearing' of the words (in other words, having an auditory image without any detectable motor accompaniment), and finally, in a comparatively few exceptionally fast readers, to an instantaneous flash of meaning that seems to have no special motor or sensory accompaniment" (pp. 558–559). It might be thought, perhaps, that this gradual internalization would be eliminated if children were taught to read silently from the beginning, as in McDade's (1937) nonoral method. However, Buswell's (1945) research found that the nonoral method failed to eliminate lip movements as the theory had predicted. The proportion of children exhibiting actual lip movements in the nonoral classes was almost the same as in the classes learning by regular oral methods. As was noted earlier, when these speech movements become only vestigial they may continue to provide internal feedback cues.

Our list's next item (number 16) noted that *perceptual units of increasing size* are utilized as the performer's skill improves. This is widely accepted in reading. Smith and Dechant (1961) stated: "The good reader is not limited to word-by-word reading. He has become proficient in seeing meaningful relationships among the words that he reads. Such reading may be called thought-unit reading" (p. 217). Dechant and Smith (1977, p. 124) further explained that "thought-unit reading" should not be wrongly identified with the concept of phrase seeing or the suggestion of seeing three or four words per fixation. Quoting results of reading eye–camera studies, they pointed out that thought units "must consist of a series of fixations." Gibson and Levin (1976) have emphasized this feature more strongly:

> Written words, like spoken ones, are of course combined into still higher-order structures, like phrases and sentences and paragraphs. Higher-order structures, once detected by the learner, provide him with larger units of information that he may be able to process as wholes or "chunks," a very great cognitive economy. We are going to suggest and elaborate as we proceed the proposition that *the reader processes the largest structural unit that he is capable of perceiving and that is adaptive (has utility) for the task he is engaged in* (p. 23).

Bond and Tinker (1973) indicate that learning to read in thought units can be observed already in first grade and that this subskill develops steadily through the primary and intermediate grades.

The distinction between larger units of perception and *larger units of action* is less clear in the research literature on reading than it is in publications about other skills. Possibly this is because the distinction between perception of the text and the reading reaction to it is harder to distinguish in this skill. But Drever's (1964) *Dictionary of Psychology* defines *perception* thus: "The process of recognizing or identifying something" (p. 206). His definition of perception might be acceptable as a possible definition of reading itself. Furthermore, perception in general is by no means a passive taking in of external stimuli. Thus Piaget (1969a) asserts:

> The subject does not submit himself to the constraints of the object but directs his perceptual activities as if he were solving a problem. . . . What is more remarkable is the number of steps involved in making even the most elementary estimation, such as size; far from remaining receptive, the subject proceeds by a method of sampling, selecting the most profitable point of concentration, hoping to multiply encounters and co-ordinate them by an exercise of couplings (p. 363).

The relevance of these remarks for reading is even more obvious as Piaget continues: "When it becomes a question of the identification of objects, even more complex activities are required."

Nevertheless, no matter where we try to draw the arbitrary boundary between reception of the visual stimuli of the text and the process of translating them into action in getting meaning, the total effect is that the reader copes with larger and larger chunks of text as skill develops.

Cue reduction and addition was number 18 in our list of characteristics of skills in general. It was the fourth way in which sensitivity to cues changes as skill develops. This type of change is clearly recognizable in reading also. Anderson and Dearborn (1952) devoted several pages to the topic. They wrote: "Cue reduction refers to the refinement of a skill and to the elimination of waste motion. In the case of reading, the concept of cue reduction applies not only to the motor side of the performance but also to the sensory side, in that, with time, fewer cues from the printed page or less of the original pattern of stimulation is required to get the meaning" (p. 162). Harris and Sipay also make explicit reference to cue reduction which they say is "a gradual process" that leads to the "attainment of true silent reading" (p. 558). Wheat and Edmond provide a specific example of cue reduction when they note that "the beginning reader uses many graphophonic cues which decrease in use as he reaches proficiency" (p. 525). Indeed, the same authors point out that "to use all of the cues available would be inefficient" (p. 524). When this is attempted, it "causes slow and nonfluent reading" (p. 525).

Wheat and Edmond mention also the phenomenon of cue addition when they declare: "To become a proficient reader it is necessary, then, to increase the use of nonvisual information (syntactic and semantic cue systems) and decrease the use of visual information (graphophonic cue system)" (p. 525). There are many other ways in which cue addition takes place; for example, in learning the significance of different print styles such as italics.

As to our characteristic number 19—that the ability to *cope with stress* increases as skill develops—there appears to be little discussion in the reading field. Sherman (1968) remarked that "the emotional disturbances of the poor reader . . . increasingly interfere with reading ability" (p. 348). The way in which the stress of failure in reading may produce disintegration of the level of skill already acquired is described by Zolkos (1958):

> Difficulty or failure in learning to read may lead to such a degree of fear-conditioning that the sight of reading material causes a disorganized emotional response which further inhibits concentration, perseverance, and motivation (p. 256).

But there does not appear to have been any study of the effects of reading under stressful conditions among highly skilled and less skilled readers.

General skill characteristic number 20 in our list had to be discussed at some length because of the confusion that is attached to the concept of skill as a *hierarchy of subskills.* Concerning the skill of reading there also appears to be much ambiguity and controversy regarding the hierarchical nature of subskills.

Artley (1980) is critical of the popular "preoccupation with skill teaching" (p. 546) which he traces to its origins in the "accountability-behavioral objectives-criterion referenced testing-management system movement" (p. 547). Downing (1981), in his review of Holmes' substrata-factor theory, argues that this overuse of the word *skill* has debased its meaning and is causing confusion among educators. It is not only that *skill* is used where *subskill* would be more accurate. Unfortunately, *skill* is used sometimes when writers are referring to activities that are not even subskills. For example, Gross, Carr, Dornseif and Rouse (1974) write: "A critical part of any reading or language arts program is the teaching of the skills underlying the reading process. Without the basic skills of word discrimination, vocabulary development, and comprehension, it is virtually impossible for a student to read new material with success" (p. 782). They go on to list a "set of behavioral objectives [that] comprises the skills programs" (p. 783) such as: "Given a sentence with a heteronym, the student will identify correctly, from the context, the syllable that is accented" (p. 784). Gross et al. seem to use *skill* to mean something like *task*. This vague use of the term *skill* is very common in the reading field.

Lansdown (1974) states the widely held view that "reading is a skill . . . organized in a hierarchy of subskills, with the very simple, like recognition of patterns, coming first and the very subtle, for example, skimming a page to gain a quick impression, coming last" (pp. 4–5). But Lansdown expressively points out how this term *hierarchy* may prove disappointing in its hint of a neat fixed order of development: "Unfortunately, this hierarchy of skills does not unfold, layer after layer, like an onion. It is more like a plate of spaghetti, with a recognizable top and bottom and many overlapping bits in the middle" (p. 5). This comment from Lansdown serves to warn us of what we are about to find when we study this notion of reading as a hierarchy of subskills.

One theorist who takes this view of reading is Samuels (1976b). In his article, "Hierarchical Subskills in the Reading Acquisition Process," he quite appropriately links the reading skill to psychological research on skills in general. However, what was pointed out earlier in this chapter must be borne in mind when evaluating Samuels' theory—namely that there is a considerable division of opinion among psychologists as to what the term *hierarchy* implies in relation to the subskills that are said to comprise a given skill. The following quotations from Samuels' article show his use of the classical concept of a hierarchy of subskills:

- Psychologists have known for a considerable length of time that in learning complex skills, mastery of subordinate units must precede final goal attainment (p. 168).
- smaller units are mastered prior to mastering the larger units (p. 170).
- subskill mastery is necessary prior to achieving skill in reading (p. 170).
- successful attainment of the final task may be facilitated by helping the student to master the lower-order units (p. 171).

But Samuels is the most searching critic of his own theoretical position and, as we shall see shortly, he does not adhere to the simplistic view of the fixed sequence of instructional steps that is promoted by so many methods experts. Nonetheless, Samuels' final paragraph in this article states:

> Although at the present time we do not have validated learning hierarchies in reading, we do have a fairly good idea of what the necessary subskills may be. We need to continue our work on validating a minimal set of subskills and on determining their optimal sequence (p. 177).

Earlier in the same article, Samuels states: "Despite the fact that . . . commercial reading series, with their scope and sequence charts, order the reading tasks as if we did know the nature of the learning hierarchy in reading, the sad truth is that the task is so complex that a validated reading hierarchy does not exist" (p. 174). Stennet, Smythe and Hardy (1975) arrived at a similar conclusion: " 'What to teach?' and 'In what order?' All commercially available kindergarten and primary-level reading programs have answers to these questions implicit in them; none provide a sound rationale or adequate documentation for either the relevance of their skill content or the sequence of instruction" (pp. 223–224). The same authors could find "little consensus about either what the essential subskills are or what the nature of the hierarchical organization is" (p. 223).

Bourque (1980) compared two methodologies for establishing hierarchical relationships (the Dayton and Macready (1976) model, and the White and Clark (1973) procedure) using criterion-referenced data. Reading experts were asked to express opinions to establish an hypothesized hierarchy. Bourque found that these experts' opinions were less stable than the hierarchies based on the empirical data obtained with either model. Thompson and Dziuban (1973) reviewed criterion referenced tests that focus on allegedly specific subskills in reading. They concluded that these tests are based on an "unsubstantiated assumption . . . that there exists an empirically derived hierarchy of reading skills. Certainly, this hierarchy is implicit when students must pass one skill before proceeding to the next. But, as yet, this assumption is faulty since no evidence is available to support this contention" (p. 294).

The way this assumption has frequently been made is illustrated by a statement from the Stanford Research Institute (1977): "Basic skills in reading can be identified by *defining* the reading tasks needed in everyday life (basic literacy), by *listing* those skills that are the basis of all reading (basic decoding skills), by *delineating* the reading level of printed materials at various grade levels and *defining* basic reading skills as the ability to read these graded materials (functional reading levels)" (p. 189, italics added to note nonempirical basis). O'Donnell (1980) contrasts this statement with Farr's (1979) testimony at Senator Thomas F. Eagleton's hearings on the teaching and learning of basic academic skills in schools:

> We are demanding a "return to the basics" without knowing exactly what we mean by the basics in terms of reading skills and subskills or content control (p. 10).

Some researchers have conducted scientific experiments to test the validity of some of the alleged subskills in reading. McNeil (1974) tested 150 children aged seven to nine on competence in oral reading and on fifteen highly valued subskills in word attack. Three subskills were found to be false prerequisites (for instance: "distinguishing meaning of homographs") and a fourth subskill was on the borderline of being categorized as a "false prerequisite" by the data. Four other subskills were identified as "possibly necessary but not sufficient" (e.g., one of these was "matching of rhyming words"). The seven remaining subskills had been mastered by nearly all the competent readers and by only a few incompetent readers (for instance: "determining the number of syllables"), but McNeil points out that "it is possible that competent readers acquired some of these skills after or as a concomitant in learning to read, not as a prerequisite" (p. 426). Friend's (1980) small experiment found that even literal and inferential comprehension could not be differentiated empirically as separate subskills.

A research technique that has been used a number of times to try to identify the important subskills in reading is factor analysis, including other variations of this statistical procedure for analyzing the correlations between tests. In factor analysis proper, a matrix of intercorrelations between a variety of tests is studied to determine if there are distinct factors in the overall skill and what their order of importance is in explaining the level of performance. It is inferred that this order reflects the level of the subskill in the hierarchy.

For example, Davis (1968) conducted a large-scale study of eight subskills of reading comprehension among twelfth grade students. His factor analysis procedure led him to conclude that five of the eight subskills were distinct: (1) "recalling word meanings"; (2) "finding answers to questions answered explicitly or in paraphrase"; (3) "drawing inferences from the content"; (4) "recognizing a writer's purpose, attitude, tone and mood"; (5) "following the structure of a passage." Thorndike (1971) reanalysed Davis' data by a different statistical method and claimed that 93 per cent of the nonchance variance could be accounted for by one factor alone which he believed to be mainly a measure of reasoning. Only one of Davis' tests was distinguishable from the others—that of "recalling word meanings." Spearritt (1972) made a further refactorization of Davis' data with yet another statistical method and verified that Davis' original conclusions had been technically correct, except that the subskill of "finding answers to questions answered explicitly or in paraphrase" was not distinguishable. But Spearritt added that "it must be stressed that, although the four skills are distinguishable, some of them are only just so." Spearitt's conclusion is that "although certain comprehension skills can be differentiated, present types of reading comprehension tests . . . largely measure one basic ability, which may well correspond to the label of 'reasoning in reading' " (p. 110).

These types of results are frustrating to anyone hoping to discover the basic subskills of reading from such research methods. Samuels (1976b) believes that a fault in their design has produced misleading results. He points to the studies' "failure to differentiate between good and poor readers in the analysis" (p. 173). The intercorrelations among subskills were high because the good readers had mastered them all. Guthrie (1973) did analyze intercorrelations separately for good and poor readers. He found that, while intercorrelations were high among good readers, they were low among the poor readers, indicating that the separate subskills had not been mastered in the latter group. But this does not overcome McNeil's objection that one cannot tell by such methods whether the subskills are the cause or effect of a high level of reading skill.

Stennett et al. (1975) in their review of statistical approaches to this problem note a vital logical weakness. "A correlation technique . . . does not allow one to conclude that mastery of one skill is *dependent* upon mastery of another" (p. 224). They conclude that, by these statistical methods, "The problem of elucidating the hierarchical organization or functional interdependence of the key subskills underlying the complex skill of reading is a major and unanswered one" (p. 227).

Some writers are highly skeptical of the existence of any fixed hierarchy of subskills in reading. Jansen (1968), in his article "How Long Will We Go on Waiting for 'the Great Pumpkin'?", expressed impatience with the common notion that there exists any one correct scope and sequence of methods of reading instruction. Hoskisson (1975) writes: "Perhaps one of education's greatest delusions is that we teach children to read. All that may really occur is that materials are presented to a child in one form or another and he uses them to solve the reading problem" (p. 446). Goodman (1970) specifically rejects these implications of the concept of reading skill as a hierarchy of subskills: "There is no possible sequencing of skills in reading instruction since all systems must be used independently in the reading process even in the first attempts at learning to read" (p. 25).

However, as we noted in discussing the concept of a hierarchy of subskills, under number 20 in our list of characteristics of skills in general, more recent writings have suggested that the hierarchy may exist in degree of control over skill usage without there being any necessary sequence of either learning or performance. Samuels (1976b), an important advocate of the search for subskills and their hierarchical organization, recognizes that "it makes no difference to the final outcome in which order they are introduced" (p. 174) in reading instruction. With regard to the performance of reading skill itself, Posner, Lewis and Conrad (1972) believe that although it is perfectly feasible to isolate subsystems of reading skill these do not operate in a "successive and additive" manner "especially in tasks like reading" (p. 160). They cite Levin and Kaplan (1970) in support of their own view that "complex visual processing moves ahead of, as well as being simultaneous with, other components of the reading task." Posner et al. conclude that "we must avoid the human predilection for single orderings (DeSoto, 1961) by recognizing that different children may find their strengths in different subskills" (p. 186).

One of the most interesting of all theories of reading dealt with this problem of the organization of subskills exceptionally well. It was put forward by Holmes in several publications in the 1950s and 1960s. Holmes (1970) expressed his "Substrata-Factor Theory of Reading" in appropriately formal, precise, premised statements. For example, he wrote:

> *In essence, the Substrata-Factor Theory holds that, normally, reading is an audiovisual verbal-processing-skill of symbolic reasoning, sustained by the interfacilitations of an intricate hierarchy of substrata factors that have been mobilized as a psychological working-system and pressed into service in accordance with the purposes of the reader* (pp. 187–188).

Holmes' theory takes account of many problems in explaining both the reading process and the learning-to-read process. For example, his concept of "mobilizers" explains how reading may be influenced by neurological dysfunctions even though reading is far too new historically in the repertoire of human behavior for it to have evolved any specific neural system or organ of its own. Holmes states that mobilizers are "conative tendencies . . . that function to select from one's repertoire of subabilities those which will maximize one's chances of solving a specific problem . . ." (p. 188). These subabilities may be modules of behavior generally available for human behavior other than reading.

The concept of a *working-system* in Holmes' theory provides a much more feasible description of how subskills may be organized for hierarchical control. He wrote: "A working-system may be described as a dynamic set of subabilities which have been mobilized for the purpose of solving a particular problem. Neurologically, a working-system is conceived of as a nerve-net pattern in the brain that functionally links together the various substrata factors that have been mobilized into a workable communications system" (p. 189). This makes it perfectly possible that "different individuals may perform the same task to an equal degree of success by drawing upon different sets of subabilities. In other words, we hypothesize that there is more than one way to solve an intellectual problem" (p. 189).

The *reasoning* in the reading process was of central importance, in Holmes' view. Holmes was one of the first people in this field to recognize that children's cognitive clarity about the purposes and techniques of reading depends on clear understanding of the tasks that they are given in reading instruction. Here is his strong plea to teachers on this matter:

> The point I wish to drive home is this, the careful selection of meaningful material, the logic of our explanations, the continuity of our theme in the classroom lesson, the unit, and the total curriculum are important not only because they foster clarity and understanding at the time, but because the logic-and-fact of the sequential input is the essential element in teaching that leads the child *himself* to develop those habits of cortical association which determine not only the nature and efficiency of recall, but also the degrees of freedom or versatility a child may have for reorganizing his working-systems later on when, in fact, reorganization is necessary and desirable, if the process of symbolic reasoning is to be both logical and creative—that is, if it is to maximize creativity in the transfer of training process (p. 191).

Holmes used a type of factor analytic technique to try to identify the *subability* elements that can be mobilized into different *working-systems*. In his 1960 paper, he had isolated thirteen crucial variables. (Other analyses were made subsequently). These elements seem to have a similar status to the *subskills* in other theories. Here we need not concern ourselves with the specific subskill-variables identified in Holmes' analyses. They have been subjected to methodological criticism by other researchers concerned with statistical formulae (for example, Carroll, 1968b). Holmes' chief contribution to the debate on the hierarchy of subskills in reading is his theoretical explanation of how subskills may be mobilized as needed to cope with a wide range of problems of reasoning that arise one after the other in rapid succession as a reader plays the psycholinguistic guessing game with an author.

Singer has continued this work on the substrata-factor theory. Singer (1964) clearly describes how a hierarchy of elements can be flexibly organized. He writes that underlying "speed and power of reading" is "a complexly interwoven hierarchy of elements and processes. The elements are mobilized into substrata factors and organized into working-systems that function at various substrata levels according to the momentary purposes of the reader and the demands of the material. Hence, as the individual reads he constantly organizes and reorganizes the elements . . ." (p. 315). With reference to progressive development, Singer (1971) states: "As an individual's subsystems improve in variety, magnitude, and intercommunicability . . . he becomes more flexible in organizing and reorganizing his subsystems" (p. 108).

In recent years, there has been an increasing interest in naturalistic observational studies of what people actually *do* in reading and what children *do* when learning how to read. Some of these studies seem to fit Holmes' theory of skill development in reading. For example, Francis (1977), in a study of beginning readers' oral reading errors, concluded that "children seem to bring to initial reading those analytic, mostly intuitive, problem-solving skills that characterize human learning in general" (p. 125). This confirms Singer's (1966) proposition that: "Children have learned to read by means of a wide variety of methods and materials. . . . However, all the necessary elements for reading are present in the materials employed by each method so that pupils in learning to read through any of these methods could have used their capabilities for selecting their own unit of perception, their own conceptualized mediational response systems, and developed their own mental organization for attaining speed and power of reading" (pp. 116–117).

Thus, in reading, as in other skills, the hierarchy of subskills seems likely to be *modular* in organization. Once a subskill element is mastered, it becomes a module available for use in a variety of working-systems for solving specific reasoning problems during reading. This modular organization may be hierarchical in terms of control without there being any necessity for a fixed sequence of either learning or performance.

Summary

In this chapter we have summarized the wealth of psychological research evidence on the characteristics of skills. We found twenty-one major generalizations about the acquisition of skills in general that an eclectic psychologist would be likely to accept. Then we went on to examine whether observations of behavior in reading and in learning to read fit these twenty-one generalizations. We found that the fit is very good. Therefore, we conclude that psychological research findings on skill acquisition in general can be applied with confidence to the specific skill of learning to read.

Principles of Skill Acquisition in Reading

CHAPTER 3

In the preceding chapter, it became clear that reading in every respect fits the description of a skill as defined by psychologists. Therefore, we can confidently apply what psychological research has discovered about skill acquisition in general to learning to read in particular.

Phases of Skill Development

Fitts' (1962) review of the research on skill learning in general led him to conclude that there are three phases in the development of any skill. We shall call them the *cognitive, mastering,* and *automaticity* phases. They occur in that order, although, of course, they are really one continuous process without any distinct boundary between them. Also, it should be noted that, in a very complex skill like reading, these three phases must be continually recurring as each new subskill is encountered by the learner during the many years needed to become a fully skilled reader.

The initial *cognitive phase* is the stage in which the learner, according to Cronbach (1977, p. 396), "in an unfamiliar situation must find out what to do." Thus the beginner "is getting in mind just what is to be done" (p. 398). Therefore it is important when teaching a skill to make the task clearly understandable in the initial stages. In research on learning to fly a plane, for example, it was found that the average number of hours needed to learn to fly solo could be reduced from eight to four, if special attention was given to helping students to understand their tasks (Williams and Flexman, 1949; Flexman, Matheny, and Brown, 1950). The usual length of this phase in adults is comparatively brief—a few hours or days, but it may be much longer in children learning to read.

In the *mastering phase,* learners work toward a perfect performance of the skill. They practice until they achieve a high level of accuracy with almost no errors. This stage may last for days, months, or even years, depending on the complexity of the skill and opportunities for practice.

Once the skill is mastered, however, there is still a very important stage ahead. This is the *automaticity phase* which comes about through overlearning. *Overlearning* is practice beyond the point of mastery. When overlearning is accomplished, expert performers can run through the skill effortlessly, with rare errors—automatically, and they do so, unless some unusual problem arises that makes it necessary for them to become conscious of their activities.

Vernon (1957) was among the first psychologists to stress the importance of the cognitive phase in learning to read. Her review of the extensive research on the causes of reading disability led her to conclude: "Thus the fundamental and basic characteristic of reading disability appears to be cognitive confusion" (p. 71). She commented in passing that this confusion seemed to be similar to that found in normal beginning readers. Downing (1971–72) obtained objective evidence of beginners' cognitive confusion in experiments with five-year-olds in England. His results are summarized by Downing and Thackray (1975):

> These children's responses, as the year moved on, could be compared with the clearing of fog. Gradually out of confusion came a clearer and clearer understanding of the nature of the learning and problem-solving tasks they were required to undertake (p. 65).

Numerous other studies confirm that it is normal for children to appear confused in the initial cognitive phase of learning to read.

Cronbach mentions another significance of the cognitive phase. He states that, "The change from conscious step-by-step direction to an automatic performance is in large part due to the dropping out of *mediating responses*. . . . Each of the mediating responses at this early stage is a thought leading the performer one step along the way. In a chain such as this a response is also a stimulus for the next step. The beginner's performance, broken into steps, is clumsy. With practice the separate mediating responses become unnecessary" (p. 271).

These mediating responses often require the development of new concepts and associated terminology. De Cecco and Crawford (1974) note that "the student's own descriptions of the skill may be an important aid to learning" (p. 277), and they cite Ozolin's (1958) experiment as evidence. In it, an experimental group was given special training in the terminology of complex gymnastic exercises. They learned more effectively than a control group that was given no special attention regarding these technical terms.

In reading instruction, a very complex set of special technical terms and their underlying concepts is used by teachers. Downing (1980b) gives this example of the way in which the child's thinking may become confused by the terminology of reading instruction. Imagine the effect on the child who hears something like this:

> *This is how you sove the zasp "bite." It is tebbed with the rellangs fly, ear, milk, wow. The last rellang is the holy wow. When you have a holy wow at the end of a zasp the ear says ear not ook like it does in the zasp "bit"* (p. 17).

Yet this may not be such an uncommon experience for beginners in the cognitive phase of learning to read, as the translation of the nonsense words into standard terminology shows:

> *This is how you* write *the* word *"bite." It is* spelt *with the* letters bee, eye, tea, ee. *The last* letter *is the* silent ee. *When you have a* silent ee *at the end of a* word *the* eye *says* eye *not* i *like it does in the* word *"bit"* (p. 36).

Beginners have nothing to translate to. The nonsense of unknown terminology remains nonsense to them. Francis (1973) found that, for the English primary school pupils she studied, "the use of words like *letter, word* and *sentence* in teaching was not so much a direct aid to instruction but a challenge to find their meaning" (p. 22). Similarly, in Russia, Egorov (1953) found that "the conceptual difficulties of this initial period of reading instruction are serious. Therefore, the teacher must take special care to avoid adding to the pupils' difficulties by introducing any unnecessary complications. For example, a common teaching error in the pre-primer period is flooding young beginners with too many new concepts, such as 'sentence,' 'word,' 'syllable,' 'sound,' 'letter,' and so on." Numerous other investigations have confirmed that young beginners enter the reading acquisition task with a paucity of metalinguistic concepts. Two recent research reports both contain extensive reviews of the theoretical and research literature—Dopstadt, Laubscher and Ruperez (1980), and Templeton and Spivey (1980).

The technical terms used in discussing writing and reading belong in what DeStefano (1972) has called the "Language Instruction Register." This is the special language used for the social purpose of teaching language skills. DeStefano (1980) writes that a lack of understanding of this register "can have important instructional consequences, especially if the teacher has formed the prior belief that a student's definition of terms in the Language Instruction Register 'fits' the teacher's" (p. 812). This register is sometimes referred to as "metalinguistics." However, it is not the register itself which is of primary importance. More significant are the concepts which are labeled by these metalinguistic terms. It is these concepts that are needed for reasoning about the learning tasks in the cognitive phase, although the terminology, once it is understood, becomes effective in mediating responses.

Marcel (1980) stresses the need to distinguish between "*use* of language and our *reflexive awareness* of language. The first in no way implies the second." He notes "the fact that all people who adequately perceive and produce speech are at some level of description segmenting and combining phonemes stands side-by-side with the fact that not only are most people unaware of this but that many people have great difficulty in understanding what they are doing" (p. 389). As Fischer (1980) comments: "The child's success in internalizing the strategies for reading may, at least in part, depend upon his overt awareness of the formal properties of language" (p. 35). It needs to be added that this awareness can stem from the child's own natural experiences of written language. Wiseman and Watson (1980) conclude from their review of several studies of children's early spontaneous experimentation with writing that "these four- and five-year-old children show us that knowledge about print production occurs before formal instruction" (p. 753).

But learners' development of skill in the cognitive phase depends not only on their concepts of its distinctive features. It depends also on their concepts of its functions. Downing (1979a) emphasizes that concepts of the purposes of literacy are an integral part of the skills of reading and writing. The *way* one reads and the *way* one writes depend on one's purposes, and the link between purpose and technique needs to be understood and mastered to automaticity. Smith (1980) also stresses this point: "Children come to understand how language works by understanding the purposes and intentions of the people who produce it, and they learn to produce language themselves to the extent that it fulfills their own purposes or intentions" (p. 155). Klein and Schickedanz (1980) have described how children in their kindergarten study learned the purposes of written language: "Perhaps the most important discovery that children made was that writing is functional. Children learned that print is a tool for communication and that writing has a purpose" (p. 748). This discovery occurred through the children's writing of messages. Other reading educators have asserted that teachers should structure the classroom situation so that students will develop concepts of the varied purposes of literacy (for a review, see Shanahan, 1980). Thus, Page (1980) believes that, "Reading instruction should include helping youngsters to understand how it feels to make sense of an author's message. We can do this by helping our students to find, formulate, and solve problems for which using written language is a solution, problems that they see as important although we may not" (p. 231). Golden (1980) is another writer among many who affirm that "The teacher who creates a rich environment with authentic purposes for writing will help to assist the child in developing an awareness of writing as a natural process for communication" (p. 762). Downing's (1979) *Reading and Reasoning* provides numerous examples of teaching methods that have been created specifically to develop children's concepts of the functions of literacy and their concepts of the linguistic features of speech and writing.

During the 1970s, more and more research findings pointed to the need for greater emphasis on cognitive rather than on perceptual factors in learning to read. For example, the study by Rupley, Ashe and Buckland (1979) concluded that "the epistemology of interpreting word recognition reading problems as being due primarily to perceptual processing handicaps may be contraproductive. Learning difficulties may be more closely related to cognitive variables than they are to perceptual abilities" (p. 123). Downing, Ayers and Schaefer (1978), in a study of 300 Canadian kindergarten children, compared measures of their cognitive and perceptual development as related to learning to read. They found evidence that attention should be given in school to children's cognitive needs, since most children were already fully capable of coping with perceptual aspects of the reading task. This shift of emphasis in teaching is increasingly being recognized by reading specialists. For example, Greenslade (1980) writes that "teachers must focus on the conceptual tasks faced by the learner" (p. 195). We have devoted rather a large amount of space to the cognitive phase of the acquisition of reading skill because, despite its great importance, it is often neglected in the teaching of reading. The mastering and automaticity phases will be treated further, as we study the details of psychological principles of learning a skill.

Basic Learning Principles

It is assumed that students reading this book will have already completed basic courses in human learning. In the sections that follow, only those learning principles that are especially relevant for skill acquisition in general and learning to read in particular will be discussed.

Knowledge of Results

Cronbach (1977, p. 404) recognizes two different aspects of feedback: "Internal feedback (knowledge of the act itself) shades over into 'knowledge of results' (from outside). . . . Knowledge of the end result—that his arrow hit the target, or was six inches too high—affects his next shot." It is this second aspect of feedback that concerns us here. It produces improvement in learning a skill in two ways—cognitively and affectively. Cognitively, feedback provides learners with information about their performances that allows them to make adjustments to improve their accuracy. Affectively, feedback may encourage or discourage performers and affect their motivation for future learning.

McDonald (1965) succinctly summarizes the psychological research findings on the cognitive effect of feedback: "Experimental evidence clearly indicates that knowledge of correct performance or performance errors rapidly improves the learning of a performance pattern." This is because, "As the learner attempts responses, he can revise his performance only on the basis of information about its accuracy. Without this information, he may continue to make the same error over and over again" (p. 400). This principle is very well understood by teachers of reading. For example, the cloze procedure with feedback can be used to break the habit of slow reading. The cloze procedure consists of presenting pupils with reading passages with every fifth word (for instance) deleted. Downing (1976) writes: "It is probably most useful as a remedial technique for slow readers who are inhibited from guessing by their early conditioning. The cloze technique, *with feedback about the positive results of their guesses,* seems likely to overcome their inhibitions and encourage them to develop and use the subskill of intelligent use of context clues" (pp. 58–59).

One of the problems in teaching skills is that feedback information may not be obvious to the learner. As reading skill develops, direct feedback increases as readers learn to more rapidly detect their own failure to understand the author's message and adjust their efforts accordingly. In the early stages of learning to read, as is the case in the beginnings of many other skills, feedback clues are not recognized. Borger and Seaborne note, "The only criteria which the learner understands and can recognize may be a long way, in time, from his present activity" (p. 139). In this situation, "the provision of a usable criterion becomes important" (p. 138). McDonald gives an example: "Some other person or mechanical device must inform the learner about his accuracy—a child attempting a multiplication problem cannot tell whether he has made a mistake unless the teacher checks the correctness of his answer" (p. 401).

Annet (1964) distinguishes between these two types of feedback as *intrinsic* (directly observable results of one's own actions) and *extrinsic* (indirectly provided by the teacher or teaching device). Annet states that it is preferable that pupils be taught to employ indicators of successful performance that will be available to them when they will not have their teacher present to guide them. De Cecco and Crawford indicate that, as skill acquisition moves from the mastering phase into the automaticity phase of development, "we rely less on extrinsic and more on intrinsic feedback. In this way our skill learning becomes self-evaluative" (p. 260).

The application of these findings of psychological research to classroom teaching is brought home to us by Bruner (1971):

> There is a very crucial matter about acquiring a skill—be it chess, political savvy, biology, or skiing. The goal must be plain; one must have a sense of where one is trying to get to in any given instance of activity. For the exercise of skill is governed by an intention and feedback on the relation between what one has intended and what one has achieved thus far—"knowledge of results." Without it, the generativeness of skilled operations is lost (pp. 113–114).

Purposeful activities in reading and writing at the beginning stage are vital for three reasons. First, as Bruner argues, skill learners must know what they are trying to accomplish. Second, there is the factor of motivation. Purposeful reading is intrinsically motivating. Third, knowing the purposes of reading is an essential part of the skill because the psychological process changes with the purpose.

Motivation is enhanced by children's understanding of the purposes of reading. Downing and Thackray (1975) give this example:

> If children are unready for reading because they do not understand its *purpose,* then, the "reading" we introduce them to must be fitted to this need in the child. Clearly, the child should meet real-life examples of the communication and expressive purposes of written language. In all schools, reading can be integrated naturally with other activities which children understand more immediately. For example, five-year-olds enjoy making things to eat. If they share the experience of looking up the recipe with their teacher or with older children who already can read, they learn

through such realistic experiences the true purpose of written language (p. 88).

Hunter and Harman (1979) observe that practical experiences in literacy projects in third-world countries provide a lesson for combatting adult illiteracy in the United States. They show us that the illiterates themselves must participate in designing and conducting such educational efforts and that these efforts must be directed to the needs that these people themselves perceive, not to objectives set by others. We would go even further and generalize this principle to the child beginning in school.

The third important reason for purposeful reading from the beginning stage onward is the well-established fact in psychological research that the purpose of the reading act is inextricably interwoven in its technique. Purpose in reading is like the gear shift system in an automobile. The total process cannot be separated from the essential shift system that changes dynamically according to the driver's (or reader's) purpose and the level of difficulty of the road (or book).

An indication of the key significance of purpose in reading was also given by two classical studies. Both Gray (1917) and Judd and Buswell (1922) found that eye movements in reading change according to reading purpose. As we shall see in Chapter 8, the eyes are literally extensions of the brain and provide us with an opportunity to observe changes in brain processes. When eye movements change, there is a change of brain process; such changes occur when readers change their purposes for reading. Eye movements also change when the level of difficulty of the reading material changes (Buswell, 1926; Tinker, 1958, 1965). This reflects a modification in the reader's intentions: for example, to slow down because the material is more difficult.

Research by other methods also shows how the reader's purpose influences the processes of comprehension and retention. For example, Postman and Senders (1946) showed by experiment that college students' reading comprehension was significantly influenced by the purpose they were instructed to adopt. Rickards and August (1975) found that college students "who were free to underline any one sentence per paragraph recalled significantly more incidental material than those explicitly instructed to underline the one sentence per paragraph that was most important to the overall meaning of each paragraph" (p. 864). The Rickards and August study suggests that setting one's own purpose may bring the highest returns in comprehension. Russell (1970), in his last book, concluded: "The dominant factor in comprehension, accordingly, is the purpose of the reader, stated or unstated" (p. 170).

Different purposes require different reading techniques. Therefore, Burmeister (1974) states that secondary school pupils need to learn to "use different rates for various types of materials and/or when reading for different puposes" (p. 239). Russell also concluded that "one of the most important reading heights we can gain is that of flexibility of reading in different ways for different purposes" (p. 152). But consciousness of purpose in reading needs to be developed from the earliest stages of instruction, according to Malmquist (1973).

Another concept related to feedback and motivation is *reinforcement.* This term has a special meaning in psychology. It does not mean repeating a lesson by a different teaching technique—as it often does among specialists in curriculum and instruction. In psychology, reinforcement carries connotations of what is popularly known as "reward." McDonald states the commonly accepted principle in the psychology of learning: "If the consequences of a response have reward value, either by indicating to the learner that he is making the correct response or by obtaining need satisfaction for the person, the response pattern is strengthened, and it is likely to occur more frequently the next time the response pattern is attempted." On the other hand, "Responses that are not reinforced are usually dropped" (p. 401). It needs to be mentioned also that reinforcement is usually most effective when it follows rapidly after the response.

An experiment by Gates (1947) showed how feedback reinforced some (but not all) children's early attempts at reading. The subjects were young children without previous experience of reading. They were presented with five boxes, each of which had a different word printed on its top: *ball, bolt, bell, fall, roll.* Each child was told that a real ball was in the box with the word *ball* on it, and that, if he correctly selected this word three times without making a mistake, he could keep the ball. This purpose for learning to read provided the initial motivation, and every one of the children started the game enthusiastically. Some quickly succeeded, and their learning was so reinforced that they moved on rapidly to playing the game with new words. But other children who failed with *ball* became very discouraged, and with repeated failure their motivation faded away.

Practice

There cannot be any feedback if the learner does not practice performing the skill. De Cecco and Crawford conclude that "Considerable evidence in skill learning proves that practice leads to perfect performance" (p. 256). One reason for this is that learners reason about how they can improve their performances, and then use judgment to evaluate the feedback that they get as a result of their own activities. This view is implicit in several theories of learning to read. For example, it is fundamental to the theories of Goodman and of Smith that children learn to read by reading. Bamberger's work in Austria has given great impetus to this idea. One of Bamberger's (1976) studies revealed the paradox: "Many children do not read books because they cannot read well enough. They cannot read well because they do not read books" (p. 61). Bamberger's point is that children become skilled readers only through practicing reading. Samuels (1976b) too concludes that, "Students will learn to read only by reading" (p. 325). Holmes (1970) explained this seeming paradox in terms of his theory of substrata factors:

> They are thought of as neurological subsystems of brain cell-assemblies, containing various kinds of information; such as, memories for shapes, sounds, and meanings of words and word parts, as well as memories for vicarious and experiential material, conceptualizations, and meaningful relationships stored as substantive verbal units in phrases, idioms, sentences, etc. Such neurological subsystems of brain cell-assemblies gain an interfacilitation, in Hebb's sense, by firing in phase. By this means, appropriate, but diverse, subsets of information, learned under different circumstances at different times and, therefore, stored in different parts of the brain are brought simultaneously into awareness when triggered by appropriate symbols on the printed page. These substrata factors are tied together in a working-system, and as their interfacilitation in the working-system increases, the efficiency of the child's reading also increases. Here is an explanation, then, of what may take place when the child learns to read better by reading (p. 188).

Although it is generally agreed that practice is the foundation of skill acquisition, there are many questions about the kind of practice that is most beneficial to the learner.

How Much Practice?

According to Underwood (1964), the more time students spend on learning, the more they will learn. Underwood's conclusion was based on a review of laboratory experiments on verbal learning. But a similar conclusion was reached by Carroll (1975) in his research on classroom learning of French as a foreign language in eight different countries. Carroll suggests that the amount of time allocated to the study of French should be fitted to the level of proficiency desired. However, while this may be true for the study of a content area in general, it must be recognized also that subskills may differ in the amount of practice needed to bring them to mastery and automaticity. For example, Cronbach (1977, p. 425) notes that "a small amount of overt practice suffices if the explanation can be very clear and the cues obvious. More is needed when a response is hard to explain or demonstrate. A skill that requires delicate discrimination or exact timing needs much practice."

Mednick (1964), while recognizing that a skill may still improve even after years of practice, emphasizes that sheer amount of practice may not produce higher levels of skill if it is not goal-oriented. "Higher levels of skill are not reached by repetitious, half-hearted performance. Monotonous repetition, in fact, does not increase skill; it seems only to make lower-level performance more automatic" (p. 67). E. L. Thorndike (1930) placed great emphasis on practice in his Law of Exercise, but he recognized that practice was effective only because it can provide favorable conditions for learning. If the materials or methods of practice provide unfavorable conditions, then learning will not be enhanced. The Bullock Report complains that there are many basal readers "in widespread use whose language is stilted and unnatural, and far removed from anything the child ever hears in real life or uses himself" (p. 105). Thus, "They produce prose so unrealistic that it can no longer be regarded as an effective basis for reading instruction" (p. 106). Similarly, with regard to worksheets or workbooks that are designed to provide practice for subskill development, the following comment from the Bullock Report is highly pertinent: "They provide too restricting a context and do not take account of the fact that reading should satisfy some purpose on the part of the reader" (p. 120). In summary, plentiful practice is desirable, but only if the activities provided are perceived as worth practicing.

Realistic Practice

McDonald states the general rule of practice in skill learning: "Realistic practice—practice under conditions similar to those where the skill will be used—is ultimately the most beneficial and efficient kind of practice" (p. 411). McDonald recognizes that schools are limited in their facilities for providing realistic practice conditions for all skill learning. Even so, they should "approximate realistic conditions."

But Cronbach (1977) generalizes less on this point. He writes: "The cues that direct significant action should be realistically reproduced; irrelevant aspects of the situation need not be" (p. 418). Cronbach also is discerning about whether practice should take place in a realistic context: "Using a response in a significant context is often advantageous" (p. 416).

Applying this to the acquisition of the skill of reading, we may summarize as follows. As far as possible, practice reading should be similar to real-life reading. Reading materials in school should include some practical matter from the outside environment—product packages from stores, TV listing, airline schedules, and so on. In addition, real-life reading situations can be simulated in the classroom—a classroom store, cooking with a recipe book, planning an imaginary trip. Some basal reading series incorporate written language that children meet in their environment outside school—for example, street and traffic signs.

However, there may be a need for short periods of practice of some specific subskill, such as phoneme discrimination or morpheme analysis. Even so, as one of the present authors (Downing, 1979) has proposed, "all instruction in subskills such as letter-sound associations should be organized so that it appears to arise quite naturally from the pupil's desire to learn the easiest and most efficient ways of getting meaning from print" (p. 45). But, in general, realistic practice of the whole skill is more beneficial than practice on isolated subskills. An important psychological characteristic of all skills is the organization or integration of the many different subskills into a total complex pattern, and effective integration is the chief characteristic of proficient reading. Therefore, it is very important to practice realistic reading because it provides opportunities for integrating a variety of subskills to reach the target of comprehension of the author's message. Walker and Meyer (1980), following their review of current theories of integrating information from text, draw the practical conclusion that, if integration is the goal, the learning situation should be structured accordingly.

It is considered probable that improvements in the integration process are occurring in the periods known as *plateaus.* A plateau is a period when there is negligible or no progress in a student's level of skill performance. After the plateau, the performance again improves for a time until the next plateau is reached. Bryan and Harter (1897) first observed these learning plateaus in their classic study of learning telegraphy. A common theoretical explanation of this phenomenon has been that, during the plateau period, the learner is in some way integrating the components of the response.

McDonald sums up for us this point: "If a pattern is broken up into discrete responses to be practiced separately, the individual responses may be practiced in a way in which they will never be used." Then the danger is created "that the learner may never see the importance of integrating these responses" (p. 413). Such failure in the integration process is a well-known feature of reading disability—for example, in pupils who can decode letters to sounds or printed words to spoken words but cannot integrate these subskills in fluent reading.

One problem that may be raised in discussing how to make reading practice realistic is that real-life reading is usually silent and therefore difficult to monitor. Nevertheless, it is of the utmost importance for children from as early an age as possible to be given extensive practice in silent reading. Hunt (1970) has proposed a way of insuring that schools provide regular daily practice in silent reading. He calls it *USSR* for *uninterrupted sustained silent reading.* In schools that use USSR, everyone does silent reading for a certain period every day. Some teachers reject the USSR approach as too artificial. They prefer the more natural way of giving practice in silent reading that is commonly found in modern "open schools," where children engage in research projects that involve much silent reading. Another natural way of getting children to practice silent reading is through Bamberger's method of "luring" children into literature. The teacher tells or reads a sample from a book and then provides copies for the pupils to enjoy silently.

Scheduling Practice Time

There has been considerable controversy among learning theorists in psychology about the question of "massed versus distributed (or spaced) practice." In *massed practice,* a skill or subskill is practiced without interruption or rest. In *distributed practice,* the schedule provides rest periods between shorter bursts of practice. In Duncan's (1951) experiment, one group practiced a motor skill continuously. This massed practice group had three times the amount of practice as the distributed practice group that used part of their time for rest periods. The distributed practice group performed better, even though they had only one third the practice. When both groups were given an equal period of rest, the distributed practice group remained superior when they began to perform again. McDonald gives the general conclusion from the numerous experiments on this problem: *"Experimental evidence strongly favors the conclusion that spaced practice is more beneficial than massed practice for the learning of skilled performance"* (p. 410). The reason is that long periods of practice may produce fatigue or boredom. Also it is theorized that unwanted and incorrect responses tend to drop out during the rest period.

However, it is unwise to apply this general conclusion unthinkingly to skill learning in school. De Cecco and Crawford point out that "The effects of rest periods undoubtedly vary with different skills" (p. 259), and cite Deese (1958) as stating that the length of work period depends on the nature of the task. Underwood (1961) gives one clue to the problem in his review of the research. If the probability of *forgetting* is very high, massed practice is more efficient. McDonald also gives two situations in which massed practice is more beneficial: (1) "When the task to be learned is simple, and the time required to learn it is comparatively short," and (2) "When the learning task requires considerable exploration to discover the correct responses" (p. 411). Cronbach (1977, p. 430) warns that there is only so much time in the school year and, therefore, increasing intervals between practice reduces the total time for practice. Also, "intervals can become so long that forgetting is excessive."

Simplifying the Beginner's Task

So long as the practice does not become too unlike the real-life situation, it is generally agreed that it is beneficial to simplify skill learning tasks for beginners. Thus, Cronbach (1977, p. 420) believes that "Usually, the best sequence for training is to begin with easy discriminations that help the learner to identify major cues, and then to move gradually toward more subtle discriminations."

This is one aspect of the concept of *readiness.* Downing and Thackray give this definition:

> The term "readiness" for any kind of learning refers to the stage firstly, when the child can learn easily and without emotional strain, and secondly, when the child can learn profitably because efforts at teaching give gratifying results (p. 9).

Downing and Thackray point out that a lack of readiness "implies some kind of gap between the psychological state of the human being and the task he must accomplish. . . . The gap can be narrowed either by changing the individual or by changing the task, or, of course, by doing both these things." These authors continue: "If we look at the various attempts to facilitate the early learning of reading we shall see that they can be classified according to whether they try *either to fit the child for reading or to fit reading to the child"* (p. 72).

Cronbach's concern seems to be more with fitting the task to children's levels of understanding. Teachers generally have been intuitively aware of this need to simplify the tasks of reading instruction to make them suitable to the pupil's level of development. For example, reading instruction has traditionally been introduced at age five in Britain, but at age six in North America. If one examines the typical reading materials used in the schools of these countries, one finds that the British are generally much simpler, as befits the needs of the younger beginners there.

Experimental evidence for the facilitation of learning subskills in reading was provided by two studies by Carnine. In the first experiment, he created an easy-to-difficult progression of learning letter-sound correspondences by separating similar sounds from each other in the order of introduction (Carnine, 1976). Carnine's (1980) second experiment sequenced visual discriminations (the letters *b, d, p,* and *q*) in an easy-to-difficult progression. In both experiments, "sequencing discriminations from easy to difficult . . . reduced the number of training trials required in distinctive-feature training" (p. 46). Carnine proposes that the children had learned to attend to the relevant dimension more readily because of the easier examples. They were then able to apply this understanding to cope more rapidly with the more difficult discriminations.

The effects of simplifying the learning task for beginning readers were rather dramatically demonstrated in the experiment with Pitman's (1961) *i.t.a.* (initial teaching alphabet). The i.t.a. codes English words so that the letter-sound relationships are more consistent than in the conventional system. This code gives children a simpler initial task when learning how speech is related to print. For example, the simple sentence *I like my pie* contains the vowel sound of the personal pronoun "I" in each word, but it is spelled in several ways. In i.t.a.'s ie liek mie pie the same letter represents the same sound every time. Similarly, the different vowel sounds in the sentence dω sum wimen gœ tω ŧhe mωn are more easily perceived as being different than in the conventional form *Do some women go to the moon?* Again, the concept of phoneme is more readily understood when the word cof, for instance, has three letters for its three phonemes than when it has five letters for three phonemes as in *cough.* Furthermore, the principle of decoding only from left-to-right is easier to learn when phonemes are always represented in left-to-right order in words like biet, than when the decoding order has to be reversed in such spellings as *bite.* The large-scale longitudinal experiment with i.t.a. in England found that simplifying the task for beginners in this way led to more rapid acquisition of the skill of reading and reduced the incidence of reading failure (Downing, 1967, 1977a; Warburton and Southgate, 1969).

Even more directly to the point are the two studies of the effects of i.t.a. on *reading readiness.* Downing (1963) found that in the control group, children aged five made significantly better progress in learning to read than children aged four. But, in the i.t.a. group, the four-year-olds learned just as well as the five-year-olds. He concluded that, "The majority of four-year-olds may not be able to learn to read traditional orthography, but this does not appear to be true of their ability to learn to read i.t.a." (p. 25). Thackray's (1971) experiment confirmed that i.t.a. does, to an important degree, narrow the gap between the child's ability and the intellectual problems of learning to read by making the task simpler. Thus simplification of the learning task can be effective in reading acquisition.

Certainly, we cannot agree with Hunter-Grundin's (1979) view that "The confusion, ambiguity, and misrepresentation connected with 'reading readiness' are so entrenched that it would be a good thing if the concept were abandoned altogether" (p. 21). Readiness remains a viable concept despite its current unpopularity. When teachers are mindful of readiness, they can prevent unnecessary failures in learning to read. For example, Southgate's (1980) study of the books read by seven-, eight- and nine-year-olds revealed that "large numbers of children were . . . struggling with books which were too difficult for them to understand" (p. 16).

Meaningfulness

A very well-established conclusion from psychological research on verbal skills is—the more meaningful the materials, the more rapid the learning (Underwood, 1964). Research has shown also that, "Not only is meaningful material more rapidly learned than meaningless material, but also it is remembered for longer periods of time" (De Cecco and Crawford, p. 214). *Meaningfulness* is defined in experimental psychology as "the number of different associations elicited by a verbal unit. . . . The more frequently a word occurs in the language, the greater its familiarity, and the greater the ease with which it can be attached to other words" (De Cecco and Crawford, p. 211). Cronbach (1963) comments that "The value of meaningful teaching has been demonstrated repeatedly. . . . Greater understanding of what is taught produces more rapid learning, better retention, and better adaptation to new conditions" (p. 350).

To the definition of meaningfulness quoted from De Cecco and Crawford, we must add after *language—of the child.* This has often been overlooked in selecting samples of language for children's practice tasks in learning to read. It is sometimes argued that children should be taught first to read the words that are most common in the language as a whole, because these are "key words" that open up the language found most often in books. Unfortunately, these key words include such words as *the* and *and* which are notoriously difficult to teach. They are hard because they contain very little meaning. Even the more meaningful key words may not be very frequent in *the child's* experience.

The best way to ensure that the vocabulary for reading is meaningful and well known to children is to let them choose the words that they want to learn how to read and write. For example, Ashton-Warner (1963) in her "key vocabulary" method asked each pupil daily to tell her the word he or she wanted to take home and learn. Many teachers follow the same principle in using the *language-experience approach* to reading. Briefly, this consists in using the child's own language and experiences to construct his or her personal materials for reading. In the beginning, the teacher writes down what each child wants to express about his or her experiences. When children start writing independently, they write more and more of the words they want to communicate. The language-experience approach may be used individually, as a group activity, or the whole class may create a combined composition. Individuals and groups of pupils become authors of their own books which they share with each other.

The importance of meaningfulness of reading materials is stressed by several writers on the language-experience approach. Goddard (1974) states that "children should meet reading and writing as a part of their own (as distinct from other people's) lives, in situations where the written or printed word has real meaning for them" (p. 12). Hall (1976) writes that, "As children see their spoken thoughts put into written form they can understand the nature of communication in reading in addition to recognizing words" (p. 2).

Allen (1976) stresses that meaningful reading activities provide more consistent exemplars for the child to develop concepts about language and literacy in the cognitive phase of acquiring the skill of reading. He writes that the language-experience approach develops such concepts as: "(1) 'I can think about what I have experienced and imagined'; (2) 'I can talk about what I think about'; (3) 'What I can talk about I can express in some other form'; (4) 'Anything I record I can recall through speaking or reading'; 'I can read what I can write by myself and what other people write for me to read' " (pp. 51–52). McCracken and McCracken (1979) point out that language-experience activities provide intrinsic feedback for beginners: "It is through the meaning on a printed page that a child can determine if he is using and acquiring skills of written language" (p. 1).

Part Versus Whole Learning

It may sometimes make a task easier if it is broken down into smaller parts. However, Borger and Seaborne (1966) note a disadvantage: "We have emphasized earlier the smooth and rhythmic nature of skilled performance, and the deliberate breaking up of the performance does by itself not favour the development of continuity" (pp. 139–140). Nevertheless, they conclude that there are some advantages in breaking down a task into smaller parts. They write that, "The advisability of splitting up a task into manageable sections, each with its own clearly defined goal, is another consequence of the view that one of the most important functions of a teacher or trainer is to provide, where possible, criteria which the learner can himself use to judge the quality of his own performance" (p. 139). They add that, beside this simplification effect, "There is an additional argument in favour of the partitioning of learning tasks." This is that it makes speedy reinforcement more feasible (p. 141).

The question of whether to break a learning task into parts or to teach it as a whole is an old controversy in psychology. Naylor (1962) summarized the evidence on this issue and concluded that if the skill is highly coherent, continuous, highly organized, and moderately or very difficult, the whole method is more efficient; otherwise it is more effective to use the part method to practice the subskills that need most attention. Of course, there is a third alternative: to combine both methods. If it has been thought necessary to divide a task into parts, it is possible "to link up the various sections, gradually if there are many, by concentrating on joint performance, once the individual parts have been adequately mastered" (Borger and Seaborne, p. 140).

This controversy in psychology has spilled over into reading instruction. Belief in part learning methods has generally been associated with *phonic* techniques, while the philosophy of wholes is usually thought to go with a *look-say* approach to reading instruction. But, in fact, there are many different methods that have gone under such labels. Chall (1967) reclassified teaching methods into *meaning emphasis* and *code emphasis* approaches, because she found that teachers and authors of reading textbooks placed more importance either on teaching children the meaningful communication aspects of written language or on the technical linguistic elements of the printed code for the spoken language. Downing's

(1973) international studies of this aspect of reading education confirmed Chall's conclusion. No matter what the language of instruction, educators everywhere discuss the relative merits of meaning emphasis versus code emphasis approaches.

This controversy over part versus whole methods continues in the debate over the *psycholinguistic* theories of Smith and of Goodman. Goodman (1976b) shows clearly why the part method is anathema for educators who prefer the meaning emphasis approach. He attacks "instructional reading programs that begin with bits and pieces abstracted from language, like words or letters, on the theory that they're making learning simpler," but "in fact make learning to read harder," because it "isn't language any more" (p. 59). The essence of reading is a "constructive . . . search for meaning" (p. 58) in which the readers' "language competence enables them to create a grammatical and semantic prediction in which they need only sample from the print to reach meaning" (p. 59). The "search for meaning is itself what makes it possible for the reader to predict the grammatical structures" (p. 64).

However, it is questionable if the learning-to-read process is directly derivable from the fluent reading process, as Goodman and Smith both imply. It is a characteristic of skills that they change in the course of their development. Behavior appropriate to the beginning stage drops out later as mastery progresses. New behaviors are incorporated as attention is freed from acts that have become more automatic. Elkonin (1973b) writes:

> It is only the summarized, abbreviated and highly automated nature of the perfected form of this skill that gives the impression of a simple association between speech and print. Prior to this level of performance, the skill must go through a long period of development and its initial form is not in the least like its final one. One of the most flagrant errors in methods of reading instruction, in our view, is the belief that the initial and final forms of any skill are identical. Their processes are always very different (p. 17).

Transfer of Learning

The phenomenon of "transfer of learning" or "transfer of training," has been well established in psychological research. Drever defines *transfer of training* as "the improvement of one mental or motor function, by the systematic training of another allied function" (p. 302). Cronbach (1977, p. 435) gives this example: "The young person who can ride a bicycle learns to slow down when he observes children at the edge of the street, to correct steering on the basis of visual feedback, to estimate how soon a car in a side street will reach the intersection he is approaching. When he begins to drive an automobile, all these interpretations will be helpful." This is *positive transfer of learning.* But we must also take account of *negative transfer.* That is, when the learning of one skill or subskill is interfered with by the learning of some related activity. A common example of negative transfer is what happens when a student takes French and Spanish classes at different times during the same day. Words like *que* and *de* occur in both languages, but they are pronounced differently. Negative transfer causes many mistakes when students move from one language lesson to the other.

Psychologists also distinguish between two other categories of transfer. Travers (1972) writes: "When the effect of transfer is on subsequent learning, the term *proaction* is often applied or one refers to *proactive transfer.* When the effect of transfer is to enhance or depress the retention of some previous learning, then there is said to be *retroactive transfer"* (p. 155).

Several of these transfer phenomena can be seen in the effects of reading instruction of one kind or another that have been discussed earlier in this chapter. For example, in the i.t.a. experiment, the use of this simplified orthography during the first one or two years at first produced negative proactive transfer in children's abilities to spell correctly in conventional English orthography. Later this situation was reversed and the result at the end of five years was positive proactive transfer. At that stage Downing (1977a) found nearly twice as many poor spellers in the control group that had used conventional spelling than in the experimental group that used i.t.a. in the early stages. This result may seem strange on first consideration, but if we apply the psychological concept of transfer of training, the result no longer seems paradoxical. We must escape from our preoccupation with the surface structure of written language—the specific graphic shapes of print, and penetrate more deeply into the abstract features of the skill of reading—understanding literacy learning tasks, attitudes toward these tasks, subskills such as the segmentation of speech into abstract units, and so on. *All these deeper features of reading skill are universal to all languages quite irrespective of their often very different specific surface structures. These deeper features of reading skill are the essential characteristics that must be considered in understanding the psychology of the learning-to-read process.* Thus, in the i.t.a. experiment what got transferred in both the experimental and the control groups was the effect of the initial experiences on these deeper features of reading skill. Transfer of training is just as important in reading instruction as it is in other forms of skill acquisition.

Readiness and Transfer

Another topic that has already been discussed and that is related to transfer is readiness. During the prereading period, children are learning language and other skills needed for reading. Thus Chapman and Hoffman note that "primary reading skills have their origin in the child's own language and his developing perceptual skills" (p. 80).

Reid (1973) cites the studies of children's reading errors made by Goodman (1967), Clay (1969), Weber (1970b) and Beimiller (1970). She concludes: "All four studies show that the greater proportion of errors in the reading of children in their first year are syntactically correct—that is to say, they consist of an acceptable part of speech in terms of the preceding words in the sentence" (p. 32). In other words, the way in which children read in the beginning stages is influenced by the language that they have learned in the preschool years. There is proactive transfer of training from their speaking and listening skills to their acquisition of reading skill. This proactive transfer, as usual, may have positive or negative influences on learning. For example, if the language samples used by the reading teacher are closely matched to the preschool language experiences of the child, positive transfer can be anticipated. But, if there is a mismatch between the pupil's language and the language samples of reading instruction, negative transfer must be expected.

There are many situations in which the pupil's mother tongue *(L1)* is different from the language of instruction *(L2)*. Then, the metalinguistic description of language used by the teacher may employ linguistic concepts related to *L2* that may be meaningless in the child's own experience with his or her *L1*. In reading instruction, for instance, the teacher may refer to *L2* phonemes that do not exist in the child's *L1*. Thus it is in the area of the development of language skills that the greatest difficulty might be anticipated in bilingual settings of this type. In addition to the cognitive difficulty of comprehending instruction given in *L2*, positive or negative affective factors must be taken into account (Downing, 1978).

Transfer in the Curriculum

Educators usually can only adapt their teaching to the children's preschool language development that has already occurred. Once children arrive in school, the curriculum can be planned so that positive transfer is maximized and negative transfer is minimized. Elkonin (1973b) writes:

> Teaching methods specialists of the past were meeting a purely pragmatic objective—simply to teach children the practical skills of reading and writing by the most effective means possible, without any complicating consideration of its influence on other broader aims. Nowadays, in contrast, the initial teaching of reading and writing is just a part of the general cycle of teaching language. Therefore, the methods of beginning reading instruction must be evaluated also with regard to the general orientation to language and its laws that they give. That is, to what extent do they prepare the pupil for an understanding of scientific knowledge about language (p. 14).

Cronbach's (1977, p. 420) view is that the student should "practice reflectively in the greatest variety of situations he can cope with. . . . Variation requires him to isolate the essential elements and respond to them." Cronbach (1963) has also pointed out that "we are never training a response alone; we are always developing ability to adapt to diverse situations" (p. 288). How can this insurance policy for skill acquisition be implemented? Borger and Seaborne answer that "effective transfer of training to a variety of tasks is best encouraged by an emphasis on *variety* in the training situation, as opposed to concentration on one particular use of skill, or one particular set of circumstances" (p. 147). Cronbach (1963) put it like this: "More desirable is practice in a naturally varying context, so that the performer learns to recognize recurring cues in an ever-changing setting" (p. 310).

This variety policy can be applied, for example, to the early readiness activities for developing the auditory discrimination subskill in preparation for learning the relationships between individual letters and their associated individual sounds. Egorov (1953) has written about the need for variety in the examples used in developing children's concepts of phonemes. He points out that the "pure" phoneme that is represented by an alphabetic letter is an abstraction that has no concrete reality in any particular word. A phoneme is really a family of sounds—an abstract category into which we sort the sounds that we learn to perceive as belonging to that family. Objective recording and analysis of speech in linguistic and phonetic science laboratories shows that phoneme boundaries are not clearly definable because phonetic segments are co-articulated (Liberman, Cooper, Shankweiler and Studdert-Kennedy, 1967). For example, in the word "dog," we perceive three phonemes, but objectively it consists of a single acoustic segment. The phoneme /d/ in this word is actually different acoustically from /d/ in such other words as "din," "aid," or "Fido."

The beginner's problem is to learn to categorize these objectively different sounds as being "the same," and to be able to recognize that each of the variants of this phoneme is a kind of /d/. In phonics, students have to learn that the letter *d* does not represent one sound only (as some teachers wrongly declare) but a range of variations of the phoneme /d/. The sound represented by letter *d* changes according to the sounds of its neighboring letters.

Hence, drilling pupils on one example of *d* in a key word such as *dog* in a picture alphabet display is undesirable because it produces a stereotyped response to letter *d* that is only one of the variants in the family of sounds it represents. This is one of the causes of the "blending difficulty" so often discussed by reading teachers. The child, through this type of poor teaching technique, is unable to synthesize the units because their combination does not sound like any word known in the listening vocabulary and does not feel like any known movements of the speech organs in the speaking vocabulary. Therefore Egorov (1953) suggests that analysis and synthesis of phonemes in auditory discrimination exercises should be conducted on a variety of words that children know in their listening and speaking vocabulary. As well as being closer to the objective reality of the concept of the phoneme, this variety policy prepares pupils for meeting the letter and its sound in all its different guises.

As a second example of the application of the variety policy for maximum proactive positive transfer in acquiring the skill of reading, let us consider the very severe problem of overly slow pace in reading that is commonly reported by older students and adults. Downing (1976) notes that "this complaint is an oversimplification of their real problem. This is a *lack of flexibility*" (p. 81). Bond and Tinker state: "A rapid rate of reading has no particular value. The proficient reader will have several speeds, each of which can be used as the occasion demands" (p. 451). Karlin (1972) sums up what is desirable: "A good reader knows how to shift gears when he reads and lets the nature of his materials and his purposes for reading control his speed of reading" (p. 238). This analogy is extended by Parker (1970): "A good reader is like a good driver. He doesn't move at the same rate all the time; he is flexible" (p. 212).

But unforunately many children with normal or superior intelligence do not acquire this ability to change gears in reading. They carry this handicap into their secondary and college education and find themselves in difficulty in coping with the reading required for their higher level studies. Several causes have been suggested for inflexibility in reading rate. Among them is negative proactive transfer from methods of instruction in the primary years of schooling. Thus, Burmeister mentions "excessive attention to details" (p. 239) which may be due to the early "conditioning to slow careful reading" mentioned by Strang, McCullough and Traxler (1967, p. 271). Carrillo (1973) explicitly states that "too much attention in the early stages of reading instruction to phonics, structural analysis, structural linguistics, and/or oral reading, will interfere later with flexibility of rate" (p. 66). These educational mistakes are caused by teachers' failure to consider transfer of learning effects.

To prevent these difficulties of inflexibility in reading, it is essential to plan for positive transfer and to bear in mind the long-term purposes of communication through the written form of language. From the very beginning the teaching of reading should have these long-term goals in view. Bond and Tinker recommend that, "The basic program should itself reflect the kind of reading [the beginner] is expected to do in the entire curriculum" (p. 421). Positive proactive transfer for flexibility in secondary school and college level reading can be planned for best by providing a variety of different purposes for reading from the very beginning.

Rate of Progress

Bryan and Harter (1897, 1899) found that the rate of progress in skill development is not constant, and their findings have been confirmed in many other studies over the intervening years. Cronbach (1963) summarized the evidence that in progress in skill learning one can observe six characteristics:

1. *Negligible progress.* Very little improvement in score.
2. *Increasing gains.* The rate of learning increases as the learner grasps the essentials of the task.
3. *Decreasing gains.* The rate of measured improvement is slower.
4. *Plateau.* A period of no systematic change in score.
5. *Renewed gains.* Performance again rises.
6. *Approach to limit.* Progress becomes negligible (pp. 298–299).

Cronbach pointed out that these were only theoretical generalizations about the kind of cycle of progress that has often been observed in skill acquisition. Different subskills have different characteristic cycles of progress in improvement. More recently Cronbach (1977) comments: "Individual learning curves are characteristically irregular, reflecting transient shifts in interest, energy, rhythm, and so on" (p. 432).

In reading instruction, experienced teachers recognize these phases of development of a skill. For example, the first grade teacher is not unduly disturbed by the period of negligible progress at the very beginning. Children then are in what Fitts called the *cognitive phase* of trying to comprehend what they are supposed to do in their reading tasks and why. Having grasped the point, there is a sudden leap forward in progress. Williams (1976) reported this phenomenon in the Schools Council Project in Compensatory Education in South Wales. Regular measurement of the development of reading subskills was made over the period of the first three years in school, beginning at age five and continuing through to age eight. The measure used was a word recognition test of a sample of words from the *Concise Oxford Dictionary.* Williams reports that "the growth of reading vocabulary usually began very slowly, and then proceeded through a stage of rapid growth. The rapidity of some of the growth spurts that were shown was astonishing. The growth tailed off, to complete an s-shaped curve" (pp. 294–295). Williams found that, "For most children, the peak of word recognition growth occurs when the word recognition vocabulary is between 20 and 29 per cent or about a quarter of the dictionary vocabulary" (p. 296).

Another of Cronbach's generalizations also is confirmed by Williams' data. That is Cronbach's (1977, p. 431) point that "parts of a skill develop at different rates or at different points in training." In Williams' study the same children were also tested at regular intervals on the *Swansea Test of Phonic Skills* (Williams et al., 1971). This test assesses the child's performance in attaching the correct pronunciation to sixty-five of the most frequent letters or letter combinations used in early reading. The results of the phonics test were quite different from those found with the word recognition test. There were more individual differences in the children's performances on the phonics test. Also, "the rate of growth of phonic skills did not show quite the same peak as was the case in the rate of growth of word recognition skills" (p. 297). Williams also examined the relationship between the children's attainments in phonics and in word recognition. Most of the children "reached their maximum rate of growth in phonic skills before their maximum rate of growth in word recognition skills." The remainder appeared to reach the peak score in both skills simultaneously. "No child showed maximum growth of word recognition skills before maximum growth of phonic skills. It seems that a child needs considerable facility in phonic skills, a good grasp of the phoneme–grapheme relationship, before he can enter the word recognition growth spurt . . ." (p. 298).

The experienced and knowledgeable reading teacher also will not become overanxious when a child goes through a brief period of negligible progress at a later stage. This is a plateau when, as we noted earlier, the process of integration of a skill may be improving.

Reduction of Errors

One of the ways in which improvement in a skill progresses is through reducing errors in performance. An experiment by Lindahl (1945) showed how people make fewer and fewer errors as they become more skillful. Vince's (1953) experiment uncovered the way in which errors are corrected progressively. Vince's subjects were required to learn the skill of drawing a line through a series of circles presented on a moving band. They could observe the circles only through a narrow slit.

The direction of the circles changed after every fourth circle. Errors occurred at these points when the direction of the line of circles changed at these corners. The subjects overshot the corner. Gradually such errors were reduced, as the subjects developed a conception of the whole pattern in the line of circles. This was confirmed by the subjects' reports of their own thoughts during the learning of the skill. They began to anticipate the changes of direction and were thus able to avoid errors.

Merritt's (1970) work on *the intermediate skills* in reading has shown the importance of reduction of errors in the higher levels of improvement in reading skill. He writes: "Intermediate skills have an additional function in reading . . . in that they assist in the discovery of errors of word recognition. . . ." Merritt describes how in reading, too, just as in Vince's laboratory experiment, this error reduction is vitally dependent upon the subskill of prediction. Merritt argues as follows:

> If we are anticipating on a basis of many cues that one or a very small number of words may follow, we are, as it were, arousing in the brain a set of models of some kind against which to match each successive unit we perceive. The act of reading therefore appears to be one of prediction and model-matching. . . . The intermediate skills, then, function in advance of the recognition of individual words by making readily available to the reader a limited number of possibilities against which each successive word may be checked. Because they provide so much information, only the briefest inspection of the predicted word is often necessary. Missing words, missing letters or misspellings then provide little hindrance to the fluent reader, as is demonstrated in the following passage: If yuo are a fl--nt reodur yu wlll heve no difticllty reod:ng th:s (p. 54).

Different Stages Require Different Abilities

Merritt's identification of the important intermediate subskills reminds us of a conclusion about skill acquisition in general that has been drawn by De Cecco and Crawford: "One of the most important findings in the research on skill learning is the following: As the student moves through the various stages of skill learning, the particular combination of abilities which the skill requires changes. . . . The combination of abilities required early in the training may be quite different from the combination required later" (p. 268).

The intermediate subskills are different from primary subskills. Merritt (1970) states that "there is now ample evidence that there exists a separate set of skills which provide the essential basis of fluent reading. These are the . . . 'intermediate skills' " (p. 43). Merritt's studies with three different types of text "demonstrate quite clearly the decisive difference between reading separate words (using primary skills), reading fluently with comprehension (using higher order skills) and reading fluently with little or no comprehension" (p. 44). However, although they are distinguishable, the primary and intermediate skills are not entirely separated in time of development. Chapman and Hoffman (1977) state that *"the interaction of primary and intermediate skills is essential even in the earliest stages of learning to read"* (p. 67). But there is an important difference in the rate of progress of their development. "The intermediate, like the primary, skills have their origins in the child's language. Unlike the primary skills, however, they continue to develop over the years," report Chapman and Hoffman (p. 80). Of great importance, they propose, is the reader's sensitivity "both to *word-class* (i.e. adjective, noun, pronoun, etc.) and to *word-form* (i.e. the spelling of verb inflections, plurals, etc.). The fluent reader is also sensitive to *syntactic relations* and is able to *anticipate the possible class and form of successive words.* This narrowing of the range of grammatical possibilities plays a very important part in fluent reading. . . . In illustrating this in greater detail, however, we cannot emphasize too strongly that it is the automatic aspect with which we are concerned" (p. 67).

Another writer who has urged educators to distinguish between different types of reading skill is Pugh (1975). He argues that, historically, the move from oral reading to silent reading, "demanded that a mode of reading be developed which was not only nonoral but which also had its own distinctive qualities and applications" (p. 110). Pugh complains that "certain writers have failed even to make a clear distinction between silent reading and oral reading. Thus doubtful inferences are sometimes made from one mode of reading to another. For example, Weber (1968), reviewing the literature on miscues, remarks on the dangers of drawing conclusions about cues used in silent reading from errors made in oral reading" (p. 114). Pugh's article provides a quite detailed description of the subskills of silent reading of which the following is only a list of their names: "scanning," "search reading," "skimming," "receptive reading," and "responsive reading" (pp. 112–113). In another more recent article, Pugh (1980) reviews research on strategies in silent reading and his own investigations of silent readers' strategies for locating information in a book.

Is Early Performance Predictive?

One consequence of recognizing that different levels of skill development involve different abilities is that individuals may differ in the extent to which they possess the various abilities. This leads Cronbach (1977, p. 432) to conclude that, "Performance early in training is not a dependable predictor of ultimate proficiency in a psychomotor skill. . . . Those slower to understand a complex situation often overtake the early star performers. Differences later depend on co-ordinations and speed." Unlike the other psychological generalizations on skill performance and its acquisition that we have reviewed in this and the preceding chapter, this conclusion of Cronbach's does not match what is generally found in learning the specific skill of reading. Generally, children who make a good beginning in reading go on to become the better readers in the later stages of education. For example, many studies have found that children who are poor readers in the primary grades very rarely develop normal reading attainments in later years. How can we explain this discrepancy between general research on skill acquisition and our knowledge of learning to read?

There are two probable causes of the difference between reading skill and other skills in respect of the predictive significance of early performance. First, although reading includes important motor activities such as eye movements and speech muscle movements, nevertheless it is primarily a mental skill. Many psychologists have stressed the importance of reasoning in reading—for example, Holmes' (1970) statement that "reading is an audiovisual verbal-processing-skill of symbolic *reasoning*" (p. 187, italics added). Thus, what makes reading different from other psychomotor skills is that reasoning is very important both for acquiring the skill and for its later performance. This is quite unlike the type of skill described by Cronbach, in which the beginner with rather low reasoning ability makes a slower start but may catch up and overtake other pupils with superior reasoning abilities, once the skill no longer depends so much on reasoning. In reading, reasoning continues to be of great importance. Therefore, the student with good reasoning power makes a more rapid start and continues to get further and further ahead of students who are less gifted in this respect. This is what is commonly observed in reading development.

However, there is a second probable factor in this characteristic of the acquisition of reading skill. This is what Downing (1977b) refers to as "society's critical period" (p. 275). This is the school deadline by which time every child must have developed a basic competence to a certain level in reading skill. The deadline varies from one country to another but, generally, if pupils do not succeed in reading at that point, they are considered to be failures and they are given remedial reader status. Possibly, if educators were more flexible in their expectations of pupils' progress and allowed children to develop reading skill at their own individual pace, the phenomenon of slow starters catching up and overtaking the early star performers would occur more often in reading.

Individual Differences

The view of De Cecco and Crawford on this matter coincides with that of Cronbach. They state: "Any prediction about the student's ultimate success based on the initial combination of abilities alone would be very misleading. As the ability requirements of the task change during practice, individual differences in these abilities affect the student's learning and performance." Therefore, "Rarely can the student make the same rate of progress in all stages of skill learning" (p. 269). Certainly there is evidence of individual differences in subskill development in reading. For example, in Williams' (1976) study of the development of subskills during the first three years of schooling it was found that, in learning phonics: "Some children showed little progress throughout the period of assessment; others had acquired a reasonable competence by the time they entered the infant school. Other children showed a dramatic increase in knowledge of phonic skills during a very short period of time" (p. 297). Yet the whole research literature of reading readiness is dominated by the search for the best predictors of later progress in learning to read. The general assumption has been that, if a boy or girl performs well in letter-name knowledge or in auditory discrimination, for instance, he or she will perform well later in the reading skill as a whole. In fact, there are quite high correlations between the results of readiness tests such as auditory discrimination and later achievement in reading, but even so, they are only in the order of .5, which leaves a great deal of room for variance. The assumption that the pupil's ability to learn is the same for all subskills should be questioned seriously in future research. Also needing examination is the related assumption that the differences in rate of progress in reading skill development that are observed in the primary years must set the pattern for later years.

However, there is no doubt whatsoever that very large individual differences in pupils' level of development of reading skill as a whole do exist. Bond and Tinker remark that, at any level, "it is reasonable to expect that there will be a wide range in reading ability" (p. 49). Downing (1976) estimates that, "In a comprehensive secondary school one can anticipate that twelve-year-olds will have a range in reading age from eight years to sixteen years. By age fifteen the range will be from ten to the adult level of reading ages" (p. 68).

Most of the discussion of individual differences in reading are of this global kind, whereas psychologists in their studies of skill acquisition in general emphasize the need to take account of individual differences in the different abilities required at the various stages of learning. Thus, De Cecco and Crawford recommend that "the teacher must know all the abilities required by the practice of the skill so that he can determine where each student will make the most rapid and the slowest progress and so that he can supply the necessary help for the periods of slowest progress" (p. 269). Some authors have made such recommendations for reading instruction. Harris and Sipay (1975) write: "Pupils differ widely in every significant trait that can be observed. An effective plan of teaching reading must take account of variations in intelligence, in language and conceptual skills, in maturity, in interest, and in the presence or absence of handicaps to learning. If a reading program is to succeed with all pupils, it must be flexible enough to give different pupils the kinds of instruction they need" (p. 86).

Burt (1967b) went further when he wrote that "the general look of the visible word or the phrase, taken as a whole, directly suggests its meaning without analysis into letters or sounds. Many children, particularly those who are visualizers, learn to read in this way from the very start. . . . Some children, however, seem almost devoid of visual imagery. Of these many are audiles; and their natural method of tackling a new word is to translate it letter by letter into its component sounds. There is, however, a third type of child, less commonly recognized—the motile. For him, what the teacher calls 'sounds' are really the movements needed to produce the sounds, or the 'mental images' of such movements" (p. 103).

Remembering and Forgetting

Here space permits us to do little more than remind students to consider again what they learned in their educational psychology courses. Therefore, let us just note the chief causes of failures in remembering.

One of the main features of forgetting is *retroactive interference*—a new activity interferes with what has been learned earlier. This phenomenon was demonstrated in the classic experiment by Jenkins and Dallenbach (1924). Their subjects learned nonsense syllables that had to be recalled after varying periods during which they had been either asleep or awake. Recall after sleeping was very much better than recall after being awake. For the shorter periods of one and two hours, the amount forgotten was similar for both the sleeping and awake conditions; but for longer periods, forgetting was significantly greater when the subjects were awake. This finding indicates that forgetting is not caused merely by fading away through the passage of time. Rather, what happens is that the other activities going on in the waking state interfere with what has been learned earlier. Borger and Seaborne sum up the general conclusion as follows: "Whatever the precise form of the process underlying this form of retention loss, it is clear that interaction with the environment—new learning—in the interval between final learning trial and memory test accounts for a good deal of the forgetting usually found" (p. 158).

Cronbach (1977) states that, "The key to reducing interference is solid, meaningful initial learning" (p. 459). Similarly the comment of De Cecco and Crawford should be borne in mind: "Not only is meaningful material more rapidly learned than meaningless material, but it is also remembered for longer periods of time" (p. 214). Therefore, the student is referred again to the earlier section of this chapter where the various methods of teaching reading that stress the need for reading materials that are truly meaningful for the child were described.

Interference may be proactive as well as retroactive. *Proactive interference*—the negative influence of earlier learning on new learning is a persistent problem when some habit learned earlier has become so overlearned and automatic that it prevents a new type of response being learned. Cronbach (1977) notes that, "Serious interference with learning occurs when the new task requires a change in some part of the original response that is not under voluntary, verbally mediated control" (p. 437). This is why people who have been strongly conditioned to one single speed of reading by poor teaching methods in the primary grades find it so difficult to learn how to change gear in reading in later years.

Borger and Seaborne draw our attention to another cause of interference in learning that seems relevant for the acquisition of reading skill. They conclude from research on forgetting that "if the responses required in the first and second task are different, then *interference increases as the stimuli in the two tasks become increasingly similar*" (p. 156, italics added). This warns us to watch out for stimuli in reading that are similar, because they will be most difficult to remember. In other words, printed stimuli that look alike are most likely to interfere with one another and be forgotten. Harris and Sipay note, "Studies have shown that reversal errors are very common among young children," and they cite examples such as: *p, d, p,* and *q; m* and *w; on* and *no; saw* and *was,* and so on (pp. 23–24). In such cases, pupils easily forget which stimulus represents which sound or spoken word. Special care needs to be taken when this type of stimulus is being learned in beginning reading.

Methods of Instruction

Everything that has been said already in this chapter is related to methods of instruction. The psychological findings as to how people acquire skills that we have reviewed should be the foundations of instructional methods in reading. Fitting teaching methods to children's ways of learning is the most efficient way of obtaining the best results in teaching.

In this final section of the chapter, it may be helpful to change the focus from the learner to the teacher in the apprenticeship of reading. We have emphasized that in any apprenticeship the most important, indeed the essential, principle in learning the skill is that apprentices must *do* the action. They do it with awareness of what they are trying to achieve. They reason about how they can improve their performance and they use judgment to evaluate the feedback that they receive from the results of their own activities. But apprentices are not abandoned to their own devices. They are apprenticed to someone who is their model and their guide. So it is with the skill of reading. The pupil is the apprentice trying to understand what to do and why it must be done that way. The teacher is the model reader and the guide to better understanding. The teacher, therefore, must be not only a good performer of the skill but also a good thinker. This means analyzing the skill and recognizing what aspects of it have to be understood by the apprentice at each stage in the development of skill. Thus reading teachers must be fully skilled readers themselves and their pupils must have opportunities to see them at work in reading. Reading teachers must also have a good store of knowledge *about reading* if they are going to guide their reading apprentices.

Let us now review what is known in psychology about the methods that may be used by instructors when they give guidance to students learning a skill.

Verbal Exposition

The utility of verbal instructions depends on the particular situation at the moment and the nature of what has to be learned. Some examples from the psychological literature help us to understand the occasions for verbal exposition and its limitations.

Borger and Seaborne state: "The use of verbal instructions is effective only to the extent to which the words used in fact convey the necessary message." Remember Downing's (1980b) *"The last rellang is the holy wow."* If children do not understand technical terms like *letter,* or *silent e,* their use in verbal instructions is a hindrance rather than a help. But Borger and Seaborne are concerned with something deeper than this. They point out there are some aspects of skill behavior "which a verbal description conveys only to someone who has already mastered the skill" (p. 138). In other words, the learner has no concept to relate to the instructor's verbal description.

There are two grave errors that are commonly made by adults trying to help children to learn new concepts. The first error is to tell them some verbal formula or definition. The second common error made by adults is to test children's understanding of concepts by asking them to recite a verbal formula or definition. Evidence for this was provided by Belbin's (1956) research on road safety education in England. Children were shown road safety films, and afterwards effectiveness was measured in two ways: (1) by questioning the children about what the films said and (2) by observing the children's behavior as they left the film theatre. Belbin found only low correlations between the children's verbalizations about road safety and their actual behavior in the road. The conclusion was that the effectiveness of instruction cannot be measured by children's recall of the instruction.

Vygotsky (1934) stated the truth on this matter very clearly: "Direct teaching of concepts is impossible and fruitless. A teacher who tries to do this accomplishes nothing but empty verbalism, a parrotlike repetition of words by the child, simulating a knowledge of the corresponding concepts but actually covering up a vacuum" (p. 83). Vygotsky's comment may even be optimistic because the result often is worse than a vacuum. For example, Emery's (1975) research on the effects of religious education revealed that preschoolers learned many *incorrect* concepts rather than nothing at all.

Verbal instruction becomes more effective as pupils grow older and develop a larger bank of concepts to draw upon. Also there is a place for verbal explanation in guiding the learner's reading behavior in other respects than in concept learning. Verbal explanation and other methods of guidance should be used to clarify how a reading task should be tackled and why that technique is appropriate. Even when the learner has no conception of the task to be attempted, the teacher's carefully thought-out verbal explanation may "get the behavior approximately right, and this provides an enormous short-cut. . . ." (Borger and Seaborne, p. 138).

Demonstration

In the applied psychology of skill training in general, demonstration by the instructor is often recommended. Borger and Seaborne suggest:

> The second feature of training procedures which may be seen in a new and useful way is demonstration. In showing a learner how to do something, the demonstrator provides among other things a picture of what correct performance *looks* like. In so far as this can be remembered, this constitutes a criterion which the learner can then use for judging his own performance, it allows himself to set an appropriate goal. Seen from this point of view, the demonstration, as it appears to the learner, should resemble as closely as possible what he is likely to see when he makes his own attempt. This has obvious implications, for example, for the way the demonstrator should stand in relation to the learner (p. 139).

Demonstration obviously has limited application in reading instruction, but there are occasions when reading skill as a whole can be demonstrated effectively. Also, demonstration may be useful in training certain subskills.

For example, when the teacher reads a book to the class for enjoyment, this is a demonstration of meaningful reading and it is also a demonstration of one purpose of reading, Similarly, when a teacher reads a recipe book in a baking session with children who are still nonreaders, this is a demonstration of another purpose of reading. As Sokhin (1974) describes, in subskill development the teacher can, for example, demonstrate how *a sentence* can be segmented into *words.* The teacher can say the sentence with special pauses to separate each word. Even better, he or she can use concrete aids to make such a demonstration more comprehensible. The teacher may say, "Let's make the *sentence:* 'The cat drank its milk.' You be the word *the* [points to first child], you be the word *cat* [second child]" and so on. "Now come out to the front and make the *sentence:* 'The cat drank its milk.' We must get the *words* in the right order," and so on. Such demonstrations with concrete aids can very quickly develop the abstract concepts that children need to understand verbal instructions in reading and writing.

The point that Borger and Seaborne make about the *position of the demonstrator* is particularly important for instruction in reading and writing because of the need for the learner to become correctly oriented toward the direction of letter formation and the lines of text. For example, in the language-experience approach, teachers must be careful of the direction in which they stand when writing an experience chart in front of a class or group. Also, when writing pupils' personal dictated messages, the teacher should sit beside children so that they can form a picture of the writing act as a criterion for judging their own writing performance. Here also teachers can demonstrate segmentation subskills by exaggerating pauses between spoken words and spaces between written words to provide clear exemplars of these linguistic concepts.

When to Give Guidance

De Cecco and Crawford note that, "The purpose of describing and demonstrating is to develop a plan for the execution of the task" (p. 276). They cite several studies that show the importance of this type of guidance early in the training so that the student's attention is drawn to appropriate ways of practicing. Cronbach (1977) warns that, "The person who practices before he knows the correct general pattern of the task is likely to practice wrong actions" (p. 425).

Cronbach's next point is extremely important. It shows the desirable positioning of guidance in relation to practice. He writes: "An interplay among explanation, practice, and further explanation is called for" (p. 425). This reminds us of Southgate's (1973) comment that subskill instruction is most effective when it is given at the opportune moment in reading practice. The teacher should be ready, "when the moment for a small amount of direct teaching arrives to help the child to take the next minute step forward and so channel learning towards the ultimate goal of efficient reading" (p. 372). The best time to provide guidance is that opportune moment when the pupil is engaged in reading practice and requests the teacher's advice. This is more likely to occur in informal methods such as the language-experience approach. It is less likely to occur in formal reading instruction by whole class, or even group, methods with basal readers. Therefore, it is important that the language-experience approach should be used for, at least, a part of the time allotted to the development of literacy skills.

How Much Guidance?

We have seen that for guidance to be effective it has to be given at the right moment; it also has to be given in the right amount. Too little leads to errors being perpetuated; too much leads to overloading and confusion. Cronbach comments that lack of guidance in a complex skill may lead the learner to "settle upon a relatively inefficient pattern" (p. 290). But, on the other hand, De Cecco and Crawford comment that, "Verbal instructions should be at a minimum in the early stages of skill learning. . . . Descriptions should direct the student's attention to only the essential aspects of a skill" (p. 276). One reason why guidance should be brief is suggested by research evidence discussed by Cronbach that showed that a demonstration is most effective when the learner pays full attention to it. Attention will flag as soon as the learner becomes fatigued or bored.

McDonald (1965) sums up for us the psychological facts about the amount of guidance that is effective in skill training:

> Once the learner has clarified the character of the response required and is able to make interpretations of the learning situation, additional guidance may only confuse him. He may be given more information than he can assimilate at the time, or he may not yet be able to integrate new responses into the pattern that he has already learned. The student reaches points in learning a complex sequence of responses where he must integrate sets of responses and assimilate the information that has already been provided. Until this process of assimilation and integration is completed, addition of new information, or the demonstration of new responses, interferes with the assimilation and integration process (p. 397).

McDonald adds: "Unfortunately, no rules are available so that the teacher can know just how much information to provide at any stage of the learning of a skilled behavior" (p. 397). In opportunistic teaching, the teacher "intervenes on the basis of what is happening now plus his knowledge of the individual child" (Downing, 1975b, p. 25).

What Guidance?

We have discussed the psychology of how, when, and how much guidance should be given in the development of the skill of reading, but what should be the content of the guidance that teachers give to pupils learning to read? The answer given by educational psychologists is that we should analyze the skill learning task. De Cecco and Crawford assert to the student teacher: "Your first teaching function is to do a task analysis of the skill you plan to teach" (p. 272). McDonald writes that "we have stressed the importance of component task and behavior analysis. Nowhere is its necessity more clear than when preparing and executing an instructional strategy to produce learning of a complex performance" (p. 413). And reading certainly is a complex performance.

But task analysis is very difficult. How can we begin? Jokl (1966) suggests that it should start from observations of successful performers. Some work of this kind has been done on the reading behavior of skilled readers (for example, the eye movement studies that we have referred to earlier), and it is indeed a fruitful approach. But Borger and Seaborne note a deficiency in it. They write: "In describing a task we tend to concentrate on what is *done,* and task analysis as in motion study takes the form of recording the detailed 'units' of movement into which an operation has been broken down. All this represents the *output* of the individual; what we tend to ignore, partly because it is taken for granted, and partly because it is difficult or impossible to observe directly, is the *input*" (pp. 129–130). The input of reading behavior is extremely difficult to determine in many ways, but not in all. For example, the designers of systems of printed symbols and the authors of books have intentions about how readers will use them. A study of those intentions may provide some clues as to what is expected of readers in their task of interpreting the printed page. This is the kind of analysis of the reader's task that we turn to next in Chapters 4 and 5.

CHAPTER 4

Orthography and Reading

From the previous chapters on reading as a skill and principles of skill acquisition, we will discuss *task analysis* or *job analysis.* This approach investigates exactly what a person does in performing a task efficiently. The skilled reader may be viewed as a worker with print, while a beginning reader is an apprentice developing the skill of reading.

In industrial or occupational psychology, a variety of scientific methods has been developed to secure valid job analyses, but this kind of systematic research on the tasks involved in learning to read and reading is not found in the research literature. Also, while many reading specialists and authors of instructional materials have made known their own subjective analyses of the task, they generally appear to be more preoccupied with the job of the teacher than with that of the pupil. Nevertheless, their ideas about how to teach reading are developed around an implicit model of how a child learns to read and what this learning task involves.

In recent years the science of linguistics has made important contributions to our thinking about this problem. In particular, linguistics provides more precise concepts and technical terms for thinking about language, and systematic descriptions of language norms. One linguist, Mountford (1970), has made a penetrating and unusual approach to the problem of learning to read and write that utilizes job analysis. He says "it puts the literate's linguistic knowledge first and the perceptual and motor skills last, as an indicator, however crude, of where the emphasis should lie" (p. 306). Mountford's analysis of the task of learning to read and write takes the form of an answer to the question: what does the normal literate individual know that the nonliterate does not know? According to Mountford, there are five psycholinguistic components of standard literacy:

1. knowledge of a standard language of literacy.
2. knowledge of its standard orthography.
3. knowledge of the "technical concepts" of literacy.
4. the linguistic "habitudes" of literacy.
5. the basic skills of literacy: reading and writing (p. 301).

By *technical concepts,* Mountford means those categories of thought and language that are used to describe literacy (such terms as *word, letter, read, write,* and so on). The *habitudes* of literacy are "such things as the following. With literacy we learn to use language solitarily, engaging in linguistic communication with people not present with us and with people not known to us; to use highly drafted language both in reception and in production; and to use the impersonal and elaborated language characteristic of written communication" (p. 304). Mountford's other categories need no definition since they are more widely known. A cursory study of Mountford's list of psycholinguistic components might lead one to dismiss the first item on the grounds that the nonliterate also knows the language. But the word *standard* is deliberately used by Mountford to indicate the difference in knowledge. Furthermore, the literate has some knowledge of language, described by component three, which the nonliterate does not possess.

The Writing System

The most obvious learning task in Mountford's list is the second component—acquisition of the knowledge of standard orthography. *Orthography* is referred to as the *writing system* of a language; that is, the system of visible marks or signs used to communicate a message from the writer to the reader. One of the most important mysteries in the psychology of reading is the problem: to what extent does the learner need to be consciously aware of the rules of the writing system? Is learning to read primarily a matter of establishing stimulus-response bonds between written symbols and units of speech? Or is it more a matter of knowing concepts of writing and speech and then understanding how they are related? These two alternatives represent the two extremes in the pedagogy of reading.

One way of analyzing a job is to find out how the designer of the equipment or process intended it to be used. This certainly is a limited method because workers often find different and effective ways of employing tools from those originally intended. Nevertheless, it may provide a useful starting point for this theoretical analysis of the job of learning to read. One must consider that the "original designers" of the most widely used writing systems of today lived so long ago that their purposes may have been obscured by later institutional habits or deflected by rituals or customs. Nevertheless, it is of considerable importance to determine the nature of the writing system. As Fries (1963) wrote: "The basic 'structure' of each particular writing system will necessarily determine what must be learned as the first steps to the reading of materials written in that system" (p. 152).

Gelb's (1963) study of the history and development of writing systems concludes that: "Writing began at the time when man learned how to communicate his thoughts and feelings by means of visible signs, understandable not only to himself but also to all other persons more or less initiated into the particular system" (p. 11). These two essential features of writing systems (which includes the print in books in these studies) are spelled out by Jensen (1970): "(1) its production by the act of drawing, painting or scratching on a durable writing-material, and (2) the purpose of communicating (to others or, as an aid to the memory, to the writer himself) . . ." (p. 24). Thus, writing was developed so that writers could *encode* in visible signs their thoughts or feelings and so that a reader could reverse the process by *decoding* the visible signs to receive the writer's thoughts and feelings. All the writing systems analyzed by linguists and philologists have these features. But writing systems differ in their technical methods of coding thoughts and feelings. The aims of encoding and decoding are universal, although the techniques differ.

In the study of the history of writing systems, two difficulties occur in determining the boundaries of the category *writing*. The first is whether to include pictures, and the second is whether objects used as symbols can be classed as *writing*. These classification problems are interesting because they point to two psychological foundations for the conception of the writing system. First, pictures are to be excluded, according to Gelb, if they are "objects of art resulting from an artistic-aesthetic urge. . . ." Nevertheless, "writing had its origin in simple pictures . . ." (p. 190). This is the beginning of the idea of a two-dimensional script, and most authors are in agreement with Gelb's position. Second, Gelb asserts that objects used as code signs ought to be excluded because they are not manmade marks. However, Jensen includes them as *object-writing* because their aim is communication. For example, a Yoruba man in jail sent his wife a stone, a piece of charcoal, some pepper, and some shrivelled grains of maize, all wrapped in a rag. She decoded this "letter" as "my body is healthy" (the hard stone), "my prospects are dark" (the black charcoal); "my spirit is aroused" (the hot pepper); "my body will become gaunt with its sufferings" (the shrivelled grain), "my clothing is in tatters" (the rag). Many other instances of object-writing are known, including the wampum-belts of the Iroquois and Algonquin Indians, and the knotted cords of the Inca quippu. These are the beginnings of the idea of encoding and decoding in a visual system, although the signs were objects rather than marks.

Closer to writing as it is conceived today are the systems called *semasiography* by Gelb. This is the expression of thoughts and feelings only loosely connected with speech. A message had only one meaning to the encoder and the decoder, but its actual form if spoken was not fixed. Typical is the well-known pictography of many North American Indian tribes. Jensen calls this *idea-writing* and contrasts it with *word picture-script*. In idea-writing, the pictures are "linked only loosely to the corresponding spoken form of expression" (p. 50), whereas a word picture-sign is a code for a specific spoken word. In idea-writing, the decoding task was to unlock the thought of the writer without reference to any particular utterance. For example, Figure 4–1

FIGURE 4–1. A business letter of an Ojibwa Indian. [From H. Jensen, 1970, used by permission.]

shows a business letter of an Ojibwa Indian. The *X* at the center stands for the gesture of crossed arms, meaning a deal or exchange. The message can be decoded to the idea that the writer has skins of buffalo, weasel and otter which are offered for a rifle and thirty beaver skins.

Several developments away from pure idea-writing toward making a one-to-one written code for specific utterances have been found in the historical study of writing. A primitive step in this direction has been noted in object-writing. If a Yoruba man sent a girl six cowrie shells on a cord it was decoded as *efa,* the word for "six." But *efa* also means "attracted." Thus this "love letter" depended on that specific meaning of *efa* being read. More important was the use of idea-writing as a mnemonic device, that is, as notes to remind the reader of the exact wording of magic spells, incantations and so on. Thus the Ojibwa Indians distinguished between *kekewin* and *kekinowen* in their pictographic system. Kekewin had the usual loose connection only between writing and speech, but kekinowen were used by the medicine men to remind them of their magic chant. Each sign reminds the medicine man of the next verse in its precise form of words. Another instance is the sentence-script of the Ewe people of Togoland, of which Figure 4–2 is an example. This represents a ball of wool with a needle and a piece of cloth. The Ewes could weave only narrow strips of cloth and, therefore, had to sew these pieces together to make any larger items that they wanted. From this life experience, these people created the proverb "Needle sews cloth big" meaning that big effects can be made out of little ones. The symbols shown, however, are decoded to the precise formal wording of their proverb.

The general trend in the development of idea-writing systems is for the pictures to become more and more simple, stylized, and conventional. According to Jensen, the result is that the difference between these simplified conventional symbols and "what they were supposed to represent gradually became greater and greater, so great finally that the bond linking form and meaning could break completely, and instead the phonetic equivalent of the picture gained the upper hand: the picture was now no longer, or no longer solely, the representation of an object or of the meaning of the word naming it, but at the same time, or even solely, a colorless and meaningless fixing of a certain sound, or sound-complex. This transition is known as 'PHONETICIZATION' " (p. 51). Gelb concludes similarly: "From then on writing gradually lost its character as an independent mode of expressing ideas and became a tool of speech, a vehicle through which exact forms of speech could be recorded in permanent form" (p. 12).

Gelb asserts that a pure word script or logographic writing system probably has never existed. "Even Chinese, the most logographic of all the writings, is not a pure logographic system because from the earliest times it has used word signs functioning as syllabic signs" (Gelb, p. 193).

FIGURE 4–2. Sentence script of the Ewe people of Togoland. [From H. Jensen, 1970, used by permission.]

For example, if English were written in such a mixed system, a conventional simplified picture of the human eye might represent the word "eye" or it could be used as a phonetic rebus for the words "I" or "aye," or for the first syllable in "ideal."

Chao (1968) restricts the term *writing* to systems that have become phoneticized. He states: "Visual symbols do not begin to be writing until they have a close correspondence to language" and, "if a sign represents a specific part of language, it is writing; if it represents things directly it is not" (p. 101). Although, this is a matter of definition, it carries the important implication for the analysis of the job of reading that modern writing systems are designed to be decoded to language. Of course, the purpose of the writer as defined by Chao remains the same as the man who conveyed thought by pictures; that is to communicate a message about his ideas or feelings. But the technique of the code of writing as defined by Chao *requires that the reader arrives at the thought or feeling of the author through the medium of language.* This is the first major conclusion of our job analysis from the point of view of the user of writing. It applies to all present-day writing systems. In current usage, there are three main techniques for coding language in writing: (1) *logographs,* written symbols representing linguistic units of meaning; (2) *syllabic writing,* symbols representing the syllable units of speech sound; (3) *alphabetic writing,* symbols representing the phoneme units of speech sound. Gelb points out that there are "no pure systems of writing" (p. 199), but nevertheless one can categorize systems as being primarily either logographic, syllabic, or alphabetic.

The student of the psychology of reading will find that the effort of considering other languages with different writing systems is very worthwhile. One does not realize the significance of certain factors in reading the writing system of one's own language until one notes the absence of these features in other languages. Whorf's (1941) reason for placing such a high value on studying another, preferably remarkably different, language was that "in its study we are at long last pushed willy-nilly out of our ruts. Then we find that the exotic language is a mirror held up to our own." Therefore, the next step in our analysis of the task of the student learning to read is to consider in more detail how these different systems code the language in which writers communicate their thoughts and feelings.

The Learning Task in Different Languages

In his book, *Comparative Reading* (Downing, 1973) addressed the question: how does the child's experience of the task of learning to read vary from one language to another? Fourteen countries were compared, and many different writing systems were contrasted.

Some features of the learner's task were found to be quite different from one language to another. The most obvious is the unit of language represented by the basic unit of writing. As has been noted above, Chinese is not a pure logographic writing system. A full description of it has been provided in *Comparative Reading.* Here it is necessary only to note that Chinese has several different types of characters based on different systems of coding (one of which is phonetic). Nevertheless, the major feature of the Chinese writing system is its code for morphemes. In linguistics the term *morpheme* refers to the minimum unit of meaning in a language. This may be or may not be a word. For example, in English "boat"[1] is a morpheme which is a word, but "boater" has two morphemes of which the "-er" morpheme is not a word. Similarly, the "-s" part of "boats" is not a word, but it is a morpheme conveying the plural meaning. Written English can be analyzed in terms of morphemes, but (as will be shown later) English is not primarily a morphemic writing system. The point is that a writer using the Chinese writing system makes marks, each of which represents a morpheme. Therefore, the task of the learner is primarily to acquire knowledge of the relationships between the characters of the Chinese writing system and the morphemes of the Chinese language.

Another language studied in *Comparative Reading* was Japanese. It, too, has a very different writing system from English and other European languages. Japanese has several writing systems, but the everyday usage in books and other written or printed Japanese materials is a combination of two main types of characters—*Kana* and *Kanji.* The Kanji characters are logographic, like the Chinese symbols. The Kana characters represent the sounds of syllables of Japanese speech. It is possible to write Japanese sentences in Kana characters alone. This is done in telegrams and in the first reading materials of young beginners. Thus, the initial task of Japanese children is to relate the Kana characters to the syllables of Japanese

[1] Where the spoken word is referred to in this book, it is placed within quotation marks, thus "boat."

speech. Later they must learn more and more Kanji characters for morphemes as they replace the Kana syllabic symbols. English speech also can be analyzed into syllables, but the written characters of the English alphabet were not designed to represent syllables, as were the Japanese Kana characters.

Most other widely used world languages are written in alphabets in which a quite different unit of language is the primary subject of coding. The next chapter will examine the minority view of a number of linguists that the basic unit of the code in the English writing system is not, as is commonly held, the phoneme. For the moment, the usual view will be assumed. That is, that the unit coded in alphabetic writing systems is the *phoneme.* Phonemes are contrasted speech sounds which make a difference in meaning. For example, in English the /k/ sounds at the beginning of "cap" and "cougar" are different phonetically, but this difference is never used to make a contrast in meaning.[2] Therefore these sounds are not phonemes in English. On the other hand /b/ and /v/ are said to be different phonemes because they are used to contrast the essential difference in meaning in such words as "boat" and "vote." Different languages have different phonemes, although, of course, there is overlapping. In some languages, there is only one phoneme for what English speakers recognize as /b/ and /v/. *Phoneme* has a precise linguistic meaning, and is quite unlike the ambiguity of the word *sound* as it is often employed in teaching phonics. Another ambiguity which causes difficulty in phonics teaching is in the terminology for describing the units of the writing system. Most English teachers call these units *letters* of the alphabet. But Spanish teachers, for example, describe *ch* as "a letter," although most American reading teachers would say they are "two letters." This problem arises when the phoneme is coded by a unit larger than a single letter. A linguistic term which may be used for this basic unit of the alphabet is *grapheme.* But linguists are not all in agreement in their usage of *grapheme.* Some employ it for the individual letter. Certainly the term *letter* is inadequate for understanding the relationship between written and spoken English. Teachers and parents who rely on this unit alone for teaching phonics cannot help but cause confusion in the child's mind. Albrow (1972) states that "it is necessary to distinguish in the description between *letters* and *orthographic symbols.* The alphabet with which we write English consists of twenty-six letters, but these have to be seen as creating a much larger number of orthographic symbols" (p. 11). Albrow gives as examples the letters *t* and *h* employed in the orthographic symbols *t* as in *ten, h* as in *hen, th* as in *thin,* and the letters *c* and *h* used in the orthographic symbols *c* as in *car, h* as in *hen, ch* as in *chin.* However, *orthographic symbol* seems rather cumbersome for frequent use, and, therefore, in the following discussion, the term *grapheme* will be used consistently for that unit of the writing system which clearly represents an orthographic unit, for example, *ch* or *th.*[3]

Hebrew, Sanskrit and some other Asiatic languages have writing systems which have a transitional form between a syllabary and an alphabet. But all the modern European languages are written with an alphabet. If the graphemes in these writing systems primarily represent phonemes, then an important task for the learner in these alphabetic languages is to acquire knowledge about the way in which the phonemes of speech are related to the graphemes of writing. (It is important to note that this is not a prescription for phonic methods of teaching. This is an analysis of the *learner's* task—not the teacher's). English can be analyzed into syllables or morphemes, but these are not the main units represented by the graphemes of the orthography. The unit which seems to have been recognized throughout the history of English orthography (though not so named until comparatively recently) is the *phoneme.*

To sum up this aspect of the task analysis of learning to read, a universal task in all languages is to learn *how* the writing system represents language. The writing system is the basic tool of literacy. But the tool varies from one language to another. In Chinese, writing mainly signals morphemic units; in Japanese, the initial tool symbolizes syllables; in English, the chief units of the tool are usually assumed to be phonemes. The learner's task must vary correspondingly.

Writing systems vary in several other respects, as was shown by the *Comparative Reading* investigation. Chinese employs a very large number

[2] Symbols between slash marks, for example, /k/ do not refer to spelling. They refer to speech sounds. The symbols used in this book for this purpose are for the most part those of the International Phonetic Association (1949).

[3] Where the printed or written word is referred to in this book it is given in italics, thus *chip.*

of characters, and it is commonly supposed that the resulting burden of memorization makes it difficult to learn to read Chinese. However, the *Comparative Reading* study concluded that this burden may have been exaggerated, and that, in contrast, the burden of memorization has been underestimated in the alphabetic system. The number of graphemes in English, for example, is far greater than the twenty-six letters of the alphabet. One must take account, for instance, of such alternative graphemes as *ie, y, uy, igh, i* for the single phoneme common to *pie, my, guy, sigh, mind.* Other alphabetic writing systems have fewer alternative graphemes than English. Certainly, the load on memory represents a different task from one language to another for the literacy learner.

Another difference between writing systems is the complexity of the rules linking the written language to speech. For example, Finnish has a near one-to-one relationship between its phonemes and graphemes. In contrast, the relationship is more complex in English (as will be discussed later). Thus the task of understanding the writing system may be more difficult in English than it is in Finnish.

Yet another interesting difference noted in the *Comparative Reading* study is in the spatial representation of the temporal features of speech. Israeli children must learn to relate the order in which sounds occur in spoken Hebrew to a right-to-left representation in written Hebrew. In English, the direction is the opposite way. In Chinese, the ordering on the page is vertical instead of horizontal. In Japan, about one half of all modern printed books are printed in vertical lines and the other half have horizontal lines. A universal task is to learn the relation between the ordering of speech units in time and the order of written units in space. But the spatial arrangement differs from language to language.

Two other differences noted in *Comparative Reading* are the *complexity of the written symbols* and the *transfer value of their names.* Research cited in that book (especially that of Kawai, 1966; and Leong, 1970) indicated that extremely simple shapes are not ideal. Children seem to discriminate and remember more readily the characters which have more complex features. Simple characters are more readily confused with one another, especially if the differences between them are primarily orientational (for example, the four stick-with-loop characters of English orthography—*b, d, p, q*). Thus, although all learners must learn to discriminate visually between the characters of a writing system, it will be more or less difficult according to the design of the characters employed.

Letter names vary in the extent to which they may provide a clue or mnemonic for the unit of speech that they represent. For example, in English "aitch" and "double-you" do not even contain the phonemes that *h* and *w* usually represent. In other languages the letter names have more general transfer value in this respect. However, research on teaching children letter names (for example, Samuels, 1971) shows that it has no effect on learning to read. Therefore, learning letter names does not appear to be a primary task for the child in the initial stage of literacy acquisition. It is more likely to be a secondary task which is rather easily accomplished once children are motivated to label a symbol which they recognize as significant and useful.

This brief and simplified account of some of the more interesting differences between the writing systems of various languages already has identified some of the tasks of beginners in learning their writing system. They must learn:

1. what unit of speech is coded by their writing system.
2. a number of visually presented two-dimensional shapes.
3. the rules for relating the speech units to the written shapes.
4. the way in which the time order of speech sounds is related to the spatial order of the written shapes.

At this point it is very important to remember that, thus far, we have discussed no more than the simplest aspect of only one part of the task of learning to read—the elements of the writing system from the point of view of a linguist. Even limiting ourselves to the above four linguistic tasks, when the psychological work involved is considered, the task seems much less simple. Task number 1 requires: (a) learning that speech can be segmented into units; (b) the ability to discriminate those units appropriate for the writing system; (c) the ability to analyse a continuous utterance into those units. Task number 2 raises numerous questions about visual perception. The child must learn which differences between written symbols are relevant and which are redundant. Task number 3 requires considerable work in reasoning and memory. Task number 4 needs, in addition, general conceptual development in the matters of time and space.

These problems may become clearer if we take our analysis of the task of learning a writing system into greater depth by applying it to one language—English. To do this adequately, we must make a major excursion into history to find out what were the intentions of the people who have shaped the writing system tool over the past thousand years. We should apply the techniques of psychohistory, and look for the motivations of those who invented characters and rules for combining them to code language. Why was it decided to spell a certain word this way? Why did this particular convention become fixed? Why was it decided to change this spelling rule thus? Why do certain words have equally acceptable written forms? The motivations of the early users of English orthography and the motivations of its present-day users should provide the key to the learner's task in understanding the nature of the writing system. An important part of reading is discovering the intentions of the writer, and for the beginner this involves the elementary signals of the writing system. What does the writer intend to convey by these written symbols?

The English Writing System

No natural writing system represents all aspects of language. All that is provided is sufficient clues for the reader to work out the writer's message on the basis of prior knowledge of the language. For instance, the Aztecs used a sign which could represent either the whole of a word or only part. Thus in Figure 4–3 *snake* is "coatl" in Aztec, and *hill* is "tepec." This is the sign for the name of the town of "Coatepac." If one has never heard its name before, it is difficult to read it correctly from "coatl" + "tepec," but when one is acquainted with "Coatepec" there is no difficulty. This brings out a very important aspect of the task of reading which is that it normally involves *recognition of what is already known in speech.* The reader must make intelligent guesses based on his knowledge of *more* than what is signaled in writing.

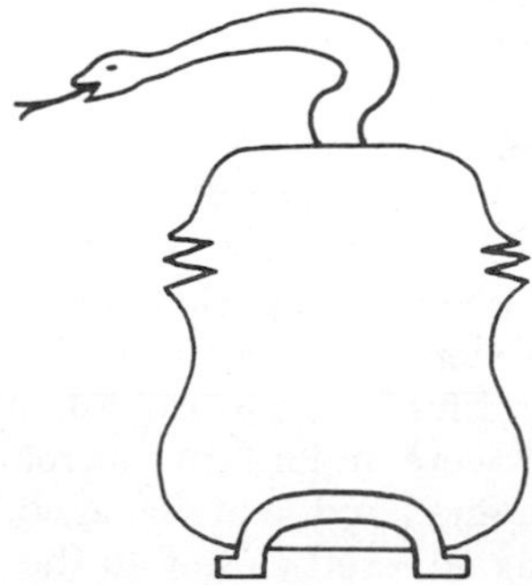

FIGURE 4–3. Aztec sign for the name "Coatepec" ("coatl" + "tepec")

Another example of this assumption of greater knowledge in the reader is the clog almanacs used in Staffordshire, England in the Middle Ages. These consisted of four-sided blocks of wood on the edges of which were cut notches to represent the days of the year. Special signs marked festivals and saints' days. For example, a harp stood for St. David's Day. But a heart was used *both* for the day of the Purification of the Virgin *and* the Annunciation of the Virgin. This was because the reader of the almanac was expected to know that these two events are separated by about seven weeks.

In the English writing system there is only scanty notation for *stress.* Written English for the most part expects readers to supply stress from their prior knowledge of the stress patterns of the language. From the beginning, this is one of the important tasks of learners. They have to learn to make intelligent guesses about things not signaled on the basis of their past experience of speech. Thus a teacher who told her pupils "never to guess" could inhibit the child from learning one of the most important truths about the writing system—its functioning as "a psycholinguistic guessing game" (Goodman, 1970).[4] Another task indicated by the above examples of partial clues is that of knowing what is signaled by the writing system and what is not. Remembering these points we may now consider what aspects of the English language are signaled directly by its writing system. This will provide a guide to this component of the pupil's task in learning to read.

To understand this complex task we must begin our journey into history because the child's task today may be better understood when we know how the present orthographic conventions came into being. Gelb (1974) has pointed out that the relationship between speech and writing "is generally stronger in the earlier stages of a certain system of writing and weaker in its later stages. This is due to the fact that a writing system when

[4] But note that listening, too, is a psycholinguistic guessing game.

first introduced generally reproduces rather faithfully the underlying phonemic structure. In the course of time writing, more conservative than language, generally does not keep up with the continuous changes of language and, as time progresses, diverges more and more from its linguistic counterpart" (pp. 297–298).

Historical Facts

Prior to the Greek alphabet, vowels were not deliberately represented as separate sounds. Around the eleventh or twelfth century B.C., the Greeks borrowed letters from one of the Semitic alphabets then in use in Syria and Palestine. At first, the Greeks imitated the Semitic right-to-left direction of writing the letters. Then they tried writing as follows: line one right-to-left, line two left-to-right, line three right-to-left, and so on. Finally, they fixed on the order left-to-right on all lines.

Two great modern alphabets are descended from the original Greek system. The present-day Russian writing system is derived from the Cyrillic alphabet which came directly from the Greek system with the addition of some new letters. The other great branch resulted in the modern Roman alphabet, used for the writing system of most European languages, including English. The Etruscans took over the Greek alphabet, and the Romans adopted it from the Etruscans as the writing system for Latin.

The Roman alphabet was introduced into England in the sixth century when Roman and Irish missionaries converted the Anglo-Saxons to Christianity. Although no earlier writing has been found in England (except Oghams used to write Celtic in the southwest) it is probable that the Anglo-Saxons were acquainted with writing before they saw the Roman alphabet. They probably brought the runic alphabet with them from Germany when they invaded England and settled there in the fifth century. This is important because two of the runic symbols were adapted to supplement the Roman alphabet for phonemes not found in Latin. One of these, þ, called *thorn,* was used to represent either the sound /θ/ as in *thigh* or /ð/ as in *thy* (the double representation in Modern English by *th* has arisen because what are now two phonemes were in fact only one phoneme in Old English). *Thorn* remained in use from the eighth century until the seventeenth century when it finally succumbed to *th.* Even today, *thorn* has a vestigial existence in such pseudohistorical names as "Ye Olde Tea Shoppe," because *y* was used by printers who did not have a þ in their equipment; hence *ye* instead of *þe* for *the.*

A comprehensive and scholarly investigation of the history of English orthography has been provided by Scragg (1974). Scragg not only surveyed what has been written about English orthography throughout its history, but he also made a careful analysis of ancient documents and old books to determine how English has actually been written through the ages. Space here permits only a brief summary of Scragg's main findings as they reveal the nature of the present-day writing system of English.

Scragg's survey is chronological and follows accepted lines of historical investigation. Here the attempt will be made to convert Scragg's historical account into a psychological analysis of the motives and other forces which have caused the English writing system to be what it is today. Changes of behavior have occurred continually in the course of the evolution of English orthography. These changes have been of two kinds—changes in speech and changes in writing. There seem to be strong tendencies to change but also a powerful force for stabilization in the orthography.

Motivation for Stability

It is popularly supposed that the conventionalization or standardization of English orthography is of comparatively recent date. Some people credit Samuel Johnson with having standardized written English in his great dictionary. Others have proposed the early printer Caxton or the King James Bible as setting the trend for standardization. Scragg's scholarly survey and analysis explode all these myths. In fact, from the earliest times there have been deliberate efforts to stabilize English orthogaphy.

The first great period of orthographic stability was in the reign of King Edgar, 959–975. Success in standardization was motivated by the needs of educated people in a period of peace and prosperity. The monasteries flourished, there was a great demand for books in English, and the monastic orders were under firm control. The scribes were well trained and well managed. Therefore, their spelling adhered closely to the convention of the *West Saxon standard* which employed the

Roman alphabet plus four additional characters (now defunct). It is interesting to note that the Roman alphabet in the tenth century did not then include *j*, *v*, or *w*, and that *q* and *z* were usually avoided. Scragg points out that this period of standardization "meant that accuracy of phonemic representation was increasingly disturbed in the eleventh century" (p. 12) because of changes in speech with which the orthography had not kept pace. Nevertheless, Scragg states: "As a whole, Old English spelling as developed in the West Saxon tradition was much nearer a one-to-one relationship with sounds than is its Modern English descendent" (p. 11). A number of present-day spelling conventions date from this early period of standardization—for example, the use of *s* for /z/, the lack of separate graphemes for /θ/ and /ð/, and the partially overlapping use of *i* and *y*. The West Saxon standardization was followed by a long period in which the motivation for a stable orthography was very weak. The main cause was the neglect of English following the introduction of French by the Normans after 1066.

Renewed motivation for standardization of English spelling came with the revival of English in the chancery, beginning about 1430. "Standard written English used today as a world language, and the spelling convention which broadly is part of that standard, were established in London in the fifteenth century . . ." (Scragg, p. 33). This standard was based on the dialect of the London area, where the royal family had decided to establish their capital.

Caxton's first English printing press was established at Westminster in 1476, but it was not the force for stabilization which is popularly supposed. Scragg found that the first printers lacked the discipline of the scribes. "Rather than further the stabilizing movement of the professional scribes, the printers in effect encouraged lack of conformity in spelling" (p. 64).

The real driving force for standardizing English orthography came from the writings of schoolmasters, which became numerous from the end of the sixteenth century. The most important of these was Richard Mulcaster's *The First Part of the Elementarie*, published in 1582. His purpose was to increase standardization by reducing drastically the number of alternatives then acceptable. Wherever a word had a stable written form, he accepted it. If there were alternatives, he chose the one closest to a phonemic rendering. But Mulcaster was influenced by analogy with other written words and also by calligraphic aesthetics. "With Mulcaster's list of recommended spellings the first step had been taken towards the provision of an authoritative work of reference for spelling . . ." (Scragg, p. 62). Thus Mulcaster became "the virtual founder of English lexicography" (p. 79).

Mulcaster's work, however, became effective through two other channels. On the educational side, it was another schoolmaster who turned Mulcaster's theory into classroom practice. Edmond Coote in 1596 published *The English Schoolemaister* which was a class workbook for the teaching of reading and writing. Its great popularity may be judged from the fact that its fifty-fourth edition was published in 1737. Coote's spelling lists were taught everywhere in schools and in classes for apprentices. The second channel for Mulcaster's ideas was through the printers. Scragg recognizes the powerful influence of the press here: "It was the printers who led the way to the orthographic regularity evident at the end of Elizabeth's reign" (p. 70). Summing up on this period, Scragg concludes: "Thus the spelling book and the primitive dictionary, with their growing authority during the seventeenth century, induced the printers to adopt a common orthography" (p. 78).

Stabilization was complete by 1700, and Samuel Johnson's *Dictionary of the English Language* was not published until 1755. Hence Johnson merely recorded what was already an established convention and "in the development of spelling he had almost no influence at all" (p. 82). But Scragg limits this to "the public spelling of the printers," and gives Johnson the credit "for the establishment of printers' spelling in private use."

With the spread of literacy and the enormous expansion of publishing in the nineteenth and twentieth centuries, even stronger motivation for standardization of English orthography has developed and been established. Motivation for change is discernible but seems weak. Changes in public spelling, therefore, are very difficult to introduce today.

Motivation for Change

At other periods in history, motivation for change has been stronger than the drive for stability. A number of different motives for changing English orthography are apparent from Scragg's historical survey.

Speech Changes

The most important motive for change has been the effort to keep the writing system phonemic. Whatever the motivations underlying changes in spoken English, the fact is that pronunciation is continually being modified. In the past, writers and printers have made frequent attempts to bring the orthography back into line with a standard pronunciation of English, and, when they have failed, reformers have urged them to return to a more phonemic representation. For example, Richard Hodges in *The English Primrose,* published in 1644, urged a clearer indication of speech sounds by orthography. He introduced his theme by the quotation "If the trumpet give an uncertain sound, who shall prepare himself to the battle?" Scragg gives numerous examples of the many perplexing problems which faced scribes and printers who tried to restore grapheme-phoneme correspondence when pronunciation shifted. Often nothing was done, leading to such results as the two different phonemic values for *th.* Another example of such a failure to adapt is the use of *gh* in words such as *high, ought, night, bough* where the corresponding phoneme has disappeared in most dialects of English. In words like *cough, laugh, tough,* the phoneme changed to /f/ instead of disappearing altogether. However, the orthography failed to adapt; hence these anomalies of the present day.

Often the scribes reacted to a change in speech by trying to adapt the redundant grapheme to represent some other aspect of language. An excellent example is that of so-called "silent *e.*" In the eleventh century, a sound-change occurred which involved the lengthening of short vowels in the open syllables of two-syllable words. For example /namə/ became /na:mə/. Then in the fourteenth century the final unstressed /ə/ was dropped and /na:mə/ became /na:m/, but the *e* remained in the written word *name* and so became "silent *e.*" The initial reaction to this change in pronunciation was not to drop final *e* but to add it to many other words quite haphazardly. Mulcaster proposed to regularize this aspect of English orthography by restricting final *e* as a device for signaling vowel length in such words as *name, mete, bite, note, mute.* But an inappropriate final *e* remains in *done, gone, have, live, love, doctrine* as a vestige of the earlier confused reaction to these changes in pronunciation.

Sometimes the change goes in the other direction, and one sees the phenomenon of "spelling pronunciation," that is, a change in the pronunciation of the spoken word based on the graphemes of the written word. For example, Dr. Johnson's dictionary in 1755 stated of *fault,* "the *l* is sometimes sounded, sometimes mute," whereas /l/ is normally pronounced today. The Middle English written version of the word was *faute.* Current spelling pronunciations more and more frequently heard are the *t* in *often, Christmas,* and *postman.* Less frequent is the *l* in *palm* and *salmon* (cf. Middle English spelling *samon*). The *b* in *debt* and *doubt* remains unpronounced as it was, of course, in Middle English *dette, doute.*

Creative Spelling

Another motive for changing the orthography has been the creativity which produced experiments and reforms of various kinds in the English writing system. At the present time, this creativity is still evident in areas where special motivations have priority over the powerful drive for conventionality. For example, advertising seems to give a special license for innovative spelling. Also certain literary conventions involve creating novel spellings.

One of the motives for creativity in spelling has been discussed already in the preceding section. It is the major one and quite universal. As Moorhouse (1946) notes, "as long ago as the days of cuneiform, the process of amending spelling gradually in order to keep pace with linguistic changes has been a regular feature of writing . . ." (p. 68). An example of successful creativity in this respect was the invention of the grapheme *ch* to cope with an ambiguity created by a change in Old English pronunciation. Originally the sounds /tʃ/ and /k/ were not contrasted to indicate any change in meaning. That is, they belonged to one phoneme. With the pronunciation change, they became separate phonemes, although Old English orthography wrote them both with *c.* Thus "kin" and "chin" were both written *cinn.* The scribes took over *ch* from foreign writings to represent English /tʃ/. Scragg comments: "The spread of *ch* is so complete and so fast that it must have fulfilled a need felt everywhere for unambiguous expression of the sound" (p. 45). In English, this type of creativity has always been left to private enterprise, and orthographic innovations have depended for their success on the taste of writers and printers and the purchasers of their products. In other languages there has been more centralized control. For example, the Académie Française was founded in 1635 and exercises this kind of control. Its power is indicated by the fact that 25 per cent of French written words were orthographically revised in the Académie's 1740 and 1762 dictionaries. Its power has continued to the present time.

The patchwork appearance of present-day English orthography is probably due to the lack of a stronger unifying force. For example, although doubling the consonant to indicate a preceding short vowel is a fairly general rule, why is *v* never doubled, except in new words coined since the power of the press was established? The double consonant convention began to be used in the late Old English period, but only inconsistently until the fifteenth century. But *v* or *u* could not be doubled in Middle English because of ambiguity with *vv* or *uu*. Modern English spelling does not have this problem because *w* is available for the related phoneme. Nevertheless, *lever, never, sever, hover, Dover, rover* all continue to have a single *v*, thus ignoring the general double consonant rule for distinguishing between the different vowel length in such words.

Another reason for creative orthographic changes has been to give clues to the etymology of words. English was less subject to this type of creativity in the Middle Ages, but some examples were found by Scragg. For example, Anglo-Norman *barun* was later spelt *baron* on the model of Parisian French. It was the Renaissance which produced the age of *etymologizing* in English orthographic reform. A great admiration for classical culture and language combined with the need for expanding vocabulary to cope with the knowledge explosion to motivate the coining of new words derived from Greek and Latin. New orthographic forms were introduced for old words which showed, by analogy, their classical derivations. "For example, from the Latin participle *perfectum,* French derived an adjective which passed into Middle English as *perfit,* also spelled in the sixteenth century as *parfit.* The Renaissance borrowing into English of *perfection* drew attention to the discrepancy between the English adjective and its classical root, and *perfit/parfit* was respelled *perfect"* (Scragg, p. 54). Vast numbers of English words were changed for this etymologizing purpose.

Many of these etymological orthographic changes remain with us today, but not all were accepted. For example, *sanct* for "saint" enjoyed only a brief popularity in the sixteenth century. *Phantasy* for "fantasy" lasted until the nineteenth century when *f* reasserted itself, and this option for reversion remains open in many words—for example, *elefant* for "elephant."

Unfortunately, as Scragg notes, "The zeal of those intent on reforming spelling along etymological lines often led them astray in cases in which their knowledge of Latin exceeded that of the history of the words they were emending" (p. 57). For instance, Middle English *yland* was changed to *island* by association with French *isle* derived from Latin *insula.* John Ray in his *Note on the Errors of Our Alphabet,* published in 1691, called these errors "false spellings." Numerous examples exist in current English orthography. For example, the *c* in *scent* and *scissors* was erroneously added on the analogy with *science* where *c* does correctly indicate the Latin derivation. The confusion is so extensive that Scragg comments: "Without recourse to an etymological dictionary, few users of English today are able to distinguish between the unetymological *b* in *crumb* and the same letter in *dumb* where it is etymologically correct . . . , or the unetymological *c* in *scent* and the etymological one in *scene* and *science"* (p. 58). The overenthusiasm of the etymologizers seems to have defeated their own purpose since their signals of etymology are so unreliable.

The Profit Motive

This motivation for creative spellings will be discussed again in a later section on economic factors in general. Here it need only be mentioned that sometimes spellings have been changed mainly or solely for financial gain. Mulcaster in 1582 wrote: "If words be overcharged with number of letters, that coms either by coutousnesse in such as sell them by lines, or by ignorance" (p. 86). He was referring to the fact that in the Middle Ages lengthened spellings were employed by lawyer's clerks who were paid by the inch for their writing.

Spacing

Variant written forms for the same word, for example *pity, pittie, pyttye,* and so on were motivated by their convenience for spacing. A printer would choose the one which best fitted the space on the line of print. This is one reason why the

King James Bible of 1611 was not the model for the standardization of English orthography which some have suggested. Pollard (1923–1924) notes that "the only consistency is that the form is always preferred which suits the spacing" (p. 6). The later Authorized Versions in 1629 and 1638 did show a gradual removal of such variant spellings but "this was the effect, not the cause, of increasing spelling stability" (Scragg, p. 73).

Aesthetic Motivation

Taste or fashion has often influenced English orthography. Indeed, some of the preceding subheadings might be included under this one. For example, in the West Saxon standard orthography *q* and *z* were usually avoided though available in the Roman alphabet then in use. Subsequently *q* came more into favor so that *cwen* became *queen* and *cwic* became *quick*. But *z* has continued to be disliked throughout the history of the English writing system.

Avoidance of Homographs

An increasing concern has been shown for avoiding homophones becoming also homographs. For example, when phonemic distinctions between *u* and *o* were eroded by imitation of the Late Latin change from *u* to *o*, one of the innovations seems to have been such distinctive orthographic forms for each member of the homophonic pairs, thus: *some, sum; son, sun; ton, tun.* Later this motivation is more clearly stated. Scragg remarks that the books by sixteenth and seventeenth century schoolmasters referred to above, "show that conscious efforts were made to avoid homophones becoming homographs also . . ." (p. 59). As will be noted later, public reading aloud gave way to silent reading as more and more people began to possess their own copies of books. Until then the listener to oral reading presumably used context to deal with any possible homophonic confusion, as he would in normal conversation.

Economic Factors

The cost of written or printed materials has had an important influence on the English writing system. Until the fourteenth century, written material was a luxury enjoyed by only a tiny minority. Every book or other written communication had to be written individually by the hand of a scribe. Writing was on expensive parchment or cumbersome wax tablets. The breakthrough for more widespread private reading came with the introduction of paper at the end of the fourteenth century. Paper was cheaper than parchment and led to an increased demand for books. This demand in turn motivated the invention of the printing press and thus escalated the spread of books. A number of the creative changes in English orthography depended on this economic factor, because, as Scragg found, "In the fifteenth century, private reading began to replace public recitation. . . . As medieval man ceased pointing to the words with his book mark as he pronounced them aloud, and turned to silent reading for personal edification and satisfaction, so his attention was concentrated more on the written word as a unit than on the speech sounds represented by the constituent letters" (p. 56). This change from public oral reading to private silent reading opened the way for such nonphonemic motivations as etymologizing, avoidance of homograph/homophone coincidence, and visual aesthetics.

Two other economic factors should be mentioned here. First, the tendency to elongate written words when clerks were paid for writing by the inch should be noted again. Second, the continuing importance of powerful economic influences on English orthography should be recognized. The scribes' conventions and the printers' spelling rules were developed and maintained because their customers had to be pleased and satisfied. The present-day extremely strong motivation for stability in English orthography is powered by publishers' and printers' belief that their customers want books and other papers printed in the conventional orthography. However, signs that this stability of spelling may be disintegrating began to appear in the 1970s. This breakdown too has an economic motive. Computerization of the press has important cost benefits. At the same time, proofreading has become extremely expensive. Therefore, printers' errors in books and newspapers are becoming increasingly common—witness the following letter from the novelist Graham Greene to the editor, published in *The Times* of London on May 24, 1978:

> *The Times,* London, England
> May 24, 1978
>
> Is this a rekord?
>
> *From Mr. Graham Greene, CH*
>
> Sir, May I suggest that the number of misprints per page in an English daily newspaper would

be a worthy candidate for the *Guinness Book of Records?* Just to establish a claim I nominate page 4 of *The Times* of May 12 which contains 37 misprints. They include two well worth preserving: "entertoinment" has a fine Cockney ring and "rampaign," combining in one word the ideas of campaign and rampage in an article on vandalism, deserves to find a permanent place in the Oxford Dictionary. I was glad to note too the firm attitude taken to juvenile delinquency—two defendents aged 3 and aged 0 were committed for trial at the Central Criminal Court.

Yours truly,
GRAHAM GREENE
Paris 17.

Environmental Influences

Some motivations for change in the English writing system were indirect results of historical events. The layman might call them "accidents of history." We have already noted that the West Saxon standard was permitted by a period of peace and prosperity. The wrecking of that standard (as will be shown in the next section) was due to the Norman invasion. Similarly the dialect spoken in the London area and the phonemic coding that went with it became the basis of the standard written English of today because the King happened to choose that area for his capital. If the King had chosen Gloucester or Oxford, a quite different standard orthography would have developed because of the localization of speech and writing in the three centuries following the Norman conquest. Another influence of the Norman conquest was the influx of French vocabulary. Scragg estimates that "about 40 per cent in a dictionary count" of present-day vocabulary would show French derivation (p. 40).

One particularly important environmental influence on the English writing system was the bilingualism and biliteracy of cultured English people in the twelfth and thirteenth centuries. Scragg shows that "many words of the vast influx from French into English were already familiar to Englishmen not only in French as a spoken language but in French writings too. What was required of such words in English writings was not an anglicised spelling (which might serve to remind readers of the pronunciation) but the spelling by which they were traditionally represented in the French, however ill that accorded with English conventions" (p. 42). Thus, the environmental fact of bilingualism and biliteracy caused the English writing system to take this particular diversion from a phonemic orthography. One may note also the motivation for preserving the linguistic norms of the victors' language over the language of the vanquished, which is an example of the influence of social status in determining linguistic conventions.

Education and Training

One of the strongest influences of all those enumerated here in this motivational analysis of Scragg's historical survey is that of education and training. When the education and training of those who wrote or printed books was good, progress toward order and stability in English orthography was made. The best example is the one given above of the establishment of the West Saxon standard at the end of the tenth century. Prosperous and peaceful times brought a high standard of training to the scribes. When William I defeated Harold in 1066 it heralded a period of chaos for English orthography because a phase of neglect of education and training in English was beginning. The French conquerors had no use for the English language. The demand for written English consequently fell greatly. The new masters of the scriptoria were often French-speaking, as were their abbots and bishops. Scragg found: "Gradually the number of scribes engaged in the copying of English writings declined, and the careful training of novices in conventional spelling, so important in the maintenance of a universal orthography, was neglected" (p. 16). Regional orthographies sprang up, but the all-pervading influence was one of neglect and ignorance. Numerous errors crept in during this period and many have been preserved in present-day English orthography. For example, *sinder* became *cinder*, *is* became *ice*, *mys* changed to *mice*, *lys* altered to *lice*, all because of poor training of the scribes. These errors occurred because of the scribes' stronger knowledge of the French writing system. Similarly, Latin provided another "set of spelling conventions to cause additional confusion in a situation already very fluid" (pp. 43–44). Under this Latin influence *u* was changed to *o* erroneously in many English words such as *come, some, monk, son, tongue, wonder, honey, worry, dove, love.* Many other examples can be cited of "the results of scribes' confusion between English, French and Latin spelling" (p. 44). The root cause of the confusion was their ignorance of English. For example, *hw* was changed to *wh* in a mistaken analogy with the use of *h* in *ch* and *th*. No wonder that Scragg refers to English orthography after the effects of the French invasion as "a curious and at times eccentric building on so simple and sound a ground-plan" (p. 14).

A second massive influx of orthographic errors occurred in a period when one might have expected improvement rather than the reverse, but the root cause is the same—a relative neglect of the English language. The etymologizing changes introduced during the Renaissance were based on superior knowledge and respect for Latin and related languages and a correspondingly inferior knowledge of the history of English. It was this period which erroneously inserted the *s* in *island*, the *b* in *crumb*, the *c* in *scent*, the *ph* in *elephant*, and produced innumerable other errors. Some of these errors are concealed today because of spelling pronunciation. Thus the true origin of many English words has been lost in their pronunciation as well as in their orthographic form. For example, *caitif* became *captive*, *cors* became *corpse*, *descryve* became *describe*, *faucon* changed to *falcon* and so on.

A third very productive source of errors was the introduction of printing. Inexpensive books were in great demand, and hasty production caused many careless errors which have later become conventionally "correct" in Modern English orthography. Caxton, for example, had lived for a long time on the Continent and was quite out of touch with English orthography. He took little care in editing copy or in supervising the setting up of the print. Furthermore, there were no English compositors, and Caxton was forced to employ foreigners in his print shop. One curious error which remains as a monument to Caxton in present-day English orthography is the use of *gh* instead of *g* in initial position of a number of words. "In the many translations he made from French, Dutch and Latin, he seems heavily influenced by his sources, the most notorious of his permanent contributions to the language being the introduction of the Dutch convention *gh* for /g/ in *ghost*, a native word spelled *gost* until the later fifteenth century" (p. 66). But not all of Caxton's errors received popular acceptance. For example, *gherle* ("girl"), *ghoos* ("goose"), *ghes* ("geese"), *ghoot* ("goat") are no longer with us in present-day English orthography.

The writings of the schoolmasters like Mulcaster and Coote raised the level of education of writers and improved the training of the apprentices. Although they could not correct the old errors made through previous neglect, they were able to establish stability in the orthography which was the residue of all the various vicissitudes described in this chapter.

This analysis of the motivations for stability and for change in the English writing system is of crucial importance in the task analysis of learning to read. If we are to answer the question—what is the nature of the reader's task?—we must know what were the intentions or expectations of those who created the written or printed symbols to be read. The motivations of the writer become the interpretive tasks of the reader. Similarly, the child learning to read has the task of finding out what writers intend to signal with their symbols on the printed page. But, before we can reach the end of this inquiry into what the symbols of the English writing system are intended to represent, we must approach the problem from a different point of view—a psycholinguistic analysis of English orthography in its present-day form. This will be the subject of Chapter 5.

CHAPTER 5

Psycholinguistic Analyses

At this point it may help the reader to recapitulate the progress of our study of the psychology of reading. From the previous chapter on the largely historical survey of orthography, we shall now turn to linguistics. It is important to keep in mind the psychological goals of these discussions of related disciplines. We have identified reading as a skill, and psychological research on skill acquisition shows that the novice's chief objective is to understand what must be done and why. In reading, the reader's task is to find out what the writer intended to convey in the way of meaning. Beginners have to learn that this is the function of literacy and, in addition, they have to learn how this function is fulfilled—what is the technique by which the message is conveyed? What features of language did the writer intend to code with those visible symbols? The historical analysis in the previous chapter has revealed the intentions of the developers of English orthography. That historical evidence is extremely valuable for our analysis of the literacy learner's task. But this problem has been approached in a different way by some modern linguists. They have tried to work out the rules of English orthography by analyzing its linguistic system in present-day usage.

The classical view of the linguistic basis of the English writing system is that its graphemes are symbols for phonemes. Thus English orthography has been said to be a graphic code for phonemes, which has lost much of its original regularity mainly because of changes in pronunciation. Some linguistic descriptions represent the orthographic code as very simple but with a great many irregularities. Other descriptions show a more complex code with correspondingly fewer irregularities of grapheme-phoneme relationships. However, in recent years a different type of description has appeared in linguistics, in which other elements of language are said to be coded by the writing system. Francis (1970) notes that a number of linguists and educators have abandoned the notion that writing is nothing more than a way of representing speech. He says they take the view, instead, that "writing is systematic in its own right" (p. 45). This has led to a controversy which is very important for the study of the psychological tasks of learning to read. The question is whether or not *English orthography either as a whole or in part is a code for phonemes.* An examination of the linguistic literature on this problem reveals that there seem to be three broad schools of thought about this question. We shall examine these in turn under the headings: *classical phonemic descriptions, structural descriptions,* and *multi-code descriptions.*

Classical Phonemic Descriptions

Bloomfield and Fries

Leonard Bloomfield (1942) was one of the first linguists to show concern for the nature of the child's task in learning to read. In a famous article, "Linguistics and Reading," he wrote: "The letters of the alphabet are signs which direct us to produce sounds of our language." He emphasized that the phonemes related to the letters do not occur in isolation in natural speech, and therefore teachers should not teach the letter-sound relationships in isolation. One effect of isolating consonant phonemes that Bloomfield pointed out was that it produces in addition "an obscure vowel sound" not present in the actual spoken word (for example, by single letter phonics, *cat* comes out as "kuhatuh"). Nevertheless, Bloomfield was quite certain that "alphabetic writing . . . directs the reader to produce certain speech-sounds" (p. 129).

Somewhat later, another linguist, Charles Fries (1963), made a more comprehensive study of English orthography that confirmed its essential nature: *"Alphabetic writing is basically phonemic,"* and the child, "just as he responds to the phonemic patterns that identify the word patterns in speech he must learn to respond to the graphic representations of these phonemic patterns in reading" (p. 155). Thus Fries expressed linguistically what users of English orthography seem to believe intuitively. Similarly when Fries wrote: "An *alphabet* is a set of graphic shapes that can represent the separate vowel and consonant phonemes of the language. All *alphabets* are phonemically based, and the procedures of teaching the process of reading alphabetic writing must take into account this essential fact of the structural base of alphabetic writing" (p. 156), he was giving technical linguistic expression of what most teachers of reading have believed intuitively to be the nature of the child's task in learning to read. (We are not concerned here with the "phonics versus look-say" controversy. This is a matter of pedagogical choice based often on educational philosophy and is not influenced by the nature of the writing system, which may be learned eventually by either teaching method).

Fries spells out the essential nature of phonemic writing as follows:

> A strictly "phonemic" alphabet would have one symbol for each of the separate phonemes of *a particular language,* that is, for each of the bundles of sound contrasts that function in identifying the word-patterns of that language. These phonemes are not separate *sounds,* but *bundles* of sound contrasts that are phonetically actualized differently in various environments. One cannot pronounce the English phoneme /t/. He can pronounce the phonetic realization of this phoneme as it occurs initially in the word *top,* or as it occurs finally in the word *pot,* or as it occurs in the initial cluster of the word *stop.* And these three pronunciations would all be different. He couldn't pronounce all these three phonetic realizations of /t/ at a single time. The phoneme /t/ is not a single physical unit. It is a single abstract structural unit (pp. 159–160).

This is the classical linguistic concept of the phoneme, which, according to Fries, is the essential unit coded in an alphabetic writing system.

Bloomfield and Fries, as well as many other linguists, accepted that English orthography is not a perfect one-to-one code of grapheme-phoneme correspondences. But this did not lead them to reject the phonemic basis altogether. Fries' view was that "the English alphabet is phonemically based but it is not, as used for English, a 'phonemic alphabet' in the sense that there is only one letter symbol for each phoneme and only one phoneme for each letter symbol. . . . Although phonemically based, the individual letters of the alphabet with which we write do not stand in a one for one correspondence with the separate phonemes of our language" (p. 160). Fries saw the many divergences from the phonemic principle in English orthography as arising out of the vicissitudes of history, spelling changes "lagging behind" changes in spoken English, the "ignorance" of the false etymological spellings, the stabilizing of spelling by printers without consideration for linguistic knowledge, and so on. But despite these divergences, English orthography remains "basically phonemic in its representation" (p. 169).

Fries preferred to use the term *spelling-pattern* for the grapheme representing a phoneme because often in present-day English orthography a group of letters has come to stand for a phoneme and often also the members in such a group of letters are not adjacent. Thus in the printed word *hate* the $a + e$ is the spelling-pattern for the phoneme /ei/. Fries was able to describe present-day English orthography in only ten pages of clear and simple exposition. Any classroom teacher with a clear knowledge of the forty or so phonemes of English can understand Fries' description on first reading. A teacher without such knowledge needs only some more time for insightful study.

Fries' analysis seems plausible because it does not, and does not claim to, explain the whole of English spelling as consisting of regular spelling-patterns. It appears as a writing system with a basic principle of regular relationships between spelling-patterns and phonemes with a considerable residue of irregularities, which is what one might predict from Scragg's (1974) historical survey reviewed in the previous chapter.

Satisfactory scientific details were not provided, but Fries claimed as evidence that subjects asked to create nonsense syllables produced spelling-patterns which almost always were predictable by his analysis. Similarly, readers were observed to pronounce nonsense words spelled according to the spelling-pattern rules "without hesitation" (p. 182).

Fries very firmly claimed psychological reality for his analysis. Not only did it explain why people spell English as they do, but it is, in Fries' view, the key to the teaching of reading: "Modern English spelling is fundamentally a system of a comparatively few arbitrary contrastive sets of spelling-patterns, to which readers, to be efficient, must, through practice, develop high-speed recognition responses" (p. 183). The child's primary task in learning to read is "learning to shift, to transfer from auditory signs for the language signals, which the child has already learned, to visual or graphic signs for the same signals. Both reading and talking have the same set of language signals for language reception. In talking, contrastive bundles of sound features represent these signals; in reading, contrastive patterns of spelling represent these same signals" (p. 188). Furthermore, "the recognition responses to be developed in the reader of the transfer stage are those of spelling-patterns consisting of sequences of letters of the present-day English alphabet. It is alphabetic writing" (p. 189).

Fries went on to make specific detailed proposals for the methods teachers ought to use in instructing children in these spelling-patterns for phonemes. But here, like Bloomfield before him, Fries ventured into the fields of child psychology and pedagogy. Their pedagogical proposals have not found popularity in the schools, but this is not the concern of this chapter. The essential point is that Bloomfield and Fries provided descriptions of English orthography which indicates its nature as being a visual code for phonemes but with imperfections in the regularity with which these sounds are represented. Their classical descriptions seem to fit quite well to the conscious experience of teachers and other current users of English orthography and with historical accounts of its development. However, phonic instruction has been by no means a universal success. One cause of the many failures may be that the classical phonemic description of English orthography is more or less inappropriate.

Structural Descriptions

Moving from the taxonomic views of classical structural linguists of the persuasion of Bloomfield and Fries, we will discuss the coding systems put forward by Noam Chomsky and Richard Venezky. In relating conventional English orthography to the structure of the spoken language, Chomsky has posited an abstract representation and Venezky an internal structure. There seems to be some similarity in their analysis of the orthography, but they differ in their conceptions of the underlying, abstract phonological representation and the manner in which phonetic representations are actualized.

Structural Descriptions—Chomsky's Lexical and Phonological Representations

From the 1950s the linguistic writings of Noam Chomsky have had considerable impact on psycholinguistics. Although he has had little to say directly on the processes of reading and writing, his theories have stimulated research in the wider areas of syntax, phonology and more latterly semantics.

Within the purview of this chapter on the relationship between the written and spoken forms of language, we will draw mainly on Chomsky's earlier works or so-called "standard theory" as set forth in *Syntactic Structures* (1957) and *Aspects of the Theory of Syntax* (1965) and his chapter on phonology and reading (Chomsky, 1970). We will also refer extensively to the seminal work *The Sound Pattern of English* by Chomsky and Halle (1968). In this book Chomsky and Halle propose a grammatically oriented phonology known as *generative phonology* and argue that English orthography is near-optimal. Chomsky's views on the broader aspects of grammar and on the relationship between deep structure, surface structure and semantic representations found in his "extended standard theory" will be discussed in the next chapter.

At the outset, it is important to understand the meaning of knowing a language. Chomsky and Halle (1968, p. 3) explain it this way: "The person who has acquired knowledge of a language has internalized a system of rules that determines sound-meaning connections for indefinitely many sentences." A distinction should be made between *competence* and *performance*. Competence refers to the speaker-hearer's knowledge of the grammar that determines an intrinsic connection of sound and meaning for each sentence. Performance is based on competence plus such factors as memory, attention, extralinguistic knowledge, and so on. The term *grammar* is used by Chomsky and Halle (1968, p. 4) to "refer both to the system of rules represented in the mind of the speaker-hearer, a system which is normally acquired in early childhood and used in the production and interpretation of utterances, and to the theory that the linguist constructs as a hypothesis concerning the actual internalized grammar of the speaker-hearer."

As utterances are infinite in number, they can form a complex system and this is not conducive to an insightful understanding of languages. It is therefore necessary to educe general principles governing linguistic structures. With this postulate of the existence of underlying linguistic representations that are abstract and not directly observable, we can systematically explain general linguistic principles and account for linguistic variations. Thus, the rules are abstract entities rather than actual sounds and these rules attempt to reach the highest-order generalizations possible.

The phonetic realizations are termed *phonetic representations.* Chomsky and Halle state that:

> a phonetic representation has the form of a two-dimensional matrix in which the rows stand for particular phonetic features; the columns stand for the consecutive segments of the utterance generated; and the entries in the matrix determine the status of each segment with respect to the features (p. 5).

For example, segments (featural complexes are shown in enclosed square brackets [ ]) such as [s] and [š] are [+ strident] as distinguished from [− strident] segments of [p], [t] and [Q] and the entries in the row corresponding to stridency would indicate a differentiated scale of such a feature. Thus the grammar of the language assigns to the phonetic representation a *structural description* that indicates how it is to be interpreted in the language (see also Chomsky, 1965, p. 9 on grammar assigning structural description to the sentence). Furthermore, "the grammar of a language must contain syntactic rules that determine phrasing and a lexicon that contain the semantically and syntactically functioning units, as well as rules that relate structural descriptions to phonetic representations" (Chomsky, 1970). The significance of this statement will be elaborated on in the subsequent sections. Suffice it to say at this point that in order to accommodate the infinite number of sentences that humans can create and within the finite capacity of the human brain, the grammar of a language must have a *recursive property.* The grammar must contain rules with new combinations and new arrangements to account for the infinite variety of structural description of sentences. According to Chomsky, that part of grammar which has the recursive property is the syntactic component.

Syntactic Component and Phonology

Chomsky and Halle (1968, p. 6) explain the *syntactic component* of a grammar "assigns to each sentence a 'surface structure' that fully determines the phonetic form of the sentence. It also assigns a far more abstract 'deep structure' which underlies and partially determines the surface structure but is otherwise irrelevant to phonetic interpretation, though it is of fundamental significance for semantic interpretation." The surface structure consists of a string of minimal elements called *formatives.* Each formative is assigned to various categories which determine its underlying abstract form. Thus, the formative *boat* belongs to the categories of "initial voiced stops," "noun," "nonanimate," "common," "countable." The information on formatives is organized into a *lexicon* which might be regarded as a dictionary with different *lexical entries.* These entries are organized into a structure, as otherwise it will be difficult to explain the phonetic representations of words such as *boy, boat* and nonwords such as *gnip* or *psik.* Chomsky (1965, p. 214) explains that a lexical entry might be taken simply as "a set of features, some syntactic, some phonological, some semantic." But "more precisely, the lexicon is a set of *lexical entries,* each lexical entry being a pair *(D,C),* where *D* is a phonological distinctive feature matrix 'spelling' a certain lexical formative and *C* is a collection of specified syntactic features (a complex symbol)" (Chomsky, 1965, p. 84, original and added italics).

Some examples from Chomsky and Halle will illustrate the relationship of phonetic variations with lexical representation. The related words *courage* and *courageous* involving vowel alternations are represented by the underlying abstract form of /Koraege/. This representation will be actualized as /kóræge/ by a stress rule, as /kóræge/ by velar softening, /kʌ́ræje/ through unrounding, as /kʌ́ræǰ/ through *e*-elison and finally as vowel reduction of the phonetic form /kʌ́rəǰ/. Another set of examples is the differentiated stress patterns of the related words *télegraph, telégraphy,* and *telegraphic.* The underlying lexical representation is + tele + graef + and the variations are shown thus (with primary, secondary and tertiary stress shown as *1, 2,* and *3* or ´, ˆ, `):

te̍ləgraef (1 on e, 3 on ae)	(in isolation)
te̍ləgraef (3 on e)	(in the context of *ic,* i.e. telegraphic)
təle̍grəf (1 on e)	(in the context of *y,* i.e. telegraphy)

Chomsky and Halle maintain that it is the underlying abstract form, rather than the phonetic variations, which enables us to better understand the relationship between *telegraph, telegraphic* and *telegraphy* and likewise other words.

An analogous argument applies to *phonological representation* which is determined from lexical representation by the application of certain *adjustment rules.* These rules provide a link between syntax and phonology and operate in a certain order; adding, deleting or modifying distinctive features. The generalized representation takes the form of:

$A \rightarrow B / X - Y$

This is read as: Element of the type *A* is actualized or rewritten as a corresponding element of the type *B* when *A* appears in the context $X - Y$ (i.e. with *X* to its left and *Y* to its right or $X\,A\,Y\,\#$ with # as the boundary symbol). Examples of verb-adjective relation such as *corrode–corrosive, submit–submissive* will explain the use of adjustment rules. Verbs ending in /d/ (with a few exceptions) and ending in /t/ preceded by /mi/ may be turned into adjectives by changing the final sounds into /s/ and adding the suffix /iv/. This is in accordance with part of the spirantization rule that converts dental stops to [s] if unvoiced or to [z] if voiced. With the examples given, the rule is:

/t d/ → /s z/ in the context of: — /iv/

Thus the /t/ of *submit* changes to /s/ directly whereas the /d/ in *corrode* changes to a hypothesized /z/ which in turn changes into /s/ by another rule:

/z/ → /s/ in the context of: —/iv/

A further example is the word *division* which has the underlying form [diviz + yVn], the underlying /d/ having become [z] by the spirantization rule and subsequently with [z] becoming palatal to derive [dəvižən], dropping the glide after [z] by a later rule.

In explaining the linkage between the spoken and the written forms of language, Chomsky and Halle postulate that the spelling and syntactic forms of a word are used to educe the lexical representation. Then rules are applied to produce a sequence of phonemes and an appropriate stress pattern. This latter is governed by complex factors of phonemic distinctions (lax versus tense vowels; weak versus strong clusters), morphemic structure and syntactic functions.

English Orthography as "Near-Optimal"

Thus, in the phonological scheme of Chomsky and Halle, there is no intermediate stage between the "absolute" representation of the sounds of morphemes in the lexicon and the phonetic representation of actual spoken sounds in the final product. In fact, Chomsky and Halle (1968, p. 11) would avoid the terms "morphophonemic representation" or "systematic phonemic representation" for the reason that the existence of a linguistically significant level of representation, intermediate in abstractness between lexical and phonetic representations, has yet to be demonstrated. In their view:

> conventional orthography is . . . a near optimal system for the lexical representation of English words. The fundamental principle of orthography is that phonetic variation is not indicated where it is predictable by general rule. Thus, stress placement and regular vowel or consonant alternations are generally not reflected. Orthography is a system designed for readers who know the language, who understand sentences and therefore know the surface structure of sentences. Such readers can produce the correct phonetic forms, given the orthographic representation and the surface structure, by means of the rules that they employ in producing and interpreting speech (Chomsky and Halle, 1968, p. 49).

This emphasis on the near-optimal system of conventional orthography for lexical representation is reiterated in Chomsky's chapter on reading (1970, pp. 13–14) and in his other works.

On the place of the phoneme as the basic unit signaled by the grapheme, Chomsky (1970, p. 15) makes it clear that "there is little reason to expect that phoneme-grapheme correspondence will be of much interest because it appears that phonemes are artificial units having no linguistic status." Furthermore, "the rules of sound-letter correspondence need hardly be taught . . . , nor is there any particular reason why the teacher should be aware of these processes or their detailed properties. These rules, it appears, are part of the unconscious linguistic equipment of the nonliterate speaker" (Chomsky, 1970, pp. 15–16).

In a similar vein, Chomsky and Halle (1968) offer their "first approximations" of reading aloud as follows:

> We assume a reader who has internalized a grammar *G* of the language that he speaks natively. The reader is presented with a linear stretch *W* of written symbols, in a conventional orthography. He produces as an internal representation of this linear stretch *W* a string *S* of abstract symbols of the sort that we have been considering. Utilizing the syntactic and semantic information available to him, from a preliminary analysis of *S*, as well as much extralinguistic information regarding the writer and the context, the reader understands the utterance, and, in particular, assigns to *S* a surface structure Σ. With Σ available, he can then produce the phonetic representation of *S* and, finally, the physical signal corresponding to the visual input *W*. Clearly, reading will be facilitated to the extent that the orthography used for *W* corresponds to the underlying representations provided by the grammar *G*. To the extent that these correspond, the reader can rely on the familiar phonological processes to relate the visual input *W* to an acoustic signal. Thus one would expect that conventional orthography should, by and large, be superior to phonemic transcription, which is in general quite remote from underlying lexical or phonological representation and not related to it by any linguistically significant set of rules (pp. 49–50).

Chomsky's (1970) evidence that the traditional orthography of English is related to lexical representation instead of phonemes consists in: (1) "conventional orthography is highly appropriate, with little modification, for a wide range of dialects" (p. 4); (2) "the level of lexical representation is highly resistant to change and persists over long historical periods. It follows, then, that it should be common to a wide range of dialects . . . correspondingly, one finds that conventional orthographies remain useful, with minor changes, over long periods and for a wide range of dialects" (p. 12). But here the empirical evidence is not unequivocal. The historical evidence reviewed in the immediately preceding chapter of this book shows that the changes that have taken place in the past thousand years of English orthography have been far from "minor." In the following section we will comment on the assertions made by Chomsky and Halle.

Commentary on "English as Near-Optimal"

Other linguists have been skeptical of the assertions of Chomsky and Chomsky and Halle that the English orthography is "near-optimal." Vachek (1973, p. 68) comments: "Clearly, as a piece of apology for present-day English spelling, the argumentation adduced by Chomsky and Halle is hardly convincing. . . ." Francis (1970) analyzes Chomsky's general assertion into three subsidiary claims: "(1) that the prephonetic level of surface structure, the level of lexical representation is linguistically meaningful; (2) that this level and the lexical representations that it includes are psychologically real, though below the level of conscious knowledge; and (3) that the standard orthography is, with minor exceptions, isomorphic with that level" (p. 48).

Francis finds that "the danger of circularity here is obvious" in regard to claim (1) but it has "much to recommend it" so long as psychological reality is not assumed. But here (and frequently elsewhere), Chomsky (1970) does claim psychological reality for his theory of grammar. He actually states: "The psychological reality of lexical representation, in this sense, is hardly open to question." This is claim (2), and Francis' reaction to it is: "I cannot find this claim 'hardly open to question' " (p. 49). Francis' reasons for questioning "the psychological reality of lexical representation" are: (a) "the assumption that all speakers store the same lexical items in the same way seems to run counter to the great individual diversity that obtains in other forms of memory. The way in which particular parts of other systems are stored may be highly idiosyncratic, probably as a result of the way in which they were learned" (pp. 49–50). (b) "If lexical representations of the form here posited are indeed psychological realities, there should be some way of getting at them by some other route than the highly ingenious analysis that Chomsky and Halle have used and that has taken them a good many years to work out." Francis even wonders if drugs or hypnosis might be used to bring them to consciousness if they are not subject to recall, and suggests that one should at least sense some intuitive recognition of lexical representations as instanced by Chomsky. Yet Francis' own reaction to such instances cited by Chomsky as being "internalized, as part of his knowledge of English by the speaker-hearer who is acquainted with this word" was "one of extreme skepticism. The response of other native speakers of English . . . has been the same" (p. 50). Francis concludes that "it is unfortunate that a brilliant linguistic demonstration is weakened by extravagant and unsupported psychological claims" (p. 51). On Chomsky's third claim that standard orthography is isomorphic with the level of lexical representation, Francis remarks: "In the light of the facts about the history of English . . . it would be indeed remarkable if his claims were true . . . ," and Scragg's historical survey certainly supports Francis' skepticism. His conclusion is that "the claim is too sweeping" that English orthography "is in virtual one-to-one correspondence with the segments of the internalized lexical representations. If this were so, why would people have so much trouble with English spelling?" (p. 51). In the same vein, Baker (1980) remarks that "all but the most fortunate of English spellers have first-hand familiarity with the existence and persistence of spelling difficulties irrespective of our level of reading attainment; and one is inclined to ask whether the second-order, high-level regularities of English spelling, which may be patent (in both senses, perhaps) to linguists, represent anything other than an obstacle course for the average speller" (p. 54). Francis' review of Venezky's (1970a) study of the structure of English orthography (see next section) leads him to add that "no one who reads it can avoid the conclusion that Chomsky's assertion must be taken with more than a grain of salt" (p. 54).

Another linguist, Hall (1975), in criticizing Vachek's theory, makes a point which seems relevant here too:

> Morphophonemic alternations (or "underlying representations") are simply groupings of phonemes which are distributed, in one way or another, in morphemes. These latter do not exist apart from their phonemic structure. There is no such thing as a disembodied linguistic form existing in some soundless Platonic ideal realm, coming down to earth and being given corporeal shape or "realized" in a sequence of sounds. Even a "zero" morph or morpheme (e.g. in the genitive plural of Russian feminine nouns . . .) is simply a bookkeeping device to indicate the absence of sound in certain forms as contrasted with its presence in others. (When a person remains silent, he is not uttering an infinity of zero-morphemes).
>
> There is, therefore, no justification for considering morpho-phonemic spellings . . . , graphic distinctions between morphemes (e.g. Fr. *cet* "this" [m.], *cette* "this" [f.], *sept* "7," *Cète* or *Sette* "a town-name," all /set/), or logographs (like *lb.*, £, &) as extraneous to spoken language. When differences in graphic shape occur, due to a loose fit or (as in Chinese writing) the absence of fit between grapheme and phoneme, they can be used . . . to indicate distinctions on any of these levels; but they are nonetheless related to differences between linguistic forms as they are spoken. Consider the difference between £, &, etc., on the one hand, and an international road-sign on the other. A logograph like £ or & can be "read off" in more than one language; but it will always be correlated with some specific form in a given language: *Pound, and* in English; *lira, e (d)* in Italian, etc. A road-sign, however, conveys a non-linguistic message. [It is] correlated, not with any linguistic form, but directly with the real-life situation. Thus, a triangular shape tells the beholder "Look out!" or "Be careful!" or "Take it easy!" or "Aufpassen!" or "Habt acht!" or "Faites attention!" and so on—i.e., to be careful, no matter how the injunction might be phrased. The shapes and images of international road-signs are true "visual morphemes," to use Bolinger's (1946) term; morphophonemic spellings, contrasts like that between *bear* and *bare*, logographs like *etc.* read as /ənsówfòrθ/, or Chinese characters, are not (pp. 462–463).

In view of the vicissitudes on the course of the long history of English orthography—especially the successive waves of spelling errors perpetrated in periods of poor education and training—it is difficult to accept Chomsky's claim for the "near-optimal" quality of the written form of English. Psychoanalysis might even extend the unconscious element in Chomsky's theory to evoke motivational mechanisms which guided careless scribes and ignorant printers' apprentices to make "near-optimal" errors rather in the manner of Freud's (1920) unconscious motivation for slips of the pen in *The Psychopathology of Everyday Life.* If one admits that orthography may change and develop in an informal, unconscious or organic manner like the continual adaptation of the norm of spoken language, then the historical evidence may seem less in conflict with Chomsky's assertion that English orthography is not based on phonemic representation. Perhaps further historical research may throw more light on the problem of the efficiency of the English writing system.

Here we must move to the firmer ground of scientific experimentation. Its results do not provide much support for the psychological reality of Chomsky's claims in other aspects of language behavior. The outcome of much experimental testing of psycholinguistic hypotheses said to be derived from Chomsky's theory is not encouraging. Part of the problem is that linguistic theories and psychological realities may not be isomorphic, and it is not always possible to verify linguistic constructs empirically. Related to this is that the differences between the various versions of pre- and post-*Aspects* generative syntax as it relates to phonology vary considerably. Chomsky (1968, p. 54, fn. 6) himself has remarked that at the time of writing "the field is in considerable ferment, and it will probably be some time before the dust begins to settle and a number of issues are even tentatively resolved."

A second problem is the misinterpretation of the word *deep* in *deep structure* and the mistaken notion of a dichotomy between this and *surface structure.* In his post-*Aspects* postulates or the *extended standard theory* Chomsky has dissociated the syntactic and semantic properties of the *deep structures* in the *standard theory* and has suggested that either category of properties might be taken as defining the technical notion of *deep structure* (see Chomsky, 1975). He has never intended *deep* to mean "deep" in the nontechnical sense of the word with the implication that the rest is trivial or unimportant. He asserts that "phonological theory includes principles of language that are deep, universal, unexpected, revealing, and so on"; and the same for the theory of surface structures and other elements of grammar (Chomsky, 1975, p. 82).

A third problem is the circularity of Chomsky's explanations. For example, Chomsky's reliance on the native speaker's intuitive knowledge to judge whether a sentence is or is not grammatical cannot be tested by experiment, according to Chomsky, because the experimental methods would have to be validated against the same criterion of intuition. This problem leads Chomsky to define a grammatical sentence as one for which the rules of the grammar in his theory would generate a sentence phrase marker—a clearly circular definition.

A fourth problem for Chomsky's theory is that it does not explain how a speaker chooses a particular sentence from all the many possible alternatives available to her/him in Chomsky's model. Osgood (1971) emphasizes the failure of generative grammar to explain how speakers adjust their language to situational conditions. Speakers and listeners share certain presuppositions and expectations which have no existence in Chomsky's model.

Attempts to test Chomsky's theory experimentally have generally proved negative. Broadbent (1970) has shown that real-life utterances do not always fit the form predicted by transformational grammar. Several experiments, for instance Slobin's (1966), have shown that in normal language it is the semantic factors that are primary and not the syntactic component specified by Chomsky's theory. Greene (1972) states that evidence tends to indicate that "the more the situation approximates to natural language use the more likely subjects are to respond to direct meaning cues, rather than going through an ordered set of transformational and decision making operations" (p. 136). This is true both of speech perception and of speech production. As Fodor, Garrett and Bever (1968) have shown, listeners have a series of options open to them *as a sentence unfolds,* whereas according to Chomsky's theory the sentence cannot be analyzed until the overall structure of the whole is available. Experiments by Wason (1965), Greene (1970a, 1970b), and Johnson-Laird (1968) have produced evidence contrary to Chomsky's hypothesis that the listener always must run through the same series of transformations when analyzing a sentence.

Further Evidence and Questions

Returning now to Chomsky's specific assertion that English orthography is not a phoneme code, it has often been noted that some English spellings seem to preserve a semantic link between the words at the cost of sacrificing grapheme-phoneme correspondence. For example, in *courage* and *courageous* the *age* syllable is pronounced differently, but the identity of its spelling may signal the semantic link. This phenomenon leads Noam Chomsky (1970) to assert: "The reader who knows English would be best served by an orthography that leads him directly to the single syntactic-semantic unit *courage* that appears in the two phonetic forms and that eliminates all irrelevant phonetic detail" (p. 13). Carol Chomsky (1970) applies this idea more directly to the reading task. She claims that "English has many kinds of surface phonetic variations which need not, and preferably ought not, be represented in the lexical spelling of words. They are wholly predictable within the phonological system of the language and are therefore best introduced within the grammar by means of automatic phonological rules. As with vowel alternations, these other variations obscure an underlying sameness which the lexical spelling is able to capture. And as with vowel alternations, these surface phonetic variations are not reflected in the conventional orthography" (p. 292).

Carol Chomsky gives as examples: medi*c*ate–medi*c*ine, prodi*g*al–prodi*g*ious, gra*de*–gra*d*ual, ques*t*–ques*t*ion, *s*ign–re*s*ign. She comments: "By being 'unphonetic' in all of these cases, by not exhibiting grapheme-phoneme correspondence, the orthography is able to reflect significant regularities which exist at a deeper level of the sound system of the language, thus making efficient reading easier" (p. 293). She points out further that stress and vowel reduction also are not reflected in the spelling. Carol Chomsky concludes: "Thus on the lexical level and in the orthography, words that *are* the same *look* the same. In phonetic transcription they look different. . . . The spelling system leads the reader directly to the meaning-bearing items that he needs to identify, without requiring that he abstract away from superficial and irrelevant phonetic detail" (p. 294).

Venezky (1970a) makes a similar plea: "Consider the forms *autumn: autumnal, damn: damnation, paradigm: paradigmatic, sign: signify.* It is not sufficient to state that *gn* and *gm* in final position correspond to /-gn-/ and /-gm-/. Such rules fail in cases like *autumns, designing* and *singer.* There is no way to avoid reference to morphemes in this case, unless one simply enumerates the words for each pronunciation. A regular pattern is present in these forms, the most important aspect of which is the preservation of morpheme identity" (p. 43).

These arguments may appear persuasive, but they fail to mention three important problems. First, why do some other semantically or morphemically related word groups have spellings which *do* reflect the phonemic changes and sacrifice the semantic or morphemic link—for example, *beast: bestial?* Also, why is it that an even greater number of such word groups have spellings that signal *both* the "surface phonetic variation" *and* the underlying semantic relationship without compromising either principle—for example, *law: lawful; learn: learning; call: recall?* Possibly both principles are at work. Often they coincide. Sometimes they conflict, on some occasions the morphemic principle dominating, at others the phonemic.

As a matter of fact, Yule (1978) has made an exhaustive analysis of the 6,385 words in the basic spelling list of the Education Department of Victoria, Australia, and she could find only 168 pairs which supported the Chomskys' notion of orthographical representation of a lexical structure that overrode apparent sound values. She concluded: "Clearly it seems pure luck whether Chomsky's principle applies or not," and she remarks that "there are too many tautological traps in emphasizing a 'meaning-bearing' value in spelling showing etymology or 'deep structure.' It is often necessary to *know* that words are related in order to recognize that they are related—or mistakes can be made, even by Carol Chomsky" (p. 11).

A second problem is—how did such lexical or morphemic orthographic conventions develop historically? A plausible answer is—through creative changes *by analogy.* For example, Scragg notes: "The fixing of *c* for /s/ in English was aided by the fact that in many words with the final sequence *se* the consonant sound represented was /z/, e.g. *lose, surprise, wise.* Use of *ce* in the final position thus clarified the representation of final /s/: *ace, pence, since.* The device was particularly useful in noun/verb pairs where the spelling difference reflects one in pronunciation: *advice, advise; device, devise,* and in the seventeenth century it was extended by spelling book compilers to similar pairs which involve no sound change: *licence, license; practice, practise.* American usage has preferred *se* in all such cases since Noah Webster" (p. 43, note). These changes by analogy was frequently the basis for modifying English spellings. It was what Mulcaster meant when he proposed that the phonemic principle sometimes must give way to "reason." The analysis of such behavior in the history of English orthography indicates the rather confused operation of newer principles such as morpheme representation on the older and more basic phonemic code, sometimes working harmoniously but sometimes with conflict.

A third problem is the concept of automaticity of phonological rules in the reader. For instance, Venezky (1970a, p. 120) states: "The orthographic preservation of morphemic identity is predicted on the assumption that the reader knows the phonemic alternations that accompany derivational and inflectional formations." Similarly, Noam Chomsky (1970) claims that sound-letter correspondences need not be taught because children arrive at the correct pronunciation because of their "unconscious linguistic equipment" (p. 16) which operates automatically. Carol Chomsky also finds phonetic details "irrelevant" in spelling because the reader can arrive at these "by means of automatic phonological rules" (p. 292). In our preceding chapter, the Aztec sign for "Coatepec" is cited as an example of the common principle of all writing systems. No natural writing system represents all aspects of language, but only just enough clues for the reader to work out the message. The reader is expected to make intelligent guesses on the basis of shared knowledge with the writer. Venezky and the Chomskys are implicitly calling on this principle of partial clues. Their only reason for minimizing the significance of phonemic clues is that readers do not need them because they will arrive at the sounds automatically through their internalized rules. Yet when hearers listen, they arrive at the semantic significance of an utterance by proceeding "automatically" from the sounds to the meaning. Why could this not be true also in reading? Why then could not the lexical or morphemic aspects be "irrelevant" in the orthography because of the "automatic" processes from sound to meaning? There is no doubt that the reading process itself becomes highly automatic in mature readers, but, as is shown in Chapter 2, this automaticity develops through much practice and is a part of the cue-reduction phenomenon in the process of skill development. It is notable that Carol Chomsky's references are to "mature readers."

This aspect of Chomsky's theory has been subjected to experimental investigation. Barganz (1974) compared the performance of forty good readers with that of forty poor readers on a series of tasks which were predicted to differentiate their abilities according to the theses of Noam and Carol Chomsky. One question that Barganz proposed to investigate was "whether conventional English orthography may be considered 'optimal' in contrast to a more 'phonemic' orthography" (p. 105). The test most relevant to this question was the "visual/visual task. . . . For example, the word 'revere' was presented by an overhead projector while a sentence, in which the word was used, was read aloud by the experimenter. The position of 'revere' in the sentence was indicated by the sound of a toy cricket. A second sentence was read aloud by the experimenter. The word 'reverence' was not said, but the position of it was indicated by the sound of a toy cricket. Four orthographic depictions of 'reverence' were presented by an overhead projector; one item was to be selected as correct" (p. 107).

This task seems hardly a critical test of the Chomskys' claim for the nonphonemic nature of English orthography. It was not a *reading* task. We cannot tell how the subjects interpreted either *revere* or *reverence* in respect of pronunciation or meaning. It is not at all surprising that poor readers performed significantly less well in selecting the correct spelling. Poor readers have less experience with the orthography and obviously are less likely to recognize the correct spelling or to guess it by analogy with other printed words in their past experience. Barganz's results could be explained more simply in terms of the differences in amount of reading practice in good and poor readers. His other tasks were even less relevant to the Chomskys' claim. Yet Barganz concluded: "By their knowledge of the phonological rules of the language and of the 'morphophonemic' nature of the orthography, good readers . . . were able to bypass the grapheme/phoneme correspondences and to relate the surface structures of words phonologically and orthographically to deep structures. The functional stimuli for the good readers appears to be the underlying form of lexical items; that is, a search for the semantic correspondence in derived words seems existent in the good readers" (p. 116). Barganz suggests that poor reading was associated with a tendency to "cling to the alphabetic principle." But again the cause-effect relationship could equally well be in the reverse direction. Barganz's subjects were fifth graders. The good readers among them had had long experience and much practice in traditional English orthography. Their lesser reliance on the alphabetic principle may have been due simply to their greater experience of its irregular implementation in the English writing system.

Simons (1975) tested an hypothesis derived from Chomsky and Halle (1968) and Carol Chomsky (1970) "that English spelling corresponds to an underlying lexical level of representation rather than to a surface phonetic level, i.e. pronunciation." A second hypothesis was "that learning to read involves learning the spelling-lexical level correspondences" (p. 49). Eighty-seven second and third grade subjects were tested on a paired-associate and reading task for two types of word pairs; morphologically related word pairs, for example, *hide–hid,* and unrelated pairs, for example, *pine–pin.* The procedure was for the experimenter to read the words (printed on individual cards) to the subject. The subject's task was to read the card presented and then respond verbally with the other member of the word pair. According to Chomsky's theory, it was predicted that all subjects would perform better on the morphologically related pairs than on the unrelated pairs, and that this difference would be greater for better readers than poor readers, and greater for grade three subjects than for grade two subjects. The assumption here is that "the organization of the internal lexicon corresponds to the way words are stored in memory" (p. 52).

The only support for the Chomskys' hypothesis was in Simons' finding of a trend in the direction of difference predicted for good as compared with poor readers. All other results were negative. Simons notes the evidence from studies by Moskowitz (1971), Robinson (1967), and Steinberg (1973) that the phonological rules, particularly vowel shift proposed by Chomsky have no psychological reality. "All three studies have shown that children and adults have great difficulty applying stress and vowel shift rules in producing the correct pronunciation of affixed words where these rules should apply. If the phonological rules have no psychological reality, there is reason to question the psychological reality of lexical level of representation." Simons points out that, in reading acquisition, "many of the words from which the child must abstract letter-lexical level correspondences are of low frequency and do not occur often in the reading material presented to children, e.g., profane–profanity, verbose–verbosity, discrete–discretion, resign–resignation, etc." Simons draws the conclusion, therefore, that "the great bulk of them are in all probability learned in the later years of school. Since many children learn to read quite well before finishing elementary school, it is not clear whether learning letter-lexical level correspondences is an important factor in learning to read well" (p. 58).

Two further empirical works should be mentioned. Anisfeld (1969) tested the generative phonological rule of the kind:

$$\left\{ \begin{array}{r} /(mi)\ t/ \\ /d/ \end{array} \right\} \rightarrow /\mathrm{s}/ \text{ in the context: } -/iv/$$

as in the derivation of *decisive* from *decide* and *permissive* from *permit*. When forced to choose between two artificial substitutes (e.g. *gasluzive* vs. *gaslushive*, or *yermizive* vs. *yermishive*), introductory psychology students chose more frequently /ziv/ endings for synthetic /d/-final verbs *(gaslude)* than for /t/-final verbs *(yermit)*. This and other findings are taken as support for the central role of rules in guiding subjects' responses. It is, according to Anisfeld, the "rule-mediated relations among sounds, rather than absolute similarities, that seem to determine judgments" of the words (p. 195).

More recently, Smith and Baker (1976) reported on two experiments which investigated the process of converting written English into speech. They aimed at deriving the most plausible rule system for the pronunciation of unfamiliar words and at relating their results to Chomsky and Halle's pronunciation rules. In the first experiment, they constructed nonsense words by systematically varying spelling and grammatical categories (e.g. *nodud* transformed to *noddud, nodude*) and asked their subjects (university students) to read aloud sentences containing these nonsense words. The location of primary stress in each nonsense word was found to depend on the phonemic form, grammatical category, and spelling of the word, in ways similar to those predicted by Chomsky and Halle's (1968) rules for assigning stress. In the second experiment, subjects judged the morphemic structure and apparent foreignness of the nonsense words used in the first experiment. Results showed that many of the interactions observed between experimental factors in their investigation could be interpreted in terms of morphemic differences between different groups of words. While there was "mild support" for Chomsky and Halle's phonology as relevant to their subjects' pronunciations, Smith and Baker did not find strong evidence for underlying, abstract forms. They maintained that orthographic devices such as final *es* (e.g. *profane* with the underlying form /profaen/ and phonetic form [proféyn] and double consonants (e.g. *coquette* with the underlying form /kōkette/ and phonetic form [kowkέt]) seem to influence performance through their effect on perceived morphemic structure, not on more abstract forms. Smith and Baker also set out some salutary implications for the English spelling system: "Linguistically unsophisticated subjects can squeeze a large amount of information out of a word's spelling, and some of this information might be lost in a reformed or simplified spelling system. We must have a clearer idea of what information can usefully be transmitted by written language before we try to reform English orthography" (pp. 284–285).

Thus, taking into account the relevant theoretical and empirical findings, Chomsky and Halle's theory of phonology has yet to be demonstrated as providing the best description of how the speaker-hearer actually processes language. This takes us back to the competence-performance distinction and is not easily resolved as linguistic knowledge and psychological postulates cannot in principle be completely isomorphic.

Structural Descriptions—Venezky's Morphophonemics

Richard Venezky (1970a, 1970b) attacks the view that the English orthography is a system for coding phonemes by graphemes. From his extensive analysis of the English orthography, Venezky maintains that the units of language coded by written symbols are "morphophonemic," from which the actual phonemes are derived. He computer-tabulated and computer-analyzed spelling-to-sound correspondence in the 20,000 most commonly used English words, with a view to "discover and describe the underlying patterns of the current orthography" (Venezky, 1970a, p. 126). This analysis takes into account the position of written symbols and sounds in the context of words and provides valuable empirical data in their own right. It is, however, important to note the one-way direction of Venezky's spelling-to-sound analysis, or how graphemes are pronounced rather than how speech sounds are written.

"Relational Units" and "Markers"

Venezky (1970a) found that two kinds of "functional units" at the "graphemic level" were significant for the prediction of the pronunciation of written English: (1) *Relational units,* each consisting in "a string of one or more graphemes which has a MORPHOPHONEMIC CORRESPONDENT which cannot be predicted from the behavior of the unit's smaller graphemic components"; (2) *Markers,* each of which "is a cluster of one or more graphemes whose primary function is to indicate the correspondences of relational units or to preserve a graphotactical or morphological pattern. It is mapped into a zero morphophoneme" (p. 50). Some examples may help to clarify this brief summary. The "*gn* in *cognac* and *poignant* is a single relational unit" which corresponds to a certain morphophonemic cluster, "but *gn* in *sign* and *malign* is not a relational unit but rather a combination of two relational units which correspond to" two separate morphophonemes. Morphophonemic rules determine whether what corresponds to *g* is silent or not, as in *signal* and *malignant.* Examples of markers are final *e* in *notice* which indicates that *c* corresponds morphophonemically to what we usually think of as "the *s* sound." In *argue* the final *e* is a marker which protects one from *argu* because word-final *u* is never allowed in the orthography. Venezky shows how these markers are "dropped before a suffix which begins with a letter that will perform the same function as the *e*" (p. 52). Thus, when *ing* is added to *notice* and *argue,* the marker *e* is not needed.

Venezky (1970a) provides a list of fifty-nine relational units, six of which have an alternative spelling—for example *oi* or *oy* (p. 54). There are four groups of markers: (1) "Markers of Consonant Correspondences"—for example, the *e* in *notice* referred to above; (2) "Markers of Graphotactical Patterns"—for example, the *e* in *argue* also referred to above; (3) "Markers of Vowel Correspondences"—for example, final *e* in *mate, mete, site, note, cute* to mark the vowels' free pronunciation in contrast to *mat, met, sit, not, cut;* (4) "Markers of Morphemic Patterns"—for example, final *e* "to avoid the appearance of a final inflectional *s*" in *moose, goose, mouse.* Several different markers exist of each type (pp. 55–58). In addition, Venezky has a set of rules describing the "graphemic alternations" *i* and *v, u* and *w, ous* and *os,* and *i* and *e* (pp. 59–62). The chapter stating these rules of the graphemic system is clearly set out and its fifteen pages should be easily understood by a specialist in the orthographic aspects of linguistics.

The next 38 pages of Venezky's (1970a) work describe the distributions, correspondences and alternations of consonants in written or printed English. Nine pages are devoted to fricative alternations and nineteen to the distributions, correspondences and alternations of vowels in written English. Here Venezky presents his evidence for the superiority of his system of description over the conventional grapheme-phoneme correspondence analysis. "When viewed from the direct spelling-to-sound standpoint, the patterns for these units reveal no regularity. *O* corresponds to seventeen different sounds, *a* to ten, *e* to nine, and the combined group to forty-eight. When the morphemic structure and consonant environments of the words in which these units appear are analyzed, however, a single major pattern emerges, from which regular subpatterns can be derived." Venezky concludes: "Exceptions still remain, large numbers of them in some cases, but the underlying pattern is so dominating that the exceptions, which were once the rule, become mere oddities, begging for historical justification" (p. 101). That this claim is exaggerated is obvious when one reads Venezky's analysis carefully. For example, a rule he quite often employs is that the consonant simply has an idiosyncratic pronunciation in the words listed, without any other reason being given.

The overall working of Venezky's system is described in the following quotation: "In the spelling-to-sound model employed here, graphemic words are divided into their graphemic allomorphs, and then these allomorphs are related to intermediate (morphophonemic) units by an ordered set of rules. Other rules then relate the morphophonemic units to phonemic forms. All rules which are based upon nongraphemic features are applied in an ordered sequence on the morphophonemic level, yielding various sublevels of intermediate forms for each word. The final morphophonemic form is then mapped automatically onto the phonemic level" (p. 46).

Commentary

Venezky's analysis of English orthography in its present-day form is ingenious and is probably the most thorough scholarly description at present available. But Venezky claims more, and clearly he had much more in mind from the outset, than mere linguistic description.

Early in his book, Venezky reveals his own value judgment: "For centuries philologists have approached the study of English orthography with the purblind attitude that writing serves only to mirror speech, and that deviations from a perfect letter-sound relationship are irregularities" (p. 11). Venezky's historical survey is rather selective. From the time of Alfred the Great nearly everyone has been overemphasizing the sounds of letters, according to Venezky. Only a few noteable authors saw beyond simple letter-sound relationships. Spelling reformers are given short shrift by Venezky: "The twentieth century reformers have in general presented an even more distorted picture of the orthography than their predecessors. Their arguments, instead of being based on the true irregularities which exist, generally are based upon non-existent patterns like the celebrated *ghoti* . . ." for "fish" (p. 32). Here Venezky's own value judgment has taken him well away from the facts. *Ghoti* was one of Bernard Shaw's literary jokes, not taken seriously by any spelling reform organization. It is also not true, as Venezky asserts, that the Simplified Spelling Society (in Britain) and other such bodies have "faded from existence" (p. 32). Actually, many are alive and well, and some are quite strong.

If the orthography of English is not a written code for phonemes, it seems odd that for more than a thousand years most people have believed that they were writing the sounds which currently have the technical name "phonemes," and furthermore did write more or less phonemically. Venezky hints at a "National Orthographic Character" which may have caused people to spell morphophonemically even though they were not conscious of doing so.

It also seems strange, if Venezky's theory (or Chomsky's) is valid, that people who have the professional job of creating new orthographies for languages that have never before been written almost invariably prefer to use a phonemic alphabet. For example, Pike's (1947) well-known chapter on "The Formation of Practical Alphabets" states: "A practical orthography should be phonemic. There should be a one-to-one correspondence between each phoneme and the symbolization of that phoneme" (p. 208). Pike's ten principles for creating a practical orthography are all based on making it easy for the native speaker to learn the writing system. An interesting example is the principle dealing with words borrowed from other languages: "If these loan words have been completely assimilated . . . , then they will not contain sounds which the native language lacks, nor will they contain familiar sounds in unfamiliar circumstances. In these instances assimilated loans should be spelled as they are pronounced by the native, and spelled with the symbols utilized for the native language and not with the traditional spelling of the second language" (p. 211). Venezky's view about loan words in English, many of which, as was shown by Scragg's historical survey, were imported in a bygone age of biliteracy and bilingualism, is that "such borrowings cannot be classed as entirely irregular since their spellings mark their foreign identities" (p. 121).

Morphemic writing and morphophonemic writing have been considered by specialists in creating new orthographies. Thus Smalley (1964) recognizes that "there are some important cases where non-phonemic writing may be of great value" (p. 7), and he cites such examples as the plural morpheme *-s* in such words as *boys* and *ships* where final *s* is pronounced /z/ and /s/ respectively. But this type of deliberate creation of nonphonemic spelling is the exception rather than the rule. More common is Crofts' (1971) behavior in developing the orthography for the Mundurukú language: "We have sets of words with two phonologically-conditioned allomorphs (forms with the same meaning, but different phonetically), i.e. post-positions that begin with *d*- following vowels and with *t*- following consonants. We could choose a base form to use throughout, but since *d* and *t* are full phonemes, we write these phonemically, not morphophonemically. We have not found that this causes any confusion" (p. 52, italics added). Thus present-day creators and users of orthography, like the scribes and printers of history, are conscious of working with phonemes rather than the lexical representations of Chomsky or the morphophonemes of Venezky.

This would not be important to this study of the psychology of reading if Venezky limited his theory to linguistic description, but he does not. Although Venezky quite properly expresses caution, he nevertheless indicates a belief that his analysis is related to the psychological reality of the processes of reading and of learning to read. Thus he states: "At a minimum it can be assumed that the classification scheme for spelling-to-sound patterns presented above could be used as a basis for the selection of words for the teaching of reading" (p. 128). Furthermore, "except where whole words are recognized, a sequence of units within the word is observed in the translation process. The relevance of this to the teaching of reading is in the instructions given to a child who is first learning to read. Should he be told to scan left to right, letter by letter, pronouncing as he goes, or is there a more efficient scheme? In the first place, a person who attempts to scan left to right, letter by letter, pronouncing as he goes, could not correctly read most English words. Many of the English spelling-to-sound patterns require, at a minimum, a knowledge of succeeding graphemic units. How, for example, is initial *e*- to be pronounced if the following units are not known (cf. *erb, ear, ewer, eight*)? This is just the beginning of the problem. In some patterns, the entire word must be seen—and this is true of almost all pollysyllabic words since stress patterns are significant for vowel quality" (pp. 128–129).

These examples of the unproductive effect of the left to right, letter by letter, scanning method may be true without any dependence on Venezky's descriptive analysis, but Venezky seems to imply that his system of analysis is directly applicable to the task of learning to read. However, the chief difficulty for anyone desiring to apply Venezky's theory in the classroom is that very few teachers, let alone children, would be able to understand or remember its seventy or more pages of rules for predicting the pronunciation of written English. Even the simpler rules seem likely to be difficult for elementary school pupils. Take for example the following:

In some cases the discrimination of a morphemic spelling from an identical, non-morphemic spelling is necessary for the prediction of sound from spelling. Consider the following two word lists.

A	*B*
boys	*melodious*
judges	*stylus*
cats	*apropos*
man's	*careless*

The pronunciation of final *s* in any column *A* word can be predicted by the following rules (these rules must be applied in the order shown here):

(1) /IZ/ after /s,z,č,ǰ,š,ž,/.
(2) /Z/ after any other voiced sound.
(3) /S/ in all other cases.

These rules, however, apply only to *s* when it is one of the following morphemes:

(1) regular noun plural.
(2) third person singular, present indicative marker for the verb.
(3) singular or plural possessive marker.
(4) any of the contractions like *John's* (from *John is*) (pp. 42–43).

Inadvertently, it seems, Venezky himself has provided an evaluation of his theory as a practical guide to the child's task of learning to read. In another publication, Venezky (1970b) discusses at length the "elusiveness of the concept of 'regularity' " (p. 30) as used in descriptions of language. He argues very effectively that *regularity is in the eye of the beholder:* "What is regular in one system may be irregular in another, and what one analyst sees as order, another sees as disorder"

(p. 30). This, Venezky claims, explains why estimates of the percentage of English orthography that is "regular" varies from study to study, one finding 80 per cent, another 90 per cent, and yet another 95 per cent.

But Venezky's insight into the perception of regularity may be applied also to the child's task of learning to read. Children too must be analysts of the written language set before them. Thus, they will also search for regularity, and one of the problems of teaching reading is that some children fail to perceive any regularity at all. As was noted in *Comparative Reading* (Downing, 1973), "The linguist's mapping of the regularities of English orthography may prove far too complex for the young child to grasp. The linguist may be able to provide a description of English orthography that is a perfectly logical proof of its regularity. But the real issue in the psychology of the learning-to-read process is the *perceived* regularity of the code. The linguist's regularity may be far too complex a system for the child to *perceive* as such" (pp. 220–221).

What is much more important is the logical implication of Venezky's view that what is regular in one analysis of the orthography may not be a regularity in another linguist's analysis. The same must be true of his own analysis, and he cannot escape from his own conclusion by relabeling *regular* and *irregular* as *predictable* and *unpredictable,* as he claims (Venezky, 1970b, p. 42). People make predictions on the basis of perceived regularities. In other words, Venezky's analysis is merely *one possible way* of *describing* present-day English orthography. It does not necessarily have psychological reality in the way in which readers past or present have perceived English writing and reacted to it.

Multi-Code Descriptions

Several linguists have suggested that English orthography primarily represents phonemes, but that it has other overlapping codes in addition. It seems quite plausible to suppose that the initial system was a code for phonemes, but that later developments created additional codes for other aspects of language. For example, in Scragg's historical survey we noted some deliberate creative spelling reforms devised for other than phonemic motivations. Lefevre's (1964) analysis seems to take this eclectic position. For example, in his book, *Linguistics and the Teaching of Reading* he concludes: "Despite the irregular and inconsistent relationships we have noted between phonemes and graphemes, an exhaustive listing would show that there are families and groups of words where the correspondences between sounds and spellings are fairly regular. Moreover . . . word-form changes, prefixes, suffixes, and other systematic clues to language structure are generally spelled quite regularly without regard to differences in sound; this regularity corresponding to important structural signals probably compensates for irregular spellings at the phonemic level" (p. 184). Examples of these nonphonemic signals in the orthography include: (1) the regular noun plural inflection *-s* in *cats,* where the phoneme is /s/ and in *dogs,* where the phoneme is /z/; (2) the regular verb inflection for the past tense spelled *-d* and pronounced /t/ in *dropped,* but /d/ in *learned.* Lefevre provides many other examples in his detailed description.

Vachek's "Functionalist" Theory

Vachek's (1973) *functionalist* theory of written language proposes that the *spoken norm* of language and the *written norm* of language each have an independent existence despite their obvious connections. They exist independently because each system has its own functional motivation. Nevertheless, Vachek accepts that the basis of the relationship between these two norms in alphabetic systems is grapheme-phoneme correspondence when he states that "hardly any written norm can be found which would implement this 'ideal' correspondence type. . . . Admittedly, most of the written norms do respect the correspondences between phonemes and graphemes to a degree (and some of them to a relatively high one) but alongside this basic type of correspondence one can also ascertain in these norms at least some specimens of correspondences on some higher language level . . ." (pp. 21–22). These "higher" levels are said by Vachek to be the word and the morpheme.

At the level of words, correspondence is produced by "the operation of the logographic principle" (p. 23). Vachek gives as examples the homophonous but not homographic words *right/rite* and *wright/write,* and several similar instances from other languages.

On the morphemic level Vachek instances "the phonological opposition of voice in word-final paired consonant phonemes" which "becomes neutralized, but the graphemic opposition remains unimpaired." Words like *Rad* (wheel)–*Rat* (advice), *Tod* (death)–*tot* (dead) in German are suggested as examples (pp. 23–24). Instances of this tendency, Vachek continues, "can also be found among the grammatical morphemes. Well-known cases of the kind are the Modern English *s*-endings of the plurals of nouns and of the third person singular present indicative: in both grammatical categories the graphemic shape of the morpheme *-(e)s* is retained despite the existence of the phonemically different allomorphs /-s/, /-z/, /iz/, alternating according to well-known morphonemic rules of Modern English" (pp. 24–25).

These principles come into conflict with the basic phonemic level. Vachek concludes that "there do not seem to exist written norms based on an exclusive correspondence on one and the same language level. It seems certain, in other words, that all written norms constitute various kinds of compromises between the correspondences established at various levels" (p. 25).

Vachek emphasizes the shift in the function of writing which took place with the spread of literacy. Then, he notes "a tendency emerges aimed at establishing a direct link between the written utterance and the extralingual reality to which it refers. Such a direct link implies that the originally existing detour via the corresponding spoken utterances is becoming gradually abandoned and that, at least to a degree, the written or printed symbols are gradually acquiring the status of signs of the first order. . . . That this is really so is evidenced by the fact of 'silent reading,' in which an experienced reader can peruse a written page at a much higher speed than if he were actually to read the same text aloud" (p. 37). It is this function which has caused the shift "from the correspondence built up almost exclusively on the basic level (phonemes—graphemes), with some interference of the morphological level, to the present state of things in which the logographic principle has come to play a hardly unimportant part" (p. 40).

These considerations of silent reading in particular lead Vachek to conclude that the task of the reader is not the same as the task of the writer. The writer may be aided by simple grapheme-phoneme correspondences, but the reader is motivated for quick silent understanding, and short-cuts the roundabout route through speech. The reader needs writing "to speak quickly and distinctly to the eyes" and this is the reason why "written norms often deviate from the correspondences on the basic level of language in the direction of logographic and/or morphological correspondences" (p. 53).

Vachek's theory seems consistent with the history of English orthography. For example, when the schoolmaster grammarians, such as Mulcaster, began to publish their proposals for stabilizing the orthography we find references to such considerations although they were given rather minor importance. Furthermore, as was noted earlier in this chapter, it is possible that shifts in written language occur rather unconsciously, as do shifts in pronunciation. Vachek makes this suggestion explicitly in discussing the tendency against two-letter words in English spelling. This tendency led to the lengthening of words such as *doe, rye, toe,* and *see,* but it did not effect another group of words—*to, of, do, no, so, be.* The first examples are "non-formal" words but the second group are "formal." Vachek comments: "It appears that the early users of the English written norm unconsciously felt the difference of the non-formal and formal words and expressed the distinction between the two categories by the susceptibility of the former, and non-susceptibility of the latter, to the tendency directed against the two-letter words . . ." (p. 54). This symbolizes "their greater semantic and communicative weight by a more impressive graphemic extent of their written forms . . ." (p. 54, note).

Another of Vachek's instances of the independence of the written norm from the spoken norm is his suggestion that spelling may signal emotion. He cites *ghastly, ghost, ghetto, ghoul,* and so on in which "the word-initial digraph *gh-* . . . undoubtedly underline[s] the strongly negative emotional colouring" (p. 55). An immediate reaction to this hypothesis of Vachek may be skepticism, but if one admits that changes in orthography may occur with the same lack of awareness as do modifications to the norm of spoken language, then his proposition may seem more plausible. This may then explain why most of Caxton's initial *gh* spellings were dropped, while those in words with "strongly negative emotional colouring" were retained. In such words the *gh* grapheme may have felt appropriate and so it stuck. Bolinger (1946) in arguing for the existence of "visual morphemes" wrote of the "semantic evolution of spellings." He claimed that "the clustering of repetitions of a given distinctive spelling about a given meaning (*passed* versus *past*) can result just as surely in establishing a fixed written sign for that meaning as can a similar clustering of sounds result in establishing a fixed morphophonemic sign (*let us* vs. *let's* . . .)" (p. 336). Vachek's case for the existence of nonphonemic conventions in orthography, which are motivated by the needs of rapid silent reading, thus seems plausible and is further supported by the evidence from historical accounts.

Albrow's Description

This possibility that the English writing system has today become a combination of several methods of coding language seems to be supported by Albrow's (1972) description. Albrow is another linguist who rejects the notion that English orthography is based on a simple representation of phonemes. Instead he proposes that it is "more closely linked to a classification of the sounds of the . . . language in relation to their various lexical or grammatical functions, and in relation to their place in phonological structure (initial, medial, final; accented, unaccented, etc.)" (p. 9). Albrow asserts that "the English writing system . . . is not one system of symbols corresponding rather superficially to sounds only (or rather to sound groupings called phonemes), but a system of systems, reflecting the phonological structure of the language, with different conventions for representing the grammatically (and lexically) different elements" (p. 10). The apparent irregularities and anomalies of English orthography, according to Albrow, are often due to the overlapping of these several systems. The same grapheme is used by more than one system. For example, in Albrow's "system 1" *g* represents the initial sound common to "get," "go," "give," but in "system 2" it corresponds to the initial sound in "gem," "gentle," "gym." Albrow describes "three systems" that "have equal status and all three together constitute the writing system in the wider sense" (p. 14). Within each system there are subsections describing the orthographic conventions for such categories as lexical monosyllables, grammatical conventions, and so on. For instance, the difference between grammatical and lexical function is used to explain the contrasted spellings of *be, me, we, he* and *bee, wee, see* in system 1. Such contrasts may have been gradually adopted under the principle of "reason" which Mulcaster used to refer to spelling changes by analogy. However, Albrow admits the arbitrary nature of his description of the English writing system, and there is certainly no evidence of any awareness of the rules of his "system of systems" in users of written English.

In summary, multi-code descriptions, such as those of Albrow, Lefevre, and Vachek accept that the primary basis for English orthography was and still is a code for phonemes. However, they recognize that other spelling principles have grown up alongside the phonemic one, and that a full understanding of English orthography involves the discovery and learning of these other systematic codes.

Nonphonemic Devices

Most discussions of the nature of the English writing system as it relates to the task of learning to read have rather little to say about anything other than the orthographic conventions for words. Thus Venezky recognizes that the English writing system has thirty-seven "graphemes"—the twenty-six letters of the alphabet, "eleven marks of punctuation," plus "space, a sort of zero grapheme" (p. 47). Lefevre indicates the importance of careful attention to punctuation in samples of writing provided by teachers for children learning to read. He is particularly concerned with all aspects of the writing system which signal intonation patterns in the language, and punctuation is one of the devices employed by the writing system for this purpose. Other functions of punctuation include: (1) the period, to mark a sentence boundary; (2) the comma, to prevent ambiguity of meaning; (3) the exclamation mark or question mark to clarify the writer's intention; (4) the apostrophe for contractions or possessives; and so on. Mountford mentions several other nonphonemic devices in the writing system. He states that "orthographies are elaborated by the complex punctuation systems, the differentiation resources of upper- and lower-case, italics, etc., the abbreviation devices, reference devices, serialization and sequencing devices, and so on, familiar in European and other orthographies. Literacy-learning in the sense of mastering the resources of a standard orthography can go on for many years . . ." (p. 302). In general, the nature and function of these other punctuational elements in the writing system have caused little controversy. The comma gives some trouble, but usually the function of each convention is agreed upon. This part of the writing system is clearly not phonemic, at least.

Certain other arbitrary conventions in the English writing system have to be learned. Clay (1974) calls these "orientation to the spatial characteristics of visible language" (p. 275). On a printed page the message begins at the top left-hand side and proceeds left-to-right along a horizontal line. The continuation then begins on the left of the next line, and so on down the page. Then the continuation is on the next page to the right. Also there is a "right-way-up" for the page, and a "beginning" and "end" to the book in this systematic spatial sequence. None of these arbitrary rules are intuitively obvious and so cannot be taken for granted in beginners. If the language were not English, the rules could be quite different. Clay found that children's understanding of these spatial conventions was related to progress in learning to read.

Conclusion

This review of some alternative theoretical descriptions of the English writing system began with the question—is English orthography phonemic? Chomsky and Venezky say "no." But more eclectic observers seem to say "partly yes, and partly no." The weight of the evidence suggests that English orthography was originally a phonemic notation and that the phonemic principle has been maintained and persists to the present day. The current spelling in English is only partly phonemic because of changes in pronunciation, accidental spelling errors, and deliberate orthographic innovations which have developed other coding principles. Hence, the present-day orthography of English is mainly phonemic. The large majority of words are spelled phonemically. But some other coding principles exist side by side with the phonemic principle.

Returning to our analysis of the task of learning to read in terms of the intentions of the creators and users of the writing system as a coding tool, we may sum up as follows. The English writing system is primarily a code for phonemes. Of course, those phoneme signals are intended to act as clues to morphemic units because the writer's purpose is to pass on a meaningful message. But the code system is primarily a set of written signs representing phonemes. This is the chief item of knowledge which children need to acquire about how the writing system works. In addition, they must cope with the task of understanding how and why the English writing system deviates from that central phonemic principle. Two other important principles have been found which sometimes conflict with the phonemic principle. First, there are consistent morphemic signals for such aspects of language as plurals and verb tenses. Second, there is a deliberate attempt to avoid homographs for homophones by creating logographic representations for whole words. Further linguistic research may reveal other coding principles. In addition, there is a great deal of what looks like chaotic irregularity to the child; and much of it is indeed chaotic irregularity, arising as it did through tinkering and errors in the course of the long history of English orthography. Many of these "errors" may be impossible to explain to the young learner, but others may be understood as children develop skill. These may even help them to remember the written form of the words and how to spell them—for example, Caxton's *ghost* replacing the original *gost*. Etymological signals are best forgotten, certainly in the initial stages, since they have only a secondary purpose and, in any case, are so unreliable.

Although the basic phonemic principle of the code is a simple one, we must not underestimate the complexity of the task of learning this code in the English writing system. The code itself is complex—by no means a simple one-to-one relationship between letters and phonemes. Fries' lists of spelling patterns are helpful guides to what needs to be learned here (though not necessarily to how to teach it). In addition, it must be borne in mind that the task of learning the phonemic code may be difficult because: (1) the phoneme unit in speech is not easy to conceptualize and discriminate as a separate entity; and (2) the concept of a code in which a symbol represents something else is not usually known to the beginner.

The other nonphonemic parts of the writing system which have to be understood and remembered are such signals as are given by punctuation marks and blank spaces, and the rules of ordering written language in space—for instance, the left-to-right direction along the horizontal line.

This linguistic analysis of the child's task in learning how to use the writing system tool is not enough. Its chief deficiency is in its assumptions about what knowledge children bring with them to this task. For example, we have discussed the orthographic conventions for representing "words," but all children seem to pass through a stage when they possess no concept of "word" and there is considerable evidence that most children begin school cognitively confused as to what constitutes "a word" (see, for example, Downing and Oliver, 1973–1974). Therefore, the student of the psychology of reading must break down this task into simpler units which reflect the psychological learning and problem-solving work of the beginner. But before undertaking this, let us return to Mountford's survey of the psycholinguistic components of standard literacy. The writing system is only one of the five components of literacy which have to be mastered.

Other Psycholinguistic Components of the Task

The Standard Language of Literacy

Mountford (1970) places this "psycholinguistic component" at the top of his list: "Initiation into a standard language of literacy is the most far-reaching aspect of standard literacy. Continuously expanding control of that standard language, or of a second standard language of wider range, accompanies growth on the educational scale." Thus, "an education system requires some degree of standardization in a language (for the training of primary teachers, production of primers, etc.) if it is to use it for initial literacy training." Even in multilingual countries where reading is taught first in the local vernaculars, "these languages will be standardized to this extent" (pp. 301–302). In other words, the language of literacy is more or less different from any individual's personal language of oracy. Mountford's reference to the policy of beginning reading in the vernacular before going on to reading in a national language reminds us that the gap between the child's language of oracy and the school's language of literacy may vary considerably in breadth. Thus this aspect of the child's task of learning to read will vary correspondingly. But the universal task variable here is adapting or relating personal oral language to the special standardized form of language used in books and other reading materials.

If the gap between the child's oral language and the school's language of literacy is small, the child may be able to understand the connection without undue difficulty; but, as that gap between these two languages widens, so the child's cognitive confusion about their relationship seems likely to increase. Despite Chomsky's contrary view, many authorities on reading education have emphasized the importance of this potential hazard in learning to read, and a considerable body of research evidence has accumulated which justifies their concern. This research will be reviewed in detail in Chapters 12 and 13, but a few brief examples here will illustrate this problem in the child's task.

At its narrowest, the gap between the child's oral language and the school's language of literacy may be only one of style—for example, if the child and teacher speak the same middle-class standard English dialect. Even then, complacency does not seem justified, for, as Reid (1971) points out, "sentence forms that belong to story-telling or to written description [such as *said he* instead of *he said*] should not be introduced prematurely into reading material" (p. 18). In other words, the acquisition of these special literary styles is one of the tasks of literacy learners, but it may be wiser to postpone it until it no longer gets in the way of their understanding the simpler relationships between spoken and written language. A more extreme mismatch between the child's oral language and the school's language of literacy may create an unbridgeable gap for the child's understanding—as when, for example, children know only Spanish but the teacher speaks to them in English about English speech and written English. An intermediate level of difficulty may be created where the child's dialect differs from the dialect of literacy used in school. But, as has been noted elsewhere, whether the difference is one of dialect or language, "when the language of reference in the teacher's instruction is different from the child's experience of speech . . . such mismatch is an important cause of reading retardation" (Downing, 1974, p. 81).

In summary, an important aspect of the task of learning to read is acquiring the more or less different language used in books and other written or printed materials. These differences may be a matter of style, grammar, or pronunciation within the same language, or in more extreme (though not uncommon) situations the two languages may be entirely different.

Technical Concepts of Literacy

The second component of Mountford's list is "knowledge of the writing-system," which was the topic of the earlier and major part of this present chapter. The third component is technical concepts of literacy. Mountford notes: "It is presumably the case that knowledge of the standard technical vocabulary of literacy is not an essential component of literacy; but in standard literacy such knowledge is certainly expected" (p. 303). *Technical concepts* refers to such linguistic elements as *word, sentence, reading, writing, letter, number,* and so on. From the point of view of our task analysis, Mountford's next comment is highly relevant: "One reason for the presence of the technical vocabulary is, of course, that literacy is imparted by instruction." In other words, children need to learn these concepts and their technical labels because otherwise they cannot understand what the reading teacher is talking about. But one might go further than Mountford and say that the child needs the concepts *to think about the task of learning to read.* Therefore, these technical concepts of literacy are necessary for developing cognitive clarity in the learning-to-read task. Furthermore, it is not only concepts of literacy that must be learned. Literacy learners are striving to relate written language to their past experience of speech, and therefore, they need to learn concepts of the elements and functions of speech which are related to literacy.

A fairly considerable amount of research on this aspect of the child's task in learning to read has been completed, and this will be reviewed in the next chapter. One or two examples should suffice here to illustrate this problem. There seem to be two broad categories of concepts needed for thinking about reading and writing. First, there are concepts of *function.* Vygotsky's (1934) research on the child's conceptions of written language led him to conclude that the child "feels no need for it and has only a vague idea of its usefulness" (p. 99). These concepts include those of purpose—why do people write and read?—and also concepts of actions such as "reading" and "writing." Parallel concepts about communication in speaking are also needed for thinking about the relations between spoken and written language. The second group of concepts have to do with the analysis of speech and writing. Such analysis requires the acquisition of concepts like "spoken word," "written word," "letter," "phoneme," and so on. That these concepts cannot be taken for granted has been amply demonstrated by research. As was concluded elsewhere, many children fail in reading because of an abrupt "immersion in a sea of undefined linguistic concepts" (Downing, 1975a, p. 31). The development of these concepts thus appears to be an important component in children's clear thinking about the task they must undertake in learning how to read.

The Linguistic "Habitudes" of Literacy

The habitudes is Mountford's fourth component: solitary use of language, receiving communication from someone not present and a complete stranger; language which is carefully rehearsed; and language which is often depersonalized. All these habitudes are rather foreign to the preschool child's experiences of language, where the communicator is present and communications are informal and personal. Vygotsky emphasized this contrast between written language and the child's previous experiences of language. He wrote: "Writing is also speech without an interlocutor, addressed to an absent or an imaginary person or to no one in particular—a situation new and strange to the child" (p. 99). Thus another task for the literacy learner is adaptation to and adoption of these conventional habitudes.

The Basic Skills—Reading and Writing

Mountford's final item is the one to which most attention has been given by psychologists and educators. Mountford describes reading and writing quite appropriately as two skills. This is how they would be treated in psychology, as is noted in our Chapter 2. Mountford's special contribution to this topic is his clarification of the role of skill in literacy. He explains how important it is for the educator to separate the concept of skill from the specifics of a particular language. Just as in learning to speak a second language we do not need to learn how to speak all over again, so in learning to read a second language we do not need to learn to read all over again. Once developed, the skill of articulacy and the skill of reading are available for application in other languages and in other writing systems. Thus the skill of reading can be studied separately from the specifics of a particular language and writing system, just as it can also be studied in relation to the particulars of language and orthography.

Summarizing, we have in this chapter examined theoretical and experimental evidence of certain psycholinguistic components—the relation between written and spoken forms of English and how the written forms are converted by the reader into sound. We have discussed the taxonomic, structural views of Bloomfield and Fries; the generative phonology of Chomsky and Halle; the internal structure view of Venezky, and the multi-code descriptions. This exposition brings us to the important question of language awareness in children and beginning readers. We will discuss both the structure and function of the English language and will emphasize the different ways in which language becomes accessible to readers.

Language Awareness

CHAPTER 6

In the preceding two chapters we have discussed the historical aspect of the English orthography and the relationship of orthography to phonological and phonetic representations. We will now turn our attention to the topic of language awareness. This burgeoning topic has been incorporated into the work of some linguists and has assumed considerable importance in recent publications of a number of psycholinguists, psychologists and educators in relating language development to reading acquisition. Within the scope of this chapter we will deal with awareness as two interrelated themes: structure and function of language. The first theme—structure—relates to the form of the language and specifically grammatical rules relating to categories of words and sentences and how these structured strings of words are comprehended. The second theme—function—deals with interpretations of language by human users. No dichotomy of structure and function or form and interpretation is implied. If there is any demarcation, it is more along the zone which divides works primarily by linguists on the one hand and by psychologists on the other. Although this book is dedicated to applying psychological theory and research to reading and learning to read, the student would be greatly mistaken if he or she were to neglect the work of the linguists. It is very important for students to study carefully the first part of the chapter on linguistic theories. An understanding of these theories is an essential foundation for the comprehension of the review of psychological work on language awareness that makes up the remainder of this chapter.

From the point of view of linguists, the fundamental problem is to explain how a person can acquire knowledge of language as a set of structural descriptions of sentences determining the sound and meaning of a linguistic expression. From the point of view of psychologists, linguistic knowledge is part of cognitive psychology and is concerned with certain mental activities involving both grammatical competence and pragmatic competence of language in use rather than language as abstractions of grammar. Especially in his later or post-*Aspects* works, Chomsky (1972a, 1972b, 1977) has emphasized the aims of assimilating the study of language to "human psychology" and "natural science." The empirical aspects of language performance will be dealt with in Chapters 9 and 10. In the survey of relevant literature, it becomes clear that it is the access of word meaning, of sentence meaning that provides the heuristics more amenable to empirical examinations.

We will take as the starting point for our discussion of language structure Chomsky's (1972b, p. 115) assertion: "that a person with command of a language has in some way internalized the system of rules that determine both the phonetic shape of the sentence and its intrinsic semantic content—that he has developed what we will refer to as a specific *linguistic competence.*" This notion of linguistic competence is one of tacit knowledge of the language. The phenomenon of language awareness is tacit knowledge that has become explicit. We will discuss the system of rules and their explicit intuitions in relation to reading.

Language Form

Background

In the early 1950s a number of psychologists wrote from a behavioristic perspective on the acquisition and use of language. Skinner (1957) predicated his work on verbal behavior on conditioning principles where an operant response is one whose strength is a function of the degree to which it has been reinforced. Osgood (1953, 1963) wrote on the mediation model in conditioning. According to these approaches, language learning, or more properly verbal learning, relates to the broad principles of classical and operant conditioning. Thus, infants are reinforced by their parents in early vocalization and the self-reinforcement of the infant leads to the child's gradual acquisition of sounds, then syllables, and then words. At first, approximations to words are reinforced, then a process of differential reinforcement of closer and closer approximations of particular words shapes the child's speech. Once children utter words, the words become response units. Children begin to match their behavior to that of others by being reinforced when, for example, saying "papa" in the presence of the father and "doggie" in the presence of a specific four-legged animal. Earlier, in the 1950s, Miller and Selfridge (1950) and Miller (1951) in his influential book *Language and Communication* emphasized the contextual dependencies between sequential elements in a string of words. Miller and Selfridge found that people could remember more of a string of words the more it approximated to standard English. However, the authors emphasized that this result is due not so much to meaningfulness per se but to the short-range associations which are familiar to the subjects. In their view, meaning is dependent on contextual constraint.

Thus, according to these early views, verbal responses relate to the stimulus complex present and are a function of the strength of a particular response relating to the strength of other competing responses at the time. Sentences are seen as acquired in linear sequences of longer and longer stimulus-response chains. Sentences are produced in a left-to-right Markov sequence conceived as a series of probabilistic events where each stimulus word in the sequence has a probability of eliciting the next word response which, in turn, acts as a stimulus for the succeeding word response. Grammar is conceptualized as a device moving through a finite number of internal "states" in the generation of sentences. It is clear that this early view of language does not attach much importance to the "innateness" of language acquisition, nor to the active way in which the learner uses language.

It is against this zeitgeist of conditioning, mediation theory, and information theory that we can better evaluate the work of structural linguists as represented by Bloomfield (see also relevant sections in Chapter 5). For Bloomfield, language (or strictly speech behavior) emphasizes precision, objective methods and classification and is analyzable as separate levels of phonology, morphology and syntax. The Bloomfieldian model is unidimensional from the bottom-up with phonetically transcribed utterances as primary data. These are analyzed in a taxonomic classification with the ordered operations of contrast and substitution. An example of the particular sounds represented by *p* in *p*in /pIn/ and s*p*in /spIn/ will illustrate this. Classical structuralists explain that the aspirated phone [pʰ] as in *p*in occurs only in the speech environment #-*V* (# being a word boundary and *V* any vowel) and [pʰ] is in *complementary distribution* with the unaspirated [p] as in s*p*in where [p] occurs in the speech environment #*S*-*V*. Moreover, the initial consonant *p* in *p*in is in *contrast* with [tʰ] as in *t*in. From phonemes, the operations are repeated at the next level of morphemes. Thus, the phonemically distinct English plural morphs /-s/, /-z/ and /-əz/ are classified together on the basis of their complementary distribution in such words as cat*s*, dog*s*, and fox*es*. For structural linguists, the emphasis is on phoneme, and syntax is relegated to a position of minor importance.

It should not, however, be assumed that Bloomfield is unaware of the importance of meaning. His classic book *Language* published in 1933 contains many references to meaning. An example will show this:

> We have defined the *meaning* of a linguistic form as the situation in which the speaker utters it and the response which it calls forth in the hearer. . . . In order to give a scientifically accurate definition of meaning for every form of a language we should have to have a scientifically accurate knowledge of everything in the speakers' world. The actual extent of human knowledge is very small, compared to this. We can define the meaning of a speech-form accurately when this meaning has to do with some matter of which we possess scientific knowledge (Bloomfield, 1933, p. 139).

Given Bloomfield's own behavioristic orientation and the prevailing concepts of language at the time, it is not surprising that Bloomfield (1933, p. 140) proclaimed that "the statement of meanings is therefore the weak point in language-study." As we shall see presently and in Chapter 10, the study of semantics, though gaining momentum as compared with phonology and syntax, remains controversial and a complex area of investigation.

Returning to the probabilistic notion of language, it is clear contextual constraint cannot explain many of the infinite number of sentences we can generate. For example, in the sentence: "The man who would be king visited the middle kingdom," the conditional probability after "who" is open to a large number of possibilities. The serial order postulated by Miller (1951) as a concatenation of strings of letters or words cannot accommodate the larger units of language so cogently set forth by Lashley (1951) in his celebrated Hixon lecture on "the problem of serial order in behavior." Lashley raised two specific objections to the associative chaining model in vogue at the time. First, serial responses can be highly complex and the rapidity with which these are made leaves little time for the nervous system to conduct an impulse from the receptor to the brain and back to the muscle. Second, in any well-organized temporal behavior, the same response patterns may occur in a variety of different sequences. He characterizes the essential problem of serial order as: "The existence of generalized schemata of action which determines the sequence of specific acts, acts which in themselves or in their associations seem to have no temporal valence" (p. 122). His much-quoted example: "Rapid righting with his uninjured hand saved from loss the contents of the capsized canoe," was first interpreted by his audience as "Rapid writing with his uninjured hand" until "capsized canoe" required a complete and amusing about-face to "Rapid righting . . . capsized canoe."

Rules of Grammar—Phrase Structure

Moving closer to some current notions of grammar, we can see from the examples below that the left-to-right Markov chain explanation cannot disambiguate the separate meanings of each of the sentences:

(1) The shooting of the soldiers is terrible.
(2) The eating of the chicken is sloppy.
(3) You have no idea how delicious Peking ducks taste.

To some extent, disambiguation can be achieved through the use of *phrase structures*. Phrase structure rules are rules of grammar which can explain or represent much, though not all, of the speaker's knowledge of the internal structure of sentences. The rationale is that sentences are not unordered strings of words. Rather, the words and morphemes are grouped into functional constituents such as subject of the sentence, the predicate and the object, etc. A sentence *(S)* can thus be decomposed into a noun phrase *(NP)* followed by a verb phrase *(VP)* in the form of $S \rightarrow NP + VP$ (the arrow signifying "actualized as" or "rewritten as"). Thus the left-hand symbol can be rewritten as the group of symbols on the right-hand side. In a *NP* the noun *(N)* will be preceded by a determinant or article *(Det)* while in a *VP* the verb *(V)* will be preceded by an auxiliary. Thus a sentence of the following kind can be decomposed in two different ways:

(4) They were entertaining people.
(4a) ((They) ((were entertaining) (people)))
(4b) ((They) ((were) (entertaining people)))

The bracketing of the constituents shows the different meanings. But if we consider the sentence:

(5) He was hit by the car,

the sentence could refer to *how* he was hit and *where* he was hit. Phrase structure grammar does not enable us to understand the relation between a sentence and a paraphrase of a sentence or between two paraphrases of a sentence. The following pair of sentences has the same phrase structure but differs in deep structure:

(6) He is easy to please.
(7) He is eager to please.

Thus, if we accept that language is a rule-governed system, we must discover what these rules are and, if appropriate, their psychological status so as to account for our language capabilities. These capabilities include:

1. the ability to understand and produce novel sentences.
2. the ability to understand and distinguish between sentences which are well-formed and those that are ill-formed.
3. the ability to disambiguate ambiguous sentences.
4. the ability to summarize and paraphrase.

5. the ability to understand sentences when part or much is unsaid.

Rules of Grammar—Syntactic Structure

In this and subsequent sections, we will delve into such aspects of linguistics as are necessary for our understanding of language processing. In particular, we will outline the earlier works of Noam Chomsky and his more refined recent views. It was in 1957 that Chomsky published his book *Syntactic Structures* in which he rejects the Bloomfieldian approach of structuralism to language learning. He postulates a system of grammatical rules to account for sentence processing. He presented in 1965 a more comprehensive theory in *Aspects of the Theory of Syntax.* Grammar in *Aspects* consists of rules for syntactical, semantic and phonological levels. Over the years, Chomsky's views have also evolved, and the syntactically-based *standard theory* postulated in the 1950s and the 1960s is further elaborated on. Interested readers should read the above works of Chomsky and his later works, especially *Studies on Semantics in Generative Grammar* published in 1972 and *Essays on Form and Interpretation* in 1977. For those desiring clear and concise views of the 1957 and 1965 versions of Chomsky's theory, the books by Greene (1972) and Lyons (1970) should be consulted. A recent two-volume work by Lyons (1977) provides a good exposition of the current literature on semantics.

As we indicated earlier, a grammar is a set of rules relating to syntax, phonology and semantics that characterizes the knowledge a person has of his or her language. Chomsky's *transformational generative grammar* refers to the grammar which is both creative and mathematically precise. Transformational rules are rules which relate or transform the deep structure of a sentence to the surface structure of a sentence. The phrase structure rules are rewrite rules of the simple form $A \rightarrow b + c$ or the *recursive form* which reintroduces the initial symbol S thus: $A - bAc$. Transformational rules take a structural description specified by the phrase structure rules and rearrange the structure by the addition and deletion of elements as well as by the reordering of elements. Take, as an example, the sentence:

(8) The funny clown, who holds a whip, chases the horse.

The *matrix sentence* is: "The clown chases the horse" and the *embedded sentences* are: "The clown is funny" and "The clown holds a whip." The relationship is diagrammed in Figure 6–1. Note the repetition of the *base structure* in the tree diagram: "The clown, the clown is funny, the clown holds a whip, the clown chases the horse." Thus we need *rewrite rules* to transform the base structure into the surface structure we ordinarily use by rearranging, deleting and inserting elements into the phrase structure. The transformational rules are applied from the bottom-up to the top of the phrase marker and reapplied at the next level if needed. Further, these rules can be reordered if necessary.

Thus we will need to apply: (a) one rule to replace or delete "the clown" by the use of the relative pronoun "who" and (b) another rule in the next sentence to delete "the clown" and to move the adjective "funny" into the adjectival position next to the noun in the higher level. These rules thus change the base structure to the surface structure that we ordinarily use. These transformational rules are an abstract formal representation of the knowledge of the speaker rather than what actually goes on in the mind. When the child acquires rewrite rules, he or she meets the requirements of creativity or productivity. This means a small number of rules for

FIGURE 6–1. Relationship of matrix and embedded sentences.

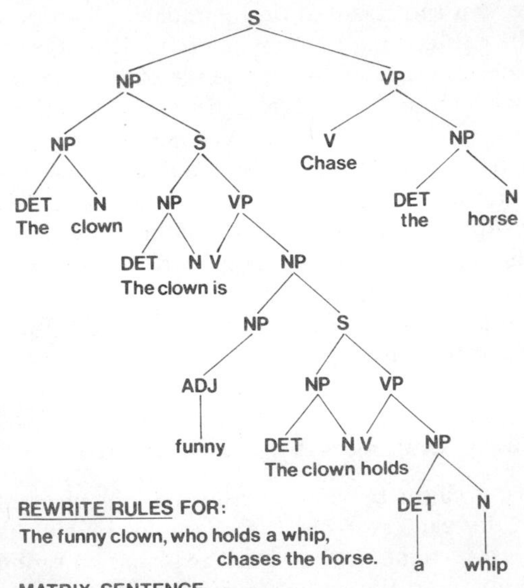

the production of a large number of different utterances conforming to them. The theory also accounts for the semantic component operating on deep structures and deriving from them the semantic interpretation of the sentence.

Compare our earlier discussion of phrase structures where a sentence can be decomposed into the form: $S \rightarrow NP + VP$. It is true that the recursive rule enables us to expand NP into the form:

$$NP \rightarrow \begin{Bmatrix} (Det+)N \\ S \end{Bmatrix}$$

as shown in the sentence:

(9) Jack said Jill thought Cinderella was a pumpkin,

and diagrammed in Figure 6–2. The same recursive rule is not able to disambiguate sentences (6) and (7). Here the same phrase structure is followed but very different deep structure applies.

The use of rewrite rules can be exemplified in the panel of active and passive sentences:

(10a) The boy will open the window.
(10b) The window will be opened by the boy.

The rewrite rule takes the form of:

$$NP_1 - Aux - V - NP_2 \rightarrow NP_2 - Aux + be + en - V - by + NP_1.$$

The plus signs give part of the information needed to construct the phrase marker for the output

FIGURE 6–2. Recursive rule for "Jack said Jill thought Cinderella was a pumpkin."

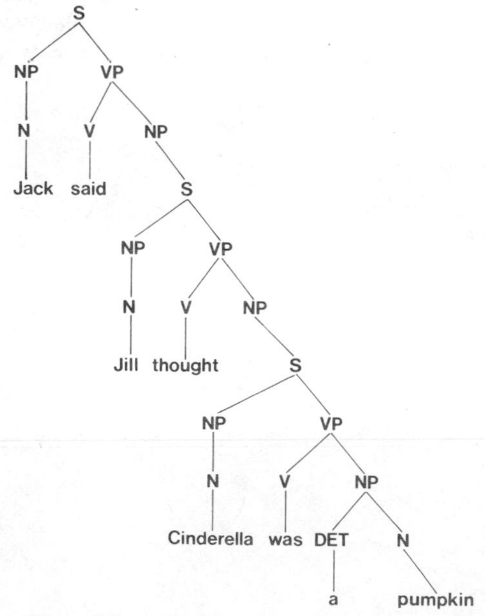

string of the passive transformation. Thus *be* + *en* are attached to the *Aux* rather than *V* and that *by* is to be attached to NP_1. From the notations above we note:

1. There is more than one element appearing to the left of the arrow and the operation performed by the rule is rather complex.
2. There is a permutation of the two *NPs* and the addition of the elements *be, en* and *by* at particular points.
3. A single symbol may refer to a string of more than one element as transformation rules operate on phrase markers rather than strings of elements.

A further illustration of the more creative and precise nature of transformational rules over phrase structure *(PS)* rules relates to our understanding of well-formed and ill-formed sentences. If we write *PS* rules which will generate all the well-formed sentences and no ill-formed or unacceptable sentences we will need a very complex set of rules taking into account the sentential environment. Examine these two sentences:

(11) * I like yourself.
(12) * You like myself.

The reflexive "myself" may occur if and only if the form "I" appears to its left. Similarly for "yourself" when "you" appears to its left. In this way, the *complementary distribution* (i.e. neither of two items can occur where the other can) of reflexive and nonreflexive provisions will be correctly accounted for. One simple way, but not the only way, for transformational grammars to deal with *reflexivity* is to postulate two levels: deep structure where simplicity exists and surface structure where the unacceptable forms such as *"You like myself" have been converted into acceptable forms such as "You like me" by transformation. Thus transformation helps to filter out ill-formed sentences, to convert deep structures of the form "Claire$_1$ loves Claire$_1$" into "Claire loves herself" if the two Claires are co-referential. The formalized version of the "myself" reflexive can be approximated as:

PRONOUN → *myself / X I Y – Z*

This is read as: A pronoun is rewritten as "myself" only in the environment "I" when "I" may be preceded or followed by nothing, or anything, and "myself" may be followed by nothing, or anything. The next rule is:

$$\text{PRONOUN} \rightarrow me\ /\ X \left\{ \begin{array}{l} \text{he} \\ \text{she} \\ \text{they} \\ \cdot \\ \cdot \\ \cdot \\ NP[-\text{PRONOUN}] \end{array} \right\} Y - Z$$

This reads: A pronoun may be actualized as "me" in an environment (shown by dash to specify the place in whose environment expansion occurs) where it is preceded by "he," "she," "they," or any nonpronominal *NP* and when "he," "she," "they" . . . may be followed by nothing, or anything and the "me" may be followed by nothing or anything.

"Deep Structure, Surface Structure and Semantic Interpretation"

Borrowing the title from one of Chomsky's essays, we will attempt to summarize the main arguments in Chomsky's theory. He views the grammar as consisting of a *base* composed of the lexicon (theoretical or mental dictionary as discussed in Chapter 5) and phrase structure rules, or more correctly, *categorical subcomponent* with a set of rules similar to phrase structure rules. Syntax has a component consisting of a set of transformational rules, which occur after the phrase structure or *PS* rules but before the phonological rules. The output of *PS* rules is usually referred to as deep structure which is the input to both the semantic component and transformational component.

Deep structure is explained in *Aspects* (Chomsky, 1965) as a phrase marker which contains all the lexemes (lexical entries) whose forms appear in the surface structure of the same sentence. In the *standard theory* of Chomsky, deep structures require certain conditions:

> First, they determine semantic representation. Second, they are mapped into well-formed surface structures by grammatical transformations (without any subsequent insertion of lexical items). Third, they satisfy the set of formal conditions defined by base rules, in particular, the rules of the categorical component define the grammatical functions and order of constituents, and the contextual features of lexical entries determine how lexical items can be entered into such structures (Chomsky, 1972a, p . 66).

From the transformational component is derived a set of rules known as surface structure, which in turn, is input to the phonological rules (see also relevant sections in Chapter 5). The semantic component of the grammar interprets the meaning of the base sentence by means of projection rules which combine the word meanings into a whole sentence. The semantic aspect is referred to as *interpretive* because the complex of symbols of the base phrase markers representing structural relationships among ideas is interpreted by the semantic component through the use of lexemes in the base component.

The above discussion of Chomsky's grammar can be approximated in Figure 6–3. Unlike the earlier work of Chomsky where surface structure is held to be of little importance in semantic interpretation, the schematic portrays the role played by surface structure as evident in *Aspects* and

FIGURE 6–3. Schematic of Chomsky's surface structure, deep structure, and semantic interpretation.

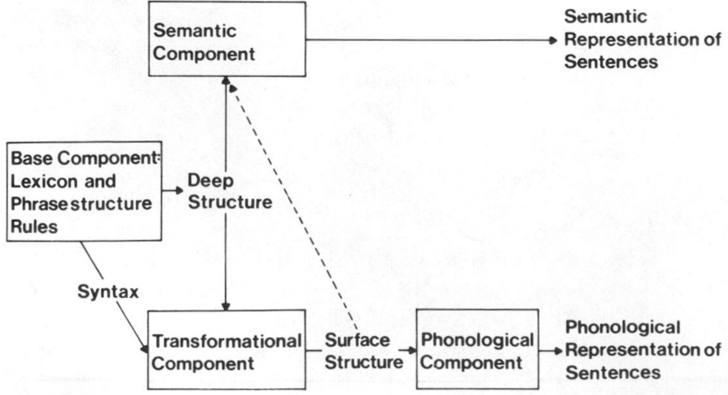

later works. In his clear exposition "Form and Meaning in Natural Languages" Chomsky (1972b, p. 107) makes this clear: "surface structure also plays a role in determining semantic interpretation. The study of this question is one of the most controversial aspects of current work, and, in my opinion, likely to be one of the most fruitful." He goes on to elaborate:

> the generative grammar of a language specifies an infinite set of structural descriptions, each of which contains a deep structure, a surface structure, a phonetic representation, a semantic representation, and other formal structures. . . . It seems that both deep and surface structure enters into the determination of meaning. Deep structure provides the grammatical relations of predication, modification, and so on, that enter into the determination of meaning. On the other hand, it appears that matters of focus and presupposition, topic and comment, the scope of logical elements, and pronominal reference are determined, in part at least, by surface structure. The rules that relate syntactic structures to representations of meaning are not at all well understood. In fact, the notion "representation of meaning" or "semantic representation" is itself highly controversial. It is not clear at all that it is possible to distinguish sharply between the contribution of grammar to the determination of meaning, and the contribution of so-called "pragmatic considerations," questions of fact and belief and context of utterance. It is perhaps worth mentioning that rather similar questions can be raised about the notion "phonetic representation." . . (Chomsky, 1972b, pp. 110–111).

The above quotation sets forth Chomsky's views on deep structure, surface structure and their relationship to semantic representation and also draws our attention to topics of current interest. The question of "the meaning of meaning" is one of perennial interest to philosophers, linguists and latterly psychologists (see, for example, Ogden and Richards, 1923). Furthermore, the extralinguistic contribution to meaning should not be overlooked as shown in the following sentences:

(13) * Stones get headaches.
(14) Our four-year-old son told his friends that stones get headaches.

It is clear that (13) is anomalous as it stands, but is acceptable in the total context of (14). The current approach of cognitive psychology to meaning is well represented by the assertion of Bransford and McCarrell (1974, p. 215) that "a person may . . . have knowledge of a language and yet fail to comprehend an utterance because he is unable to make the necessary cognitive contributions." They emphasize that an adequate theory of meaning must consider the cognitive contributions of the comprehender as well as the linguistic characterizations of input sentences. They show that people could not understand such sentences as "If the balloon popped, the sound could not carry" in isolation but could do so in the context of a loudspeaker suspended on a balloon by means of which the modern-day Romeo plays a guitar for his Juliet, who is listening to him from a skyscraper window. This pragmatic aspect of language will be dealt with more fully in the section on language function and especially in Chapter 10 on comprehending prose materials.

Two notions of importance to Chomsky's argument of the role of surface structure in semantic interpretation are: *focus* and *presupposition.* The focus of a sentence is that part of it which presents new information and is often marked by stress, whereas the presuppositions of a sentence are those propositions not asserted directly, which the sentences presuppose to be true. Chomsky (1972a) explains his position this way:

> Rules of phonological interpretation assign an intonational contour to surface structures. Certain phrases of the surface structures may be marked, by grammatical processes of a poorly understood sort, as receiving expressive or contrastive stress, and these markings also affect the operation of the rules of phonological interpretation. If no such processes have applied, the rules assign the normal intonation. In any event, phrases that contain the intonation center involve expressive or contrastive stress, as noted. Choice of focus determines the relation of the utterance to responses, to utterances to which it is a possible response, and to other sentences in the discourse. The notions "focus," "presupposition," and "shared presupposition" . . . must be determinable from the semantic interpretation of sentences if we are to be able to explain how discourse is constructed and, in general, how language is used (pp. 99–100).

Further: "The focus is a phrase containing the intonation center; the presupposition, an expression derived by replacing the focus by a variable. Each sentence, then, is associated with a class of pairs *(F,P)* where *F* is a focus and *P* a presupposition, each such pair corresponding to one possible interpretation" (Chomsky, 1972a, p. 100, italics added).

Some examples will explain the relational aspect of meaning. The use of *intonation* in these sentences is evident:

(15) Who won the hockey game?
(16) It was the NEW YORK RANGERS who won.

The second sentence presupposes that there was a hockey game and the contrastive stress brings out the meaning. Similarly:

(17) Did John give Terry the PRESENT?
(18) Did John give the present to TERRY?

For (17) the focus is "the present" and the presuppositions are "give Terry the present" and "John gives Terry the present." Similarly, for (18) the focus is "Terry" with "give the present to Terry" and "John gives the present to Terry" as presuppositions. Thus, in sentences (15) to (18) meaning is determined also by surface structure.

Pronominalization plays a part as shown in this pair of sentences:

(19) Each of the men likes his sister.
(20) The men each like his sister.

In (19) "his" may refer to one of the men, while in (20) "his" *must* refer to some other person.

Active-passive pairs of sentences provide different interpretations:

(21) Chinese cook Peking ducks.
(22) Peking ducks are cooked by Chinese.

These sentences differ in the range of meaning. Sentence (21) states that it is the property of Peking ducks that they are cooked by Chinese. But this interpretation is false as some Peking ducks are not cooked by Chinese. Such an interpretation is not possible, at least under normal intonation. Sentence (21) states that Chinese have a certain property, namely, they cook Peking ducks but the sentence does not imply that they cook all Peking ducks. Thus the position of the words "Peking ducks" in surface structure plays a role in determining the meaning of sentences (21) and (22). To understand (22) we must know that the *NP* "Peking ducks" is the subject of the sentence. But we must also know that the *NP* "Peking ducks" bears the grammatical relation of direct object to the verb "cook." Thus the subject-predicate relation is defined in surface structure.

As a further illustration of the role of surface structure in meaning, Chomsky has provided the example of:

(23) "John has lived in Princeton,"

with the presupposition that John is alive. Chomsky suggests that one would not say:

(24) "Einstein has lived in Princeton,"

knowing Einstein is dead. The correct version for (24) is "Einstein lived in Princeton." Thus, the presupposition is that the person denoted by the surface subject is alive. In this sense, the surface structure contributes to the meaning of the sentence as it is relevant to determining what is presupposed in the use of a sentence. In this regard, the descriptions by Jackendoff (1972) are appropriate. He defines *focus* in a sentence as "information in a sentence which is assumed by the speaker not to be shared by him and the hearer" and "presupposition" as "the information in the sentence that is assumed by the speaker to be shared by him and the hearer" (p. 230).

To return to the "questions of fact and belief and context of utterance" (Chomsky, 1972b, p. 111) to explain meaning, Chomsky's *selectional rules* should be noted. To explain the anomalous sentence:

(25) * "Sincerity may admire the boy."

Chomsky (1965, pp. 82–86) invokes the concepts of categories and features. Each lexical formative is associated with a set of syntactic features (e.g. *boy* has the features of [+ common], [+ human], [+ countable], and so on). The symbols representing lexical categories *(N, V . . .)* will be analyzed by the rules into complex symbols. Each complex symbol is a set of specified syntactic features just as phonological segments consist of a set of phonological features. The subcategorization rules serve as their function the development of category *N* into a set of features. Among these rules are

1. N → [+N, ± Common]
2. [+ Common] → [± Count]
3. [+ Count] → [± Animate]
4. [− Common] → [± Animate]
5. [+ Animate] → [± Human]
6. [− Count] → [± Abstract]

Thus, every member of the category *Noun* has the feature of being "common" or "noncommon" (± common); all categories with the property of "plus common" are either "countable" or "noncountable," and so on.

Given this formalization of the syntactic properties, we can organize the lexicon thus:

sincerity: [+ N, − Count, + Abstract]
boy: [+ N, + Count, + Common, − Abstract, + Human]

Assuming the verb *admire* only goes with animate objects, we can formulate a selection rule in terms of the features [+[+ Human] Aux —]. Chomsky treats selectional restrictions as a matter of syntax rather than as semantics though he makes it clear that the two aspects are not sharply distinguishable (1965, p. 72). Some linguists (e.g. Bierwisch, 1970), however, formulate such selectional specifications as a condition for well-formedness on semantic representations rather than on syntactic structures as suggested by Chomsky. Fodor, Fodor and Garrett (1975) have moved away from decomposition of lexical items into features in the direction of a more integrative approach to meaning. They now suggest that a more holistic approach through meaning postulates probably is more useful. To explain the oddity of such an anomalous sentence as (25) "Sincerity may admire the boy," Chomsky invokes selectional restrictions on the insertion of lexical items into a deep structure representation. But this principle can be violated with a negative which would make the co-occurrence of *S* and predicate acceptable:

(26) Sincerity may not admire the boy.
(27) Stones do not get headaches.
(28) Colorless green ideas do not sleep furiously.

Similarly, nonlinguistic elements are important. The selectional restriction principle can be violated without leading to oddity of the entire sentence:

(29) The fairy said stones get headaches.
(14) Our four-year-old son told his friends that stones get headaches.

Given our knowledge of the world that many things would be possible in a make-believe realm of fairies and in the fantasy of young children, sentences (29) and (14) could be accepted. According to this "world view," semantic deviance is due not so much to the way in which language is structured but more to the way the world is structured. However, this view of cognitive contribution does not force the conclusion that oddity or anomaly cannot be accounted for within semantics.

Semantic Relational "Cases"—Case Grammar

Charles Fillmore (1968) has developed a *case grammar* as a variant—a radical variant—of transformational grammar to explain basic semantic relations. Such concepts as subject and object which are defined in Chomsky's standard theory as *NPs* dominated by *S* and *VP* respectively are replaced by the specification of semantic roles and functions. Fillmore (1968, p. 21) explains that "the sentence in its basic structure consists of a verb and one or more noun phrases, each associated with the verb in a particular case relationship. . . . The arrays of cases defining the sentence types of a language have the effect of imposing a classification of the verbs in the language. . . ." An example will illustrate the role of conceptually required number of arguments in verbs in English sentences. Conceptually the verb *rob* has three arguments predicating someone taking something (unlawfully) out of some place or from someone else. Similarly, *buy* and *sell* are each four-argument predicates representing the buyer, the seller, the goods or services rendered, and money changing hands. Fillmore (1971a, 1971b) emphasizes that conceptually necessary arguments to a predicate cannot always be matched on a one-to-one basis with the "cases" associated with the same predicate. Thus sentence (30):

(30) He bought it (from Joe) (for ten dollars),

shows the optionally present arguments marked off by parentheses.

In essence, case grammar takes the form of *propositions in deep structure.* A proposition is marked for tense, mood, negative, aspect, interrogative and consists of a verb and case categories involving the nouns. Propositions refer to: *who* did it, *who* it happened to, *what* was done and *where* it happened or *cases* of *agentive, instrumental* and *dative* cases. Fillmore (1968) suggests:

> In the basic structure of sentences, then, we find what might be called the proposition, a tenseless set of relationships involving verbs and nouns (and embedded sentences, if there are any), separated from what might be called the "modality" constituent. This latter will include such modalities on the sentence-as-a-whole as negation, tense, mood, and aspect (p. 23).

Examine these sentences:

(31) The vase broke.
(32) John broke the vase.
(33) A stone broke the vase.

The deep structure to sentences (32) and (33) is identical except for the lexical entries. Such a deep structure analysis designating "John" as subject of the first sentence and "stone" as subject of the second sentence would miss certain relationships in deep structure, which are understood by native speakers. In case grammar, "John" is classified as *agentive* and "stone" as *instrumental.* This classification is held to explain why (33) is not acceptable whereas the instrumental case can be expressed by *with:*

(34) John broke the vase with a stone.

The structures of the above sentences are:

(31a) ([*V,* break], [Object, the vase]).
(32a) ([*V,* break], [Agent, John], [Object, the vase]).
(33b) ([*V,* break], [Instrument, a stone], [Object, the vase]).
(34c) ([*V,* break], [Agent, John], [Instrument, a stone], [Object, the vase]).

The semantic case relationship (case grammar) is shown diagrammatically in Figure 6–4(a). The standard theory analysis is represented in the tree diagram of Figure 6–4(b) for comparison.

We will need to refer to Fillmore again for a clear exposition. "The case relations comprise a set of universal, presumably innate, concepts which identify certain types of judgments human beings are capable of making about the events that are going on around them, judgments about such matters as who did it, who it happened to, and what got changed" (Fillmore, 1968, pp. 24–25). In Fillmore's original formulation the cases needed include: Agentive *(A),* Instrumental *(I),* Dative *(D),* Factitive *(F)* ("resulting from the action or state identified by the verb"), Locative *(L)* (spatial orientation) and Objective *(O)* or the "semantically most neutral case." In his recent writing Fillmore (1971a) suggests that case relationships relevant to the subclassification of verb types include:

> Agent *(A),* the instigator of the event
> Counter-Agent *(C),* the force or resistance against which the action is carried out
> Object *(O),* the entity that moves or changes or whose position or existence is in consideration
> Result *(R),* the entity that comes into existence as a result of the action
> Instrument *(I),* the stimulus or immediate physical cause of an event
> Source *(S),* the place from which something moves
> Goal *(G),* the place to which something moves
> Experience *(E),* the entity which receives or accepts or experiences or undergoes the effect of an action (earlier called . . . 'Dative') (p. 376).

FIGURE 6–4. Case grammar and "standard theory" analyses of "John broke the vase with a stone."

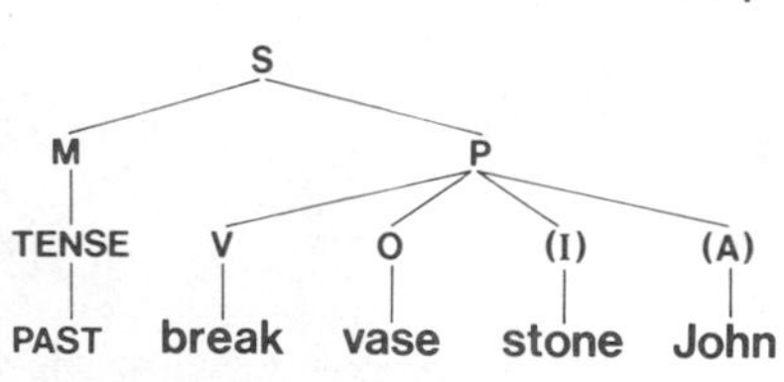

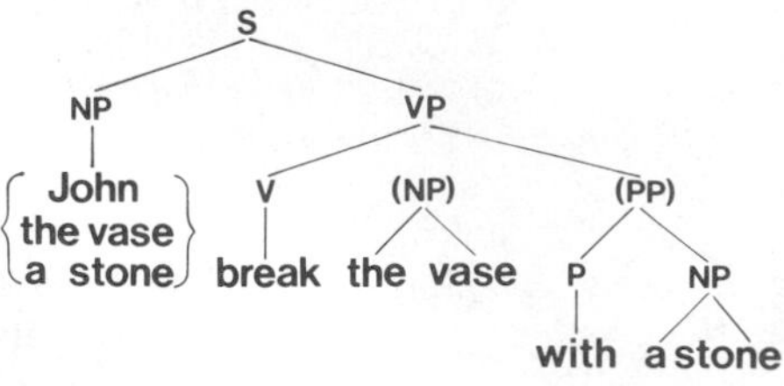

Note that each proposition has no more than one case of the same kind. In order to achieve this, some reanalysis may be needed and there is a hierarchical order of cases. These may be obligatory or optional. For example, the "break" requires an object, while agent and instrument are optional, as shown in sentences (31)–(33). Furthermore, there may be constraints upon the deletion of cases. For example, MOVE needs either an agent or locative or both if it has an object, though neither agent nor locative are obligatory in the absence of an object for MOVE, as shown in "I moved," "I moved to the west side of town," and "I moved my furniture to the living room."

With the use of the verb as the central organizing unit, case grammar apparently offers some advantages over transformational grammar [see explanation for sentences (31) to (34)]. A further example will show how case grammar can describe some relations among sentences which are difficult to handle on syntactic grounds:

(35) Bill seems to me to be silly.
(36) I regard Bill as silly.

Both *I* and *me* share the same case relationship of experience *(E)*, and this analysis probably is in closer accord with our intuitive understanding of sentences. Chomsky (1972a), however, wonders if case relationships differ empirically from standard theory. He sees very little difference and suggests perhaps the case system expresses semantic facts in a "direct way" through relational content, while the standard system does so only "indirectly" by identifying the constituents. To some extent, the linguistic generalization that needs to be expressed in sentences (32) to (34) can be accommodated with the *lexical redundancy rule* (Chomsky, 1965). This rule states general properties and regularities of all lexical entries in the range of environments in which members of a given category of items (usually verbs) can occur. This, however, does not weaken the psychological conception of relational units and propositions as basic to memory and hence to comprehension. Shafto (1973), for example, showed that sentences similar to one another in their case relations are more confusable than sentences with the same "empty" categories of nouns and surface subjects and objects.

On psychological grounds, a case grammar has certain advantages over transformational grammar. Perfetti's (1972) comment in his review on some cognitive aspects of structural meaning that "the psycholinguistic implications of case grammar are only beginning to be investigated" serves to highlight some significant work using the model. Fillmore's case grammar is used by Greenfield and Smith (1976) to provide a framework to examine the combinatorial meaning of one-word and holophrastic utterances in sentential and extrasentential contexts. They show that the child can use single words in relation to concrete situations to express semantic ideas analogous to the various "cases." Fillmore's case grammar is also the basis for much of the work of Kintsch (1974) on text grammar, and much of Meyer's (1975a, 1975b, 1977a, 1977b) system for analyzing the organization of information in textual materials. We will return to the topic of prose comprehension and structure in Chapter 10 on other cognitive aspects. Central to much of comprehension and memory is the question of the propositional unit in the form of: verb, subject, object. If we accept the premises that sentences consist of propositions, and that propositions are multi-arguments with the verb as the main term, then the verb must come early in the comprehension process and must carry a great deal of information. From the "action" conceptualized by the verb, the hearer/reader can build up a "semantic network" (see Lindsay and Norman, 1972) with links to account for relations among concepts. It is the relationship among propositions (agent, instrument, location, time, quality, and so on) which is critical to comprehending. We will return to this aspect in the sections on cognitive contributions to comprehension in Chapter 10.

Bridge from Language Structure to Language Functions

It is painfully obvious that the preceding sections have only sketched the structure or form of language on a canvas which needs to be much larger to include other significant works. Our purpose has been to provide a clear understanding of the rules of grammar which enable humans to comprehend and produce an infinite number of sentences, to distinguish well-formed from ill-formed sentences, and to disambiguate ambiguous ones. From the point of view of linguists, sentences in isolation should be the basic subject of analysis. They provide many readings for the listener/reader to select from in a proper context. Katz and Fodor (1967, p. 405) make this clear: "a theory of settings must contain a theory of semantic interpretation as a proper part because the readings that a speaker attributes to a sentence in a setting are a selection from among those that the sentence has in isolation." For psychologists, knowledge of language is necessary but not sufficient to understand utterances unless the listener/reader can also activate his/her prior world knowledge. We should thus note Chomsky's (1972b, 1975, 1977) assertion of linguistics as a branch of cognitive psychology. By this he means that linguistics has an important contribution to make to our understanding of mental processes. For example, Chomsky (1975, p. 4) has commented: "By studying language, we may discover abstract principles that govern its structure and use, principles that are universal by biological necessity and not mere historical accident, that derive from mental characteristics of the species. . . . Thus language is a mirror of mind in a deep and significant sense. It is a product of human intelligence, created anew in each individual by operations that lie far beyond the reach of will or consciousness."

How the child learns language is the topic for the next part of this chapter. The linguist Halliday (1975) has alerted us to the distinction between acquiring a language and learning a language; the first has the sense of something "out there" for the child to acquire, and the second is the process itself with the child as the active participant in the learning process. Halliday also implies that the child in "learning how to mean" is making or creating language from the total linguistic resources—phonological, syntactic and semantic—available to him/her. To the child, the language system, as we have discussed in Chapter 5 and in this chapter thus far, is a system for making meanings and meaning relationships in the environment. Halliday's view of language development as an interactive process away from purely descriptive aspects and towards explanatory aspects of language in terms of cognitive theory characterizes much of linguistic studies in the 1970s.

Halliday's distinction between the *pragmatic* function and the *mathetic* function is a valuable contribution to our understanding of how the child moves into adult language. The pragmatic function refers to "that of language as doing, that creates the conditions for the development of interpersonal meanings, those expressing the speaker's role in and angle on the communication process" (Halliday, 1975, p. 88). The mathetic function "is language enabling the child to learn about his social and material environment, serving him in the construction of reality." Further, "this function is realized, in the first instance, through the child observing, recalling and predicting the objects and events which impinge on his perceptions" (Halliday, 1975, p. 75). Thus:

> A child learns a symbolic behaviour potential; that is what he "can mean", in terms of a few elementary social functions. In the process he creates a language, a system of meanings deriving from these functions, together with their realizations in sound. The meanings are, in turn, the encoding of the higher-level meanings that constitute the developing child's social system; first his own relationships with people and objects, then the relationships among the people and objects themselves, then relationships among symbols, and so on (Halliday, 1975, p. 80).

The textual component, essentially an adult system, is structured on the pragmatic and mathetic functions.

In the course of learning language the child is also learning *through* language. Halliday (1975, p. 121) provides a beautiful example of how a young child learns his language and learns through language in the exchange between Nigel (2:11) and his mother:

> MOTHER [having fetched Nigel home from school]: How on earth did you get all that sand in your hair?
> NIGEL: I was just standing up and I threw the sand to it [= "at it"; referent unspecified] and it got in my hair.
> MOTHER: And what did the teacher say?
> NIGEL: No . . . because it was time to go home and have your [= "my"] pieces of meat.

This exchange illustrates the gap between the child's world of meaning and that of the adult. To Nigel, the sand got into his hair because things just happened that way and he was told not to throw sand because it was time for "pieces of meat" (lunch). Thus the child has to learn the social or *semiotic* system and concurrently the means of learning this sociocultural system through language.

Thus, to linguists of the persuasion of Chomsky, meaning is defined in terms of the mind. His transformational grammar is marked by a high degree of logic, of idealization and is focused on intralinguistic rules and regularities. To linguists like Fillmore and Halliday (if we can bracket them), case relation of intralinguistic elements and the syntagmatic relation or structure of text materials are important. Halliday has further emphasized meaning potentials less in terms of abstractions of the mind but more in terms of actualized potentials, of what the child can do. While we will not go into the sociological aspect of Halliday's "learning how to mean" as implicit in his theory, we will examine the "communicative competence" of children. From an inquiry of how children make use of their competence in listening and speaking, we will better understand how they acquire the activity of reading print.

Language Functions

In this part of the chapter we will discuss the functions of language or how language is used in context. This "communicative competence" referred to earlier is succinctly put by Hymes (1972, p. xix) in his introduction to a volume on language functions in the classroom: "The functions of language in the classroom are a special case of the general problem of the study of language in its social context . . . an adequate theory of the functioning of language would not 'start' from either language or context, but would systematically relate the two within a single model." It is only by viewing the relationship between language structure and language form that we can understand better how language is acquired, is taught and learned, and how language underpins reading acquisition. In the following sections we will be concerned with such issues as the meaning of language awareness; the different forms it will take; its development in children and specifically its relationship to learning to read.

What is language awareness? Obviously there is no one answer to this question which has occupied the attention of linguists, psycholinguists, experimental and child psychologists and educators. Recall early in the chapter our reference to Chomsky's (1972b, p. 115) conception of *linguistic awareness* as referring to the language user having internalized a system of rules in relation to their phonetic and semantic representations. Compare this with Cazden's (1974b, p. 29) explanation: "Metalinguistic awareness, the ability to make language forms opaque and attend to them in and for themselves, is a special kind of language performance, one which makes special cognitive demands, and seems to be less easily and less universally acquired than the language performance of speaking and listening. . . ." It is clear from even these short references that Chomsky conceives of language awareness as abstract, idealized systems, while Cazden and many others view them in more pragmatic terms.

In the survey of the literature there seem to be two related strands of works in recent years—one strand has a linguistic or psycholinguistic orientation with Chomsky (1957, 1965) and Chomsky and Halle (1968) as the reference and the other strand is psychological or psycho-educational. The psycholinguistic strand is best represented by an earlier paper by Mattingly (1972) in the volume *Language by Ear and by Eye* (Kavanagh and Mattingly, 1972) and his more recent paper directly on the topic and reading (Mattingly, 1979). Underpinning this work is the active support of NICHD ([U.S.] National Institute of Child Health and Human Development) for basic and applied research into communicating by language as evidenced by an early volume with that name (Kavanagh, 1968) to the more recent work on language in the laboratory, school, and clinic (Kavanagh and Strange, 1978), and the cross-national study on orthography, reading and dyslexia (Kavanagh and Venezky, 1980). The psychological or psycho-educational strand encompasses two quite distinct sources of work—one source emanating from a group of Russian psychologists and pedagogues and the other source from some very penetrating work by other psychologists outside the U.S.S.R. The hitherto little-known Russian work on literacy acquisition in children is represented by the writings of scientists in the Academy of Educational Sciences (e.g. Redozubov in Rozhdestvensky (1961)), the Scientific Research Institute of Schools of the Ministry of Education, Egorov (1953) and the more familiar Elkonin (1973a, 1973b). The other group of psychological writings include such works as the proceedings of the Nijmegen Max-Planck psycholinguistic project on the child's conception of language (Sinclair, Jarvella, and Levelt, 1978); the monograph by Hakes (1980) on language intuition in children; Donaldson's (1978) powerful book on young children's "disembedded thoughts" and social values; the ongoing research and writing of I. Liberman and her associates (e.g., I. Liberman, Shankweiler, A. Liberman, Fowler, and Fischer, 1977) on linguistic awareness and reading; the Summer 1979 University of Victoria Conference on the same theme (see Mattingly, 1979); and Downing's (1979a) cognitive clarity theory set out in his *Reading and Reasoning*.

These burgeoning psychological and pedagogical interests are best encapsulated in the various converging explanations of language as a skill (see Chapters 2 and 3 of this book), as a conscious repairing. Thus language awareness is explained by the Nijmegen project participants as "metacognition," "reflective abilities," "general development of consciousness and self-consciousness" and "objects of reflection" over and above language as a formal system. One participant, Read (1978), a linguist, summarizes the concept well: "We might say that a speaker exhibits metalinguistic awareness when that speaker is attending to some part of what he or she knows about the language, and also knows that he or she possesses that knowledge" (p. 65). His further explanation brings us directly into the realm of reading:

> The performances of adapting, manipulating, segmenting, correcting, and judging language seem to play an important role in at least three processes: learning to read and write, learning a non-native language, and responding to social expectations. In short, they have a great deal to do with using language effectively un-

> der varied circumstances. Whether they are conscious or can easily be brought to consciousness appears to be of secondary importance (Read, 1978, p. 66).

In the following sections we will elaborate on these various views—linguistic or psycholinguistic, and psychological or psycho-educational—all bearing on how children have access to language and hence to reading.

Mattingly's Linguistic Awareness

The earlier NICHD report (Kavanagh, 1968) summarizes much of the theoretical findings on communicating by language and in a sense foreshadows a number of significant issues still being pursued. Highlighting the relationship between speaking, listening and reading, the report emphasizes reading as "parasitic on speech" as a central theme. Built around this are discussions on such significant issues as: errors of reading are patterned phonemically or subphonemically rather than syllabically and are verifiable in confusion matrices; segmentability of some phonemes especially the nonsegmentability of the stop consonants /p/, /t/, /k/, /b/, /d/, /g/ (see Chapter 7 in this book); "thinking without speech" in deaf individuals; access to the lexicon for "grammatical and semantic correlates" (see Chapter 9 in this book for experimental evidence); dyslexia and reading processes generally. By taking up and/or continuing these lines of studies, researchers have done much to enhance our understanding of reading processes in the early years.

Thus much of the *Language by Ear and by Eye* volume published in 1972 is an elaboration of this empirical tradition. Mattingly's 1972 paper and his 1979 keynote address on language awareness and reading at the Victoria Conference with this name reflect much of this line of thinking and the influence of Noam Chomsky's work. Agreeing that listening and reading somehow employ the same linguistic processes, Mattingly (1972, pp. 134–135) is emphatic that "it does not follow that the two activities are directly analogous" or parallel. Research by Mattingly and his colleagues at the Haskins Laboratories has shown that the speech code is complex and multidimensional, and speech cues and print carry different levels of linguistic information. The language cues for speaking-listening are largely phonetic; the writing-reading cues involve the more abstract phonological coding (see Chapter 9) and both listening and reading are linked by phonological rules. More specifically, the speaker must produce a phonetic representation (perceived pronunciation) of a sentence with a semantic representation. The listener must synthesize a sentence which matches a particular phonetic representation and recovers the semantic representation. The reader must know the rules of the phonological, graphological, syntactic and semantic cues to produce, construct and reconstruct what is contained on the printed page. Mattingly suggests that not only does the speaker-hearer need to synthesize a particular utterance, "he is also aware in some way of having done so, and can reflect upon his linguistic experience as he can upon his experiences with the external world" (Mattingly, 1972, p. 139). But much of the process of synthesis is "beyond the range of immediate awareness" (p. 139) and is not evenly distributed over all phases of linguistic activities. Mattingly claims that linguistic awareness can become the basis of various language-based skills including reading and the broader aspect of thinking as well. His conclusion is that reading be regarded "as a deliberately acquired, language-based skill, dependent upon the speaker-hearer's awareness of certain aspects of primary linguistic activity. By virtue of this linguistic awareness, written text initiates the synthetic linguistic process common to both reading and speech, enabling the reader to get the writer's message and so to recognize what has been written" (Mattingly, 1972, p. 145).

In his 1979 paper, Mattingly refines and elaborates on his earlier concepts of linguistic awareness. He now suggests that metalinguistic awareness is not so much a matter of consciousness but of access. This access is not to the linguistically aware person's linguistic activity but to "his knowledge of the grammatical structure of sentences" (p. 2). Further, reading is just as natural an activity as listening and speaking, albeit more "linguistic" than these two primary activities. Basing his linguistic and psycholinguistic assumptions largely on Noam Chomsky's transformational generative grammar (see earlier part of this chapter), Mattingly suggests that the speaker-hearer's grammatical knowledge is also tacit knowledge but is accessible in the same way that the speaker-hearer has intuition about grammaticality. Following Chomsky's competence and performance distinction, Mattingly stresses that grammatical knowledge is intuitive knowledge and hence accessible while strategies to use such knowledge (strategies such as speech perception, parsing mechanisms) are inaccessible empirically, if not linguistically. He also holds that individuals' grammatical knowledge far exceeds the functional requirements of performance and that those people who continue to acquire grammar beyond what is needed for ordinary communication are also likely to be proficient readers.

To answer the question of how the intuitive grammatical knowledge of listening and speaking are related to reading acquisition, Mattingly discusses the role of the "practical orthography" and experimental evidence on phonological coding during reading. He holds that:

1. Practical orthographies are not phonetic but would be based on semantic representation of sentences.
2. Orthographies do not transcribe information about phrase-markers representing syntactic structure.
3. In practical orthographies lexical items are transcribed morphemically as a morpheme carries both semantic and phonological values.

Here, as elsewhere, we can see the influence of Noam Chomsky on the role of English grammar and his concept of English as an optimal orthography (see discussion in Chapter 5). In fact, Mattingly (1979) emphasizes that "the conventional spellings of . . . English words correspond to the morphophonemic rather than the phonetic forms" (p. 9) and that "differences in orthography reduce to whether a morpheme is written as a single symbol or as a sequence of symbols corresponding to morphophonemes or morphophonemic syllables" (p. 11). It follows that the language-learner/reader has to exploit the morphophonemic representations in practical orthographies which presuppose the learner's/reader's access to such representations. Mattingly then cites empirical evidence on the role of phonological coding even with a morphemic writing system such as Chinese. Phonological coding is a generic term for the transformation of printed words into any type of speech-based code, whether it be articulatory, acoustic, auditory imagery or a more abstract code. Phonological coding is necessary for short-term representations of information—temporary storage needed for listening, speaking and reading. Subsequent representations in long-term memory are semantically structured.

Comments on Mattingly's Theory

Mattingly has done valuable service in his theory of linguistic awareness in relation to reading and in bringing to bear linguistic and psycholinguistic evidence on his conceptualization. Some issues will need to be clarified and questions raised.

On the question of orthographies, Chapter 4 has discussed historical and some cross-national aspects of writing systems while Chapter 5 has examined the phonemic, structural or morphophonemic and multi-code natures of the English orthography as set forth in the writings of Bloomfield, Fries, Chomsky and Halle, Venezky, Vachek and Albrow, among others. Whether the English orthography is "optimal" or "practical" is not easy to answer. There are criteria other than the orthography representing sentences by transcribing words morphemically and not phonetically. Klima (1972, p. 61), for example, states that "the optimal orthography for a language would be expected to reach the proper balance in minimizing arbitrariness, minimizing redundance, and maximizing expressiveness while still maintaining a standardized spelling" and discusses these criteria at some length. The linguist Y. R. Chao (1968) expounds on these ten requirements for "good symbols": simplicity, elegance, ease of production, suitability of size, balance between number of symbols and size of symbol complexes, clarity of relation between symbol and object, relevance of structure of symbol complexes, discrimination between symbols, suitability of operational synonyms and universality. As an example, it is clear that traditional Chinese orthography rates rather low on the Klima or Chao criteria, its main advantage being "elegance." It is with the view to achieving an "optimal" or a "practical" orthography for a more literate populace, among other reasons, that the mammoth, ongoing Chinese language reform is being undertaken. This should not be taken to mean that an orthography with a "surface phonology" or a close morphophonemic representation to a phonetic representation is necessarily felicitous or facilitating for literacy acquisition. This latter is as much a linguistic, philosophic or an empirical question. As yet, there is no convincing evidence as to whether Finnish and Serbo-Croatian (usually regarded as more "phonetic") or the Japanese syllabary are more conducive to reading acquisition or less linked to reading disabilities. One finding seems well accepted in the relative "optimality" or "practicality" of orthographies: the more efficient alphabetic writing system likely requires a higher degree of language awareness in comparison with the morphemic or syllabary systems because phonological segments are less obvious than morphemes or syllables.

Mattingly's contention that readers use their grammatical knowledge to access the morphophonemic information in the printed text leads to the question of how such morphophonemic information "triggers" the hearer-reader's performance mechanisms that ordinarily operate on auditory information. These mechanisms are said to be inaccessible, as we have been able to learn only a little about them. What is inaccessible to conscious analysis, however, is not necessarily inaccessible to internal representations of linguistic stimuli. Parenthetically, we may note that Mattingly is using morphophonemic information or representation in the sense of Chomsky's lexical representation and Venezky's internal structure as discussed in Chapter 5. Mattingly's concept of phonological representation as a means of storing incoming information while it is analyzed syntactically and semantically will not be discussed here. Experimental evidence for and against phonological access and visual access will be presented and discussed in some detail in Chapter 9. As we shall see then, the crux of the argument is whether or not phonological coding is optional or obligatory and at what stage of lexical access this coding occurs.

Mattingly's conception of individual differences in learning to read as related to how actively the individual has maintained his or her language learning capacity also seems hard to reconcile with what is known about child growth and language development. According to Mattingly, the child who is still actively acquiring language will have greater access to his or her grammatical knowledge and for such a child reading would seem reasonable and relatively easy. The child at this stage has access to morphophonemic representations and is "linguistically aware." Mattingly suggests that, in children who do not pursue language acquisition beyond what is needed for ordinary usage, their language awareness will atrophy and that this is likely to make it difficult for them to learn how to read. However, we would comment that language awareness may be continuous and developmental. Given proper linguistic stimulation, such awareness should continue to flourish. But, of course, the continuous and developmental nature of the language awareness phenomenon is also an empirical question.

This brings us to the central concept of consciousness and accessibility. The term *conscious* or *consciousness* without explicit operational analysis would be difficult for psychologists to accept. Nevertheless, complex mental operations involving long-term memory without involving some "conscious" element are not impossible. Quite clearly, Mattingly draws heavily on N. Chomsky. For example, Chomsky (1965, p. 8) states that "any interesting generative grammar will be dealing, for the most part, with mental processes that are far beyond the level of actual or even potential consciousness; furthermore, it is quite apparent that a speaker's reports and viewpoints about his behavior and his competence may be in error. Thus a generative grammar attempts to specify what the speaker actually knows, not what he may report about his knowledge." In the same work, Chomsky (1965, p. 58) stresses: "language acquisition is based on the child's discovery of what from a formal point of view is a deep and abstract theory—a generative grammar of his language—many of the concepts and principles of which are only remotely related to experience by long and intricate chains of unconscious quasi-inferential steps." Thus the question becomes one of making intuitive grammar explicit or accessible to the child.

The question of accessibility is also discussed by Klima (1972) in the *Language by Ear and by Eye* volume. At the psychological and philosophical levels, the concept of accessibility is central to memory and learning and also the larger issue of knowing and development of knowledge. There is a large body of evidence from cognitive and developmental psychology and machine intelligence studies all converging on the process of gaining access to rule-based components already in the head and on the flexible use of information so accessed. Much of the extensive work of Ann Brown (e.g. 1978) on memory and metacognition, and Flavell (1970, 1976, Flavell and Wellman, 1977) on uncovering children's awareness of knowledge available to the system already "wired" in the head is in this direction. Flavell (1976, p. 232) explains that "metacognition refers, among other things, to the active monitoring and consequent regulation and orchestration of these processes in relation to the cognitive objects on which they bear, usually in the service of some concrete goal or objective." Flavell gives some examples: "I am engaging in metacognition (metamemory, metalearning, metattention, metalanguage, or whatever) if I notice that I am having more trouble learning *A* than *B;* if it strikes me that I should double-check *C* before accepting it as a fact; if it occurs to me that I had better scrutinize each and every alternative in any multiple-choice type task situation before deciding which is the best one; if I become aware that I am not sure what the experimenter really wants me to do; if I sense that I had better make a note of *D* because I may forget it; if I think I should ask someone about *E* to see if I have it right . . ." (Flavell, 1976, p. 232).

This is essentially the view of the general problem of knowing when, knowing how, and knowing that you know and do not know, and it reminds us of the summary views presented at the beginning of this chapter on language awareness as "conscious repairing," as "reflection" on language. Here Mattingly offers some practical suggestions for clinicians and practitioners. Linguistic stimulation beyond listening and speaking and in the form of word games, puzzles, riddles, storytelling are valuable in keeping alive the psycholinguistic mechanisms so essential to reading. What good parents and good teachers have been doing for years is thus validated against a theoretical framework.

Awareness as Cognitive Representation

The work of Flavell and Brown cited in the preceding section reminds us of the importance of knowing about knowing. As children develop, they not only learn language but learn *about* language. Language awareness should not be taken to mean introspection. Language awareness is a mental activity that interacts with other cognitive activities on which it depends and which it can modify in turn. Studies of awareness usually refer to situations where children will perform actions the results of which are obvious to them and where they are encouraged to verbalize about how they perform these actions. Generally, awareness is shown to lag considerably behind success in action—the case of the child knowing more than he or she can tell. Awareness thus refers to cognitive structure not directly observable, not directly inferrable from a person's actions or conceptual representations and it is relatively unconscious. The crux of awareness is construction of knowledge which is deeply rooted in "biology." The term *biology* or *biological* here does not refer to maturational or to innate factors. The term is used in the Piagetian sense of developmental epistemology or how we come to know.

From the Genevan perspective, Sinclair (1978) has addressed this problem and emphasized that when Piaget discusses self-regulation, assimilation, and accommodation, Piaget is concerned with the interactive mechanisms governing the formation, development and functioning of cognitive structures. She goes on to say that: "When Piaget speaks about awareness, he means the subject's gradual awareness of the how and why of his actions and their results and of the course of his reasoning—but not of what makes his way of acting or thinking possible, impossible or necessary. Thus the research on 'becoming aware' is to be interpreted as 'becoming aware' of the how, and eventually the why, of specific actions and of the how, and eventually the why, of certain interactions between objects" (Sinclair, 1978, p. 193). In invoking Piaget to explain *consciousness* or *becoming aware*, we should bear in mind that he and his colleagues regard the innate mechanisms of language with some suspicion. They postulate that these mechanisms are not preformed but arise through the child's activities (Inhelder, Sinclair, and Bovet, 1974).

Within this cognitive-developmental context, awareness manifests itself at different levels of cognitive development but the deep-rooted biological source is closed to consciousness. The developing child gradually draws on the biological regulatory mechanisms, unconsciously using them to construct the actions. In this sense, the biological sources of language remain inaccessible to conscious conceptualization and the question of access becomes one of knowing about cognition and regulating (planning, monitoring, testing, repairing and evaluating) cognition (see Brown, 1978). Sinclair (1978) draws on two of Piaget's (1974a, 1974b) recent books to explain how awareness proceeds from very simple beginnings. "According to Piaget, in all intentional actions . . . the acting subject is aware of at least two things: the goal he wants to reach and, subsequent to his action, the result he has obtained (success, partial success or failure). From these modest beginnings awareness proceeds in two different, but complementary directions. Especially when the action fails, but also when the subject is pleasantly surprised by success, or, at the ages where this can be done, when he is asked questions, or when he questions himself, he will construct a conceptual representation of at least some of the features of the actions he has performed and of some of the reactions and properties of the objects he acted upon" (Sinclair, 1978, p. 195). This quotation brings up the different levels of awareness and the use of quasi-experimental and quasi-interviewing techniques to tap awareness. We will return to both of these issues shortly.

The conceptualization of awareness within the Piagetian framework links language including reading and symbolic processes to underlying cognitive representations. The importance of cognitive aspects is shown in: (a) perceptual strategies such as scanning, nonverbal training in reading and (b) the concept of conservation linked to reading. In other words, reading does not become an *operative* or an "agent" in children's thinking until they achieve Piaget's formal operational stage. For example, Briggs and Elkind (1973) found that early readers of the same sex and matched on IQ and SES were more advanced in concrete-operativity tasks than those children not yet reading. This line of investigation of cognitive aspects of reading (see also Elkind, 1976) emphasizes Piaget's model of perception in guiding research and practice of reading and also the progressing of different "kinds" of reading. However, any rigid interpretation of stages of reading overlooks the robust interpretation of the basic concept of understanding, of "knowing about knowing" and "knowing how to know." Acceptance of such a rigid position would mean that, until children reach formal operation, they would have difficulty in solving complex verbal problems, although they might be able to apply logical thought to concrete problems. Features of operational thought can be present in the reading process itself. For example, processing print from left-to-right is a form of seriation, recognition of words having spoken and written forms is equated with decentration, and recognition of relational aspects of words is equated with class inclusion. Thus Furth (1970) suggests that propositional thinking does not usually develop until about the ages of eleven or twelve and that it is during formal operations that reading can become a meaningful and challenging operative activity.

Advocacy of this position by Piagetian theorists should not be taken to mean that reading instruction for children should begin at later years than is the current practice. This will be an extreme interpretation of Elkind's or Furth's works. What it does mean is that emphasis in the early years should be on the child learning to read rather than the teacher teaching reading. Reading should be treated as high-level self-motivating thinking activities. An external guide such as a teacher or a parent can at best serve as a facilitating agent whose role it is to help the child to develop a spontaneous interest in reading. This interest will in turn provide its own reinforcement. A good example of this child-controlled rather than teacher-dominated approach to reading is the "organic reading" of Sylvia Ashton-Warner (1963), as discussed in an earlier chapter. Her approach combines reading, writing and spelling, and allows the child to figure out the meaning of reading.

Another interpretation of the position that verbal thinking will attain operativity only after preadolescence (about age eleven) is that language may not structure high-level thinking, such as logical arguments, but is structured by it (see Piaget and Inhelder, 1969). Furth (1978) and Furth and Wachs (1974) are emphatic that reading be linked to the Piagetian framework of the development of intelligence, the highest level of which is broader than reading and language. They maintain that there is also a "thinking-reading gap" as children know more than they can verbalize in spoken or written language. Extending the argument of the all-encompassing higher level intelligence and the "thinking-reading" gap, Furth suggests that children of beginning school age should be exposed to more than reading-related tasks. They should be helped to foster "theoretical intelligence" which can separate self, action and object, and hence will assist children to reflect on objects symbolically free from external constraints. Reading should thus be treated as developmental acquisition rather than things to be copied and written symbols should be regarded as objects of reflection for high level thinking.

The point that reading should be considered within a developmental context rather than as a single process has been made by a number of researchers and practitioners. The main distinction is usually between beginning readers and skilled or mature readers. The recent "modest proposal" of Chall (1979) to consider reading within Piaget's general cognitive theories is a further extension of the concept. Along with Elkind (1976), Furth (1978), Waller (1977) and perhaps E. L. Thorndike (1917), Chall hypothesizes reading as "a form of problem solving in which readers adapt to their environment (as per Piaget) through the processes of assimilation and accommodation" (p. 36). Individual readers will thus progress through the stages by interacting with their environment—the home, the school and the community at large. At each stage, a balanced experience is needed so that readers are sufficiently challenged and can move on to the next stage. This also carries the presupposition that subskills acquired in the previous stages are well mastered. While the stages have advantages in both research and instruction, their characteristics and age and grade equivalencies have yet to be worked out. There is another important issue in predicating reading on Piagetian concepts. Murray (1978) reminds us that Piaget had no theoretical position on reading as such. Furthermore, there are cases of early readers who are able to read presumably without attaining operativity. How is this explained by the stage concept of reading? Murray (1978, p. 60) offers the plausible answer that "the data such as they are indicate that although operativity is not necessary for reading acquisition, it could be sufficient for it."

To sum up this discussion of language awareness as cognitive representation, Gallagher (1979) rightly stresses Piaget's "biological explanation of knowledge." While language is necessary, it may not be sufficient for logico-mathematical operations and knowing is more than the development of logic. Reading is seen as a process of coordination, of relationship of phonologic, syntactic and semantic elements. Citing evidence of linkage between syllogistic reasoning and reading ability, Gallagher suggests that syllogistic or transitivity reasoning is likely rooted in simultaneous processing in Luria's (1966a, 1966b) simultaneous-successive paradigm. This is an intriguing concept and one we will return to in our discussion of reading disabilities. From the evidence reviewed, it seems to us that the "biological foundation" of language is one way to bring together the concepts of consciousness, awareness and accessibility, especially as propounded by Mattingly (1972, 1979).

Levels of Language Awareness

Mention has been made of explaining language awareness in terms of repairing. This line of argument is adopted by Marshall and Morton (1978). Using awareness in a restricted sense, they suggest that awareness arises out of devices for "fault finding." As language processing is highly complex, there must be mechanisms to detect any dysfunction, to signify that dysfunction has occurred, where it has occurred and what kind of dysfunction or malfunction it is. Thus language awareness is visualized as "a hierarchy of monitoring, control, and repair processes" (Marshall and Morton, 1978, p. 228). These researchers posit some kind of "mysterious apparatus" EMMA as a monitoring device for normal language processes (NLP) to detect language failure and dysfunction. Disruption of NLP can be caused by difficult lexical items or partial semantic information. An illustration can be given from the exchanges between the seven-year-old daughter (S.L.) of one of the authors at Christmas when address labels printed by war amputees were affixed to greeting cards. When told these labels were from the war amputation group, S.L. asked what amputation was and who the amputees were. When told that these were soldiers who had been injured in the war and were now making the address labels, she mused for a while, then wondered if she had to wait for another war before she could have her own address labels printed by war amputees! This is clearly a case of difficulties in "communication" and not so much a failure to understand. In the man-machine terminology of Marshall and Morton the sheer complexity of language programs is such that there must be an internal monitoring system to assess the state of the rules of language. Using this kind of terminology, we may better understand the exchange between child and mother in McNeill's (1966, p. 69) work:

CHILD: Nobody don't like me.
MOTHER: No, say "Nobody likes me."
CHILD: Nobody don't like me.
(Eight repetitions of this dialogue).
MOTHER: No, now listen carefully; say *"Nobody likes me."*
CHILD: Oh! Nobody don't likes me.

McNeill's point about the "relatively impenetrability" of child grammar to the adult model can be seen in terms of the child's tacit discovery of the rules of language through the interaction with adults and the linguist's explicit formulation of those rules.

In her empirical studies of what children do and say when they reflect on language, Clark (1978, p. 34) summarizes different types of metalinguistic awareness. They are

1. monitoring one's ongoing utterances.
2. checking the result of an utterance.
3. testing for reality.
4. deliberately trying to learn.

5. predicting the consequences of using inflections, words, phrases or sentences.
6. reflecting on the product of an utterance.

Included in "monitoring one's ongoing utterances" are such activities as practicing sounds, adjusting speech to different groups, ages and status; and in "checking the result of an utterance," such activities as commenting on and correcting the utterances of others. In a series of studies, Read (1971, 1975, 1978) has provided us with a fascinating account of young children's phonological awareness. Their "invented" spellings are shown to have a consistent and plausible phonetic basis with an apparent hierarchy of phonetic features. Preschoolers may represent the past tense "married" in its [perceived] phonetic form MARED; while school-age children may adopt a *-D* spelling as WALKD for "walked." There is thus a progression towards the direction of standard orthography. The different levels of "abstractions" in the child's spelling as found by Read provide a basis for both research and instruction. Under Clark's (5.) "predicting the use of inflections, words, phrases or sentences" are included such activities as judgment of utterances. Under (6.) "reflecting on the product of an utterance" we will include disambiguation of ambiguous sentences, understanding of jokes, riddles and humors, and explaining anomalous sentences.

Of the various kinds of metalinguistic awareness discussed by Clark, the last two named, "predicting" and "reflecting," are the later emerging. This developmental trend is evident with older children who are better able to reflect on language than younger ones and who have a greater appreciation of more complex ambiguities. In the next section we will discuss some research findings on how children become aware of ambiguities.

Awareness of Ambiguities

Studies of how children become aware of ambiguities and disambiguate ambiguous sentences are not only interesting in their own right, but also help us to understand the processing of sentences in general. Garrett (1970) pointed out that it is usual to encounter ambiguous sentences but it is not usual to notice their ambiguity. An example is the possible ambiguity of "I took his picture." There must be some way that we can cope with ambiguities. Could it be prior context? Could it be an option that we choose until it is disconfirmed? Garrett suggested that ambiguity must be dealt with by the normal language routine. It is likely that all meanings of ambiguous words are accessed, transferred to working memory, and evaluated for some kind of goodness of fit. Chapter 9 will elaborate on the access of word meaning.

With children, Bever (1968) suggested that they first understand surface structure and only later deep structure of sentences. He gave such examples of the five-year-old's joke: " 'Why can't you starve in the desert?' 'Because of the sand which is [sandwich] there.' " Five-year-olds are amused by the play on words at the surface structure level. Ten-year-olds can appreciate such verbal tricks as in:

> I can jump higher than the Empire State Building.
> How come?
> The Empire State Building can't jump!

Bever provided no evidence for his assertion. The assumption is that lexical ambiguities could be processed faster than surface ambiguities, which, in turn, are processed faster than deep structures. There was some support for this assumption from MacKay (1966), MacKay and Bever (1967) who found that adult subjects were able to detect and/or complete lexical ambiguities more quickly than syntactic ambiguities. But this result was not replicated by Bever, Garrett and Hurtig (1973). This progression from lexical to surface and deep ambiguities, however, was obtained by Shultz and Pilon (1973) with children six, nine, twelve and fifteen years of age, who were asked to detect various types of linguistic ambiguity. The results show that children's ability to detect phonological ambiguity (e.g. "The doctor is out of patience (patients)") appeared first with the largest improvement occurring between six and nine years of age. Next was the detection of lexical ambiguity, while detection of two different types of syntactic ambiguity did not appear until around age twelve.

The primacy of lexical over syntactic processing may be explained in terms of lexical items being processed before an analysis of the syntactic structure is completed (Schlesinger, 1968). What about the relative ease of phonological over lexical processing? It is possible that homophonous words are stored separately from polysemous words (see Katz and Fodor, 1963) and hence locating homophonous ambiguities is relatively rapid compared with the search for the different features of polysemous words. It could also be that the difference between phonological and lexical ambiguities in the study of Shultz and Pilon was blurred (e.g. "eighty cups" vs. "eight tea cups"). This was commented on by Hirsh-Pasek, Gleitman and Gleitman (1978) especially as Gleitman, Gleitman and Shipley (1972) had found earlier that even five-year-olds could give judgments and paraphrases in quite difficult syntactic circumstances.

The Bever (1968) suggestion that ambiguities could be processed faster at the phonological, then lexical, and finally syntactic levels seems to be at variance with the assumptions of sentence comprehension evolving from underlying structure to surface structure and finally lexical items. Several studies should be mentioned. McNeill (1968), for example, provides evidence from both English and Japanese children that what is learned is the deep structure of the language. Kessel (1970) carried out a thorough study of children's understanding of lexical, surface-structure and deep-structure ambiguities. The fifty children, ten from each of the following classes: kindergarten, first, second, third and fifth grades, with ages from six to twelve years, were asked to select a picture to go with a spoken sentence. Two of the four pictures presented were appropriate for ambiguous sentences of the kind: "The eating of the chicken was sloppy." Two of the three linguistic constructions in Kessel's study were first investigated by Carol Chomsky (1969).

Chomsky found that children between the ages of five and ten showed incomplete mastery of certain syntactic forms. Among the structures that she studied were complement clauses of the kind:

(a) John told Bill to go.
(b) John ordered Bill to go.

In both sentences the subject of the complement verb *go* is not expressed. To understand the sentences, listeners have to fill in the subject in order to decide that it is Bill who does the going. The listeners must have learned such a rule of the form:

Noun Phrase$_1$	Verb	Noun Phrase$_2$	to	Infinitive Verb
NP_1	V	NP_2	*to*	*Inf. vb*

or: for sentences of the form $NP_1 V NP_2$ to *vb*, assign NP_2 as subject of the infinitive verb. Such a rule Carol Chomsky refers to as the *minimal distance principle (MDP)*. According to this principle, the subject of a subordinate complement clause is the noun referent which most nearly precedes that clause. But the *MDP* is violated with a verb of the semantic class such as "promised" in "John promised Bill to go" as it is the NP_2 which is the subject of the infinitive verb. A more subtle difference is in the contrast pair "I told him what to do" and "I asked him what to do." The child must know to employ the *MDP* with the first sentence to mean "I told him what *he* should do," whereas the *MDP* must be violated with the second sentence to mean "I asked him what I should do." Hence, the correct interpretation for the second kind of sentence follows later than that for the first. Carol Chomsky found that about a third of her samples had not mastered the *promise* construction and that the children's mastery of the *ask* construction was even less complete. In addition to *promise, ask,* Chomsky also found *easy, and, although* to evoke the type of confusion as in "The doll is easy to see." Here the person doing the seeing is not specified.

While Chomsky's study is a good illustration of the psychologist's use of linguistic notions as a general guide to research, it should be noted that her choice of the particular syntactic structures was to some extent arbitrary. Moreover, the use of a blindfolded doll and the subsequent questions of: (a) "Is this doll easy to see or hard to see?" (b) "Would you make her easy/hard to see?" (the choice of easy/hard being determined by the child's answer to (a)), and (c) if the child answered "hard to see" he/she was asked, "Why was she hard to see in the beginning?" and "What did you do to make her easier to see and why did you do that?" could relate to the *saliency* of the doll. In other words, the child must realize that the blindfold is irrelevant in answering the question and must disregard this cue to arrive at the correct answer.

In Kessel's study, two of the three linguistic constructions were first studied by C. Chomsky: (a) *Ask–tell,* (b) *Eager–easy* and the third was a group of *ambiguous sentences* (lexical, surface structure and deep structure ambiguities). With the *ask–tell* sentences of the kind "John asked Bill what to do" and "John told Bill what to do," Chomsky found that it was not until the age of ten that children were consistent in distinguishing complement subject assignment in these sentences. With the *eager–easy* construction of the kind "John is eager to please" and "John is easy to please" Chomsky found that most nine-year-olds could distinguish subject assignment for the two sentences. By improving on task demands, Kessel found that his children acquired both the *ask–tell* and *eager–easy* results earlier than Chomsky had found. For *ask–tell,* the number of errors made by seven-year-olds was small, and the distinction was almost completely mastered by the eight-year-olds. For *eager–easy* more than half of the six-year-olds could master the construction and almost all the nine-year-olds could comprehend correctly. Kessel further found that lexical ambiguities were comprehended much earlier than both surface and deep structure ambiguities. Only his twelve-year-old subjects showed a good understanding of surface and deep structure ambiguities. The qualitative difference between the answers given by the younger and the older children was striking. The six-year-olds might choose the two appropriate pictures that matched the double meanings of a sentence, but they did so for the wrong reason. An example is the responses to the ambiguous sentence, "The eating of the chicken was sloppy." The six-year-olds would choose the appropriate pictures with the answer, "These pictures both have chickens in them." Older children would say, "The people are eating, not the chicken." Thus, along with others, Kessel's study of ambiguous sentences is a means of clarifying the nature of the comprehension process and also of understanding language development in children.

Current research on sentence ambiguities is directed towards determining how ambiguities are resolved. Does a listener/reader analyze all possible interpretations of a sentence and then in some way choose the appropriate one? Does the listener/reader recognize an ambiguity and wait until it is resolved later in the sentence? Does the individual accept one meaning of a sentence and consider another meaning only when conflicting information is processed which requires a different interpretation? Research findings are not unequivocal.

The appreciation of a variant form of linguistic ambiguity—riddles—has also been investigated. A riddle usually takes the form of a question followed by a surprising or incongruous answer and the listener is required to figure out the ambiguity. Much of the understanding of riddles depends on the "bias" of listeners or their state of epistemic knowledge. This is shown in the earlier example that the speaker can jump higher than the Empire State Building as this building cannot jump!

Shultz (1974) tested children six, eight, ten and twelve years of age with a series of "original," "resolution-removed" and "incongruity-removed" riddles of various types. As an example, to the question, "Why did the cookie cry?" the original answer was "because its mother has been a wafer so long." The resolution-removed form was "because its mother was a wafer" while the incongruity-removed form was "because it was left in the oven too long." Results showed that children eight years and older appreciated the resolvable nature of incongruities, while six-year-old children did not. There seems to be an early stage characterized by the appreciation of pure incongruity and a later stage by a differential preference for resolvable incongruity.

Support for the above Shultz work came from a recent report by Hirsh-Pasek, Gleitman and Gleitman (1978) with much more refined riddles given to children in grades one to six. The riddles were classified as phonological (e.g. cracker/quacker), lexical (bark/bark), surface ((man) (eating fish)/(man-eating) (fish)), underlying structure (make me a milkshake—with two meanings), morphemic boundary (e.g. let's hope/let's soap). Ambiguities of lexical interpretation and underlying structure are the easiest. Superficial representation of the sentence is harder and phonological and surface ambiguities are the hardest with the break-up of the morphemic boundary also quite difficult. This variant result from that found by Shultz and Pilon (1973) probably reflects the finer control of the Hirsh-Pasek et al. study over their stimuli and is likely a better reflection of processing difficulties. The large and consistent difference found by Hirsh-Pasek et al. in the metalinguistic tasks is also a function of reading proficiency. Thus along with the Kessel work, there are age-independent significant effects of verbal abilities as measured in reading ability in children's appreciation of ambiguities and riddles. Detailed discussions of the development of children's humor and its cognitive processes are presented by McGhee (1979).

Some Russian Research on Language Awareness

The earlier discussion of language awareness in children brings us to a similar line of work carried out in the Soviet Union. Understandably, literature in English on the subject is sparse. What there is available can at best only sample the vast area of Russian work with a view to obtaining an orientation of Russian psychological and pedagogical studies of child language. In an appendix to Smith and Miller's (1966) *The Genesis of Language,* Slobin provided abstracts of "Soviet methods of investigating child language" in the 1940s and 1950s. The outlines included topics of phonological competence, grammatical and lexical competence and pragmatic functions, an often-cited work being Karpova's (1955) study of preschoolers' realization of the lexical structure of speech.

For background study of works in the 1960s and to the mid-1970s *The Psychology of Preschool Children* by Zaporozhets and Elkonin (1971) and especially the anthology *Soviet Developmental Psychology* edited by Cole (1977) are valuable. From the sampling of a vast literature on developmental psychology and paedology (the science of child study) there is clearly a great concern for the acquisition of literacy. The seminal work of Vygotsky (1934) on child psychology has influenced Soviet psychological thinking to the present day. The emphasis on child interaction with the social environment and on the important role of language as a means of acquiring knowledge is all-pervasive. The methodology of combining experimental and observational approaches with small groups of children to tease out complex psychological functions is also quite unique. In fact, this clinical method has long been used by Piaget and his associates and is also gaining ascendency in many child language studies. It is against this background of the concern for literacy, the influence of Vygotsky, and the use of quasi-experimental, quasi-interview methods for data collection that Downing's anthology (in preparation) on reading research in the Soviet Union should be read. What follows is a brief discussion of some of the key works and authors on how Russian children learn reading. Of the institutions that may be singled out are the Academy of Pedagogical Sciences and the Scientific Research Institute of Schools of the Ministry of Education. Of the individuals, such influential researchers/scholars as Egorov (1950, 1953) and Elkonin (1973a, 1973b) must be mentioned, among others.

Historically, a key figure in the development of reading education in the U.S.S.R. was Ushinsky (1949). It was over a century ago that he introduced his method of teaching reading in Russia (the date 1949 relates to the publication of Ushinsky's *Collected Works*). Ushinsky wrote that his aim was to utilize "those common psychological processes that are effective in all languages and to children of all nationalities." In particular, Ushinsky aimed at making children familiar with the phonemic system of the language and to make reading instruction one of *language study* linked to mental development of children.

Another well-known name in Russian reading is Redozubov (1947). His book *The Methodology of Russian Language Instruction in the Primary School* covered all sections of the methodology of teaching children the Russian language. His most important achievement was probably his strong call that learning to read must be regarded as a developmental skill emphasizing phonemic knowledge of the language and requiring instruction beyond the initial primary years.

In his influential book *The Psychology of Mastering the Skill of Reading,* Egorov (1953) has applied Vygotsky's general theory of child development to the problem of how children can develop a conceptual framework in reading. He writes of the role of language awareness:

> When the child arrives in school he can already differentiate very well all the sounds of his language and he discriminates words correctly on this basis. But the child does not notice exactly what sounds occur or in what order they make up a particular word. However, he must become aware of these units of speech and their temporal order if he is to learn how to write words correctly. That is why the acquisition of writing and reading skills requires a restructuring of phonemic hearing. This makes great demands on the child's analytic and synthetic processes. It requires the child not only to distinguish words but also to be aware of their sound composition.

He goes on to emphasize the importance of concepts such as "words," "syllables," "sounds," "letters" and so on and the need to be cognitively sure of these concepts in learning to read.

Another contribution of Egorov was his emphasis on the incorporation of the *speech motor processes* into reading instruction. He discusses the role of the second signaling system in the speech-sound analysis and synthesis—a clear example of the Pavlovian tradition and the influence of Vygotsky. The second signal system is seen as organizing, directing and controling the activities of the first signal system as is evident from this quotation:

> If our sensations from the surrounding world are for us the first signals of reality, concrete signals, then *speech, and above all the kinesthetic stimuli from the speech organizer to the*

cortex are the second signals, the signal of signals (Egorov, 1953, p. 232, original italics).

Thus the mastery of phonemic hearing and its speech-motor apparatus in speech-sound analysis and synthesis is paramount. Egorov suggests that teachers should begin with appropriate words familiar to the children, use rhythmic and syllabic structure of words and unravel conceptual difficulties such as ensuring that concepts like "word," "syllable," "sound," "letter" are understood. Egorov's comments on linguistic concepts in learning to read remind us of more recent work by such investigators as Reid (1966) in Scotland and Clay (1972) in New Zealand and Egorov's chapter on "The Role of Guessing the Sense" has the ring of Goodman's work (1970), though with some difference. Like Goodman, Egorov saw the value of studying children's "miscues" in reading. Egorov traces these "errors" to various sources including pupils' misunderstandings of the purposes of reading. He points out the need to plan teaching materials carefully to "follow closely the progress of the child's thoughts and problem solving in learning how to read." Thus we note Egorov's consistent concern for children's thought processes as they work their way toward a clearer understanding of the task of reading.

Elkonin (1963) acknowledges Egorov's fundamental contribution to his own studies of the psychology of the learning-to-read process. Egorov's observation that school beginners usually are quite competent in speech and listening but lack awareness of their own linguistic activities was originally stated in the "glass window theory," put forward by Luria (1946):

> The first important period in a child's development is characterized by the fact that, while actively using grammatical speech and signifying with words the appropriate objects and actions, the child is still not able to make the word and verbal relations an object of his consciousness. In this period a word may be used but not noticed by the child, and it frequently seems like a glass window through which the child looks at the surrounding world without making the word itself an object of his consciousness and without suspecting that it has its own existence, its own structural features (p. 61).

Much of Elkonin's experimental work has been directed toward finding practical methods of fostering children's awareness of linguistic acts. He believes that many traditional teaching procedures should be abandoned or at least modified because they make it unnecessarily difficult for children to understand concepts of the features of language that help them in reasoning about writing and speech. For example, Elkonin (1963) states that "children of six or seven years already know the names of many letters, sometimes the whole alphabet, but they cannot read, and if they try to do so they simply put together the names of letters. This is one of the worst habits with which many children enter school to begin learning to read and it is necessary to teach them afresh." Why? Elkonin (1973b) in a more recent article explains that "children who learn their ABCs at home by various methods such as cut-out alphabets and letter blocks, acquire little, if any, understanding of the differences in the sound packages of words. Instead, their attention is drawn to differences in the letters. This may lead to negative transfer in the further study of language."

Elkonin's theoretical position that *nothing must confuse the child's understanding of the features of speech* that are coded in the writing system leads him to propose that the study of speech should be carried out *before the introduction of written letters.* Elkonin's (1973b) view on this matter can be summarized succinctly in this quotation:

> The phoneme is not a simple sound governing particular acoustic and articulatory properties. It is a sound that belongs to a definite system of phonematic contrasts. The essential distinction that must be made in this regard is between the perceived phonemes of a language and their embodiment in the natural flow of speech. It was this conclusion in particular that led us to recognize the necessity for replacing conventional phonic analysis, which has the objective of teaching the sounds of letters, by phonematic analysis which aims at giving children an understanding of the phonematic system of language.

This emphasis on the underlying phonematic representation of letters is often not well understood (see Chapter 5 on the nature of the orthography).

Parenthetically, it should be mentioned that a recent report "The Quest Must Continue" by Goretsky, Kiriushkin and Shanko (1972) vigorously defended the traditional methods of teaching typically used in the schools in Russia and attacked Elkonin's research. Their criticism of the latter's experiments was reacted to with equal sharpness by Elkonin (1973b) from which work the immediately preceding quotation is taken. In this work Elkonin further elaborates on his definition of reading as "the re-creation of the sound form of a word according to its graphic model (representation)." He points out that this does not mean neglecting comprehension. What is more important is that re-creating the sound form of a word is a highly complex process and not a simple association between print and speech. Prior to attaining automaticity the skill must go through a long period of development and the initial and final forms of the skill are not the same. This is also the view we have taken in our discussion of reading as a skill and principles of skill acquisition (Chapters 2 and 3).

The above overview of some key Russian work spanning the last twenty years or so shows their emphasis on linking reading with speech, on the representational nature of symbols and above all on reading as reasoning. This brings us to the theory of *cognitive clarity* embodied in Downing's (1979a) *Reading and Reasoning* as basic to reading acquisition.

Cognitive Clarity

The term cognitive clarity refers to "clear thinking," "clear understanding," "reasoning" or other psychological structure needed for skill acquisition and problem solving. The two basic components relating the theory to reading are: (a) understanding the purpose of reading and (b) understanding the technical characteristics of reading. These aspects will be discussed below.

The cognitive clarity theory has its origin in the psychological work of Piaget (1959) and Bartlett (1932) and can be traced latterally to linguistic studies of Cazden (1972) and Halliday (1975). Vernon (1957, 1971) and Reid (1966) are among the early workers who have applied this basic notion to reading. Elaboration of this notion can be found in a number of studies in different countries, for example, those of Downing (1978, 1979a, 1979b, 1980a, 1980b), Ayers and Downing (1979), Downing, Ayers and Schaefer (1978, 1980), Downing and Oliver (1973–1974), Downing, Ollila, and Oliver (1975, 1977) and Leong and Haines (1978) in Canada; Downing (1970, 1971–1972), Francis (1973) and Hall (1976) in England; Clay (1972) in New Zealand; Ferreiro (1978) in Spain; Lundberg and Tornéus (1978) in Sweden; and Ehri (1975), Fox and Routh (1975, 1976), Holden and MacGinitie (1972), Johns (1980), Kingston, Weaver, and Figa (1972), I. Liberman and her associates (I. Liberman, Shankweiler, Fischer and Carter, 1974; I. Liberman, Shankweiler, A. Liberman, Fowler and Fischer, 1977; I. Liberman, A. Liberman, Mattingly and Shankweiler, 1980; I. Liberman and Shankweiler, 1979; Shankweiler and Liberman, 1976), Lewkowicz (1980), Meltzer and Herse (1969), Scholl and Ryan (1980) in the United States, Papandropoulou and Sinclair (1974) in Switzerland and Beliakova (1973), Karpova (1955) and Sokhin (1974) in the U.S.S.R.

Understanding Purposes of Reading

In the earlier discussion of "communicative competence" it is dramatically shown by Piaget (1959) that children aged six to eight years do not know the communicative function of language. In a series of experiments in which a simple object was explained to one child who then had to explain it to a second child, Piaget found that communication at this age level was ineffective. The breakdown occurred as the explaining child did not appreciate that his or her hearer knew less than he/she did and because the hearer did not recognize that the explainer possessed more information than he/she had. Both were egocentric in failing to take account of the other child's point of view. Piaget commented that children think they "understand and are understood" in contrast to adults, who "make an effort to understand and be understood." The failure to understand on the part of these six- to eight-year-old children was also found in their failure to recall stories in terms of chronological, causal and deductive relations (e.g. who is doing what to whom). Halliday (1975) has distinguished between *pragmatic* and *mathetic* functions of speech. The pragmatic functions are the intrusive, interactive and manipulative aspects of speech. The mathetic functions are the declarative and observational utterances that occur when the child attempts to understand the self and the surrounding world. Thus the line of studies conducted by Piaget shows that young children, and many school beginners, are not well equipped in communication skills, as these children lack the awareness of the communication process. Halliday's *mathetic functions* of language also emphasizes linguistic awareness.

Writing on reading backwardness more than twenty years ago, Vernon (1957) identified *cognitive confusion* as underpinning reading failure.

She explained this concept as failure to analyze, abstract and generalize linguistic materials or generally failure in the development of reasoning processes. The importance of conceptual development in reading is further emphasized in her later work (Vernon, 1971). She states, "It would seem that in learning to read it is essential for the child to realize and understand the fundamental generalization that in alphabetic writing all words are represented by combinations of a limited number of visual symbols. Thus it is possible to present a very large vocabulary of spoken words in an economical manner which requires the memorizing of a comparatively small number of printed symbols and their associated sounds. But a thorough grasp of this principle necessitates a fairly advanced stage of conceptual reasoning, since this type of organization differs fundamentally from any previously encountered by children in their normal environment" (Vernon , 1971, p. 79).

In an intensive study of twelve five-year-old children in Edinburgh, Reid (1966) described how these children's conceptions of reading and language developed during their first year of schooling. She found that they all began with a poor idea "of the purpose and use of [written language]." Downing (1970) replicated Reid's innovative study with a group of children in England and found essentially the same results—difficulty in understanding the *purpose* of written language in young beginning readers. Subsequently, Downing, Ollila and Oliver (1975) found two groups of Canadian Indian beginners were significantly less aware of the purposes of reading and writing than were non-Indian beginners attending kindergarten classes in the same school districts. This might be due to the different cultural tradition of literacy in the homes of these Indian children. In a subsequent study, Downing, Ollila and Oliver (1977) found that children from the economically poorest third of the population in a Canadian city began school with significantly less understanding of the functions of writing than children from the other two-thirds of the population in the same city. More recently, Downing, Ayers, and Schaefer (1978) conducted a structured interview with over three hundred Canadian kindergarten children to examine their concept of reading. The interview consisted of four parts: (a) recognition of acts of reading and writing, (b) concepts of the purposes of reading and writing, (c) concepts of features of printed materials and (d) "visual perception." It was found that children had most difficulties with concepts of features of printed materials (part (c)). This was followed by part (b), then part (a), while "visual perception" was the easiest. Subsequently Downing, Ayers and Schaefer (1981) published *The LARR—Linguistic Awareness in Reading Readiness Test* based on the first three of the parts of their interview. Reliability and validity studies of the *LARR Test* have been reported by Ayers and Downing (1979). Clay (1976) in New Zealand studied children's understanding of the functions of literacy and their reading attainment. She found her group of Samoan children performed better than the Maori group. She attributed the Samoans' better understanding of the purpose of literacy to the high value placed on written communication at home.

The above represents some of the studies focusing on the importance of understanding the purposes of reading in literacy acquisition.

Understanding Technical Concepts of Reading

The second component of reasoning or problem-solving tasks facing the child in reading acquisition is understanding the technical concepts needed for reasoning about the relationships between speech and writing. In learning to read, children should have clear concepts of a "word," and of a "sentence," and should be aware of their constituent parts: phonemes, syllables and phrases. They must also map the written word to the spoken word. Reid (1966), Meltzer and Herse (1969), Downing (1970, 1971–1972), Downing and Oliver (1973–1974), Downing, Ayers and Schaefer (1978), and Ayers and Downing (1979) have shown that prereaders are not aware of word boundaries and do not realize that words are spatially ordered groups of letters. Downing and Oliver (1973–1974) have shown that prereaders are not aware that words are spatially ordered groups of letters corresponding to temporally ordered sounds. Holden and MacGinitie (1972) further found that function words were more difficult for kindergarten children to isolate than content words. Ehri (1975) noted that readers, in contrast to prereaders, showed superior awareness of printed correlates (lexical items and syllabic constituents) of spoken language. Francis (1973), in her study of English primary school children, found that factors independent of a general ability to deal with abstract concepts were involved in learning linguistic concepts and that these were closely related to reading.

Understanding of the internal structure of language does not refer simply to phonemic discrimination of minimally different word pairs. In a series of experiments with nursery, kindergarten, and first grade children, Isabelle Liberman and her associates (Liberman, Shankweiler, Fischer, and Carter, 1974; I. Liberman, Shankweiler, A. Liberman, Fowler, and Fischer, 1977; I. Liberman, A. Liberman, Mattingly and Shankweiler, 1980; I. Liberman and Shankweiler, 1979; Shankweiler and Liberman, 1976) have shown the ability to segment a word into phonemes does not appear until about age five. One reason for this is that phonemic boundaries are not clearly marked and that consonant segments are encoded at the acoustic level into the vowel. This difficulty of phoneme segmentation is also observed by other researchers (Calfee, Chapman, and Venezky, 1972; Elkonin, 1973a; Gleitman and Rozin, 1973; Helfgott, 1976; Leong and Haines, 1978). Leong and Haines (1978) further noted that their grade one, two, and three children had difficulty in repeating "high complexity" sentences compared with "low complexity" ones. Savin (1972) suggested that children who failed to learn to read by the end of grade one were unable to analyze syllables into phonemes, were insensitive to rhymes and had difficulty manipulating sounds as in Pig Latin. Fox and Routh (1975) found a developmental progression in the ability to analyze spoken sentences into words, words into syllables and syllables into speech sounds in children aged three to seven years. In their more recent study, Fox and Routh (1976) noted that the ability to segment syllables into sounds was a good predictor of children's performance in decoding unknown written words. Lewkowicz (1980) categorizes various phonemic awareness training tasks and suggests ways of teaching them.

Thus there are clear indications that beginning readers are not at all clear about the communication process and may experience cognitive confusion in moving from audible to visible language. It should not be assumed that as children grow older, this cognitive confusion will automatically give way to cognitive clarity which is essential to reading. They need to develop their awareness of language with the help of such activities as language games. Papandropoulou and Sinclair (1974) showed how children made an active search for concepts when asked to say a long word and a short word. The usual answer was to name large objects as "long words" and small objects as "short words." Similar findings were obtained by Lundberg and Tornéus (1978) with Swedish children. Ferreiro (1978) found developmentally ordered categories of responses in her study of meaning attached to written sentences in Spanish children. Thus development of concepts of linguistic materials is more difficult than identification or discrimination of visual shapes. Gleitman, Gleitman and Shipley (1972) demonstrated how to help young children to monitor their own language behavior, to objectify it in words, to operate on it in various ways, and to know that they know. This awareness of language includes reflection on sounds in the words, on the grammatical structure children use and hear; and the deliberate, conscious judgments they make (see also McNeill and Lindig, 1973). What is needed in reading is a theory of instruction that should give appropriate weight to meaning and decoding without overemphasizing one or the other according to the ability of the children and the stage of reading they are at. In this way, we can help them to understand better the reading task and to integrate both meaning and decoding. Doehring's (1976) important developmental study of levels of rapid, efficient processing of print provides some insight for further research. While decoding subskills are necessary in grade one, they are not sufficient for discourse comprehension. Children can acquire sentence processing and read for meaning from early grades on, if properly guided.

To summarize, in relating the cognitive clarity theory to reading acquisition Downing (1979a) formulates these eight postulates:

(1) Writing or print in any language is a visible code for those aspects of speech that were accessible to the linguistic awareness of the creators of that code or writing system.
(2) This linguistic awareness of the creators of a writing system included simultaneous awareness of the communicative function of language and certain features of spoken language that are accessible to the speaker-hearer for logical analysis.
(3) The learning-to-read process consists in the rediscovery of: (a) the functions and (b) the coding rules of the writing system.
(4) Their rediscovery depends on the learner's linguistic awareness of the same features of communication and language as were accessible to the creators of the writing system.
(5) Children approach the tasks of reading instruction in a normal state of cognitive confusion about the purposes and techniques of literacy.
(6) Under reasonably good conditions, children work themselves out of the initial state of cogni-

tive confusion into increasing cognitive clarity about the functions and technical characteristics of written language.

(7) Although the initial stage of literacy acquisition is the most vital one, cognitive confusion continues to arise and then, in turn, give way to cognitive clarity throughout the later stages of education as new subskills are added to the student's repertoire.

(8) The cognitive clarity theory applies to all languages and writing systems. The communication aspect is universal, but the technical coding rules differ from one language to another (p. 37).

The above formulation requires further experimentation, especially on a cross-national basis, if the theory is to provide some universality as an explanation of reading acquisition. The formulation is also meant to provide some testable hypotheses and does not pretend to exhaust the complexity of relationship between speech and print and language awareness and reading.

Summary

In this chapter we have attempted to unravel the structure and function of language and the relationship of both. We have discussed Noam Chomsky's formal description of grammar in his pre- and post-*Aspects* works and Charles Fillmore's case grammar. From the description of language as abstractions of rules of the mind, we have moved into the related area of the use of language in learning "how to mean" by children. Specifically, we have discussed the concept of language awareness in relation to reading acquisition. Beginning with Mattingly's earlier and more recent formulations, we have addressed ourselves to the central questions of awareness and accessibility from the cognitive-developmental perspective. The different levels and kinds of language awareness have been reviewed and their significance for language learning is noted. A resumé of some important Russian studies on the pragmatic functions of language and reading acquisition is presented. The Downing cognitive clarity theory with its theoretical and empirical support is seen as providing a coalescing view bringing together form and interpretation of language learning and reading acquisition.

If we accept the assertion, as set forth in the preceding sections, that language awareness relates to the monitoring, control and repair of and general reflection on language, we may find it somewhat curious to move from Chomsky to the cognitive pragmatic aspects. Yet the apparent distinction between the internalized mentalistic view of language as structure of the mind and the communicative competence of language use is not as rigid as is usually claimed. Feldman (1977) has argued for the implicit assumption in Chomsky's work of the communicative function of language. We will sketch some of these and other viewpoints to show how both structure and function can provide insight into language learning and beginning reading.

One source of the structure-function differentiation relates to Chomsky's (1965) claim of innate language acquisition mechanisms, which are probably universal in the structure of the languages of the world. This notion does not have general acceptance. To the extent that recent studies have shown anatomic and physiological mechanisms in the human central nervous system predisposing specialization for language (see Chapters 7 and 15, also Segalowitz and Gruber, 1977), it is reasonable to accept that an innate and "preformed" language structure subserving language functions exists. Following from the innate language acquisition device, Chomsky's rejection of the principles of imitation, modeling, reinforcement and association in general has not found favor with those scientists of the traditional behavioristic persuasion. They have in turn countered that the Chomskyan approach is too mentalistic, too much given to formulation of rules without regard for environmental variables such as parent–child, child–child social interaction. The more radical of the behaviorists have also found it difficult to reconcile the abstract concept of language with the procedures and analysis of language learning in language-deviant children. However, a rapprochement is possible as set forth in the *neopsycholinguistic* approach of Staats (1974). Deploring the separatism between psycholinguistic and learning theories of language, Staats suggests ways for the furtherance of a cognitive-linguistic approach by reference to a learning theory of language. There is concrete evidence of this coming together in intervention programs and strategies for the language deviant, the mentally retarded (see Schiefelbusch and Lloyd, 1974).

Of more central concern to the theme of this chapter is Chomsky's position that language is rule-governed, is highly logical, is idealized and focuses on intralinguistic regularities. A few quotations will further illustrate this concept. The "study of structure, use, and acquisition may be expected to provide insight into essential features of language" (Chomsky, 1975, p. 56). Language is a "branch of cognitive psychology," has a "central place in general psychology" and deals with mental processes. Moreover, "the empirical study of linguistic universals has led to the formulation of highly restrictive and, I believe, quite plausible hypotheses concerning the possible variety of human languages, hypotheses that contribute to the attempt to develop a theory of acquisition of knowledge that gives due place to intrinsic mental activity" (Chomsky, 1972b, p. 99). But it will be a rigid, separatist position we will be taking if we infer from these and other statements that Chomsky's notion is distinct from those who emphasize the functional, contextual approach to language. Chomsky at least agrees in part that understanding of syntax also entails understanding the communicative use of language. He does state, however, that the contribution of "pragmatic considerations" to language is not at all clear for the simple reason that the wider realm of meaning, of "semantic representation" is not as yet well understood. Even with the better-understood phonetic representation, he raises the issue "whether a deeper understanding of the use of language might not show that factors that go beyond grammatical structure enter into the determination of perceptual representations and physical form in an inextricable fashion, and cannot be separated, without distortion, from the formal rules that interpret surface structure as phonetic form" (Chomsky, 1972b, p. 111). Here, as in his other works, Chomsky is concerned with the centrality of "knowledge of language" or "linguistic competence" as a "working hypothesis about the nature of the mind when we try to study the use of language." Failing the systematic working hypothesis, we may be faced with platitudes or findings without identifiable integration.

This interpretation explains why Chomsky suggests Kintsch's (1974) criticism of the "strict separation" between competence and performance is only one of "a conceptual distinction; knowledge of language is distinguished from behavior (use of this knowledge)" (Chomsky, 1976, p. 15). In his formalism of memory processes of meaning, Kintsch finds the competence-performance distinction incompatible with psychological processing of meaning and difficult to explain individual differences. Chomsky, however, sees little evidence of an alternative framework being proposed. As to Chomsky's (1975) claim that he can use language in the strictest sense with no intention of communication, except communication with himself, Feldman (1977) quite rightly likens this to Vygotsky's (1934) interpretation of communicative function as essentially private rather than social. The attribution of "inner speech" probably explains Chomsky's assertion of the noncommunicative function of language. For Vygotsky, "inner speech" is internalized thought with rules corresponding to grammatical categories. With external speech, it is "the turning of thought into words, its materialisation and objectification"; with inner speech "the process is reversed: speech turns into inward thought" (Vygotsky, 1934, p. 131). Vygotsky further suggests that inner speech resembles a dialogue between two people who understand each other with complete mutuality and cites examples from Tolstoy's *Anna Karenina* to illustrate the psychology of understanding. May it not be that Chomsky's communication with himself represents a form of deictic relations akin to Piaget's decentration with full recognition not only of contexts but of intentions? In short, if it is the formal linguistic system that determines mental operations, it is likely that social interactions trigger off and elaborate on these operations.

To conclude this chapter, it is relevant to bring up again Donaldson's (1978) powerful book *Children's Minds*. In this, she has shown through a series of dramatic studies that given a setting and a language that makes "human sense" (p. 23), even very young children can perform tasks often thought to be beyond them. She suggests that before we can master any formal system we have to learn to take some steps "beyond the bounds of human sense" and that the problem of helping children to do this early in their schooling has not been properly recognized (p. 82). The strategies that schools can adopt include: more awareness of the spoken tongue, development of reflective skills in the early years, guidance of child ren to manage a set of options when unknowns are encountered. The latter particularly refers to the teacher's "capacity for decentering," to see the child's point of view, to inculcate "disembedded thought." She firmly believes that "education should aim to encourage the readiness to come to grips with incongruity and even to seek it out in a positive fashion, enjoying challenge" (p. 112). This will require understanding and sensitivity on the part of parents and teachers, when they are guiding their children's development either of language or of reading.

Neurological Substrates of Language and Reading

CHAPTER 7

It is often said that it is not the eye that reads but the brain. In this chapter we will outline some of the characteristics of those areas of the central nervous system involved in information processing in general, and language and reading in particular. We will attempt to provide a readable, though necessarily condensed, discussion of the structure and functions of various neurologic elements of interest to the psychology of reading. Students who are stimulated to inquire further in this area may consult, among others, the work of Dimond (1978), Kuffler and Nicholls (1977), Teyler (1975), Wittrock et al. (1977), Woodburne (1967) and the complete September, 1979 issue of *Scientific American,* which is devoted to various aspects of the brain. These sources elaborate in depth on various technical mechanisms of the brain and brain-behavior relationships.

The Nervous System—Nerve Cells

The nervous system is composed of about a hundred billion (10^{11}) highly specialized cells or *neurons.* These basic building blocks of the system have a variety of forms but generally each neuron consists of a cell body ranging from five to one hundred micrometers in diameter with a nucleus. The cell has one long fiberlike extension known as the *axon* along which the nerve impulse travels outwards. The axon may be branched to allow the impulse to be transmitted to several other neurons at the same time. Each neuron also has a number of other extensions or *dendrites* (from "dendron" meaning "tree") whose function is to receive stimulation from the axons of neighboring neurons. The nervous system always operates by the formula: dendrite → cell body → axon → dendrite, and so on as illustrated in Figure 7–1. Incoming information travels via dendrites and outgoing information via axons. The nerve impulse is an electrical current that jumps from node to node (nodes of Ranvier), in a fashion known as "saltatory conduction" in myelinated axons. In Figure 7–1 the dendrites of the first neuron on the left are stimulated and an electrical impulse passes down the axon towards the dendritic tree of the cell on the right; the axon of this neuron is stimulated and so on along the chain of nerve cells.

Each neuron is completely separate from all other neurons, but there are places where the dendrites of one neuron come close (1/50,000,000 of a meter gap) to the axon of another neuron. These places of near "contact" are the *synapses* and the gaps are the *synaptic gaps.* Synapses are the primary sites for intercellular communication. When a *nerve impulse,* usually called an *action potential,* in an axon reaches a synapse, it releases a chemical substance termed the *neurotransmitter* from the axon terminal. This substance may then stimulate the dendrites of a neighboring neuron. The synapse acts like a switch with only two positions, either "on" or "off." If it is "on,"

FIGURE 7–1. Diagram of neuron.

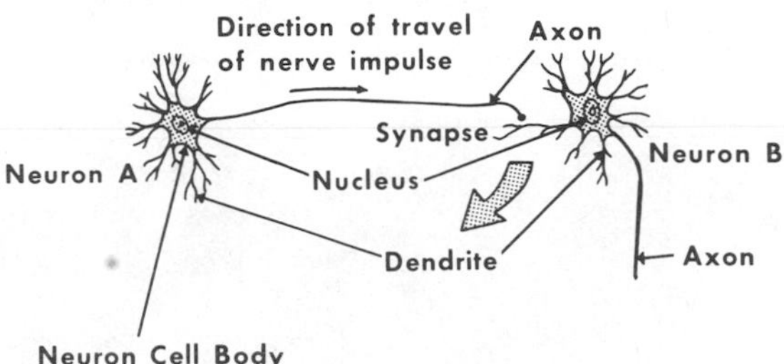

the impulse passes. If it is "off," the impulse is stopped from crossing to the next neuron. Another important feature of this process is that the nerve impulse never varies in strength; the neuron either "fires" (conducts an action potential down its axon) or it does not. It never fires weakly or partly. More correctly, a neurotransmitter released by the axon of a neuron will either arouse (excite) or will depress (inhibit) the action of the adjoining neuron. When the total amount of excitatory transmitter input exceeds that of the inhibitory transmitter input by a critical amount, firing will take place.

Whether or not an impulse crosses a synapse depends on variability in its readiness for transmission. One way in which this readiness is influenced is by the number of axons stimulating an adjacent neuron. For example, sometimes the impulse from one axon may not affect the neuron sufficiently for it to fire its dendrites; in other words, the incoming stimulus is below the "firing threshold" of the neuron. But if two or more axons are firing simultaneously to the same neuron, the additional stimuli may be sufficient to produce a response as an outgoing axonal impulse. In short, this is known as the "summation effect." Neurons have characteristic "firing thresholds," and impulses have to be summated or added above the theshold for that neuron to fire. This kind of variability allows for a very wide range of response patterns, despite the basically simple mechanism of these units of the nervous system. It has billions of these "on-off" switches permitting enormous possibilities for permutations and patterns in the organization of the firing of individual neurons.

In addition to the neurons, the nervous system also contains a large number of *glial cells.* Their role seems to be to synthesize and store materials for use by the neurons and to hold the neurons together. Hydén and Egyházi (1963) have conducted a number of experiments in which biochemical changes in glial cells have been related to learning behavior in rats. They claim that changes in the base ratio of the components of ribonucleic acid (RNA) in the glial cells are associated with learning and that neurons and glial cells operate as functional units.

Structure and Function of the Nervous System

The human nervous system receives information from the environment through the sense organs. Bundles of nerve fibres called *afferent nerves* transmit this information to higher centers for such activities as analysis, organization, storage, and response. The system also contains bundles of nerves called *efferent nerves* that transmit impulses to and initiate responses in muscles, viscera and glands.

The *central nervous system* can be divided into these three parts: the spinal cord, the brainstem, comprising a collection of structures at the base of the brain, and the forebrain, consisting of the thalamus, hypothalamus, pituitary, limbic system, and cortex. Figure 7–2 illustrates the main parts of the central nervous system. The functional parts of the system will be discussed in the following sections. We will begin at the level of the

FIGURE 7–2. Main parts of the central nervous system.

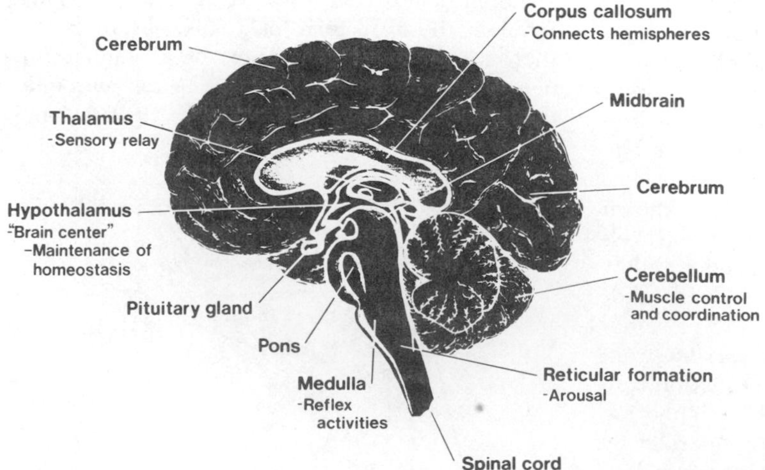

peripheral nerves and work up to the cortex.

Peripheral nerves are defined as those lying outside the spine and skull (except for those nerves forming the autonomic nervous system which is traditionally treated separately). The peripheral nerves are either afferent fibers carrying sensory information (for instance, touch and temperature) to the spinal cord or efferent fibers sending motor impulses from the spinal cord to muscles and glands. Afferent fibers carry sensory information from the surface of the body and from within the body. Nerves conveying sensory information from within the body are called *proprioceptives* ("proprio" meaning "of one's own"). They bring feedback information about activity in muscles, tendons, joints and viscera. Of special interest to students of reading are those proprioceptive nerves which transmit sensations of movement, the kinaesthetic sensation. For example, when the child is writing or tracing, the hand movements produce proprioceptive positional feedback impulses which are transmitted to the spinal cord.

The spinal cord is the main trunk line to which the peripheral nerves are connected. The spinal cord is protected by three layers of tough, fibrous tissue (dura mater, pia mater and arachnois) and also by the vertebral bones of the spine. Impulses from afferent peripheral nerves travel upwards through the cord to the brain and enter the *conscious level.* Some impulses, upon entering the spinal cord, will synapse with neurons at the same, or adjacent (above and below), level and produce an efferent impulse towards the peripheral nerve endings. This process is unconscious and is known as a *reflex action.* There is a correlation between the segments and the different parts of the body.

The medulla is the first level of the brain. Here the segmentation of the nervous system for particular body regions ceases and the first center for coordinating sensory information is found. Several separate nerve pathways are combined before going on to higher levels. There is also a rearrangement of motor pathways traveling downwards at the level of the medulla. The main motor pathway, the pyramidal pathway, crosses over from one side of the medulla to the opposite one. In other words, fibers originating in the left cerebral motor center will cross to the right side of the medulla and descend into the spinal cord as the right pyramidal pathway. In addition, many of the peripheral nerves of the head connect with the nervous system here, in the pons and in the midbrain. These nerves are not specialized for segments of the head region but operate rather as functional units for one type of sensation such as smelling, or motor behavior such as facial expression. The medulla is also an important center for pathways to and from the viscera; for example, the centers for respiration, digestion and circulation are found here.

The pons receives its name from the Latin word "pons," meaning bridge, because its fibers form a bulge which bridges the two sides or hemispheres of the cerebellum. This provides a direct link between each of the two halves of the cerebellum. As was noted above, some of the peripheral nerves in the head area connect with the central nervous system at the pons level.

The midbrain is the next section in this upward progress. It is formed by all the ascending pathways to the diencephalon. The midbrain contains the red nucleus which is of critical importance in maintaining balance in locomotion. Of interest are the four colliculi or protuberances on the dorsal surface of the midbrain; two of these colliculi are reflex centers for hearing while the other two are reflex centers for vision. Synchronized eye movements have their control center here.

The reticular formation or *reticular activating system* is an ill-defined group of neurons that extends throughout the brain stem (medulla, pons and midbrain) and the diencephalon. Sensory signals from all parts of the body relay into the reticular formation on their way to the cortex. This is shown in Figure 7–3. From the reticular activating system, impulses are projected into all areas of the cortex. These impulses have the function of *arousing* or *activating* the cortex. Without them, activity in the higher centers falls off and a state of torpor results. If the impulses from the

FIGURE 7–3. The reticular formation. [From J. D. French, 1957, used by permission.]

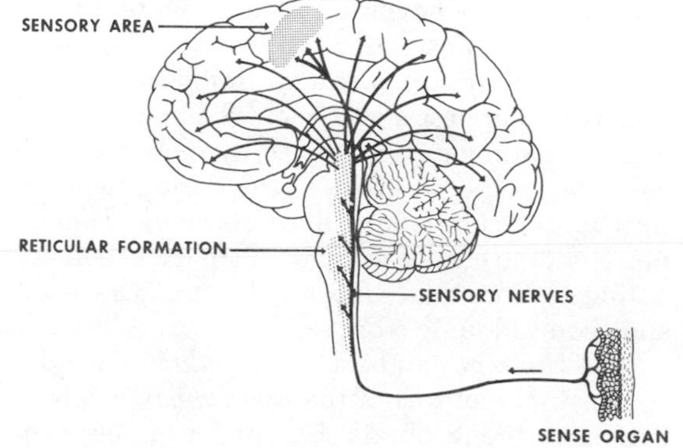

reticular formation become excessive, a condition of great excitement is produced. The output of the reticular formation upwards depends on the inputs from the sensory nerves. For example, when people prepare for sleep they close their eyes and lie still; this reduces the inputs into the reticular formation and consequently reduces reticular output to the cortex, thus lowering its activation. This is a reciprocal process since the cortex also excites the reticular formation, which, in turn, sends impulses down the spinal cord to influence motor activity. Thus the reticular formation has a critical function in maintaining alertness, and in sending arousal signals to the cortex. The reticular formation also influences motor activities of the body, to modify muscle movements, and visceral functions such as respiration, digestion and circulation.

The cerebellum is a bulb of nervous tissue that lies behind the pons and medulla. Only about one-sixth of the cortical surface of the cerebellum is exposed; the remainder is concealed by folding. The chief function of the cerebellum is to control the position and movements of the body. To this end, the cerebellum has extensive connections with all parts of the body and many sense organs. Eccles, Ito, and Szentāgothai (1967) draw the analogy between the cerebellum and a computer. Vast quantities of data come into the cerebellum from peripheral afferent nerves from surface areas and from proprioceptive afferent nerves in muscles, tendons and joints. These signals are evaluated, filtered and discriminated in order to end up with an efferent impulse that will modify the motor impulses traveling downwards in the brain stem and spinal cord towards the periphery.

The cerebellum also receives data from other sources such as vision, hearing, the vestibular balance system of the middle ear, and impulses from higher cortical levels in the brain. In computer fashion, all these data are coordinated to produce smooth motor behavior through its efferent functions. All this information is stored and organized so that the system is poised for immediate action. Like the computer also, the cerebellum does not display continuous neural activity such as can be observed in the cerebral cortex during thought. Instead, the cerebellum, upon receiving stimulation from the cortex, engages in a burst of activity lasting no more than a few hundredths of a second and then suddenly stops.

The *thalamus* and the *hypothalamus* are the two main structures of the *diencephalon,* which lies above the midbrain. Except for impulses related to smelling, all the sensory information must pass through the thalamus before reaching the cerebral cortex. It also receives information sent down from the cortex (see Figure 7–2). The thalamus is thus the final "relay station" for afferent impulses. However, it is not merely a junction. Woodburne (1967) states that the thalamus functions rather "as a huge shunting yard where different combinations of freight cars are made up for different destinations." Fusion and coordination of sensory information in the thalamus results in the original impulses losing their separate identities beyond this point when the coordinated sensory inputs are projected onto the cerebral cortex. Without the thalamus, we are incapable of sensory information such as vision, hearing, touch, and so forth.

The other major structure of the diencephalon is the *hypothalamus.* This is situated below the thalamus and it is vital for maintaining certain balances in physiological functioning such as hunger, thirst, sexual behavior, body temperature and fluid balance, sleeping and waking, and, in general, emotional behavior. The thalamus relays impulses to the hypothalamus to maintain an appropriate internal balance or homeostasis. Because of this regulating behavior, the hypothalamus is considered as the visceral brain center.

Alongside the thalamus is a broad band of fibers known as the *internal capsule.* These fibers are the main motor and sensory connecting route between the cerebral cortex and lower centers, the thalamus, spinal cord, and so on. The internal capsule is of interest because it is very susceptible to the slightest damage by cerebral hemorrhages or tumors.

The pituitary is connected to the hypothalamus by a thin stalk of neural tissue. The chemicals manufactured by the hypothalamus are then transferred to the pituitary for release into the bloodstream.

The limbic system, phylogenetically an older, more primitive part of the human nervous system, is concerned primarily with emotional and motivational experiences. It has three subsystems: (1) structures functioning in the sense of smell (very important motivationally in lower animals); (2) structures including the amygdaloid nuclei which relate to eating, sleep–wakefulness rhythms, defense–flight reactions; (3) structures including the hippocampus which has an important function in enabling the cortex to lay down permanent memory traces. This third subsystem also plays an essential part in the arousal of certain parts of the cortex (more specifically than the reticular activating system). More recently, Lamendella (1977) has produced anatomic, physiologic and behavioral evidence to suggest that the limbic system is responsible for a variety of human communication patterns at three levels. These are the "appetite" level related to automatic sign behavior, the "affective" level related to emotional and motivational states, and the "volitional" level of intentional signal behavior of an individual with respect to the environment.

The cortex or cerebral mantle is the outer covering of the cerebrum. It contains billions of neurons and the processes connecting the neurons. The cortical surface of the human brain is extensively folded. The major folds and fissures provide convenient dividing lines between the four main lobes: the *frontal, parietal, occipital* and *temporal.* These regions are illustrated in Figure 7–4. Each lobe has somewhat specialized functions. All lobes can be divided into: (1) zones that are either *motor* or *sensory;* and (2) zones that are *associational.* The motor zones produce the stimuli for muscular contractions. The sensory zones receive bodily sensations such as pain, temperature, and touch. The association zones are particularly developed in humans and this development, which parallels the increase in cognitive abilities, is one of the facts that separates us from the rest of the animal kingdom (Wittrock et al., 1977). Association zones, as the name indicates, are connected reciprocally (they receive and send information) with neighboring cortical areas. In this manner, the information arriving to an area of cortex may modify the output of a different cortical zone. The *frontal lobe's* four main functional areas are association cortex, frontal eye fields for coupled eye movements, premotor cortex, and motor cortex. The *parietal lobe's* functional areas are somatic sensory cortex, association cortex, and visual association cortex. The main function of the *occipital lobe* is visual reception. The *temporal lobe's* functional areas are the sensory receptor area for hearing, and an association area which seems to be concerned with higher mental processes. In addition, buried in the folds of the temporal lobe is *the island of Reil* which has as its main function the reception of taste impulses and sensations from the alimentary canal.

The human brain is divided into two cerebral hemispheres and is not fully symmetrical physically and functionally. Exchange of information takes place via commissural fibers, the most important of which is the *corpus callosum* (see Figure 7–2). That there is a certain specialization of functions for each hemisphere can be gauged from at least the phenomenon of handedness. Most of the human population favors the right hand. Since the motor pyramidal pathway crosses over in the medulla, a right-sided person shows a preference for the left cerebral hemisphere and is described as having a "dominant" left hemisphere. The "dominant" hemisphere not only specializes as the preferred center for hand, eye, and

FIGURE 7–4. Three views of the human brain.

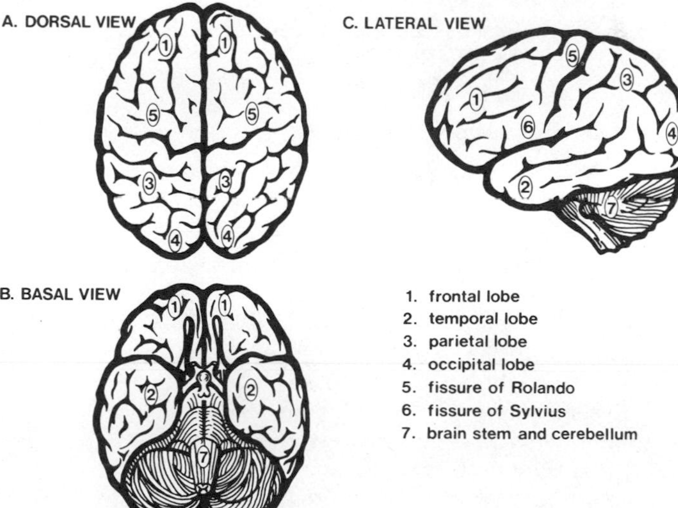

foot actions, but it also shows specialization for language processing. The right hemisphere in comparison is "dominant" for musical aptitude and recognition of complex visual patterns as well as the recognition and expression of emotion. Thus so-called cerebral "dominance" is now seen as reciprocal specialization of the hemispheres. This concept will be further explored in the discussion of laterality and reading retardation in Chapter 15.

Thus language depends on several kinds of associative functions involving wide areas of the cerebral cortex. Cerebral dysfunction and various brain lesions may cause one type or another of language disturbance including loss of reading and/or writing ability. One school of thought attributes acquired language disturbance in adults to "disconnection" between the temporal-parietal-frontal lobes of the hemisphere "dominant" for language or to disruption of the callosal fibers between the two hemispheres or to the combined mechanisms (Geschwind, 1965). The Russian neuropsychologist Luria (1973) has discussed the functional organization of the brain for processing and interpreting language. The retention of various elements of a sentence involves the temporal region of the left hemisphere. The elements must be simultaneously analyzed and synthesized, for which process the parieto-occipital areas of the left hemisphere are involved. The integration of the elements for the detection of meaning and structure involves the frontal lobe, which is responsible for planning and decision-making as a whole. While there are specialized regions for certain functions, Luria emphasizes that any conscious activity is always a complex functional system and takes place through the combined, concerted working of all brain areas.

Broca's Area and Wernicke's Area

In the middle of the nineteenth century two surgeons in France, Bouillaud and later Broca (1861, 1888), claimed to have discovered "the cerebral organ for language" through their postmortem examinations of the brains of patients who had developed aphasia after recovering from an apoplectic stroke. Broca's evidence related to two patients, both right-handed, who had lost their ability to speak almost entirely before they died. Subsequent postmortem study of their brains showed that they both had brain damage involving the posterior part of the third frontal convolution in the left hemisphere. This area of the brain in the inferior frontal gyrus of the language dominant hemisphere became known as "Broca's area" (see Figure 7–5), as other case histories produced evidence that this area was involved in aphasia or dysphasia. Here the reference is to *expressive* aphasia, the loss or disturbance of speech. In Broca's aphasia, speech is slow and labored and response is not fully grammatical. This inability to form sentences was described by Broca as "aphemia" suggesting that ideas were present but no words were available to clothe them.

Broca attributed the patient's loss or disturbance of speech to: first, his loss of ability to form concepts; second, his loss of the function to make connections between concepts and words; and third, his inability to produce words through his motor system. That aphasia should be regarded as a disturbance of intellectual or conceptual activity was shared by Marie (1926) and Goldstein and Gelb (1918), though Marie suggested the locus of Broca's aphasia was more diffuse. The attribution of Broca's aphasia to paralysis of motor muscles relates to the fact that Broca's area lies immediately in front of the motor cortex that controls the muscles of the face, the jaw, the tongue, the palate and the larynx. It must be noted, however, that damage to the corresponding area on the right side of the brain does not cause aphasia, although there is a similar weakness of the facial muscles.

Hécaen and Angelergues (1964) studied the language disturbance (articulation, fluency, naming ability, comprehension, reading, writing, repetition of spoken sentences) in over two hundred patients with brain damage to different parts of the left hemisphere. They found that greater language disability was produced after larger lesions

FIGURE 7–5. Broca's Area and Wernicke's Area.

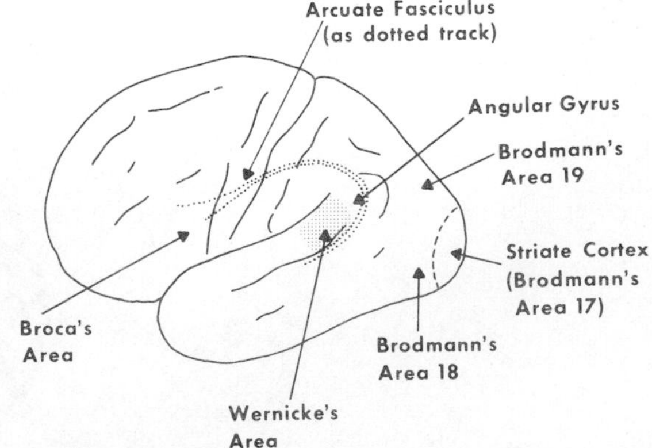

which damaged more than one area of the cortex, but that the relationship between types of disability and the location of the damage was not specific. In an evaluation of negative evidence, that is, evidence of destruction of Broca's area reportedly without any expressive aphasia, Whitaker and Selnes (1975) concluded that this area is an important part of the neurological substrate of language. More recently, Mohr (1976) has addressed himself to Broca's area and Broca's aphasia as a controversial issue in neurolinguistics. From personal and retrospective autopsy case studies and from a review of the literature, he suggests that Broca's aphasia arises from a considerably larger brain injury than the more circumscribed component in the inferior frontal region. However, it should also be noted that the exact boundaries of Broca's area have been difficult to establish as there are striking individual variations in the amount of cortex devoted to a particular cytoarchitectural area. There is also the interpretation that regions bordering on Broca's area may share its specialized function in some form.

Another kind of aphasia was investigated by a Viennese contemporary of Freud, Carl Wernicke (1874). Wernicke concluded that *receptive* aphasia was the result of damage to the posterior portion of the superior or first temporal convolution. This region of the auditory association cortex, which shows considerable individual variations and about which there exist conflicting views as to its exact location and size, became known as Wernicke's area (see Figure 7–5). In Wernicke's aphasia, speech is phonetic and may even be grammatically acceptable, but meaning is expressed in a roundabout way.

While the most important cortical areas for language functions are Broca's area (expressive language) and Wernicke's area (receptive language), the *angular region* (see Figure 7–5) is important for crossmodal association. The angular gyrus mediates between visual and auditory forms of information. Damage to the angular gyrus has the effect of disrupting communication between the visual cortex and Wernicke's area. Patients thus affected may speak and understand speech but have difficulty with written language. There is also some evidence that certain *subcortical structures* (especially the thalamus) are involved in expressive language and language behavior generally. This was demonstrated by Penfield and Rasmussen (1950) and Penfield and Roberts (1959) in their artificial electrical stimulation of the exposed cortex of epileptic patients undergoing brain surgery. They hypothesized that the thalamic center served in an organizing role and that this center could be employed for the "ideational mechanisms of speech." Then, interconnections of different cortical areas play a part in language behavior. Primary cortical areas communicate mainly through their surrounding association areas from which the *fasciculi* or long association tracts originate. One of the most important of these association tracts for language is the *arcuate fasciculus,* (dotted track in Figure 7–5) which interconnects the frontal language area (Broca's area) with the posterior language area (Wernicke's area). When an utterance is heard, the acoustic signal is first received in the primary auditory cortex and is passed through Wernicke's area. From thence it is transferred through the arcuate fasciculus to Broca's area for vocalization. When a word is read, the graphic signal is first received through the primary visual cortex, then sent to the angular gyrus and further transmitted to Wernicke's area. Thus proper language functioning depends on the integrity of the language area and surrounding cortical areas, as well as their interconnections. Lesions of these pathways lead to disruption of language activities.

Studying Cerebral Functions

The general principles of language perception and language production formulated by Broca and Wernicke some one hundred years ago are still generally valid, although much new information has been added. An example is the mapping of the various regions in the brain responsible for a number of functions, as found by Penfield and Roberts in their electrical stimulation of the cortex. The advance in knowledge of cerebral functions is also facilitated by other procedures: surgical, bioelectrical, chemical and, more recently, computerized X-ray scan of the brain. A brief discussion of these advances follows.

Surgical procedures developed for the control of severe epilepsy and invasive brain tumor have contributed to our understanding of the functions of the separated hemispheres. In one procedure, *commissurotomy,* the commissures or neural fibers connecting the two cerebral hemispheres are severed to control epilepsy. In the other method, *hemispherectomy,* the entire cerebral cortex of one hemisphere as well as some subcortical tissues is surgically removed to excise the tumor. Sectioning of the commissures severs much of the integration of the two sides of the brain and leaves each hemisphere to recognize only contralateral sensory input. In this way, the right and left hemispheres can be studied independently on the same task. Sperry and Gazzaniga (1967, see also Gazzaniga, 1970) made detailed studies of cerebral specialization of these commissurotomized or split-brain patients. Their reports show the "minor" or right hemisphere lacking in expressive language. Their split-brain patients were not able to name verbally or in writing objects felt in the left hand or words seen in the left visual half-field, although nonverbal testing indicated that the right hemisphere "knew" what it had felt and "comprehended" the nature of the test items. Thus it appears that *expressive language* in these commissurotomized patients is a left hemisphere skill. There is, however, some evidence that at least some split-brain patients can produce a correct verbal response to a left visual half-field stimulus if the stimulus is limited in number (e.g. single digits and letters) and if longer time is allowed for (Gazzaniga and Hillyard, 1971; Teng and Sperry, 1973). With hemispherectomized patients, neuropsychological testing shows how the remaining hemisphere copes with the loss of the other brain-half and hence the limits and capabilities of the hemispheres.

While both commissurotomy and hemispherectomy procedures enable direct examinations of cerebral functions, it is difficult to ascertain how intact the two hemispheres are in their premorbid states in view of the patients' history of severe epilepsy or of invasive brain tumor.

Temporary anesthetization of one side of the brain with the *sodium amytal* test originally devised by Wada and Rasmussen (1960) enables intrasubject comparisons of hemispheric functions to be made. The procedure involves the injection of sodium amytal into the internal carotid artery supplying blood to one hemisphere and paralyzes that hemisphere temporarily (for two or three minutes) until the drug works through the system. During this brief moment of mimicked incapacitation of one hemisphere the subject's language abilities can be tested. The thoroughness and complexity of the neuropsychological tests are of course limited to the fleeting period of unconsciousness. The technique, however, does allow for the capacities of the left or right hemisphere functioning to be tested separately.

The different functions of the two cerebral hemispheres have also been studied with electrophysiological procedures such as the *electroencephalogram (EEG)*. The *EEG* has been developed as a result of technical advances in amplifying the very low voltage (50 microvolts or less) of the brain's normal electrical activity. Electrodes are placed on the scalp on both sides of the head symmetrically, usually in accordance with the International 10–20 system. Bioelectrical signals are usually recorded from the frontal, temporal, parietal, and occipital regions of the brain (see Figure 7–4) and these signals show different wave patterns of electrical bursts and rhythmic waves. Electrical activity in the *alpha* frequency band of 8 to 13 Hz (Hertz or cycles per second) is usually used in EEG research. This is because alpha has the distinctive quality of occurring in well-defined bursts and stands out from other activities in high amplitude, rhythmic waves. The faster *beta* activity (13 to 30 Hz) is also distinctive but is of low amplitude and occurs during aroused conditions. The experiment by Wood, Goff and Day (1971) is a good example of the use of recordings of electrical activities to study neural responses of the two hemispheres during speech perception of specially prepared stop consonants /ba/ or /da/ with identical duration, initial fundamental frequency, frequency and intensity contours. They used the *auditory evoked potential (AEP)* procedure which is time locked to the onset of some specific stimulus compared with the EEG which records continuous, ongoing neural electrical activity relatively independent of any reference point. They found that an equal amount of electrical activity occurred in both the left and right hemispheres during the task which did not require linguistic analysis, but significantly greater electrical activities occurred in the left than in the right hemisphere when linguistic decisions had to be made. The results indicate that different neural events occur in the left hemisphere in analyzing linguistic versus nonlinguistic events.

Attempts to demonstrate that asymmetry in alpha activity is tied to handedness have not been entirely successful. For example, a recent research report by Herron, Galin, Johnstone and Ornstein (1979) has shown that electroencephalograph alpha asymmetry measures at central and parietal leads differentiated right-handers from left-handers, but not left-handers using the "inverted hand position" (hand held above the line and pencil pointing towards the bottom of the page) from left-handers using the noninverted position (hand held below the line with pencil pointing towards the top of the page). The EEG differences between hand posture groups did appear only at occipital leads during reading and writing tasks. The inverted and noninverted hand positions during writing relates to the hemispheric motor control model of Levy (1974). In her controversial proposal, hemispheric motor projections that control the fine movements of the distal musculature are viewed as primarily contralateral in noninverted writers and ipsilateral in inverted writers. Hence Levy argues that the language-dominant hemisphere is on the same side as the writing hand in inverted writers, and on the opposite side in noninverted writers. The Herron et al. EEG study provides very modest support for the claim that the two hand postures might indicate different patterns of brain organization among left-handers but the data also suggest that hand posture does not appear to indicate the "language hemisphere."

With EEG studies it should be noted that quantification and analysis of data pose considerable methodological problems. There is a relatively high incidence of "abnormal" EEG in control subjects. It is not easy to compare EEG output from each hemisphere using the usual alpha power measures (amplitude and wave duration). There is also the added problem that bioelectrical indices do not tell us how information is processed.

Recently, Risberg and Ingvar (1973) and Lassen, Ingvar and Skinhøj (1978) have related cerebral functions to *cortical blood flow* in response to specific mental activities. Different sensory, motor and mental tasks bring about different neuronal activities. These in turn affect the corticovascular system to bring about changes in the amount of blood flow in areas of the cerebral cortex. The changes can be measured with the use of a radioactive isotope and observed in cathode-ray tube images. For example, a digit-span backward task produced increased blood flow mainly in the anterior, frontal, prerolandic, and posterior temporal regions; while a visual reasoning task brought about increases mainly in the occipital, parietal, and frontal areas. Lassen, Ingvar and Skinhøj have further shown that reading silently and reading aloud involve different patterns of cortical activities. Reading silently activates these areas: the visual association area, the frontal eye field, the motor area, and Broca's speech center in the lower part of the frontal lobe. Reading aloud activates two more centers: the mouth area and the auditory cortex. This powerful, integrative technique of measuring regional cerebral blood flow has advantages over other direct measurements such as electrical stimulation or electroencephalography. The blood flow is a direct measure of intact cortical activity and hence a more direct approach to the study of cerebral functions. In their analysis of cortical activation during reading, Lassen, Ingvar and Skinhøj have shown that such a complex task is carried out by several circumscribed cortical regions brought into action in a specific pattern. Their series of studies support Luria's (1976, p. 53) basic assumption that "complex psychological processes are carried out by functional systems, based on certain component factors; being systems, these factors are not 'localized' in circumscribed areas of the cortex but are distributed in the cortex (and subcortical formations); moreover, each area of the cortex (or subcortex) makes its own specific contribution to the organization of every complex functional system." This statement makes it clear that neither "narrow localizationism" which regards a complex psychological process as a function of a localized group of cells, nor the atomistic view of the brain as a single undifferentiated entity is tenable.

The development of *computerized axial tomography* (*CAT* scan) of the head further advances our understanding of brain asymmetries and brain functions through computerized X-ray readings or pictures of different angles or "slices" of the brain in a more or less horizontal plane (see Galaburda, LeMay, Kemper, and Geschwind, 1978; Geschwind, 1979). In these X-ray projections it is shown that in most right-handed people the right frontal lobe is usually wider than the left, while the left parietal and occipital lobes are wider than the right. In applying this approach and technique to children with delayed speech, Hier, LeMay, Rosenberger, and Perlo (1978) have reported on findings of a subgroup with reversal of the usual pattern of cerebral asymmetry. There is a higher than expectancy proportion of these children showing a wider right posterior region than is found in normals. The Hier et al. study raises the intriguing possibility that at least some language delayed children have an unusual pattern of neurological organization or pattern.

The Case of the Equipotentiality Hypothesis

The surgical, bioelectrical, chemical and computerized tomography procedures discussed in the preceding sections have delineated the functions of the two hemispheres, including the right hemisphere's capacity to understand language greatly exceeding its capacity to express it. These findings remind us of Lashley's (1929) principle of equipotentiality. From his experiments on the surgical removal of the cortex in rats and their subsequent learning of maze paths, Lashley proposed that in the rat the whole cortex is equipotential for such functions as learning and problem solving. However, Lashley's principle has not been supported by modern research on mammals more advanced than rats. Furthermore, Lashley's hypothesis conflicts with well-established observations of "localization" at a grosser level, such as damage to the occipital lobe resulting in blindness but never the loss of motor ability.

With humans, the concept of hemispheric equipotentiality refers to the purported equivalence of the two cerebral hemispheres for basic language capacity. Data from clinical case studies (Basser, 1962) showed that damage to the language dominant (usually left) hemisphere is much less deleterious to language acquisition in young children than it is in older children and adults. From Basser's and other studies and from his clinical observations, Lenneberg (1967) postulated that the left and right hemispheres are equally good substrates for language processing in the early years. He noted that right hemisphere damage produces some language impairment in children much more frequently than in adults and that unilateral cerebral insult in early years seldom leads to permanent language impairment. He suggested that hemispheric equipotentiality would hold until the onset of speech or to around the age of two. This critical period of approximately age two is extended by Krashen (1973) to about the age of five. Krashen supports his hypothesis with data from the smaller incidence of speech loss associated with right-hemisphere lesions sustained after the age of five. There are also data from Zaidel (1976) supporting the importance of age five in the neurologic representation of language.

Recently, Dennis and Kohn (1975) and Dennis and Whitaker (1977) directly tested the theory of equipotentiality by examining the language performance of hemidecorticated individuals. These were patients with surgical removal of one brain-half. Each person possessed only a right or a left hemisphere. The Dennis and Kohn study dealt with matched groups of left and right hemiplegics whose hemidecortication dated from the first year of life. Those hemidecorticates functioning with a left hemisphere made more correct responses with shorter latencies in their comprehension of spoken sentences. This reflects the finding that the child with impairment of the left hemisphere, though not aphasic as an adult would be, functions linguistically at a disadvantage compared with the child with a right impairment. The Dennis and Whitaker study involved three children with surgical removal of one brain-half predating the beginning of speech. When tested at the age of nine on the Illinois Test of Psycholinguistic Abilities (Kirk, McCarthy and Kirk, 1968), the children showed considerable within-test variation, although their overall psycholinguistic ages were comparable. The ITPA profile of the three hemidecorticates reflects in general a right hemisphere superiority for visuo-spatial tasks and a greater left hemisphere superiority for auditory language. Dennis and Whitaker suggest that infantile left hemisphere damage disrupts an ongoing course of language development. The case studies show that right hemisphere control of language, as in left hemidecorticate infant hemiplegics, causes difficulties with language structure even in adulthood. Dennis and Whitaker (1977, p. 103) state that, "hemispheric equipotentiality does appear to make an untenable supposition about the brain because it neither explains nor predicts at least two facts about language—that the two perinatal hemispheres are not equally at risk for language delay or disorder and that they are not equivalent substrates for language acquisition." More technical discussion of language development and neurological theory can be found in the work edited by Segalowitz and Gruber (1977).

It should be noted that because of his sampling of the cases and his criteria of language disturbance, Basser's data do not give unequivocal support to hemispheric equipotentiality. The general principle of the possible assumption of language functions by the right hemisphere for children up to a certain age, as proposed by Lenneberg (1967), also seems to have been overstated. Molfese, Freeman, and Palermo (1975) recorded the responses to speech and nonspeech stimuli from infants, school children, and adults. The results indicated hemispheric differences at all ages with speech stimuli producing greater auditory-evoked responses in the left hemisphere. Infants showed the most lateralization effects. Thus, the responsivity to and specialization for language in the left hemisphere seem to be present long before evidence for the emergence of language in infants (see also Molfese, 1977). More recently, Woods and Teuber (1978) reported on their detailed study of 65 children with unilateral hemisphere brain lesions occurring after speech acquisition any time from the second through the fourteenth year. They also critically surveyed the literature on childhood aphasia, which is generally defined as a disturbance or loss of ability to comprehend, elaborate, or express language concepts. From these sources, they suggested that the higher incidence of bilateral pathological damage in patients in the early studies in the literature, probably including Basser's data, might be partly explained by the lack of the benefit of antibiotics and other modern treatment. Specifically, they proposed that cross aphasias (aphasia after right hemisphere lesions) may not be more frequent in children than in adults and that even though recovery from aphasia is more likely to occur after early than after later lesions, the time taken for recovery of language is not well correlated with the onset of the disturbance. The Woods and Teuber report also points out that in assessing language functioning of brain-damaged children, such characteristics of the subjects as age of onset, the site and severity of the lesion and the nature and timing of the language assessment need to be taken into account.

To conclude this part of the discussion ranging from the central nervous system to the duality of the brain and its functions in relation to language, it is appropriate to mention Ornstein's (1972) interesting book, a kind of foil to much of the foregoing neuropsychological findings. Ornstein suggests that the different information-processing styles used by the two hemispheres reflect an underlying difference in their modes of consciousness. Using the right brain/left brain theme, he provokes a philosophical discussion of the functional duality of the brain. The left hemisphere is seen as being rational, verbal in consciousness, while the right is seen as intuitive, spatial and receptive. We are thus reminded of the "propositional" and "appositional" modes of thought discussed by Bogen (1969) and the duality of the brain that Hughlings Jackson (1874) wrote about more than a hundred years ago. In analyzing the complementary-different function of the brain, Bogen wrote that the acceptance of the right hemisphere being dominant for certain higher functions could lead us to the view that "every higher function is distributed unequally between the hemispheres, and that we might hope to determine the ratio or gradient of distribution for each function" (p. 145).

Hearing and Speaking Mechanisms

The foregoing discussion of the structure and function of the nervous system in humans provides information on the neurological and neuropsychological mechanisms underlying language and a background against which to evaluate language acquisition and dysfunction. In the following sections we will examine some of the hearing and speaking mechanisms which may affect language and reading.

At the outset, we must recognize the interrelated nature of the speaking-hearing communicative function. The speaker has something to say, arranges his/her thoughts and puts them into some linguistic form. The choice of the right words, right phrases, and right sentences to convey a certain meaning in a certain context is associated with activities in the speaker's brain and it is in the brain that appropriate impulses are sent to the muscles of the vocal organs, the tongue, the lips and the vocal cords. The nerve impulses set the muscles into motion, which, in turn, produces minute pressure changes in the form of acoustic signals. These signals in turn will activate the hearer's learning mechanism and will produce nerve impulses travelling to the listener's brain. Activities in the latter's brain will bring about recognition and understanding of the speaker's message.

It seems logical to begin with hearing behavior because reception usually occurs before production in children's language development. In learning to read they relate their previous experiences of heard language to its visual form in written or printed language.

Structure of the Ear

The anatomy of the organ of hearing, the ear, is shown in Figure 7–6. The ear is an instrument for detecting vibrations in the air (or water). These vibrations, sound waves, are collected by the *pinna* which leads to a tube through which the sound waves pass to strike the *tympanic membrane (eardrum).* The eardrum is a tightly stretched membrane which seals the rest of the ear from the outside air in the direction of the pinna. The *Eustachian tube* connects the middle

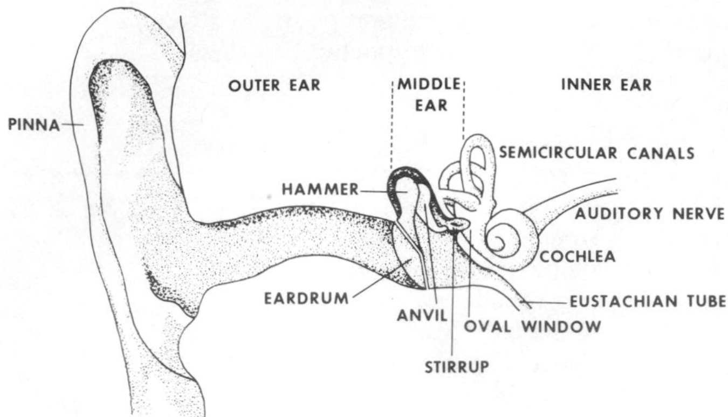

FIGURE 7–6. Parts of the ear. [From G. von Békésy, 1957, used by permission.]

ear to the mouth for purposes of equalizing pressure, but this tube is normally closed except for swallowing or yawning. The sound waves in the air vibrate the eardrum and its motion moves a chain of three very small bones in the middle ear known as the *ossicles.* One of the ossicles, the *malleus* (or *hammer*), is joined over about half of its length to the tympanic membrane, while the other end rests against the *incus (anvil),* which carries at its extremity the *stapes* (or *stirrup*). The foot of the stirrup fits tightly to the *oval window* of the *cochlea* in the inner ear, and this enables the motions of the middle ear bones to produce oscillations in the fluid contained in the cochlea. Thus the middle ear functions to transfer airborne vibrations into vibrations of the fluid of the cochlea. The complexity of the middle ear's mechanism serves to prevent loss of the energy of the original vibrations.

The cochlea is a spiral-shaped channel which makes about two and a half turns and is filled with viscous fluid. The *basilar membrane* divides the duct of the cochlea in half horizontally. When the vibrations reach the oval window, they become fluid-borne in the form of waves which influence the basilar membrane. Then the vibrations in the fluid are transferred into nerve impulses by the *organ of Corti.* This structure rests on the basilar membrane. In it, tiny hair tufts penetrate beyond the membrane surface of the hair cells, and these tufts are slightly embedded in the *tectorial membrane,* which is a thick, heavy, viscous covering over most of the organ of Corti. When the basilar membrane is vibrated by sound waves, the hair cells get pushed against the tectorial membrane and the hairs are pulled or bent. This movement of the hairs sets off nerve impulses. Even the most minute movements initiate impulses and this produces the astonishing sensitivity of hearing.

The movements of the hairs caused by the incoming sound waves are transmitted by the auditory nerve cells in code. The intensity or loudness of sound is signaled partly by the rate of firing and partly by which fibers are involved. The greater the number of impulses, the louder the sound is the general code rule. Some fibers, however, are less sensitive than others and only fire for louder sounds, while some other more sensitive fibers decrease their firing rate beyond a certain level of intensity. The pitch of the incoming sound is most likely coded on the basis of differential responses at different places on the basilar membrane to sounds of different frequency. While loudness and pitch discriminations probably are all performed below the level of the brain, the discrimination of the timbre of sounds and the ability to locate the source of a sound both depend on analysis of the incoming auditory impulses in the brain.

The hearing mechanism is susceptible to different kinds of disorders. Colds often affect the middle ear through the spread of inflammation into the Eustachian tube (see Figure 7–6). This causes it to close so that air can no longer reach the middle ear, and a partial vacuum builds up. This allows increased pressure on the eardrum from the outer ear, and the small bones of the middle ear cannot operate properly. Often the infection spreads into the middle ear producing *otitis media,* a condition in which pus forms to cause outward pressure on the eardrum. Drainage of the pus often becomes imperative, and this is sometimes achieved by a surgical puncture of the eardrum. A frequent result is damage to the small middle ear bones as well as the eardrum. Otitis media is the most common cause of malfunctioning of the middle ear. Other causes include: congenital malformations, accidental injuries, cysts, and *otosclerosis,* a disease producing a bony growth that progressively impedes the action of the stirrup bone.

The cochlea may also be affected by otitis media or otosclerosis. The damaging effect of the latter disease may spread to the cochlea, or infection from otitis media may reach it. The cerebrospinal fluid surrounding the brain is directly in contact with the cochlea's fluid. Thus any infection may be passed on. A *sensory-neural* hearing deficit is one caused by disorders of the organ of Corti and/or in the auditory nerve. Other diseases which may lead to sensory-neural deficits in hearing are encephalitis, influenza, measles, meningitis, mumps, scarlet fever, and whooping cough. The child may suffer sensory-neural deficit at birth if the mother contracted a virus disease such as rubella, influenza, or mumps during the first few months of pregnancy. Sensory-neural hearing deficit may also be caused by blood-group incompatibility between the fetus and the mother. Furthermore, the possibility of sensory-neural deficit from an hereditary trait must be mentioned. In addition, the physiological organ of hearing and its connections in the nervous system can be damaged through physical injury. At the higher levels in the nervous system, hearing abilities may be destroyed or disturbed by damage to the brain. Some of the effects on language have been discussed in the preceding sections.

Children's Auditory Perception of Speech

The perception of speech in languages like English depends on the ability to discriminate between *phonemes,* the elementary and basic sound units of speech which determine differences in meaning (for example, the initial sounds of "bat" and "cat" represent a phonemic difference). Phonemic discrimination cannot depend only on the hearing apparatus because the pure phoneme as we think of it in the teaching of reading does not exist in reality. It is an abstraction from a wide range of differing sounds. A phoneme differs according to what other phonemes it is associated with in a word or neighboring word. Also, the sound of a phoneme varies with such factors as intonation, mood, accent, syntactic structure, and so on. Furthermore, each individual pronounces the same phoneme in a slightly different way from everyone else.

It is not surprising, therefore, that children up to the age of about six years make many mistakes in their hearing of language. For instance, Midgeley (1952) is cited by Vernon (1957) as having shown that six-year-olds made frequent mistakes over the words "house" (often confused with "mouth"), "rose," "cage," "hen," "lid," "mug," and "frock," in an experiment in which children had to identify pictures from words heard through headphones. Thompson (1963), too, found that six-year-olds often showed inadequate auditory discrimination between words. Seven-year-olds still confused words which differed in only one phoneme in an experiment by Tikofsky and McInish (1968). Thus Vernon (1971) remarked, "it is clear that the language which the child understands is very closely related to that which he speaks, although the vocabulary of the former exceeds that of the latter."

Most children usually grow out of these difficulties after the age of six to seven years, probably because of their increasing interest in the spoken language of their peers and their ever-expanding experience of hearing and producing speech. Garnica (1973) provided some preliminary data to show that phonemic speech perception might develop with semantic development in as early as the second year of life, though there is considerable individual variation. However, a minority of children continues to exhibit symptoms of inability to hear differences in some speech sounds. Vernon (1957) stated that "some degree of hearing loss should be suspected when these defects appear in children of 6 years and older," referring specifically to such speech problems as pronouncing /t/ or /θ/ instead of /s/ or omitting it altogether, and pronouncing /l/, /j/, or /w/ instead of /r/. She also commented that the child retaining these or other speech defects after the age of entering school would likely have difficulty in learning to read. In her later book, Vernon (1971) cited, for example, Thompson's (1963) longitudinal finding that approximately 25 per cent of children aged eight years showed poor discrimination between words with similar sounds and half of them were disabled readers. In contrast, most good readers at age eight had entered school two years earlier with adequate auditory discrimination for words. Dechant and Smith (1977) have pointed out the importance of auditory discrimination skill for successful achievement in reading: "If the child cannot hear sounds correctly, he normally cannot learn to speak them correctly. A child cannot pronounce distinctions that he cannot hear. Furthermore, if he confuses or distorts sounds in speech, it frequently is impossible for him to associate the correct sound with the visual symbol. Thus, inadequate auditory discrimination leads to improper speech and ultimately to an incorrect association of sound and printed symbol" (p. 105). Much of the research evidence on hard-of-hearing children learning to read supports this view. We must, however, also recognize that the maturation of the auditory system is a slow process. Fior (1972) has provided some recent data to show that maximum acuity for the central audiometric frequencies (1, 2, and 4 KHz) is reached only at about seven years of age and that children do not attain some auditory functions before the age of seven to eleven years.

Speech Perception Characteristics

It is not only the sensation of hearing which is linked so closely to the motor behavior of speaking. The kinesthetic sense is also inextricably involved. The *kinesthetic system* is that part of the central nervous system which provides information about the position and movements of one's own body. The system includes the receptors in muscles (proprioceptors) which provide feedback about their movements and which provide kinesthetic sensation for the brain.

In learning to speak, therefore, infants associate the sounds they hear themselves making with the kinesthetic impulses received from their muscles when they move them to produce the sounds. These auditory and kinesthetic patterns of sensation are gradually modified as infants adapt their speech sounds to those they hear from the adults near them. At the very fundamental stage when the neural foundations of language are being laid, kinesthetic, motor, and auditory impulses are closely connected. Hence, Brain (1961) described speech as being "fundamentally . . . a sensorimotor-sensory activity," pointing out that "whereas congenital deafness interferes grossly with the development of speech, when once normal speech has been established acquired deafness disturbs it relatively little" (p. 151). Thus the deaf child's dysfunction in speech production is due more to incapacities in speech perception than motor disabilities. Even with adventitious deafness, speech production shows disintegration because of lack of support of speech perception. Brain posed an important question:

> To go back to the beginnings of speech in the infant, we have seen that this is based upon a sensorimotor-sensory circuit, by means of which the child reproduces the sounds which it hears and regulates its own motor activity in doing so. We saw also that the child hears what we call *the same sound* produced in many different ways by different people, whereas its own production of this sound is relatively stereotyped. Physiologically, therefore, the first problem is how these widely varying stimuli can produce the same response, that is, by what physiological mechanism the brain responds to a common pattern in the stimuli and disregards the irrelevant elements (pp. 155–156).

The production apparatus for speaking and hence the kinesthetic feedback system are complex. The three main parts of the speech apparatus are

1. The breath stream which constitutes the energy source created by the lungs, diaphragm, and the primary respiratory muscles.
2. The vibrator system including the larynx, vocal folds and laryngeal muscles which together create phonation.
3. The resonator and articulators that shape speech, including the lips, tongue, teeth, palate, and the mouth, throat, and nasal cavities.

Normal speech is dependent upon the precise coordination of these three systems. The resulting highly refined muscular movements take place extremely rapidly. During speaking, the airwave pattern produced by a speaker depends on the air forced from the lung past the vocal cords in the larynx, or through the pharynx and out through the oral cavities. The vocal chords will open and close (vibrate) at a rapid rate as air is forced from the lungs and thus produce one *fundamental frequency* (vibration) and harmonics of that fundamental frequency. The fundamental frequency and its harmonics then pass through the vocal tract which acts as a resonator to reinforce or amplify certain frequencies.

The speed of input and output in hearing and speaking is so great that this in itself is difficult to explain. Liberman, Cooper, Shankweiler, and Studdert-Kennedy (1967) at the Haskins Laboratories noted that up to about 25 to 30 phonetic segments per second can be perceived. Although not all the phonemes are necessary for decoding the spoken message, nevertheless the rate of input remains much higher than can normally be processed sequentially by the nervous system. Liberman et al. propose that this higher rate of processing is achieved because several channels are transmitting and receiving speech information in parallel, each channel operating at the normal speed for the nervous system. Thus the several cavities of the resonator can be tuned in a relatively independent fashion by appropriate actions of the muscles of the tongue, lips, and face and other parts of the vocal apparatus.

Several speech characteristics of relevance to language and reading acquisition need to be explained. *Acoustic* cues are patterns of specific events, and not whole sound. Through a complex encoding connection, acoustic cues reflect features that characterize articulatory gestures. When these features are properly combined, they form the equivalent to the segments of the phonetic representation. *Articulatory* or *subphonemic* features refer to the movement of some specified articulator or a set of articulators in some specified way or the relationship in time between these movements. The realization of a phoneme is the result of the joint working of a number of articulatory features, all of which it shares in common with other phonemes.

The Haskins Laboratories researchers have shown that acoustic cues for individual phonemes are context-dependent (see Liberman, Cooper, Shankweiler, and Studdert-Kennedy, 1967; Studdert-Kennedy and Shankweiler, 1970). This means that the cues change for a particular phoneme in different contexts. For example, in a classic study, Liberman, Delattre, and Cooper (1952) demonstrated that a synthetically produced burst of noise at 1,800 Hertz (Hz) was heard as /p/ before /i/, /k/ before /a/, and /p/ before /u/. Another example is the perception of the voiced stop consonant /d/ in /di/ and /du/. The steady-state *formants* (a formant is a concentration of acoustic energy within a restricted frequency range) are sufficient to produce the vowels /i/ and /u/. But it is the *formant transitions* (a rapid change in the position of the formant on the frequency scale) that are important acoustic cues for the perception of the consonants. The *first* or *lower formant transition* is the cue for the *manner* and *voicing* of the consonant and tells the listener that the consonants belong to the class of voiced stops [b, d, g]. The *second formant transition (upper formant transition)* carries the important acoustic cue for the perception of consonants according to their *place* of production. Figure 7–7 shows the essential acoustic cues for the stop consonant /d/ plus vowel syllables. The schematic spectrogram shows that only steady-state formants are needed to synthesize the vowels [i] and [u], at least in slow articulation, while the rapid changes in formant frequency at the beginning of the speech patterns carry important information. Note also the different transition cues for [d] in the two different vowel contexts. Thus, successive phonemes are merged in the sound stream as a parallel transmission. It is this parallel transmission of two or more phones that characterizes the phonological or speech code and is an important condition for its efficiency. In fact, most of the information of the phonetic representation of the speech signal is carried by the first two or three formants, the fundamental frequency, the plosive bursts and the fricatives.

One consequence of the parallel transmission is that the acoustic cues cannot be divided on the time axis into segments of phonemic chunks. The acoustic cue for the same perceived consonant /d/ is different in two different vowel contexts /di/ and /du/ and there is no acoustic segment corresponding to the consonant segment /d/. Thus acoustic cues are presented in contrasts in terms of articulatory features. In the English language, place of production has three values (labial, alveolar, velar), while voicing has only two (voiced, voiceless). Examples of *place contrasts* are: /b,d/, /b,g/, /d,g/, /p,t/, /p,k/, /t,k/. Of *voicing contrasts* are: /b,p/, /d,t/, /g,k/. Of *place and voicing contrasts* are: /b,t/, /b,k/, /d,p/, /d,k/, /g,p/, /g,t/. The cues for manner, place and voicing for /b/ in /ba/ are acoustically different from those of /b/ in /ab/. Liberman, Delattre and Cooper suggest that the determinant for a consonant heard is "the articulatory movements which the listener would make in attempting to repro-

FIGURE 7–7. Simplified spectrographic patterns sufficient to produce /di/ and /du/. [after Liberman, 1970, used by permission.]

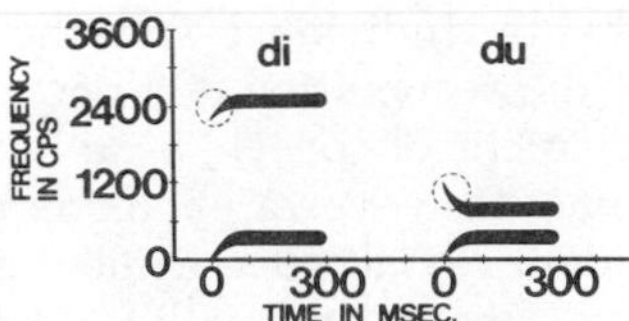

duce these acoustic patterns . . . or perhaps only the short-circuited neural equivalent of these movements, with the result that the initial schematic phonemes *p* and *k*, which can be entirely identical as acoustic stimuli, become clearly differentiated in proprioceptive terms . . ." (p. 514). They concluded that their research results gave "some additional support for the assumption that the perception of speech depends in any final analysis on the proprioceptive stimuli which arise from the movements of articulation." Similarly, Liberman et al. (1967) indicated that different sounds are heard as being "the same phoneme" because the neural instructions to the vocal muscles and the proprioceptive feedback are similar. Thus the close link between hearing and speech probably exists because they have some common neural basis, at least in part. It seems likely that in the babbling stage of infancy, associations are formed between auditory, motor and kinesthetic impulses because of overlapping experience in the cortex.

Thus the motor theory of speech perception proposed by the Haskins Laboratories researchers (Liberman, Cooper, Shankweiler, and Studdert-Kennedy, 1967) argues for the close link between speech perception and production. Their argument, as discussed in the preceding paragraphs, is based on: (a) the speed of processing speech sounds as compared with nonspeech sounds, (b) the perception of different acoustic signals as the same phoneme, (c) the perception of the same acoustic stimuli as different phonemes in different speech environments, (d) the "categorical" perception of speech sounds (at least consonant sounds) because of some special speech mechanisms and (e) the differential perception of speech and nonspeech sounds in the different hemispheres. In one sense, it is the tacit knowledge that listeners possess of certain properties of the vocal tract, of speech and language that renders possible the perception of such a complex code as speech.

Brain's (1961) concept of a *schema* to explain speech activities is appropriate: "The schema . . . is an unconscious physiological standard of comparison . . . ," and "most speech schemas, when established, remain stable parts of the permanent equipment of the individual. Thus the physiological basis of the recognition of a phoneme, i.e. of the basic element of speech, is an auditory phoneme schema. However a phoneme may be uttered, we identify it at once without any process of conscious comparison with a standard: the schema is therefore purely physiological" (p. 156). Brain also identifies word schemas and, in sum, schemas as responding to, and patterns in, varying stimuli. This concept of a schema reminds us of Bartlett's (1932) suggestion that experience is represented in memory by "schemata." The Haskins Laboratories studies have drawn attention to the complex process of conversion from speech sounds to phonetic messages and the different representations in memory of the complex code for transmission and subsequent incorporation into experience for long-term storage. This relates to language awareness of the primary activities of listening and speaking on the one hand and the phenomenon of paraphrase for semantic representation on the other hand. Language awareness has been discussed in the preceding chapter; the question of comprehending will be taken up in a subsequent chapter.

Some Speech Disorders

These four aspects of speaking disorders are often mentioned in the literature as having a bearing on language and subsequent reading behavior: (1) articulation, (2) fluency, (3) voicing and (4) language.

Articulation problems are the most frequently diagnosed type of speech defects. In order to produce the sounds in the "correct" pronunciation for their language and dialect, children not only need to be able to control the movements of their speech organs but also they must be able to hear differences between speech sounds distinctly if they are going to be able to shape their own speaking to the speech of those around them. One problem for beginning reading instruction at age five or six is that many children have not reached maturity in these respects at that early age. Another aspect of learning to articulate is that the sounds must be produced in a certain order. One error sometimes made by young children is pronouncing "basket" and "biscuit" as "baksit" and "biksit." Such errors may be caused by faulty perception in hearing or by the tendency of the tongue to fall more easily into the other pattern.

In addition to misordering of sounds, four other types of articulation errors are frequently noted: (1) *Omissions*, for example, saying "do'" for "dog," "'at" for "cat," or "ba'y" for "baby." (2) *Substitutions*, for example, saying "train" for "crane." The substitution of /t/ for /k/ is common in English-speaking school beginners. Others are

/k/ for /t/, /b/ for /v/, /f/ for /θ/, /θ/ for /s/ (lisping), /w/ for /l/ or /r/. (3) *Distortions* may be distinguished from substitutions in that the former include sounds not normally produced at all in the child's language or dialect group. For example, some children make a friction noise between the lips or between the upper teeth and the lower lip when trying to produce the sound /r/. The result sounds like a cross between /w/ and /v/. (4) *Additions* are less common but sometimes occur in such examples as "furog" for "frog" or "habist" for "habit."

Several studies have established an association between articulation defects and reading retardation. Yedinack (1949) studied seven- to nine-year-old children who had been referred by their teachers because they were defective in the pronunciation of at least one phoneme. Children with a hearing deficiency were excluded from the sample. Yedinack found that children with defective articulation were, in comparison with normal subjects, about six months retarded in oral reading and (to a less extent) in silent reading. The study of Crookes and Greene (1963) examined a group of five- to eleven-year-olds who had been referred to a clinic for speech difficulties. In eight of these twenty cases, articulation was defective, but auditory perception and memory and language development were normal. The other twelve children were normal in articulation. Their problem was in other aspects of language development. All the children were seriously retarded in reading for their level of intelligence.

Fluency disorders have drawn the attention of therapists, theorists, and researchers more than any other type of speech problems. In particular, "stuttering" or "stammering" has been given greatest attention. "Cluttering" is another commonly recognized fluency disorder.

In stuttering behavior, the dysfluency appears as blocks, repetitions, prolongations and hesitations which disturb the normal flow of speech. Blocks may occur at any point in the utterance. The child may not be able to get out the first word or may get stuck in mid-sentence or mid-word. Sometimes the stutterer sticks on a particular sound which then gets prolonged. Repetition may be of phrases, words, syllables, or phonemes. Frequently stutterers' dysfluent speaking is accompanied by other motor behaviors which usually have no connection with speech. They may stamp their feet, blink their eyes, make facial grimaces, or breathe pantingly. These are secondary symptoms.

Cluttering is similar to stuttering in only some ways. Clutterers speak so rapidly that they cannot control their fine articulatory movements. Therefore they leave out or transpose syllables or phonemes, particularly in the middle or at the end of words, and they omit smaller words. But, when clutterers take special care to talk slowly and deliberately, they can speak clearly and fluently. In contrast, stutterers become more dysfluent when they try especially hard to avoid stuttering.

Nine per cent of Monroe's (1932) 415 reading disability cases exhibited stuttering behavior, whereas only one per cent of her control group did so. However, the causal relationship is not clear. The stuttering may have been caused by the reading disability, for example. Burt (1937) found that the incidence of stuttering increased with the age of school children. Despert (1946) also reported that the onset of stuttering often occurs at the age when children first start to attend school. Vernon (1957) notes: "It seems possible therefore that this increase was due to the difficulty experienced by many children in learning to read and write, rather than that stammering made reading difficult" (p. 65). This suggestion that stuttering may be the effect, rather than the cause, of reading difficulties deserves further study.

It may be thought that the reading achievements are bound to appear poor if they are tested orally. However, Murray (1932) produced evidence of a relationship between stuttering and *silent* reading difficulties. Murray found that abnormal variability in the amplitude and duration of inspiration and expiration in breathing, which is characteristic of stuttering behavior, occurred during the silent reading of stutterers. Characteristic tonic spasms of the breathing muscles also occurred. The disintegration of breathing control increased as the reading material became more difficult. Furthermore, in a group of eighteen stutterers there was a correlation between the amount of breathing disintegration and the level of poor reading achievement. The average degree of retardation of reading development was 1.5 years in comprehension and 2.5 years in rate. Ketcham (1951) attempted to improve both breathing control and reading ability in an experiment with 32 boys, aged seven to ten years, who were seriously retarded in reading development. They were given special training in breathing control and in understanding printed words. They gained 6.2 months in oral reading age and 9.9 months in silent reading age. A control group of other retarded readers who received no special training made no significant improvement. Unfortunately, from the point of view of understanding the causal relationship between stuttering and reading, it is impossible to determine whether it was the breathing control exercises or the training in understanding printed words which produced the improvement.

Other authors have proposed theoretical explanations of stuttering which emphasize an *organic* basis for a failure in feedback behavior. These theories have been reviewed by Webster and Lubker (1968) and by Timmons and Boudreau (1972). The general consensus of these theorists is that stuttering is caused by some defect in the timing of the process of transmitting auditory feedback from the individual's own speaking. Timmons and Boudreau concluded:

> Such factors as individual geometry and density of the skull with special attention to the oral cavity and surrounding bone and tissue structure, as well as time of arrival of sound through air conduction at the cochlea should be considered. If this is done, at least nine possible combinations of temporal receptive disturbances can result from internal and/or external feedback discrepancies. If one accepts as probable individual difference variables, it follows that some individuals while learning to speak have to adapt more than others in order to use the feedback they receive (p. 481).

They further suggested that "stuttering and DAF reaction are manifestations of attempts to compensate for the discrepancies described above." DAF or *delayed auditory feedback* artificially induced in the laboratory has been shown to mimic stuttering (see Van Riper, 1971).

Webster and Lubker (1968, p. 763) also concluded that "aberrant temporal interactions between components of auditory feedback underlie stuttered speech." Webster and his colleagues, however, specify a rather different physiological basis for the defect: ". . . middle ear muscle reflexes could be responsible for distorting or momentarily cancelling auditory feedback cues that are important for speech guidance" (Webster, Schumacher, and Lubker, 1970, p. 49).

In the search for the organic basis of stuttering it is worthy of note that recently Travis (1978a, 1978b) reassessed his cerebral dominance theory of stuttering first articulated in 1931. Citing current studies of slow potential shifts in relation to speech onset, evoked potentials and other studies, he still finds his cerebral dominance postulate a viable explanation for stuttering. While admitting that conclusive evidence on the constitutional or acquired origin of stuttering is lacking, Travis suggests that vigilance on the part of the stutterer might help.

Voicing problems in children's speech are less frequent. Voicing is produced by vibrating the vocal chords in the larynx; the sound is amplified and given quality by resonance in the chest below and the pharynx, mouth, nose, and facial cavities above. Various abnormal voicing behaviors are recognized. Most commonly mentioned are weakness of voice, hoarseness, and denasality. An abnormally weak voice tends to produce imprecision in articulation. Denasality produces the kind of speech usually associated with head colds, "names" becomes "dabes," for example.

Language deficiencies will be discussed briefly with the focus on the neuropsychological foundations of language behavior. Many reading specialists have asserted that language deficiencies are an important cause of reading disabilities. For example, Buckingham (1940) believed that children labeled as disabled readers ought more properly to have been recognized as deficient in language growth. Artley (1953) mentioned "enriching oral vocabulary," "strengthening meaning associations," "formulating sentences," "organizing ideas into language units," "using narrative expression," "developing sensitivity to inflectional variants," and "developing awareness of sentence structure," as well as "improving articulation" as special preparation to be given to children before they are introduced to reading. Harris (1956) asserted that the child's vocabulary and mastery of sentence structure, as well as his clarity of articulation, are vital factors in readiness for learning to read. Betts (1935) included "meagre vocabulary" in his list of "reading disability correlates."

As for actual research evidence, most of it supports these rather common-sense beliefs. Two studies provide negative evidence. Martin (1955) could find no relationship between oral language and either reading readiness test scores of school beginners or their reading attainments at the end of the first school year. Martin's measures of oral language were: quantity of words used, breadth of vocabulary, and sentence length. Silver (1968), according to Vernon (1971), asked severely backward readers to select pictures to match spoken words and found no evidence that they lacked understanding of word meanings, but this needs to be substantiated.

In contrast, there are many studies providing positive evidence for a connection between language development and progress in learning to read. The research of de Hirsch, Jansky, and Langford (1964) might be cited. They studied the language abilities of a group of five-year-old prematurely born children compared with a control group of full-term children. The premature children were normal in intelligence and were equal to the full-term children in three linguistic abilities: auditory discrimination, memory, and articulation. But in several other aspects of language behavior, the premature children were significantly inferior: vocabulary, naming familiar objects, understanding questions, length and complexity of sentences, and spontaneous spoken language. When they began to learn to read, this premature group achieved at a significantly poorer level. In a later publication, de Hirsch, Jansky, and Langford (1966) reported that tests of memory for words, naming the class to which a group of objects belongs, and the quantity of words used to tell a story were effective predictors of subsequent failure in reading. Sampson (1962) reported two interesting correlations between earlier spoken language ability and later achievement in reading comprehension. The amount of correctly phrased speech at age 2.5 years, and the vocabulary and language development scores on the *Watts English Language Scale* at age five were all correlated significantly with reading comprehension attainments at age eight. Ravenette (1968) found spoken vocabulary as measured by the *Crichton Vocabulary Scale* and the *N.F.E.R. Picture Vocabulary Test* to be associated with reading achievement at ages seven to eight.

Several studies have attempted to unravel the connections between language development and reading achievement by use of the 1961 experimental version of the *Illinois Test of Psycholinguistic Abilities* (ITPA) (Kirk, McCarthy and Kirk, 1968). Spache (1968) found that reading achievement was more closely related to the group of subtests measuring automatic sequential abilities than it was to the group of subtests sampling abilities related to understanding and reasoning. Ravenette (1968) cites research by Kass on severely retarded readers aged seven to ten years which arrived at the same result, except that the association test in the first group of subtests was also related to reading failure. Two investigators have reported that disabled readers perform particularly badly on the sequencing subtest in the automatic group: Doehring (1968), and Naidoo (1970). But Clark (1970) in her study of Scottish retarded readers at nine years of age found that "neither the boys nor the girls in this study *as a group* scored particularly low on these sequencing tests" (p. 95). Indeed, she remarks that "disappointingly little discrimination based on sub-test analysis was found" (p. 93) on the ITPA. What Clark found was that her group of retarded readers scored significantly lower on the whole test. The ITPA is an American test whereas Clark's subjects were Scottish children, but Mittler and Ward (1970), in their study of twins in Britain, reported that the twins scored according to the expectations of the American norms. However, Mittler and Ward conducted a factor analytic investigation which seems to lend some strength to Clark's finding that the ITPA subtests did not specify particular psycholinguistic disabilities in her retarded readers. A single general factor accounted for a large part of the variance in test scores. Other minor factors were related to particular subtests but their nature was difficult to determine.

Several linguistic subtests were included in the *Canadian Reading Readiness Test* developed by Evanechko, Ollila, Downing, and Braun (1973). The test has four parts: (1) the child's concept of the reading task; (2) perceptual ability; (3) linguistic competence; and (4) cognitive functioning. Each part has three subtests. Several of the subtests are closely related to the literacy learning task itself. Others are concerned with language development quite apart from literacy. The "linguistic competence" set consists in tests of semantics, syntax, and morphology. As recognition of letters by name has been found to be a good predictor of reading achievement in the first year of school, such a subtest is included in the "perceptual ability" set of this test developed by Evanechko et al. They report correlations of 0.4, 0.4, and 0.3 between this predictor and their tests of semantics, syntax, and morphology respectively. A factor analysis found one general reading readiness factor which accounted for almost 50 per cent of the variance. Three other relatively narrow factors were found: one on the morphology subtest, another on the semantics subtest and the third on the syntax subtest. The authors conclude: "This result lends support to the contention, commonly expressed, that success in reading is not predicated on any single competency but demands a total readiness on the part of the child" (p. 72).

From this review of the research evidence, we can concur with Vernon's (1971) conclusion: "It is obvious that there is much variation between the findings of different experimenters as to the relation of linguistic processes to reading achievement. It is clearly difficult to specify, differentiate and measure exactly the different types of linguistic skill."

Summary

This chapter aims at providing some basic understanding of neurological substrates subserving language and reading as part of the language continuum. The structure and function of the nervous system in humans and of the cerebral hemispheres have been discussed. Procedures of studying cerebral functions—surgical, bioelectrical, chemical, radiological—have been outlined and the reciprocal specialization of the left and right hemispheres is emphasized. The interrelated hearing and speaking functions have been discussed in relation to the perception of the complex speech code and to reading behavior. Speech perception is seen as predicating on language awareness and the schemata of comprehending linguistic codes.

CHAPTER 8

Seeing and Reading

The ability to see printed symbols is an obvious prerequisite for learning to read. In this chapter the essential physiological and neurological foundations of such seeing behavior will be described. From the outset, we must recognize the ongoing nature and the complexity of much of the research data in this area, especially on the neurological aspects of seeing. This is an extremely active area of research, but, as Blakemore (1973) has remarked, "Seeing is more of a mystery than ever. The whole field is a bit like a scientific bombsite—attacked from all sides and much in need of some theoretical reconstruction."

The Eye

The apparatus for seeing depends on a pair of specialized organs—the eyes—the neural receptors of which, strictly speaking, are said to be part of the brain which has extended outside the skull. Each of the two eyes has the same anatomy, which is depicted in Figure 8–1. The eye refracts light rays, acts as a transducer to convert electromagnetic energy to nerve impulses, and performs a great deal of information processing. The analogy drawn between the eye and a camera, often found in school textbooks, is at best misleading. True, both are receptive to light rays and there is some similarity in their functioning; but the analogy fails completely to bring out the *active* searching behavior of seeing. The eyes are continually alert and seeking visual stimuli, whereas the camera is, of course, passive.

Referring to Figure 8–1, light passes through the *cornea* which is transparent and curved so that it acts as a convex lens to focus light roughly on the *retina*. Behind the cornea is the *lens* proper which, through changing its curvature, provides fine focusing adjustments of the light rays onto the retina. The retina is the light-sensitive inner surface of the eyeball consisting of nerve cells which produce impulses in the *optic nerve*.

The lens of the eye is particularly important in reading since it allows the focusing of closer objects on the retina (strictly speaking, much of the focusing is done by the cornea, as evidenced by the fact that people with their corneas removed need very strong glasses to read). The lens is suspended by a series of zonule fibers from another muscular ring, the *ciliary muscles,* which lie just under a strong elastic membrane called the *sclera* and to the outside of an opaque membrane, the *iris.* For seeing distant objects, the ciliary muscles are relaxed and this allows the pressure of the fluid in the eyeball to flatten the

FIGURE 8–1. The human eye.

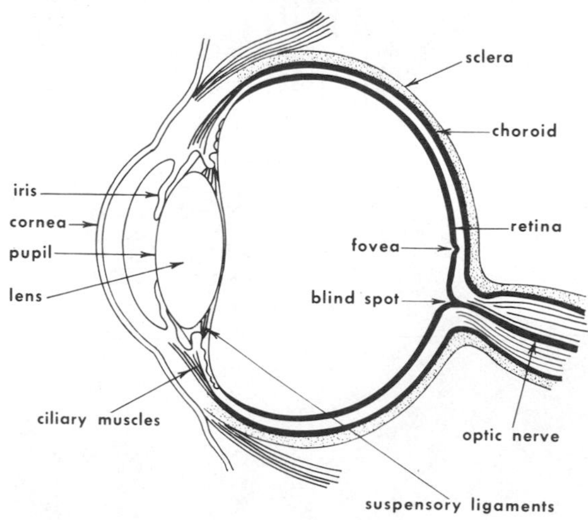

shape of the lens. For closer vision, the ciliary muscles contract to take off some of this pressure on the lens so that it can assume more of its natural spherical shape. These adjustments of the ciliary muscles are automatic and reflexive and their functioning is quite remarkable. The change in focal length of the lens is termed *accommodation,* which is also aided by convergence of the two eyes. Aging causes the lens to lose some of its flexibility so that it does not respond properly to the contraction of the ciliary muscles. This loss of flexibility in aging is explained by the increased tautness of the zonule fibres, which overcomes the natural elasticity of the lens. Assistance is needed from an artificial lens in the form of spectacles.

The *pupil* is the aperture of the eye, and it too is subject to modification by a light reflex and by muscles. The iris consists of muscular bands which control the size of the pupil. Constriction of the pupil reduces blurring of the image and increases the range of distances at which objects are simultaneously in focus. Dilation of the pupil increases the amount of light entering the eye. Visual acuity is reduced as a result of blurring of the image when the pupil size increases.

The light rays collected from the outside environment are focused upon the retina, which is a complicated structure in both its anatomy and its physiology. The retina consists of three main neural layers as shown in Figure 8–2. In addition, there is a backing of light-absorbing pigmented tissue customarily known as the *choroid layer,* which cuts down reflection and scattered light. The *rods* and *cones* are the receptors which form the first layer next to the choroid layer. Their light-sensitive outer segments point away from the lens. The second layer contains the *bipolar cells.* These have dendrites making contact with the rods and cones. The axons of the bipolar cells are in synaptic contact with the *ganglion cells* which form the third layer. These have axons which converge from the different parts of the retina at the *optic disk* (the "blind spot") where they pass through the other layers as the optic nerve (see Figure 8–1), which consists of about a million nerve fibers. It is the set of ganglion cells which sends its fibers—the optic nerve fibers—to the brain.

FIGURE 8–2. Schematic diagram of the human retina.

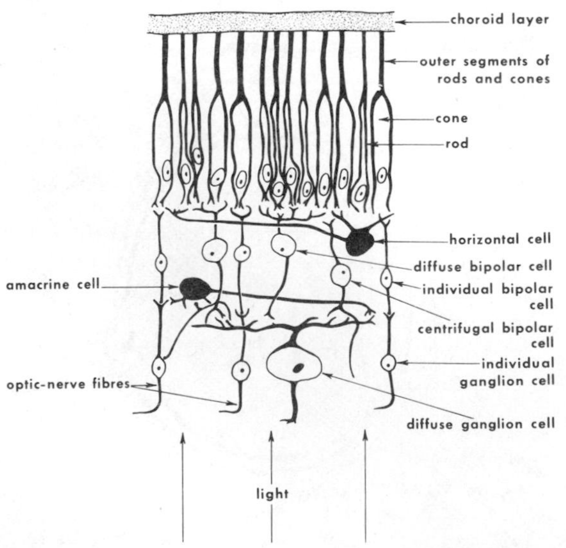

Beside these three layers, there are two kinds of cells running laterally (see Figure 8–2). The *horizontal cells* link dendrites of bipolar cells lying some distance apart and link receptors together. The *amacrine cells* are found in the area on the border between the ganglion cell layer and the bipolar cell layer. Horizontal and amacrine cells play a part in regulating the flow of impulses through the retinal paths to the optic nerve, and these cells serve to integrate information from neighboring areas on the retina. In addition, there are *centrifugal bipolar cells* connecting ganglion cells and they may also connect with efferent optic-nerve fibers to the rods and cones layer.

The *fovea* (see Figure 8–1) is a small depression in the retina which is not obstructed by cellular material as are other parts. The fovea also differs from other parts in other ways. Almost all the receptors at the fovea are slender cones. With distance from the fovea, the density of cones decreases and the frequency of rods increases (up to 20° from the fovea, when the density of rods also decreases to the edge of the retina). In each retina as a whole there exist approximately 125 million rods and about 6 million cones. Still another difference between the fovea and other parts of the retina is the relative incidence of ganglion cells. There are approximately one million of these in each retina. In the fovea there are nearly equal numbers of ganglion cells and receptor cells, whereas toward the periphery the ratio is more like 100 receptors to each ganglion cell. It is the equal number of ganglion cells and receptor cells in the fovea that accounts for the fovea being the center of greatest visual acuity.

Peripheral vision is not nearly as acute as that in the central foveal region, which is obtained for about two degrees of the total visual field. This is out of a total range of vision of about 180° horizontally and 60° vertically and results from the comparatively few foveal data-gathering receptors. The rest of the field of vision serves primarily as an alerting system signaling movement of objects not being "looked at" through the sharp foveal vision and their relative position. If it is the intention to see the moving objects, the eyes must be positioned to center the object of interest on the fovea, and the brain uses all available data to perform the act of cognizing. The two degrees of clear vision is probably related to the balance between economy and utility. The two degrees of clear vision uses up about ten per cent of the total channel capacity in the optic nerve and this would seem to be what the visual system could afford for clear vision (Kabrisky, 1966). Beyond the fovea and subtending about 10° of visual angle around the reader's fixation point is the *parafoveal region.* Both parafoveal and perifoveal vision may be important in guiding a reader's eye movements.

The rods and cones not only have different distributions in the retina, but also have distinct functions. The rods permit discrimination of brightness or shades of gray, while cones serve in the discrimination of wavelengths or hues and permit fine discrimination of detail. Both rods and cones have pigments which absorb light and undergo photochemical reaction as a result. These chemical reactions lead to changes in the membrane potential of the receptor and form the basis of nerve impulses. The exact process of transmitting the signal from the receptors to the ganglion cell is complex, but important changes in the signal have already taken place. When a single ganglion cell is stimulated by the effects of light stimulus, the burst of impulses is termed the "on" response. The burst of impulses coincidental with the termination of the light stimulus at the end of a period of lateral inhibiton is known as the "off" response of a ganglion cell. The "on" and "off" responses can also be obtained by stimulating different neighboring areas of a cell's receptive field in which light alters the firing rate. Thus a single ganglion cell acts as a clearing house for information coming from receptor cells in the retina. Ganglion cells fire regularly at the rate of about 5 per second even when the retina is in total darkness. When light stimulates the rods and cones on the retina, their signals converge on the associated ganglion cell, and within a fraction of a second there is a marked increase in the latter's rate of firing. Within another fraction of a second, the rate of firing drops off almost to its normal background rate. When the light stimulus ceases, the ganglion cell stops firing altogether for a fraction of a second and then gradually over a few seconds returns to the normal background rate of impulses. But these are not the only effects. In the *receptive field* of the retina around the ganglion cell, which increases its firing from the effect of the light stimulus, other ganglion cells are completely inhibited and stop firing altogether. When the light stimulus ceases, these neighboring cells begin firing again, at first at an above normal rate for a fraction of a second before returning to the regular background rate. This lateral inhibition is probably produced by the horizontal cells and the amacrine cells as well (Figure 8–2). This process of lateral inhibition serves to enhance contrast of the visual signal by maintaining sharp boundaries between excited and nonexcited areas of the retina.

Even this abbreviated account of the structure of the human eye brings out its enormous complexity. Those readers who desire greater details may refer to Hubel's (1963) article on the visual cortex, a recent article by Hubel and Wiesel (1979) on the processing of sensory information in the brain by studies of the primary visual cortex, a work on the nervous system by Guyton (1976) and a recent comprehensive and readable text on sensation and perception by Coren, Porac and Ward (1979), among others. In these sections, we shall concern ourselves with only those aspects of the visual system and its functioning that relate to the psychology of reading.

The brief description of the structure of the eye may be summarized by noting the route taken by light energy from the outside environment before it stimulates the retina and the subsequent passage of impulses through the different neural layers. Light passes through the transparent cornea, the aqueous humor (a fluid), the lens, the vitreous humor (a fluid) and falls upon the receptor cells of the retina. The light energy is then transformed into a chemical change in these cells, and this photochemical reaction produces, in turn, changes in the electrical potentials of their membranes. Impulses pass to interconnecting neurons. Thus the features of the light energy are coded into patterns of neural impulses in the optic nerve. It should be noted that the coding of light energy into patterns of nerve impulses may take place at various levels in the system. Clearly, some of the coding must take place already in the retina itself. For example, even for peripheral vision there must be considerable compression of visual data when the ratio of receptors to ganglion cells is 100 : 1. Overall, the 130 million receptors in the retina are handled by less than one million fibers in the optic nerve.

Visual Pathways

The neural pathways from the eyes to the brain are represented in Figure 8–3. In order to understand the reading process fully, we need to know the structure of the eye and also what happens "between the eye and the brain."

The retina in each eye has half-retinas or hemiretinas: the *left hemiretinas* and *right hemiretinas.* From both eyes for humans, about half the optic nerve fibers cross at the *optic chiasm* to pass to the opposite hemisphere of the brain while the remaining half continue to the same side in the brain. This process is known as *decussation.* For lower animals (e.g. birds), the optic nerve from the right eye crosses completely to the left side of the head and vice versa. Because of the split of the channels in humans, destruction of an optic nerve after decussation would result in blindness in one-half of each eye about a vertical axis through each fovea. Thus, the brain connections are quite different in the case of "eyedness" from what they are in "handedness." Handedness is associated with "dominance" of the opposite cerebral hemisphere. But in eyedness the "dominant" eye has afferent connections to both hemispheres.

FIGURE 8–3. Simplified representation of visual pathways.

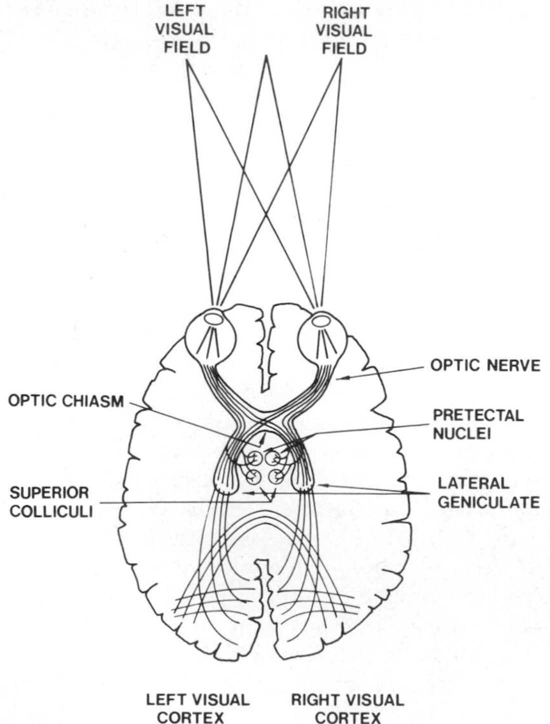

The anatomy in the eyes of humans is such that impulses from the left hemiretina of both eyes travel to the left hemisphere, and the impulses from the two right hemiretinas go to the right hemisphere. The left hemiretina is responsible for the right field of vision, and the right hemiretina for the left field of vision. At the cortical level, objects to the right of the fixation point in the environment are eventually represented in the left hemisphere, and similarly objects in the left field of vision are primarily represented in the right hemisphere. Obviously, in normal seeing behavior there is considerable overlap as most objects in the environment produce responses in both hemiretinas of both eyes. Both hemispheres therefore receive data on the same object. Furthermore, in each eye there is some mixing of the fibers of the two hemiretinas on their borderline.

Beyond the chiasm the pathways are called "optic tracts." Most of these nerve fibers are adjacent to the *lateral geniculate nuclei* of the thalamus, but some go to the *pretectal nuclei* and the *superior colliculi.* Each lateral geniculate has six layers and the fibers from the contralateral eye and from the ipsilateral eye project to different layers. Thus there is little significant interaction between them there, although there is some inhibitory interaction. The majority of the neurons of the lateral geniculate nuclei project on to the *primary visual cortex* (known also as *"Brodmann's Area 17"* or the *striate area*). There is a very close similarity between the signals recorded in these relay neurons and those recorded in the retina's ganglion cells. Thus the data from the optic nerve seem to be relayed to the primary visual cortex with little alteration. But one difference has been detected. The boundaries between excited and nonexcited areas have been sharpened, indicating that further lateral inhibition probably takes place in the lateral geniculate body.

It is in the primary visual cortex that the main convergence occurs between the data from corresponding hemiretinas in the two eyes, the right halves of both retinas connecting with the right cortex and the two left halves connecting with the left cortex. The complex relationship between the stimulation of cells in the eye and neural activity in the brain is discussed in a technical source on psychobiology of sensory coding edited by Uttal (1972). It is clear the layman's notion of "a picture" in the brain is quite erroneous. As Gregory (1972, p. 7) remarks, "There is a temptation, which must be avoided, to say that the eyes produce pictures in the brain. . . . What the eyes do is to feed the brain with information coded into neural activity—chains of electrical impulses—which by their code and the patterns of brain activity, represents objects. . . . When we look at something, the pattern of neural activity represents the object and to the brain *is* the object. No internal picture is involved." The nature of this neural coding of information picked up by the retinas has been a challenging problem and continues to exercise the research ingenuity of neurophysiologists.

The experiments in artificial electrical stimulation of the exposed cortex of humans conducted by Penfield and Roberts (1959) provided some evidence for spatial representation of the retinas upon the visual cortex. When the primary visual cortex was stimulated, the patient would report "seeing" a flash of light. If the electrodes were moved slightly, the next stimulation was "seen" as a flash in a correspondingly different location in the visual field known as the "visual projection area." But as the point of cortical stimulation was moved away from this central region, patients reported more complex sensations. At first, they "saw" flashing, swirling, colored shapes. Then, still further out in the visual association areas, the artificial stimulation produced hallucinations of complete scenes. The general conclusion drawn from these investigations has been that the primary visual cortex relays the information it receives to other areas of the cortex where "perceptual judgment" takes place.

Further understanding of the nature of the neural code for visual stimuli has been provided by experiments on animals. Hubel and Wiesel (1962) implanted microelectrodes to record nerve impulses in individual cells in the visual cortex of cats, whose visual system is much like that of humans. These researchers confirmed the Penfield and Roberts finding of a link between a position on the retina and a specific point in the cortex. They also made the discovery that the cell in the cortex fires only if a particular pattern appears in the "receptive field" of the corresponding part of the retina. Subsequently the same results were obtained in monkeys. When cortical cells are mapped in this way, the "on" and "off" regions found in ganglion and geniculate cells are not present. The particular pattern is a line or edge at a certain angle. Some cells fire only for horizontal edges, others only for vertical, and still others only for diagonal lines or complex stimuli such as moving shapes. These features seem to be some of the basic units of the neural code for visual stimuli, but other elements have been reported in a number of experiments on cats and monkeys (reviewed by Milner (1970) and Blakemore (1973) in relevant chapters). Hubel and Wiesel thus infer a neuronal "wiring" diagram as follows. The visual system is organized in a hierarchical fashion with lines of retinal ganglion cells feeding into single cortical simple cells via the geniculate nuclei. The serial processing is thus from ganglion cell to *simple cell* to *complex cell* and then *hypercomplex cell.* Simple cells generally do not respond to diffuse illumination; complex cells have larger receptive fields than simple cells; and hypercomplex cells respond not only to the orientation of movement of the stimulus, but also to the length, the width or selective features of shape. There are also cells of *spatial frequencies* which respond to changes in luminance in adjacent areas in the visual field. Recently, the *inferotemporal cortex,* which is located in the temporal lobes of the brain, has been shown to be involved in the visual process of monkeys (Coren, Porac, and Ward, 1979). Thus, the Hubel and Wiesel early discoveries show that we see the world as we do because our visual system is "wired" in a certain way and that functional change can be brought on by the environment. Their feature detection theory emphasizes the importance of the single cell as the functional unit in perception and the serial nature of processing from ganglion cell to simple cell to complex cell to hypercomplex cell and (in the monkey at least) to the inferotemporal cortex.

Recent data, however, seem to suggest the feature detection and extraction theory may only apply to the initial processing of visual information. It is possible that complex cells respond more quickly to stimuli than do simple cells, a fact difficult to explain with the hierarchical ordering of simple to complex and hypercomplex cells (Coren, Porac, and Ward, 1979). John (1972) has criticized the feature detection theory on methodological grounds for recording only from single cells and thus missing intercellular relations or ensembles of cells. There is also some doubt that neural processing begun in Brodmann's Area 17 progresses serially on through Areas 18 and 19. To Pribram (1971), for example, a great deal of perceptual processing is parallel and cells are organized as cortical columns acting as feature analyzers which are laid down holographically. Recently, Henry (1977) has offered a reassessment of the hierarchical explanation of cortical function.

Evidence from other kinds of research also provides more insight into the feature detection theory. Injury to the human primary visual cortex, such as may be caused by penetration of bullet wounds, for example, causes a precise blind spot which can be detected and mapped by careful testing, but the patients are often not quite aware that they have any blindness at all. More extensive brain injury causes a generalized loss of perceptual ability such as poor visual memory or less appreciation of spatial relationships, but practically never does it cause the patient to fail to recognize one kind of object rather than another. For example, in *visual agnosia,* the disturbance of seeing following brain injury is usually in the parieto-occipital area. Williams (1970) notes: "The defect consists not so much in non-awareness of the stimuli as in misrecognition of their meaning." Also, "it is more usual for a patient who shows difficulty in recognizing one type of stimulus to have difficulty in recognizing others, too" (p. 58). We should, however, note that the absence of a class or type of feature analyzers may not preclude the recognition of an object. Alternatively, the class of feature analyzers may be present in more than one area of the cortex and a circumscribed wound may not destroy all the available analyzers.

Experimental destruction of the visual cortex in subhuman species also has produced surprising results. For example, Humphrey (1972) reported that a monkey with no visual cortex reached for small objects quite accurately and easily moved through a series of obstacles. Milner (1970, p. 201) reviewed a number of other experiments and concluded that the primary visual cortex "appears to be essential for form vision, but a small remnant can function quite effectively for that purpose, a phenomenon that has provided a longstanding puzzle for physiological theorists interested in vision. The visual cortex is probably not necessary for making discriminations based upon total luminous flux at the eye or upon movement or amount of contour of the stimulus, at least in some animals." We should, however, bear in mind the global tests used, as more refined tests may indicate significant deficits not apparent with crude tests.

There are puzzling findings also about the *visual association areas,* whose location is mapped in Figure 7–5. This shows the *primary visual area* as *Brodmann's Area 17,* or *striate cortex,* and the *visual association Areas 18 and 19.* These latter two areas—Areas 18 and 19—have available binocular information from both halves of the visual field, although binocular neurons have also been found in Area 17. Neuroanatomical research shows Areas 18 and 19 to be the chief destination of fibers leaving Area 17, and postmortem examinations of human patients have generally indicated that damage to Areas 18 and 19 is an important cause of visual impairments. However, as was noted earlier, brain damage is rarely confined to the area of theoretical interest. It is more diffuse and damage to Areas 18 and 19 is usually accompanied by subcortical damage. Chow (1952) ablated Areas 18 and 19 in monkeys and found no permanent deficit in form discrimination. Even though critics of this experiment may be justified in doubting if all connections from Area 17 to Areas 18 and 19 were cut because of the inaccessibility of some of them in surgery, yet with such massive ablation it seems difficult to maintain that these neural connections play a major role in vision. We may, however, again note the negative findings may be attributed to the crudeness of the test. If binocular vision is tested after ablation of Areas 18 and 19, it is likely that significant visual impairment will result.

There is also some evidence of the effects of temporal lobe damage on seeing. Direct neural connections from Area 17 to the temporal lobe are almost, if not totally, nonexistent. Yet there is a considerable amount of evidence both from surgical experiments on animals and from studies of human patients undergoing surgical treatment or accidentally brain-damaged that the temporal lobe is more important for vision than Areas 18 and 19 which have many connections to Area 17. The effects of damage to the temporal lobe in humans are particularly interesting to the student of the psychology of reading. They produce a condition of visual agnosia in which patients have no loss of visual sensation, yet what they see has no meaning for them. Serious visual agnosia is more frequently associated with vascular accidents in the occipital lobe, but some cases of temporal lobe lesions have been reported, and Milner (1970, pp. 202–205) reviews a number of experiments on animals. He concludes from the human research that damage in the right temporal lobe "often results in mild but detectable deficits of visual learning and of comprehension of visually presented material like cartoons. Left temporal damage has little effect upon visual performance, except in the case of verbal material; no cases of bilateral temporal lesions confined to the neocortex have been reported" (p. 208). This human defect of visual agnosia is similar to the "blindness" found in monkeys whose inferotemporal cortex is affected. The animals could reach for and pick up objects but could not identify them by sight.

Even the classical mapping of the brain, conventionally used for descriptive purposes as it is in this text by Brodmann's Areas, is in doubt. Brodmann (1909) classified the areas mainly on the basis of size and shape of nerve cells and fiber bundles. More recently, Zeki (1970) has been tracing degenerating nerve fibers from tiny areas of damage in the monkey's cortex. He has already found ten more different visual areas than the three or four usually mapped in Brodmann's system.

Earlier in this description of the neural system for seeing, it was mentioned that fibers carrying information from the retina do not go only to the lateral geniculate nuclei and thence to the primary visual cortex. Some have their destinations elsewhere, including the superior colliculi which are, among other things, reflex centers for the visual system. The evidence from experiments on animals in which the visual cortex has been removed suggests that the superior colliculi allow some kind of vision to be retained. Blakemore (1973) reviews this evidence and notes two possible speculative explanations regarding the normal function of the superior colliculi in seeing: (1) "Cells in the colliculus detect the presence of novel objects in the periphery of the visual field and automatically produce eye movements to look at them," or (2) "the colliculus may be involved in determining whether objects are important and speeding up the eye movement if necessary" (p. 677). Blakemore notes that there may be "two visual systems in the brain: the 'where' system in the colliculus and the 'what' system in the cortex." The superior colliculi are generally considered to mediate "visual grasp" (visual orientation) responses.

Another kind of "where" information needs to be considered also—the spatial relations between several objects seen at the same moment. This problem is usually treated under the theme of "depth perception" and will not be dealt with here.

The theme of this book permits only a brief expedition into these regions of the neurology and physiology of vision, but these glimpses do provide a clear picture of its state of knowledge—much complexity, rather like a jungle whose charting has only just begun. The simple brain maps of the past have long since proved as illusory as the ancient maps of the world.

Eye Movements in Reading

Seeing is an active process. There is much active neural information processing even before the signal leaves the retina. This active searching behavior of human vision is repeatedly emphasized. One important aspect of this activity is eye movement, which also is a subject of special concern to students of the psychology of reading. However, before they can consider the specific problem of eye movements in reading, it is essential to understand the basic capabilities of the eyes for movement and how these are controlled in the physiological structure of the nervous system. Two kinds of movement have importance for the act of reading: first, actual movements of the eyeballs; second, changes in the accommodation size of the pupil of the eye.

Movements of the eyeball are controlled by three distinct pairs of muscles shown in Figure 8–4: (1) the *medial and lateral recti* contract re-

FIGURE 8–4. The extraocular muscles and their nerve pathways.

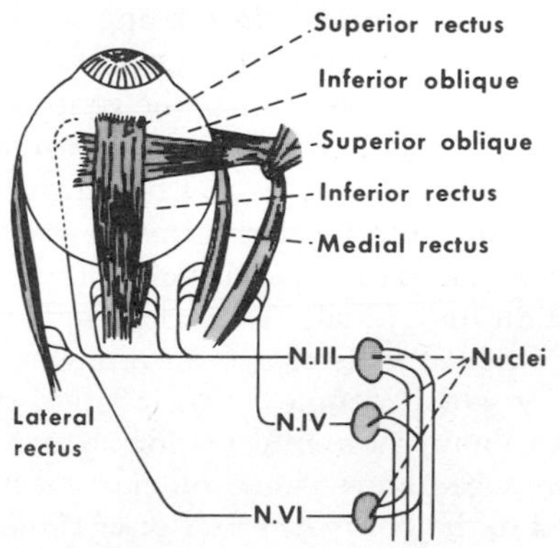

ciprocally to produce side-to-side movement; (2) the *superior and inferior recti* contract reciprocally to produce up-and-down movements; (3) the *inferior and superior oblique muscles* serve chiefly to rotate the eyeballs in such a way that the visual fields maintain an upright position when the head is tilted towards the shoulders. Each of these three sets of muscles is controlled by nerve connections which act reciprocally to cause one muscle of the pair to relax while the other contracts. The nerve pathways controlling these muscles are shown also in Figure 8–4. They are the third, fourth, and sixth cranial nerves which have their respective nuclei in the brain stem.

These nuclei are controlled by complex interconnections with other parts of the brain and certain principles are clear. For example, *conjugate movement* of the eyes—that is, movement of both eyes in the same direction—is a response to sensory information from the retinas. This illustrates the typical active, searching behavior of seeing. It is a constant combination of incoming visual data, their analysis, and hunting for more data, what Gregory refers to as the brain's "groping towards organizing the sensory data into objects" (p. 8), and "a dynamic searching for the best interpretation of the available data" of the "visual Gestalt" (p. 11). For example, an object is registered on the periphery of the field of vision; this information is received in the cortex, and the appropriate nuclei in the brain stem receive impulses that produce eye movements that bring the object onto the fovea. This is the normal relationship between eye movements and seeing. Eye movements are part of the person's active searching for more information. Eye movements are the servants of vision—not its masters. Eye movements of reading are not specific to reading. They are the application of general eye movement abilities to the task of reading.

Fixations of the eyes in reading similarly are not specific to reading. Fixations in reading occur as a result of the application of the general fixation processes of vision to the task of reading. For skilled readers, the average fixation duration is about 200 to 250 milliseconds (msec.) ± 20 msec. but there is a great deal of variability between and within individuals. These fixation processes, like all other aspects of eye movements, are the means by which people fix their vision on some object to obtain more information about it. There are two quite different neurological mechanisms involved in the control of fixations: (1) the *voluntary fixation mechanism* which is used to move one's eyes at will to seek out something upon which one desires to fix one's vision; (2) the *involuntary fixation mechanism* which automatically locks the eyes on the object when it has been found. These two mechanisms are controlled by different areas of the cortex. Impulses from an area in the frontal eye fields (Brodmann's Area 8) control the voluntary searching movement, and the automatic "locking" mechanism has its control center in the eye fields of the occipital cortex (mainly Area 19).

What is experienced as the "locking" of vision on an object is in reality not so simple, because actually the eyes are imperceptibly in continuous movement. There are three categories of involuntary movements of the eyes: (1) slight *tremors* occurring at a rate of from 30 to 150 per second, (2) a *slow drift* of the eyeballs, (3) sudden *flicks* occurring every second or so. These movements have the effect of moving the point of stimulation across the receptors in the retina. When a light stimulus has become fixed on the fovea (the center of greatest visual acuity), the tremors cause the stimulus to move back and forth across the cone cells, and the slow drift also causes a slow movement of the stimulus across the cones. When the stimulus approaches the edge of the fovea, the sudden flick brings the stimulus back in the direction of the center of the fovea. These movements of the eye have the function of preventing the image from fading. Milner has reviewed the research on the perceptual effects of these movements and concludes "that the signal from the retina is drastically reduced if the receptors are prevented from frequently crossing the contours between light and dark." Thus, "the image on the retina must be moved to a different set of receptors every second or so, in order to provide the optimum signal to the rest of the visual system" (p. 190). The research of Ditchburn, Fender, and Mayne (1959) found that tremors are not very effective in preventing fading, whereas flicks are. These flicking movements are automatic and are controlled by the involuntary fixation mechanism during the process of maintaining fixation on an object.

The so-called "voluntary" searching movements of the other neurological mechanism also are in the nature of flicks. Indeed they have been labeled *saccadic* movements, from the old French word *saccade* meaning the flick of a sail. Saccadic eye movements are the rapid conjugate movements by which we change fixation from one point to another voluntarily with "seeing" actually impaired (but not blinded as usually thought) during the saccadic trajectory. Saccadic movements include the "jump and rest" fixation movements observed in scanning a visual scene or reading. The duration of a saccadic eye movement varies from 30 to 120 msec. and this is a function of the distance covered. The purpose of the saccadic eye movement system appears to be fixation of the image of the target on the fovea, the high-acuity region of the retina. In reading, it is estimated that saccades take up about 10 per cent of the reading time and the average saccadic extent is about 2° of visual angle across the foveal region (Rayner, 1978a). It is further observed that the eye movements in reading take on a similar form to the eye movements in other kinds of visual search behavior. This indicates that *reading is active searching,* in which the movements of the eyes serve the purpose of locating appropriate data to increase available information.

Perceptual Span in Reading

Very early in the study of the psychology of reading, Dodge (1907) noted that *peripheral vision* plays an important role in reading. When the eye fixates on an area of the line of print, a segment of only about seven to ten letter spaces is covered by the area of fairly clear vision in and around the fovea. But, in addition and at the same time, there is some less distinct vision to the left and right of the fixated area. Dodge showed that in reading English these indistinct images to the right of the area of fixation help readers to begin to forecast what they will see after they make the next saccadic eye movement to the next fixation. Tinker (1965, p. 72) states that this hazy peripheral vision "yields premonitions of coming words and phrases as well as stimulates meaning premonitions. That is, word forms indistinctly seen in peripheral vision begin the perceptual process much in advance of direct vision." In another pioneer investigation in this field, Hamilton (1907) presented a line of print in a *tachistoscope*—an apparatus used in the psychological laboratory for controlling the length of exposure of an object and its illumination. She flashed the printed words for such a brief amount of time that the reader could make only one fixation. The subjects were instructed to try to read as far as possible to the right and to guess the words which they would see indistinctly. The guesses were not merely random but typically approximated the words that had been displayed in the tachistoscope. It must, however, be pointed out that the use of a cognitive "map" or Hochberg's (1970) *cognitive search guidance* in addition to peripheral vision is more characteristic of practiced readers. They sample text materials and have learned to respond to the features seen in clear foveal vision by anticipating a new word or phrase. They also make more use of peripheral information and are likely to be more impeded than beginning readers when peripheral information is reduced, such as in deleting the space between words.

The extent of peripheral vision would be expected to influence the total amount of print that can be seen in a single fixation of the eyes. This amount is variously termed the *visual span, perceptual span,* or *span of apprehension* and this span is related to cognitive processing in reading. The perceptual span can be measured by testing how much of a printed message can be seen in a single tachistoscopic exposure, though this span could be greater or smaller than in a normal fixation in everyday reading behavior. Greater because of the isolated presentation of stimulus materials and smaller because of lack of redundancy as found in actual reading. *Recognition span* is computed by measuring the number of fixations made by the reader in reading a passage and then dividing the total number of words in the passage by the number of fixations made in reading it. All words in this measure are recognized or understood, thus it is applied at a rather high level of reading skill and not at the initial stages of learning to read. But Taylor (1957) asserts that a narrow span of recognition makes it difficult for the child to look ahead for the next words beyond the present focus. However, in the more primitive difficulties of severely disabled readers neither the span of recognition nor the visual span seems likely to be important. As Vernon (1957, p. 123) noted: "Narrowness of perceptual span cannot be supposed to limit the reading capacity of a child who stumbles through print, one word at a time." Thus it may not be surprising that Rizzo (1939) obtained only a low correlation between span of recognition and reading achievement in 310 children between the ages of seven and seventeen. However, Rizzo found that the poorest readers had particularly narrow recognition spans, and concluded that narrow span was a contributory cause of their reading disability. But the causal connection could have been in the reverse direction, and Vernon's point makes Rizzo's conclusion seem improbable. A more ecologically valid technique involves monitoring readers' eye position while they read text displayed on a cathode-ray tube (CRT) controlled by a computer (see Rayner, 1977; Rayner and McConkie, 1977). Rayner and McConkie concluded that readers obtain different types of information from different regions within the perceptual span during a fixation in reading. They suggested that information on the fovea is processed for semantic content and information on parafoveal vision is processed for gross featural information.

The recognition span measure is tied to the measure of fixations in reading, since one must measure the number of fixations in order to determine the divisor in the formula for the total number of words recognized in a passage. But fixations are the outcome of eye movements. Hence the problem of limited peripheral vision may be related to *abnormal eye movements.* The physiological conditions mentioned earlier—damage to the foveas of both eyes, vestibular damage, and cerebella damage—are all very rare and no evidence has been reported regarding their influence on reading. Earlier (and misguided) thinking led to attempts being made to improve reading ability by training subjects to make more appropriate eye movements. For example, Taylor (1937) developed the *metron-o-scope,* an instrument which exposes words and phrases in sequence at a speed which can be adjusted to compel the reader to process these chunks of reading material at a regular speed. Another example was Sievers' and Brown's (1946) *Manual for Improving Your Eye Movements in Reading.* However, the efficacy of all these ocular trainings has yet to be proven. Freeman (1920) in his description of a case history of severe reading disability noted very irregular and uncoordinated eye movements during attempts to read. Gray (1921, 1922) and Hincks (1926) also found abnormal eye movements in the reading of their reading disability cases. All of these authors observed that eye movements became more orderly and efficient, when the reading disability was more or less overcome through regular remedial teaching.

Morgan (1939) put forward the hypothesis that there are individual differences in eye movement ability which are determined by heredity. He obtained data on the eye movements, IQ, reading age, grade position, and socioeconomic status of 35 pairs of identical twins and compared them with similar data on 33 pairs of fraternal twins and 40 pairs of unrelated children. His results showed a correlation of from .66 to .72 between the eye movement scores of the identical twins, but only from .24 to .53 for the fraternal twins, and .04 to .24 for the unrelated pairs. Morse's (1951) study of the eye movements in reading of 54 fifth grade pupils and 54 seventh grade pupils seems supportive of Morgan's position. There was little relation between the relative difficulty of the reading materials at the two grade levels and eye movements. Instead, eye movements seemed to be due more to inter- and intra-individual differences in the children.

However, there is much more research evidence that the relationship between eye movements and reading ability has a different explanation. Most studies, unlike that of Morse, have found that eye movement patterns are determined directly by the difficulty of the material being read. For example, Ledbetter (1947) investigated the eye movements of 60 eleventh grade pupils when tested with five passages of 300 words on a variety of topics. The eye movements were clearly determined by the nature of the reading material. Evidence that fixation duration is affected by the processing demands of reading materials was found also by Tinker (1951) and Abrams and Zuber (1972). Tinker's (1965, p. 107) own extensive research on eye movement behavior in reading and his review of all the work in this field led him to conclude that "in practically all cases faulty eye movements are merely symptoms rather than causes of poor reading."

Eye Movements Reflecting Cognitive and Linguistic Processing

Traditional studies of eye movements and reading have been more concerned with the oculomotor aspects of processing. This is reflected in studies of fixation durations, regressions and magnitudes of saccades within the framework of little cognitive or stimulus control of eye movements. More recently, there is a shift from the oculomotor aspect of processing to the information processing of text materials (Gaarder, 1970; Hochberg, 1970; Part I "Eye Movements in Search and Reading" in Kolers, Wrolstad, and Bouma, 1979; McConkie and Rayner, 1976a, 1976b, Part VI and Part VII "The Role of Eye Movements in Reading" in Monty and Senders, 1976; Rayner, 1977, 1978a, 1978b; Rayner and McConkie, 1977; Wanat, 1971, 1976a, 1976b). While eye movements are under oculomotor control, there is a great deal of variability in saccadic lengths and fixation durations according to the skill of the reader and the demand of the task. The locus of control of eye movements in reading is well discussed by Haber (1976) and Rayner (1978a). Along with this emphasis on cognitive processing, there have also been technological advances in eye movement recording methods, such as the use of on-line computers to experimentally manipulate parafoveal information to determine how far specific cues in the periphery are processed in a single fixation (McConkie and Rayner, 1976b; Rayner, 1977, 1978b). Young and Sheena (1975) have provided in a technical paper a comprehensive survey of most of the known eye movement recording techniques including electro-oculography, corneal reflection, tracking of the limbus (position of the iris-scleral boundary), pupil and eyelid, and contact lens method. The same authors have analyzed different types of eye movements and suggest that in work with children a system with minimal subject training and one amenable to analysis should be used. A brief account of the Young and Sheena full technical report is provided by Young (1976).

Current work on eye movements in reading from the information processing perspective has been critically reviewed by Shebilske (1975). He found evidence that both duration of fixation and spacing of saccades are influenced by processing time, although it is difficult to say what recognition processes are mainly responsible. He suggested interfixation distance (average number of fixations excluding regression divided by the total number of words in a passage) seems to be influenced by processing considerations rather than by oculomotor factors. Skilled readers not only rely on visual information for primary recognition, but also make use of redundant nonvisual information such as orthographic, syntactic and semantic rules. Shebilske further found partial support for Hochberg's (1970) peripheral search guidance hypothesis that peripheral information guides eye movements for gross physical cues, such as blank spaces, which can be used quite apart from meaning extraction. In addition to the Shebilske review, chapters in *Eye Movements and Psychological Processes* edited by Monty and Senders (1976) have discussed the role of eye movements in reading. In a recent comprehensive review Rayner (1978a) has emphasized eye movements in reading as a specific example of the more general phenomenon of cognitive processing. He has also discussed the basic topics of perceptual span, eye guidance, saccadic movements, fixation durations as they relate to reading and has presented data from on-line computer displays to show the role of eye movements in cognitive and linguistic processing.

The other current development is a number of works relating eye movements to explicit linguistic variables (see Gibson and Levin, 1975; Rayner, 1977, 1978a, 1978b; Wanat, 1971, 1976a, 1976b). Some of these studies can be traced to eye-voice span (EVS) studies, which have a long history in reading research. The eye-voice span is the distance, usually measured in words, that the eyes are ahead of the voice. A consistent finding of EVS investigations is that EVS increases with age and is affected by the difficulty of the reading material (shorter EVS for more difficult texts). The effect of text on word perception and as a source of partial information for the reader has been explored by the Cornell Project Literacy group (see Gibson and Levin, 1975). Wanat (1971) carried out a careful study of eye movements of adult readers as they processed sentences differing in grammatical structure, the subjects being those on which the Cornell group had EVS data. Wanat found a reasonable match between the EVS findings and the pattern of eye movements and that readers selectively allocate their visual attention to different sentence areas. For example, they took more time in the area of the main verb of the sentence and they read active sentences more smoothly (with fewer and briefer forward fixations and less regressions) than they read simple passive sentences. This finding that the main verb in simple active sentences received longer fixation durations than other parts of the sentence is also confirmed by Rayner (1977). Wanat (1976a, 1976b) summarizes some of the findings of his research program this way:

> A sentence type which is less structurally predictable requires more visual attention. A sentence's immediate constituent analysis affects the way the reader's visual attention is distributed across sentence. Varying the structural predictability of items inserted into the same immediate constituent framework affects the amount of visual attention required. Differences in the kinds of linguistic cues (i.e. content words versus function words) to the same underlying sentence relations affect the reader's allocation of visual attention. Differences in the immediate constituent analysis of sentences affect forward scanning, while differences in the structural predictability of items within a given immediate constituent framework affect re-

> gressive scanning. Oral reading requires more visual attention than the silent reading of the same type of materials, and linguistic factors affecting the reader's allocation of visual attention may behave differently in oral reading than they do in silent reading (1976a, p. 133).

Predictability here refers to both the sentence level and the word level. At the sentence level a right embedding sentence is more predictable than a left embedding one and requires less visual attention. At the word level, agent-included passive (e.g. "The letter was brought by the man") differs in predictability from agent-deleted passive (e.g. "The letter was brought to the man"). Wanat suggests the "line-of-sight" approach has raised some interesting questions on the role of grammatical structure and other linguistic variables "behind the eye." Mackworth (1977) has recently demonstrated the usefulness of line of sight fixations in the study of reading and reading difficulties. Those children who experience difficulty in processing the printed word show prolonged eye fixations, which indicate difficulties with cognitive strategies. Poor readers are likely stimulus-bound as shown by their inefficiency in visually linking words, while good readers are sensitive to context and can predict what will come next. Thus, teaching must be done from the cognitive end, according to Mackworth, rather than training these children to move their eyes faster. Serious investigations have confirmed Tinker's (1958) finding that eye movement training does no more than well-motivated reading practice even though these training programs may reduce the number of eye movement fixations and regressions (Levy-Schoen and O'Regan, 1979).

Thus there is considerable evidence converging on the cognitive and linguistic processing of eye movements in reading. This aspect of information seeking is further stressed by Kolers (1973c, 1976). Drawing on empirical work of eye movements of students reading and of speed readers, he showed that reading print need not be serial as usually supposed. On the other hand, reading pictures need not be holistic or simultaneous, as Kolers illustrated from the studies by Yarbus (1967) of people's eye movements while looking at objects or pictures. Kolers emphasized that in reading print and pictures there is a marked similarity in the acquisition of information from a series of eye fixations. In reading text, subjects look for and are sensitive to certain syntactic, semantic relationships holding the sentence together, albeit this performance is not conscious. In reading pictures, the spatial relations or structural details connecting the objects are examined. Thus reading print is more constrained by the rules of syntax and semantics, while reading nonprint is affected by the richness (e.g. contour, motion in a picture) and alternative possible interpretations of pictures. Gould (1976) has discussed four factors important in fixation-integration in reading pictures: peripheral vision, efference copies, short-term memory and knowledge of the world. The implication that Kolers drew from these and his own studies is that, in reading, written words are both pictorial or graphemic displays and also linguistic displays. Hence children "might profitably be taught something about the idea of representation itself and something about the role of symbols in that process" (p. 39). One component of learning to read is thus seen as symbol manipulating activity. This is consonant with the current concept of language awareness (see Chapter 6 for discussion).

Reading Behind the Eyes

It may seem common sense that seeing is an important ability in reading. Is not the ability to see clearly the letters and words on the printed page an essential prerequisite of the reading act? Many reading teachers have believed the answer to be "yes," and therefore they have concentrated efforts on improving children's so-called visual perception for readiness to learn to read. But the act of reading requires more than the child's natural seeing abilities. To investigate this issue, we must study the research on the question—how is children's reading affected by defects in their physiological apparatus for seeing? We must form a judgment of the relative importance of the visual component of reading in comparison with other psychological aspects of the process.

Because the physiological apparatus for seeing is so complex and elaborate, the possibilities for many types of malfunction exist. For example, defects may occur in the optical system of the eyes, the muscle apparatus for their movement, or in the neurological systems of the brain. Such defects may arise from congenital malformations, accidental injuries or diseases. The question of the effect of visual defects on the child's ability to learn to read requires us to consider what happens when the degree of clear visual acuity deteriorates from normal seeing to mild weaknesses or blurring, and then to the more severe conditions of partially seeing, and finally to the severest defects classified as blindness. In addition, certain special kinds of seeing behavior need to be considered, such as seeing objects correctly orientated and seeing a series of objects in their correct serial order. These visual perception abilities may become defective also.

Visual Acuity and Reading

Visual acuity refers to the sharpness or clearness with which a person sees an object. The common means of testing acuity is the *Snellen Chart* (Farrell, 1958). Charts in current use have rows of capital letters, each row getting progressively smaller from the top to the bottom. The top row letters are actually each about 3.5 inches square. This size was chosen so that at a distance of 200 feet the letters would appear to be the same size as normal print when viewed from 20 feet—the standard testing distance. At a distance of 20 feet, light from the letters tends to be parallel, and the normal eye can focus on them while the eye muscles are at rest. The basis of measurement is what a person with normal vision can see at a particular distance. Thus when individuals have normal vision they are said to have "20/20" vision, the first figure being the test distance, and the second figure denoting the normal distance at which those symbols can be recognized. An example of abnormal vision would be a person with "20/70" vision because at the 20 feet test distance, he or she could see only what would be clearly recognizable by a normal person standing 70 feet away from the chart.

In the hands of a properly trained specialist in a well-equipped modern clinic, with controlled conditions of distance and lighting and good rapport with the patient, measurement is accurate. (However, this type of measure is often used with less carefully controlled conditions.) The modern eye clinic also has a number of other tests at its disposal for determining visual impairments and their treatment.

It has been customary to use the basic Snellen Chart rating as a measure of visual acuity. Thus, better than 20/70 vision is said to be "correctable"; between about 20/70 and 20/200 is said to constitute "partially seeing"; and below 20/200 is said to be "blindness." However, as will be shown later, such mechanical classification fails to take into account other factors which may influence the individual's ability to cope with his/her condition.

A relationship between visual acuity and the ability to read printed words is indicated by the results of Jones' (1961) survey of the 14,125 children registered as legally blind in the United States. The frequency of reading materials printed in ink fell steadily from 80 per cent of children with 20/200 vision to 30 per cent of those with 2/200 vision and finally to zero at total blindness. But even at the level of the more severe deficiencies in visual acuity some children were reported to be reading print only. Furthermore, another kind of reading increased with the severity of the handicap; this was the reading of braille. Thus even total blindness does not rule out the possibility of learning to read. It can be accomplished in another sensory mode.

Braille reading *is reading*. It is the interpretation of symbols in the tactile mode. In place of printed shapes on paper which the readers examine with their eyes, the readers of braille symbols examine raised dots with their fingers. Braille has 63 possible combinations, each consisting of a braille cell of six raised dots. Almost any literary, numerical, scientific, or musical material can be presented in braille. It is as complete a reading and writing medium as the alphabetic system of ink printing. According to Ashcroft (1960), the skills of reading and writing braille have the same basis as the skills of reading and writing visible symbols expressing and communicating meaning. Ashcroft (1967) even went so far as to assert that "the same principles which apply to teaching and learning reading and writing in print apply to developing these skills in braille." He observed that in "the primary grades the braille reading pupil is not at a great disadvantage in speed as compared to his sighted peer" (p. 448). It is only later when silent reading becomes regular that the braille reader is at a disadvantage in speed of reading, and this is probably due, at least in part, to the sighted reader's ability to make use of redundancy in text materials.

From this consideration of the reading behavior of blind people, it is clear that obtaining and conveying meanings through a system of arbitrary symbols (as in braille) representing language does not depend only on the ability to see. Even if the eyes are unable to search out meaning from a visual code, a parallel search for meaning can be made in a tactual code. Thus the essence of the psychological processes of reading and learning to read cannot be in visual ability itself. This fact is of very great importance when considering theories of reading and learning to read.

Ocular Defects

Although the severest form of visual handicap, blindness, does not prevent the child from becoming a reader, provided that we recognize that print reading is only one special kind—albeit the most common kind—of reading, it is useful to study how deficiencies of sight affect visual reading.

The simplest and best-understood deficiencies of seeing are those produced by structural anomalies of the eyes and the muscles controlling their movements. First, there are three common *refractive defects*, which can arise from injuries, disease, or hereditary abnormalities in the lens or the cornea. Figure 8–5 illustrates *emmetropia* (normal vision) where parallel light rays focus on the retina and also these three refractive difficulties. These difficulties relate to the process of visual accommodation by which the lens of the eye adjusts to focus light from a near object on the retina for near-point viewing and to the maintenance of proper convergence alignment of the muscles of the eye so that the images in the two eyes are formed on corresponding retinal points.

FIGURE 8–5. Parallel light rays focus on the retina in emmetropia (normal vision), behind the retina in hypermetropia, in front of the retina in myopia and as a refractive error in astigmatism.

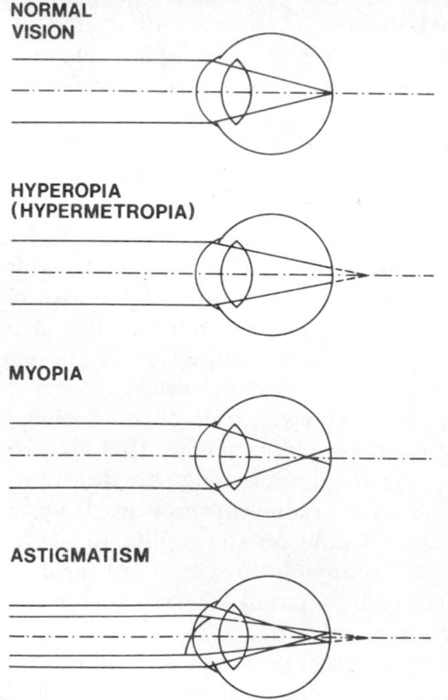

If the eyeball is too short, the lens, even when completely relaxed, fails to focus light reflected from near objects onto the retina. The focus would be behind the retina. Because of the lack of refractive power of the eye when this inappropriate focusing occurs, a condition of farsightedness or *hyperopia* (also *hypermetropia*) occurs. If accommodation is adequate, hyperopia can be corrected with convex lenses which produce a sharply focused image, but this treatment may cause discomfort, especially if the user is engaged in near vision for lengthy periods of time, as, for example, when reading. Hyperopic persons have reasonably good distant vision with a small amount of accommodation, but must exert a greater amount of accommodation when reading. The greater amount of accommodation, while enabling them to read, may result in visual symptoms of blurred vision, inability to concentrate, and general discomfort. These symptoms in turn will deter the hyperopic person from reading and therefore the visual accommodation process should be investigated.

In *myopia* or nearsightedness, the eyeball is too long from front to back, so that the point of focus falls inappropriately in front of the retina. The myopic reader may try to overcome this difficulty by bringing the book abnormally close to the eyes. Correction for myopia is made by use of concave lenses that diverge the light rays for proper focus on the retina.

The other prevalent refractive anomaly is *astigmatism*. This condition is caused by irregular or unequal curvature in one or more dimensions of the cornea or lens. Uncorrected astigmatism results in visual blur and distortion, which may become limiting factors in reading proficiency. Correction can be made with an appropriate lens of opposite power difference—usually a cylindrical lens.

Another common ocular defect is lack of appropriate coordination of the two eyes in binocular vision. In *strabismus* or "squinting" the eyes aim in different directions because of the muscular imbalance caused by incoordination of the muscles of the two eyeballs. In one common form the person affected uses either eye for fixation and in another form one eye is used for fixation while the other eye is not used. Treatment may be the prescription of spectacles, eye exercises—orthoptics—or surgery. If the deviant eye is not trained to fixate, the vision fails and *amblyopia* or "lazy eye" results. The basis for this condition is as complex as that for strabismus and seems to be age-dependent. Amblyopia usually occurs in the first six to seven years of life and early treatment is imperative. There is now some evidence that amblyopia can be corrected in late childhood. If there is a critical period for treatment, it is the first two years of life for children who have suffered oculomotor and visuosensory embarrassment in infancy (see Young and Lindsley, 1970).

In connection with strabismus several other technical terms need to be known to follow the research literature: *heterophoria* is the general term for any tendency for the eyes to deviate from normal coordination of direction; *exophoria* is deviation outward; *esophoria* is inward deviation; *hyperphoria* is the focusing of one eye higher than the other. *Aniseikonia* is experienced as a difference in the size of the images from the two eyes and is caused mainly by an inequality in their respective refractions.

Serious defects of vision and visual impairment are produced by deformity or opacity in the refractive media of the eye. For example, *cataract* is a frequent problem of this kind. Opaque areas form in the normally transparent lens of the eye. Cataract is more common in older people. In children an operation called *discission* is performed to break up these opaque formations. Powerful convex lenses are then required to replace the lens function of the eye. Congenital cataract prevents the normal development of foveal fixation and acuity. Fortunately, this condition is rare in humans.

Another ocular defect which may affect reading behavior is *limited peripheral vision.* This is tested by having the person fix the eye on a central point. Then the peripheral vision is evaluated in terms of degrees of visual angle in which a standard visual stimulus can be seen on a black background when viewed from about 39 inches. A person is considered legally blind when, among other things, the widest angle in which this stimulus can be seen subtends an arc of 20 degrees or less in the better eye with correction.

In the act of reading itself, poor readers show *abnormal eye movements* in making fixations on the printed page. These are the function of the voluntary fixation mechanism referred to earlier in this chapter. However, there is no evidence that they are caused by abnormalities in the eye muscles or their neural control systems. Rare conditions of damage to both foveas, damage to the vestibular apparatuses for maintaining balance, or severe damage to the deep nuclei of the cerebellum can cause abnormal eye movements (see Guyton, 1976).

In addition to the specific ocular defects, we should also watch for near *visual discomfort, fatigue, or stress.* Bedwell (1972) found that, even if any basic errors have been properly corrected, "with most young patients discomfort appears to be due to a difficulty in maintaining a comfortable accommodation/convergence relationship. If this convergence cannot be comfortably maintained, so that images fall on customarily used retinal correspondence areas, the eye(s) may tend to diverge relative to the fixation point. The image(s) will then fall outside these corresponding areas." The result is "binocular confusion" (presumably diplopia or double vision) unless "the patient makes an effort to contain his convergence within preexisting limits." The ensuing discomfort may become chronic and cause a more permanent habit of eccentric fixation of one of the eyes in binocular vision. Near visual discomfort arising from such difficulties in binocular coordination often appears to cause the eyes to become *photophobic*—oversensitive to light. Such patients prefer only just enough light to manage their seeing task and express dislike of bright illumination.

Finally, it needs to be mentioned that in some *psychosomatic disorders,* such as migraine, there is an increased probability of visual discomfort.

Defective Vision and Reading Ability

A rather large volume of research has been conducted to investigate the relationship between ocular defects and either reading ability or the ability to learn to read. These studies may be classified according to the types of defects described in the previous section, although some investigators have worked on a more general basis.

As might be anticipated, poor reading has been found to be more closely related to farsightedness than to nearsightedness. Eames (1935) compared one hundred cases of reading disability with 143 unselected children. Fifty-three per cent of the former as compared with 27.6 per cent of the latter were placed in the category of *hyperopia.* In a later study on a larger scale, Eames (1948) found 43 per cent of one thousand poor readers (median age 9.5 years) were hyperopic, whereas only 12 per cent of his 150 control subjects had this particular ocular difficulty. Similarly, Farris

(1936) and Taylor (1937) found farsightedness to be more common among poor readers than among good readers. Robinson (1946) too noted many cases of hyperopia in her group of disabled readers. In a later study comparing 63 good with 60 poor readers, Robinson (1968) found greater amounts of hyperopia in the latter group.

Starnes (1969) using optometric examination techniques on third grade pupils found that good readers tended to be nearsighted whereas poor readers tended to be farsighted. Similarly, Wold (1969) found that above-average achievers tended toward *myopia* but below-average pupils usually showed normal refraction or mild hyperopia. Eames (1935), and Witty and Kopel (1936a, 1936c) all found no difference between samples of good and poor readers. Farris, in the study referred to in the previous paragraph, suggested that myopia was associated with above-average achievement in reading. This is confirmed by the two studies of Starnes and of Wold. Eberl (1953) concluded that myopia may be an adaptation to the demands for close vision made in learning to read, and that children who fail to develop myopia may avoid reading as an uncomfortable visual activity.

Several studies indicated that the blurred vision of astigmatism causes reading difficulties. Thus Eames (1932) found a significantly higher degree of astigmatism among 114 clinical cases of reading disability than among 146 unselected pupils. Gates (1947) cited evidence of about twice as many cases of astigmatism among poor readers as among normal readers at the age of 8.5 years. Wolfe (1941) and Schonell (1942) both found more astigmatism in disabled readers than in control groups of normal readers. Betts (1934) considered astigmatism a serious handicap in learning to read. However, in several of these studies involving the visual conditions of disabled and nondisabled readers, there was no indication if the refractive errors were corrected or uncorrected at the time of the studies. If the refractive anomalies were corrected, the subjects would have emmetropic or normal vision. It would thus be difficult to pinpoint the role of astigmatism in reading proficiency and reading disability.

Turning to the binocular difficulties, *strabismus* has been found to occur frequently among reading disability cases. Two-thirds of Robinson's (1946) thirty cases of severe reading disability, and 45 per cent of 133 reading disability cases studied by Park (1948) had problems of muscular imbalance. Schonell (1942) too found a higher frequency of strabismus among disabled readers than among normal readers. Spache (1940) found an abnormally greater degree of muscular imbalance in his group of fifty cases of reading disability. In Eames' (1932, 1935) investigations referred to earlier, 44 per cent of the reading disability cases, but only 18 per cent of the unselected pupils, had fusion difficulties. However, three more recent investigations all found no significant differences between good and poor readers with regard to the heterophorias. This was the result in the two studies of Starnes and of Wold referred to earlier in this section. The third study is that of Gruber (1962) who found that there was no correlation between reading ability in poor readers, and binocular coordination, eye muscle balance, and fusion ability. Cogan and Wurster (1970, p. 75) reported from their ophthalmological studies that "contrary to popular belief, strabismus itself causes little impairment of a child's visual functions" and that the condition "has no bearing on dyslexia." However, they went on to stress the importance of preventing amblyopia before the vision in the strabismus eye is irretrievably lost. Harris and Sipay (1975) note the lack of agreement among research findings on the significance of visual defects for reading but state their belief "that positive findings outweigh negative findings" (p. 283).

Exophoria was found to be associated with reading disability in several earlier investigations. Eames' (1932, 1935, 1948) studies all found a greater incidence of exophoria among his reading disability cases than among the unselected controls. For example, in the 1935 investigation of one thousand poor readers, 63 per cent were exophoric as compared with 16.7 of the controls. Park and Burri (1943a) obtained a correlation of −.631 between exophoria ratings and reading achievement in a study of 225 children, aged six to thirteen years. Park's (1948) study, mentioned in the previous paragraph, found exophoria especially associated with reading disability in his 133 cases. Spache's (1940) study of muscular imbalance in reading disability particularly stressed exophoria as a problem. Empirical evidence on the incidence of *esophoria* and *hyperphoria* in reading disability is lacking.

Aniseikonia has been linked with reading disability in two studies. Dearborn and Anderson (1938) compared one hundred severely retarded readers with one hundred control cases, and found aniseikonia in 51 per cent of the former but in only 23 per cent of the latter. Spache's (1940) study cited in the two preceding paragraphs noted aniseikonia as a problem among his fifty reading disability cases. But Rosenbloom (1968) reported contrary findings from his comparison of the incidence of aniseikonia exhibited by forty retarded readers in grades four to eight with its incidence in a control group of average readers matched for size, age, and intelligence. There was no significant difference in the incidence of one per cent or more of aniseikonia.

The effect of *cataract* and other causes of severe deficiencies of visual acuity has been indicated in the previous section on *measurement of visual acuity*. There is a steady drop in the proportion of visual readers with the falling off of acuity (Jones, 1961). But it is interesting to note that "visual reading" is only completely nonexistent in the totally blind. Right up almost until the point where this condition is reached even with extremely limited sight, some legally blind children were reported to be reading visually in Jones' survey.

The connection between *near visual discomfort, fatigue, or stress* and reading disability has been shown in several investigations. Thus Clark (1935, 1936) found that exophoria in young adults is associated with abnormally greater divergent eye movements during reading. Normal readers tend to overconverge their eyes when they move them from the end of a line to the start of the next line and have to compensate for this by making divergent movements. Clark's subjects with a high degree of exophoria made this same compensatory movement but in an exaggerated form. Vernon (1957) comments: "Such excessive movement might be very fatiguing" (p. 121). Vernon notes also more generally that any of the deficiencies of binocular coordination may have caused "excessive fatigue which impeded practice and further progress" in learning to read. The negative effect of visual stress or fatigue on learning to read has been shown to be important by the results of two recent studies. When Schubert and Walton (1968) experimentally induced astigmatism in adult subjects, they reported, not only that their reading materials were blurred and distorted, but also that they wanted to stop reading and felt weary and exhausted. More than two-thirds of the subjects reported these experiences and a similar proportion reported experiencing headaches as a result of the experiment.

There is, however, no *direct* research evidence on the relationship between *psychosomatic disorders,* visual defects, and reading disability, but from what is known more generally of the effects of psychosomatic disorders on behavior it seems reasonable to believe that the stress caused by anomalies of the visual apparatus would be heightened in psychosomatic problems.

Several investigators have studied the effects of ocular deficiencies in general. Park and Burri (1943b) believed that many children of the age when school begins have immature visual systems. They found 50 per cent of a group of six- to seven-year-olds had visual acuity below 20/20. Furthermore, the eleven nonreaders in this group had especially poor visual acuity. On the other hand, in their other report (Park and Burri, 1943a), a correlation of only .24 was found between acuity scores and reading scores. Russell (1943) noted that coordination of accommodation and binocular fusion is still developing in the primary years of schooling, and Robinson (1953a) cited research evidence that these visual abilities continue to improve between ages nine and twelve. Vernon (1957) suggests that the causal connection between poor reading ability and slow development of this visual coordination ability may be in the opposite direction:

> Thus it is possible that poor reading may retard the attainment of this coordination, and that incoordination is the effect rather than the cause of poor reading (p. 121).

Most of the more general surveys of visual deficiencies in good and poor readers seem to provide negative or inconclusive evidence. For example, Fendrick (1935) found that 44 per cent of poor readers as compared with 30 per cent of good readers had visual deficiencies as revealed by an optometrist's examination. Farris, in the research referred to earlier in this chapter, found 44 per cent of 1,685 seventh grade pupils tested had eye defects. Relating reading proficiency to various ocular defects in 188 fourth grade pupils, Edson, Bond, and Cook (1953) found no significant connection. In 16 of Robinson's (1946) 22 reading disability cases there were ocular defects, but she concluded that in only 11 of these 16 cases did the visual anomaly contribute to the reading disability. In summary, while many reading disability cases have ocular defects, many do not, and in those that have such defects it is not always the cause of their difficulty. Furthermore, ocular defects are common among normal readers. For example, Money (1966, p. 33) notes: "There are many cases, nonetheless, of severe optic or ocular defect in which reading progress is average or even superior."

Some authors have reviewed relevant research and come to the conclusion that, contrary to what might seem common sense, defective vision is not the cause of reading disability. Thus Vernon (1971, p. 37) concludes: "There is no reliable evidence that such disorders affect the capacity to learn to read . . . , provided that the child is not suffering from such gross refractive errors or diseases of the eye that he is unable to see the print." However, this conclusion may need to be qualified by a point made by Bond and Tinker (1973) in their review of the research findings in this area. They comment that, although ocular defects do not clearly differentiate poor and good readers, good vision still could be an important factor in reading because it can never be known if average readers with visual deficiency would not have been better readers if they had had normal vision.

Returning to the more specific ocular defects, it seems possible to make some judgment of the probability of the effect of each on reading disability according to the weight of evidence from the different investigations. Myopia appears to have a facilitating influence. Hyperopia, astigmatism, cataract and other serious disorders affecting the clarity of reception in the retina all seem to be hazardous for learning to read. Though discomfort, stress, or fatigue of the visual mechanism are sometimes implicated, the relationship is not clearcut. It is, however, likely that the child's motivation to learn to read and to practice reading will become negative as a result of these unpleasant experiences.

Limited peripheral vision and abnormal eye movements have not been found to cause reading disability. On the contrary, it is poor reading ability which seems to produce inefficient eye movements and a narrow span of recognition.

The evidence on strabismus and aniseikonia is conflicting, and as causes of reading disability the verdict seems to be "not proven." More research is required to settle the question of their effects.

Complicating Factors

One reason why the research evidence on the effects of ocular deficiencies on reading development has often been inconclusive may be the confounding influence of other variables.

Research methods often have limitations which may produce misleading or conflicting data in this field. Two particular problems should be mentioned: the sampling of behavior in vision tests, and the sampling of the population being evaluated. With regard to the first problem, Ashcroft (1967) points out that clinical tests of vision "are usually only representative of a very small sampling of the visual behavior of individuals in very special circumstances. The complex physical and psychological characteristics of vision make ineffective for many purposes characterization of total visual efficiency solely in terms of such a short clinical test, no matter how carefully it might be obtained" (p. 417). This limitation is particularly relevant in connection with other confounding variables to be mentioned below. As regards the second methodological problem, many of the studies do not specify how the samples of subjects were obtained or how representative they may be of "poor" or "good" readers. This problem is especially important at the secondary and tertiary levels of education, by which time many pupils have dropped out of school. It is possible that severe reading disability cases and/or serious ocular handicaps are underrepresented in these studies.

Ashcroft's insightful observation suggests that more refined techniques are needed to sample the vast, complex visual behavior. This is well borne out by Bedwell and associates (Bedwell, 1972, 1978; Bedwell, Grant and McKeown, 1980) in a series of studies of visual function under static and dynamic viewing conditions in infant, junior and middle school children in England. Some of Bedwell's clinical and experimental studies confirm earlier findings, while others reveal more relevant data are needed. As an example, Bedwell et al. point out that the conventional Snellen chart only tests static viewing. In their study of binocular function and reading in thirteen-year-old readers, they added dynamic viewing conditions of "range of fusion" or the degree of out-of-alignment that the eyes could contain while looking at an object and yet maintain binocular vision. This was done with two photographs superimposed on each other and viewed through polarized goggles. The polarized vectograms can assess the ability of the eyes to diverge or converge relative to each other and still see a single image in depth or stereoscopically. Results showed that neither suppression nor the ability to maintain fusion on convergence or divergence is significantly related to reading performance, thus confirming earlier results. But dynamic viewing both during changing fixation and actual reading revealed that such aspects as eye coordination on looking from left to right; unequal eye movements while reading; divergence, overconvergence, indecision in eye control and compensatory head movements during reading all have an effect on reading performance. While these findings need to be substantiated, they point to the fact that any simple or static study of vision must be supplemented with much fuller investigation.

Identification of ocular handicapped children is also a source of unreliability. Sometimes defects go undetected and it is not known that the child has a visual problem. This is more of a general practical problem than one affecting the research reviewed in this chapter, most of which employed sophisticated technical equipment. However, failure in detecting visual handicaps may influence teachers' judgments based on classroom experience.

Detection is important in preventing reading difficulties. For example, if an ocular defect is corrected before reading instruction begins there is less danger of visual discomfort, stress, or fatigue becoming associated with the activity of reading. A program of vision screening tests together with a careful watch for physical and behavioral symptoms of eye problems will help to uncover cases of visual defects. These children should then be followed up with clinical diagnosis and appropriate remedial measures. But screening tests should not be given exaggerated importance in teachers' and parents' thinking about visual difficulties. Of equal importance is the "continuous observation for behavioral and physical signs and symptoms of potential difficulty" (Ashcroft, 1967, p. 421). He lists the following behavioral symptoms: reading material being held or placed abnormally close to or distant from the eyes; walking overcautiously, faltering or stumbling; bumping into objects not in the direct line of vision; rubbing the eyes; frowning or distorting the face when looking; shutting or covering one eye; unusual posture of the head; oversensitivity to light; difficulty in telling colors or estimating distance. Physical signs mentioned by Ashcroft include: red-rimmed, encrusted, or swollen eyelids; frequent styes; watery, red, or bloodshot eyes; dizziness, headache, eye pains, nausea; double vision or blurring; and the eyelids itching or burning.

Clinical screening tests can be given by teachers or school nurses. The schools' screening equipment includes the Snellen Chart test of visual acuity, the *Eames Eye Test* and a telebinocular and slides from the *Keystone Visual Survey Test* for detecting nearsightedness, farsightedness, astigmatism, muscular imbalance, and lack of near- and far-point fusion. In doubtful cases, specialists should be consulted and their advice be followed through. Strang and Bracken (1957) list practical questions the reading teacher should have in mind at this stage: Does the specialist need to examine the student again? Have glasses been prescribed? Should they be worn all the time or only for close work or viewing at a distance? Does the pupil need special lighting and, if so, what kind? Should he/she be seated in a particular part of the classroom, for instance, at a certain distance from the blackboard? Does he/she need special equipment, for instance, larger print?

Definitions of visual handicaps differ. Unsatisfactory definitions of visual handicaps cause problems for the schools as well as for researchers. For example, for legal purposes the *blind* are defined as persons having 20/200 vision or less in the better eye with the best possible correction or with a field of vision restricted to an angle subtending an arc of 20 degrees or less. The *partially seeing* are defined traditionally as persons with visual acuity between 20/200 and 20/70 in the better eye with the best possible correction or who may benefit from special educational facilities. In the past, it was conventional to follow these definitions and to think in terms of teaching reading in braille to blind children and in enlarged print to partially seeing children as defined by the acuity tests. However, educators who have specialized in teaching children with such severe visual handicaps have found these definitions unsatisfactory for practical purposes. Ashcroft (1967) gives the reason: "While persons may be described as having the same vision characteristics in terms of clinical vision tests, their visual behavior may vary widely because of physical, psychological, social and environmental factors." For instance, Jones' survey referred to earlier in this chapter found many legally "blind" children reading print only. These considerations led the American Foundation for the Blind (1957) to propose new definitions based on behavior rather than on clinical measures of visual acuity. For example, the blind child is one who can and should use the braille system, and the partially seeing child is one who needs special educational provisions but can use print to read. This problem of defining visual handicaps for practical educational purposes alerts us to the parallel theoretical problem in the psychology of reading—the way in which other psychological variables interact with visual defects in determining the outcome in learning to read.

Intelligence, or the child's general scholastic aptitude or ability to learn, reason, and solve problems is one such variable. It is difficult to assess the intelligence of visually impaired children as it is necessary to use verbal tests or performance tests in the tactile and/or kinesthetic mode. The general consensus of research findings is that there is no special relationship between visual handicap and general intelligence. For instance, Hayes (1950) found that the range of intelligence among blind children is similar to the normal range. Kirk (1972, p. 309) states that ". . . in spite of the deprivation of experience through limited or no vision, the visually handicapped child shows approximately the same distribution of scores on intellectual tasks as the seeing child, when tests like auditory-vocal or haptic-motor channels of communication are used." Thus in the design of research the difficulty of assessing intelligence in visually handicapped pupils should be noted. For practical educational purposes the teacher needs to consider the child's general intellectual ability in planning the instruction of children with defective vision.

Personality factors also affect the extent to which a child may overcome a visual defect. This variable is described vividly by Ashcroft (1967, p. 413): "Blindness and lesser visual impairments such as those of the partially seeing may have dramatically varying effects on children. To many younger people, extreme loss of vision, even total blindness, seems to be merely an incidental inconvenience. To others, lesser losses seem almost catastrophic in their effects on education, normal activity, and adjustment." Research on the relationship between visual anomalies and reading disability rarely take account of individual differences in personality, emotional development, or motivation. In some of the studies with small samples in particular, the results may be confounded by such variables. In general, there seems to be no systematic relationship between visual handicap and maladjustment, although there is some evidence that children with severe visual deficiencies are more likely to develop negative self-images (Murphy, 1960). However, Cowen, Underburg, Verrillo, and Benham (1961) found no differences in adjustment in their comparison of blind and normally seeing children. But partially seeing children showed greater adjustment difficulties than the blind. Similar consideration of the effects of such interacting variables needs to be given in evaluating the findings of research on the reading abilities of children with less severe correctable ocular defects.

Summary

In summary, defective abilities in seeing have much less effect on learning to read than one might anticipate from a commonsense view of what reading behavior constitutes. Many people with defective vision become average or superior readers of print. Furthermore, all reading does not depend on the eyes. Blind people can read braille with their fingers. Telegraph operators can read the Morse code with their ears. Of course, blurring of the reception of the signal through deficiencies in any of the neurophysiological systems involved is likely to cause difficulty in seeing the print, or feeling the braille, or hearing the "dots and dashes," but the essence of reading is not in these peripheral reception mechanisms. This must be sought elsewhere.

In this chapter and the preceding ones, the roles of hearing, speaking, and seeing in learning to read have been examined. The focus has been on the neurology and physiology of these functions in what traditionally has been thought of as "sensation" in these areas. But the neurophysiological foundations of sensation continue to develop through maturation and learning in the preschool and school years. The ability to see printed words depends to some extent on the forms and patterns of the physical stimuli. The visual input during visual perception is not continuous but is interrupted by eye jumps several times a second. This visual information is divided into chunks which are integrated spatio-temporally in the brain—the sequencing of visual data in space and auditory data in time. The ability with which the child can encode visually perceived symbols such as letters or words into some auditory form is of relevance to the reading process. In the next chapter these visual and phonological coding processes in accessing word meaning will be discussed.

Perceptual and Coding Processes

CHAPTER

9

In the preceding chapters we have discussed the physiological foundations of hearing, speaking, and seeing and the relationship of these activities to reading. We have sketched the functional organization of the brain for processing and interpreting language. Relevant literature shows that neither the narrow *localization* theory nor the view of the brain as a single undifferentiated entity helps us to understand reading processes. Various sensory activities often have a cognitive basis. Take, for example, visual perception. The line between problem solving and visual processing of stimuli is hard to draw. Processes such as selection of relevant information, hypothesis testing and creative synthesis would have to be invoked to explain even simple perceptual processes. The perceiver plays an active role in integrating incoming information and in its interpretation.

The Information Processing Approach to Word Perception

The interplay of seeing, speaking, and listening is highlighted as a backdrop to this chapter. The focus here is on word perception as a basic subskill system in the learning to read process. The actual way in which we recognize words is not well understood because the whole process of pattern recognition is highly complex. How do we, for example, recognize and discriminate shapes like triangles, circles, letters and words? Somehow, we learn to recognize and discriminate shapes even if they are rotated to different orientations. We recognize and discriminate, with varying degrees of accuracy, letters and words. With regard to the young child's perception, Vernon (1957, p. 16) stated that "there seems to be general agreement: that he does not observe, or only observes and remembers with difficulty, the orientation of shapes. . . ." One piece of evidence for this was the kind of errors children make in learning to read. In reading, children are faced with the problem of responding differentially to different kinds of lines—horizontal, vertical, curved and others. And yet they manage. Vernon (1957, p. 27) further suggested that if children are given sufficient time to perceive the letters carefully they can differentiate them "with fair accuracy by the age of 6–7 years." She went on to say that "the real difficulty lies in remembering which of the reversible letter shapes corresponds to which sound; and this difficulty persists up to 7–8 years, even in normal readers."

The broad area of pattern perception has long excited and puzzled psychologists and others. The specific aspect of letter and word recognition in young children is one that has interested both researchers and practitioners. For many years, work on perception and reading dealt more with the surface aspect of recognition and discrimination (e.g. so-called "reversal" errors). More current studies have related word perception directly to the extraction of meaning, which is the essence of reading. Modern research on getting meaning from printed words generally follows an information-processing model. It seems to be the Zeitgeist to compare higher mental processes, of which reading is one, to the working of the computer.

More than thirty years ago, Wiener (1948) saw striking parallels between the computer and the nervous system, such as the apparent similarity of neurons and relays. Up to a point, the brain–machine analogy is valid. Some of the all too well-known parallels include the ability for receiving and storing information and the capacity for solving problems. But there are also striking dissimilarities. For example, the high speed with which the computer, once programmed, can solve problems and its large memory load for storing information, far surpass those of the human. It can of course be said that since the efficient working of the machine depends ultimately on human ingenuity, the analogy should be from computer to human, and not the other way around. The oft-voiced opinion that a computer can do only what it is instructed to do by a specific program, and no more, is technically correct but misleading. The machine is capable of divergent thinking. The computer can be enabled to play a game of chess, and better than its programmer at that. The versatile General Problem Solver (GPS) devised by the Nobel Laureate and psychologist Herbert Simon and associates is known to solve a variety of logical problems including proofs in trigonometry (see Farnham-Diggory, 1972; Kessen and Kuhlman, 1962; Reddy and Newell, 1974). The protocols of the GPS of computer simulations of stages and sequences of human reasoning have shown the direction of the analogy is from machine to human.

There is another neglected point raised by Wiener (1948). Humans as processors normally retain their experiences, whereas it is possible to wipe the memory clean from a computer and reduce it to a tabula rasa. In an early key paper on computing machinery and intelligence, the English mathematician Turing (1950) approached the human–machine problem this way. He asked, "Could we envisage a situation such that we should not be able to tell the difference between the thinking of a man and a machine from the answers either gave us to our questions?"

The works of Farnham-Diggory (1972), Kessen and Kuhlman (1962) deal specifically with the child as an information processor within a developmental context. More recently, Farnham-Diggory (1978a) emphasizes the contribution of information-processing technology to research into reading acquisition. She discusses protocol analysis—the matching of sequential data emitted by a person to a theoretical simulation of the data. For example, the patterns of errors of word reading in poor readers can be reproduced in normal readers by manipulating experimental variables such as displacing the temporal order of letters and masking the exposure of individual letters of words. Farnham-Diggory also provides data on converging operations such as relating reading (generally grapheme to phoneme) and spelling (generally phoneme to grapheme) as an heuristic in understanding what goes on in the child's head when reading. Thus simulation by the computer can explicate the complex interactions of visual input, storage in short-term memory, retrieval from long-term memory, and the accessing of meaning, and can provide us with information on what goes on in reading. This is the third metaphor of Miller (1974) of procedures involved in using language.

An important note of caution about simulation studies that are conducted without a full knowledge of what is being simulated is sounded by Guthrie (1978a) in his discussion of Farnham-Diggory's work. Specifically, Guthrie points out that an adequate simulation of reading should have two features: (1) the components of the computer program should be the same as the components of human cognitive operations, and (2) the parameters that influence one should influence the other. Guthrie draws attention to the interrelatedness of the components of reading. Thus, to understand reading, one needs to know what happens to one component when another is increased or decreased in proficiency. An example is the interaction (not just the correlation) between decoding and comprehension in readers of varying reading proficiency.

The diverse but complementing views of Farnham-Diggory and Guthrie on information processing in reading acquisition may seem difficult for students of the psychology of reading to reconcile. This is because the child as an information processor has to work within the limits of his or her storing, processing, and retrieving capabilities to process a wealth of information. Simon (1972, p. 4) has pinpointed what is known of the important components or subsystems in processing information:

1. At the sensory end—the eyes and the ears—the detail of physiological mechanism determines, to a great extent, the ways in which information is processed. The sensory organs and their central connections form a complex interface between man and his environment.
2. As we move through perception to cognition, we find that central processes are less affected by detailed features of the system's construction, and seem to be shaped mainly by its broad architectural outlines and a few key parameters.
3. In describing this architecture, particularly as it affects development and learning processes, we

need to give special prominence to these features:

a. the short-term memory, limited in capacity to holding a few chunks;
b. The mechanisms of attention that determine what small fraction of the sensorily available information will be selected for central processing;
c. The long-term memory, potentially unlimited in capacity; probably organized in terms of quite general systems of associations and directed associations; slow to store new information;
d. Hemispheric specialization in long-term memory for storage of information relating to different modalities—visual and auditory, for example;
e. The control of behavior, including the internal behavior of thinking, by stored, learnable and modifiable, strategies or programs.

The above is quoted at some length because these very components and their interaction are basic to our understanding of the reading process. Also, such components as the memory system (e.g. working memory, semantic memory), attentional mechanisms and the use of differential strategies are the central concern of this chapter. To study how meaning is derived from words, we must deal with the related phases of acquisition, storage, and retrieval, or in the terminology of Wickelgren (1972) with coding, retrieval, and dynamics. Central in this trichotomy for our purpose is coding.

Coding Processes

Coding refers to the abstract, internal representation in memory of events and relations between events. It refers to the structure of memory, its components, and their organization into a system. Coding is thus concerned with the central question of "What is learned?"

The concept of coding was introduced by Miller (1956). He suggested that, when people are presented with information sets for retention, one way that they can facilitate their remembering is to recode subsets of more than one item into a single higher-order code. An illustration is the remembering of a string of binary digits in terms of pairs recoded into decimal digits. Thus the binary sequence of 01 00 10 11 could be reduced to 10 23 (the pair 00 being the decimal digit 0, 01 being 1, 10 being 2 and 11 being 3). This makes a saving of 50 per cent of the number of items that have to be held in memory storage. The subset of response items that are recoded into the same higher-order code is referred to as a *chunk*. Thus the first two binary digits in the above sequence together would form a chunk as they are represented in memory by the same code. The pair of decimal digits could be further recoded into a higher-order recoding scheme with the use of letters. For example, a 00 pair could be remembered as A, a 01 pair as B, a 02 pair as C and so on. In this way people may increase their immediate memory span for binary digits to facilitate their remembering. In a string of letters like MISHAP, the sequence could be organized into MI as one chunk, SH as another chunk, AP as a third chunk. Alternatively, the sequence could be organized as MIS, HAP and then these chunks could be further recoded into a higher-order code. Another example is in encoding a word like DRAINING. The principle of coding by letters or clusters of letters is illustrated in Figure 9–1. Clearly, the organization of a sequence of letters can be defined as the pattern of recoding.

This process of reorganizing or restructuring information, in whole or in part, is a matter of coding the information in a new form. Miller's work, referred to earlier, reminds us of the "restructuring" emphasis of the Field Theorists or Gestalt Psychologists. The difference is that these

Figure 9–1. Encoding of the word DRAINING.

theorists tended to discuss visual problems that can be presented in pictorial or diagrammatical forms. Thus they talked of "seeing," "visualizing," "form," "structure," "missing relations" and so on. Even in visual forms, patterns other than visual ones exist. Visual problems can also be recoded into words. Getting the solution into words can help us to: (1) verify it, (2) make it more precise, (3) use it for further thinking and (4) use it for communication with others. An example of the work of the Field Theorists who demonstrated the difference between memorizing and organizing was given by Katona (1940). Subjects were told that the U.S. federal expenditure in a certain year amounted to 5812151922.26 and they were asked to memorize this figure. On being tested a week later, they could remember the figure as being *about* 5.81 billions, but they could not recall the precise number. Another group of subjects was instructed to try to remember the following series—5–8–12–15–19–22–26. These subjects discovered that the difference between successive numbers is 3, 4, 3, 4, 3 and 4. By discovering this principle, they were able to remember the answer when asked a week later. The process of coding and recoding operates in our daily lives. We witness an event that we want to remember. We cannot recall all the details and, therefore, we select the information that is salient or critical, recode it in words and then try to remember the words.

Several tentative coding models of word perception in reading have been put forward (see Wathen-Dunn, 1967). Usually these models consider word perception to be a subset of pattern recognition and, as such, the models are more concerned with the contour or geometry of the stimulus. Earlier studies also considered a *template* hypothesis (see Selfridge and Neisser, 1960). In *template-matching,* when a previously perceived stimulus is recognized, it is supposed that it is identified by noting its congruence with a basic model held in memory. However, this hypothesis has been found to be inadequate to account for even simple recognition processes (see Neisser, 1967). A form can be recognized even in a new retinal position and despite its changes in size, shape, or rotations, despite the fact that these operations destroy the congruence necessary for recognition according to the template theory. More complex models have dealt with various specific features. The details of these features are complex: they might be letters, parts of letters, clusters of letters, or higher units. But specific features models also fall short of explaining the complexities of the reading process. Hence current models have sought to explain the nature of the *coding processes* involved in word recognition (see Singer and Ruddell, 1976). Also, current models increasingly insist that what the perceiver (the reader) already knows is an essential contribution to the reading process. Thus, the explicit stimulus represents only cues to the underlying semantic structures. According to this view, reading a word for meaning consists in extracting some form of information from signs and using this information to reach the word's entry in what is termed the *lexicon.*

Internal Lexicon and Lexical Access

The question of how words are read for meaning was often discussed in the past under the topic *vocabulary.* Children were said to "have" a word in their "vocabulary" if they "knew" it. Numerous studies based on this vague concept cluttered the literature of reading research and even resulted in such spurious claims as that Russian children were better served by their basal reading books because they contained a richer vocabulary of words that children "know" than did American basal readers. What "knowing" a word means was usually never discussed in these vocabulary studies—not even whether the word was known as an auditory stimulus or a visual one. The modern student of the psychology of reading can draw on the development of the disciplines of psychology and psycholinguistics. Their clearly defined, sensitively precise concepts and empirical data make it possible to study the problem of how a person reads for meaning in a more scientific manner.

One such central concept in word recognition is the *internal lexicon.* The concept of the internal lexicon or internal mental dictionary was proposed by Treisman (1960, 1961) and further developed by Oldfield (1966). The *lexicon* is defined as an abstract, associated network of information. In it, each event or concept has a unique internal representation. These internal representations have different degrees of association with one another, depending on how frequently they have been contiguously activated. Thus the lexicon consists of all the information that the reader has acquired about the words of his or her language. There are subsystems or *lexical entries* including specifications of the meaning of the word, of its pronunciation, and of its spelling. The successful operation on the part of the reader to reach the word's lexical entry is termed *lexical access* (see also Chapter 5 for a linguistic view of lexical representation). This access furnishes the reader with the meaning of the word since semantic information forms part of the word's lexical entry. Lexical entries of semantically related words are interdependent with facilitatory connections in the lexicon.

Forster (1976) has provided a discussion of lexical access based on the assumption that locating and retrieving information that we have stored in an internal mental dictionary is not unlike looking up a word in a printed dictionary. Forster points out that the lexicon has to be accessed under three different conditions: when we are reading, when we are listening, and when we are talking. (Writing is regarded as a different condition.) In reading, it is likely that lexical items are organized in a system that may be likened to pages of words of similar *orthographic* properties. In listening, the entries are more likely to be organized by *phonological* properties. In sentence production, it is probable that entries are organized by *syntactic* and *semantic* properties. As well as these three *access files* for orthographic, phonological, syntactic/semantic entries, there is a need for a *master file* both for economy and for coordination. The entry for a word in the master file contains all the information that we have about the word, whereas the entry for the same word in each of the access files simply contains a description of the stimulus features of that word (the *access code*) and a "pointer" to the relevant entry in the central, master file. Thus accessing the entry for a word involves "preparing a coded description of the target item (the stimulus word) and then searching through the access file, comparing the description of the target item with the access codes in each actual entry. When a sufficiently accurate match between these is obtained . . . the search terminates, the pointer specified in that entry is used to access the master file, and then a detailed comparison between the properties of the stimulus item and the properties of the master file must be made" (Forster, 1976, p. 268). Forster further extends access in sentences. He suggests that there are two possible access functions: one that makes a search on the basis of sensory functions and one that makes a search for semantic properties. It is likely that both sets are searched simultaneously and that the semantic search is the fastest.

Writing on access to the internal lexicon, Coltheart, Davelaar, Jonasson, and Besner (1977) point out that we need specific ideas about how a reader proceeds from the information that he or she extracts from a target stimulus word to the relevant internal lexical entry. They pose these two principal questions:

1. What is the access *code?*
2. What is the access *procedure?*

The first question pertains to the nature of the information extracted from a printed word for use in lexical access. The second question relates to the way in which the stimulus information is made use of in order to gain access to the appropriate lexical entry. Coltheart et al. claim that only the *lexical decision task* research method is suitable for investigating the above questions because:

> Tasks involving visual search, naming latency, same–different matching, and so on are . . . open to the objection that they are not necessarily relevant to the question of lexical access; any effect observed in such tasks may be nonlexical (it is possible to pronounce nonwords; therefore it is possible to pronounce words without necessarily using the lexicon) or postlexical (phonological codes can be generated as a consequence of locating a lexical entry) instead of lexical (Coltheart et al., 1977, p. 539).

Lexical decision tasks involving word/nonword discrimination overcome the above objections. Judging illegal nonwords like RZQ, PJK as not being English words does not involve consulting the internal lexicon. However, deciding if legal nonwords like SLINT, FON, PRONK are English words requires lexical access. Coltheart et al. acknowledge that there is a difference between the experimental situation of lexical decision tasks and the reading act. In the former, full analysis of the stimulus is needed to reach a decision with certainty (e.g., BR_BE could be BREBE, BRABE, BROBE, *BRIBE*, BRUBE). In everyday reading, *partial analysis* is often sufficient for the reader to decide that the word is BRIBE. This is aided also by the fact that reading usually involves only real words, whereas in experimental lexical decision tasks nonwords (legal and illegal) are used. Despite this difference, which is a quantitative one, there is no suggestion that qualitatively different access codes or procedures are used. Thus lexical decision tasks provide a suitable and viable means of studying the access code during normal reading.

From the above discussion, it is clear that lexical access events take place covertly. They are events that do not have any overt or observable behavioral component and cannot therefore be directly observable. But there is one property of mental events that can be studied directly, *while* the events are taking place. That is their duration. Reaction time (RT) measures in human information-processing studies have been used increasingly for this purpose.

Reaction time is usually defined as the duration or time interval that has elasped between the presentation of a stimulus to a subject and the subject's response. Operationally, this refers to the period between the *onset* of the stimulus presentation and the *initiation* of the subject's response. Thus reaction time measures avoid the arbitrary use of variables such as test scores as surrogates of some underlying construct for which they purport to measure. But there are definitional and methodological problems in the use of reaction time measures. Firstly, visual stimuli may be presented serially or simultaneously, whereas auditory stimuli (at least overtly observable ones) must necessarily be presented serially or successively. Secondly, the definition of onset of auditory stimuli is by no means straightforward because the beginning of phonation is not marked by a single event having a conspicuous acoustic correlate (see Leong, 1975a). This is of some importance because reaction times usually are concerned with short durations, quite often intervals of fractions of seconds. The instant of onset of an auditory stimulus has been described by Studdert-Kennedy and Shankweiler (1970) as the first excursions above noise level in an oscillographic record that is sustained and followed by clear periodicity.

Another problem with reaction time measures hinges on the assumption that the subject uses only the minimum time needed to produce the correct response. This problem relates to the speed-accuracy trade-off. It is difficult to know exactly what the *intention* of the subject is. In actual practice, it is likely that the speed-accuracy trade-off leads an individual to use a strategy of neither wasting time nor rushing the response. One way to ensure that the assumption is valid is to arbitrarily eliminate "too fast" or "too slow" responses and to work with only correct responses. Statistically, reaction time measures tend to be skewed in distribution and are loaded with outliers. This can probably be adjusted with different statistical transformations.

Of the several methods used in reaction time studies, the Additive Factor Method developed by S. Sternberg (1969) should be mentioned. This method is a set of converging operations (Garner, Hake, and Eriksen, 1956). These must include several conditions, none of which uniquely identifies the effect of the process under study, but when all are taken together they define such an effect. The Sternberg method attempts to identify processing stages from a pattern of data which result from a set of converging operations. The nature of the input and output of each stage is independent of underlying factors that influence its duration. It is the durations of these stages and the factors or factor sets affecting their durations that are the primary concern of the Additive Factor Method. The Sternberg model is outlined here as there are some recent studies based on this model, which are concerned with componential processes in reading. This aspect will be discussed in a section in the chapter on Reading Difficulties (Chapter 14).

The above discussion of the internal lexicon, lexical access, and the prevalent use of reaction time measures prepares us to examine those two important questions raised by Coltheart et al. (1977), as mentioned earlier. These questions deal with the *access code* or the nature of the information extracted from the printed word and the *access procedure* by which the internal representation is used to find the word's entry in the lexicon. Discussions of these questions usually revolve around three views: (1) that the access code during reading is phonological and indirect; (2) that the access code is visual and direct; and (3) that there are dual (parallel) phonological and visual codes. In the following sections these complementary views will be discussed and the relevant research literature will be reviewed in some detail because it is vital for the modern student of the psychology of reading to be conversant with this basic research on coding processes.

Phonological Coding

In his classic book, Huey (1908) devoted no less than two whole chapters to the "inner speech of reading." On the basis of evidence from experiments with adult readers he stated, "Although it is a foreshortened and incomplete speech in most of us . . . it is perfectly certain that the inner hearing or pronouncing, or both, of what is read, is a constituent part of reading . . ." (pp. 117–118). The terms *inner speech, silent speech, subvocalization, acoustic recoding, phonemic recoding* and *speech recoding* are sometimes used interchangeably and often not clarified.

Gibson and Levin (1975) use the term *subvocalization* for speech ranging from audible sound such as whispering to movements of speech musculature that can only be detected through the use of amplifying apparatus. They state, "The important point is that the reader normally does not want to make sounds, but at some levels he does" (p. 340). Thus subvocalization implies translation to sound or its surrogate. Goto (1968) uses the term *inner speech*. Rubenstein, Lewis and Rubenstein (1971b) and Meyer, Schvaneveldt and Ruddy (1974) have used the term *phonemic recoding*. They are inclined to agree that the nature of the code is unknown (i.e. whether it is auditory, articulatory or in terms of some abstract verbal system that may be neither auditory nor articulatory). Hence their use of the term phonemic recoding. Kleiman (1975, p. 323) uses *speech recoding* as a "generic term for the transformation of printed words into any type of speech based code, whether it be articulatory, acoustic, auditory imagery or a more abstract code." Whichever term is used, the central questions are: Does all reading involve speech, and does reading aloud merely add sound? Is there a direct visual access or do we have to say words, whether covertly or overtly in order to understand their meaning? In this and other places, we will use the term *phonological coding* in the same way as Kleiman uses "speech recoding" to encompass the generic transformation of printed words into some form of speech-based code.

Evidence for Phonological Coding

Work of Linguists

One source of support for the phonological coding in reading viewpoint is the logic of the structural linguists of the persuasion of Bloomfield (1942) and Fries (1963), who were among the early linguists to interest themselves in reading. In their work, they related the alphabet to the speech sound. For Bloomfield, the printed letter was equated with the speech sound to be spoken. For Fries, language itself is not meanings. His view was that a language is a code of signals. He suggested that "an alphabet is a set of graphic shapes that can represent the separate vowel and consonant phonemes of the language" (p. 156).

Another source of support for the phonological coding position is derived from the view that there is a common decoding mechanism for verbal material in both visual and auditory modalities. This view is implicit in the argument of N. Chomsky (1970), Chomsky and Halle (1968), that English orthography is a better fit to the phonological than to the phonetic level of the language. The speech-to-sound correspondences exploit the linguistic rules that show how the phonological representation of a morpheme is to be realized. Thus the regular plural morpheme /ṡ/ is written *s* even though this morpheme is phonetically [ez], [z], [s]. In the chapters on psycholinguistics and the English writing system (Chapter 5) and on language awareness (Chapter 6) we discussed the works of Bloomfield and Fries and Chomsky's theory that English orthography is a near-optimal system for representing the spoken language.

Electromyographic Studies

Edfeldt (1960), using needle electrodes inserted directly into the speech musculature, measured and recorded electrical activity in the speech muscles of the laryngeal area of university students who were reading easy and difficult passages, as well as texts physically clear and blurred. This procedure is known as the electromyographic technique (EMG). Edfeldt found that there was more electrical activity for difficult passages and more subvocalization for blurred passages than for clear ones. McGuigan (1967, 1970) has discussed his own EMG experiments on covert oral behavior during silent reading. The fact that silent reading is accompanied by electrical activity in muscles required in the production of speech sounds, though no oral speech is directly observable, is viewed as evidence for the occurrence of silent articulation of speech during silent reading. But it is not known whether silent speech, as measured by electrical activity in the speech muscles, necessarily accompanies phonemic or phonological recoding. Phonological recoding may occur as an auditory phenomenon and yet take place without measurable activity in the speech muscles.

Related studies use *suppression of vocalization*

and *feedback training.* An example of the first kind was an early investigation by Pintner (1913). He asked his subjects ($N = 2$) to count or to pronounce the syllables "la—la—la" while reading prose. This verbal accompaniment had little effect on the subjects' reading. Pintner concluded that his subjects did not require subvocalization for comprehension and that they could suppress vocalization. However, it is possible that phonemic coding would deter wandering thoughts and help the subject to concentrate, even though the rate of reading might be slowed. With this study, the small number of subjects and the lack of control should be noted, of course.

Hardyck, Petrinovich, and Ellsworth (1966) trained their college subjects to stop subvocalizing by giving them feedback on the activity of their own speech muscles. In a subsequent study, Hardyck and Petrinovich (1970) gave difficult and easy materials to their subjects to read with similar feedback training. They found that, when laryngeal activity was decreased with feedback training, comprehension of the difficult passage, but not the easy one, suffered. McGuigan (1971) found that feedback training given to subjects aged from seven to nineteen years helped to eliminate subvocalization with little loss of comprehension and an increase in reading speeds. However, the effect of feedback training was short-lived and subjects reverted to their pretraining level of vocalization when the feedback was omitted. These suppression and feedback studies show that subvocalization is *not necessary* for the reading of easy materials and that readers can be trained to give up subvocalization, at least for a while.

In their evaluation of EMG and related studies, Gibson and Levin (1975) state that the body of research is neutral regarding the effect of subvocalization in reading. Teachers of reading seem to be divided in their opinions on the question. Some think that subvocalization is an extension of reading aloud and that it indicates that the child is thinking about reading (see Sokolov, 1972). Conrad (1972, p. 209) suggests that there seems to be an aggregate of evidence that reading is accompanied by articulation. He raises a pertinent point: "What is far from proved is that articulation is *necessarily* involved in silent reading." Even if articulation is absent, it does not preclude the use of speech imagery. On the other hand, there is no conclusive evidence that EMG responses are related to the actual words used. In rapid reading it is likely that articulation occurs only at eye fixations and also at those points where enough words can be seen and articulated for adequate comprehension.

Short-Term Memory Studies

Conrad (1962, 1964) found that, when subjects were shown six letters, for example, *B, C, P, T, V, F,* one at a time, and then were required to write them down, the errors they made were similar to the kinds of errors made in identifying the names of the letters heard in the context of "white noise" (a random mixture of many frequencies, heard as a hissing or roaring sound). In these studies, Conrad was more interested in the decay of memory processes. Conrad (1972) took a less direct way in approaching the problem of whether or not comprehension in silent reading depends on an articulatory input. His rationale was that, if subjects use a phonological code, then silent reading of phonologically similar items would lead to impairment in recall.

Some experiments by Corcoran (1966, 1967) are cited by Conrad as evidence for his acoustic scanning theory. In Corcoran's first experiment, adult subjects were required to mark rapidly all the letters *e* in a passage of printed prose. Corcoran (1966) found that the subjects missed "silent *e*'s" nearly four times as often as "pronounced *e*'s." In Corcoran's (1967) second experiment, adult subjects had to mark as quickly as possible places in a printed prose passage where letters were missing. He found that the "absent silent *e*" went undetected significantly more frequently than an "absent pronounced *e*." Corcoran (1967) concluded: "The importance of the acoustic factor in visual scanning is clearly demonstrated in the present experiment. Apparently, both the detection of an existing *e* and the detection of its absence are determined in part by whether or not the *e* is pronounced. Thus the process of acoustic scanning and the consideration of evidence from the two modalities would appear to be a phenomenon of some generality" (p. 851). Conrad (1972) commented: "Here is an almost pure visual task, but using verbal material, and with neither a need to memorize nor to comprehend meaning. The evidence is that, just the same, silent speech . . . occurs . . ." (pp. 214–215).

But Downing and Timko (1981) point out that neither Corcoran nor Conrad defined what each meant by "silent *e*." The closest to a definition from Corcoran comes when he writes: "Thus when an acoustic event was lacking, that is, when an *e* was silent . . ." (Corcoran, 1967, p. 851). But he gives no examples. Asked for a definition, Corcoran (1977) responded: "I use it simply when in normal reading there is no phoneme uttered which is temporally correlated with the spatial position of the particular *e*. This means that the *e*'s in *hate* and *have* are 'equally' silent." Conrad gives *hope* as an example of "silent *e*" and *seat* of "pronounced *e*." But if "an acoustic event is lacking" (sic) at the *e* in *hate* and *hope* why are these printed words not read as "hat" and "hop" whereas *have* is read as "have"? Such questions raise doubts about the psychological reality of "silent *e*" as employed in Corcoran's experiments and Conrad's theoretical review.

These considerations led Downing and Timko to conduct an experiment in which 42 university students were asked to read aloud 60 three- and four-letter nonsense syllables. When the letter *E* was added to each of the 20 stem trigrams (e.g. JUM), the subjects significantly more often produced a different pronunciation, but, when the fourth letter *B* or *K* was added, subjects significantly more often retained the same pronunciation that they produced for the trigram. Downing and Timko conclude that the subjects who missed final *e*'s in Corcoran's experiments could not have done so merely because they were "silent" or "unpronounced."

Smith (1980) reviewed other research evidence on *e* cancellation tasks and concludes that Corcoran's original claims are disproved by data from other experiments. For example, Smith and Groat (1979) found that subjects instructed to ignore meaning cancelled more *e*'s in *the* in a text than subjects not so instructed. Also the *e* in the past tense morpheme *-ed* was missed much more frequently than other *e*'s in similar positions in words. Smith concludes that "syntactic and semantic factors are important in determining what features of a text a subject pays attention to. Phonetic factors also play a role in this task but not in the direct way that Corcoran originally claimed" (p. 44). That phonetic factors play a role in the *e* cancellation task is clear. Both the Smith and Groat study and one by Frith (1979) found that unstressed *e*'s (e.g. OFTEN) are more frequently missed than stressed *e*'s (e.g. OFFEND). Frith's letter cancellation tasks and reading of misspelled and graphically distorted text provide evidence against prior phonological encoding, although phonological coding in writing appears to be necessary and primary. But, as Smith points out, "the data suggest a richer theory in which the boundaries between graphemic, phonemic and lexical information are not sharply drawn" (p. 44). Smith and Groat analysed their data in terms of seven different roles of letter *e* and found quite different omission frequencies among them in the *e* cancellation task. This suggests that the *e* cancellation task taps information at several different levels, some associated with pronunciation, some with meaning, and so on.

Further doubt is thrown on Conrad's acceptance of Corcoran's claims by the results of an *e* cancellation experiment on deaf subjects conducted by Brooks (1980). He had 17 profoundly, prelingually deaf children cancel *e*'s in text of suitable readability. The results paralleled those that have been obtained with normal hearing adults. Brooks concludes that this effect cannot be a phonological one. "It seems more probable that both the deaf and the hearing show this effect for orthographic reasons: silent *e*'s carry less information than pronounced ones, and those in the definite article least of all" (p. 102).

These several studies make it quite clear that Corcoran's results can no longer be regarded as valid evidence in support of Conrad's acoustic scanning theory. Furthermore, the *e* cancellation task is not necessarily evidence that phonological coding is a preliminary to lexical access.

Conrad conjectures that, at a *simple* level of explanation, our initial language experience is aural. Therefore it is likely that our initial reading experience is also vocal reading. He further conjectures that initial reading is linked to the development of the short-term memory system in that, even though a child of about four years of age may have a good visual perception system, his or her phonological system is probably not well-developed. Furthermore, a visual code is a poor vehicle for storing percepts. Conrad found that adults presented *visually* with like-sounding and unlike-sounding verbal items used a *phonological* code in recall. Also when children had to recall pictures of names which were homophones (e.g. cat, rat, bat) and nonhomophones (e.g. train, horse) they were found to be saying the names to themselves and using that phonological information as a memory code. In addition, Conrad's study of deaf subjects showed that they may have been using a "phonological code very ineffectively, or they could be using some other code or codes that are in themselves less efficient for the purpose than is a phonological code" (Conrad, 1972, p. 226). Such "other codes" could include processes such as finger-spelling, signing and lip-reading. This phonological impairment explains in part why deaf individuals read poorly. Conrad concludes that ". . . STM thrives on a speech like input" and that "reading is most certainly possible with no phonology involved at all, but that, with phonology, it is a great deal easier" (p. 237). It must be noted, as does Furth (1974) in discussing processing of the hearing-impaired child, that Conrad's evidence for the role of phonological coding in short-term memory (STM) is weak since he tested only for phonemes.

In his insightful discussion of Conrad's paper, LaBerge (1972) draws the distinction between the strong form and the weak form of Conrad's hypothesis. The strong form refers to the *obligatory* recoding of written material into the phonological form to be comprehended. The weak form refers to an *optional* coding. Conrad tests his strong version of the hypothesis with data from the profoundly deaf, who were classified by him into articulators and nonarticulators by the kind of confusion errors that they made in recall from short-term memory. The finding that "reading aloud" reduced the comprehension of the nonarticulators more than that of the articulators provides evidence that the deaf probably use a visual code in reading. Hence the strong claim is rejected. LaBerge (1972) states:

> I would like to suggest that the code in which visual written material eventually is cast en route to the comprehension processes need not be exclusively auditory *or* exclusively visual for a given individual reader. It is conceivable that both the auditory and visual codes may make contact with comprehension processes, and that during reading they may make this contact in parallel, or one at a time by fluctuating in some fashion between the two modalities (p. 242).

(This dual coding or parallel coding position is one that is favored by some other researchers, and we will take this up again in later sections).

The Deleterious Effect of Homophonic Similarity on Lexical Decision Tasks

While Conrad's findings are interesting, they simply show that phonemic recoding could be a result of rehearsal for storage in short-term memory. Some researchers have taken the direct line of studying the deleterious effect of homophonic similarity on lexical decision tasks. This is related to the general finding that, when subjects are asked to decide if a letter string forms a word, it takes longer to reject a nonword string like BRUME if that string *sounds* like a real word (Rubenstein, Lewis, and Rubenstein, 1971a, 1971b; Spoehr and Smith, 1973). Apparently, this task requires the subjects to obtain access to their internal lexicon in order to arrive at a correct decision.

An early experiment on pronounceability by Gibson, Pick, Osser, and Hammond (1962) could be taken as evidence for phonemic recoding. They constructed a series of orthographically legal nonsense words by placing typical English initial consonants or consonant clusters at the beginning and at the end with a vowel or vowel cluster in the middle (e.g. SLAND). A control list from inverting the consonant clusters in each of the pseudowords to yield an unpronounceable, orthographically illegal string of letters was also constructed (e.g. NDASL). The two lists of words were presented tachistoscopically to college students and written reproductions were used. Results showed that the percentage of pronounceable words read correctly was greater for all exposure durations, which ranged from 30 milliseconds to 250 milliseconds. This suggests, first, that pronounceable words were perceived more accurately and, second, that both phonological and orthographic regularity is effective in facilitating recognition of units of word size when meaning and familiarity are absent. Since the pronounceable words were also orthographically legal and the unpronounceable ones were orthographically illegal, the difference in accuracy could reflect the sequential dependencies between letters as well as the difference in pronounceability. This confounding of experimental results because of the "coincidence of the phonological and orthographical rule systems" is also pointed out by Gibson and Levin (1975).

Gibson et al. (1962) hypothesized that readers use their knowledge of letter order to group letters into an intermediate functional unit called the *spelling pattern*. This is explained as a cluster of letters with an invariant pronunciation according to the orthographic and linguistic rules of English. A similar unit defined in phonemic terms was proposed by Hansen and Rodgers (1968). This psycholinguistic unit called *vocalic center group* (VCG) corresponds to a letter sequence centered around a vocalic element with consonants or consonant clusters preceding and/or following the vocalic elements. This concept is further extended by Smith and Spoehr (1974). This and related aspects will be taken up in the section dealing with units of processing in the chapter that follows.

In contrast to previous workers who focused on short-term memory, Rubenstein, Lewis, and Rubenstein (1971a, 1971b) concerned themselves with long-term memory of the internal lexicon. Rubenstein et al. (1971a) suggested a word recognition model that includes four important processes: (1) *Quantization* which is the division of the stimulus into segments and the assignment of these segments to letters and phonemes; (2) *Marking*, which is that stage when quantization output distinguishes some subset of lexical entries as being in agreement with it; (3) *Comparison* of the subsequent quantization output with the marked entries; and (4) *Selection* of the marked entry which meets the accuracy criterion adopted by the subject. According to this model, for a stimulus word like STIR, the first quantization outputs could be /st-/ and entries like STAB, STEM, STUB would be marked. While this marking is in progress the entries already marked are compared against the second output of the quantization process. If this output contains enough information to eliminate all marked entries but one, the search process is over.

The Rubenstein, Lewis, and Rubenstein (1971b) study will be discussed in some detail because this is an early and theoretically important study of lexical access that supports the view of phonological coding. In their first experiment, the subjects (university students) were presented with real words, orthographical and phonological legal nonsense (e.g. DRILK, MELP, JUND), illegal nonsense words of higher pronounceability (LAMG, TRUCP, BLACF) and illegal nonsense of lower pronounceability (TRITV, FLIPB, GHOSJ) in a lexical decision task. Results (correct responses only) showed that response latency for legal nonsense was longer than response latency for illegal nonsense of higher pronounceability, which in turn was longer than the response latency of illegal nonsense words of lower pronounceability. The finding that the pronounceability of illegal nonwords influenced reaction time was taken as evidence that the phonological representation of a letter string was being compared with a subset of phonological representations stored in lexical memory. The large difference in reaction time between legal and illegal types supports the hypothesis that deciding if a word is nonsense when it is orthographically and phonologically illegal does not require the exhaustive search of the internal lexicon that is necessary for considering legal nonsense words. Rubenstein et al. (1971b) take this finding as evidence in support of their word recognition model and they conclude that phonemic recoding and the deletion of phonological illegality occur during quantization.

The second experiment of Rubenstein et al. (1971b) used either real English words or legal nonwords that were homophonic with real words (e.g. BRANE with "brain," TRATE with "trait") or nonhomophonic (e.g. MELP, SHARF). Their argument was that, if phonological coding had not occurred, then BRANE and SHARF would have been rejected as nonwords with equal speed. The more precise rationale was as follows. If "marking" and "comparison" are carried out using the phonemic representation of lexical entries and the phonemic recoding of the visual stimulus, then the recognition of nonsense words which are homophonic with real words could be expected to be retarded by false matches. A nonsense homophonic word like BRANE recoded phonemically into /breyn/ would be accepted as a match with the phonemic representation of "brain" and then rejected when the orthographic representation of "brain" was checked against the orthographic form of the stimulus. As these nonwords are legal, the search for an appropriate match must continue exhaustively through all the "marked" entries before subjects can decide that they are nonsense words. Recognition of the nonhomophonous legal nonsense would also go through a similar *search process*, but, since the search process is not sidetracked by false matches, the latency would be shorter than the latency for the homophonic cases. Results showed that the effects of homophony were significant. Reaction times for nonhomophonic words were faster than for homophonic ones.

The third experiment of Rubenstein et al. (1971b) was analogous to their second one. The stimuli were all real English words. Both the homophones and nonhomophones were divided into low frequency (e.g. YOKE) or high frequency (e.g. SALE) for homophones and low frequency nonhomophones (e.g. MOTH) and high frequency nonhomophones (e.g. LAMP). Again it was found that homophones have a longer latency and that low frequency homophones have a longer latency than high frequency ones. This will be made clear by an example. The stimulus word WEAK (frequency 243) has the confuser WEEK with a frequency of 1278. Whichever of these two stimuli is presented, the lexical search will first stop at

WEEK, the more frequent word. If the word presented is WEEK, the spelling check will succeed and the response "yes" will be made at that point. The existence of another lexical entry with the same phonological code, further down in the lexicon, will have no effect. But if the word WEAK is presented, there will be a time-consuming stop, spelling check and restart in the search down from WEEK to WEAK. So WEAK will suffer by being a homophone, while WEEK will not. In comparison, the stimulus SALE (frequency 251) has a less frequent confuser SAIL (frequency 119). We would expect the latency of WEAK to be greater than the latency of SALE since in the search for WEAK the confuser WEEK will be encountered first with a resulting mismatch. In the search for SALE the correct representation will be encountered first, since it has the greater frequency and will be accepted. Thus the procedure is characterized as a search process, proceeding from high-frequency to low-frequency items. When a lexical entry has been successfully found, the search ends and a positive response follows. When no entry is found, the search terminates only after every entry has been examined.

Thus both experiment two and experiment three support the hypothesis that it is the phonemic form of the stimulus and of the representations in the internal lexicon that are compared in order to recognize a printed word presented visually. Unpronounceable stimuli are detected faster because they deviate more from phonological well-formedness. Rubenstein et al. suggest that the speed with which the illegality of a phoneme can be detected may depend on the number of distinctive features on which it is illegal. An example is the unpronouncable word IIKJ which deviates from legality by three distinctive features. But more important is the fact that sometimes it is the particular distinctive features involved rather than the number of features, which are signs for pronounceability.

Results similar to those of Rubenstein et al. (1971b) have also been obtained by Stanners, Forbach, and Headley (1971). However, the Rubenstein et al. work has been criticized by Clark (1973) for failing to establish generality over both items of words and subjects simultaneously. He recalculated the data by treating the stimuli and subjects as a random rather than a fixed effect and found the results to be nonsignificant. To counter this criticism, Rubenstein, Richter, and Kay (1975) asked a panel of judges to rate the legality of the consonant clusters and the pronounceability of the nonwords and also used the more stringent min F′ test as suggested by Clark in their statistical analyses. The results confirmed that the less pronounceable nonsense words were more quickly recognized as nonsense words. However, the real words yielded the fastest response times. This seems difficult to explain, as the unpronounceable nonwords should show faster response than words, since the former could be rejected before lexical search begins, according to the Rubenstein recognition model. Meyer, Schvaneveldt, and Ruddy (1974) criticized the Rubenstein et al. experiments on the ground that graphemic properties of the letter strings may have been confounded with phonemic properties. It is possible that homophonic nonwords look most like English words while unpronounceable nonwords look least like English.

Coltheart et al. (1977) point out that, in the Rubenstein et al. study, homophones and nonhomophones, which were used as comparison groups, were not equated on such factors as word frequency and part of speech. Both these have been shown to effect lexical decision times (Forster and Chambers, 1973). In the case of nonwords, it might be that those items that sound like English words also look more like English words than those items that do not sound like English words. In other words, the pseudohomophones should be equated for visual similarity. Incorporating these criticisms into their design, Coltheart et al. replicated the Rubenstein et al. (1971b) experiments and obtained slightly different results. Coltheart et al. found that reaction times or decision times to pseudohomophones like BRANE were again slower than nonpseudohomophones like BRONE (with visual similarity controlled). The reaction times to less frequent members of pairs of homophones (SAIL) were no different from the decision times to a set of matched nonhomophones controlled for frequency and part of speech. These authors suggest that while phonological recoding may play a role in the rejection of nonword items, it is doubtful if similar recoding is carried out for words.

Coltheart et al. emphasize that their finding is not evidence against the view that the access code for the lexicon is phonological; it is only evidence against the *joint* assertion that the code of the lexicon is phonological and that the procedure is serial search. Davelaar, Coltheart, Besner, and Jonasson (1978) carried out four experiments to examine the effects of homophony (e.g. SAIL/SALE) on response latencies in lexical decision tasks. Results showed that an effect of homophony was evident only if the nonword distractors consisted of legal, pronounceable strings (e.g. SLINT), but that this effect disappeared if the nonwords sounded like real English words (e.g. BRANE). The explanation is that while both graphemic and phonemic encoding occurred simultaneously, naive subjects tended to rely on the outcome of the phonological route. However, when this led to a high error rate, these subjects were able to abandon the phonological strategy and would rely on the graphemic encoding procedure instead. Thus, Coltheart et al. and Davelaar, Coltheart, Besner, and Jonasson (1978) propose that lexical access is a *parallel process* involving the active interplay of the phonological and visual codes in the lexicon during reading. This interplay between visual and phonological access routes to the lexicon is characterized as one of cooperation. The view of lexical access as involving the summation of visual and phonological information rather than as a serial search using the phonological code will be further examined in the section on "coalescing view."

Manipulation of Grapheme–Phoneme Relation

Meyer, Schvaneveldt, and Ruddy (1974) designed two experiments to test the roles of graphemic- and phonemic-encoding in visual word recognition by manipulating graphemic and phonemic relations within various pairs of letter strings. On each trial, the subject was presented with two letter strings instead of just one. The stimulus included a pair of words, a pair of nonwords, or a word paired with a nonword. This is depicted below (extract from Meyer et al. 1974, Table 1, p. 314):

Type of Stimulus Pair	Graphemic Relation	Phonemic Relation	Examples
Word–Word (1)	Similar	Similar	BRIBE–TRIBE FENCE–HENCE
Word–Word (2)	Dissimilar	Dissimilar	BRIBE–HENCE FENCE–TRIBE
Word–Word (3)	Similar	Dissimilar	COUCH–TOUCH FREAK–BREAK
Word–Word (4)	Dissimilar	Dissimilar	COUCH–BREAK FREAK–TOUCH
Word–Nonword	Similar	?	RUMOR–FUMOR HEDGE–PEDGE
Word–Nonword	Dissimilar	Dissimilar	RUMOR–PEDGE HEDGE–FUMOR
Nonword–Word	Similar	?	SOIST–MOIST FRUNK–DRUNK
Nonword–Word	Dissimilar	Dissimilar	SOIST–DRUNK FRUNK–MOIST
Nonword–Nonword	Similar	?	DEACE–MEACE CULSE–GULSE
Nonword–Nonword	Dissimilar	Dissimilar	DEACE–GULSE CULSE–MEACE

NOTE: Question marks indicate some nonwords with more than one phonological representation.

In the first study the strings were displayed simultaneously with one string shown horizontally above the other in capitals. The subject had to judge whether or not both strings were English. This simultaneous presentation aimed at separating the effects of graphemic and phonemic factors on recognition. The critical factors were the graphemic and phonemic relations within the pairs of words.

Meyer et al. (1974) postulated that under the graphemic-encoding hypothesis the following should hold because only the visual properties of the stimuli ought to influence recognition.

Time (2)	—	Time (1)	=	Time (4)	—	Time (3)
(FENCE–TRIBE)		(BRIBE–TRIBE)		(FREAK–TOUCH)		(FREAK–BREAK)

In contrast with either the phonemic encoding or the dual-encoding hypothesis then, the reaction time of lexical decision would be influenced by the phonemic relation between words. Recognition might be facilitated by phonemic similarity in addition to graphemic similarity. Thus:

Time (2) — Time (1) > Time (4) — Time (3)

In the second experiment, two strings of letters were presented successively. The subject had to classify each string separately as a word or a nonword. Reaction times were measured for the individual strings. This method provided better control over the order in which the subjects examined the stimuli.

Both studies showed that performance depended on the phonemic relation within pairs of words, not just the graphemic relation. In particular, the difference between mean reaction times for the graphemically similar words and their controls also depended on the phonemic relation involved. It is likely that the graphemic and phonemic properties of preceding words may influence the phonemic encoding of subsequent words. There is thus a series of *successive operations* in the graphemic and phonemic relations between words. Meyer et al. proposed an *encoding-bias* model to explain their data. During the initial encoding stage, grapheme–phoneme correspondence rules are applied to form a phonological representation of the first letter string in the stimulus. Then a lexical decision (word–nonword) is made by accessing memory to determine if or not the representation has been stored there previously. If it is not found in lexical memory and if the string has more than one possible representation, then the encoding and decision operations are repeated until either a positive outcome occurs or all of the alternatives have been checked. The series of operations is analogous to the way a person might use a dictionary to decide if a string of letters is a word or not. The total reaction time would be the sum of the times taken by the three stages (*encoding, lexical memory* and *response execution*):

Reaction Time (RT) =	$Time_1$	+	$Time_2$	+	$Time_3$
	(Encoding Stage)		(Retrieval Stage)		(Response Stage)

It is possible that the facilities observed for the graphemically and phonetically similar words were due to the use of both graphemic and phonetic information in lexical access.

Loci of Influence of Semantic Context

In further studies, Meyer et al. (1975) investigated how the recognition of words in a pair depends on the context established by the first word in a pair. They asked their subjects either: (1) to classify successive strings of letters as words and nonwords, or (2) to pronounce the strings. Both types of responses to words (e.g. BUTTER) were consistently faster when preceded by associated words (e.g. BREAD) rather than unassociated words (e.g. NURSE). There were also fewer errors. The difference in reaction times for the two kinds of stimuli is reliable across both the individual words and subjects. As there is a corresponding difference in error rates, the variation in reaction time is probably not caused by a speed-accuracy tradeoff. A larger association effect occurred for visually degraded words than for words displayed intact. Reaction time was also affected by the phonemic relation between words. These results suggest that semantic context may influence an early stage of visual word-recognition in which strings of letters are encoded graphemically and transformed to phonemic representations used for accessing lexical memory. This depends on the phonemic and graphemic relation between words. The assumption is that words are stored in distinct "locations" or files (see section on Internal Lexicon and Lexical Access earlier in this chapter; also Forster, 1976) in lexical memory and the memory is organized semantically. Thus associated words like BREAD and BUTTER are relatively close together, whereas unassociated words like NURSE and BUTTER are further apart. This is, of course, only an approximation to the complex working of the internal representation. Meyer et al. make the further claim that accessing information from a given memory location produces residual neural activity that spreads to nearby locations. This temporary increase of excitation then produces the faster recognition of associated words. This they term a *spreading-excitation model.* From this concept of spreading excitation, Meyer et al. conjecture that, under certain circumstances, other operations besides graphemic encoding are affected by semantic context.

Evidence from Nonalphabetic Script and from Serbo-Croatian

There is evidence from nonalphabetic languages that phonetic recoding may be possible and in fact sometimes necessary. A weak piece of evidence for this view is the study by Klapp (1971) who found that the time taken to press a key to indicate that a pair of numbers was the same was much shorter for two-syllable numbers (e.g. 15 and 15) than for three-syllable numbers (e.g. 17 and 17). However, the limited set of numbers does not compare with the richness of language and the Klapp findings should be interpreted accordingly.

In an earlier section of this chapter, the work of Conrad (1972) was cited to illustrate how confusions in short-term memory and the retention of alphabetic materials are more often due to phonetic similarity between presented and recalled items than to visual or semantic similarity. To test the hypothesis if the silent reading of Chinese characters is accompanied by phonetic activity, Erickson, Mattingly, and Turvey (1972) of the Haskins Laboratories used a probe short-term memory paradigm with 12 Asian university students (10 Japanese, 1 Chinese and 1 Korean). The subjects were presented with a set of Japanese kanji characters. On completion of the presentation of the list, one item from the list was presented as a "probe" and the subject was asked to identify the item that appeared immediately before the probe in the list: the "probed-for" item. Results showed that the subjects resorted to a phonetic strategy because there was a significant difference between phonetically similar characters and those with no systematic similarity.

One explanation of the Erickson, Mattingly, and Turvey results is that the primary phonetic aspect of the letters produces phonetic short-term storage effects. This distinguishes the phonetic activity from the more abstract phonological, morphological and syntactical factors. The other explanation is that phonetic short-term storage is only one component of a more general system for processing linguistic information. In this latter view, phonetic activity evoked by nonphonetic symbols would not be incompatible.

It can also be argued that ideographic and alphabetic systems of writing differ only in degree and not in kind. Leong (1972, 1973) has argued from a linguistic perspective and some type-token studies that, in Chinese, which is usually regarded as morphemic rather than phonemically based, there are also phonemic components that readers make use of. There is neurological evidence from a series of studies in Japan (Sasanuma, 1975; Sasanuma and Fujimura, 1971, 1972) that differential damage to the brain affects the differential processing in Japanese of the phonetic kana characters and the morphemic kanji characters. There is also evidence (Biederman and Tsao, 1979; Tzeng and Hung, 1980) that there may be some basic differences in the perceptual demands in recognizing Chinese characters and English words. Thus Erickson, Mattingly, and Turvey suggest that phonetic activity depends on the essentially linguistic nature of the experimental task. The Haskins group regards *primary linguistic activity* as a process of constructing a semantic representation and a phonetic representation. The phonetic representation will enable the listener and the reader to hold shorter segments of print (e.g. words) in some short-term store so that the meaning of longer segments (e.g. sentences) can be extracted and processed (see also I. Liberman, Shankweiler, A. M. Liberman, Fowler, and Fischer, 1977). This position is consonant with Conrad's (1972) work cited earlier on short-term memory. Information processing takes time, even in registering an icon. Thus some kind of work space is needed in which the representation of a sentence can be stored and updated in the course of processing.

Erickson et al. are careful to point out, just as Conrad has done, that there are alternatives to phonetic processing. They are also careful to recognize that reading is a highly complex skill that cannot possibly be explained merely by extrapolating from short-term memory experiments. Reading as a secondary linguistic activity is based on the primary linguistic activities of listening and speaking and also on explicit linguistic awareness. The Haskins group suggests that phonetic short-term storage is a part of primary linguistic activity whereas inner speech seems to be associated with linguistic awareness. Primary linguistic activity takes time, and phonetic short-term storage may serve as a kind of buffer in which sentences can be represented while linguistic processing goes on. They further interpret the Japanese studies as reflecting a difference at the level of *linguistic awareness* without hypothesizing that there are different kinds of primary linguistic activity with the two Japanese writing systems.

A study by Tzeng, Hung, and Wang (1977) using Chinese subjects reading Chinese characters also showed that visual processing of Chinese characters involves phonetic recoding in short-term retention as well as in a sentence judgment task. But, as this study aims at showing that phonemic recoding takes place at the working memory stage, it will be discussed in connection with that model of word perception in subsequent sections.

In a series of experiments, Turvey and associates (Lukatela, Savić, Gligorijević, Ognjenović, and Turvey, 1978; Lukatela, Savić, Ognjenović, and Turvey, 1978; Lukatela and Turvey, 1980) have found in adult Yugoslavian readers that in lexical decision tasks on Serbo-Croatian letter strings the phonological coding is automatic, rapid, and obligatory. Serbo-Croatian is bi-alphabetic with a Roman alphabet and a Cyrillic alphabet. The Roman and Cyrillic alphabets map onto the same set of phones and semantic structure but still comprise two sets of letters that are, with a few exceptions, mutually exclusive. Serbo-Croatian is thus considerably more transparent than English in that individual letters have phonetic representations that remain consistent throughout changes in the context in which they are embedded. Results of the experiments suggest that in lexical decision tasks Serbo-Croatian letter strings receive simultaneously two phonological representations (Roman or Cyrillic). Whether or not this phonologic bivalence impedes lexical decision in the assigned alphabetic mode depends on whether or not the letter string has a lexical entry in one of the alphabets. Turvey and associates emphasize that the full implication of their data for a general theory of word recognition remains to be further explored. They suggest that for English the evidence for phonological coding is not unequivocal.

Summary of the Evidence for Phonological Coding

In this section, the relevant literature that supports the view that phonological coding occurs during reading has been discussed at some length. A vestige from the work of classical structural linguists tended to favor this view. Electromyographic studies do not provide unequivocal findings. Short-term memory studies suggest that the phonological code facilitates storage and the retrieval of speechlike input. Empirical experiments that examine the effect of homophonic similarity on lexical decision tasks, the manipulation of grapheme–phoneme relations, and the influence of semantic context all provide successive and converging operations to support the possible use, and sometimes the necessary use, of the phonological code in lexical access. There is also some supportive evidence from studies of the phonetic processing of written Chinese, usually regarded as a morphemic writing system, and the interpretation of phonetic coding of this language within the context of linguistic awareness. Empirical results from Serbo-Croatian with its bi-alphabetic Roman and Cyrillic systems suggest the need for phonological representation in such a transparent language. But implications for the role of phonological coding are not unequivocal or direct.

Conditions under which Visual or Phonological Coding Occurs

The central problem in the study of lexical access is not whether or not speech recoding does or does not occur. The essential problem is rather to determine the conditions under which visual or phonological coding occurs and to localize the subsystems under which speech recoding may occur and from what cause. Kleiman (1975) attempts to explicate these conditions. He points out the confusion between the reading process and lexical access, which is a substage of reading. He divides reading into the subprocesses: (1) *visual encoding,* (2) *lexical access* and (3) *working memory.* Visual encoding refers to the perception of letter strings (see Smith and Spoehr, 1974 for review). In lexical access, readers retrieve the semantic and syntactic information that they already possess in memory about the individual words being read. In working memory, there is a storage component and a processing component for comprehension. Kleiman suggests that the storage component is needed to hold, until processing is completed, the individual words of the sentence with their lexical information. Other information such as syntactic-semantic information also needs to be stored. Kleiman argues that it is difficult for this form of information to be either explicitly visual or explicitly phonological. He considers that it is at the working memory stage that phonemic recoding is needed. He posits speech recoding as an "overload" system to help comprehension. This is used when sentence parts must be held long enough for semantic integration or interpretation to occur. This "speculative" model of Kleiman's is illustrated in Figure 9–2.

Kleiman conducted three experiments to explore whether recoding to speech during reading occurs *before* lexical access, *after* lexical access,

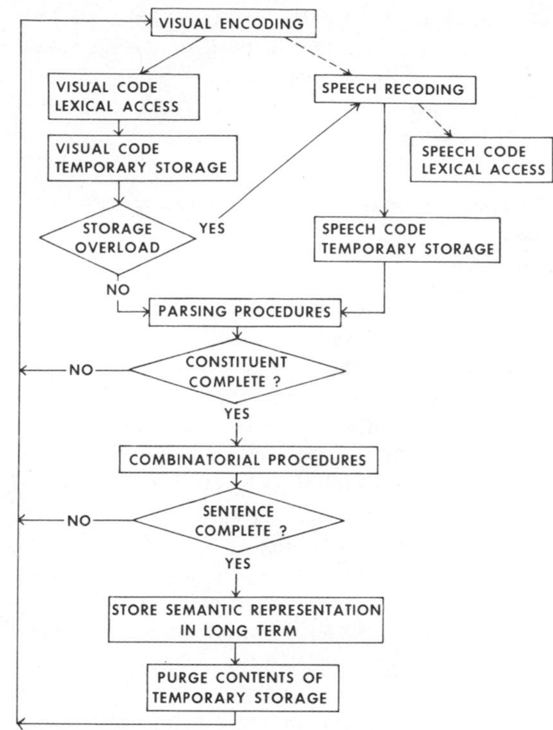

Figure 9–2. Kleiman's "speculative" model. (From Kleiman, 1975, used by permission).

or not at all. Using a reaction time measure, Kleiman demonstrated that requiring subjects to shadow aurally presented digits (to suppress speech reading) while making decisions about word pairs (phonemic, graphemic and semantic) or sentences, had a more severe effect on phonemic and comprehension judgments than on graphemic or simple synonymity judgments. He argued that lexical access can occur without recoding (e.g. in simple synonymity judgment) but that the semantic integration needed to understand whole sentences requires speech recoding to keep the word units available in working memory. Results showed that speech recoding occurs *after* lexical access and facilitates the temporary storage of words necessary for sentence comprehension.

In the *graphemic decision* condition, subjects were presented with word pairs such as NASTY–HASTY and SHADOW–FALLOW and asked to press the "true" button if the two words were spelled alike after the first letter, and to press the "false" response button otherwise. Recoding would not be useful for this decision and it should not show a large shadowing effect. For the *phonemic decision* condition, subjects were asked to respond if the two words such as TICKLE–PICKLE sounded alike after the first word (i.e. if they rhymed) or if they did not sound alike (LEMON–DEMON). The words in each pair, whether they sounded alike or not, always had identical spellings after the first letter. For the *synonym decision,* the subjects were asked to respond "true" if the two words had approximately the same meanings, and "false" otherwise (e.g. INSTANCE–EXAMPLE, BRAVERY–QUANTITY). As hypothesized, results showed that reaction time was influenced about equally in the semantic and graphemic decisions, and for each of these was much less than for the phonemic decision. This suggests that subjects retrieved the necessary *lexical information* for the synonym decision without using speech recoding.

To further test if speech recoding is used in the graphemic decision, subjects in experiment two made graphemic decisions with and without concurrent shadowing. There were two types of stimuli: phonemically similar (e.g. BLAME–FLAME) and phonemically dissimilar (e.g. HEARD–BEARD). The aim was to determine if shadowing had different effects on these types of stimuli. If subjects used speech recoding on the nonshadowing task, it should facilitate the decisions about the phonemically similar pairs relative to the decision about the phonemically dissimilar pairs. Results showing that shadowing hinders both stimulus types by the same amount support the assumption that speech recoding is not used in the graphemic decision condition. Both experiments one and two thus provide evidence that speech recoding is not needed for the retrieval of lexical information. The next question is: Does speech recoding occur at the working memory stage? Experiment three aimed to answer that question.

The third experiment determined the effects of shadowing on four types of decisions: graphemic, phonemic, category and acceptability. The stimuli for each trial contained a string of five words as shown below (Kleiman, 1975, Table 3, p. 333):

Graphemic
BURY
YESTERDAY THE GRAND JURY ADJOURNED (True)
Phonemic
CREAMY
HE AWAKENED FROM THE DREAM (True)
SOUL

THE REFEREE CALLED A FOUL (False)
Category
GAMES
EVERYONE AT HOME PLAYED MONOPOLY (True)
Acceptability
PIZZAS HAVE BEEN EATING JERRY (False)

For the graphemic, phonemic and category decisions, subjects judged whether a target word was present in the sentence. The category task required the subjects to decide if the sentence contained a word belonging to the category named by the target word and thus required lexical access plus some memory load. The acceptability decision required subjects to judge if the sentence was semantically correct. The operation needed lexical access, comprehension, and memory storage. The effect of shadowing was larger for the acceptability and phonemic conditions relative to the graphemic and category conditions.

All three experiments suggest that speech recoding occurs in the *working memory* stage. Kleiman points out that although this stage contains both storage and processing components, the working memory hypothesis does not specify which of these require recoding. He also points out the difficulty in separating these components.

Kleiman cites the short-term memory experiments of Conrad (1972) in support of his argument that speech recoding occurs in the working memory, rather than in lexical access. Further, as mentioned earlier, Hardyck and Petrinovich (1970) showed that EMG activity increased when subjects read more difficult passages and that, when subvocalization was suppressed in the feedback condition, comprehension of the difficult but not the easy passage was reduced. These results suggest the possibility that speech recoding is used only when necessary, i.e. when the capacity of temporary storage for visually coded words gets overloaded, as illustrated in the model in Figure 9–2. Recoding would enable new words to be stored without losing any words already in storage. Recent data from the Haskins group (Mann, I. Liberman, and Shankweiler, 1980; Shankweiler, I. Liberman, Mark, Fowler, and Fischer, 1979) have shown new support for the involvement of phonological representation in the reading process. In these studies, poor readers' inferior recall of phonetically confusable letter strings, word strings, and sentences varying in syntactical dimensions and meaningfulness (e.g. "Jack and Mack stacked sacks on the track in back of the shack" is a meaningful, phonetically confusable sentence compared with "Fred and Ed read sleds on the thread instead of the bed" which is a meaningless, phonetically confusable version) reflects failure to make full use of phonetic coding in working memory.

Suppression Phenomena in Support of Kleiman

Levy (1975) asked subjects to count while reading, thus hindering speech recoding. She showed that the detection of both wording and meaning changes in sentences was markedly and consistently worse following counting than when subjects had read silently. In an analogous listening task, the detection of lexical and semantic changes was little affected when subjects counted, rather than listened quietly. Levy took these results to mean that subjects relied on speech processing even when reading meaningful passages. She suggested that the *speech-based* process may be related to a holding code which keeps the word units active until they can be understood or they can be related to an integration mechanism that brings together individual words into the syntactic-semantic gestalt of the sentence. The finding that there was a larger and more consistent decrement when subjects counted while *reading* rather than when they were *listening* also allowed her to evaluate a *divided attention* postulate. Can speech recoding be due to divided attention? The answer is "no." The reasons are: (1) Counting has no effect on memory if passages are presented auditorially. The attention position should predict memory deficit in *both* listening and reading, but no deficit occurs in listening. (2) Practice does not lead to attenuation as it should with the memory position. (3) Even with unlimited time, suppression decrement still is found. It may also be pointed out that the modality comparison is a difficulty as it was made across experiments.

Levy (1977) overcame the flaws in her 1975 experiments and used a within-subject modality manipulation. Her second experiment examined if the interference effect in her first experiment was a divided attention problem due to unfamiliarity with the tasks. If so, subjects should be better able to divide their attention between counting and reading as they became more familiar with both tasks. Both the first and second experiments showed a reading deficit in fluent readers (university students) by using reading tasks as defined by Gleitman and Rozin (1977): "the skill of extracting meaning from print to the same degree that one extracts it from the sound stream." That is, the material used is meaningful and grammatical, and the deficit is nontrivial as it does not disappear when practiced subjects are used or when subjects are free to adopt an optimal strategy.

Levy (1977) performed a third experiment to relate to the *cognitive control* problem in the interactive model of reading. This is done by using *theme-related* sentences, rather than isolated sentences as Kleiman (1975) did, to create the *thematic* or *cognitive* expectancy in relation to speech recoding. The third experiment replicated findings of the first two experiments and further showed that meaningfulness influences reading, making it easier to detect changes in meaning (but not in wording) when the sentences bear a thematic relationship to each other. The important point is that meaningfulness and speech suppression effects were independent. When subjects read for meaning, which they must have done with thematic passages, they were no less influenced by the speech interference. Thus the cognitive system probably analyzed for meaning and was aided by thematic context, while the stimulus processors worked away on speech analysis, being impeded by counting. Thus, both the "top-down" (concept driven) and "bottom-up" (data driven) kinds of processing helped in the memorizing of what was read.

The 1977 work of Levy provides strong evidence *against* the direct access hypothesis that speech recoding does not occur during fluent reading. That hypothesis is not consistent with such results as those of the third experiment because the subjects were fluent readers who were clearly processing for meaning. Levy (1978a, 1978b) has provided further data to show that the working memory approach to reading needs to be clearly defined as to how the components of the reading process operate. She suggests that the sequential stage view of Kleiman does not seem to be able to explain a suppression decrement independent of the thematic effect. A more flexible approach within the working memory framework is provided by Baddeley (1979). He draws the distinction between the central executive component and the articulatory loop of working memory. The central executive is responsible for information processing, while the articulatory loop deals with such events as speech suppression in thematic effects. Baddeley suggests that the articulatory loop plays an important part in learning to read but is less essential in fluent reading.

Support for Kleiman from Morphemic Writing

Tzeng, Hung, and Wang (1977) investigated whether phonemic similarity affected the visual information processing of Chinese characters presented to Chinese subjects. In the first experiment the researchers showed the effect of phonemic similarity on short-term memory retention of Chinese characters. The second experiment showed that the phonemic similarity also affected the reaction time in a sentence (in Chinese) judgment task. The experiment's paradigm was a retroactive interference paradigm similar to that of Wickelgren (1965).

In the first experiment, Tzeng et al. presented lists of characters of same-consonant (SC), same-vowel (SV), same-consonant and same-vowel (SCSV). The target lists were presented visually and the interference lists of shadowing were presented orally (a six-character list sampled exclusively from the SC, SV and SCSV lists). The subjects were required to write down the correct characters. In the second experiment, subjects were required to judge if a single sentence was a normal sentence or an anomalous one. Normal sentences were both grammatical and meaningful, whereas anomalous ones were both ungrammatical and relatively meaningless. The major independent variable was reaction time needed for making the correct judgment. In both experiments, subjects' performance was impaired by the introduction of phonemic similarity into the test materials. Apart from showing that phonetic recoding was involved in processing visually presented Chinese characters, the Tzeng et al. results also lend support to Kleiman's contention that lexical recognition is only a subprocess of the whole reading process and that phonemic recoding takes place at the working memory stage. This recoding is needed to facilitate temporary storage of lexical information, or text comprehension, or both (see also Tzeng and Hung, 1980).

Visual Coding

Earlier sections in this chapter have discussed one way in which the reader might derive meaning from the printed word. This indirect path assumes that access to meaning is via the use of sound representation. Another way might be through the direct path from visual analysis to meaning without having to go through the phonological route. Evidence for this direct access hypothesis is presented in subsequent sections.

Speed Reading

Though some people find reading difficult, many read very proficiently. The average speed of adult readers is about 400 words per minute. Readers reading at the rapid rate of 1000 words or even 2000 words per minute with complete understanding have been reported. This has led to the suggestion that reading can be an entirely visual process, without involving phonological mediation which necessarily slows down reading (see Bower, 1970). Bower asked Greek-English bilinguals to translate into English an altered Greek text in which many of the words had been changed visually to pseudowords by replacing one letter with another having the same phonetic value. A parallel example in English is reading words like *phast* and *fotografy*. Bower interpreted the much longer time his subjects took to translate the altered text into English as evidence that phonological coding does not usually occur.

In claiming direct access to meaning from print, one must remember that the English language is redundant. Visual texts contain information that specifies both syntax and semantics with high probability. There are many contextual clues that eliminate character-by-character processing and that enable the reader to read rapidly with understanding. Even taking this into account, reading is many times faster than speaking and any phonological recoding would have to occur at a very abstract level.

Reading as Uncertainty Reduction

Cattell's (1886) classic finding that, with a ten msec. tachistoscopic flash, adult subjects could recognize three or four random letters, or two unconnected words or as many as four short words making up a meaningful phrase was erroneously taken as the basis for the whole-word approach to teaching and learning reading. Cattell attributed his results primarily to meaningfulness of a word and familiarity with its meaning. From an information processing point of view, his readers processed the same amount of visual information in each case, but they were able to use the varying orthographic constraints (distribution and sequential redundancy) inherent in print to produce these different responses. The uncertainty of an event refers to the number of times (measured in "bits" of information) a "yes" or "no" question would have to be asked and answered (assuming each answer would reduce uncertainty by half) in order to reduce all uncertainty. The concept owes a great deal to Shannon's (1951) "guessing game" technique whereby a single subject was asked to guess successive letters composing a message. From the guesses, Shannon worked out an empirical estimate of the letter redundancy of printed English. This technique became the basis of the *cloze* procedure first used by Taylor (1953). Carterette and Jones (1963) extended the idea and showed that contextual constraint with the printed word as the unit is related to readability. From the above and related works, McLeod (McLeod and Anderson, 1970) devised an uncertainty reduction index to assess reading ability and further explored this method with a multilingual reading comprehension test (McLeod, 1975). Thus in the case of Cattell's readers, or for that matter other readers, uncertainty among 26 alternatives of the alphabet (given by $-\log \frac{1}{2}$ with two alternatives) is 4.7 bits of information if each letter is equiprobable and 4.03 bits if the distributional redundancy is considered. This uncertainty will fall to about one bit when context is meaningful. Thus twice as many words can be identified at a single glance when they are embedded in a meaningful context. It is this meaningfulness aspect of context that helps to overcome the bottleneck in memory and reduces uncertainty.

Similar perspectives have led Goodman (1967, 1968, 1976a) to postulate reading as a selective, active "psycholinguistic guessing game" involving interactions between thought and language. These ideas have led him also to reject the letter-by-letter or word-by-word search process. Goodman (1967, p. 127) states that, "Efficient reading does not result from precise perception and identification of all elements, but from skill in selecting the fewest, most productive cues necessary to produce guesses which are right the first time. The ability to anticipate that which has not been seen, of course, is vital in reading, just as the ability to anticipate what has not yet been heard is vital in listening."

For F. Smith (1975, 1977, 1978), reading is the reduction of uncertainty. Readers do not need letter names, phonic rules, or language lists. They need to use "nonvisual information" or prior knowledge of the way in which words go together to derive meaning. This ability to use sequential redundancy is shown early in young readers (Lott and Smith, 1970). It has been found also that fourth grade children may be as efficient as adults in making use of letter redundancy in both nonwords and words (Krueger, Keen, and Rublevich, 1974). For the beginning reader, Smith (1977, 1978) emphasizes two main insights the child needs to acquire: (1) print is meaningful and (2) print does not equate with speech. Just as children learn language for a purpose within the context of language function, so they read written language for meaning. The linguist Halliday (1973) has set out various categories of language use, which can apply to both adults and children. There is the *control* function of language (e.g. "Clean your hands"). There is *general encouragement* (e.g. "That's a lovely picture"). There is *running commentary* (e.g. "You are drawing a nice train. Here is the engine . . ."). There is the *extension of play activities*. Smith sees an analogy between the functional use of language and the meaningful basis for learning print. Thus reading is not decoding letters to sounds but bringing meaning to print. In his argument in favor of direct access of meaning from print rather than going through speech, Smith (1975) provides an interesting example in the reading of the following sentence:

> THE NONE TOLLED HYMN SHE HAD SCENE BEAR FEAT INN HOUR RHEUM. (The nun told him she had seen bare feet in our room).

The fact that the spelling anomalies in the sentence at the top are so evident clearly indicates that visual aspects of words distinguish their meaning independently of their sounds. F. Smith (1978, p. 184) further contends, "Immersion in functional language, the possibility of making sense, a plentiful experience, and the opportunity to get feedback to test hypotheses would seem to be just as easily met with written language as with speech." One way to achieve this is to arrange for children to listen to written language read aloud.

While there are some dissimilarities in their conceptions of reading, both Goodman and Smith emphasize the holistic (from the Greek *holos* for whole) approach to reading and the direct access route.

Reading as Selective Patterning

In a series of elegant research programs, Kolers (1970, 1973a) studied visual operations in letter recognition, sensitivity to grammar, and reading bilingual connected discourse. In his presentation of text as a temporal succession of letters, each letter must be exposed for 250 milliseconds or more. This rate of about 42 words a minute is only about one-tenth of the speed of reading of an adult reader, and is far too slow to explain the normal reading process. When letters were presented at short durations of 125 msec. or less, subjects reported all the letters correctly but got the order wrong. This shows that identification and seriation are not the same. Kolers further found that, in the reading of geometrically transformed text (e.g. text rotated in the plane of the page, inverted text), errors are predictable from visual appearance, rather than similarity of sound. Thus it is likely that subvocalization is not essential. In his study of mixed passages with English and French juxtaposed ("His horse, followed de deux bassets . . ."), bilinguals fluent in English and French were required to read aloud these passages. The subjects were subsequently tested for their understanding of such bilingual passages as compared with their understanding of similar passages in English or in French only. The subjects could read and understand the bilingual passages quite well. But when they could not remember particular sequences of words they substituted for a word in one language an appropriate word in the other (e.g. *porte* for *door*). Earlier, Kolers (1966a, 1966b) found that, with bilingual adults as subjects, both isolated words and connected discourse printed in two languages are perceived and remembered in terms of their meaning rather than their appearance or sound. Kolers suggests that it is meanings and not word forms that the reader comprehends. Brown (1970) in his discussion finds it a more interesting interpretation that words are stored in memory only as meanings and not as forms or sounds.

Reading by Deaf Subjects

Deaf individuals with their impaired phonological system still manage to read, even though poorly. They must be using visual and other means. Gibson, Shurcliff, and Yonas (1970) reported an experiment in which deaf and hearing subjects were compared in their ability to read pseudowords presented tachistoscopically. Both the deaf and the hearing subjects were more successful in reading the pronounceable than the unpronounceable ones. Thus orthographic rules and other visual cues were used by both types of subjects. As mentioned earlier, Conrad (1972) suggested that reading is possible, though not optimal, in the absence of phonological coding and that, in this case, visual coding is used. This also points to the difficulty of generalizing results of performance in reading in the deaf without equating appropriate means of testing. Balow, Fulton, and Peploe (1971) studied the reading comprehension skills of 157 severely to profoundly deaf adolescents and found that their mean vocabulary scores were in the mid-fourth-grade level and that their mean comprehension scores were in the early fifth-grade level. More encouraging results were found by Simmons-Martin (1972). They reported on average word meaning, sentence meaning, and paragraph meaning scores of 132 deaf children who were tested in each of five consecutive years from age eleven to age fifteen. Initially, the children achieved a mean grade equivalent of slightly over third grade at the age of ten, but they progressed to almost a sixth grade level score at age fifteen.

In England and Wales, national data on the level of reading development of deaf children have been obtained. Conrad (1977) surveyed virtually all children aged fifteen to sixteen in special schools for the deaf. Their median reading age was around nine years. Kyle, Conrad, McKenzie, Morris and Weiskranz (1978) extended this survey to the same age group in partially hearing children in special classes. Their median level was about eleven years of reading age. These two national surveys clearly establish the detrimental effect on reading of the hearing handicap.

Effect of Homophonic and Heterophonic Words

Baron (1973) argued that a visual analysis is *faster* than phonemic encoding for skilled readers and is thus normally used when readers are free to choose their strategies of analysis. He asked college students to classify phrases as either sense or nonsense and reaction time was measured. In the first experiment, the stimuli were visually and phonologically congruent phrases (e.g. I KNEW HIM and MY NEW CAR), phonologically congruent but visually incongruent phrases (e.g. MY KNEW CAR and I NEW HIM) and phonologically and visually incongruous phrases (e.g. I AM KILL and OUR NO CAR). If phonological coding is used, then MY KNEW CAR and I NEW HIM which sound but do not look correct should be rejected more slowly than I AM KILL which neither sounds nor looks correct. Results showed that, though there was no difference in reaction time, there were more errors on the phonologically congruent but visually incongruent phrases than the phonologically and visually incongruous ones. This higher error rate points to the possibility that phonological recoding might have taken place some of the time by some subjects. In the second experiment subjects had to say "yes" if the phrase "sounded like it made sense," irrespective of its orthographic form. They made more errors and took longer reaction time on the phonologically congruent but visually incongruent phrases relative to those that were both visually and phonologically correct. Thus visual information is available early in the analysis of each phrase. One criticism of the Baron study by Meyer, Schvaneveldt, and Ruddy (1974) was that there may have been a speed-accuracy trade-off. When subjects were asked to say whether phrases such as MY KNEW CAR and OUR NO CAR "looked meaningful," there was no difference in response latencies although only the latter phrase is phonemically anomalous while both phrases are visually incongruous.

From the Baron (1973) findings, one would expect the speed of visual analysis to be a better predictor of an individual's reading speed than his speed of phonemic analysis. Baron and McKillop (1975) carried out a study to test this expectation by examining individual differences in phonemic analysis, visual analysis, and a basic reading task in which subjects were free to use either strategy. In each task the subject was required to distinguish two different kinds of phrases, mixed together randomly in a list, by putting a check mark (√) next to one type and an X next to the other as *fast* as possible. One task, the sense-versus-homophone (SH), required the subject to place a check mark next to the sense phrases and an X next to the homophone phrases. This forces the subject to rely on the direct pathway, so that differences in speed of performing this task reflect differences between the subjects in the speed of this pathway. The homophone-versus-nonsense (HN) task required the subject to use the indirect path, since both phrases would not make sense if judged according to the direct path. The speed in performing this task thus provides a measure of the speed of the indirect path. In the third task, the sense-versus-nonsense (SN), the subject could use either path. In this sample of experienced and competent readers the results showed that those who were better at the phonemic strategy than the visual strategy were slower than the readers who were better at the visual strategy. This further reinforces the earlier Baron (1973) finding that the visual strategy is a generally superior one, when the subject is free to use either one. Subjects' speed on the direct path is a better predictor of their reading speed than is their speed on the indirect path measured independently. It is also possible that those subjects using the indirect path were less mature readers.

In reviewing his own earlier work, Baron (1977b) pointed out these limitations: (1) The experimental tasks differed from real reading which involves short-term memory as an intermediate stage in sentence comprehension. As well, storage in long-term memory is needed in addition to understanding materials; (2) The assumption that homophones have the same representation in the phonemic code that is used in the indirect path may not be valid. Baron (1977b, p. 193) states, "There might well be a kind of representation that is phonemic in terms of what interferes with it and what capacities it draws on, yet that is closer to spellings than to sounds in terms of the relations of similarity and identity that exist within the code. This code might be in essence what Chomsky (1970) has called a deep phonemic level, as opposed to the surface phonemic level within which homophones are in fact identical."

Building from his earlier (1973) studies, Baron found there is considerable evidence for the use of the indirect path (with a phonemic code that may differ from that used in speech) to meaning for even the simplest task. This was shown in a number of studies he performed (Baron, 1977b) with artificial alphabets and "Greek" letters and "Roman" numerals. This seems puzzling. Baron suggests that probably the advantage of accessing meaning with sounds instead of direct access is sufficiently great to compensate for the extra time required to get the sound in the first place. But the most plausible explanation is that the indirect path, when memory is not required, is used in parallel with the direct path. This also assumes that some of the subskills have attained automaticity, as postulated by LaBerge and Samuels (1974) (see also our Chapter 2 on Reading as a Skill, and the relevant section in Chapter 10).

Analogous studies using *heterophonic words* (words very similar in spelling but not in pronunciation such as HORSE–WORSE, MOWN–DOWN) were carried out by Bradshaw and Nettleton (1974). They measured times for initiating and completing the vocalization of the pair, the first alone or the second alone. Overt vocalization of the first was found to be needed for any delay in initiating vocalization of the second. It was not sufficient to observe or store the first of the pair of heterophonic words. This suggested that articulatory interference depended on the establishment of a pronunciation set with actual vocalization and that a word could be recognized, identified or stored without phonological recoding.

Green and Shallice (1976) investigated if phonological recoding is obligatory in reading for meaning or whether direct access is the general rule. Experimental materials consisted of combinations of rhyming versus nonrhyming words (e.g. DOTE, STOAT vs. POISE, WISE) and spelling pairs (correctly spelled vs. incorrectly spelled words). In one study it was found that the time taken by university students to make a semantic decision about the pair of words was much more delayed by misspelling (e.g. URGE, VERGE became ERGE, VURGE) than was the time to make a phonological one. In another study, reaction time varied with the semantic difficulty of the category decision (e.g. WASP, GRASSHOPPER for the category "insect") but not with syllable length. Green and Shallice argue that reading for meaning generally uses a direct route from visual form to semantic representation and does not usually involve prelexical phonological recoding. They further suggest as more plausible the argument of Kleiman (1975) that for phonological effects to occur at all, they would be more likely at the working memory stage after lexical access.

Frederiksen and Kroll (1976) have argued against the phonemic recoding hypothesis. They compared those factors that affect naming latency and those factors that affect lexical decision times. They assumed that, if phonological recoding occurs prior to lexical access, then those factors that affect naming must also affect lexical decision time in the same way. For example, they predict that, if the number of letters in an item can be shown to affect the time required to begin to say the item, then that factor should also affect decision time if phonemic recoding occurs. Their results demonstrated that none of the factors that were observed to affect naming latencies affected lexical decision times (e.g. number of letters, size of initial consonant cluster, and complexity of vowel translations). Frederiksen et al. therefore concluded that phonemic recoding is not a prerequisite for lexical retrieval.

Stroop Effect

A number of researchers (Ehri, 1976, 1977; Golinkoff and Rosinski, 1976; Rosinski, 1977; Rosinski, Golinkoff, and Kukish, 1975) have exploited the Stroop (1935) word-color interference task to show that readers (mainly second to sixth grade children with a small number of college students) are capable of accessing word meaning without phonemic recoding. In essence, subjects were asked to name pictures of common objects aloud while ignoring distractor words superimposed on the pictures. In the *congruent condition* the words were the names of the objects (e.g. the label PIG superimposed on the picture of a pig). In the noncongruent or *Stroop* condition, there was a mismatch between the picture and the label printed on it (e.g. the word PIG was superimposed on the picture of a dog). In the *control condition* consonant–vowel–consonant (CVC) trigrams were printed on the pictures. Despite instructions to ignore the superimposed words, semantic characteristics of the distractors affected the rate at which both adults and grade-school children could name the pictures. Subjects were more rapid in naming pictures in the congruent word condition; they were the least rapid in the noncongruent or Stroop condition while the control nonsense trigrams condition was intermediate in response times. The general reasoning, especially by the Rosinski group, was as follows: (1) There could be an input interference in which the presence of the superimposed noncongruent words distracts the subjects from the pictures. (2) There could be a response interference in which both pictures and words are processed and both initiate a motor response. (3) It could be that both the meaning of the picture and the distractor word were picked up and the discrepancy between these two semantic referents led to interference. In the case of the first alternative, the Stroop and the control nonword conditions should not have differed as both increased processing load. In the case of alternative (2) responses in the nonword trigrams condition should have taken longer than those in the Stroop condition as the unfamiliarity of the nonsense words would make them harder to read. With alternative (3) the control nonsense word condition should have been intermediate between the other conditions.

The general finding of the third alternative above led the researchers to suggest that word meaning cannot be ignored because of rapid and direct semantic access without phonological reading. It was found that beginning readers process meanings of printed words rapidly, automatically, and involuntarily. Even skilled comprehenders who appeared to possess poorer decoding skills experienced semantic interference from meaning of the single words. Another finding was that decoding and semantic processing are separable processes and that, although less skilled comprehenders have difficulty decoding, this does not result in difficulties in decoding meaning. Further, the organization of semantic processing is similar across age levels and not specifically tied to reading levels.

To further test if extraction of meaning from single words can proceed without phonological coding, Kerst, Vorwerk, and Geleta (1977) asked college students to engage in picture-naming tasks similar to those used by Rosinski, Golinkoff, and Kukish (1975). Specifically, the subjects were required either to ignore the distractors, read them silently, pronounce them covertly or say them aloud. The phonetically novel nonwords retarded picture-naming performance more than did real words when phonetic processing was explicitly required, but not during silent reading. In addition, covert pronunciation required more time than silent reading. The overall pattern of results tends to support the hypothesis that there is direct access of meaning from print without going via the phonological route. The results are also consonant with those obtained in a study by Forster and Chambers (1973), who found pronunciation for words was more rapid than for nonwords. These researchers suggested that naming and categorization are independent events taking place *after* the completion of a lexical search and that lexical access occurs before the availability of phonological information. The latter is determined by the former.

Recently, Posnansky and Rayner (1977) and Rayner and Posnansky (1978) performed a series of experiments with a modified Stroop task to evaluate the direct-semantic-access model, the visual-features stage model and the phonemic recoding stage model of word identification. They criticized the Rosinski group for using gross dependent variables (total time needed to name a sheet of pictures) and hence the difficulty in determining the degree to which visual or phonological factors are important. Rayner and Posnansky varied visual-threshold exposure durations for the time needed for subjects to name a picture and then presented pictures within the modified Stroop paradigm, both at threshold and with various constant amounts of time added to the threshold duration to tap stages of processing. Examples of stimulus materials can be illustrated with the different conditions/labels printed in the center of the picture HORSE. For the word condition, the actual label *horse* is used. For the nonword with overall word shape preserved condition, the label is *hcnre*. The other conditions are: *hgple* (nonword with initial and final letters preserved); *bcnre* for nonword plus overall word shape; *pynrk* for nonword with neither word shape nor any letters preserved and for *radio* as a Stroop word. In all the experiments, nonwords that preserved more of the visual features of the picture label resulted in faster naming times than those that did not, especially when the stimuli were presented at any brief durations. When exposure duration was very brief, even Stroop words that preserved a number of the visual features (e.g. *loaf* printed on the picture LEAF) were named faster than conditions that changed a number of the features of the picture's label. Rayner and Posnansky suggest that the results support the visual features stage model. However, the possibility exists that phonemic recoding en route to word meaning was used and this might be related to the verbal responses required. It is also possible that, in concentrating on vocalic quality, there was some confounding visual and phonemic features in the initial letters.

Neurological Evidence—Paralexic Errors

Another source of evidence in support of the direct visual route hypothesis of word recognition comes from studies of paralexic errors of acquired dyslexia in adult patients. Paralexic errors are those where the relationship between a stimulus word and response can be classified as derivational (e.g. *courage* to "courageous"), visual (e.g. *dug* to "bug") or semantic but nonderivational (e.g. *dream* to "sleep"). It should be pointed out that some caution is needed in applying results obtained from brain-damaged patients to the normal population. Postman (1975, p. 308) stated that such data "do not impress us as unequivocal" and that "extrapolations from pathological deficits to the structure of normal memory are of uncertain validity." However, the wealth of experiments and research findings from patients who have suffered damage to the left cerebral hemisphere resulting in aphasia and in reading impairment known as "deep" or "phonemic" dyslexia is compelling. It certainly has added to our cumulative understanding of reading processes.

In their research program, Marshall and associates (Marshall, 1976; Marshall and Newcombe, 1966, 1973, 1977; Marshall, Newcombe, and Marshall, 1970) reported on and discussed the rather unusual occurrence of semantic errors (e.g. *speak* read as "talk", *suit* read as "coat") but not grapheme–phoneme errors. In an important paper, Marshall and Newcombe (1973) detailed three types of dyslexic errors with two case studies each. One type consists of *visual errors* (e.g. *dug* read as "bug", *beg* as "leg"). *Surface dyslexic* errors or grapheme–phoneme conversion errors occur where the wrong phoneme is chosen for a potentially ambiguous grapheme. This type of errors can take these forms: unvoiced consonants used for voiced ones (*disease* read as "decrease"), neologisms (*hiss* as "hish"), loss of whole syllable (*banishment* as "banment"), consonant cluster difficulties (*applaud* as "apollo"), nominalizing of verbs (*govern* as "governor"). In contrast, *deep dyslexia* is characterized by semantic errors (e.g. *speak* read as "talk") rather than grapheme–phoneme errors. The impairment of the ability to give a phonological representation of a printed word by nonlexical grapheme–phoneme rules is of particular interest to our discussion of word meaning.

These "central" errors contrast with peripheral errors. It is the disturbance of the central lexicon that explains the semantic relationship between the erroneous response and the stimulus item. Early studies of this kind included those of Franz (1930), Goldstein (1948) and Schuell (1950). Franz reported on a patient's errors such as *hen* read as "egg", then "chicken, chick, turkey"; or *cat* read as "mice, dog, rat". Goldstein discussed similar errors. Schuell classified errors into: (1) coordinate type such as *cream* read as "milk"; (2) subordinate type such as *garden* read as "flower"; (3) supraordinate type such as *farm* read as "country"; and (4) contrast type such as *his* read as "her". Luria (1947) noted both single word substitutions and long paraphrasic circumlocutions as illustrated by the response to the stimulus word *Holland:* "Well . . . yes . . . I know. . . . It's a country . . . not Europe . . . not Germany. . . . It's small. It was captured . . . Belgium!" The *deep dyslexic* errors reported by Marshall and his associates, and others since, are characterized by: (a) striking, selective response bias toward producing nouns and this much better than adjectives or verbs; (b) predominantly semantic substitutions (*sick* read as "ill", *city* as "town", *pray* as "chapel", *cheer* as "laugh"); (c) derivation errors (*height* as "high", *depth* as "deep", *heat* as "hot", *truth* as "true"); and (d) nominalized verbs (*entertain* as "entertainment"). Furthermore, deep dyslexics cannot read nonsense syllables and their errors are never nonexistent lexical forms. Their semantic misreading is sometimes preceded by a partially erroneous visual analysis of stimulus as shown in *sympathy* being read as "orchestra" (by analogy with symphony) or *symphony* read as "tea" (by analogy with TEA and SYMPATHY). Marshall and associates emphasize the essential "normality" of the semantic errors. These are interpreted in terms of a "functional analysis of normal reading process" in both adults and children (Marshall and Newcombe, 1973, p. 188). Marshall and Newcombe invoke Morton's (Morton, 1964; Morton and Broadbent, 1967) theory of logogens (lexical entries) and excitation of thresholds to explain paralexic errors. The theory itself will be discussed in subsequent sections. It is not uncommon that errors of functional equivalence occur in adults reading under time pressure (e.g. MOST–MANY). Clay (1969) in a study of beginning readers noted such errors as "Mother ASKED . . . Mother SAID". It must, however, be pointed out that semantic errors due to deep dyslexia differ from semantic errors in other situations. In the former, semantic errors arise from single words as a result of impairment of the nonlexical route from print to phonology. In normal reading or in developmental dyslexia, semantic errors are of a "surface" rather than a "deep" nature. They are much more context-dependent and likely reflect misapplication of grapheme–phoneme conversion rules.

Shallice and Warrington (1975) discussed a case of acquired dyslexia (case "K.F."). K.F. generally read nouns better than adjectives, which in turn were read better than verbs. Other grammatical categories were still more poorly read. Visual errors predominated and phonemic errors did not occur. A significant number of errors contained a semantic component of which the majority had the same root as the stimulus word. There was also a difference between abstract and concrete words with a sharp drop in performance as concreteness diminished and a somewhat less sharp drop as frequency decreased. The reading performance of K.F. did not seem to be constrained by grapheme–phoneme correspondence rules (see also Albert, Yamadori, Gardner, and Howes, 1973) and was similar to the performance of the two phonemic dyslexics in Marshall and Newcombe (1973). There is thus further support for the direct encoding route hypothesis. Shallice and Warrington suggested that concrete and abstract words are semantically processed in different cerebral systems so that the two systems can be differentially impaired (cf. also Sasanuma, 1975; Sasanuma and Fujimura, 1971, 1972), but they pointed out that the basis of this differential remains obscure.

Further evidence of the effect of word imageability in acquired dyslexia was provided by Richardson (1975a, 1975b). Following Paivio (1971), Richardson distinguished between imageability and concreteness. The imageability of a word was found to be a good predictor of the probability that a dyslexic subject would be able to read it, while a word's concreteness did not appear to have this capacity when imageability was partialled out or controlled. Results similar to Richardson's findings of deep dyslexics' selective inability to read words rated low on imageability were also obtained by Patterson and Marcel (1977). Imageability was shown to affect left visual field (LVF) presentation but not right visual field (RVF) in normal subjects, a finding which seems to mimic the deep dyslexics' performance. Patterson and Marcel (1977) also found that their two severely aphasic males were largely successful in *repeating* orthographically regular nonwords (e.g. DAKE) that were presented auditorily but that they were almost totally unsuccessful in *reading* aloud such stimuli given visually. Further, the two patients showed no effect at all of the phonological status of nonwords, whether in response latencies or in error rates, although they could perform lexical decision tasks (making word/nonword judgments) reasonably well. These case studies suggest that non-lexical routes from graphemes to phonemes are essentially inoperative in patients with phonemic dyslexia. Results further show that purely visual access to the internal lexicon is possible and usable and explain how these patients could read what they could (see also Marcel and Patterson, 1978).

Saffran and Marin (1977) question whether, in the Marshall and Newcombe (1973), and Shallice and Warrington (1975) studies, the grapheme–phoneme impairment arises *after* grapheme-to-phoneme conversion since the difficulties are inferred from oral reading. In their case report of a fifty-one-year-old acquired dyslexic "V.S.", Saffran and Marin attempted to show that there was a *pre-lexical* grapheme-to-phoneme impairment, although she had a rather extensive reading vocabulary, V.S. retained an extensive vocabulary of at least 16,500 words that could be processed for meaning, although they could not always be read aloud. This observation supports the view that there are separate visual and phonological pathways in reading. Specifically, V.S. was not able to perform operations that critically depend on grapheme-to-phoneme conversion of the following categories: (1) She could not read nonsense words like WID (read as "widow") although she could read aloud complicated words like "chrysanthemum"; (2) In *visual* rhyming tasks (e.g. for HOPE the choices were "hop, choke, heap, soap") her performance was 50 per cent correct, although, given her own choices in an auditory rhyme discrimination task, she performed perfectly; (3) She performed poorly in finding the word that sounded exactly the same as the sample (e.g. WRITE, writ, right, ride), while visual presentation was 38 per cent correct.

Performance in the above tasks suggests there was phonological impairment but not conclusively, as V.S. might use a visual mode of lexical address. In accessing lexical entries from homophonic spellings as *kote,* V.S. was given 60 homophones of real words, mostly concrete nouns (e.g. KAT, NITE) and asked to identify the lexical item corresponding to each of the homophones. Acceptable identification responses included pronouncing or writing the word, providing a semantic response (e.g. reading BOOTS as "shoes"), or pointing to an appropriate object (as in the case of DESQ). Later, she was asked to read aloud, or otherwise identify, the same list of words in their usual spellings. Many of V.S.'s responses are phonologically remote from the stimulus word (e.g. "blood" for BLOO, "weasle" for WEALE). They are rather closely related orthographically. Orthographic factors could also account for a number of correct responses to homophones that depart from the conventional spelling in more than one letter position. These results suggest that V.S. relied on an orthographic strategy that was probably used to read familiar graphemes as well. In other words, the graphemic information is referred to the internal lexicon and matched against stored orthographic representations without prior conversion to phonological form. This leads to the question whether the orthographic match was a holistic method of word recognition. This was discounted because typographic variation (such as mixed case presentation) did not interfere with reading performance (e.g. cAbiNeT, n + i + g + h + t) or D
O
G. Thus V.S. was processing words as strings of letters that must be encoded as such before lexical identification can occur. The total performance pattern of V.S. suggests that she identified words by matching particular letter strings with their corresponding meanings. Saffran and Marin are careful to point out that the "orthographic reading mechanism may . . . be difficult to acquire without some basis in phonology" (p. 524).

Allport (1977) suggests that the paralexic errors of phonemic or deep dyslexic patients indicates that they must have some means of access to the semantic system for visually presented words that does not require mediation by a phonemic code. It is unlikely that these patients would have acquired since their injury a specific visual-semantic route not also available to normal readers. In his own research, Allport has studied errors generated by normal adults in attempting to read arrays of unrelated words, followed at brief delays by a *graphemic pattern mask* (an array of densely distributed letters or letter fragments succeeding the display of words and in the same retinal position). He finds that such errors are comparable to the types of reading errors produced by brain-damaged deep dyslexics. Among other findings, the discovery of semantically related reading errors (e.g. BLUE reported as "jazz", DRINK as "wine") under severe pattern-masking conditions leads to a reconsideration of the relation between processes involved in conscious perception or explicit report of a word's identity and processes sufficient for a reader to be influenced by a word's meaning. A similar phenomenon was described by Bradshaw (1974). A word presented peripherally and briefly without a pattern masking can influence the semantic interpretation of a centrally presented homograph even though the peripheral word could not be reported explicitly. The central question is why pattern-masking prevents lexical information from becoming available for explicit word production, granted the pattern-masked words access the lexicon/semantic systems. Allport suggests that Morton's (1964, 1968, 1970) logogen model may account for such a performance (see section "Coalescing View" in this chapter). Allport also puts forward a model for the perception of printed words which are processed asynchronously and in parallel through a system of visual codes, a system of whole-word pattern analysis and grapheme–phoneme conversion. The effect of a graphemic pattern masking thus preempts or interrupts the relatively slow process of grapheme–phoneme conversion and also disrupts information represented in the visual code.

It should be noted that Allport's (1977) semantic error rate of 6–9 per cent (a "relatively cautious criterion") of all whole-word error responses was largely verified in a replication by Ellis and Marshall (1978). These researchers went on to caution the need for baseline data of semantic errors to estimate chance levels of performance. In their view, Allport's 9 per cent "cautious" error rate or even the 20 per cent morphemic or derivation error rate (e.g. SLEEP reported as "asleep" or ARMY as "arms") might be within the "danger" zone of chance. They also point out that the instance of true cases of deep or phonemic dyslexia does not affect their argument because subjects in the Marshall group of studies may produce an excess of 50 per cent error rates in response to randomly selected and individually presented words. These various studies of paralexic errors made by phonemic dyslexic patients in reading single words aloud point to the failure of different components in the process of word recognition and production (see Patterson, 1978). Patterson (1979) has shown further, in her clinical study of two deep dyslexic adults that, despite the general severity of the patients' deficits, some aspects of their processing of written words were relatively well-preserved (e.g. recognition of function words). That these patients comprehend more than they can read aloud suggests that their reading impairment cannot be reduced to a comprehension deficit but that their comprehension "has not gone seriously wrong" (p. 126. See also Albert, Yamadori, Gardner, and Howes, 1973.) Thus the various sources of data on deep dyslexia suggest that different routes of lexical access of graphemic stimuli—one via phonological codes and the other via semantic codes—can be demonstrated (see Allport, 1979 for further information).

In view of the contemporary interest in the access of the internal lexicon and the extraction of word meaning at the deep level, relevant empirical evidence for and against visual coding and phonological coding has been discussed in some detail. The extensive available literature precludes an exhaustive review, but what we have attempted is representative of studies from psychology and neuropsychology. Additional references can be found in an important review paper by Bradshaw (1975), book chapters by Rozin and Gleitman (1977) and Barron (1979). In his review of "three interrelated problems" in reading, Bradshaw (1975) concludes that skilled readers, when dealing with relatively simple materials, are capable of extracting meaning from text without a prior stage of phonological recoding. The condition under which direct visual access occurs is not known precisely, but probably depends on familiarity of the material, skill of the reader and the purpose of the reader. Barron (1979) prefers to regard phonetic recoding as a strategy rather than as an obligatory procedure, which is used when the reading situation places demand on memory. Also, direct visual access to meaning might be regarded as a strategy which is used when processing speed is important and when familiarity is high and memory demands are low. The Bradshaw, Rozin and Gleitman and Barron reviews and the large number of experimental studies discussed here all point to the existence of multiple strategies for accessing word meanings. There are individual differences in fluent adult readers in the extent to which they know and rely on spelling-to-sound correspondence rules in pronouncing printed words. With beginning readers, the use of rules also supplements decoding skills. This brings us to the importance of dual coding or parallel processing.

Dual Coding—Multiple Paths

It is often thought that children in comparison with adults are not as skilled and are more prone to use the indirect path or phonological coding in word recognition (see Gleitman and Rozin, 1977; Rozin and Gleitman, 1977). Much of this argument is based on the evidence of the importance of decoding subskills (Calfee, Chapman, and Venezky, 1972; Perfetti and Hogaboam, 1975). While there are strong arguments for both visual and phonological coding, there is also persuasive evidence for the dual coding and multiple paths theory.

Successive Stages of Word Recognition

In a series of experiments, Baron (1975) asked subjects to compare two strings of letters for visual identity. He found that the time taken was not affected by whether or not the strings were words, or whether or not they were homophones but it was affected by their conformity to orthographic regularities. The time taken to search for a letter in a string was also affected by orthographic regularity but not "wordness" or meaning. But wordness did influence the time for comparing the sounds of two strings. It is suggested that visual comparison and letter search rely on a stage of visual coding which precedes that which is necessary for phonemic comparison. It should be pointed out that the lack of effect of meaningfulness on visual tasks relates to some methodological preconditions: use of large, bright, and well-formed letters, emphasis on speed, forced-choice procedure, span of visual memory of subjects not exceeded. Baron suggests that "It is possible . . . that different visual features are extracted for the visual tasks than for the phonemic tasks. It is also possible that the extraction of the visual features in the phonemic task is influenced by such factors as meaningfulness, which do not affect the visual tasks. In proposing that successive stages are involved, we are assuming that this is not the case, that the visual features used for both tasks are of the same sort, and that their formation is influenced by the same factors and the same sort of prior experience" (pp. 572–573).

In a study of the relative efficiency of direct and indirect path change with progress through elementary schools, Barron and Baron (1977) used a sound task and a meaning task with grades one, two, four, six and eight children. They were given a list of five picture-word pairs consisting of a word next to a picture. In the meaning task, the children were asked to point to those picture-word pairs that "went together", such as the picture of a pair of pants and the word *shirt*. In the sound task, the children were asked to point to those picture-word pairs in which the word rhymed with the name of the picture (e.g. a picture of a horn and the word *corn*). The aims were to compare: (1) the time for the sound and the meaning tasks; (2) the performance of the two tasks done with and without concurrent vocal interference (the assumption being that this would tie up articulatory and auditory mechanisms); and (3) confusable conditions with distractor items. It was further assumed that, if children show developmental change from phonetic to graphemic information to get meaning, then vocalization should influence both the meaning and the rhyme tasks early in development, but only the sound task later in development, as the older children begin to use direct visual access.

Barron and Baron found that there was no interaction between task and age variables, and that concurrent vocal interference produced more errors in the sound task than in the meaning task at all five grade levels. But vocal interference had no influence upon decision times or errors for the meaning task at any of the grade levels including grade one. Barron and Baron took the vocal interference results as suggesting that meaning of a word or a picture does not rely heavily on auditory or articulatory mechanisms. It is also possible that rhyme decisions were based on visual rather than sound similarity as many rhyme pairs are also visually similar, although there are exceptions (e.g. chair/pear). While confusability increases both the time and error percentages, it appears to influence both tasks equally across all age groups. The effect of confusability is most likely due to similarity on an irrelevant dimension, either sound or meaning, that might influence speed and accuracy of children's decision. Barron and Baron suggest that some children will use the direct access path while others will employ the indirect one. With practice, which is positively correlated with age, both paths come to be used in parallel by all readers. This is shown by the small variance of the lag times for each separate task. They emphasize that young children learn the print-meaning direct relationship very rapidly, perhaps with several exposures. This is consistent with studies by Brooks (1977) with adults in their rapid acquisition of print-meaning. Barron and Baron caution that their claim should not be generalized to units larger than single words.

Orthography and Lexical Rules

Baron and Strawson (1976) distinguished between an *orthographic mechanism,* which makes use of general and productive relations between letter patterns and sounds and a *lexical mechanism,* which relies on specific knowledge of pronunciations of particular words and morphemes. In the orthographic mechanism, the effective units for accessing pronunciation are letters or letter groups; in the lexical mechanism, the units are whole words or morphemes. The orthographic mechanism may make use of analogies with the spelling of similar words or of direct rules concerning relations between letters and phonemes. The lexical mechanism can include the use of letter identities (disregarding their associated phonemes) to access pronunciation or meaning codes, and the use of the relation between spelling patterns and meaning compounds. In other words, readers must use both mechanisms—the orthographic mechanism in pronouncing words that they have not seen before and the lexical mechanism for words for which no rules are available such as *lb, Ag*.

In two experiments with university students, Baron and Strawson found that words which conform to spelling–sound correspondence rules (e.g. SWEET) are read aloud more quickly than words which do not so conform (e.g. SWORD). This suggests that these rules are used in reading a word, and speed its association, despite part-learning of the association between the word and its entire pronunciation. This effect is large in subjects who rely heavily on the rules, as determined by independent tests.

The Baron and Strawson study using real words was extended by Baron and Brooks (Brooks, 1977) with a six letter artificial alphabet in which they wrote six four-letter words. In one condition, the subjects learned to pronounce the words according to the orthography, the same symbols always standing for the same letters. In the other condition, the six printed words were randomly paired with the six spoken words, so that the orthography was no longer useful. Baron and Brooks found that, even after 400 trials with each stimulus, pronouncing the words was faster in the condition with the orthographic relationship. Spelling-to-sound correspondence rules thus can facilitate reading words aloud, despite extensive practice that would encourage the use of word-specific association. This view of the role of orthographic rules in addition to knowledge of association between whole words and their respective pronunciations leads to a number of questions. These include: how rules could be used, how meaning is extracted, the mediation of deep phonemic representation and whether knowledge of correspondences can be acquired implicitly.

Analogy Rules

Baron (1977a) examines the rules used in reading and the way in which we use rules besides orthographic ones. He suggests three ways in which people might make use of the existence of rules: (1) the component-correspondence method uses knowledge of letter-sound relations; (2) the analogy method makes references based on the changes in whole words; and (3) the similarity method takes over the entire response from a similar word. With the first method, the person uses knowledge of letters to sounds or clusters of letters to sounds. Thus one must know the rules in some sense, though one may not be able to state these rules. By knowing the pronunciation of whole words and the general strategies for forming analogies the person might be able to read new words. The similarity method (such as pronouncing "cap" for CAB) is occasionally useful.

Baron asked adult subjects to pronounce 35 nonsense words such as CAWS, SAIF, WIGHT and found that they relied heavily on analogy strategy. For example, TEIGH could be pronounced so as to rhyme with either PEA or PAY. In principle, the analogy strategy can be taught or facilitated without changing any specific knowledge about pronunciation of words or letter groups. After training in the use of analogy rules, the subjects increased their correctness in pronouncing the nonsense words. Thus training in itself, rather than mere repetition, was crucial. Also, errors of phonological illegal sequence such as pronouncing K and N in KNIF, G and N in BIGN were much reduced. This also argues for the greater efficiency of analogy rules. Baron raises further the interesting point about the use of analogies rather than rules as such. With analogies, a "rule" need not have been previously "productive" in order to be psychologically real. The analogy strategy can be used to invent new rules that make sense in terms of what we know. He gives an example that if LB is pronounced as "pound", then the pronunciation of LT as "pount" is acceptable as T is to D as P is to B (labial changed to dental). Similarly, SAIF is pronounced as "said." The results of several experiments with adults involving the use of introspection led Baron to suggest that the analogy strategy often wins out over the direct application of rules.

One advantage of the analogy strategy is that it allows people to learn the correspondence rules between letters and phonemes without ever having to produce the phonemes in isolation. In the case of beginning readers, they might also abstract the rules through "trial and error." In meeting with a new word like DIGN, the child will recall from memory words with similar properties such as IGN. This "learner-as-linguist" strategy is analogous to the hypothesis of language awareness: generate-a-rule-and-test-it. The importance is to teach the learner to transfer the rules. Reading is then seen as part of the process of intellectual development. Children cannot be expected simply to pick up the rules incidentally by practice or drill. We must make sure that they have the learning sets required to make use of this information.

Transfer of Learning in Related Words

Baron (1977b) reported some results of instructing young children to improve their ability to decode new words on the basis of similarities and differences with old ones. The subjects were five-year-old children (nonreaders who could not segment words). The aim was to measure the use of strategies by looking for transfer of learning between related pairs of words. For example, the child was asked to learn the pair of words MAT and MUG to criterion; then AT and UG under exactly the same conditions. Transfer was measured by subtracting the number of errors made while learning the second pair from the number of errors made with the first pair. To encourage subjects to learn the analogy strategy, they were given hints in the learning of the second pair and encouraged to think of a similar word that they had just heard. The results of experiments with adults confirmed the results of this child experiment. Instruction will improve the ability to decode new words on the basis of similarity and difference with old ones. The transfer effect from related words was also reported by Pick (1978) in a study with kindergarten children to determine the units of words detected and used by beginning readers. Pick reported that children did begin to abstract useful units larger than single letter-sound relationships and suggested the possibility that "after children learn the *idea* of decoding when they are learning to read, further emphasis on decoding per se instead of on learning the relevant graphic units for maximum efficiency in acquiring meaning may be uneconomical" (p. 118).

Baron (1977b, p. 213) suggests trying to teach children relevant strategies of learning and transfer before trying to teach them how to read. In a research program, Farnham-Diggory (1967, 1972, 1978b) investigated cognitively synthesized behavior involved in artificial reading of logographs by young children. The ability to connect visually apprehended logographs to the spoken word is related to development. As children learn to read, they must simultaneously apprehend and comprehend a number of units and integrate these units in the visual-auditory speech chain. In her recent work, Farnham-Diggory (1978b) reiterates the importance of synthesizing hand, eye, and mind behavior as precursors to reading. She asks children to perform pattern-drawing (simple geometric forms) from memory and monitors their behavior with cameras. Specifically, these behaviors and their latencies are recorded: tracking behavior, in which the eye looks ahead and the drawing hand catches up with it; monitoring behavior, in which the hand and eye are in the same place so that the eye is watching the hand. From these observations, Farnham-Diggory would expect that children who could not rhythmically coordinate eye, hand, and mind in pattern-drawing might also be unable to coordinate eye and mind in reading.

In three experiments, Baron (1979) has further confirmed that children differ in their ability to use rules rather than word-specific associations to read words and that they differ in the extent to make meaning-preserving errors (e.g. *cloth–clothe, seat–sit*) versus sound-preserving errors (e.g. "literal" pronouncing of *tint* by analogy with *pint* or *prey* by analogy with *key*). Reliance on rules is found to lead to sound-preserving errors while reliance on specific associations produces meaning-preserving errors. A further study by Baron and Treiman (1980) replicates the major finding that children differ in their use of rules and word-specific associations (direct path from whole printed words to whole spoken words and the indirect path from print to meaning to sound) in reading words aloud. Failure to use spelling-sound rules is seen as a failure to use strategies that would be helpful for rule learning. The series of studies by Baron and associates has shown that both analogies and smaller-unit rules are used in reading and that children can be taught intentional strategies and incidental strategies in learning rules (see also Baron and Hodge, 1978; Brooks, 1977, 1978; Brooks and Miller, 1979). Brooks claims that an alphabetic spelling system can help readers (college students) learn to pronounce a set of words even though they may not know the explicit rules of pronunciation. Their implicit knowledge is made possible through correspondence between overall similarities of stimuli and responses, as words that look alike sound alike.

With children, the difficulty is in determining what constitutes similarity. However, the possibility that implicit word knowledge is organized differently from explicitly given rules has implications for reading instruction. In terms of the abstract, internal representation in word reading, Baron (1977b, pp. 213–214) has well summarized the argument: "In activating one code or representation on the basis of other codes, there may be different paths connecting the relevant sets of codes. . . . In cases in which two pathways between one set of codes and another set receive extensive practice, both pathways will tend to become automatic. As a consequence, the use of one pathway will not take capacity away from the use of another, and both paths will be used. If, further, the two paths are nearly equal in effectiveness, both will contribute to the speed of activating the codes they lead to. This is especially true if we imagine both paths adding information to the critical codes continuously over some time span, rather than in an all-or-none manner."

Coalescing View

Mention has been made of the critique that Coltheart, Davelaar, Jonasson, and Besner (1977) wrote on the work of Rubenstein, Lewis, and Rubenstein (1971b). In their own studies, Coltheart et al. found that a letter string's similarity to English words influenced the "no" response latency, but not the "yes" response latency. It is argued that this result favors the view that lexical access is direct rather than requiring search. The other experiment showed that a nonword's phonological features influenced the time taken to say "no" to it. Thus, phonological encoding is occasionally involved in these experiments. To explain this parallel access to the lexicon, they invoke Morton's (1964, 1969, 1979a, 1979b, 1980) and Morton and Broadbent's (1967) logogen theory. This model is illustrated in Figure 9–3 (1977 version in Morton and Patterson, 1980).

The Morton *logogen* model (from *logos* meaning word and *genus* meaning birth) explains a great deal of data in accessing word meaning and in deep dyslexia, although the author modestly calls his model a "useful expository device" (Morton, 1979a, p. 109). The central features of the logogen theory are the sets of neural units called logogens. A logogen is not a word; it is the device or process which makes a particular word available as a response by collecting information or evidence, regardless of source, concerning particular word responses. A logogen is thus the memorial representation of a word. This representation consists of three parts: two input logogen systems, one for visual and one for auditory categorization; and one output logogen system. The output logogen system is the source of phonological information which is sent to the response buffer. There is also a pathway from the input analysis via a grapheme–phoneme conversion route to the response system to permit the reproduction of nonsense words.

As a neural unit, each logogen has a stable level of activation and a threshold—in fact, two thresholds. When the level of activation exceeds the first threshold, the logogen fires. In other words, when sufficient evidence has been collected within a particular logogen, the logogen passes its threshold value and the corresponding word

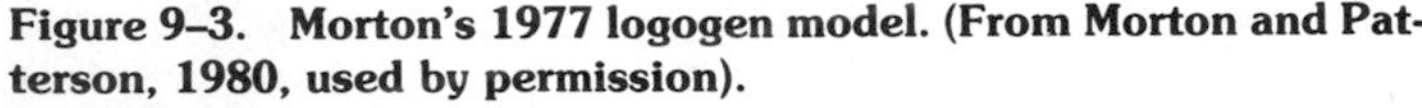
Figure 9–3. Morton's 1977 logogen model. (From Morton and Patterson, 1980, used by permission).

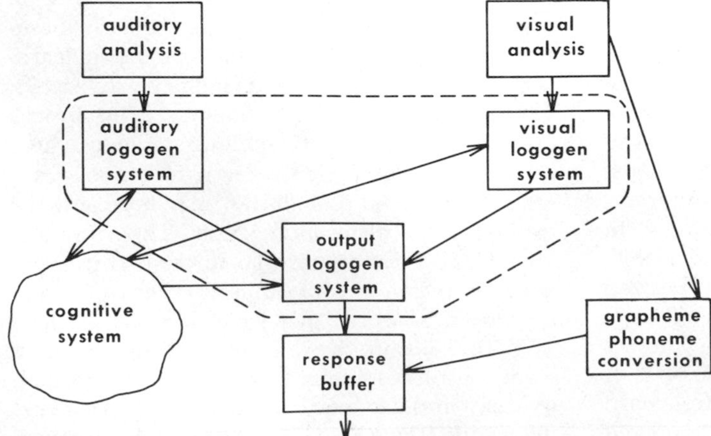

response becomes available. When a logogen fires, its resting level of activation is increased sharply and decays more slowly. An example will illustrate this. The visual logogen PARK has a little memorial representation from a stimulus PERK, a great deal more from BARK and maximally from PARK. Thus the logogen for PARK is scarcely excited by PERK, considerably excited by BARK and maximally by PARK. If excitation of an input logogen reaches threshold, the first stage of lexical access has occurred and information can be sent to the cognitive system where semantic information may be obtained, or to the output logogen where the phonological code may be found. It is possible for the first threshold to be exceeded without the second threshold being exceeded. Thus it is possible to understand a word, as in the case of deep dyslexia, without knowing what the word is. With deep dyslexics, it is likely that the level of the second threshold is raised abnormally high. Another word which is visually or semantically similar to the target and which has a lower threshold than the correct word may be produced as a paralexic error.

When a word is presented in isolation, a certain amount of evidence must be produced by the sensory analysis systems before evoking a response. When a word is presented in context, less information is required from the stimulus for the word to be recognized. Thus context helps to increase the likelihood of responding with certain words, using knowledge from the cognitive system. Also, logogen threshold is inversely related to word frequency, as common words do not require as much information from the stimulus as rare words do. It is possible to use the logogen model quantitatively to predict contextual effects on the basis that a particular logogen responding to a stimulus is affected not only by the amount of evidence collected, which is relatively constant for a stimulus, but also by random variations on the part of the individual. Morton (1969, 1979a) provides the mathematical derivation of the probability of making the correct response as the result of both stimulus and context information. With contextual feedback from the cognitive system to the input logogen systems both sensory evidence and contextual information combine directly to produce a response.

To return to the coalescing view, Coltheart et al. (1977) have emphasized lexical access as a parallel procedure. They have invoked the logogen model to explain the way in which stimulus information is made use of to gain access to the lexical entry. The first, GRONE, produces more overall excitation in the lexicon than a word like BRONE. The reason is that GRONE is homophonous with GROAN and this implies that at least part of the input to the lexicon is phonological, even when presentation is visual. But, if the lexicon dealt only with phonological input, GRONE and GROAN could not be discriminated and a lexical decision would not be possible. Hence some use must be made of visual information. Thus the *interplay* between phonological and visual information in the lexicon during reading is used.

This interplay is characterized by Meyer, Schvaneveldt, and Ruddy (1974) as a race. Lexical access is thus viewed as a *discrete* event rather than a continuous *incremental process* as increasing logogen excitation. Coltheart et al. emphasize the relationship between phonological and visual inputs to the lexicon as one of *cooperation*, rather than of competition. They state, "We suppose that the level of excitation of a lexical entry can be raised by appropriate visual input and also by appropriate phonological input, and, as this level rises during the process of reading a word, the lexical entry is *summing* phonological and visual evidence . . ." (p. 550). Their data show that differential effects of accessing nonwords of the kind of SLINT and GRONE can be explained by this optional encoding procedure and by the abandoning of the phonological strategy when an unacceptable level of errors occurs. Davelaar, Coltheart, Besner, and Jonassen (1978) further extend the dual coding and multiple paths hypothesis. They state: "an explanation in which decisions as to lexicality may sometimes be based on the outcome of a phonological encoding procedure and sometimes on the outcome of a graphemic encoding procedure would most satisfactorily account for all of the observed effects" (p. 399). This interpretation of the simultaneous phonemic and graphemic encoding allows for: (1) the optional nature of phonemic reading which is under the control of the subject, (2) a visual spelling recheck to be carried out after lexical access, and (3) a temporary inhibition after a lexical entry via a phonological code and an unsuccessful spelling check. The Coltheart et al. (1977) view of accessing the lexicon in parallel contrasts with the serial search view proposed by Rubenstein et al. (1971a, 1971b). Within the framework of the logogen theory, the optional rather than obligatory nature of phonological coding explains why the more frequent member of a homophone pair will reach threshold before the less frequent member on the basis of phonological input to the lexicon. However, the phonological strategy is likely abandoned in favor of graphemic coding when there is a high error rate. Whenever this visual spelling check fails, indicating access of the wrong entry, the inhibitory mechanism will temporarily reduce the availability of the lexical entry. This inhibition explains why presentation of a low-frequency homophone will impair the "yes" response to subsequent presentation of a high-frequency homophone.

The preceding detailed arguments for and against the alternative direct visual coding, the indirect phonological coding and the integrative dual coding hypotheses are summarized schematically in Figure 9–4. In brief, Figure 9–4A shows that visual processing of a printed word is constrained through some kind of phonological coding before meaning is accessed. Figure 9–4B suggests that words are processed directly from visual features to meaning with the minimum of intervening stages. The distinction between 9–4A and 9–4B, however, is not well-defined. Figure 9–4C illustrates the visual access stage model with a number of visual operations between feature extraction and interpretation (see Smith and Spoehr, 1974). Figure 9–4D summarizes the parallel coding, multiple paths model and shows the interplay between the different routes in accessing word meaning. It must be emphasized that the reader as an information processor has the option of sometimes using the one route, sometimes the other route, in accessing word meaning. This flexibility is a function of, among other things, the purpose of reading, the demands of the task, and the skill of the reader.

Figure 9–4. Phonological, visual and integrative coding of lexical access. (A.) Phonological coding. (B.) Direct visual access. (C.) Visual access stage. (D.) Dual coding—multiple paths.

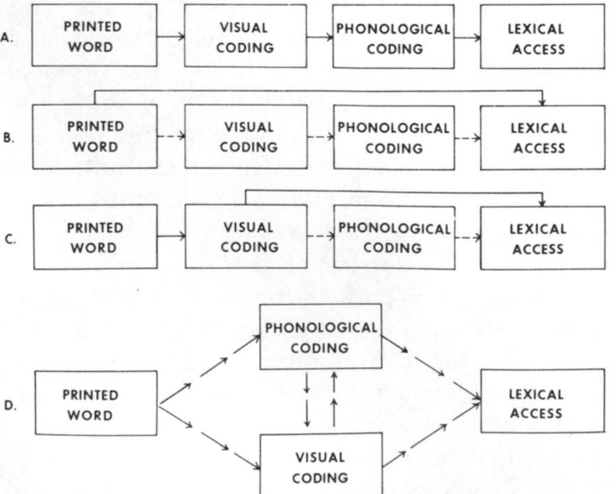

Summary

In this chapter, the discussion on the perceptual and coding processes that occur during reading has revealed the complexity of this problem. Empirical studies and scientific analyses aimed at understanding lexical access of word meaning do answer some of the research questions posed by the Modeling the Reading Process Panel on studies in reading convened by the U.S. National Institute of Education (Venezky, Massaro, and Weber, 1976). There are still many other unresolved issues. At the same time, we should be aware of the fact that much of the basic research on reading processes, such as some of the works discussed here, is done with adult subjects, not children. The performance of skilled readers with their overpracticed reading abilities may not be entirely applicable to the reading processes of beginning readers. There is a need for more research with beginners (e.g. work of Farnham-Diggory, 1978a, 1978b; Pick, 1978), with skilled, unskilled, and other poor readers. We would agree with Venezky's (1977) reminder of this in his review of historical perspectives of reading research: "Most present-day studies on reading processes are not motivated by an interest in reading per se. Much of the work on word recognition, for example, is aimed toward the construction of information-processing models for visual processing, rather than toward reading models or even toward an understanding of how words are recognized in normal reading. Although the results of these endeavors might eventually contribute to the improvement of literacy, the lack of focus on reading often leads to ignoring the relationship of laboratory-derived processes to what occurs in the reading task" (p. 343).

Venezky's concern would apply to some of the studies that we have reviewed in this chapter. But we are inclined to be more optimistic in this regard. Writing in a volume on knowledge and cognition, Forehand (1974) indicated the potential of information processing psychology for the understanding of complex human behavior. He stated, "That rapid success encourages me to speculate that within a comparable short time the approach will have as much of an impact on psychology in the field as it has had on psychology in the laboratory. In particular, its potential for illuminating recalcitrant problems in education seems excellent" (p. 159). Relevant works in recent years have included the volume by Klahr (1976) on cognition and instruction, the volume by LaBerge and Samuels (1977) on perception and comprehension in reading and the volume by Lesgold, Pellegrino, Fokkema, and Glaser (1978) on cognitive psychology and instruction with chapters on reading processes. These are but some of the concrete examples of the advances and the extent to which theoretical and methodological developments in information processing might provide useful knowledge and heuristics with regard to the design and management of instruction. Other cognitive aspects of reading processes with implications for instruction will be discussed in the next chapter.

CHAPTER 10

Other Cognitive Aspects

Writing in 1903, Binet (1969, p. 93) defined intelligence this way: "That which is called intelligence, in the strict sense of the word, consists of two principal things: first, perceiving the exterior world, and second, reconsidering these perceptions as memories, altering them." According to this view, intelligence is a process that includes organizing, directing and adapting external stimuli which differs greatly among individuals. In his classic work *Cognitive Psychology* Neisser (1967) writes of cognition as follows:

> the term "cognition" refers to all the processes by which the sensory input is transformed, reduced, elaborated, stored, recovered and used. It is concerned with these processes even when they operate in the absence of relevant stimulation, as in images and hallucinations. Such terms as *sensation, perception, imagery, retention, recall, problem-solving,* and *thinking,* among others, refer to hypothetical stages or aspects of cognition (p. 4).

Thus what was at one time considered sensation, perception and memory would all be subsumed under cognition. The emphasis is on the active, integrative role of the individual. Take, for example, the visual perceptual system. The perceiver can function flexibly in an analog, spatial manner or in a digital, serial manner (see Attneave, 1972). This interplay parallels the complex working system of the human brain (see Chapter 7).

This chapter deals with some of the issues arising from the previous chapter on coding processes in accessing word meaning. It has been shown that word comprehension involves memory search of the abstract, internal lexicon and that there are parallel coding processes involving multiple neural pathways. Readers seem to know that CHAIR is an English word before they know it is the name of an item of furniture and that fact before recognizing its other meaning of "chairing a meeting." Understanding certain aspects of a word seems to take longer than others, while recognizing ambiguous words takes longer still. In this chapter, we will discuss some "bottom-up," "top-down," and parallel, interactive models of reading comprehension. We will identify units in levels of processing: features, syllables, words, and sentences. We will examine the interdependence of cognitive processing involved in reading. Comprehension is conceptualized as going beyond syntactic knowledge and involves active construction and reconstruction of text materials by readers. This emphasis on the cognitive, representational approach dovetails into the cognitive clarity theory and tacit knowledge. The theme of reading as reasoning and the reader as an active information processor of discourse runs through this book. The term *discourse* (from the Latin "discurrere" meaning running to and fro) is used to denote any utterance larger than a sentence and may or may not comprise the full text of a given situation. Before discussing units of processing and textual comprehension, we will examine the reading-listening relationship and the role of visual imagery in reading comprehension.

Reading-Listening Relationship

One view of the reading-auding relationship is that there is one holistic ability to comprehend language by ear and by eye. The further corollary is that one should be able to comprehend equally well by listening or by reading, if one has learned auding and reading equally well. The holistic view seems to be at variance with the work of Spearritt (1962) who found separate listening and reading comprehension factors from his factor analysis. However, there are some methodological aspects of Spearritt's work such as the nonequivalence of reading and listening time leading to different interpretations of the factors. In reviewing this study, Sticht (1972) suggested that Spearritt's different factors should be interpreted to mean modality variables and task differences under different test conditions, but could find no support for "a special kind of language comprehension which is different when used in conjunction with listening than with reading" (p. 294).

Sticht (1972, 1978a, 1978b; Sticht, Beck, Hauke, Kleiman, and James, 1974) himself has studied the relationship between reading and listening in literacy acquisition. Specifically, he examines pragmatic aspects of language use in adults in conjunction with on-the-job behaviors involving motor skills. In this sense, his work relates reading and listening to real-world activities. Sticht (1972) found that poorer-reading men prefer to learn by listening rather than by reading. He suggested that much of their reading difficulty may result from reduced ability to comprehend language rather than (perhaps in addition to) lack of ability in decoding written symbols into the language of speech. In his military training program on reading and auding, Sticht (1978b) has integrated literacy skills and job skills training for marginally literate members of the U.S. armed forces. He identifies "reading-to-do" tasks and "reading-to-learn" tasks. The former tasks involve reading in which information is looked up and applied. This takes place when the persons already know how to do a particular job but need specific additional information. Reading-to-learn tasks include the use of rehearsal, focus of attention, and problem-solving skills. Thus Sticht not only has shown how a person performs a reading task but also has linked the cognitive aspect of reading to real-life problems.

In the case of children, Sticht presented evidence that comprehension by listening is greater than comprehension by reading in early school years. Beyond this stage, the two subsystems should be highly correlated. Specifically, "learning to language by eye as well as one can language by ear may require as long as 7 school years or thereabouts" (Sticht, 1978a, p. 138). Sticht presents his own data to show that it is at or about the seventh grade that auding ability is greater than reading ability, or the other way around. He also finds some support from "tenuous pieces of evidence" in that eye movement records generally show it is not until the eighth grade that the adult pattern of eye movements during reading is achieved, as found by Tinker (1965). Further, Durrell and Brassard (1969) showed in a large norming sample that auding and reading performance on paragraph comprehension became equal during the sixth grade, auding surpassed reading on vocabulary knowledge subtests through the eighth grade and that auding and reading performance became equal on the combined vocabulary and paragraph test scores. In a review of research, Sticht, Beck, Hauke, Kleiman, and James (1974) found that of the studies reviewed beyond the eighth-grade level, less than 50 per cent showed an advantage to reading comprehension compared with listening comprehension.

Sticht (1978a) suggested a conceptual model to guide research on reading and auding. This should deal with the questions of how people listen, how they process information for recall at the different language levels—sound, syntax and meaning. Sticht emphasizes teaching *learning* by listening just as we should teach *learning* by reading, rather than reading per se. This is cast within the context that oracy subskills of speaking and auding subskills of listening are part of conceptual development and that the same conceptual base and rules apply to both modes.

Not everyone will agree that listening and reading are one and the same skill. This disagreement was voiced by the discussants of the earlier Sticht (1972) work in which he argues that "there is only one, holistic ability to comprehend by language, and one should be able to comprehend equally well by listening or by reading, *if one has been taught to decode well and other task variables are equalized*" (pp. 293–294). One implication of this line of research is that initial reading involves the mastery of decoding to the point of automaticity (see section on LaBerge and Samuels (1974) model).

Another implication is that reading can be defined in relation to auding. Poor readers are those whose auding is significantly better than their reading; good readers are those for whom the reading-auding gap is not significantly different from zero; and excellent readers are those whose reading is significantly better than auding (see Mosberg, 1978). This seems to be also the view of Gleitman and Rozin (1977). They define fluent readers as those performing equally well in understanding spoken and read materials. Kintsch and Kozminsky (1977) provided evidence that reading and listening involve identical comprehension subskills. They found that adult readers' performance in reading and listening is remarkably similar when reading time equals listening time. This similarity holds at least for short texts and in answering short factual questions (see also Kintsch, Kozminsky, Streby, McKoon, and Keenan, 1975; Sachs, 1974). Young (1973) also found no difference between the comprehension scores of college readers and listeners when the time variable was controlled by presenting the written material on film at the same rate as the presentation of the oral versions. Kintsch and Kozminsky (1977) emphasize that the results are restricted by the subjects and the relatively easy texts used and that there may be thresholds beyond which reading and listening do not produce comparable results.

The findings of Sticht and of others suggest that one of the goals in reading education should be to narrow the gap between oral comprehension and reading comprehension. In this connection, it is significant to note that in Britain, the Schools Council sponsored a project from 1967 to 1972 on the whole field of speaking and listening with reference to school children. A good example of this important work and the research reports emerging is *The Quality of Listening* by Wilkinson, Stratta and Dudley (1974). These authors investigated linguistic communication, the reception and interpretation of listening and its role in reading and writing (see also Wilkinson, 1971). More recently, Carver (1977–1978) has proposed a theory that reading comprehension be considered a more general language comprehension called *rauding* which involves the two primary linguistic activities of *rauding* and reading. Pearson and Kamil (1977–1978) have critically reviewed Carver's theory of reading comprehension and rauding and have interpreted it as a mathematical, serial model.

Another important implication of the Sticht program is that it conceptualizes reading as involving alternative modes of *representation*—one mode being aural and the other mode being written. This accords with the broader definition of reading as interpretation of symbols or symbol systems. The position of Sticht has encompassed the concept of reading as "learning to language by eye as well as one can by ear by considering reading as linguistic-to-linguistic transformations of printed words into spoken words" (Sticht, 1978a, p. 156). The qualitative aspect of "languaging" as contrasted with the quantitative aspect of comprehension test scores was recently examined by Walker (1975–1976, 1977). He studied the precision of recall of materials presented either as formal writing or spontaneous speech in eleventh grade and college students. He found a difference in the sampling of linguistic cues and meaningful reconstruction in favor of the readers rather than the listeners, and suggested reading as a more precise form of language processing, at least for mature readers. Neville and Pugh (1976–1977) have shown that skilled readers exploit the precision and permanence of written texts by extracting the information they need when this arises, but poor readers may not do so.

The research of Sticht and associates should be seen in the broader perspective of relating reading to literacy acquisition, especially so in his training program for adult "exliterates." The social significance of literacy as a key tool for acquiring knowledge is emphasized by Halle (1972) and the summing-up by Miller (1972) in the conference on "language by ear and by eye." Carroll (1968a) has provided a perspective of the importance of "learning by being told" and has discussed (Carroll, 1974) the potentials and limitations of print. Carroll (1968a) suggests that learning by being told is characterized as a variety of *epistemic knowledge*. This is "the acquisition of knowledge through experience; learning through language is the acquisition of such knowledge vicariously—through the experience of one who formulates a sentence or a discourse. Overt *responses* on the part of the person receiving a message comes into the picture only when the message itself, or some external demand, requires him to make those responses; these responses, in turn, are based upon whatever kind and degree of epistemic competence the individual has acquired as a result of receiving and apprehending the message" (p. 9). There is a continuum of epistemic knowledge which can be acquired through visual, auditory, kinesthetic and other modes and which can range from perceptual to propositional learning.

In a wide-ranging "manifesto for visible language," editor Wrolstad (1976) discussed the relationship among three components of literacy acquisition: inner organization of language (comlang), and its expression as visible language, and as audible language ("speech and language glotto genesis"). He suggests a closer affinity between a person's internal information processing and the visible language system. In his developmental model, Sticht (1978a) is emphatic on the role of knowledge as foundation for the acquisition of new knowledge. To Sticht (1978a, p. 136), "development of the oracy skills requires the development of the cognitive content through the intellectual activity that we call conceptualizing ability." We should further compare the theoretical position of Sticht that reading and listening are parallel, analogous processes with Mattingly's (1972, 1979) concept of language by eye as "parasitic" on "language by ear" as discussed in Chapter 6, "Language Awareness."

While Mattingly has emphasized the psycholinguistic basis of reading and listening and Sticht has considered both activities within the larger context of literacy acquisition, contributors to the special issue of *Visible Language* (Winter, 1978, Vol. 12, No. 1) have used an information-processing model to explain how language is processed, and not just what the reader or listener must know to understand language. Language processing is viewed as involving internal processing components that occur between the language stimulus and meaning and these mental operations can be analyzed through reaction time studies (Massaro, 1978). Levy (1978a, 1978b) extends and clarifies her earlier work (see section on suppression phenomenon in Chapter 9) on the locus of speech suppression effect during reading. She explores the view that speech recoding occurs in working memory, where word units are held in a phonological form until comprehension of sentences occurs. She views language processing as involving different levels—perceptual, syntactic and semantic. Thus, the question of whether reading is an "analogous process" with, or parasitic on, listening may best be viewed as level-by-level processing.

Similar reasoning is put forward from a psycholinguistic perspective as well. From studies of children's comprehension of syllogisms, Mosenthal (1976–1977) suggested that a common language competence underlies both silent reading and aural processing but not reading aloud and that both silent reading and aural processing are facilitated by iconic and enactive representation. He has extended his investigation of aural and visual processing competence to the semantic level (Mosenthal, 1978). He used the Given-New Strategy of Clark and Haviland (1974) to test grade two, four, and six children in their visual and aural comprehension and presuppositive negatives. The results suggest that children use different strategies in comprehending aurally and visually, the tendency for children to treat more information as "given" in the aural process and more information as "new" in the visual processing. These "processing routines" are "disparate even as late as sixth grade" (p. 275). The Mosenthal psycholinguistic studies underpin the importance of sublevels of processing and raise the question of the type of processing most useful for pedagogic purposes.

Visual Imagery and Reading Comprehension

Understanding spoken or written discourse involves relating the words, phrases and clauses in the sentence or prose material to other information in the preceding part of the discourse or information in the world (epistemic knowledge). Understanding discourse involves an abstract semantic representation. This representation is most likely propositional but it can also be imaginal or pictorial or both. We will first discuss the role of visual imagery in reading.

Paivio (1969) found that information embedded in concrete words is easier to learn than information conveyed in abstract words. He suggested that imaging should facilitate recall of meaning by forming a "thema" (Paivio, 1971) and that dual coding (verbal and imaginal) is superior to single coding in pair associate learning. Experimental evidence for the facilitating effect of imagery comes from several sources. Using two methods with 100 ESN (educationally subnormal or retarded) children aged nine to sixteen, Riding and Shore (1974) tested the hypothesis that imaging and slower rate of presentation of text material would facilitate prose comprehension. Both methods (imaging and slower rate of presentation) produced significant improvements in recall performance that were large enough to be of practical usefulness. What is difficult to determine in this study is whether the slowness in recoding by ESN children is due to the use of inefficient recoding strategies or to a general slowness of reaction or to both. The size of the code and the speed of recoding will also have to be determined. This study with retarded children reminds us of the discussion of *phonemic dyslexia* (Marshall and Newcombe, 1973; Richardson, 1975a, 1975b; Shallice and Warrington, 1975) in Chapter 9. In these rare cases of acquired dyslexia with paralexic errors, imagery and frequency have been found to be good predictors of reading retardation. Note also that Richardson rejects the idea that word imagery simply facilitates direct access to semantic information on the grounds that word imagery is a better predictor of reading performance than word concreteness. Thus, it is not necessary to assume that in reading readers must elicit a mental picture. Kintsch (1974) has offered a viable explanation of the role of mental imagery. He suggests that high imagery words are represented in a subjective lexicon by a few strong relations while low imagery words enter into more relations with other words and these latter relations are more diffuse. When learning to associate a high imagery word with a printed form, readers should have a smaller pool of strong cues to choose from, making the correct response easier for them to encode and to retrieve.

In a study of imagery and prose-learning in high-school seniors, Anderson and Kulhavy (1972) instructed them to form mental images while reading a 2,000 word textlike passage. They recalled no more "factual" text than did a noninstructed control group. However, on a post-experiment questionnaire more than half of the control group reported using imagery, while about one-third of the experimental group did not use imagery as they were instructed . Those who said they used imagery learned more than nonimagery learners. The study raised at least two questions: (1) The question of how to evoke and maintain imagery needs more study; (2) It is likely that high-school students have already developed a procedure for remembering text.

Kulhavy and Swenson (1975) studied imagery and text comprehension in 119 fifth- and sixth-grade children. They read a twenty paragraph text entitled "The Island of Ako and its People," which described the life and culture of a fictitious people living on a remote Pacific island. Half of the group was tested immediately after reading and all children were given a delayed test one week later. The test measured both *verbatim* and *semantic* (lexical paraphrase) recall of materials seen during the initial reading. An example of a lexical paraphrase item to the question:

> "The islanders construct their clothes from . . . (palm leaves)."

was:

> "Garments worn by the natives are made with . . . (palm leaves)."

Half of the children received instruction to form mental pictures of the text events during reading. It was found that imagery learners performed better than nonimagery ones in the recall tasks and the former also recalled more semantic test items. The performance differences were less pronounced between immediate and delay measures, but the pooled delay scores showed a decided superiority for image learners. Thus image instructions act to increase the amount of text content available over time.

From the studies of imagery and prose-learning in high-school students, retarded children, and grade-school children, the next question is whether children can be trained to use imagery effectively. Training can be externally imposed or internally induced. McCabe, Levin and Wolff (1974) found that five-year-old children can benefit from observing or constructing *external* pictorial mediators. However, children at that age do not benefit from *internal* mediators or visual imagery instructions (Wolff and Levin, 1972). Children at age six do not benefit from subject-generated overt pictorial augmentation (by selecting plasticized figure cutouts) of aural prose except when they are given the correct illustrations (Lesgold, Levin, Shimron and Guttman, 1975). By age seven or eight, children begin to acquire internal elaboration ability (Levin, Davidson, Wolff and Citron, 1973), and they can be trained to elaborate without external prompts even earlier (Varley, Levin, Severson and Wolff, 1974). Further study by Lesgold, McCormick and Golinkoff (1975) aimed at examining the effects of coordinating verbal and pictorial representation by having third- and fourth-grade children read passages, illustrate them with stick-figure cartoons and by using the cartoons as prompts in recalling prose passage content. It was found that after this "imagery" training, performance in a paragraph-recall task improved, but only when explicit imagery instructions were given with the task. The authors suggested that the effects of imagery training lie in the organization and storage of information in providing a more retrieval memory representation of prose. Pressley (1976) improved on the Lesgold, McCormick and Golinkoff study by training third-grade children in several minutes instead of the four-week period of Lesgold et al. The aim was to develop internal mediation in the recall of a 950-word story. Pressley suggested that perhaps skilled readers process prose so well spontaneously that the use of mental imagery may not greatly improve their information processing. This was also observed by Levin and Divine-Hawkins (1974), who further suggested that imagery instruction does not necessarily improve the memory of middle-childhood children (fourth-graders). Levin (1973) showed that while *internal visual imagery* facilitates story comprehension, this strategy is differentially effective for two different kinds of poor readers. Poor readers with adequate vocabulary subskills benefitted more from imagery instructions than those with inadequate vocabulary subskills. Then Guttman, Levin and Pressley (1977) examined the effects of various imagery and pictorial strategies on young children's oral prose-learning performance. Their findings showed that : (1) There are developmental differences in the ability to profit from a completely self-generated imagery strategy; (2) Children, including kindergarteners, can benefit from experimenter-provided cues to generate imagery; and (3) The type of cue provided is related to the kind of information recalled. Partial pictures may help in situations in which completely induced imagery may not. Thus Guttman et al. demonstrated that the period between the ages of five and eight is important in the development of imaginal mediation of prose-learning and that this learning progresses from externally imposed pictures to internal images as children grow and develop.

From the evidence reviewed it seems that in a large number of learning tasks including prose learning, children benefit by the use of pictures or visual imagery. There are some reservations. Samuels (1967) applied the principles of cue selection and least effort of Underwood, Ham, and Ekstrand (1962) to the area of word recognition by children. He found that pictorial redundancy seemed to be distracting when preschoolers were presented with common words on flash cards alone or on cards accompanied by appropriate pictures and also in a classroom experiment with a story accompanied by an illustration. This distracting effect of pictures on word acquisition was replicated by Braun (1969) and Singer, Samuels, and Spiroff (1973–1974).

Samuels (1970) further reviewed other evidence and found pictures of limited usefulness in helping children learn a sight vocabulary. Willows (1978a) found that reading performance of second- and third-grade children was less efficient in terms of time and errors if pictures were shown in peripheral vision. Less skilled readers were more susceptible to the distraction, and unrelated pictures produced more interference than related ones. It was found also that less skilled third-grade readers were influenced by pictures shown with words of all levels of difficulty and that this susceptibility to distraction showed marked individual differences (Willows, 1978b). Contrary evidence for kindergarten children was obtained by Arlin, Scott and Webster (1978–1979), who found that simultaneous presentation of pictures with concrete sight words facilitates rather than impedes learning and that this facilitating effect outweighs any distraction. In light of recent evidence, which has moved towards the "processes" associated with the picture-phenomenon, the early views of Samuels may need to be modified except when pictures and text present conflicting information (see review by Pressley, 1977). However, these early results can be reconciled as the use of pictorial information is not incompatible with the operation of partial trade-offs which facilitate both word identification and word learning. Denburg (1976–1977) has found that beginning readers can achieve this trade-off and can integrate information with ease with the assistance of pictures.

The weight of the evidence from the research program of Levin and associates (Lesgold, de Good, and Levin, 1977; Levin, 1973, 1976; Levin, Bender, and Lesgold, 1976; Ruch and Levin, 1977 and Pressley, 1977) have shown the facilitating effect of illustrations to prose-learning especially when pictures are interfaced with important information and clearly represent facts. To the extent that pictures divert children's attention from text, comprehension will not be complete. There is a clear advantage for pictorial representation of certain kinds of information (e.g. spatial and analogic information). Illustrations including less-than-complete pictures are effective for both simple and complex stories of both long and short lengths, especially for younger children and less skilled readers. Children can be trained to induce imagery and their ability to generate effective imagery is closely related to their cognitive development. In prose-learning, imagery strategy is differentially effective for different tasks and different children (see also Levin, Divine-Hawkins, Kerst, and Guttman, 1974). For reading materials, pictures must be carefully designed to ensure a good match between pictorial and print information.

At the conceptual level the dual coding process of Paivio has been critiqued by Pylyshyn (1973). The latter argued that imaginal representation must be imaginal and the only viable representation is propositional in nature. Norman and Rumelhart (1975) suggest that arguments about verbal or imaginal representation resolves to the type of relations that are encoded. They state:

> We believe that the human cognitive system is capable of flexibility in the way it represents the information that it uses. Propositional representation would appear to be well suited for permanent storage of the meaning and interpretation of the events that a person experiences. At times, analogical representations would appear to be better suited for the operations that one wishes to perform upon mental structures (p. 20).

This brings us to units of levels of processing and the larger issue of discourse comprehension.

Units of Levels of Processing

Before dealing with text comprehension, it is useful to pause for a while to examine the units of processing at the various levels—features, letters, letter clusters, words and sentences. The treatment is selective and only the main issues pertaining to the perception and processing of units of printed English will be discussed. One difficulty with the search for a fundamental unit in speech or language perception may be tantamount to what Bradshaw (1975) calls the "search for an elusive entity." Reviews of processing units of various sizes can be found in Gibson and Levin (1975), Massaro (1975a), Smith and Spoehr (1974), among others.

Distinctive Features and Letters

We will begin our discussion with *features* and move our way "up." These units of information are *relational* and *contrastive* and serve to differentiate more complex materials from simpler ones. In the case of graphemes, visual features take the form of straight or curved lines. Compelling evidence for feature detection comes from the series of physiological investigations by Hubel and Wiesel (1962, 1963, 1965). The reader may like to refer to the relevant sections in our chapter on Seeing and Reading. In essence, the feature detection account states that the single cell is the functional unit in perception, that processing is from simple cells to complex and hypercomplex cells, that anatomically distinct regions in the brain are activated in processing, such as Brodmann's Area 17 for simple cells, Areas 17 and 18 for complex cells and Areas 18 and 19 for hypercomplex cells.

Studies of visual features in reading are an analog of the *distinctive feature theory* of the phonemes of human speech developed and elaborated by Jakobson, Fant and Halle (1952) and Jakobson and Halle (1956). Jakobson et al. suggest that children first acquire contrasts between vowels and consonants, between nasals and oral consonants, then contrasts among sounds along a front to back place of articulation continuum (labials vs. dentals, velopalatals vs. labials and palatals vs. velars). An example of dental vs. labial consonants is the contrastive pair /t/ vs. /p/, of velopalatal vs. labial and dental consonants is the pair /k/ vs. /t/ and of palatal vs. velar consonants is the contrast /s/ vs. /k/. In their fuller system of classification, Jakobson, Fant and Halle (1952) used eight binary features to describe twenty-one English consonants. These binary features are indicated: vocalic–nonvocalic, consonantal–nonconsonantal, grave–acute, diffuse–compact, strident–mellow, nasal–oral, continuant–interrupted and voiced–voiceless. The consonant /m/, for example, is assigned a PLUS value in each of these binary features: consonantal–nonconsonantal, grave–acute and nasal–oral and given a MINUS in each of: vocalic–nonvocalic and compact–diffuse features. Take another example. The set of features that define voiceless stop consonants such as /p/, /t/ and /k/ are "+ consonantal," "– vocalic," "– continuant," "+ tense," "– strident," and "– voice." The consonant /p/ is further distinguished from /t/ on the "+ grave" (for /p/) and "– grave" (for /t/), dimension. The Jakobson et al. system of classification is based on linguistic and acoustic information of speech sounds from many languages and is *invariant* even when the sounds are produced by many voices. In their classification, Chomsky and Halle (1968) presented thirteen articulatory features with anatomic referents and five major classes including: major class features, cavity features, manner of articulation features, source features and prosodic features. The thirteen articulatory features representing twenty-two English consonants are: vocalic, consonantal, high, back, low, anterior, coronal, voicing, continuancy, nasality, stridency, round, and tense. Recently, Massaro (1978) has referred to some of his experiments based on the assumption that the acoustic features are "fuzzy" or continuous rather than present or absent in the binary phonetic system.

In her development of visual distinctive features, Gibson (1969) aims at achieving a psychologically and perceptually adequate account of the characterization of the English alphabet, the simple Roman majuscules. The overall goal is to arrive at an objectively derived set of features which are in fact used in distinguishing one letter from the other (see Gibson and Levin, 1975). Based on neurophysiological evidence such as the research program of Hubel and Wiesel, Gibson sees one basic distinction of letters of the alphabet as straight and curved lines. Another set of basic differences among straight line segments distinguishes between vertical, horizontal and various diagonals. It should be noted that the distinctive features of letters apply only to parts of the letters. Thus "P" and "R" are assigned the feature "PLUS straight-vertical line" because they each contain a straight vertical line. The letter "C" is assigned the feature of open-curve while "B" the feature of closed-curve. The rationale is that for any two letters the higher the probability of features they have in common, the more likely these letters are to be confused. The probability of confusing two letters is used to form a *confusion matrix* which can then be analyzed mathematically (e.g. through cluster analysis) to discover the contrastive features in each cluster or at each level of the hierarchical cluster. By examining the "nodes" of this treelike structure, or the intersections, it is possible to determine which features are critical for the differentiation of letters. In their research program on confusion errors in letter recognition, Gibson and her colleagues (Gibson, 1969; Gibson and Levin, 1975; Gibson, Osser, Schiff, and Smith, 1963) have consistently found that errors and reaction times increased as the number of features shared by two different letters increased. They have also consistently demonstrated the relational and contrastive nature of the features as straight vs. curved, vertical vs. horizontal or diagonal, and open vs. closed. The invariance of events is underlined.

Thus perception of a string of letters involves the processes of *differentiating, categorizing* and *interpreting* input stimuli. This is illustrated in Figure 10–1. The example is the processing of the capital letter "D". The extraction of visual features is along the lines of straight, curved, redundant and symmetrical features. The reader will have to compare this input with the stored visual representation of various letter categories and make an appropriate decision in the response. The decision may be made via the phonological route. The extraction and interpretation of single letters thus also bear some similarity in general conception to the visual and phonological access in word perception discussed in Chapter 9. It may be pointed out that research by Bouma (1971) in the Netherlands showed that the features for upper-case letters may not apply to lower-case letters (see also Dunn-Rankin, 1968, 1978), and that a priori expectation plays a part when few features are extracted and the probability for errors is high. Readers may give less to what they "see" and more to what they expect a priori when they see very little. Analogous to some recent work in speech perception, the notion of "fuzzy" information has also begun to be applied to visual features (Massaro, 1978). According to the "fuzzy"

Figure 10–1. Differentiating, categorizing and interpreting capital letter D as an input stimulus.

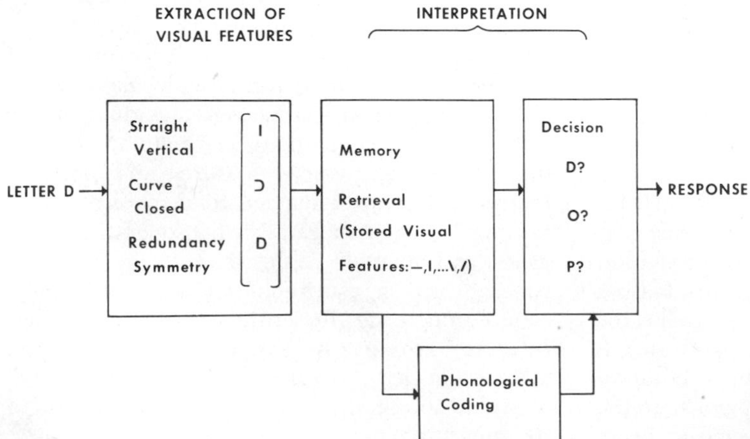

concept, visible features are detected in degrees of continuity rather than the PLUS or MINUS binary classification.

There has been some criticism of perceptual processing as espoused by E. Gibson in her research program on reading. The main question raised is whether perception is an atomistic, differentiating process or one of construction and integration of stimuli. This kind of query is no doubt influenced by cognitive theories dealing with computer simulation. In a recent article, Gibson (1977) reiterates her position that perception is an *abstraction* process carried out at a relatively high level. This level can also be attained by infants as shown in their ability to abstract phonemic contrasts in continuous speech (Liberman, Cooper, Shankweiler, and Studdert-Kennedy, 1967). Gibson points out the extraction of information varies with species (e.g. birds are well-equipped to extract visual information from spatial layouts), follows a developmental course and depends on learning the relational and contrastive aspects of information. While most children seem to be able to distinguish letters, some may find it hard to distinguish sequences of letters (e.g. *three* and *there*) and hard to differentiate succession, such as segmenting the language whether read or heard. In learning to extract information from printed words children learn the relational properties of rulelike structures and meaning. Gibson (1977, p. 171) suggests that "we should speak of learning and development in perception as differentiation rather than construction; that the relevant processes are more akin to discovery and abstraction than to association and integration; and that man evolved as a seeker of information. . . ."

The question of what visual cues people use when they look at letters or words has been explored by Dunn-Rankin (1978) in his research program. He views reading as a progressive feature-recognition process in which a few basic models of form (e.g. curves, angles, vertical lines, and so on) serve as cues for the recognition of letters, which in turn serve as cues for the recognition of syllables and words, which then serve as cues for recognizing phrases. The process is seen as parallel rather than serial as the combination of featural units is stressed. Dunn-Rankin suggests that children in as early as the second grade and very likely by the fourth grade use context and phonetic cues to "guess" what the words are in their reading. For very young children or inexperienced readers, graphic stimuli are complex and are likely processed in featural units. For older and experienced readers, visual features are only one aspect of successful reading acquisition.

Letter Clusters and Words

The above discussion of featural units has also touched briefly on *letters* and *letter clusters.* Note the later section on Gough's (1972) letter-by-letter processing in his one second of reading. A study by M. Mason (1975) with good and poor sixth grade readers may be mentioned as an attempt to distinguish between sequential redundancy and spatial frequency redundancy. Mason argues that spatial redundancy or the relation between the visual features of letters and the spatial position of their location in words helps in the identification of individual letters. Hansen and Rodgers (1968) have proposed the *"vocalic center group"* (VCG) as the perceptual unit in reading. The VCG is a letter sequence centered around a vocalic element. The basic idea is that in producing and synthesizing speech, units of at least VCG size are needed to specify phonemes, which are transmitted, not serially in isolation, but in parallel. This assumption of the vocalic center group as the unit of perception in reading was tested by Spoehr and Smith (1973). They compared the accuracy of recognition of one- and two-syllable words equated for length, frequency, and initial letters, and each word containing one or two VCGs. They found that letters in one-syllable words were recognized better than in two-syllable words and took this as evidence in support of the vocalic center group model. Spoehr and Smith (1975) further found that the vocalic center group added to the accuracy of letter-storing recognition. The VCG model, however, has been criticized by Massaro (1975b) on the grounds that the model assumes that letters are recognized before parsing begins, without any help from orthographic rules. The observation that readers usually have partial letter information before parsing is not accommodated in the model.

Gibson and her associates studied the role of letter clusters that map to an invariant pronunciation in a given speech environment. Gibson, Pick, Osser, and Hammond (1962) termed this perceptual unit larger than a single letter *spelling pattern.* They found that pronounceable words (e.g. SLAND) presented tachistoscopically were perceived more accurately than unpronounceable words (e.g. DSORBL) so presented. They suggested phonological and orthographic regularity facilitates recognition of letter clusters in the absence of familiarity and meaning. Gibson, Shurcliff, and Yonas (1970) further tested the recognition of pronounceable and unpronounceable nonwords and applied these to congenitally deaf subjects. The finding that deaf subjects could read just as well the pronounceable nonwords led to the view that the two types of nonwords might have been differentiated by orthographic structure. We should bear in mind that in studies of the kind carried out by Gibson and associates it is difficult to disentangle pronounceable and orthographic effects. This question is also related to the phonological and visual access of word meaning discussed at length in the preceding chapter.

Recently, Gleitman and Rozin (1973, 1977) and Rozin and Gleitman (1977) have suggested the use of the *syllable* as an introductory approach in beginning reading with some readers. Their view is based on the premise that ontogenetically language preceded writing and pictorial representations preceded the highly abstract symbol system of alphabetic notation. They maintain that it is easier to be aware of meaning than of syntax, and easier to move "down" to words, then to sounds. They claim that "the acquisition of reading will be made more coherent for the learner if the task is dissected in terms of successively more abstract encodings of meaning, beginning with relatively concrete visual representations (of words) and progressing by steps toward the phonological representations that underlie alphabetic writing" (Gleitman and Rozin, 1977, p. 4). This plan of progressing from more concrete to more abstract representations was bolstered by a study of Rozin, Poritsky, and Sotsky (1971) in which they showed the successful use of the syllabary with a small number of inner-city schoolchildren. Gleitman and Rozin make it clear that the syllable is "neither where the child begins, nor is it where one would want him to end up, in reading; words and phrases are the units with which the child begins . . ." (Gleitman and Rozin, 1973, p. 463), and emphasize the need to acquire phonological principles. In his critique of the earlier view of Gleitman and Rozin, Goodman (1973) rightly pointed out that syllabification has its inherent difficulties. For one thing, overemphasis on syllabification goes against the principle of economy of information pickup of the English alphabet, as there are many more syllables than there are letters of the alphabet or phonemes. For another, syllabification is not merely going by "what the sound says." An example is the hyphenation of the word "drummer" where "drumm-er" with the morpheme "er" is often hyphenated as "drum-mer." Shuy (1969) has outlined some "semiordered syllabification rules"—lexical, grammatical and phonological—to highlight difficulties in defining limits of a syllable. The *syllabic curriculum* proposed by Gleitman and Rozin with the use of the rebus thus poses a number of theoretical problems yet to be resolved.

The issue of *word* preception will not be dealt with here. The topic is extensively reviewed in the preceding chapter. Probably there is no such entity as an ideal segment in learning to read. Before we move on to sentence processing, it is helpful to conclude this section by drawing on the comments of Bradshaw (1975) and Gibson and Levin (1975). Bradshaw (p. 132) suggested, "Both syllables and phonemes appear to be useful abstract concepts and, in fact, to interrelate closely with each other. If meaning is extracted through such transparent entities, this in itself is compatible with the suggestion . . . that semantic information but not necessarily phonological or graphological information may be available from words beyond fixation." The term *transparency* as used here is in the sense used by McNeill and Lindig (1973) who in turn drew on Polanyi (1964). McNeill and Lindig found that, in listening to speech, people are not always aware of phonological and syntactical structures even though these might have been perceived. The structural information that listeners are usually not aware of is described as *linguistic transparency*. This is the case of "we do not know we know" about certain things compared with "knowing about things we do not know we know about." The question of tacit knowledge and linguistic awareness in relation to reading will be further elucidated in later sections of this chapter.

Another perspective to the search for the elusive processing unit is provided by Gibson and Levin (1975). They state that:

> A *multilevel* approach is essential. What the child reads must make sense. At the same time, it must not be so hard that he fails. Whatever the segment, it must be the most economical one that he is capable of processing. Practice with it must yield transfer to new words. . . . We want to present real information in real sentences. . . . So learning to read at the beginning must involve sentences, even if the child does some guessing. It must also include learning to segment words. Words included in the

> sentence should often be polysyllabic, since syllabic segmentation is easy and may get across the idea of analysis. They could well be words like *cowboy* and *Sunday,* so the child will learn about intraword morphemic segments. The latter is important, because English orthography is morpho-phonemic, not just phonemic. And there must be intrasyllable analysis, at some point, not just letter by letter, but by way of constrained letter rules and patterns . . . (p. 289–290, Gibson and Levin's italics).

The above is quoted at some length as it presents a coalescing view. This ties in with some of the theoretical discussions in preceding sections on both the parallel, interactive processing and units of processings. The flexible, multilevel approach has implications for teaching situations.

Doehring's Study of Rapid Processing of Print

A recent study by Doehring (1976) of different levels of rapid, efficient processing of print during reading acquisition commands attention. The work compares response latencies to a number of verbal stimuli with a wide age range of children. Doehring aimed at assessing systematically acquisition of subskills for rapid processing of letters, syllables, words and word sequences in 150 children (75 girls and 75 boys) from kindergarten (first and second halves), grades one and two (first and second halves each) to grade eleven inclusive. The children were required to perform visual matching to a visual sample tasks, visual matching to an auditory sample tasks, oral reading, and visual scanning tasks and their response latency was measured. The visual matching to sample tasks involved samples of number; upper- and lower-case letters; familiar CVC and CVCC words (e.g. "did" and "long"); unfamiliar CVC syllables (e.g. "sig") and CCC letter strings (e.g. "kzd"). The auditory-visual matching to sample tasks involved letters; familiar CVC, CVCC words; and CCV, CVC and CVCC syllables (e.g. "cla," "pin," "sild" respectively) orally presented (syllables spoken as unitary sounds rather than separate sounds) to be matched with printed choices. Oral reading included the rapid reading without errors of upper- and lower-case letters separately and in combination (e.g., "OLESMP . . . ," "uj gybm . . ." and "Mzlh OndS . . ."); random words ("the age over end made for years"); second-order and seventh-order approximations to discourse and words in meaningful discourse.

Overall results of the Doehring study showed that response latency on all tasks decreased significantly until grade five to six or about ages ten to eleven and relative speeds of response changed systematically from grade to grade. Data also showed that children in as early as grade one can use information for groups of words as relational units to increase their rate of processing print. They would, however, require several years to develop fully the relative response speeds for processing different perceptual units for skilled reading. In other words, several different levels of rapid, efficient processing of print are developed in parallel during reading acquisition. Increasing orthographic regularity, syntactic regularity and meaningfulness facilitates speed of processing. Doehring (1976) suggests that:

> Letter-by-letter processing may usually develop earliest, and syllable, word, and sentence processing may usually begin to develop during first grade. Once development has begun, sentence processing is more efficient than word-by-word processing and becomes even more efficient over the years; word processing is more efficient than syllable processing at first, but visual syllable processing may eventually become as efficient as visual word processing (p. 39).

The Doehring finding can be considered with reference to the levels-of-processing framework of memory research of Craik and Lockhart (1972) and Lockhart, Craik and Jacoby (1975). These researchers proposed a continuum varying from visual pattern recognition to semantic elaboration of stimuli. They view perception and memory as forming a single system in which the output of perceptual analysis becomes the memory representation. They also state that products of the higher level of perceptual analysis are retained longer. Craik and Tulving (1975) have extended the level-of-processing concept to a "spread of processing" approach. The surface level deals more with simple perceptual analyses, while the deeper level of processing is more related to the analysis of meaning. Stimuli processed at the semantic level are more durable and remembered better. Superordinate ideas are more resistent to forgetting than subordinate ones. Thus the level-of-processing or its extension the spread-of-processing framework lends itself to a unifying explanation of prose recall. Doehring's finding is compatible with this view. The parallel development of processing subskills also fits the automaticity model of LaBerge and Samuels (1974), the multilevel processing of Gibson and Levin (1975) and the parallel, interactive formalism of Rumelhart (1977a, 1977b). In the next section we will turn our attention to the perception of discourse —the cognitive aspect of prose comprehension.

Models of Reading Acquisition—An Overview

The terms *model* and *theory* are often used interchangeably. The difference is relative. Rudner (1966, p. 25) explained "which is regarded as the model, and which the theory of primary concern, will not depend on any structural feature of the two theories, but merely on which subject matter we are primarily interested in." One might use the theory of the flow of water through pipes as a model for a theory of electric currents in wires. In this sense, models function as heuristic devices. Thus, a model or a theory "is a unified system of principles, definitions, postulates, and observations organized in such a way as to most simply explain the interrelationships between variables" (Campbell, 1957, p. 120). A good theory or a viable model should define the relevance of facts and develop systems of classification and a structure of concepts. A model should summarize *previous* facts parsimoniously. It should help to understand *current* knowledge and should also predict *future* events and point to further research. As well, Maier (1960) adds that if certain facts do not conform to a particular model, they should be verified as there is the danger of a nonviable model built on facts which may have paled in significance because of changing events or concepts.

In Search of Models of Reading

Writing in the comprehensive literature of research on models of reading, Williams (1971) discussed the congruence of several approaches (e.g. operant, cognitive and psychometric perspectives) to building reading models extant to the late 1960s. She found the following consensus:

1. The models should have a cognitive framework.
2. The component subskills of reading and their relationship to one another are important.
3. Reading is a communication or language process and reading models will have to include the complexity of the language system.
4. Reading acquisition will need to take into account the developmental status of the child.
5. The affective factor should be incorporated into reading acquisition.
6. Reading models should take into account individual and group differences.
7. Models of reading acquisition should also be used for developing instruction.

Williams felt that as yet "a comprehensive model of learning to read" or of mature reading had not been developed and emphasized the need for partial models or models dealing with limited aspects of reading. Since Williams' review was written, there have been considerable developments in models of reading along the lines of her comments. Some sixty years ago, Gray (1919) drew attention to some of the purposes of reading, especially reading comprehension. He listed reading for coherent reproduction, for central thought, for information, for understanding and solution of problems, and for the determination of the validity of statements. This view of *reading for some purpose* was reiterated forcefully by Gibson (1972) and Gibson and Levin (1975). As reading differs for different purposes and as there is no one single reading process but rather many processes, it follows there can be no single model for reading.

It is beyond the scope of this section to discuss in detail the various models of reading. This has been ably done elsewhere, notably in the work by Singer and Ruddell (1970), the review by Mackworth (1972), the compendium volume by Davis (1971) and more recently the update by Singer and Ruddell (1976). Instead of attempting to be exhaustive, we will focus our attention on a small number of models which seem to us to explain reasonably well the reading processes. The selection is thus partial and not complete and to some extent reflects our predilections. These models, however, have been formalized and can generate further testable hypotheses. The heuristics can provide implications for instruction.

The Substrata-Factor Model

The Substrata-Factor Theory of Holmes (1953, 1970) has been discussed in connection with the chapter on reading as a skill. The Holmes model relates to neurological, psychological and psychometric aspects of reading with emphasis given to the latter two. The substrata factors are defined as neurological subsystems of brain cell-assemblies, which are facilitated by firing in phase. The substrata factors can be flexibly combined into working systems which are organized by mobilizers to be triggered by print symbols. There has been some criticism of Holmes' use of the statistical method of multiple regression. However, his conceptualization of reading as consisting of complex subsystems which can be subsumed under higher-order working systems emphasizes the holistic nature of reading. Chapter 2 in this book has further expanded on this need for integrating subskills into an organized whole skill.

Mackworth's Model

The model by J. Mackworth (1971, 1972) discusses the sequence operating in processing reading stimuli. The visual input taking place during fixation pauses is an active process involving selection, attention, expectancy and prediction. The sensory visual trace lasting for about 250 milliseconds is processed in parallel. Recognition of input occurs by matching it to long-term memory traces and the input occurs as an icon lasting for about 1000 to 2000 milliseconds. From the iconic store, words are coded into short-term memory by motor speech programs before storage in long-term memory. Visual and auditory systems contact at the point of coding. Thus what is perceived results from two processes: the sensory input and the comparison with the stored pattern. As a result of this matching, a percept is formed that is stabilized and simpler than the primary store. The comparison becomes more efficient when the stored word has been activated by the previous input. Attention pays a central role in retaining materials in short-term memory. There, materials are recoded and stored in long-term memory. With children, the coding and recoding aspect is likely to be more important than the retrieval aspect. With adults, they may encounter more difficulty in retrieval as the internal lexicon (dictionary) is considerably larger and more complex. The J. Mackworth model has the merit of being less involved than some of the other models and at the same time it encompasses the cognitive processes involving sensory, motor, language, attention, and coding aspects in reading. Where the model falls short is in its treatment of reading comprehension. This topic will be discussed under the interactive approach and in subsequent sections.

Gough's Model

In his *one second of reading* Gough (1972; Gough and Cosky, 1977) proposes a letter-by-letter model of reading. He stated in the original formulation that the model was "detailed by choice, speculative by necessity, and almost certainly flawed" (Gough, 1972, p. 331) and educed arguments to support his theory. In the 1972 work he described exhaustively the chain of events taking place during one second of reading and related the model to reading acquisition. Gough suggests that, as reading begins, the initial fixation will set in motion a chain of events. From the visual pattern reflected onto the retina, a relatively direct visual representation or an icon is formed. This lasts for a short duration after the fading of the stimulus and corresponds to neural activities in the striate cortex (see Chapter 8). An icon may contain materials corresponding to 15 or 20 letters and spaces. This icon will persist until it is replaced by the icon arising from the second fixation some 250 milliseconds later. From the time the icon is formed, letters are identified and read out at the rate of 10 to 20 milliseconds per letter. With an icon persisting for some 250 msec. and with at least 3 fixations per second, Gough estimates that the rate of reading can be in excess of 300 words a minute (assuming about 7 letters to a word). In order to explain the time-consuming passage through some kind of speech loop that his model might imply, Gough speculates that the grapheme–phoneme mapping is not onto speech but onto a string of systematic phonemes. He is not explicit on this apart from saying that systematic phonemes are "abstract entitites that are related to the sounds of the language—the phonetic segments—only by means of a complex system of phonological rules" (Gough, 1972, p. 337). This abstract phonemic representation of the original character serves as an input to the internal lexicon or mental dictionary. There a search is initiated until a lexical entry is made and the lexical search yielded by each successive word is deposited in a temporary repository. This is the primary memory, which would become the working memory for sentence comprehension. Gough sees lexical search as a parallel process with the race going to the swift one (see also section on Dual Coding—

Multiple Paths in the preceding chapter). The four or five lexical items deposited in the primary memory serve as input to "some wondrous mechanism" dubbed *Merlin* which applies its knowledge of the syntax and semantics to determine the deep structure of the input. By this time, Gough estimates some 700 milliseconds will have elapsed and the reader is likely into the third fixation. The material from the first fixation is in the final memory register *TPWSGWTAU* (The Place Where Sentences Go When They Are Understood). When all inputs of the string have been posited in this ultimate register, reading is complete.

Gough thus sees the reader as essentially a "plodder" and not a "guesser" or an "explorer." The plodder literally plods through text "letter by letter, word by word," converting letters to a system of phonological representation, which in turn contacts what is previously learned. Rozin and Gleitman (1977) have discussed the two views of the reader: the plodder and the explorer.

Gough has done valuable service in his detailed, systematic account of the sequence of events taking place during one second of reading. He has provided a millisecond by millisecond account from the first fixation of the words ("suppose the eye . . .") through the process until the word "suppose" is uttered. Pointing out some reservations and flaws, Brewer (1972) acknowledges the "provocative" nature of the model and Gough's "courageous" attempt. Massaro (1975b) lauds the testable nature of the work while Gibson and Levin (1975, p. 448) state the model "is a bold and valuable one" susceptible of "proof or disproof—at least disproof." Even the skeptic will admit that a theory is not a good theory unless it can be proved, or disproved, either way.

One of the flaws of the model is the difficulty for the reader to get from letters to "systematic phonemes." As this is an abstract representation, it is difficult to teach a child this internal system. Gough acknowledges this:

> We cannot show him that this character goes with that systematic phoneme, for there is no way to isolate a systematic phoneme. We cannot tell him, "this goes with that," for we have no way of representing that. In short, we cannot teach him the code. This is not to say that he cannot acquire it; every reader before him has done so. But the child must master the code through a sort of cryptanalysis rather than through memorization (p. 348).

The concept of the child as a cryptanalyst is an interesting one. The problem for beginning readers becomes one of mapping and not the teaching of explicit rules as in some so-called phonic programs. This mapping problem relates to cognitive clarity and tacit knowledge as we have elaborated earlier. Another problem of the Gough model is that it cannot accommodate the familiar word effect (see Thompson and Massaro, 1973) and context effect. At the oculomotor level, there is no provision for different linguistic materials interacting with rate and duration of eye fixations and different eye movement patterns. At the syntactic-semantic level Gough's hypothetical and real readers as plodders rather than guessers will have difficulty with homophones such as BRAIN and BRANE or phrases like THE NUN TOLD HIM and THE NUN TOLLED HYMN. Brewer (1972, p. 360) comments on "the paradox of having higher order linguistic processes find their way downstream. . . ." This is a real problem that other researchers also grapple with. The "wondrous mechanism" Merlin or TPWSGWTAU does not quite explain how meaning is acquired.

In his recent writing Gough (Gough and Cosky, 1977) maintains his 1972 position. He suggests that not much has been learned about how meanings are combined into propositions or how exactly context affects comprehension. He points out the physiological basis of some of his stages of learning to read: the preperceptual stage can be equated with Brodmann's Areas 17 and 18 of the visual cortex and information from the two eyes are first integrated at Area 17. He educes additional evidence to substantiate the claim that readers search through the mental lexicon in a phonological form as this code is the most efficient and cognitively economical (see also Chapter 9). In proofreading, Gough finds readers make more errors in typographical errors homophonous with the intended word than those typographical forms pronounced differently. He also found in a Stroop effect experiment that nonwords homophonous with color words provide interference as great as the color words. One might say, nonwords which sound like color words produce a Stroop effect as great as these words themselves. Thus the proofreading and the Stroop experiments suggest that the phonological route is followed in converting print to meaning. Gough and Cosky (1977, p. 281) suggest, ". . . we tentatively cling to the view that the reader automatically converts letters into phonological form, and then searches the lexicon for an entry headed by this form," but acknowledge there are difficulties. To accommodate the phonemenon found since Cattell (1886), that familiar words are named faster than letters, they differentiate between reading and naming. They argue that naming a word must take longer than naming a letter only if the time it takes to produce a word is comparable to that of a letter. They further argue that isolated letters are less familiar than common words. This is an empirical question and can be tested by comparing words of different lengths with identical frequencies of occurrence.

Cosky (1976) gathered evidence addressed to the question of whether we read letter by letter. He reasoned that if word recognition involves letter recognition, then the difficulty of recognizing a word should vary with the difficulty of recognizing its letters. This was tested by comparing 15 adult subjects' visual recognition latency to 72 empirically determined "easy-letter" words and to 72 similarly determined "difficult-letter" words. Word length and word frequency were also manipulated. Results show no effect for letter difficulty, although recognition latency decreased reliably with word frequency and increased monotonically with word length. Gough and Cosky (1977, p. 283) explain their results this way. "The fact that recognition latency is virtually identical for words composed of easy and hard letters does not encourage one to believe that we read letter-by-letter, either serially or in parallel. But the fact that it increases with word length suggests that we do read in units smaller than the word." While it is likely that we do not read letter-by-letter, it is possible that word recognition does not necessarily involve letter recognition difficulty. But this needs to be tested.

In their study of the word identification process, Theios and Muise (1977) dismiss Gough's letter-by-letter reading as inconsistent with reality and suggest that good phonology without either familiar orthography or meaning would slow down articulation. In their view, letters and other features of a visually displayed word are operated on in parallel leading to the extraction of orthographic, phonetic, and semantic information. They maintain there is very little hard experimental evidence to support the contention that orthographic information is processed before phonetic information which is processed before semantic information. The topic of "bottom-up"—a linear series of analyzing stages from the sensory representation through to meaning—and "top-down"—a cognitive system directing information abstracted from the visual signal—models of reading is one receiving much current interest. This will be discussed in subsequent sections. The suggestion by Cosky (1976) that the units in word recognition are smaller than the word and correlate with word length in letters also deserves attention. The topic of "building blocks" of reading will be examined in the section dealing with "Processing Units."

The LaBerge-Samuels Automaticity Model

LaBerge and Samuels (1974) have proposed an information-processing model of reading which attempts to explain how a person moves from the surface structure of the printed page to the syntactic-semantic aspect. The elaboration of this model is further given by LaBerge (1973, 1975), while an easily understandable account is provided by Samuels (1977).

Central to the LaBerge-Samuels model of reading is the role of *attention.* This implies the reader has to be alert to the source of information, to be selective and to use the limited capacity of attention to advantage. LaBerge and Samuels assume that a person can attend to only one task at a time but can perform other activities simultaneously if these activities do not require attention or if they have attained *automaticity.* The importance of automaticity is emphasized in our Chapter 2, "Reading as a Skill." The criterion for deciding if a skill is automatic is whether or not it can function while attention is focused on other acts. Another criterion is that, if two tasks are to be performed at the same time and each requires attention, can the tasks be performed simultaneously? If so, then at least one of the tasks is operating automatically. When readers attain automaticity in decoding subskills, they can concentrate on meanings or implications of what is read rather than the mechanism of reading itself. Thus reading is seen as a *two-stage process* comprising decoding and comprehending. In order to comprehend even simple prose, attention is required. With beginning readers, the dilemma is how to attain a balance between attending to decoding and also comprehending. Undue attention to decoding may impede comprehension. Thus, beginning readers need to switch attention back and forth from decoding to comprehension. In so doing, the reading act is slow and laborious. When decoding becomes automatic, the reader can concentrate on comprehending. The La-

Berge-Samuels model is illustrated in Figure 10–2.

The LaBerge-Samuels model has the advantage of being flexible in accommodating a variety of processing routes (see also Chapter 9 on coding processes). These components or processing stages are involved: *visual memory* (VM), *phonological memory* (PM) and *semantic memory* (SM), with feedback loops going from the one component to the other. The processing stages are described in the following paragraphs.

Visual Memory

This is the first processing stage. The printed word strikes the surface of the eye where detectors process features such as horizontal, vertical lines, angles and intersections. Each letter is treated as a set of unique features. Because of previous learning the features are combined to form letters, letters will form spelling patterns *(ch, sh, dr)* and the spelling patterns feed into word codes. Within this component of visual memory, there are other features such as word length and word configuration which may be used in conjunction with other sources of orthographic information in word recognition. In Figure 10–2 various codes are represented by either filled or empty circles. An empty circle represents a code that is not well-learned and consequently it can only be activated with attention. A filled circle represents a well-learned code that does not require attention for its activation. To the extent that mappings from features to letters, letters to spelling patterns, and spelling patterns to words are stored in long-term memory because of previous learning, the recognition of these units can occur automatically without attention. Attention can help in the construction of a new code by activating subordinate input codes. Attention of a code prior to the presentation of its corresponding stimuli will increase the rate of processing.

Phonological Memory

Figure 10–2 shows that input into phonological memory comes from various sources: visual memory, episodic memory and feedback from semantic memory. It is generally assumed that phonological memory contains both acoustic and articulatory representations. Acoustic cues are patterns of specific events, and not whole sounds.

Figure 10–2. LaBerge and Samuels' automaticity model showing different ways a visually presented word may be accessed for meaning. The major stages of processing shown are: visual memory (VM), phonological memory (PM), episodic memory (EM), and semantic memory (SM). Attention is momentarily focused on comprehension in SM, involving organization of meaning codes of two word-groups. (From La-Berge and Samuels, 1974, used by permission.)

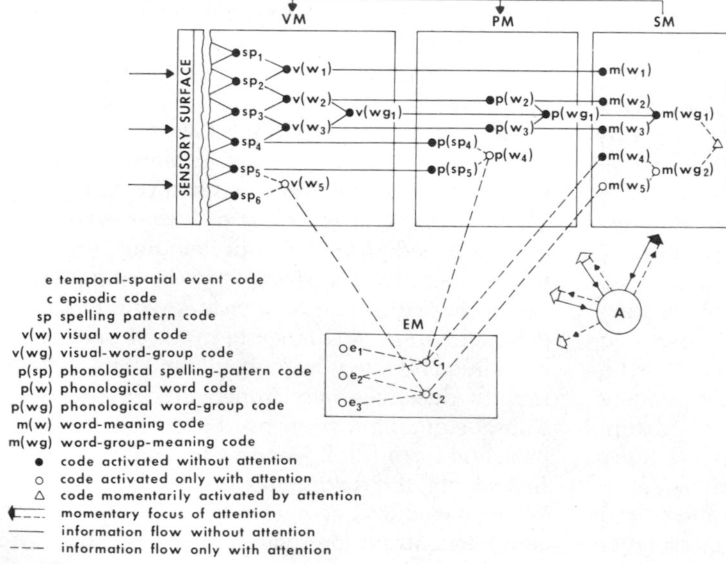

Articulatory features or subphonemic features refer to the movement of some specified articulator or a set of articulators in some specified way. The realization of a phoneme is the result of the joint working of a number of articulatory features. The units of acoustic representations are features, letters, spelling patterns and words and parallel the features, letters, spelling patterns and words in the visual memory. The articulatory inputs are considered to be part of the phonological memory system. It is the *episodic memory* which provides appropriate association links to facilitate mastery of a skill or a subskill to the automatic level.

Semantic Memory

This is concerned with the comprehension of written messages. Semantic memory is distinguished from episodic memory in that the latter is concerned with personal experiences in a given context whereas semantic memory extends to the more abstract generalizations of knowledge. With skilled readers, decoding will become automatic. Comprehension, however, does not occur automatically under most conditions and requires attention. This is used to organize words into sentences or other grammatical units and to determine relationships in meanings existing within and between grammatical units. Samuels (1977) provides a clear account of the role of attention in comprehending a sentence such as "The fierce dog bit the tall man." This is illustrated in Figure 10–3. Attention is used to decode the sentence into grammatical units to determine the agent, the action, and the object. The reader must then decide the meaning within each grammatical unit and the meaning of the sentence as a whole. The process is an active, constructive one requiring attention as an integral part.

The *feedback loop* (Figure 10–2) from semantic memory to phonological memory to visual memory should be noted. It is possible to go directly from visual memory to semantic memory. While the information flow is from VM → PM → SM, this can vary according to the difficulty of text and the ability of the readers. They can change their processing strategy and use the feedback from SM to VM. It is possible that context has its main effects through feedback processes which reduce alternatives and structure expectancies.

Thus according to the LaBerge-Samuels model, attention serves to activate specific codes, to facilitate association from one code to another,

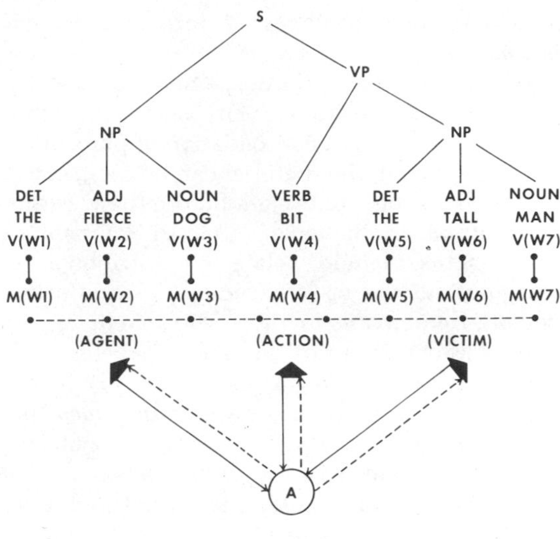

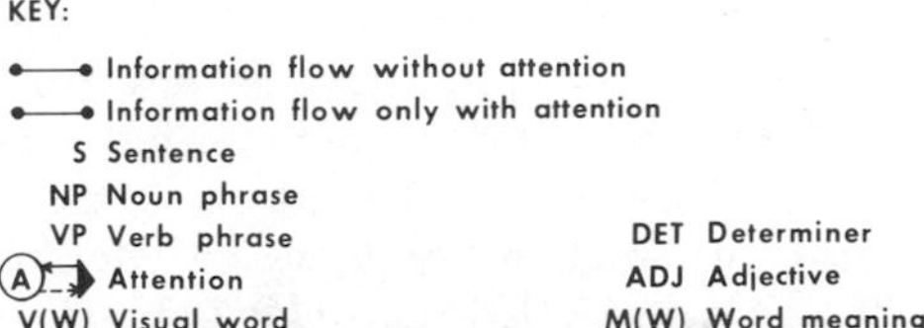

Figure 10–3. Extension of automaticity model to the role of attention in comprehending a sentence. (From Samuels, 1977, used by permission.)

to activate perceptual codes at one level into a code at a higher level and to participate in the organization of codes into new ones. Reading acquisition thus involves a program of managing attention and not just concentrating on perceptual events. As post-criterion learning (usually termed overlearning) of subskills progresses attention is gradually withdrawn so that it can be focused on comprehension which is of central concern in reading. More on the role of attention and school achievement including reading will be discussed in Chapter 11 under "Affective Bases."

LaBerge and Samuels have acknowledged the derivation of their model from the work of Estes (1972, 1975). Estes has proposed a hierarchically structured memory to interpret the effects of orthographic context. The Estes model is primarily one of sifting sensory information through a succession of levels of memory comparisons. As with Estes' model, it is difficult to predict word-letter difference with the LaBerge-Samuels model because of its hierarchical nature. This, according to Massaro (1975b), is a minor flaw. Massaro points out that the automaticity model has taken a large step in defining the stages of information processing in reading.

The suggestion by LaBerge and Samuels that practice leads to automaticity should be interpreted as more than consolidation of perception. In consolidating, the material can be reorganized into higher-order units even before the lower-order units have achieved a high level of automaticity. Practice should relate to distribution of learning and the use of feedback. When a task becomes automatic in the sense that it can be done without attention, it can be processed relatively smoothly and almost effortlessly. A distinction is made here between *accuracy* and *automaticity*. Accuracy is necessary but not sufficient for advancement to higher levels of skill building on subskills. LaBerge (1975) draws attention to this with findings from the familiar Stroop effect, in which subjects are asked to name the color of a stimulus when the stimulus is a word denoting a different color. Generally, interference occurs for subjects who have learned these associations to automaticity. Willows and McKinnon (1973) and Willows (1974) provided some evidence to support this claim. They asked subjects to read stories printed in black with alternating lines of text in red, which were to be ignored. The red lines contained wrong answers to questions following the story. Good readers showed more comprehension errors that were intrusions from the to-be-ignored lines than poor readers. A possible reason was that the good readers relied more heavily on automatic processing and hence could not prevent processing of the interfering lines which were also competing for meaning. Children who are accurate but not yet attaining automaticity in reading these words do not seem to show as much interference as adults on this task.

In terms of implications for reading research and instruction, LaBerge and Samuels (1974, p. 318) state, "We view reading acquisition as a series of skills, regardless of how it appears to the fluent reader. Pedagogically, we favor the approach which singles out these skills for testing and training and then attempts to sequence them in appropriate ways." (See our Chapters 2 and 3 on reading as a skill and principles of skill acquisition). Further, the need to integrate subskills into a higher-order holistic process or system is emphasized. Another implication from the automaticity model is the use of hypothesis/test procedures for word recognition and reading comprehension. This is demonstrated in two experiments carried out by Samuels, Dahl and Archwamety (1974) with 60 retarded children and 40 nonretarded children respectively. The experimental subjects were taught hypothesis/test word recognition subskills. These included such subskills as: training on the ability to say a word when given an initial sound (e.g. a word (any word) beginning with /p/); training on the ability to use auditory context to predict words that could follow logically (e.g. the utterance "My mother sleeps on her ________."); training on the ability to use visual context to predict word(s) that could logically follow in a sentence when given the initial letter of the target word (e.g. "The girl ate the b________."). Results of both experiments showed that hypothesis/test training produced significantly superior word recognition and comprehension. This kind of training is found to be more effective for intermediate levels of reading ability and less for high reading ability as it takes a considerable amount of time to generate prediction to effectively accommodate fluent reading (Samuels, Begy, and Chen, 1975–1976).

Samuels et al. (1974) emphasize the need to develop subskills and strategies beyond the accuracy level to automaticity so as to permit comprehension. One corollary is the role of speed in word recognition. In two experiments, one with fourth grade good and poor readers, and one with college juniors and fourth-graders, Samuels, Begy and Chen (1975–1976) found that more fluent readers were faster in word recognition and superior in generating target words given proper context. In their experiments it was determined pre-experimentally that the fluent and less fluent readers were equal in word accuracy. Thus, they might have differed in word-processing strategies. The more fluent readers probably can accomplish decoding with little or no attention (i.e., automatically) and can use their attention for comprehension.

In their study of short-term memory function in ten-year-old good and poor readers (12 children in each group) Farnham-Diggory and Gregg (1975) found their data entirely compatible with the LaBerge-Samuels viewpoint. Their poor readers showed deterioration of short-term memory function over time, a lag in the visual scanning speed compared with auditory scanning rate, and a lack of the concept of letter patterns. Farnham-Diggory and Gregg suggest that poor readers' tottering management of the flow of attention, their shifts between auditory and visual materials may result from incomplete automaticity of certain subprocesses. It is likely that the poor readers may remain at an earlier level of reading/language development, while the good readers are able to guide their reading by forming hypotheses and expectancies and testing them.

Thus what Huey (1908, p. 104) advised us more than seventy years ago, "repetition progressively frees the mind from attention to details, makes facile the total act, shortens the time, and reduces the extent to which consciousness must concern itself with the process," is capable of being empirically tested as subsumed under the LaBerge-Samuels model. From both the research and instruction points of view the production and utilization of post-criterion learning to automaticity should prove useful. Samuels (1977) suggests the supplementary method of repeated reading will improve students' reading speed and comprehension. The procedure consists of rereading a specific, meaningful passage a number of times until a certain level of fluency is reached before attempting a new passage in a similar way (see also Samuels, 1979). The practice afforded students and the motivation provided by teachers will lead to automaticity. Samuels, Miller and Eisenberg (1979) have provided further data to suggest that repeated exposure to a word leads to an increase in the size of the processing unit used in word recognition, although the perceptual learning that occurs is limited to the specific words repeatedly presented. C. Chomsky (1978) has reported on the facilitating effect of this procedure for "slow and halting readers" in increasing their fluency with ease. Thus the "method" of repeated readings can be part of a developmental or remedial reading program.

An Interactive Model of Reading

From the survey of literature, it would appear that researchers would not entirely disagree with the hierarchical analysis of reading. In general, the Mackworth, Gough and (to a considerable extent) LaBerge-Samuels models involve serial, level-by-level analyses. These are referred to as *bottom-up* or *data-driven* models. They work their way from sub-subskills, through subskills to the integration of skills or from sensory representation to the syntactic-semantic level. In contrast, the direct access models of Kolers (1970) and Frank Smith (1978), as outlined in the preceding chapter, may be classified as *top-down* or *concept-driven* ones. The two terms "bottom-up" and "top-down" are derived from computer usage and refer to the way in which an internal representation of some events (e.g. strings of words) is arrived at. Bottom-up analyses begin by analyzing the stimulus (e.g. features and letter clusters) and work their way up to "higher levels." Top-down analyses start with hypotheses, attempt to verify them by checking the stimulus (e.g. Is there a verb phrase here?), and work their way "down." Thus bottom-up analysis is stimulus-driven, whereas top-down analysis is concept-driven. These two approaches can be visualized, at least partially, with the "tree" diagram illustrated in Figure 10–3. In a crude way, the sentence (1–1) "The fierce dog bit the tall man" can be equated with the superordinate structure at the "top." It can be decomposed into subordinate structures of noun phrases, verb phrases and still further into individual words "lower down." This is at best a generalized analogy as the sentence derives its meaning from words and also from the relationship of words and groups of words. Consider the sentence:

(1–1) The dog (agent →) bit (action →) the man (object).

It is both grammatical and meaningful. If the order is reversed to:

(1–2) *The man (agent →) bit (action →) the dog (object).

The sentence is grammatical but is anomalous. It is deviant according to "world views." We accept canines biting humans as a possible course of events, but the reverse is an oddity.

Thus the meaning or semantic functions of agent, action and object are not easy to define. Compare sentence (1–1) with sentence (1–3) below:

(1–3) The dog bit nobody.

The mapping problem is not clear-cut. The word "man" does not mean "person acted upon" in the same sense as "nobody," since nobody was acted upon. A further comparison with sentence (1–4) will bring out the mapping problem involved:

(1–4) *The book bit the man.

In the four sentences the same syntactical structure is followed except for the lexical or dictionary entries. But structures do not necessarily represent the required agent-action-object relations and cannot differentiate these relations. Chomsky's (1965) distinction between CONCRETE,

ANIMATE, and HUMAN syntactic features helps to explain the constraints. Thus, the difference between sentences (1–1) and (1–4) would be accounted for in terms of the feature ANIMATE. The verb "bit" would require a [+ ANIMATE] subject. "Dog" would be marked [+ ANIMATE] and would qualify; "book" would be marked [− ANIMATE] and so would not qualify. Thus well-formedness of the above sentences depends on semantic properties of the whole noun phrase rather than just the syntactic properties of the head noun. Our short discussion explains that what is "up" and what is "down" cannot be in terms of linear progression. Before we proceed, it will be helpful to refer back to the sections on transformational grammar and case grammar in Chapter 6 ("Language Awareness").

Another way to explain the top-down, bottom-up relationship in reading is in terms of *propositions.* A proposition is an assertion about the relation between information entities. A proposition is the underlying semantic representation of a sentence. Consider the sentence:

(2) If a single figure is needed to represent central tendency, the mean is the best.

We can write a number of propositions and the main ones are as follows:

(a) The mean is a good representation.
(b) There is another good representation (e.g. the mode).
(c) There is still another good representation (e.g. the median).
(d) The mean has more "goodness" than the mode.
(e) The mean has more "goodness" than the median.
(f) The mean is the best *if* and *only if* a single figure is needed to represent central tendency.

Of the above assertions, proposition (f) unites and integrates the other propositions. Going back to the tree diagram analogy, consider the diagram at top right of this page. The sentence "If a single figure is needed . . ." also brings out a number of points. It is meaningful only to those who understand the metalanguage or, in this example, the statistical usage being talked about. For those without some understanding of statistics, the sentence would not be meaningful. In fact, the phrase "If a single figure is needed . . ." as it stands may conjure up the picture of a statue or an object. As we move to subsequent sections

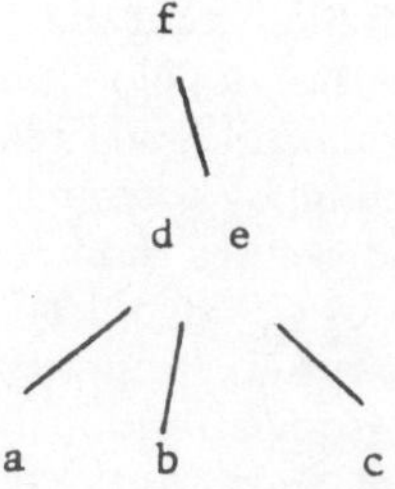

in this chapter we will realize more and more that the "meaning of meanings" of a stretch of discourse is much more than the sum total of its individual components (Miller, 1965). In the bottom-up model a component at any level can be included in different combinations of higher-level concepts without knowing what may result next. Thus the bottom-up model is too passive to account for reading, which is both flexible and dynamic. On the other hand, the top-down control structure may generate expectations which may not be satisfied or confirmed at the lower level. There is a need to use both bottom-up and top-down systems (see Adams and Collins, 1979; Lesgold and Perfetti, 1978).

The question of how higher-order events such as meaning can affect the identification of lower-order ones such as words, to which higher-order properties are related, is not easily answered. This is analogous to saying that with certain events we know what these events are without knowing their identity. One answer is that higher-order events can be accessed directly. In the previous discussion of coding processes of word perception (Chapter 9) we have examined the pros and cons of direct access routes. Recall our discussion of the accumulation of neurological evidence on phonemic dyslexics. These are adults with acquired dyslexia who make semantic errors rather than grapheme–phoneme errors. This phenomenon of paralexic errors has been mimicked in normal adults reading arrays of unrelated words, followed at brief delays by a grapheme pattern mask (Allport, 1977). Thus, it is likely that the phonemic dyslexics and Allport's experimental subjects must have some means of access to the semantic system of visually presented words, even though these are not mediated by a lower-order phonemic code.

Recall also our discussion of the loci of influence of semantic context in connection with coding processes of word perception (Chapter 9). Meyer, Schvaneveldt, and Ruddy (1975) have shown that reaction times to lexical decisions about a pair of words are faster when the words are semantically associated (e.g. BUTTER preceded by BREAD) as compared with unassociated words (e.g. BUTTER preceded by NURSE). This is interpreted as semantic context influencing an early stage of visual word-recognition in which strings of letters are encoded graphemically and transformed to phonemic representation before lexical access. The study by Klapp (1971) showing reaction time to indicate that a pair of numbers was the same was shorter for two-syllable numbers (e.g. 15 and 15) than for three-syllable numbers (e.g. 17 and 17) could also be interpreted to mean general expectancy of the category of digits. In other words, the visual pattern of 15 or 17 must first be identified and some knowledge or expectancy of the configuration is set up before actually knowing what the pair of digits is. In an early study, Miller, Heise, and Lichten (1951) found that people could hear words but not nonsense syllables at specified noise levels. Results showed that humans can use information at various levels of abstraction.

The studies of Meyer et al. (1975), Klapp (1971) and Miller et al. (1951) indicate that a higher level of processing (e.g. the semantic level) can influence a lower level of processing (e.g. the word level). In his research with visual perception, Turvey (1973, 1975) has suggested a parallel-serial processing for the visual system. To exploit the different procedures and the highly flexible mechanisms involved in processes such as reading, he prefers the term *heterarchical* or *coalitional* rather than hierarchical. He explains the main features of the heterarchy thus: "First, many structures would function cooperatively in the determining of perception although not all structures need participate in all determinations. Second, while it is certainly the case that a coalition system has very definite and nonarbitrary structures, the partitioning of these structures into agents and instruments and the specifications of relations among them is arbitrary. . . . Perhaps the main emphasis of the coalition formulation is the flexibility of relations among structures" (Turvey, 1975, p. 148). Turvey cites Winograd's (1972) computer program called PROGRAMMAR as a concrete example of how natural language is understood and produced. The Winograd system processes language by using both syntactic rules and semantic features interdependently. The system is based on the heterarchy or coalition premises that understanding sentences necessitates an integration of grammar, semantics and logic or reasoning. For example, consider the sentence:

(3) David caught the thief making off with the money.

The PROGRAMMAR would first parse "David" as a noun group and "caught the thief making off with the money" as the verb group. The phrase "making off with the money" is further parsed from the noun group parsing. Similar programs may be recalled to parse phrase structures according to phrase structure rules. The system is thus concerned more with meaning representation than it is with grammatical structure of discourse. Semantic features will determine how a particular group of words is parsed and will make another attempt if a parsing does not make sense semantically. Turvey (1975, p. 148) sums up the complex operation of the Winograd system thus: *"each piece of knowledge can be a procedure and thus it can call on any other piece of knowledge."*

In the field of reading it would seem Massaro's (1975a) *"primary and secondary recognition"* would fit into Turvey's formalization of concurrent-contingent representation. Very briefly, the primary recognition process transforms visual features into letter units synthesized in visual memory. The primary recognition process is seen by Massaro as operating in parallel on a number of letters, using rules of orthography of the language. The secondary recognition process serves to transform the visual information into meaning and is aided in this transformation by syntactic and semantic expectancies. Thus, it is not necessary to identify some letters before orthography information can be applied at the word recognition stage, just as it is not necessary to identify some words before syntactic-semantic information can be used. Massaro points out that the difference between orthographic and syntactic-semantic redundancy is that the latter information facilitates recognition of a perceptual unit at least the size of a word whereas the former (orthographic) information can facilitate the identification of letter clusters independently of meaning. Massaro suggests that the temporal course of rehearsal and recoding operations is central in reading. At this point, the reader may also want to refer to the section on successive stages of word recognition in the preceding chapter (Chapter 9) and compare the similarities and differences of processing mechanisms.

In his research program, Rumelhart (1977b) has developed a formalism based on *parallel, interactive processing of reading.* In reviewing models of reading, he finds most of them emphasize the bottom-up, stage-by-stage approach and are not amenable to accommodating the influence of higher-up processes. The Gough model and to a larger extent the LaBerge-Samuels automaticity model may be immune to such a criticism "if they assume that partial information is somehow forwarded to the higher levels of analysis and that the final decision as to which letters were present is delayed until this further processing has been accomplished" (Rumelhart, 1977b, p. 581). Rumelhart argues that there is considerable evidence supporting the view of reading as a process utilizing simultaneously constraints at the featural, letter, letter cluster, lexical, syntactic and semantic levels to interpret the input stimuli. This parallel interactive process is illustrated schematically in Figure 10–4. The example is from reading the phrase THE CAR.

In formalizing his development of a reading model based on language processing by computer, Rumelhart postulates a *message center* and a set of independent *knowledge sources.* The message center is the communication center, while the knowledge sources specialize in various aspects of the reading process. The message center maintains a running list of hypotheses about the nature of the input string and each knowledge source scans the message center for the most relevant hypotheses. These are analyzed, confirmed or rejected, and new hypotheses are added. These are further tested and integrated with existing knowledge sources. Figure 10–4 shows the interacting of the various levels of processing at the message center. Rumelhart conceives of a three-dimensional representation: position along the line of text, levels of hypotheses and alternative hypotheses at the same level. Hypotheses can be generated at any level and their probability of occurrence determined mathematically. At an early stage of processing, subjects may develop the expectation for a noun phrase, or they may look for the letter "t" from the features, or they may look for the determinant (DET) "the" or they may expect the lexical entries of "fat," "cat," "car" following the determinant "the." The lexical entry "fat" will be rejected, so also "cat" as being anomalous with information given and expectancies engendered.

Figure 10–4. Interactive process of reading. (From Rumelhart, 1977, used by permission.)

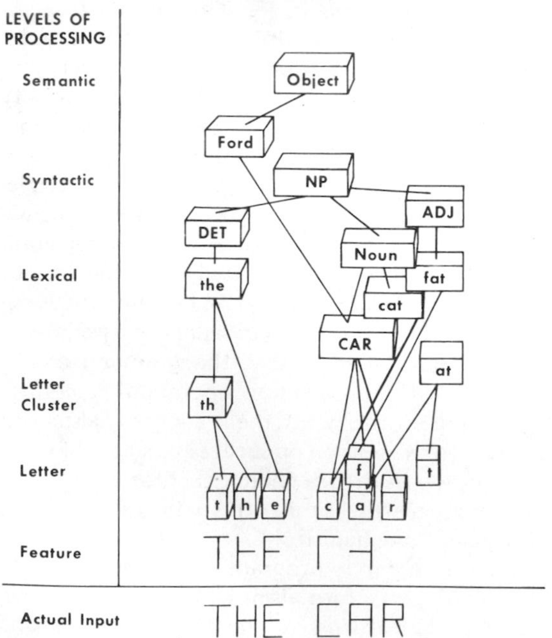

Rumelhart is careful to point out that the interactive model of reading still needs to be tested. Earlier in his research program, Rumelhart (1975) discussed top-down strategies for parsing text materials that included coherent wholes. The use of discourse materials is assumed to demand a higher level of organization than that found in the parsing of a sentence string. One of Rumelhart's rules is the identification of the time, place, and main characters of a story (e.g. "Once upon a time, in a far away land, there lived a good King . . ."). The setting often terminates with a *stative proposition* and a semantic rule joins what follows (an *episode*) to the setting. An episode leads to an *event* and a *reaction* and these can be linked to an external event and described by an appropriate semantic rule. The rationale is to match the identification of elements of a story with external events and an internal mental response. The relationship between the events is seen as the first event making the second possible, but the first event does not cause the second. An example provided by Rumelhart is that of an episode of the wind catching Margie's balloon and carrying it into the tree, thereby making it possible for the balloon to be broken. From "Margie cried and cried," the mental response is one of "sadness." The assumption here is that syntactic and semantic structures can be used as analytic and heuristic devices which will generate the structure of a story summarization congruent with the subject's recall. The conceptualization of understanding and summarizing short stories as problem solving episodes is further formalized in Rumelhart (1977a).

In a recent review, Stanovich (1980) concludes that the literature indicates that the interactive model of reading appears to provide a more accurate portrayal of reading processes than do strictly bottom-up or top-down models. This is especially so when combined with a compensatory assumption that inefficiency or deficiency in any knowledge source will place a greater reliance on other knowledge sources, irrespective of levels of processing.

Understanding short stories takes the following structure: something happens to the main character of the story and sets up a goal. The remainder of the story is a description of the protagonist's problem-solving behavior in attaining this goal. There are rules governing the relationships among the initiating event, the goal, and the attempt to accomplish that goal. Thus, the process of comprehension takes the form of the selection of abstract representation (schema) of an object, event, or situation. If a high-level representation can be found and will organize the story, the story is easily comprehensible and recallable. In fact, Rumelhart (1977a, p. 268) defines the process of comprehension as "identical to the process of selecting and verifying conceptual schemata to account for the situation (or text) to be understood." The general ideas of the schema (plural "schemata") are consonant with the notions presented by Bartlett (1932), Sachs (1967), Bransford and McCarrell (1974), among others, and will be further discussed in the next section of this chapter.

Very briefly, *schemata* are mental structures or abstract representations which provide interpretations for inputs in different modalities. Such inputs include linguistic, contextual and situational factors. It is the schema which is essential for comprehension, storage, and retrieval of input information. It is the schema which permits the *prediction* and *inference* of as yet unobserved input information. Comprehension calls for the convergence of information directly from the input in combination with expectations—a convergence of bottom-up and top-down processes. These procedures operate simultaneously (see Adams and Collins, 1979; Doehring and Aulls, 1979; Lesgold and Perfetti, 1978; Rumelhart and Ortony, 1977). Rumelhart and Ortony (1977, p. 128) explain that "in general . . . schemata activated by their own constituents are activated from the bottom up, so that bottom up processing is the activation of dominating schemata. Top down processing, on the other hand, arises from schemata activating their constituent subschemata." They further state that "information (including both the 'stimulus' and the context) enters the system and directly suggests certain plausible candidate schemata to account for it. At the same time as this data driven processing is going on, such postulated schemata activate their dominating schemata, which in turn look for other as yet unsuspected aspects of the situation. This conceptually driven processing allows internal contextual constraints to be effective. A schema is said to provide a good account of (aspects of) the input situation when it can find good evidence for itself."

From the emphasis on terms like *activation* and *invocation,* it is evident that Rumelhart (1975, 1977a, 1977b, Rumelhart and Ortony, 1977) conceives of a memory system in comprehension with a vast amount of schemata but with only a small number needing to be activated. The search for the most likely schemata must be guided and often by context. Rumelhart's "message center" (Figure 10–4) where hypotheses about text materials are derived by several levels of knowledge source (lexical, syntactical and semantic) parallels in many ways Morton's (1964, 1969, 1979a, 1979b; Morton and Broadbent, 1967; Morton and Patterson, 1980) logogen theory. Reference has been made to the logogen (from "logos" meaning word and "genus" meaning birth) model of word recognition in connection with the discussion on deep dyslexia and paralexic errors in Chapter 9 (see also Figure 9–3). We will elaborate on this aspect as Morton's work provides a powerful psychological model which accounts for a great deal of data.

According to Morton, every word has a "logogen system" or "counter" which is stimulated by semantic priming (including word frequency and context effects). These sources of stimulation increase the activation level of the correct word response. When the logogen system exceeds a predetermined threshold value, the reader has identified a word. Subsuming all processing is the cognitive system. In the words of Morton (1979a, p. 112): "A logogen is not a word; it is the device which makes a word available as a response and it does so by collecting evidence that the word is present as a stimulus, appropriate as a response, or both." Further, "the evidence for the presence of a particular word can come from the outside world, by vision or hearing, or from other processes in the brain such as those concerned with context, which we can globally term the Cognitive System" (p. 122), and the amount of evidence necessary for an appropriate response to a word is called the threshold of the logogen. Given relevant context, the cognitive system produces semantic information which interacts with the sensory information in the stimulus. Morton (1969, 1979a) has provided a quantitative account of the interaction between stimulus and context in probabilistic terms of predicting the correct response. The Morton model thus proposes that stimulus and context information combine directly to produce a response. The most recent version of the model as shown in Figure 9–3 consists of three elements: visual input logogens, auditory input logogens and output logogens, and a separate picture recognition system. The modification of the original model to include two input logogens and an output logogen is needed to accommodate modality-specific effects in facilitation (Morton, 1979a). The two levels of input (visual and auditory logogens) and the two-way independence of picture and word recognition provide a convincing account of the processing of written words by deep dyslexics and normal readers (see also Patterson, 1978). As discussed in Chapter 9, access to word meaning is a dual procedure involving auditory and visual processing. There is a constant interplay between phonological and visual information during reading and in Rumelhart's conceptualization there is an interplay between logogens on the various levels of knowledge according to associated probability estimates.

A Schema View of Reading

Nature of a Schema

In his interactive model of reading, Rumelhart (1977a) suggests that when readers read a story they use a cluster of schemata to discover its meaning. On finding a suitable schema or a set of schemata, readers will construct or reconstruct the story from stored representation of the interpretation of the original story. In summarizing and recalling an aurally presented passage, the listener/reader is aided by the propositions in the "tree" structure. The higher-up the proposition is in the structure tree, the more likely it is to be represented in the summary or the recall. What then is a schema and what is its role in reading?

A *schema* is an abstract representation of a generic concept for an object, an event, or a situation. According to Werner and Kaplan (1963), the notion of a schema dates back to formulations by the philosopher Kant (1781). Piaget (1926) and Bartlett (1932) are credited with introducing the concept to psychology to denote knowledge structure. Bartlett has shown that what people learn must be some kind of an abstract system or schema rather than a discursive list of simple instances. Concepts can be learned from a small set of special instances, which might be called prototypes or exemplars of the concepts. The remembering of semantic information from prose appears not to be based on a literal remembering of exact words and paraphrase is the normal mode of recall. The contemporary psychological equivalents of the Piaget and Bartlett schemata are the "plans" of Miller, Galanter, and Pribram (1960), the "strategies" of Bruner, Goodnow, and Austin (1956). The current artificial intelligence counterparts are the concepts of "frames" of Minsky (1975) and the "scripts" of Schank and Abelson (1977). Thus Bartlett (1932, p. 201) defines a schema as "an active organization of past reactions and experiences which are always operating in any well-developed organism." Bruner (1957a) speaks of the "surprise value of the environment" as important in cognitive development and of the need to go beyond the information given (Bruner, 1957b).

In a *schema-theoretic view of reading,* Adams and Collins (1979, p. 3) explain the goal of schema theory as "to specify the interface between the reader and the text—to specify how the reader's knowledge interacts with and shapes the information on the page and to specify how that knowledge must be organized to support the interaction." This assumes that the listener/reader has to use his/her own previous knowledge to construct or reconstruct meaning from discourse. The reader will sometimes use the bottom-up process and sometimes the top-down one, but both processes are occurring at all levels of analysis simultaneously (Rumelhart, 1977b).

Adams (1979) has proposed a model of the visual processing of words, pseudowords, and orthographically irregular nonwords in the spirit of the schema theory. Her model assumes that any set of schemata repeatedly activated facilitates the activation of other schemata and that the extraction of visual information is related to the interactions between the schemata against which the visual information is mapped. This structure thus predicts considerable perceptual advantage of words and pseudowords over orthographically irregular nonwords, given that the extraction of visual information proceeds in parallel. Thus Adams' version of word recognition provides a variant explanation of the *criterion bias* model of Morton (1969). (See preceding section and sections on deep dyslexia in Chapter 9). Adams posits two kinds of interactive processes taking place simultaneously in recognizing words: (1) Interconnections between schemata at the letter level where individual-letter schemata activate appropriate word-schemata and (2) the structure of the word schemata. One advantage of the Adams model is its possibility of being extended to the syntactic-sematic level, as word schemata facilitate other word schemata and words themselves are subschemata within these higher-level schemata.

Adams and Collins (1979) explain the extension of their "schema-theoretic" view with reference to the likely processes of understanding "Stone Soup" from Aesop's Fables. This fable is about a poor man begging for food who is first turned away by the maid of a large house. Using the clever ploy of drying his wet clothes, he is allowed entry to the house. Using a further subterfuge of teaching the cook to make "stone soup," he is given a lot of meat scraps for his stone soup and thus attains his goal of getting food. In coming to comprehend this passage, the reader needs to impose or interpret a structure on the passage as a whole. Adams and Collins explain that bottom-up and top-down processes operate simultaneously at all levels of analysis. Bottom-up processing includes schemata of letter identification, word identification, the man begging for food suggesting the schema for perseverance, and the latter the schema of the moral, "where there's a will, there's a way." Top-down processes include problem-solving schemata for goals, for propositions, and the fable schemata for the moral of the story. The process of comprehension is aided by and integrated with such world views as: ways of making soup (liquid, ingredients, heat), work of a maid (serving her master/mistress and protecting his/her goods), ways of obtaining goods (asking, tricking, and other suitable means), ways of tricking the naive, and the nature of a fable. Thus a "schema theory provides a way of integrating our understanding of text with our understanding of the world in general" (Adams and Collins, 1979, p. 21).

The importance of world knowledge or encyclopedic knowledge was discussed by Carroll (1968a) in an earlier and important article on some deep problems of "learning by being told." In discussing learning from meaningful discourse through the retention of sentence comprehension, Carroll emphasized *epistemic learning.* This he defined as: "The acquisition of knowledge through experience; learning through language is the acquisition of such knowledge vicariously—through the experience of one who formulates a sentence or a discourse" (Carroll, 1968a, p. 9). In a subsequent important work edited by Freedle and Carroll (1972), the contributors (linguists and psychologists) focused their attention on discourse comprehension. They emphasized that much of the semantic content of discourse is to be found beyond the spoken or written words themselves, this including the prior knowledge that the speaker or writer of the stretch of discourse assumes the hearer or reader to have. Carroll (1972) in that volume pointed out that comprehension contains an element of problem solving and that both memory and inferencing co-occur with comprehension. This wider interpretation of discourse comprehension is also variously stressed by Anderson (1977, 1978), Anderson, Reynolds, Schallert and Goetz (1977), Bransford, Barclay, and Franks (1972), Bransford and Franks (1971), Bransford and Johnson (1972, 1973), Bransford and McCarrell (1974), Freedle (1979), Pearson (1974–1975), Pearson and Spiro (1981) and Sachs (1967), among others. A recent, comprehensive volume on reading comprehension from the Center for the Study of Reading (Spiro, Bruce, and Brewer, 1980) has integrated perspectives from cognitive psychology, linguistics, artificial intelligence and education and has emphasized the multilevel, interactive and hypothesis-based characteristics of reading comprehension.

This bring us back to the influential work of Bartlett (1932) on memory and meaning. In his studies of prose comprehension in adults, Bartlett found that recall is a reconstructive process rather than the mere passive reproduction of stored memories. In his informal analyses of recall of the story "The War of the Ghosts," Bartlett found that recall was susceptible to a high proportion of inaccuracies in the form of omissions of ideas, transformations, embellishment, and condensation of major themes. He found that his subjects did not appear to be aware of these inaccuracies and that the latter increased over time. In Bartlett's view, remembering prose begins with the impression of the whole story, which is used to reconstruct the details and hence the schemata for understanding. Meaning is thus not the same as context but is found in context and in other situational variables. Meaning results from an individual's active cognitive efforts to fit the material (prose), within the context of the time and space, into the person's knowledge system, so that some conscious awareness of the material is possible. We should note that Bartlett's concept of schemata is rather general, as he did not explain the organizational structure of prose. His work in fact was found to be difficult to replicate (e.g. Zangwill, 1972) until more recently when researchers from related disciplines have come to better understand processing of prose materials. In the following sections, we will discuss how college students, grade-school children and kindergarteners make use of schemata in comprehending discourse.

Uses of Schemata in High-School and College Students

In their research program at the Center for the Study of Reading in Illinois, Anderson and associates (Anderson, 1970, 1972, 1973, 1974, 1977, 1978; Anderson and Ortony, 1975; Anderson, Reynolds, Schallert, and Goetz, 1977; R. Anderson, Spiro, and M. Anderson, 1978) studied the role of schemata in sentence and prose comprehension in college and high school students.

In his early work, Anderson (1970) argued that readers encode text materials first at an orthographic level, then a phonological and a semantic level. The levels are defined by the nature of the stimulus features perceived and encoded at each level. Anderson maintained that retention of prose material would improve as one moves from orthographic to semantic encoding. To test this, he provided an operational distinction between two levels of comprehension—paraphrased and verbatim questions. Paraphrased questions and answers in his early studies referred to substitution of lexical entries for context words of a text in forming a particular question. Anderson (1973) showed that high school students were able to comprehend a principle from reading textual material and to apply the principle to a new instance. These students read a paragraph explaining the principle that intermittent reinforcement causes resistance to extinction. Then they took a test that required them to apply that principle to particular instances which were "identical," "similar" or "dissimilar" to the text example. The experimental group performed better than the control group, and scores were the highest on the identical items and lowest on dissimilar ones. An expectation thus guides the mapping from grapheme to meaning and the developing of hypotheses that are tested against incoming visual data.

Similarly, Wisher (1976) examined the role of expectation as a catalyst in the interactive process of reading. He conducted two experiments to examine the effects of knowing the syntactic structure of a sentence before reading it. The first experiment required the reader to remember irrelevant material (single-digit numbers) while reading a sentence. The assumption is that the greater the effort is devoted to reading, the less is the effort devoted to remembering. When the syntactic structure is known beforehand, subjects are able to devote more effort to rehearsing the numbers while reading the sentence. Consequently their recall of the number sequence should be better. This was tested with "syntactic constant" and "syntactic mixed" conditions of sentences. In the syntactic constant condition, all sentences were segmented as:

Noun phrase/Prepositional phrase/Verb/Noun phrase/Relative clause.

An example was:

"The old man/in the big home/saw/the tired baby/who was crying."

In the syntax-mix condition, the sentences were of various syntactic forms. Results showed that prior knowledge of the syntactic structure of a sentence allows it to be read faster and understood better.

The early study by Anderson and the study by Wisher are only two of the illustrations of how readers use their knowledge of language (an internal factor) and knowledge of the world (internalized external factor) to develop hypotheses about meaning and to verify these hypotheses in the course of reading. The more recent and current research program on comprehension undertaken by the Illinois group aims at finding out what people do when they comprehend and the underlying mental representation during reading. For example, Anderson (1974) found subjects recalled whole sentences when protocols were scored for substance. Anderson and Ortony (1975) designed an experiment with college students in which a sentence could be recalled given a certain cue only if the subject's encoding of the sentence included details and involved distinctions in the senses of words which could not have been part of the correct dictionary readings of these words. The assumption is that language comprehension involves *elaboration* and *particularization* and that semantically most-relevant cues would not be differentially effective until they relate to the internal mental representation of the listener/reader during the process of encoding. Thus the cue *hammer* would be more effective than *fist* for recall of "The accountant pounded the stake" but less effective for "The accountant pounded the desk" as this assumes that *hammer* was encoded as the instrument at the time the sentence was originally processed. *Fist* would be an effective cue for "The accountant pounded the desk" only if it were "associatively related" to both "accountant" and "pounded the desk" (Anderson and Ortony, 1975, p. 176). Thus understanding a sentence depends on analysis of context and knowledge of the world. Meanings of words and sentences interact in the process of constructing an elaborated mental representation. Anderson and Ortony (1975, p. 179) stated that "models of memory should invoke understanding, and that understanding is not just parsing; it is processing to a level whose depth depends on the degree of interaction with the context and the existing knowledge base."

Thus a schema is an "ideational scaffolding," a building block, for mental structure. A schema contains "slots" into which some of the specific information described in a message will fit. In one study, Anderson, Reynolds, Schallert and Goetz (1977) asked 30 physical education students and 30 music education students to read a passage that could refer to a convict planning his escape from prison or a wrestler trying to break the hold of an opponent, and another passage with distinct interpretations of an evening of card-playing or a woodwind ensemble session. Multiple choice and free recall test results showed striking relationships to the subjects' background. In another study, R. Anderson, Spiro and M. Anderson (1978) tested the use of schemata in college students who read narratives about a meal at a fancy restaurant or a trip to a supermarket. The same items of food attributed to the same characters were mentioned in the same order in the two stories. As predicted, items of food from categories determined to be part of most people's restaurant schemata were better recalled by students who read the restaurant narrative. These same students were also more likely to recall the characters to whom particular items of food had been attributed. However, participants were equally likely to reproduce food-order information whichever passage they had read.

In a recent study, Steffensen, Joag-Dev and Anderson (1979) provided a crosscultural perspective of the role of knowledge of social reality over and above textual schemata in reading comprehension. They asked adult American and Indian subjects to read letters about an American wedding and an Indian wedding and to recall both letters following some interference tasks. Comprehension was scored for reading time, amount of text elements recall, amount of important and unimportant text elements recalled, and modifications to the text. It was found that subjects read the native passage more rapidly, recalled more information from the native passage, and produced more culturally related elaborations of the native passage, but more distortions for the nonnative passage. The researchers emphasize both linguistic and extralinguistic schemata in comprehension.

From the Anderson research program on comprehension with adolescent and college students, a number of conclusions should be noted. One is that high-level schemata play a role in the learning and remembering of text information. The high-level schemata serve both "slot-filling" and attention-directing functions to facilitate the understanding and recall of prose—slot-filling in that, if information fits a slot, "it will be instantiated as part of the encoded representation of the text" (R. Anderson, Spiro, and M. Anderson, 1978, p. 438). Attention-directing to other elements and specificity of textual material facilitate understanding (see also Johnson, 1974). Anderson (1978) has summarized some of his research on interpreting, organizing and retrieving text information in terms of high-level schemata, which should be an important source of individual differences in reading comprehension.

These important findings also throw light on the pioneer researches of Bartlett. Anderson, Reynolds, Schallert and Goetz (1977, p. 377) suggest that "distortions and intrusions will appear only when there is a lack of correspondence between the schemata embodied in the text and the schemata by which the reader assimilated the text." Anderson (1977, 1978) views the use of schemata in the same spirit as Piaget's assimilation, as people have stored different schemata for different situations. Different sequences and different prose passages may involve different assimilative uses of schemata and hence processes of construction and reconstruction. By necessity, schemata are abstract representations which can be used to cope with the many and different situations, sequences, and messages. In language comprehension, people have some abstract understanding of the words, the sentences, and the concepts involved. They have to relate these abstract concepts to particular situations, time sequences, or messages. Thus Anderson (1977, p. 422) explains that "The meaning is not in the message. A message is a cryptic recipe that can guide a person in *constructing* a representation. The representation which accounts for a message will usually include elements that are not explicitly contained in the message. These imported elements will be the ones required to maintain consistency with the schemata from which the representation is built. . . ." Anderson (1977, p. 423) further explains that "abstract schemata program individuals to generate concrete scenarios" and that the locus of understanding resides in the schemata, at different levels and pervades the whole system.

It is also suggested that schema change is maximized when a person realizes difficulties and that the difficulties can be resolved within a different schema. The problem-solving structure is akin to the high-level organization of text to be discussed in connection with the work of such researchers as Kintsch (1974), Meyer (1975a, 1975b, 1977a, 1977b) and Mandler and Johnson (1977). Anderson's (1977, pp. 427–428) suggestion that "Socratic teaching would appear to force students to deal with counter examples and face contradictions" reminds readers of our discussions in Chapter 6 "Language Awareness," especially the view that both students and teachers need to decentrate from the embedded thought.

The finding by Anderson and associates of the assimilative nature of schemata in comprehension is also discussed by other researchers in terms of integrating new ideas with pre-existing knowledge. Sulin and Dooling (1974), for example, showed that context can increase the amount of information learned from prose. Meyer and McConkie (1973) showed that the height of ideas in the structure of prose passages could account for most of the variations usually attributable to serial position effects in comprehension and that ideas high in the structure were remembered more frequently. Seemingly nonmeaningful passages could be memorized better if paragraphs were preceded by pictures or titles as appropriate context (Bransford and Johnson, 1972). In an often-quoted study, Bransford and Johnson sought to manipulate subjects' ability to comprehend by varying the availability of pre-existing information. They read the following passage to the subjects:

> If the balloons popped the sound wouldn't be able to carry since everything would be too far away from the correct floor. A closed window would also prevent the sound from carrying, since most buildings tend to be well insulated. Since the whole operation depends upon a steady flow of electricity, a break in the middle of the wire would also cause problems. Of course, the fellow could shout, but the human voice is not loud enough to carry that far. An additional problem is that a string could break on the instrument. Then there could be no accompaniment to the message. It is clear that the best situation would involve less distance. Then there would be fewer potential problems. With face to face contact, the least number of things could go wrong (p. 719).

Here listeners/readers may have knowledge of the language and yet fail to comprehend the passage. It is only when they are shown pictures—of a modern-day Romeo serenading his Juliet, who listens to him from her window in a modern high-rise building, with guitar music emanating from a microphone attached to a set of rising balloons—that the message becomes easily comprehensible. In the words of Bransford and McCarrell (1974, p. 204), the listener/reader must be able to "activate a linguistic knowledge" and also "an adequate approach to comprehension must consider the cognitive contributions of the comprehender as well as the linguistic characterizations of input sentences." The nature of the cognitive contributions is further elucidated by a number of researchers.

Schallert (1976) manipulated task instructions and exposure duration of prose passages to induce different levels of processing and to affect the amount of information retained. She constructed ambiguous paragraphs permitting two semantically different interpretations (problems of a losing baseball team manager or the manager of a glass factory worrying about a possible strike). To influence the interpretations of the ambiguous paragraphs, different contexts in the form of biasing titles accompanied the text. Results showed that weak-meaning-related and strong-meaning-related contexts influenced recall and recognition. Thus context was shown to be a powerful determinant of which meaning was remembered from ambiguous paragraphs when incoming information was processed at a deeper, more semantic level, as proposed by Craik and Lockhart (1972). While Bransford and Johnson (1972) have shown that context can increase the amount of information remembered, Schallert has extended their findings to show the biasing effect of context and how this can be manipulated for subjects to comprehend passages with two or more meanings.

The *integration* of new and old information leads to the prediction of the time it takes to comprehend a sentence in texts experimentally manipulated. The rationale is that listeners or readers will not feel they have fully understood a sentence until the new information is integrated with the old. The closer the new information matches the old the quicker they will comprehend. Compare the pair of two-sentence texts:

(4–1) Jack was given several classics books. He liked the Iliad the best.
(4–2) Jack was given a lot of things. He liked the Iliad the best.

In (4–1) the antecedent "books" helps the understanding of the second sentence. In (4–2) the inference that one of the "things" was a book has to be made before comprehending the second sentence. Hence the inferential step would likely delay processing time.

To test the above assumption, Haviland and Clark (1974) presented subjects with pairs of sentences where the first sentence (the context) provides a context for the second (the target) sentence. It was found that a target sentence with a definite noun phrase presupposing existence took less time to comprehend when its given information had a direct antecedent in the context sentence than when it did not. The sentences were of the kind:

(5) We got some beer from the trunk. The beer was warm.

and

(6) We checked the picnic supplies. The beer was warm.

The instruction to the subjects (university students) was "deliberately vague": "Press the button as soon as you understand what the second sentence means." The processing time for the kind of sentences in (5) was shorter as predicted. That the mere repetition of the critical noun is not sufficient to account for the above results is shown in:

(7) Andrew was especially fond of beer. The beer was warm.

Sentence (7) would replace (6). Again the first panel (No. 5) was faster than panel (7) as there is no direct inference in panel (7) despite the definite pronoun. Results with the adverbs "still, again, too, either" also supported the phenomenon for target sentences.

Thus to understand discourse we need to know:

1. The content of the sentences explicitly.
2. The circumstances surrounding the discourse.
3. The time and spatial relationship of the mental processes involved.
4. The tacit understanding between the speaker/writer and the listener/reader.

The tacit understanding between speakers and listeners or writers and readers is what Clark (1977), Clark and Haviland (1974, 1977, 1978) and Haviland and Clark (1974) call *Given-New contract.* This is a strategy dealing with integration of information and is based on the assumption that language is primarily used for imparting new information. Sometimes not all information is available and listeners/readers must attempt to introduce an antecedent to connect the information already in memory.

In the following two-sentence text:

(8) Jones vanished for more than a year and was not seen. His murderer was not found.

the inference is that Jones was murdered. This process is known as *bridging* (Clark, 1977) and this results in the addition of a set of one or more propositions to memory, a set called an *implicature.* Thus the listener/reader would likely add this implicature to memory:

He (Jones) was murdered.

With this addition, listeners/readers could pass from a certain proposition (the *premise*) to another proposition (the *conclusion*) because they understand, or believe they themselves understand, there is certain evidence relating the premise and conclusion. This evidential relation may or may not be conclusive and the listeners/readers may falsely believe they are inferring a true evidential relation when no such relation exists. Clark further distinguished between *authorized inferencing* and *unauthorized inferencing*. An example of the former was when John walked into Dick's room without closing the door and while there were several people talking in the corridor. When Dick remarked, "It's noisy here," John understood this to mean a polite hint for him to close the door. He is said to have drawn an authorized inference. This may be contrasted with the situation in which a suspect tries to establish an alibi when he was actually at the scene, and the jury thus drew an unauthorized inference. Clark emphasizes the following:

1. The *Given-New contract* helps listeners/readers to identify referents.
2. Certain *bridging* assumptions—authorized inferences or implicatures may need to be added to identify these referents.
3. Implications are arrived at through a process of *problem-solving*.

Thus inferencing serves the function of filling in missing "slots" in the structure of discourse and of connecting events in order to provide a higher level of organization. Warren, Nicholas, and Trabasso (1979) suggest these different classes of logical inferences: (a) motivational, (b) psychological, (c) physical cause and (d) enactment. They emphasize the *event chain* as a formalization of story relations linking people, things, time, place, and general context of a given event. Thus inferences stem from the logical relations between events in the text, between informational relations linking events such as "who, what, when and where" and the integration of the comprehender's world knowledge about events so specified. The listener/reader not only makes inferences relevant to the progression of narrative materials but also induces a mental structure on the materials.

An extension of the chronometric studies of Clark and Haviland (1974, 1977) was carried out by Lesgold, Roth and Curtis (1979) into the *foregrounding* effects in discourse comprehension of adults. Lesgold et al. explained foreground as "a possible status of concepts at points in the text that come after those concepts are first introduced. At such a point, a concept is *foregrounded* if the conventions of the language community allow a speaker to assume that the listener has the concept actively in mind at that point . . ." (p. 291). The main argument of the researchers is that, in comprehending discourse, that portion comprehended must be matched with the "reinstatement" of previous text memory. Much of the reinstatement will depend on how well all the propositions held in current temporary memory are directly integrated with previous knowledge or how well "inferential bridges" are generated by the reader.

To return to Bartlett's (1932) reconstruction theory that remembering prose involves the reconstruction of past events at the time of recall, Spiro (1977) attempts to provide a detailed model of the reconstructive process. He argues that the alternative theory known as *constructive theory* which holds that remembering is jointly determined by perceptual experiences, current knowledge of the learner, and context in which the event is preceived is inadequate to account for some data. Spiro suggests that "Accuracy can be the result of either the differentiation of information in the discourse from cognitive structures or the absence of schema modification, rather than being *general* support for abstractive-trace [constructive] retrieval theory. Inaccuracy can be the result of active elaborative processing in comprehension or merely bad guessing, with low confidence, to fill gaps in memory, rather than being the high confidence product of a natural and common process of inferential reconstruction which would generate accurate recall in exactly the same way that inaccurate recall was generated" (p. 140). He puts forth a *state of schema* (SOS) approach which incorporates these contextual factors: prior linguistic context, context of the situation, speaker/listener-hearer/reader relationship, intents and attitudes, cognitive and affective correlates, task demands, linguistic cues and the nature of the discourse. Spiro points out that many laboratory studies make the peculiar demand on a subject to disregard his/her previous knowledge when this is needed for comprehension. He gives for an example—"The hippie touched the debutante in the park," to show that in an experiment the subject is implicitly or explicitly disregarding truth values and other factors, though these should have all been included. The integrating nature of a schema theory is aptly expressed by Anderson (1977, p. 418): "the mental representations which are used during perception and comprehension, and which evolve as a result of these processes, have a holistic character which cannot be understood as simple functions of their constituents."

Uses of Schemata in Grade School and Kindergarten Children

From the studies of college students one would ask if children are able to form and use their schemata in a manner similar to, or different from, adults in comprehending. To some extent, this question is closely related to the concept of language awareness which is discussed in some detail in Chapter 6. There it is pointed out that the underlying concept of accessibility to language is central to memory and learning and that there is a large body of evidence from cognitive and developmental psychology and artificial intelligence, all converging on the process of gaining access to rule-based components already in the mind. The problem of comprehending is thus linked to the general problem of knowing when, knowing how, and knowing that you know and do not know, and of using flexible strategies in seeing relations and solving problems. Over the years there has been a considerable number of works on how young children use their old and new knowledge to comprehend, recognize, reconstruct and recall discourse materials, as evidenced in the research program of Brown and associates (Brown, 1975a, 1975b, 1976; Brown and DeLoache, 1978; Brown and Murphy, 1975; Brown and Smiley, 1977; Brown, Smiley, Day, Townsend, and Lawton, 1977), the studies of Mandler and Johnson (1977), and of Stein and Glenn (1979), among others.

In two experiments, Brown, Smiley, Day, Townsend, and Lawton (1977) tested the memory and comprehension of prose passages of children from second through seventh grades. Both experiments provided the children with different background information which could be used to disambiguate and enlarge on vague or ambiguous sections of prose passages. In one experiment, the children listened to repetitions of a passage concerning an escape. Half of the children were led to believe that the main protagonist was an escaped convict named George, while the other half was told that the main character was Galen the chimpanzee hero of the television series "Planet of the Apes." In this experiment, recognition of theme-congruent and theme-incongruent foils was the main test. In the second experiment all children listened to the story of Tor, a young man of the Targa tribe. Some children had been told previously that the Targas were Eskimos; some were told they were American Indians of the desert; while the rest had no previous knowledge of the tribe. In this experiment, intrusions in recall and postrecall interviews were used to measure the influence of pre-existing expectations on story recall and comprehension.

Results of the Brown et al. experiments showed that, by third grade, children do integrate their pre-existing knowledge into the prose passages so as to elaborate on them. The most striking finding is the lack of strong or compelling trends where similarity rather than differences between younger and older children is quite marked. Not unlike adults, younger children incorrectly identified congruent foils as part of the original story. They also show the effects of prior expectation and knowledge. They can and do use induced frameworks to disambiguate prose passages. Brown et al. emphasize that though older children do make more use of their previous knowledge in recalling prose materials, the "evidence is not overwhelming" (p. 1464). The older children did, however, produce "significantly more theme relevant intrusions" and they did recall "more of the actual story units" (p. 1464).

These findings thus extend the earlier studies of Brown (1975a, 1975b, 1976), Brown and Murphy (1975), and Brown and Smiley (1977), with subjects ranging from kindergarteners to fourth-graders and stories adapted to suit different age groups. The general conclusion is that subjects tend to extract the main theme of a story and disregard trivial items. This pattern of recalling essential event sequences runs across different ages. Brown (1975a) carried out four experiments to examine the ability of kindergarten and second-grade children to regenerate the order of events expressed in narrative sequences by using recognition, reconstruction, and recall as the response modes. The narrative sequences were either imposed by the experimenter or induced by the children themselves. The children were told that they would hear some stories about animals and were asked to try to remember the stories so as to be able to retell them. In the "ordered condition" the experimenter described a logical narrative sequence beginning with the actor and including each item of line drawings shown to the subjects in the order these items appeared. For example, the children were shown drawings of a cat, then of glasses, a plane and lightning while these items were accompanied by the narrative "The cat put on his glasses and went for a ride in his plane and then the weather got bad and he was struck by lightning." The "random condition" did not follow any logical sequence.

In the "own story condition," the children could make up their own stories. The findings showed that for all the children logical and self-imposed sentences were retained better than arbitrary sequences. Thus the failure of preoperational children to maintain correct narrative sequences when retelling a story is due less to their inability to comprehend and remember the ordered relations in sequences than to their general problems with recall tasks and their immature expository power.

The Brown (1975a) studies do not so much point to whether retelling of narrative prose materials requires reversibility of thought or otherwise or that reversibility is within the cognitive structure of young children. Rather, Brown has shown the preconditions for tasks to be developmentally sensitive to different degrees of mature, operational concepts of order. She explains: "Simple order-reconstruction tasks, where spatial and temporal cues are in correspondence, and where the child is not required to make assumptions concerning ordered relations, are within the problem-solving capacity of young children" (Brown, 1975a, p. 165). More complex tasks such as those requiring the ability to dissociate temporal and spatial orders and those requiring the retracing of an ordered sequence backward and forward demand a more mature concept of temporal order (see also Brown and Murphy, 1975). In further experiments with kindergarten, second and fourth grade children, Brown (1975b) examined how young children memorized items and order in a progressive elaboration pair-associates task. She showed that the difficulty that kindergarten children have with order reconstruction tasks because of immaturity in forming internal representation could be explained on the grounds that they fail to notice the cumulative nature of the events in a sequence chain. For such tasks children can be trained. According to these results, Piaget's (1969) estimate that the reconstruction of order involves reversibility and is too difficult for children younger than the age of seven years would need to be re-examined.

The question of the cognitive structure needed for children to comprehend discourse and the developmental course of such structure can be answered in terms of the differential strategies of children and their metacognitive control over these strategies (Brown and DeLoache, 1978). As children develop, they become able to predict in advance the essential organizing features and important elements of text materials (Brown and Smiley, 1977). With simpler texts, children can pick out the main ideas at a much earlier age. Further, the findings that children also make intrusion errors implies that pre-existing knowledge can be manipulated to help comprehension. These errors should not be considered mistakes as the intrusions add to the cohesion of the material and help to make it interpretable. Thus teachers should provide suitable backgrounds and should help pupils to generate an appropriate context and framework to incorporate a story. The same findings are in line with those of adult studies which show meaning cannot be entirely expressed by the semantic content of prose. This is evident in the work of Bransford and Johnson (1973) in their oft-quoted passage about the modern-day Romeo serenading his Juliet who is perched in the high-rise and the studies of Bransford, Barclay, and Franks (1972) and of Bransford and McCarrell (1974). It is likely that both adults and children integrate the meaning and relationship perceived in individual sentences into whole situations. Through the process of semantic integration the listener/reader also disambiguates and elaborates on comprehension. With young children they must be told clearly and explicitly how to elaborate on meaning cumulatively and how to remember the chains of events (Brown, 1975b). If information becomes an integral part of the pre-existing schemata, then the level of recall will be increased (Brown, 1975a, 1975b).

There is, however, one important finding from the series of studies by Brown and associates that differs from the studies with adults by Fraisse (1963) and Piaget (1969). Fraisse suggested that, in reconstructing narratives, adults use their logical, reasoning ability in their knowledge system to produce the probable order of events. They will then reconstruct items that follow some logical sequences or cause-effect relationships (see also Anderson and Ortony, 1975). Fraisse further suggested that children need to be capable of reversibility in order to reproduce stories. This presupposes preoperational children should perform equally in remembering logical or arbitrary sequences of events. The results of Brown and associates do not support this assertion. Like adults, children have difficulties in reconstructing *isolated* instances, although they are capable of using logical connections to form inferences. They can integrate their previous schemata into holistic semantic relationships in memory.

Corroborative evidence is also provided by Paris (1978), Paris and Carter (1973), Paris and

Lindauer (1976), and Paris and Mahoney (1974). Paris and Carter observed that second- and fifth-grade children can integrate spontaneously semantic information given in short paragraphs and can identify meaning-distorting new sentences. The spontaneity with which children can construct and retain implicit or explicit information in memory was further shown by Paris and Mahoney (1974) in their study of the way in which seven- to eleven-year-old children extracted and integrated information from sets of pictures and sentences. When second-grade and sixth-grade children were compared in memory organization skill, the older children showed significantly more spontaneous reconstruction of remembered information (Paris, 1978). Eleven- and twelve-year-old children were better able than six- and seven-year-olds to infer new information from pre-existing knowledge (Paris and Lindauer, 1976). The various studies by Brown and by Paris and their associates show that, while children in comparison with adults are not as proficient in abstracting underlying relationships and are more dependent on specific lexical information such as words and word-order, nevertheless they can store and retrieve items in their internal representation. Furthermore, a developmental study of reading comprehension in second and sixth grade children by Chi, Ingram, and Danner (1977) throws some light on the Paris and Carter and Paris and Lindauer results. Chi et al. found that their children's ability to make inferences from prose in terms of accuracy and latency did not show developmental changes. They did find, however, that the processing times for both premises and inference questions related significantly to reading comprehension for their twelve-year-old children.

Related to the use of schemata is children's understanding of figurative language. It is usually maintained that children cannot comprehend proverbs and metaphors as variations or extensions of meaning until the age of twelve or so. Recently, Honeck, Sowry and Voegtle (1978) tested the comprehension of seven-, eight- and nine-year-old children by having the subjects compare proverbs against thematic pictures consisting of a nonliteral interpretation and a foil for each proverb. Their results showed that seven- and nine-year-olds can understand proverbs and that pictures serve as a framework for organizing the common meaning of both pictures and proverbs. The findings imply that children are aware of the reality and apparent violations in the communicative act and can attempt to reinterpret the violation. To do this, they must first figure out the literal meaning of discourse to check it against context and to derive the implied meaning. An example is a recent news item reporting an unexpected surplus of chickens and the head of a government social service agency purchasing the fowls at bargain price for hospitals and senior citizens' homes. The headline of "A Plucky Business" is later elaborated on as adding "a feather to the administrator's cap."

In their study of comprehension of proverbs by adults, Verbrugge and McCarrell (1977) reasoned that understanding of metaphors involves inferring an implicit comparison between the "ground" or "topic" and the metaphorical "vehicle." An example is "Billboards and warts on the landscape," where the metaphorical topic is "billboards" and the vehicle is "warts." In understanding metaphors, subjects will need to make inferences about the topic and hence will need longer processing time because of their attention directed to aspects of the topic. This line of reasoning makes it possible to test the psychological realities of comprehending metaphors. Verbrugge and McCarrell postulated that relevant grounds are effective recall cues of figurative language and they did find that subjects in their experiments made use of such grounds for high-level recall. Recently, Ortony, Reynolds, and Arter (1978) have critically reviewed theoretical and empirical research into metaphors, and have emphasized their role in language comprehension and cognition. They find that propositional models and schema-theoretic models make different predictions about the comprehension of metaphors, with the former treating metaphors as anomalies and the latter viewing them from the input aspect. They suggest that a fruitful approach for research might be the manipulation of contexts to induce differential interpretations, as metaphors should be considered "contextually anomalous." This view of comprehension implicating both memory and inference may be compared with Scriven's (1972) concept. He suggested that comprehension involves both a "redundancy filter" to operate on previously stored "templates" and an "error-detecting filter" to prevent contradictions. To the extent that listeners/readers achieve a high-level of matching between the schema discourse and their previous knowledge, they can be said to understand. To the extent they can repair "inconsistencies" or apparently disparate elements in figurative language they would prevent storing contradictions and hence would better comprehend. The Scriven argument provides some philosophical underpinnings for the comprehending of comprehension and knowledge.

Thus the schema approach to comprehension is especially illuminating when discourse materials are well organized and cohesive and when these materials require more than mere rote memory for their recognition, reconstruction, or recall. In remembering logical narrative sequences, adults and children retain the theme or gist of the material in an integrated representation rather than as a series of unconnected events (Bransford and Franks, 1971; Brown, 1976). The importance of propositions being recalled better is well illustrated by Bransford and Franks (1971). They presented subjects with a number of sentences derived from sets of four propositions:

(9–1) The rock rolled down the mountain.
(9–2) The hut was tiny.
(9–3) The rock crushed the hut.
(9–4) The hut was at the edge of the woods.

The presented sentences contained either one or two or three of these four propositions in various combinations, but never all four propositions. Later, however, when given a recognition task, subjects claimed the sentence with the four propositions ("The rock which rolled down the mountain crushed the tiny hut at the edge of the woods") as old information, even though they had never seen it. Bransford and Franks explained that subjects had built the information structures containing the four propositions. This integration of high-level structure is illustrated in Figure 10–5.

The schematic representation brings us back to Fillmore's (1968, 1971a) case grammar (see relevant sections in Chapter 6) which discusses the verb-noun relationship and its extension. The concept of role relationship and how the protagonist of prose can be traced through a plot has also been discussed by linguists such as Fries (1952) and Pike (1967). However, it remains for psycholinguists and cognitive psychologists to unravel the psychological realities of the nature of the relationship of sentences in discourse. This relationship can be accommodated within the Given-New strategy of Clark and Haviland (1974, 1977), as the definite article "the" might have helped to hold the sentences together. Bransford and Johnson (1972, 1973) and Pearson (1974–1975) explain that grammatically more complex or longer statements could equal or even outperform their simpler or shorter counterparts. Pearson suggested a possible trade-off relationship between explicitness on the one hand and simplicity on the other. In the panel:

(10–1) The food ran short. The people were starving.
(10–2) The people were starving because food ran short.

sentence (10–2) is the more explicit though grammatically more complex, whereas (10–1) is simpler but implicit.

This discussion brings us back to the central role of the schema in reading. During the days of the ascendency of transformational grammar, it was argued that syntax plays an important role in sentence perception. Studies have shown how deep structure affects remembering sentences (Blumenthal, 1967; Blumenthal and Boakes, 1967; Perfetti, 1969), how syntax helps to organize text (Miller and Isard, 1963; Miller and Selfridge, 1950), and that passive sentences are harder to understand than active ones (Gough, 1965, 1966). While much of the findings has revealed how children comprehend syntactical structure (see Palermo and Molfese, 1972; Stotsky, 1975, for review), it is also fair to say that the emphasis of this period of work was mostly on the compre-

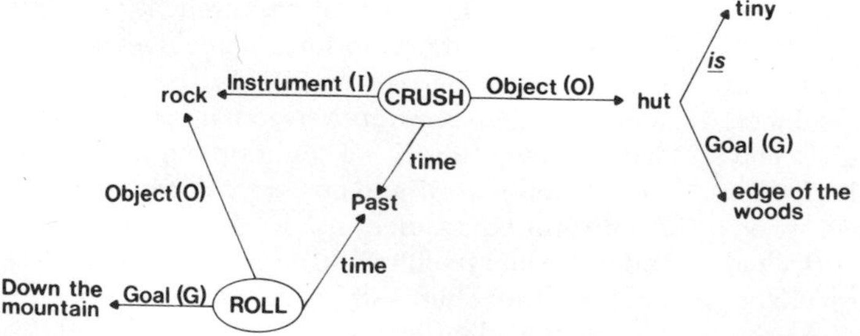

Figure 10–5. Structure of: "The rock which rolled down the mountain crushed the tiny hut at the edge of the woods."

hension of single sentences, as it was assumed that sentences need to be understood before text materials. The current literature has emphasized what people have to *know* in addition to what they actually do in prose comprehension and production. Performance in comprehension and memory tasks has a broader base than simply semantically interpreted deep structure relations underlying linguistic inputs. Some linguists have even argued that meaning of text materials is not determined exclusively by lexical and syntactical information and is related to human knowledge (e.g. Chafe, 1972). Other linguists have argued that the competence-performance distinction is too narrow as psychological factors, such as processing time and limitations and intents of communication, have to be taken into account (e.g. Lakoff, 1972).

The observation of the psychologist George Miller (1974) of the different *root metaphors* (paradigms) characterizing language learning is appropriate. He suggested that, until about the 1950s, the root metaphor was *association,* because language learning emphasized connections between words and things. During the 1950s to the mid-1960s, the *communication* metaphor focused on alternative signals, and generative grammar helped to explain syntax when attention shifted from words to sentences. The third metaphor should focus on what people do when they produce or understand linguistic signals. Miller (1974, p. 404) commented: "Whereas the first metaphor led us to look for *connections* between words and things, and the second led us to look for *rules* characterizing acceptable signals, the third should lead us to look for *procedures* involved in using language." As we have seen in the preceding sections dealing with comprehension in adults and children, Miller's metaphor of procedures needs to include human thinking and the acquisition of knowledge in coming to comprehend.

Current theories and empirical studies converging on the concept of the *schema* as ideation building blocks for comprehending discourse are important for schooling. Schema use must be seen as flexible and involving constructive and interactive processes, so as to help "dissolve the seeming paradox between abstract linguistic competence, on the one hand, and the rich particularity of the mental representation which arises from any specific instance of language comprehension, on the other" (Anderson, 1977, p. 429). In this section, we have drawn heavily on the research program of Brown and associates to show that in listening/reading, listeners/readers expect certain patterns of information from discourse materials, attend to sequences of information, and integrate input information into their existing schemata to obtain new knowledge. The studies from the Illinois group of researchers are of particular interest as they examine developmental trends by using tasks (such as picture narratives) appropriate for young children and by teasing out different comprehension protocols (recognition, reconstruction or recall). They show that young children not so much fail to comprehend as they have difficulty with mature, internal representation (schemata) or with appropriate organization of their schemata materials. How children as well as college students make use of their semantic and episodic memory to integrate the thematic structures of materials listened to or read is further investigated by a number of cognitive psychologists and psycholinguists. These have included: Poulsen, Kintsch, Kintsch and Premack (1979) in their study of young children's comprehension of stories; Meyer's (1975a, 1975b, 1977a, 1977b) analysis and experiments with college students in their recall of prose; Tierney, Bridge, and Cera (1978–1979) in their examination of the extent and type of information rendered by children during recall of connected discourse; Marshall and Glock (1978–1979) in their study of how certain aspects of text affected comprehension of college students; Mosenthal (1979) in his verification of types of schema in children's recall of text; Mandler and Johnson (1977) in their developmental analysis of the recall of stories by grade-school children and university students within a detailed framework of story grammar and Stein and Glenn's (1979) refined investigation of elementary-school children's knowledge of the structure of stories. As almost all these empirical studies relate to elegant, systematic story-specific or paragraph-specific rules based on or associated with Kintsch (1974), Meyer (1975a, 1975b, 1977a, 1977b), C. H. Frederiksen (1975a, 1975b, 1977, 1979), Thorndyke (1977), Mandler and Johnson (1977) and Stein and Glenn (1979), a further discussion will be provided in subsequent sections.

Some Linguistic Devices in Text Cohesion

From the discussions in the preceding sections on how schemata enter into and are integrated with the psychological processes involved in comprehension, we will examine the linguistic structure of discourse and how this structure is organized in discourse materials. Much of the current literature on this topic is directed toward providing answers to such questions as: Is there a discourse grammar analagous to sentence grammar? What are the linguistic devices that integrate discourse? How will a theory of discourse account for various relationships among discourse elements such as propositions? What are the psychological realities of discourse processing? (see Hurtig, 1977).

From the psychological perspective, the question of *cohesion* of discourse is an important one. Studies from anthropology and linguistics have provided psychologists with the underpinning for the latters' theory and empirical work. For example, one source that is often mentioned is the story schema of the Russian linguist Propp (1928). He studied folktales at an abstract level according to the functions of their characters because functions serve as stable content elements. This identification of functions of characters in folktales may be compared with Fillmore's emphasis on the function of information in sentences. As folktales stem from an oral tradition and are not written down, they must be well preserved through their retelling and through what people can remember. Thus we can understand the important role of memory of "things parsed"—their encoding, storage and retrieval. Other linguists whose work has important influence on or implications for discourse analysis include Halliday (1964), Halliday and Hasan (1976) and Grimes (1975). Halliday, for example, views cohesion as "syntagmatic relations" and as accounting for the structure of text. These relations are signaled by certain grammatical and lexical features (e.g. anaphora, subordination, substitution and other devices) and these features reflect discourse structure. Cohesion therefore does not constitute discourse structure but underpins the structure of text. For Halliday, Halliday and Hasan and Grimes the important relationships in discourse are: (1) organization of the content of discourse (Grimes' semantic grammar), (2) presentation of new information to a listener/reader and (3) expressing speaker's/writer's perspectives (Halliday's theme and Grimes' staging). These notions have underpinned much of the current theory and research into comprehension (e.g. Clements, 1979; Meyer, 1975a, 1975b, 1977a, 1977b). What follows in the next section is a brief discussion of a number of linguistic devices needed for prose comprehension. For detailed studies, readers are referred to Halliday and Hasan (1976) and Grimes (1975).

Indexing Linguistic Information

The following passage will provide some illustrations of the devices useful for comprehension:

> An absolute ruler for the past twenty years, the president obviously was not born yesterday. Yet he has been taken in. He has been swindled in a business deal and relieved of one million dollars. The swindler is said to be a close friend of his and is still at large. The ruler's agents, who have no great respect for due processes, are determined to get him. This may cost the swindler dearer than the million dollars he had netted.

The following devices should be noted:

1. The first sentence "The president . . ." sets what is termed the *discourse pointer* to the proposition or symbols in the comprehender's mind indicating the current topic of the discourse.
2. Key words such as "taken in," "swindled," "swindler" are *repeated* a number of times in different ways.
3. The use of *intersentential connectives* relates sentences one to the other. The word "obviously" leads to another argument. Without this word, the proposition in the second half of the first sentence is tautological. Without the word, the first sentence is analogous to "The red rose is not red." This latter proposition is an *inconsistency.* The word "yet" in the second sentence introduces an element of surprise and material opposite to what has just been said. The word "still" implies the ruler's agents have tried to catch the swindler but have not been successful.
4. The use of *contrastives in time* shows temporal relations. The assertion that the ruler has ruled absolutely for twenty years shows he is all-powerful and not considered gullible. The word "yet" also introduces another item in a time series; there may have been attempts at taking him in before, but this time the attempt carries off. The recency of the swindle is shown by the phrase "has been" rather than the past tense "was".
5. The use of *anaphoras* as devices to refer back to previously mentioned concepts. An

example is the pronominalization "he" to refer to the ruler and the use of "him" in the last sentence to denote the swindler. The discourse pointer in the first three sentences is set to the "absolute ruler"—the president—being swindled. The anaphoric referent, the pronoun "he," thus refers to the president. In sentences 4, 5 and 6 the discourse pointer is set to the swindler and so the second "he" refers to the swindler. This second referent is further disambiguated with the repetition of the key word "swindler" in the last sentence.

6. The use of *polysemous* words such as "take in" (cf. take, take on, take up, take off and others), "at large" (cf. large with small) and "get him" (cf. get a book).
7. Other devices include *direct reference* with an epithet (the president is one and the same person as the absolute ruler) and *set membership* ("a close friend of his").

The text material here ("An absolute ruler . . . he had netted") is the writers' adaptation of a news item with the heading "The Cuban Coffee Caper." The item outlines how the Cuban ruler Fidel Castro is reported as having been swindled in a big coffee transaction. Readers who have some world knowledge of the Cuban leader and the general state of affairs in Cuba will find it easier to comprehend the text. They are aided by the heading which summarizes the gist of the text. Thus, comprehending text goes beyond the language competence-performance distinction. The grammar of the language cannot be separated from psychological factors. The structure of the passage is made all the more cohesive by the linguistic devices outlined above.

Carpenter and Just (1977) discussed *dovetailing, repetition of key words,* the use of *intersentential connectives* and *discourse pointers* as being among the devices integrating memory structure. In this process there is a thorough search through the working memory to find information related to the current phrase, sentence or stretch of discourse. What a linguistic device marks as old information is to be matched with other information in memory. What is marked as new information will be added to the previous knowledge in working memory. Thus Carpenter and Just emphasize *representing, indexing* and *comparing* information. Processing difficulties found, for example, with negation (e.g. "Please do not leave cigarettes lighted" takes longer to comprehend than "Please extinguish cigarettes") are due more to a mismatch between representations and not affirmation or negation as such. This continuous psychological dimension of congruence/incongruence is also the approach other researchers have taken to consider perceptual, linguistic or crosschannel conjoined cognitions (see Hoosain, 1973, 1974; Osgood and Richards, 1973).

Space permits only a brief discussion of some of the linguistic devices useful for comprehension. We will deal briefly with anaphoras and polysemy.

Anaphora

An anaphora denotes a structure in a sentence with no fixed semantic interpretation of its own but derives its meaning from a previous sentence or an earlier part of the present sentence. Bloomfield (1933) in his *Language* discussed "substitution" at some length, much of which is concerned with anaphora, while Gleason (1965, pp. 344–345) saw anaphora as an important device, "as a signal for connectedness between clauses or sentences." Halliday (1967, p. 206) wrote that "in any information unit that is noninitial in a discursive, recoverable information tends to be represented anaphorically, by reference, substitution or ellipsis."

Turning from the linguistic to the reading literature, Robertson (1968) found in her studies that children aged nine to twelve years increased their ability to perform sentence completion tasks requiring connectives such as "when, although, therefore." As these connectives relate to clauses and phrases of sentences, it may be inferred that improvement on this task represented an increase in syntactic ability. Bormuth, Manning, Carr and Pearson (1970) investigated the understanding of syntactic structures and found a low level of performance among fourth-grade children on many basic sentence structures. Different structures (*intrasentence, intersentence,* and *anaphora*) were comprehended with different levels of proficiency. Bormuth et al. argued that these categories may be related to stages in a learning hierarchy for comprehension. They used questions mostly of the *wh-* type (what, who, when, where, by whom) to tap the understanding of a given anaphora form. For example, one sentence was written and a second constructed with some reference to the first:

(11) John went to the store.
He bought an apple.

The question was "who bought an apple?" and multiple-choice alternative answers were written for the anaphora reference. Both vocabulary and syntactical complexity of the material were scaled for reading difficulty. It is possible that there might be a confounding of syntax with semantics in the kinds of paragraphs given and questions asked. An example of the confounding is:

(12–1) He won the race.
(12–2) John knew he had won the race.

Most young children would know that "he" in (12–1) refers to the person most recently talked about and would assume that (12–2) refers to two different people whereas "John" and "he" may or may not be coreferential.

The use of a pronoun to denote a concept presupposes that the concept is known to the listener/reader. Cooper (1974) studied discourse comprehension involving the use of pronouns. The subjects listened to a passage about a trip to Africa with the mention of a dog and zebras. At the same time, they were looking at a set of pictures that included these objects. It was found that subjects tended to fixate the referential picture when a pronoun occurred. Looking at the picture might correlate with the memory search for the referent of the pronoun. When two sentences are linguistically related by *pronominal reference,* they tend to be comprehended and remembered together. Lesgold (1972) found that sentences conjoined with pronominal reference as in (13) were better recalled than those conjoined with *and* as in (14).

(13) The blacksmith was skilled and he pounded the anvil which was dented.
(14) The blacksmith was skilled and the anvil was dented and the blacksmith pounded the anvil.

It is likely that for (13) information is integrated in memory.

The article *the* is another anaphoric reference and indicates that the modified noun has been referred to in the preceding context. An example will illustrate this:

(15–1) The doctor and philanthropist received the outstanding citizen award.
(15–2) The doctor and *the* philanthropist received the outstanding citizen award.

In sentence (15–1) the "doctor" and "philanthropist" are coreferential and refer to the same person, whereas in (15–2) they refer to two different persons. The article "the" in "the outstanding citizen award" implies the award has been referred to earlier.

The different studies by Bormuth et al. (1970), Lesgold (1974) and Richek (1976–1977) have all shown that school-aged children experience difficulties in understanding anaphoric forms. All the results suggest that children need to be taught specifically about anaphoras and that writers of reading materials will need to pay more attention to both the cohesion and structure of sentences. Webber (1980) has discussed some of the factors operative in anaphor resolution. She has shown that the choice between possible antecedents for anaphoric expressions comprising pronouns, pro-verbs, certain noun phrases and ellipses may demand sophisticated syntactic, semantic, inferential and pragmatic understanding on the part of the reader.

An excellent example of identical structures *(enation)* taken from Shakespeare is the well-known oratory of Brutus when he explains why he has killed Julius Caesar:

> As Caesar loves me, I weep for him; as he was fortunate, I rejoice at it; as he was valiant, I honour him; but, as he was ambitious, I slew him. There is tears for his love; joy for his fortune; honour for his valour; and death for his ambition. . . .
>
> WILLIAM SHAKESPEARE: *Julius Caesar,* ACT III, SCENE II.

From anaphoric forms, we will move to polysemous words.

Polysemy

Polysemy refers to the different uses or senses of the same word. While we have been emphasizing relations among words and sentences we should not overlook that polysemous words are as necessary for comprehension of discourse. Examine the word *take,* for example. The following sentences are just some of the different senses possible:

(16–1) I take the book home.
(16–2) The meeting takes thirty minutes.
(16–3) I will take up residence in Toronto.
(16–4) The taxi driver took the visitor for a ride.
(16–5) I took him for a gentleman and found out I was wrong.
(16–6) I took up his offer.
(16–7) I was completely taken in by the ploy.
(16–8) I was taken by surprise.

Or take that unjustifiably maligned word *Dutch*. For no apparent reason, *Dutch* seems to suffer the "slings and arrows of outrageous" usage:

(17–1) Let's go for lunch and go Dutch.
(17–2) He showed Dutch courage.
(17–3) He talked like a Dutch uncle.
(17–4) It was all double Dutch to me.
(17–5) The guest took Dutch leave.

How should polysemous words be represented in an internal lexicon? Fillmore (1971a) suggested that different uses of the same word should appear as a single lexical entry when one use results from the extension of the other. Then the metaphorical use of words can be taken to represent the normal situation in assigning different senses to words. This will provide for cognitive economy. Caramazza and Grober (1976) reported on the use of 26 senses of the word line (e.g. "He typed the first *line* of his paper." "I am no longer in that *line* of business." "The official was able to *line* his pocket with money."). The above can be likened to the use of a computer system that can understand English. The core of the system is an internal lexicon that contains all *sense-instances* of the words of the language. With new words, the new sense value can be "computed" from its context and added to the internal lexicon (see also Figure 10–5 and discussion of the Figure). Caramazza and Grober found evidence for a single core meaning from cluster analysis and multidimensional scaling of similarity judgments among the senses of *line*. Of the five groupings of the 26 senses of *line*, one cluster was labeled a SEQUENCE or ORDERING of constructs. The senses were found in these sentences:

(18–1) Ford is coming out with a new *line* of hard tops.
(18–2) I am no longer in that *line* of business.
(18–3) They came to different conclusions, using the same *line* of reasoning.
(18–5) Sam owned the local bus *line*.

It would appear that the underlying concept with *line* is EXTENSION. From their cluster analysis, Caramazza and Grober argued for a *process view of meaning* to explain how some sense values are not found from stored representation but must be computed. This reminds us of the earlier discussion of the interactive model of reading by Rumelhart (1977a, 1977b). While the general process of "computation" is still vague, there are these components:

1. There is an abstract, internal linguistic dictionary that contains a phonological matrix, a meaning part and a conceptual representation. These parts correspond to core meaning in a computer and the core varies in degrees of abstraction. The core can also be visualized as a semantic tree specifying an n-space predicate.
2. There is a set of instructional rules analogous to syntactic-semantic rules.
3. There is an encyclopedic dictionary-knowledge of the world with both denotative and connotative meaning.

Recently, Mason, Kniseley, and Kendall (1979) investigated the ability of children in middle elementary grades to recall polysemous words and to identify their meanings after having read the words in sentences. Results showed that the children did not know the secondary meanings of some words; they did not choose the less common meanings from disambiguating contexts and would even choose common meanings in violation of context. Mason et al. suggest polysemous words as a "potential source" of comprehension difficulties. They stress the need to teach multiple meanings of words and proper discrimination of "fuzzy" meanings supported by context.

Representation of Meaning in Prose

From the role of linguistic devices in reading comprehension, we turn our attention to the organization of text. Even before the current interest in discourse analyses contributed by cognitive psychologists and linguists, there were attempts by researchers to specify the contents of a text and to show how that content is related to learning. Some of the earlier studies should be mentioned.

Rothkopf (1965) suggested that under certain conditions prequestions might exert a selective effect on learning and that "testlike" events might help people to read and listen with greater understanding (Rothkopf, 1966). Frase (1968) found that questions with control over processing in close proximity to the related text would facilitate retention and that textual materials may be represented in terms of networks of set relations (Frase, 1969). Frase (1972) further presented data to show that children as young as second-graders are sensitive to the organizational properties of text, which can facilitate or obscure the organization of text. Verbal directions affect learning outcomes which reflect the amount of information to be processed. Thus the analysis of structure and processing activities is important for instruction and learning.

Towards this goal, psychologists and educators have long sought to identify, to analyze organizational structure that facilitates prose comprehension and to provide both the theory and the testing of comprehension (see Anderson, 1972; Bormuth, 1970). It is only more recently that systematic procedures have been developed to analyze the organization of information and the representation of meaning in prose. These procedures make possible the comparison of similarities and differences of the internal structure of text materials and throw more light on what it is that enables listeners/readers to recognize, reconstruct and recall these materials. In this section some of the current procedures and their applications will be outlined.

Kintsch's Prose Organization

We will begin by attempting the well-nigh impossible task of sketching the theory of Kintsch (1974, 1977, 1978). In the *Representation of Meaning in Memory,* Kintsch (1974) provides us with a comprehensive presentation of text processing. He deals with the representation of knowledge, which is represented in terms of propositions which are "n-tuple of word concepts, one serving as a predictor, the other as argument." An example is the word concept FEEL which is used as a predictor in the sense of "to touch" and "to perceive." In the first concept, an acceptable proposition might be: "Jane feels the rough surface" in the form (FEEL, AGENT, OBJECT). The second concept might be in the proposition "John felt he was right" to denote experience. In these two examples, the predictor (the verb FEEL) is written first in a proposition and arguments are separated by commas. FEEL can also be used as arguments rather than as predictors. In addition to verbs, connectives, quantifiers, time and location predictors also are used. An example of time predictor is "The wind blew yesterday" (TIME; YESTERDAY (BLOW, WIND)). Reading is characterized as the extraction of propositions from the text and the organization of these propositions into a coherent and cohesive sequence for ease of comprehension. This will then enable a more precise, though not necessarily more explicit, means of testing how meaning is acquired.

The basic assumptions of Kintsch's work are: *word concept, proposition* and *text base.* Word concepts are abstract entries in our internal dictionary and are specified by propositional frames. A text base is an "ordered list of propositions" from which a text is generated. Thus ideas are represented in the form of propositions. Representation of meaning of a text in memory is an abstraction which is derived from the actual text but which differs from it. Propositions can be classified according to their level in a hierarchy from superordinate to subordinate ones. Superordinate propositions are better recalled than subordinate ones. The reason given by Kintsch is that superordinate propositions introduce new arguments into the text whereas subordinate propositions repeat the arguments of the higher-level propositions. It is the implicit processing and reprocessing of superordinate propositions that facilitate recall of higher-level materials. Compare this line of argument with Samuels' (1977) suggestion of repeated reading as a supplementary method and Clark and associates' (Clark, 1977; Clark and Haviland, 1974, 1977; Haviland and Clark, 1974) Given-New strategy. Kintsch has further extended concept repetition to proposition repetition as a basic strategy to text comprehension. An example from Kintsch (1978) will illustrate this:

(19) A heater exploded. The house burned down.

Kintsch explains that the above sentence contains two explicit propositions: (EXPLODE, HEATER) and (BURN, HOUSE) and since these propositions do not form a text base a connecting proposition must be inferred. Readers might construct the following text base for (19):

(20) (CONSEQUENCE, (EXPLODE, HEATER), (BURN, HOUSE)).

Texts in which propositions are explicit are easier to comprehend and to remember than texts in which some implicit propositions must be inferred. The nature of inferencing discussed earlier is thus given a more elegant explanation. In his book, Kintsch (1974) has formalized rules for generating texts from a text base and for constructing a text base for a given text.

In his "interim conclusions" Kintsch (1974) cautions that representation of meaning in memory provides only general notions of psychological processes. The difficult question is *how* we should or could represent meaning. Some of his main results are:

1. Something like case structure might be the basis for sentential memory (see section on "case grammar" in Chapter 6).
2. Text material is analyzable into propositions to generate testable hypotheses to test recall and comprehension.
3. The notion of semantically acceptable propositions is central.
4. Word concepts are not decomposed (e.g. "builder" rather than "one who builds") but are used as arguments in propositions. If the word concept corresponding to the word appears as an argument in many propositions of a text, it should be a more successful recall cue.
5. The rate of reading can be expressed as a function of the number of propositions processed during reading.
6. How readers process a text is related to the structural relationship among the propositions in the text base. Superordinate levels in the hierarchy of propositions are recalled better than subordinate ones.
7. Recall of text involves both constructive and reconstructive processes—processes of inferencing. Inferences are not just logical or formal operations based on truth values but are derived from schemata or knowledge of the world. As such, inferences are *fuzzy* (varying continuously from one schema to another) and dynamic rather than static.

The above account is at best an imperfect summary of Kintsch's tour-de-force in his experimental work and formalism of the interactive effect of memory on text processing and the effect of text processing on memory. Before steeping themselves in the theoretical and experimental papers of the main work (Kintsch, 1974), readers may like to read the lucid chapters by the same author in other sources (Kintsch, 1977, 1978). Similar analyses of organizing, interpreting text materials in terms of propositions and schemata have been proposed by other researchers, but not many have provided the integrative approach to semantic processing for paragraph and discourse materials. More recently, Kintsch and van Dijk (1978) have described a psychological processing model to examine the mental operations that underlie the processes occurring in text comprehension and the production and recall of text summarization protocols. The model deals with semantic structures at both the microstructure and macrostructure levels or how sets of propositions are structured relative to one another. The microstructure covers the structure of the underlying propositions and their relations. The macrostructure characterizes discourse as a whole. These levels are related by a set of semantic mapping rules. The Kintsch and van Dijk paper elaborates on how discourse comprehenders actually construct text bases or coherent structure units, which are developed and formalized in Kintsch (1974).

The work of Kintsch relates to Fillmore's (1968, 1971a, 1971b) case grammar and accords with Craik and Lockhart's (1972) levels of processing. Kintsch (1974, p. 256) summarizes his views on prose comprehensibility and recallability thus: "memory for text becomes a two-level affair: a surface level, which might be viewed as the leftover from the initial processing of the text, which involves semantic, that is propositional, information as well as linguistic information and various stimulus attributes of the original message, and a second, deeper level, which is mainly propositional and can be considered as the meaning of the text, is reconstructed during the comprehension process." Thus the general idea is that text will provide a schema and the listener/reader will bring his/her own schemata to bear on text materials and hence generate the macrostructure needed for comprehension. There is considerable information on the use of schemata as discussed in preceding sections. In addition to this evidence, Kintsch, Mandel, and Kozminsky (1977) showed that a goodness of match in the readers' schemata and in the temporal order of events in a story facilitated its reconstruction.

In a recent study of the recall of well-structured picture narratives in four- and six-year-old children, Poulsen, Kintsch, Kintsch, and Premack (1979) have both probed the development of a story schema in young children and have provided an analysis of their recall protocols based on the procedure of Kintsch (1974). For scoring, each proposition was classified in five ways: (1) response classes of core propositions (essence of the story as determined by adult consensus), extra propositions and spurious or wrong propositions, (2) nature of the propositions—whether they are picture propositions (responses to some features of the stimulus picture, which formed the majority of responses), story or narrative propositions, (3) descriptive propositions or cognitive and affective statements, (4) the assignment of each picture as exposition, complication or resolution and (5) the form of responses in terms of one-word, two and three or more word responses. Kintsch et al. gave an example in analyzing the response statement of "The boy is sad" in the Whiskers story about a dog who runs away from a boy, then is chased by a fox, and finally is reunited with the boy. The authors stated that the response would be scored as core proposition (by adult consensus), as picture proposition (because of the dependency on the saliency of the picture showing a sad boy), as affective proposition, as resolution category and as a two-concept phrase (relating boy and sad).

With this kind of refined and objective analyses, Poulsen et al. provided converging evidence that children as young as four-year-olds can acquire and use adultlike schema to comprehend stories. The four- and six-year-olds showed *qualitative* and not so much quantitative differences in their responses: the younger children labeled or failed to respond; the older ones tended to make a logical sequence out of their pictures. The researchers concluded that "the availability of a story schema affects the way children describe and recall picture stories. The effect is not revealed in the quantity of responses, but in the quality. The schema guides the subjects' responses. In the absence of such guidance, responses tend to be less appropriate and frequently spurious" (Poulsen et al., 1979). Thus, from their detailed analyses of recall protocols, Poulsen et al. have further shown that those parts of discourse that were well integrated into a story were best recalled. Moreover, they showed that there is a noticeable developmental change in qualitative forms of comprehension between the ages of four and six. They also further clarified the schemata inherent in stories and those inherent in the individual for better interpretation of discourse materials. The researchers have pointed to the educational implications of schema studies: the provision of appropriate schemata for comprehension, the training of schemata, the inappropriateness of many children's materials and television programs consisting of unorganized sequences and other kinds of schemata that need to be studied.

Meyer's and Clements' Analyses

While the paragraph grammar of Kintsch (1974) helps to elucidate children's comprehension of stories, Meyer (1975a, 1975b, 1977a, 1977b) has provided a conceptual framework and a system for analyzing the organization of information in textual materials. Her classification is based on Fillmore's (1968, 1971a, 1971b) case relations and Grimes' (1975) rhetorical relations and analyzes the hierarchical relationships between the elements in a text in terms of their ideational prominence. Meyer constructed a number of short texts and experimentally varied the relative position of elements within the overall content structure of the text to show the interrelations of ideas and the subordination of some ideas to others and how the content structure of a text affects learning. The aim of her investigation is to determine why some ideas from prose are easier to learn and to show the overall importance of prose structure in predicting recall of prose materials.

The Meyer procedure shows a hierarchically arranged tree structure with nodes containing content words from the passage and lines showing how the content is organized. The "labels" which classify relations can be grouped as "role relations" and "rhetorical relations." Role relations relate to content words in the structure and rhetorical relations show the overall prose organization. Propositions are composed of a predicate and its arguments and there are predicate rules and argument rules governing prose structure. Thus predicates or rhetorical relations are found at the top levels of the content structure and connect ideas together. The simple sentence example given by Meyer (1975b) ROGER RODE THE HORSE is a lexical proposition. The predicate is RODE which is related to its arguments which are content words. ROGER is related to RODE as an agent and HORSE is the object acted on. Meyer (1975b, p. 15) explained that "a rhetorical proposition has as its predicate a rhetorical predicate and as its arguments other lexical propositions or other rhetorical propositions. In other words, a rhetorical proposition is usually used to relate together larger segments of text than the segments of a simple sentence, and its arguments are often other propositions represented as sentences or paragraphs in the text. . . . Thus an entire passage can be thought of as the very complex proposition which is composed of subordinate propositions which are also composed of subordinate propositions. This chaining of propositions continues to the depth necessary for a particular passage."

From this basic rationale of case grammar and

semantic grammar of propositions, Meyer (1975a, 1975b) has provided a systematic analysis of the organization of information in prose. One procedure is the bottom-up parsing from simple sentences to higher levels of structure to show interrelationships of these sentences. The other procedure is top-down parsing from propositions down to simpler levels. Using this detailed scheme, Meyer (1975a, 1975b, 1977a, 1977b) conducted experiments with university students to test their written immediate recall and delayed recall of specially constructed passages. Her findings emphasized the importance of the content structure of prose passages. She found that information high on the content structure was recalled better and information low on the content structure was subject to loss of accessibility to force recall. Thus the Meyer analysis has provided both researchers and practitioners with another systematic and detailed device for classifying types of prose passages and for gauging content structures. Meyer, Brandt, and Bluth (1980) found in their study of ninth-grade students' use of a reading strategy (the structure strategy) that there is a strong relationship between top-level structure in text and comprehension skill.

In connection with Meyer's hierarchical structure of text bases, Clements' (1979) study of the effect of *staging* on recall of prose materials should be noted. Staging is defined as that component of prose, which identifies the relative prominence of various parts of prose materials. This is also the notion of theme and rheme or topic and comment in Halliday (1964, 1967) and in Grimes (1975). The topic/comment indicates the perspective of the speaker/writer as shown in this panel of sentences:

(21–1) Food was the problem for the stranded travelers.

(21–2) The stranded travelers' problem was food.

Clements has provided some basic rules for staging (topic rule, old/new rule and coordination rule) and the theoretical background for identifying topics, old/new distinctions and coordination. He conducted experiments with pairs of prose passages with identical content and different staging to test the effect on recall and the mechanism affecting recall in university students. Results showed that staging has an influence on information acquisition and retrieval. Clements suggested the need to study staging analysis during a reader's processing of prose passages.

Frederiksen's Network of Text Processing

In his research programs, Carl Frederiksen (1975a, 1975b, 1977, 1979) has proposed a system of analyzing data structure in terms of labeled network for both memory and text processing. The network consists of a set of concepts and the semantic relations of the concepts. The semantic structure of text is classified into the semantic network and the logical network with the former relating to concepts and the latter to all the propositions consisting of related propositions. Frederiksen (1975a, p. 148) analyzed text as a set of "conceptual classes connected by set relations" and studied the effect of context-induced processing operations on semantic information. The contextual effects on the subjects' recall of text generally supports the constructive model as first proposed by Bartlett (1932).

Frederiksen (1975b) presented a representation of propositions underpinning comprehension and production of discourse materials. In a recent exposition of his theory and empirical work, Frederiksen (1979) has focused his attention on discourse inference. In analyzing children's discourse comprehension, he raises the important question of the form of abstract, internal structure or representation at the different levels of processing. In agreement with Rumelhart (1975), Frederiksen emphasizes the interactive process in comprehension—incorporating both bottom-up and top-down processing. The constructive view of reading is top-down as readers make inferences to "instantiate" a schema. Frederiksen suggests that one source of individual differences in comprehension is the readers' ability to adopt more "text-based" or "schema-based" controls on their discourse inferences. This approach can be applied to both proficient and poor reading. Frederiksen's analysis specifies the propositional content that is explicit in a discourse. This relates to: (1) the high-level organization of the content of a message, (2) the integration of new and old information and (3) the proper perspective or staging. Within this framework, prose materials can be analyzed into a list of propositions consisting of a network of concepts and it is possible to compare the list of propositions shown in the recall protocols of readers.

In the words of Frederiksen (1979, p. 170), "A propositional structure consists of a set of concepts connected into networks by labeled binary semantic relations. A relation is defined in terms of a triple consisting of a pair of concept slots and a connecting relation. For example, the relation ( ) − CAT → ( ) connects two object categories so that the object category in the right slot is a subset of the object category in the left slot, for example, (:BIRDS) − CAT → (:CANARIES). The two smallest units of semantic information are thus: lexical concepts and relational triples consisting of pairs of concepts connected by semantic relations. All higher-order units of semantic information are composed of relational triples." This *semantic network* approach is also discussed by Collins and Quillian (1972) and E. Smith (1978). Very briefly, words are represented as nodes in a treelike network interconnecting different categories (e.g., salmon, fish, and living things). Branching off from the nodes or categories are attribute relations such as "living, animate" and so on. The network approach emphasizes comparison and the attribute approach emphasizes search processes. Both are complementary in comprehension. From the level of lexical operations, Frederiksen has devised a fine-grained analysis of major *classes of text-based inference.* These classes range from lexical operations through frame operations, event generation, and macrostructure operations to dependency operations and truth-value operations. Subsumed under each category of operations are units of operations and *inference types* (e.g. lexical expansion, attribute, time, instrument, goal, source, theme, causal and logical inferences).

With the refined classification of text-based inferences, it is possible to examine the relationships in the recall protocols of subjects and in the message base of the story presented to these subjects. The Frederiksen theory and analysis have shown that discourse characteristics are important for text-based inferences. There are also implications for early reading instruction, for school texts and for the assessment of reading comprehension. A recent complex study by Marshall and Glock (1978–1979) of how aspects of text structure affected comprehension in college students provides support for the Frederiksen model of memory structure and text-based structure. Tierney, Bridge and Cera (1978–1979) have extended Frederiksen's taxonomy of text-based inferences to the comparison of good and poor readers' discourse processing. Their results show that both good and poor readers abstracted and selected textual materials so as to integrate with their own mental structure. The poor readers, however, differed from the good readers in the ability to "render more complete propositions, the propositional structure, and interpropositional structure" (p. 566). The poor readers also were less efficient in operating the latter structure. The Tierney et al. study thus contributes to our understanding of the interactive process of reading and of individual differences in reading comprehension.

The Mandler-Johnson and Stein-Glenn Story Schema

In addition to what might be called the paragraph grammars of Kintsch (1974), Meyer (1975a, 1975b, 1977a, 1977b) and Frederiksen (1977) as discussed above, story grammars have been devised by Mandler and Johnson (1977) and Stein and Glenn (1979). These researchers have generally broadened Rumelhart's (1975, 1977a, 1977b) interactive model of reading to provide both the theory and empirical base of a *story schema.* This is an idealized internal representation of the parts of a typical "simple" story and the relationships among those parts. The notion of a simple story is that consisting of a single protagonist in each episode. Thus the simple story usually has at least four propositions: setting, beginning or initiating event, development (plan or attempt) and ending or reaction. These propositions are interrelated in some kind of hierarchical network and can be logically analyzed in terms of rewrite rules. Despite some refinements in their approaches and notational systems, the Mandler and Johnson and the Stein and Glenn analyses and rewrite rules are quite similar. Hence their "grammars" will be discussed together.

On the assumption that a story has an internal structure and can be described in terms of logical relationships, Mandler and Johnson (1977) argued that the underlying story representation can be analyzed as a tree structure. This "makes explicit the constituent structure and the relations between constituents. Events in the story are related both by their place in the tree structure, i.e., the type of node which they represent, and by between-node connections which may be either causal or temporal. The surface structure of a story consists of sentences. However, it may take several sentences, or only part of a sentence, to form a proposition which corresponds to a terminal node in the underlying tree" (p. 115). In this tree structure the nodes are connected by these types of relationship: AND, THEN and CAUSE. The AND relation connects two notions when the concept of parallel or simultaneous activity is being expressed. The THEN node connects temporally ordered events. The CAUSE node shows relation when the first node provides a reason for the occurrence of the second. In remembering "things parsed" readers need to fill the structural requirements of a given node in the structured diagram and the resulting parsing system should provide predictions for the units of prose best remembered. The predictions generated include the overall extent and accuracy of recall, the likelihood and accuracy for different parts of the story to be recalled, the temporal events in a sequence chain and the reconstruction of the story. Thus the more a story conforms to an ideal structure the better it will be recalled, as "this prediction is simply a generalization from the underlying notion of the grammar that a story primarily consists of causally connected parts" (Mandler and Johnson, 1977, p. 134).

The above predictions were tested on Bartlett's "The War of the Ghosts" which is often considered "irregular" or even "bizarre." In an elegant analysis of the story into propositions and underlying structure of basic nodes Mandler and Johnson provided some detailed insight into the possible reason why Bartlett's original analyses showed omissions, distortions and inversions of sequences. In parsing the "Ghost," they found THEN-connected linkage in five of the total of six episodes and a number of major structural violations (e.g. change of protagonist in the middle of an episode, disconnection of thought sequence). It is likely that the preponderant temporal connections using THEN nodes and the looseness of the overall representation of the structure both account for the recall of stories as an active, reconstructive process involving inaccuracies rather than passive reproduction of stored memories.

Mandler and Johnson further used their story schema to test the recall of stories of first- and fourth-grade children and university students. The subjects listened to tape recordings of four stories and were tested for both immediate verbatim recall (after ten minutes) and delayed verbatim recall (after twenty-four hours). The transcribed protocols were scored for presence or absence of specified propositions, inversions of sequence of propositions within and between basic nodes and inversion of clauses within propositions. The basic or major nodes in the schema were: settings, beginnings, reactions, attempts (including action), outcomes and endings. Results showed that in general adults recalled more than the fourth-graders, who in turn recalled more than the first-graders. Further, first graders' recall formed two clusters: settings, beginnings and outcomes were well recalled while attempts, endings, and reactions were poorly recalled. These children tended to omit the internal reactions of the characters or their attempted actions as well as the final ending. The fourth-graders showed a similar pattern of recall, although the difference between attempts and outcomes was no longer significant. The adults recalled attempts as well as settings, beginnings and outcomes, although reactions and endings were still difficult. Mandler and Johnson noted that "the similar ordering among nodes in the three age groups suggests that even the younger subjects are sensitive to the structure of stories and have schemata which organize retrieval in a fashion similar to adults" (p. 145). The main difference between the recalled stories by young children compared with adults is in the greater weight placed on outcomes than on attempts. In agreement with other researchers, Mandler and Johnson emphasized that the lack of recall on the part of children does not reflect a lack of comprehension primarily. Young children tend to stress outcomes rather than the internal events motivating them. It was found that sequence inversions between nodes were rare and mostly occurred at the THEN connection, while more inversions occurred between propositions within basic nodes and again mostly between AND- and THEN-connected propositions.

In their "exploration" into story grammar with its rewrite rules defining various units and their relationships, Mandler and Johnson (1977) have delineated the schemata used in recalling stories at different developmental stages and have shown the qualitative difference in recall between children and adults. There is thus further support for the notion that children's ability to recall stories in correct temporal sequence is dependent on the degree of structure and cohesion of text.

In common with Mandler and Johnson, Stein and Glenn (1979) have elaborated on the Rumelhart (1975, 1977a, 1977b) interactive approach to prose comprehension to focus on a wider range of stories with single or embedded episodes. In agreement with these and other researchers, Stein and Glenn have used the proposition as their unit of analysis or a measure of information on internal representation. Information can be organized in nodes or categories and the categories can be described in terms of a hierarchical network. From this basic assumption, Stein and

Glenn suggest that "a story consists of a setting category plus an episode system" (p. 59) and that these two categories are connected by an ALLOW relation thus:

Story → ALLOW (setting, Episode System).

Compare this rewrite rule with Mandler and Johnson's:

Story → setting and event structure.

An episode is defined by Stein and Glenn as a behavioral sequence with some reference to: "(1) the purpose of the behavioral sequence, (2) overt goal-directed behavior, and (3) the attainment or nonattainment of the character's goal" (p. 72). This means that an episode should contain an initiating event, an action and a direct consequence. One or more episodes will make up the episodic system, which is a "higher order category and incorporates the entire story structure with the exception of the initial setting" (p. 62). The setting is defined by Stein and Glenn as "state" and activities of state (cf. EVENT in Mandler and Johnson). Each state or activity is joined by AND, THEN, CAUSE in these following rules:

$$\text{Setting} \rightarrow \begin{bmatrix} \text{State(s)} \\ \text{Activity(ies)} \end{bmatrix}$$

$$\text{Episode System} \rightarrow \begin{matrix} \text{AND} \\ \text{THEN} \\ \text{CAUSE} \end{matrix} \ (\text{Episode(s)})$$

There are other rules for rewriting episodes, initiating events, responses, internal responses, plan sequences, initial plans, plan applications, attempts, resolutions, direct consequences and reactions. Stein and Glenn emphasized the importance of relations between simultaneous episodes and also "intraepisodic structure" and the variations of the basic sequence.

Within the framework of their story grammar, Stein and Glenn have presented detailed analyses of the recall of four stories by first- and fifth-grade children. The protocols were scored for: (1) major setting statements, (2) minor setting statments, (3) initiating events, (4) internal responses, (5) attempts, (6) direct consequences and (7) reactions. The results generally support the importance of information nodes or categories and the interconnections between categories during the related but not identical processes of story encoding and retrieval. The Stein and Glenn model has further generated sets of predictions pertaining to: temporal sequencing of story information, inferencing and construction of stories. The first set of predictions concerns subskills needed to integrate statements within an episode and the ordering of the episodes in the correct temporal sequence. The second set of predictions deals with constructive thinking arising from knowledge of story schema. The third set of predictions relates to the critical difference between comprehension and spontaneous generation of stories, with logical sequence being inherent in the former but only apparently so in the latter. There is also a developmental difference in the quality of spontaneous generation of stories. In a recent study, Glenn (1980) defined two types of interaction between informational content and passage structure in prose processing. She showed that children in first and third grades could more accurately recall the structure of logically structured episodes than that of temporally listed episodes. Passage structure thus provides the parameter of information that children need to facilitate oral comprehension and reading.

To conclude this section of representation of meaning in prose, we must stress the important role of schema theory in comprehension. Various researchers have explored schema theory to characterize the structure of paragraphs and stories. The refined, systematic analyses of protocols of recall of stories in terms of propositions have provided greater insight into what exactly it is that is recalled and why it is recalled. The exploratory rewrite rules for paragraphs and stories would permit a more precise delineation of the information contained in prose and would explain how this information is encoded, stored and retrieved. We thus come to a better understanding of the interactive process of comprehension during reading.

Summary—The Well-Ordered Mind

We have discussed in this and the preceding chapters how meaning may be accessed for words and for discourse. In word perception, we have reviewed research to show that readers in essence search the internal mental dictionary, the lexicon, to access meaning. This is found to be an efficient and economical way. As an aside, there are limitations with the literal lexicon in certain languages. Take, for example, the Chinese orthography which is so formed that a search through the dictionary necessitates knowing the root or the radical and *computing* the number of strokes for both the root and the phonetic before the dictionary user can locate relevant information. While this analogy does not invalidate our argument for the internal lexicon in word perception, the concept of retrieval of meaning from long-term memory and computing for unfamiliar words is in fact the general principle extended to the comprehension of sentences.

We have sketched the role of grammar and have shown that comprehending a sentence or discourse also requires some kind of world knowledge. The concept of a search of the internal lexicon needs to be extended to an internal encyclopedia. As with word perception, the search for prose meaning need not be hierarchical; it can be heterarchical. Again, in common with word perception, where dual coding processes (visual and phonological) are employed, so an interactive, parallel processing of prose materials more likely represents what people do when they comprehend these materials. Texts need to be well organized in terms of schemata for ease of comprehension, summarization and recall. To carry our analogy further, the internal encyclopedia will need to be expanded into the internal library where information is received, catalogued and stored for ease of retrieval. While there are different systems of classification, the most efficient ones provide for crossreferencing by author, by subject and ideally by all relevant descriptors. This analogy of the internal library with a well-connected network of systems may reflect what goes on in people's minds when they access meaning in prose and store what is learned. Broadbent (1966) has written of the well-ordered mind. It is a mind, not literally full of books and their contents as in an actual library, but one with a well-organized index system so that relevant information can be accessed efficiently. The reader can thus find information under a heading, in superordinate or subordinate terms, and also laterally. Thus reading is more appropriately *learning* by reading, and teaching reading is more *teaching learning* by reading. LaBerge and Samuels (1974, p. 320) have reminded us that "the complexity of the comprehension operation appears to be as enormous as that of thinking in general." This is not surprising. Comprehension, memory and knowledge are inextricably mixed. Bartlett (1932, p. 213) reminded us of the interrelation: "[Remembering] is an imaginative reconstruction, or construction, built out of the relation of our attitude towards a whole active mass of organized past reactions or experience." This integration of the new and the old knowledge also brings out the old paradox in Plato's theory of knowledge as presented in *Meno.* The paradox is that we cannot come to know new information unless we have some prior knowledge and yet we cannot acquire this knowledge unless we have learned it. Thus, in the analogy of Broadbent, we may well ask whether the purpose of schooling is, not just to fill the library with the contents of books, but more to write an index system. With such a system, information can be processed and placed in an organized structure of knowledge.

This brings us back to Binet's concept of intelligence, which is referred to at the beginning of the chapter. All problems of human intelligence modeling, including natural language analysis, eventually revolve around the representation and access of general world knowledge. Prose comprehension should be viewed within the broad spectrum of human symbol processing, involving memory patterns, selection processes, and problem solving. From the evidence reviewed, there is a substantial convergence from psycholinguistics, artificial intelligence, and cognitive psychology on the essential components of systems for representing knowledge (see Spiro, Bruce, and Brewer, 1980).

CHAPTER 11

Affective Bases

In this chapter our focus is on learners' attitudes, emotions, and motives. McDonald provides the psychologist's approach to this problem when he writes that, "under the influence of an internal process, called *motivation,* the individual's behavior persists until a goal has been reached. . . . On attainment of the goal the behavior leading to the attainment of the goal subsides" (pp. 115–116). The motivation questions that interest reading teachers are (1) what conditions produce motivation to learn how to read and (2) what conditions produce motivation to engage in reading activities?

There are many alternative motivational concepts: "reinforcement," "drive," "need," "incentive," "motive," "purpose," "interest," "attitude," and so on. Andreas (1972) notes that in psychology there exists a wide range of concepts of motivation. They overlap rather unsystematically. Andreas brings order into this situation by reviewing psychological experiments around three main concepts: *arousal, incentive,* and *reinforcement.*

Arousal

The *reticular activating system* in the brain has the function of arousing or activating all areas of the cortex. When the reticular formation is inactive, cortical activity falls off, resulting in a state of torpor. On the other hand, if impulses from the reticular formation become excessive, a state of overexcitement is produced. The reticular formation receives inputs from both sensory nerves and the cortex.

Wittrock et al. (1977) give the following definition of *arousal:*

> A physiological state characterized by behavioral alertness, sympathetic predominance in the autonomic nervous system, and most often desynchronized electroencephalographic (EEG) activity (p. 187).

The desynchronization of ongoing brain rhythms referred to is usually associated with cortical activation. The sympathetic division of the autonomic nervous system (ANS) is associated with mobilization of the body when a person experiences stress.

According to Hebb (1955), the optimal level of arousal for the most efficient functioning is one that is neither too high nor too low but intermediate. Hebb suggested that the individual is programmed to seek this intermediate level of arousal between excessive and insufficient stimulation. For example, Berlyne (1957) showed in an experiment that humans prefer to look at pictures that are incongruous, complex, or surprising rather than normal ones not possessing these features. Vitz (1966), in an experiment with variation in frequency, loudness, and duration of pure tones in sequences, found that people rate moderate variation as most pleasant and too little or too great variation as least pleasant to their hearing. Nuttin (1976) sums up the general conclusion on this matter: "it is generally accepted that intermediate degrees of motivation create optimal conditions for learning . . ." (p. 258).

Attention

Nuttin's next point is that "the effect of motivation of major importance . . . is the 'orienting' or attentional effect . . ." (p. 258). Nuttin reminds us that this "was mentioned as an essential condition from the very beginning in Pavlov's (1927) work on conditioning. An animal has to be *alert* and *attentive* to certain stimuli and cues." Reviewing modern research, Nuttin concludes that "The facilitative effect of selective attention on learning is generally admitted" (p. 264). Burt (1968) comments on this trend in research: "A characteristic of recent psychological work is the rediscovery of attention. . . . In order to reduce incoming information to an amount that can be effectively handled it would seem . . . that something very like a 'filtering device' must be inserted in the sensory approaches to the brain" (p. 546).

Samuels and Turnure (1974), have related reading achievement to pupils' attentiveness. They had observers record grade one pupils' attentional behaviors during reading lessons and related their attention scores to their word recognition of a random selection of 45 words from the Dolch (1956) list of basic sight words. They found that "increasing degrees of attention were related to superior word recognition." Samuels and Turnure claim that attention must be the causal factor because this relationship was found in grade one before any failure pattern could have had an influence on attention. They conclude that "Instructional success clearly requires that teachers secure and maintain the attention of all their pupils" (p. 31).

While this seems true, one must recognize that there are individual differences in attentional behavior. Nuttin notes that "personality factors" influence the level of optimal motivation in learning (p. 258). Estes (1970) also suggests that individual differences in the ability to focus attention have an important effect on learning. Malmquist (1958) found that children who failed in reading in grade one were weak in ability to concentrate and persevere. Dykman, Ackerman, Clements, and Peters (1971), theorize that an "attentional deficit syndrome" is an important cause of reading disability. Evidence exists that reading disabled children even in a nonreading situation can sustain attention less well than normal readers (Anderson, Halcomb and Doyle, 1973; Noland and Schuldt, 1971). Also Strauss and Lehtinen (1947) emphasized that a major learning problem for brain-injured children is their inability to ignore distracting stimuli. Harris and Sipay, reviewing this evidence, conclude that failure in learning to read "may be due to inattention rather than to lack of the basic abilities required by the task" (p. 257).

Thus we conclude that selective attention to the tasks involved in the acquisition of reading skill is an important variable in learning to read. As we have seen from the research reviewed thus far, attention is one aspect of arousal that is subject to individual differences in children's personal make-up. But attention and arousal are influenced also by other variables. For example, as Samuels and Turnure point out, "lack of school success may lead to inattentiveness . . ." (p. 29).

Stress

The cause of this inattentiveness following lack of school success lies in the activation of the sympathetic nervous system under the experience of stress. In general, its function is to mobilize the body to cope with stressful circumstances. Nerve fibers from this system innervate the blood vessels, sweat glands and hair follicles of the skin. Other fibers innervate organs and blood vessels in the heart, lungs, gastrointestinal and urogenital systems, as well as the head. The sympathetic system is widespread in its influence because of its extensive interconnections and because the adrenal medulla releases a transmitter agent—epinephrine—into the blood stream which distributes it to all the other organs. These physiological changes focus one's physical resources on coping with an emergency. One is thereby prepared for "flight or fight." One experiences this emotional arousal by feeling such sensations as the pounding of the heart, dryness of the mouth, "butterflies" in the stomach, perspiration, breathlessness, tremors, and so on.

In the discussion that follows we shall employ Spielberger's (1972) terminology and use *stress* "to refer to the objective stimulus properties of a situation" and *threat* to refer to "an individual's idiosyncratic perception of a particular situation as physically or psychologically dangerous." Spielberger points out that "whether or not a stressful situation is perceived as threatening will depend on his own subjective appraisal of the situation. Moreover, objectively nonstressful situations may be appraised as threatening by individuals who, for some reason, perceive them as dangerous. . . . The appraisal of a situation as dangerous or threatening will be determined, in part, by an individual's personality dispositions and past experience with similar situations" (p. 30). Spielberger uses the term *anxiety* "to refer to the complex emotional reactions that are evoked in individuals who interpret specific situations as personally threatening. If a person perceives a situation as threatening, irrespective of the presence of real (objective) danger, it is assumed that . . . he will experience an increase in the intensity of an emotional state characterized by feelings of tension and apprehension, and by heightened autonomic nervous system activity" (pp. 30–31).

From these general psychological facts we may propose the hypothesis that anxiety interferes with attentiveness because failure in reading constitutes a form of stress that causes the poor reader to perceive reading tasks as threats. This hypothesis is supported by the experiment of Santrock and Ross (1975). They found that an experimental group of four- and five-year old children who were treated with negative social comparisons exhibited significantly poorer attention than children in a control group who were not treated in this way. Berretta (1970) also has noted that inability to concentrate is one of the symptoms of "children with negative self images" (p. 232). Thus, when the child has experienced stressful failure in reading tasks and perceives new reading tasks as threats of further failure, anxiety is evoked. Then inability to concentrate or lack of attention is one symptom of this emotional state.

Bruner (1963) suggests that this phenomenon is caused by "excessive drive" which leads to a condition in which "action, affect, and thought are fused in a preemptive metaphor. . . ." This "preemptive metaphor" is a "cognitive organization" that "centers upon an affective concept like 'things that can hurt me', within which any potentially disruptive or hurtful thing can then be included" (p. 136). Bruner writes that "Once an object or event is identified as related to the defensive preemptive metaphor . . . it is then avoided, pushed out of mind, 'overignored'" (p. 139). Bruner finds, therefore, that "It is not surprising, then, that teachers often report that these children are inattentive . . ." (p. 142). Although Bruner is writing about cases of more general emotional disturbance, nevertheless, the same phenomenon of "overignoring" reading instruction is often reported in the literature on reading difficulties.

Abrams and Smolen (1973) distinguish between *attention* and *concentration:*

> Attention may be defined as a relatively effortless, passive, involuntary, free receptivity to environmental stimuli. On the other hand, concentration involves an active focussing of attention—that is, a deliberate, effortful, voluntary and selective channeling of one's attentive energies (p. 463).

This distinction fits well with what is known about involuntary and voluntary behavior generally in the affective domain. Thus Milner states: "This pattern is typical: The automatic regulatory mechanism operates within its range, but once the unbalance or disturbance becomes too great for correction at that level a higher level is brought into play" (p. 300).

Abrams and Smolen relate reading failure to Selye's (1936) classic theory of the "General Adaptation Syndrome." Selye postulated three progressive stages in adaptation to stress: (1) the alarm reaction when the organism musters its resources for action; (2) resistance or adaptation; and (3) exhaustion or breakdown in the physical ability to cope with the stress. With regard to attentiveness, Abrams and Smolen state that in stage 2 the energies of the individual threatened by stress "are bound up in his defenses and therefore not available for free, passive, attending. Nevertheless, he is able to concentrate. . . . If the stress situation continues beyond a certain point, the individual is inevitably forced to exhaust his reservoir. . . . It is at this point that concentration, too, becomes impaired" (p. 463). Abrams and Smolen believe that "the child who experiences initial reading failure . . . is ultimately subjected to emotional stress. If the reading failure persists, it is almost inevitable that frustration, reduced attention, anxiety and a real sense of helplessness will be invoked" (p. 466). An extreme form of this loss of attention may be what Lourie and Schwarzbeck (1979) describe as the tendency to "disorganize in stressful situations." In this condition, children's "response to stress is for the mind to go blank. They *disorganize;* their self-experience can then be one of helplessness" (p. 136).

Physiological changes that occurred during three reading tasks were measured by Reichurdt (1977). He compared reading handicapped students with normal achievers. Although Reichurdt does not mention it, his results provide evidence that supports the "General Adaptation Syndrome" hypothesis as applied to reading disability by Abrams and Smolen. Reichurdt found "that the handicapped readers fell into two distinct and opposite groups, related to the intensity of their handicap." He called these groups the "playing dead" and the "taking flight." The "taking flight" group exhibited physiological symptoms of hypertension during reading. These students were less seriously handicapped in reading than the "playing dead" group whose physiological measures indicated hypotension. The "most disabled readers . . . exhibited a sharp drop in arousal level as they moved . . . into the reading tasks" (p. 707).

Thus the resistance level and the exhaustion level of adaptation to stress are associated with high arousal and low arousal respectively. In either case, learning is blocked by the anxiety emotion. Sherman (1968) wrote that "continued stress . . . increases the emotional turmoil . . . , and in turn, the emotional turmoil creates a greater degree of blocking and, therefore, prevents any real improvement in reading ability" (p. 349). The effects of threatened stress on children who are failing to read is well summarized by Schonell and Goodacre (1974). They also emphasize "the emotional blocking of the pupils' learning powers" while they are in "a state of emotional turmoil" (p. 182–183). This vicious cycle of failure → anxiety → more failure we shall term the "failure-threat anxiety syndrome" in reading disability.

The Failure-Threat Anxiety Syndrome

As has been described above, the basis of this syndrome lies in experiences of failure that are perceived by the pupil as stressful. Then new reading tasks are viewed as threatening. These threats evoke anxiety and the resulting emotion produces a variety of symptoms. In Selye's terms, some of these symptoms are *adaptive*—that is, they have the function of coping with the reading threat—while other symptoms appear when the pupil's energies are exhausted through prolonged exposure to failure. Descriptions of the symptoms of what we have called failure-threat anxiety are varied, but we shall try to categorize them into its most commonly described features.

1. *Overt Fear Reactions.* Strang, McCullough, and Traxler (1967) in a section on "Characteristics of Emotionally Blocked Readers" state that "Anxiety seems to be the dominant characteristic" (p. 449). Vernon (1971) writes: "Numerous studies have demonstrated the frequency of *anxiety* and *depression* in certain backward readers" (p. 117). She cites Silverman, Fite and Mosher (1959) as having found symptoms of anxiety and depression in about 67 per cent of their emotionally maladjusted cases of reading disability. Specific fear reactions mentioned by Strang et al. include "fears of making mistakes, of failing, of having people know how poorly they read, of growing up . . . " (p. 451).

2. *Non-specific Emotional Behavior.* Not only is there a wide range of emotional symptoms in failure-threat anxiety, but also there is no single pattern of response. Two cases may exhibit quite opposite emotional responses to dreaded reading tasks. Thus Strang et al. mention that some severe reading cases may be "shy and withdrawn" but others "show aggressive behavior" (p. 449). Gates' (1936) list of the most common emotional symptoms in 100 cases of reading disability included inclination to submissiveness, indifference, inattentiveness, seeming laziness, withdrawal, daydreaming and also evasive reactions. But he also listed joining gangs and playing truant. Barclay (1966), too, mentions disruptive behavior as being associated with reading failure. Laurita (1971) includes "distractibility, inattention, hyperactivity, avoidance, perseveration" as resulting from the anxiety produced by the frustration of failing in reading (p. 45). The Bullock Report in its comment on the "close association between retardation in reading and emotional disorders" mentions both "lack of concentration" and "antisocial behaviour" (Department of Education and Science, 1975, p. 269). Niles (1970) writes that the student constantly failing in reading "may just go limp . . . or he may . . . exhibit an aggressively negative reaction to a situation which he finds intolerable" (p. 43).

In summary, while emotion is always present, the manner in which it is expressed varies from case to case. But usually one or the other of two emotional reactions is prominent in external expression—escape behavior or attack behavior.

3. *Escape Behavior.* This is the more frequently observed of the two most common emotional reactions in failure-threat anxiety. Escape behavior takes several forms—withdrawal, psychosomatic disorders, rigidity, and various overt avoidance strategies.

Gates' (1936) list of symptoms included *withdrawal,* and Strang et al. state that "The majority of the severe reading cases that have been reported seem to be shy and withdrawn" (p.449). This is not surprising in view of the psychiatric definition of *withdrawal.* For example, Goodstein and Lanyon (1975) state that "whenever a person is confronted by an insoluble avoidance-avoidance conflict, one solution is to leave the situation altogether. This behavior, of handling conflict situations by leaving them altogether to avoid anxiety, can be identified with the defense mechanism of withdrawal" (p. 220). They are referring, of course, to "leaving the situation" mentally. Goodstein and Lanyon note that "Withdrawal is often closely related to fantasy." Stott (1977) points out that some reading disabled children "react to failure by specific mental strategies of avoidance. These appear to the teacher as daydreaming, inattention, the mind's flying off at a tangent, and sometimes the child's making a quite irrelevant remark, showing that he was thinking of anything but the reading" (p. 17). Morris' (1966, p. 312) survey of reading in Kent, England showed a significantly greater incidence of " 'inhibited characteristics' (withdrawal; unforthcomingness; depression)" as measured in *Bristol Social Adjustment Guides.* (Stott, 1963; Stott and Syres, 1956).

Another way for the disabled reader to escape from failure-threat anxiety is by being sick in one or other of the *psychosomatic disorders.* For example, Hickerson (1970) describes two of the cases in her "House of Last Resort" for reading disability in such terms: "One student was sick to his stomach." Another "feigned *petit mal* seizures" (p. 264).

Rigidity is a symptom of failure-threat anxiety that is probably often overlooked because it is easily mistaken for stupidity, laziness, or mental retardation. Stott (1977) found that some children avoid reading by attempting "to retreat into dullness, as an escape from pressure" (p. 16). He cites Dreikurs as stating that "The conviction of his utter inability to learn may induce a child to 'play stupid'. In such cases the child may appear mentally retarded without being actually so." Stott and Dreikurs regard this behavior as a strategy that is at least unconsciously motivated to convince others that they cannot learn and therefore should not be taught. Eisenson (1968) also has noted what he considers to be a similar form of "perceptual defense" in "developmental aphasia." He suggests that some children may generalize their perceptual defenses against the speech signals which are meaningless to them to speech signals in general.

Pavlov (1928) noted that animals reacted with panic to discrimination learning problems that were beyond their powers. He called this behavior "experimental neurosis." Maier (1961) also found that when animals were subjected to persistent and unavoidable frustration they developed stereotyped responses that were extremely rigid and resistant to the normal effects of reward and punishment. Maier named this rigidity "abnormal fixation." In experiments on humans, Maier found similar rigidity exhibited in their severely retarded ability to learn in a situation that previously had been frustrating. Laurita (1971), on the basis of this work by Eisenson, Maier, and Pavlov cited above, suggests that this type of rigidity is an important cause of reversals such as reading *b* as *d* in reading disability. Laurita states that "certain kinds of persistent behavior evidenced by disabled readers, in this specific case, reversals, may be designated as being manifestations of frustration behavior" (p. 49). This rigidity of response is reminiscent also of the blanking out disorganization response described by Lourie and Schwarzbeck that we cited earlier in this chapter.

More *overt avoidance strategies* also occur in the failure-threat anxiety syndrome. Hickerson reported that, "Many left the school grounds and went home when they felt trapped by school procedures" (p. 264). Other overt avoidance techniques are included in Stott's "fourteen styles of nonlearning" (p. 18). In addition, most teachers of children suffering in this way are familiar with the numerous excuses that they produce for avoiding reading or coming to school.

4. Attack Behavior. An alternative to escape or avoidance is to attack the perceived source of the threat of stress. Strang et al. comment that, "The retarded reader is one whose self-esteem has been damaged by experiences with adults. He would naturally feel resentful and hostile" (p. 450). The Bullock Report notes that "Several studies confirm that many backward readers display restlessness, antisocial behaviour, and a rebellious attitude" (Department of Education and Science, 1975, p. 209). A more recent example is the study on the Isle of Wight in England, by Rutter and Yule (1977). They report that "A very considerable degree of overlap was found between reading retardation and antisocial behaviour. Of the children who were severely retarded in reading, a third exhibited antisocial behaviour. This rate is several times that in the general population even when sex differences are taken into account. . . . Similarly, of the group of antisocial children, over a third were at least twenty-eight months retarded in reading (after IQ was partialled out). Again, this rate is many times that in the general population, after controlling for sex differences" (p. 102). Rutter and Yule recognize the difficulty of unravelling cause and effect. Their analysis of their data led them to conclude that "both reading difficulties and antisocial behaviour may develop on the basis of similar types of temperamental deviance but also that delinquency may sometimes arise as a maladaptive response to educational failure. Thus, the child who fails to read and who thereby falls behind in his school work may rebel against all the values associated with school when he finds that he cannot succeed there" (pp. 111–112).

Stewart (1950) found that maladjusted children who were poor readers were more self-assertive and aggressive than another group of maladjusted children who were good readers. Spache (1957) reported that four per cent of a group of poor readers were aggressive while 10 per cent were subnormal in aggression. Douglas, Ross, and Simpson (1968) also found that some poor achievers were aggressively troublesome while others were nervously well-behaved. Morris' (1966) Kent survey, in addition to finding significantly more inhibited characteristics among poor readers than good readers also found a significantly greater incidence among poor readers of "characteristics of a 'demonstrative' or 'aggressive' nature (anxiety for adult attention and affection; hostility to adults; indifference to the adult figure; anxiety to gain acceptance and prestige among other children; hostility to other children; restlessness)" (p. 312). Thus, aggression is one of the alternative emotional reactions to failure-threat anxiety.

The term *hyperactivity* has been so loosely used in recent years that its descriptive value has been diluted, but it is mentioned here for the sake of completeness. Marwit and Stenner (1972) have related hyperactivity to aggression. They note that hyperactivity or hyperkinesis involves impulsivity, low frustration tolerance, short attention span, and excessive aggression as well as overactive behavior in general. They attempt to supply criteria to differentiate between hyperactivity that is neurologically based and hyperactivity that is an emotional response to learning experiences. Stott (1977) provides a useful hint for diagnosis in this respect: "If they are capable of getting interested in something of their own choosing and are able to persevere at it, the distractibility and hyperactivity can safely be diagnosed as a reaction to failure" (p. 17).

The impulsivity mentioned above clearly is not conducive to good reading comprehension of passages that require reflection. Roberts (1980) points out that "the speed with which someone typically makes a decision in a situation of uncertainty is likely to be an important factor in an activity as fraught with uncertainty as reading" (p. 3). She cites the finding from the study by Lunzer and Gardner (1979) that individual differences in reading comprehension are associated significantly with the extent to which a pupil *reflects* on the content of the reading.

Causes of Failure-threat Anxiety

By definition, one of the obvious causes of failure-threat anxiety is failure or, more correctly, perception of failure. But there are several other causal factors that need to be considered if we are to understand the significance of this aspect of arousal in the acquisition of reading skill.

1. *Perception of Failure.* Clay (1972) writes of the pupil who fails in reading:

> The emotional reactions that arise from knowing that he is doing a poor job, compound the problem from the first time he becomes aware of it, which is as early as six months after instruction begins (p. 161).

It is generally agreed that failure in reading creates negative emotional reactions. Vernon (1971) states that "Children who find learning difficult and hence fall behind their companions—still more those who fail to learn altogether—are not unnaturally frustrated, anxious and depressed by their failure" (p. 116). Schrock and Grossman (1961) concluded that "Children who continuously fail in reading acquire a negative outlook and defeatist attitude which prevents them from achieving in the reading area" (p. 119). The Bullock Commission recognized that children who "have lost confidence in themselves and in their capacity to learn because they have already failed in school" often "cannot apply their minds to learning" (Department of Education and Science, 1975, p. 268).

But why is failure-threat anxiety so very much more prominent in reading instruction than it is in other subjects of the school curriculum? For example, Sherman (1968) remarked that:

> Psychiatrists have observed that no other inadequacy creates as great a sense of frustration and failure as a reading difficulty (p. 348).

She proposed that there were two causes of this phenomenon: (1) "everyone is expected to read adequately in order to advance in his schooling," and (2) "reading is also considered a criterion, in the cultural sense, of an individual's mental ability." Schonell and Goodacre too note that ability to read enters into every aspect of school work, and that the pupil who fails is constantly being paraded as a failure.

Morris (1966) in her Kent survey obtained clear evidence that perception of reading failure creates failure-threat anxiety. She reported that 16 per cent of her poor readers *"hated reading"* by the fifth year of schooling. As many as 9 per cent *"had abandoned all interest in books by the end of the primary course* [age 11 in England] *and were already planning future occupations for which they believed reading skill to be unnecessary."* Among the remainder of these poor readers, their attitude toward reading was found to be "lukewarm" and likely to become as negative as those who already hated reading, if no happier reading experiences were met in their future schooling (p. 311). In contrast, Morris found that "good readers" were "confident" and enjoyed purposeful reading (p. 187).

Harris and Sipay also note that poor readers' feelings of inadequacy are caused by the social significance and pervasive importance of reading skill for success in almost all school activities. "Being a poor reader is far worse then being an inaccurate speller or a clumsy gymnast or an incompetent artist, because the poor reader so often concludes that he must be generally stupid," they write (p. 316). Thus, "Some children are so deeply discouraged that they have given up trying and have resigned themselves to chronic failure" (p. 317).

Schonell and Goodacre remark that "inability to read . . . produces in every older pupil a feeling of inadequacy and inferiority" (p. 182). Lynch and Haase (1976), too, comment that "negative self-concept changes will result when children show deficits in reading performance" (p. 198).

Research evidence confirms this view that failure in reading is accompanied by negative self concepts. McGinley and McGinley (1970) compared the sociometric choices of children in three reading groups—high, middle, and low in achievement. The high group statistically made significantly more than expected choices within their own reading group. The middle group made significantly more than expected choices from the high group and significantly fewer choices than expected from the low group. The low group made significantly fewer choices from within their own group. Thus these children's evaluation of themselves and one another was influenced by their perceptions of success and failure in reading. A study by Stevens (1971) found that remedial readers are aware of others' poor opinion of them. Lawrence's (1977) experiments showed how the self concept influences performance in reading tasks. It was hypothesized that children who are failing in reading have a concept of themselves not only as poor readers but also as "inferior" people so that their failure is inevitable. Lawrence provided poor readers with counseling directed at improving their "self-images." This gradually freed them from their emotional reactions and enabled them to concentrate on their reading instruction tasks. Lawrence's results show that reading attainments were improved by this personal counseling procedure, and concluded that, "In most cases of reading retardation it should be possible to increase the general level of motivation by planning a personal counselling programme" (p. 297).

At this point we should recall the dual effect of feedback. Cognitively, feedback is essential because skill learners need the information to improve their accuracy. But affectively, feedback may either encourage or discourage the reading apprentice. McMichael's (1977) study of four-and five-year-old school beginners in Scotland found that children who began with low estimations of their own achievements "were indeed less competent than their fellows. When they agreed that they were not able to do things as well as some other children they were admitting to a reality" (p. 124). Thus they objectively recognized their own ineffectiveness. Poor performance was recognized as poor performance. Thus, the groundwork for negative emotional reactions had been laid.

This recognition of poor performance in one's own attempts to read may lead to what Diener and Dweck (1978) have termed "learned helplessness." Recently, Butkowsky and Willows (1980) reported evidence that "poor readers displayed characteristics indicative of learned helplessness and low self-concepts of ability. These included significantly lower initial estimates of success, less persistence, attribution of failures to lack of ability and successes to factors beyond personal control, and greater decrements in expectancy of success following failure" (p. 408). These findings led them to urge that "remedial efforts . . . must also be directed at teaching these children to think more adaptively about their failures" (p. 421).

The psychology of the emotional response to perceived failure can be turned to more positive use. Also evidence of the positive influence of perceived success is further confirmation of the causal connection between achievements, affective responses and future achievements. The opposite of failure-threat anxiety is success-promise confidence. As Berretta puts it, "Successful experience is one of the surest ways of achieving positive self perceptions" (p. 234). Zolkos (1958) writes, "At no time should a child be made to feel incompetent in learning to read. Although the child may lack the ability to read as effectively as his classmates he should experience a sense of satisfactory accomplishment by tasting a degree of success at his own reading" (p. 256). Strang et al. assert, "The role of the reading teacher is to provide materials and instruction that will enable the student to see his own progress and gain recognition and approval from the persons who are significant in his life" (p. 457).

Research evidence has demonstrated that, if reading disabled students are insured success, dramatic changes occur in their self concepts and a benign cycle of success and confidence can replace the vicious cycle of failure and anxiety. Gates and Bond (1936) found that success in reading following a special tutoring program produced better social and emotional development following the improvement in reading performance. Preston (1940) reported that cases of prolonged reading failure became extremely maladjusted but, when six of the twenty cases did learn to read normally, their emotional problems disappeared. Fernald (1943) also reported that maladjustment due to failure in reading cleared up when effective remedial teaching succeeded in developing their reading skill. Johnson (1955), too, found that attitudes improved with success in reading in her clinic.

One of the present writers found evidence of the change in emotional reactions following success in remedial reading in several studies of the initial teaching alphabet (i.t.a.) that he reviewed (Downing, 1977b). For example, Lane (1974) mentioned that teachers in an experiment using i.t.a. for severely disabled readers "praised their sudden interest in reading and their 'new' personalities" (p. 26). Downing cites Kearslake, Gardner and Pettican (1966) as stating in their report on the use of i.t.a. in a residential special school for cerebral-palsied children: "In each case success was achieved and good progress was made where little or no progress was being made using the traditional alphabet. In each case the success experienced led to an improved attitude, fewer emotional upsets and a greater willingness to cooperate" (Downing, 1977b, pp. 365–366).

Downing cites an experiment by Curry in a special school for delinquent boys. Curry emphasized the *rapid success* that these boys could get with i.t.a. This provided a "quick build-up of confidence in a child whose only experience of reading has been a constant succession of failures and disappointments" (Downing, 1965, pp. 80–81). Curry, in a later report, concluded that i.t.a. "lends itself to overcoming the antagonism towards school which is a common attitude of many boys committed in this age group. The failures and disappointments come to a dead stop, and a particular child may by this method settle down to enjoy the classroom for the rest of his school life" (Downing, 1965, p. 81). Stevenson (1966), too, considered that "the most significant effect of all" in using i.t.a. with illiterate adults was "the improvement in the general outlook of the student, in his confidence and in his increased self-respect" (p. 223). Again, Stevenson notes that "A substantial contribution to its effectiveness is undoubtedly the early success rate which is achieved" (p. 222).

Whether the technique used is i.t.a. or some other method of *reducing the threat of failure*, we can agree with the more general conclusion of Strang et al. (1967):

> The individual's approach to reading is profoundly affected by his self-concept. It can be changed only by repeated experiences of success (p. 457).

2. *Emphasis on reading.* We have seen that failure-threat anxiety is more closely associated with reading than any other specific subject of the curriculum, and we noted Sherman's hypothesis that this association has two causes—(1) the reliance on reading for instruction in almost all school work; (2) the cultural use of reading ability as a criterion for a person's general mental ability.

Downing (1973) found that the cultural emphasis on reading is variable from one country to another. Among the fourteen countries he compared, the United States seemed to give the highest priority to reading. Earp (1974) believes that "reading is overemphasized" in American schools. He writes: "Such thrusts as the 'Right to Read' exemplify the high emotional climate relating to this academic area. . . . Observation in the typical school setting suggests that strong emotional tones are implicit in school reading settings." Earp hypothesizes, therefore, that "pressures become strongly inherent in a situation in which a child encounters difficulty in reading . . ." (p. 562). He argues further that the overemphasis on reading is actually counter-productive because it forces the child "into protecting himself from potential psychological damage by withdrawing, deciding to fail, rationalization and so on" (p. 565).

3. *Parents' Attitudes to Learning.* In Hickerson's "House of Last Resort" for reading failures, "In almost every case, the intense disappointment and anxiety these parents felt because of their unexpectedly slow-learning, non-reading children served to compound the students' difficulties" (p. 263). There is much research evidence that pressure from parents aggravates children's failure-threat anxiety. Vernon (1957), reviewing this evidence, concluded that, "if the parents react to the child's backwardness by blaming or reproaching him, or even merely by undue pressure, urging him to work harder, a severe emotional conflict may result" (p. 133).

Young (1938) found that in two-thirds of 41 cases studied, emotional disturbances had been aggravated by unnecessary pressure from parents and teachers. Preston (1939) interviewed the parents of 100 children between the ages of seven and seventeen years who had failed in reading despite their normal or above-normal intelligence. Many of these parents said that they had felt shocked, angry or resentful. About three-quarters of them admitted taunting their children with their failure. Anxiety about the problem was found in 66 per cent of the mothers and 28 per cent of the fathers. Johnson (1955) reported that the remedial treatment of 62 per cent of 34 cases of reading disability in a clinic was hindered by their parents' attitudes. Too much pressure on achievement was the hindrance in 38 per cent of them. Davis and Kent (1955) also reported that the difficulties of some of their cases of severe retardation in reading were aggravated by the excessive demands of their parents.

Davis and Kent considered other types of parental attitudes as well as "demanding" ones. They divided their 118 eight-year-olds into four groups according to their parents' attitudes toward learning. As has been noted above, some of the children with "demanding" parents were severely retarded in reading, but those with "overanxious" parents achieved as well as children with "normal" treatment. Severe reading retardation was also associated with "unconcerned" parents. Lansdown (1974) discusses this problem in relation to the self-concept of the child learning to read. He notes "three ways in which they [parents] can affect the way in which a child sees both himself and others." These are:

> [1] by expecting too much of a child and by communicating this to the child. Children faced with this attitude see themselves as constantly failing to meet parental demands . . . .
> [2] by being actively hostile towards a child. . . . Given this situation the child is likely to fail at everything, except possibly crime, since she has so firmly received the message of her worthlessness.
> [3] Lastly there is the indifferent parent (p. 103).

Lansdown's typology of inadequate styles of parenting leads us into two new areas of study. Firstly, it reminds us that failure-threat anxiety in reading may be only a part of a larger syndrome of maladjustment that exists before the child arrives in school. Secondly, it indicates the need to consider other kinds of affective patterns that have been created at home prior to the commencement of schooling. Stott (1977) remarks that, "Over some five years some 250 children passed through our Centre [for Educational Disabilities]. One of the first things I learned was that every child, by the age of 5, has an already-developed learning style, which he brings into school with him. . . . The result of these years of observation and recording by the Centre's staff was that we identified fourteen styles of non-learning" (pp. 17–18).

Primary Emotional Disturbances

Stott also reports a survey of 1,104 children that was conducted twice—on first entry to school and again at the end of the third year. He found that the children changed little as a result of their school experiences and, therefore, Stott concluded that "the maladjustment and bad attitudes to learning of the poor readers antedated any exposure to the teaching of reading or their awareness of failure in reading" (p. 15). Wattenberg and Clifford (1964) found that some children on entry to kindergarten had already established an unfavorable view of their own competence and that measures of self concept at that stage were predictive of reading achievement at the end of the second grade.

Vernon (1971) concludes from her review of the evidence on primary emotional disturbances that inhibit learning to read that "in most cases the primary cause is some inadequacy in *parental relationships.*" She cites Fabian (1955), Ingram and Reid (1956), Ingram (1963), and Silverman,

Fite and Mosher (1959), all of whom reported research evidence of various emotionally disruptive conditions in the homes of children with severe language or reading disabilities.

But emotional maladjustment in children is found not only in connection with such severely disordered parents, Vernon points out. In other cases, "The type of disorder, aggressive or anxious and withdrawn, may bear some relationship to the type of parental treatment; though probably innate temperamental differences are involved also" (pp. 118–119). She goes on to review the evidence for a wide variety of manifestations of emotional disorders that inhibit children in learning to read. These include:

1. Refusal to risk trying to learn to read because of over-demanding parents (Ravenette, 1970).
2. Anger against demanding parents (Mann, 1957).
3. Resistance to parents (Mann, 1957; Vorhaus, 1968).

Another oft-mentioned type of problem is

4. Lack of confidence because of the overprotectiveness of parents (Monroe and Backus, 1937; Gates, 1941; Dreikurs, 1952).

But probably the most often cited type of emotional problem that interferes with reading instruction is a child's feeling of *insecurity* with a resulting *general deficiency in stamina.* Zolkos states that, "Frequently, neither the home nor the school gives the child the adequate sense of security that is fundamental for emotional stability. Emotional disturbance in the home can deaden the child's desire to learn to read" (pp. 255–256). Schonell and Goodacre write that "It is insecurity which robs the young child of successful self-expression and a sense of achievement" (pp. 28–29). They add that, "It is possible that insufficient stress has been placed on the importance of *stamina* in these early stages—that ability not only to carry on until the process does make sense, but also the courage to 'have a go,' to be willing to try a particular word in the reading context, to correct it if it does not make sense" (p. 43).

Preston (1940) estimated the degree of security in the homes of 67 matched pairs of disabled versus normal readers. Security was satisfactory for 57 per cent of normal readers but only 37 per cent of disabled readers. Vorhaus (1968) also found evidence of insecurity among severely disabled readers. Sperry, Staver, Reiner and Ulrich (1958) suggested that reading failure may sometimes be a way of seeking security. Thus children may hope to obtain the love they are lacking by demonstrating their need for help.

From this review of theory and research on the causes of primary emotional disturbances that affect the acquisition of reading skill, it is clear that there exists a wide range of personality problems that arise from many different experiences in children's home lives. We have noted also that the causal relationship is complicated by innate differences in temperament. It is not surprising, therefore, that we find marked individual differences in children's emotional reactions to the tasks of reading instruction.

It is especially important to recognize *individual differences in anxiety as a personality trait.* Spielberger (1972) gives this definition:

> Trait anxiety (A-Trait) refers to relatively stable individual differences in anxiety proneness, that is, to differences in the disposition to perceive a wide range of stimulus situations as dangerous or threatening and in the tendency to respond to such threats with A-State reactions. . . . Persons who are high in A-Trait tend to perceive a larger number of situations as dangerous or threatening than persons who are low in A-Trait, and to respond to threatening situations with A-State elevations of greater intensity (p. 39).

"A-State" refers to *State anxiety*—the actual emotional state of persons when they experience the threat of danger.

Hence, one cannot assume that the same level of failure-threat anxiety will occur in, for example, two cases of reading disability with the same level of scholastic retardation. In the regular classroom one can anticipate that the same degree of stress may produce an "alarm reaction" leading to a constructive coping response in one child but a negative "resistance" reaction in some other child. In still another child no anxiety whatsoever will be felt because failing in reading is not perceived as a threat. Vernon's (1957) view is that, while some disabled readers are emotionally disturbed, "others are emotionally stable, and are quite unaffected by it" (p. 145). Lourie and Schwarzbeck, in their article on the tendency of some children to "disorganize" under stress ("the mind goes blank") comment that to help these children, "The first step is recognizing individual differences in children's styles of reaction to stress" (p. 140). This statement has a broader application to all kinds of emotional responses that are produced when reading tasks are perceived as dangerous.

In our review of research on arousal under stress it has become clear that in some children emotional disturbance is caused by failure in reading but that in other cases the emotional problem existed prior to commencing learning to read. Robinson (1953b) states that the potentially reading disabled child "may enter school as an unhappy child who cannot free his energies for learning, or he may enter as a happy, well-adjusted child who fails to learn to read and becomes maladjusted because of his failure" (p. 25). At one period, the question of the cause and effect relationship between emotional disturbance and reading failure was a controversial question, and a number of studies attempted to prove the causal relationship was in one direction or the other. Vernon (1957) reviewed these studies and her conclusions accord with the modern view of this theoretical problem:

> It seems fairly clear that in some cases the emotional difficulties are the primary and fundamental factor in causing reading disability; whereas in others, the emotional difficulty is largely caused by the reading disability (p. 146).

In actual practice, emotional disturbance and reading failure are interactive. Vernon (1957) notes that "Even if the defects are temperamental in origin, it is likely that . . . they have become aggravated by the reading difficulties" (p. 147). In an article reporting the positive effects of relaxation training for poor readers in Germany, Frey (1980) observes: "Diagnostic studies of reading disabled children frequently reveal high levels of tension, anxiety, mood swings, reduced ability to concentrate, and poor retention" (p. 928). Zolkos writes: "In many cases, intense emotional strain and reading disability seem to interact, each adding stress to the other" (p. 255). Lynch and Haase, too, state that "studies have shown that self-concept and reading achievement changes will affect each other interactively" (p. 198).

Of practical as well as theoretical importance is the fact that, once emotions have been aroused, they influence learning no matter whether their arousal occurred prior to reading failure or as its result. As Abrams and Smolen so pertinently observe, "no matter what the basic etiology, the reading disability can be sustained by the stress reaction long after the original causal factors have lost their significance" (p. 465).

In conclusion, it is clear that arousal is as important in the acquisition of reading skill as it is in other learning activities. Alertness, responsiveness, and attentiveness are essential for coping with the complex task of understanding how to process text. If the level of arousal is too low, pupils miss points and become more and more confused. If the level of arousal is too high, their energies may be spent not directly on the cognitive task itself. Again, attention suffers. They may rally their resources for concentration, but, if the emotional arousal persists at this high level, fatigue leads to the collapse of their motivational energy.

Incentive

The second concept that Andreas uses for classifying psychological research on motivation is *incentive.* He defines it as "the anticipation of reinforcement" (p. 518). "Reinforcement" will not be treated until the next section of this chapter. Therefore, McDonald's definition (1965) may be more helpful at this point:

> An *incentive* is a reward or source of need satisfaction that a person *may* obtain. The possibility of attaining this reward or goal induces motivated behavior. An incentive is something proffered to a learner to engage him in the actions of learning (p. 146).

It is important to note McDonald's use of the term *need.* In psychology *need* is defined as "A condition marked by the feeling of lack or want of something, or of requiring the performance of some action" (Drever, 1964, p. 182). Thus the theoretical question posed for this section of the chapter is—how is the acquisition of reading skill influenced by anticipations of results that will satisfy learners' needs?

In order to study this question one must consider what are the typical common needs of children during the period when they are learning to read. Clearly they have a broad range of needs of varying importance. One theory that classifies human needs and arranges them in an order of priority is Maslow's (1943) hierarchical need system, as illustrated in Figure 11–1. The physiological needs at the base have first priority, next comes safety, and so on. Needs higher up in the priority hierarchy are not felt until more basic ones are satisfied. The highest level, "self-actualization" is only rarely felt, according to Maslow,

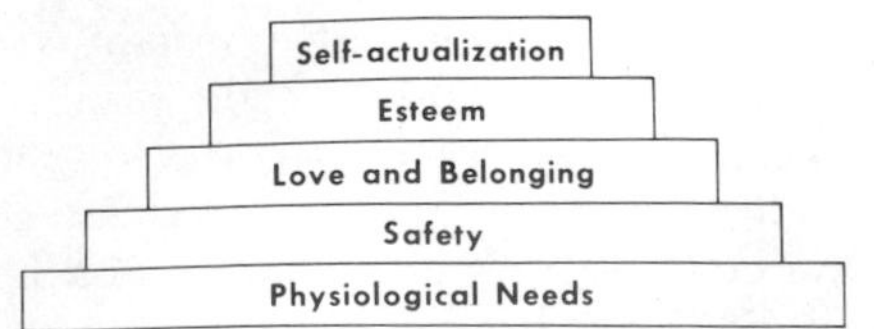

Figure 11–1. Maslow's hierarchical need system.

because it is seldom that all the more basic needs are satisfied.

Generally, one cannot expect much motivation for reading instruction when children are reacting to the two most basic needs—physiological and safety. Vernon (1971) remarks that "No individual whose mind is dominated by craving for food or by fear of danger, illness or homelessness can take much interest in school activities, or make much effort to work hard" (p. 103). In the previous section of this chapter we also noted how the danger of failure inhibits the acquisition of reading skill.

Intrinsic versus Extrinsic Motivation

Strang et al. consider that "Stars, teacher's marks, and other extrinsic rewards" are the most "temporary" and "superficial" kind of motivations (p. 23). On the other hand, behaviorist psychologists have placed much more reliance on the effectiveness of extrinsic motivation. Numerous experiments have shown how children will work hard at reading tasks for incentives such as candy or tokens that can be exchanged for toys and so on (Staats, 1968; Staats and Staats, 1962; Staats, Staats, Schutz and Wolf, 1962). Bloom (1971) has summarized the results of such experiments as follows: "It is argued that the use of environmentally attractive features as reinforcers, when made accessible to the learner, *contingent* upon the occurrence of specific reading behavior, will provide a powerful basis for particularly establishing and motivating early reading efforts" (p. 296). The behaviorists claim that if extrinsic reinforcers are used long enough, the reading activity will gain secondary reinforcement value of its own, but Gibson and Levin (1975) "doubt that this would happen." They note that extrinsic rewards "keep the child at the task. When they are withdrawn, the rate of activity at the task drops immediately and sharply. When the reinforcers are discontinued the learner seems to have no motivational basis for continuing" (p. 274).

Oliver (1976) believes that the use of extrinsic rewards for reading may give the child "a false concept of the purpose for reading" (p. 23). Oliver's hypothesis is supported by the evidence of the experiment by Lepper, Greene and Nisbett (1973). They found that extrinsic incentives had the effect of undermining the intrinsic interest that children already had in the activity. But Oliver's point is more fundamental and we must return to it again in our section on "purpose in reading."

Achievement Motivation

According to McClelland (1961), achievement itself is an intrinsic motivation. He believes that mastering a task, becoming superior to others in a skill or even just being able to perform it successfully is a strong motive. Vernon (1971) accepts that much criticism has raised "considerable doubt as to the existence of achievement motivation as an independent entity. . . . Nevertheless, the term may be employed to refer to a class of behaviour which is frequent in and characteristic of Western civilization." She states that "It is generally considered that reading achievement is increased by strong *achievement motivation*" (p. 106). She cites the study of Zimmerman and Allebrand (1965) who compared nine- and ten-year-old good and poor readers' *Thematic Apperception Test* stories. The good readers' stories stressed hard work and achievement whereas these themes were not included by the poor readers. Vernon adds: "Undoubtedly the motive to achieve is related to parental stress on achievement. . . . But parents of children with high achievement motivation, while advocating achievement and independence and rewarding children when they show these, are also permissive rather than authoritarian in their discipline. In other words, the child is attracted rather than forced by pressure to achieve; and this is reinforced by his identification with his parents and his desire to be like them" (pp. 106–107). Since there is a very wide range of attitudes toward schooling among parents, there must be a corresponding range of individual differences in achievement motivation in pupils learning how to read.

If any achievement motivation is present in a pupil, he or she must experience some success if continued effort is desired. Harris and Sipay state that "It is essential at the beginning of a remedial program to start at a level easy enough so that a successful learning experience is virtually certain" (p. 318). Collinge (1976) also emphasizes "the fundamental importance of . . . the motivation that comes from success" (p. 260). In the previous section on "arousal" we also noted the essential need for success in breaking the vicious cycle of failure-threat anxiety.

Curiosity

According to Day, Berlyne and Hunt (1971), it has been generally accepted by modern psychologists that there exists an intrinsic motivation to find things out, to understand what is not clear, to sort out muddles and so on. For example, Harlow, Harlow, Rueping and Mason (1950) found that monkeys will disassemble a mechanical device without any tangible reward other than getting it into its parts. Kavanau (1967), found similar behavior in mice. Regarding human behavior of this kind, Bruner (1968) writes: "Curiosity is almost a prototype of the intrinsic motive" (p. 114).

Strang et al. state that "Curiosity . . . is a prime motivation for reading at any age. Unless suppressed, curiosity persists throughout life and frequently turns a person to reading, which offers wide opportunities to satisfy his mood of inquiry" (p. 23). Maw and Maw (1962) found that children rated by their teachers as highly motivated by curiosity had superior scores on reading comprehension to children with low curiosity ratings. Harris and Sipay comment that "The teacher who has seen the magical effects obtainable when just the right book is placed in a child's hands cannot ever again disregard the importance of trying to match the book to the child" (p. 322).

Unfortunately, as Harris and Sipay remark, "The desirability of making reading interesting is not a controversial issue in theory. In practice it is often ignored, with teachers relying too much on drill and repetition." Collinge recognizes also that "Most graded readers are boring, some appallingly so . . ." (p. 260). Why are they so unappealing to children's curiosity? A clue to an answer to this problem is provided in an article by Bradley (1969). It states: "A major objective of the reading program is to make it more highly personalized for reaching each child's varying level of curiosity. . . . A child is more likely 'curious' when his attention is attracted by something he truly wishes to find out as a result of his own thinking about it" (p. 449). In other words, reading taps children's curiosity motivation when it is *relevant to their interests.* Otherwise, as Sinatra and Kinsler (1976) state, "When content is not relevant, children may not be motivated to learn to read" (p. 159).

Ashton-Warner (1963) recognized this essential fact in her teaching of reading to Maori children in New Zealand. She abandoned the basal readers about British culture that were quite irrelevant to her Maori pupils. Instead she introduced her "Key Vocabulary" method. Every day she asked each child "what word do you want." She wrote it on a card that the child could keep and take home as well. "They ask for a new word each morning and never have I to repeat to them what it is" (p. 29).

Ashton-Warner's technique is one variety of the "Language-Experience Approach" to reading instruction that centers on the principle that the most relevant reading materials that can be created are those that are produced by the pupils themselves. In the beginning stage the pupils dictate their text to an adult who writes or types what they say. Clearly, nothing could produce more relevant material than this since it is individually tailored to each individual child's own interests. Detailed descriptions of the language-experience approach and similar methods with their rationale have been published by Allen (1976), Downing (1979a), Goddard (1974), Hall (1976), and McCracken and McCracken (1972, 1979). Hall (1977) has published, in addition, a review of research related to the language-experience approach. She concludes conservatively that "The research does substantiate that the language experience approach is an effective way to teach reading and related communication skills" (p. 23).

Minuchin (1971) investigated the levels of curiosity in 18 Black four-year-olds in a Head Start program. She found that they varied widely in this respect. She believed that the level of curiosity was related to these children's different home backgrounds. For example, there were six children who "projected an environment characterized by sustained crisis, little coherence, ineffective and poorly defined adults; and whose conceptual grasp of order in the physical environment and of the relationships among objects tended to be poor. These children also showed limited curiosity or exploratory behavior" (p. 948). Thus, there is likely to be a broad range of individual differences in general curiosity motivation.

A wide variation of individual differences exists also in regard to the *content* of children's curiosity. What arouses curiosity in one child may be of little or no interest to another child. Nevertheless, some generalizations may be possible about what contents of books interest children at certain age levels and in certain circumstances. Such information could be useful in matching books to children's interests. This hope has led to the publication of a large number of surveys of children's reading interests.

Reading Interests

According to Drever's *A Dictionary of Psychology, interest* is a term "employed in two senses, functional and structural; (1) designating a type of feeling experience, which might be called 'worth-whileness', associated with attention to an object, or course of action; (2) an element or item in an individual's make-up, either congenital or acquired, because of which he tends to have this feeling of 'worth-whileness' in connexion with certain objects, or matters relating to a particular subject, or a particular field of knowledge . . ." (pp. 142–143). For example, a student who has a reading interest in mountaineering is one who feels that it is worthwhile engaging in the activity of reading books about mountains and climbing. Although such interests are usually learned, as Drever notes, they may have a congenital component—for instance, the sex of the reader.

Many authors in the field of reading stress the importance of interest. Thus Dechant and Smith write: "Motivation flows from interest" (p. 186). Witty (1965) too believed that lack of interest is an important cause of failure in developing full maturity in reading. Although such views are widely held among reading specialists, the evidence for the effects of interest on the development of reading skill is scanty.

In the previous section on "curiosity" we cited the finding of Maw and Maw that higher levels of curiosity were related to superior reading comprehension scores. M. Bernstein (1955) investigated the relationship between interest and reading comprehension in her study of 100 ninth-grade pupils. She gave them two passages to read. They were of equal readability but were judged to differ in degree of interestingness to pupils of this age group. The uninteresting passage, in fact, was deliberately rewritten to make it less interesting. The pupils were asked to state which story they preferred and why, and they had to write an additional chapter for each story. These measures and the reading comprehension test indicated that the more interesting story produced significantly higher comprehension scores.

An interesting phenomenon that has been observed by many teachers and parents is that children who have poor reading skill in general, sometimes, perform remarkably well when they read something that is intensely interesting for them. Shnayer (1969) studied 484 subjects drawn from 17 sixth-grade classes in one metropolitan area. He divided the subjects into seven groups according to their grade level in reading ability. Then each group was required to read stories that were two grade levels higher in difficulty (readability) than the student's actual reading ability. For example, sixth-grade pupils with reading ability at the third-grade level were assigned stories at the fifth-grade level of difficulty, and so on. The subjects also rated the stories on a four-point scale. Shnayer related the pupils' comprehension scores to their interest ratings on the stories.

Statistical data reported by Shnayer led him to conclude that, "A high interest in stories read by children results in greater comprehension than that which results from low interest", and that "Reading interest, as a factor of reading comprehension, may enable most students to read beyond their measured reading ability" (p. 700). He also found that "there is a gradual diminishing difference of the effect of interest as reading ability increases. . . . High ability students are less affected by reading interest than low ability students." Shnayer's findings indicate the special importance of providing reading materials that capture the interest of *beginners* and *older children who are disabled in reading.* Shnayer believes that his findings imply that classes should provide "an abundance of reading material" and that "the confines of reading textbooks, graded, and used in series, would seem to be a clear violation of the interest needs of children" (p. 701).

The consensus of the very large number of surveys of children's reading interests is that they vary according to the pupil's age, sex, and intelligence (Dechant and Smith, pp. 180–184). For example, a study by the Beta Upsilon Chapter, Pi Lambda Theta (1974) found (like earlier studies) that, in the early part of the elementary school, boys and girls have similar reading interests but later their interests diverge more and more. Norvell (1946, 1950, 1958) and Thorndike (1941) found that the most important variable in determining reading interests at the higher age levels in school is the sex of the reader. Beyard-Tyler and Sullivan (1980) found, in a study of children in grades seven, nine, and eleven that boys preferred stories with male protagonists while girls preferred ones with female protagonists. Boys' preferences in this regard increased with grade level whereas the girls' preferences for female protagonists decreased as grade level went up. Another study conducted in Australia by Tolley (1977) is yet another example of evidence of marked differences between boys and girls in reading interests in the later years of schooling. However, Chasen (1974) and Tibbetts (1974) both consider that such differences are derived from the differential treatment of boys and girls. Chasen had 24 prekindergarten teachers from two districts in Manhattan respond to a questionnaire. She found that "Sex-role stereotyping appeared in almost all areas in the classroom" (p. 233). Tibbetts' review of research on this question led her to hypothesize that "social pressure—or training—may be the most significant factor behind observed 'sex differences' " in reading interests (p. 281).

In view of Chasen's finding that sex-role stereotyping is part of the child's experience before entering kindergarten, the conclusion of Dechant and Smith is surprising. They believe that their review of the research shows that "among children below the third-grade, sexual differences in choice of reading interest are negligible" (p. 182). This is an important matter because Shnayer's research suggests that it is in the primary years that interest may be a powerful factor in developing reading skill.

One recent study provides evidence that contradicts the conclusion of Dechant and Smith. Kirsch, Pehrsson, and Robinson (1976) comment that "More than 300 investigations of reading preferences were published prior to the 1960s, largely in the United States. Although the surge of studies has diminished to some extent, researchers still continue their pursuit of the interest factor. Only a limited amount of research has been focussed upon the preferences of the beginning reader in the first and second years of school" (p. 302). Therefore, they concentrated on the first and second years of formal schooling (not including kindergarten). The results showed significant differences in the expressed reading interests of boys and girls in the United States both in grade one and in grade two. However, there were no significant differences between the sexes' reading interests at this stage in the nine other countries studied. Kirsch et al. listed the interests of children in the first or second year of school in the ten different countries surveyed and found them quite similar from country to country.

These reading interest surveys have some utility in making crude decisions about what categories of books to include in a library, for example, but it is doubtful if they help much in the day to day running of reading instruction. In this, the more important work of the teacher is to discover individual children's interests and help pupils to understand how they can satisfy those interests through reading. Once children perceive reading as functional in this way, it is important to make sure that an appropriate range of materials is available in the library. Then, as Berretta (1970) states, "In some instances this is simply a matter of allowing the child freedom to select his own reading material. Other times the teacher may need to help a child learn to make choices and help him become aware of what is available for him to choose" (p. 235).

Schonell and Goodacre believe that one of the important jobs of teachers and parents is "to see that reading interests do not become too narrow," and there is a "need for skilful, subtle, and persistent guidance by parents and teachers in the development of taste" (p. 171). But Baker (1968) compared children's reading interests with their teachers' predictions of them and found marked disagreement between them. She concluded: "This simply means that *teachers generally don't know what their children prefer*" (p. 106). Baker's study was specifically concerned with the representation of the experiences and environment of disadvantaged children in reading materials. Yet it has long been supposed that teachers are quite effective in guiding children's choice of books to read. Thus, Dechant and Smith state: "Wightman (1915) long ago found that teachers exert a strong influence on children's preferences. The pupils generally preferred books that the teacher was enthusiastic about" (pp. 180–181). But a more recent survey by Pugh (1971) revealed that teachers' recommendations are not highly favored by pupils. Probably, teachers vary in their skill in influencing children's choice of books.

One way of broadening children's reading interests that has proved effective in the work of many teachers is reading aloud to children. Schonell and Goodacre state that "reading aloud is one of the most effective ways of unlocking doors for many children—it is a craft that should be nurtured, practised, polished . . ." (p. 171). This is an important aspect of Bamberger's (1976) "Lure into Reading" method. The teacher tells the class a part of the story and reads some of it. This is enough to catch their interest to go on and read the book for themselves—a book that otherwise they might never have thought of looking into. "It is important to find texts which really awaken the child's interest and leave an impression strong enough to form permanent reading habits," writes Bamberger (p. 63).

Purpose in Reading

We drew attention in the preceding section to the important work of the teacher to help pupils to understand how they can satisfy their interests through reading. This understanding of that specific purpose of reading is part of the more general development of cognitive clarity about the purposes of reading. The reading process actually changes with the purpose of the reading act. Hence, children need to practice reading for different purposes and they need to practice changing from one type of purpose to another if they are to develop that flexibility of timing that is such a noteworthy feature of superior skill performance in reading.

The term *purpose* in this connection might be described as "meta-motivational," because what we are discussing here is not merely motivation to read but the reader's awareness or even conception of such motivation. Drever defines *purpose* as "The thought, in the present, of an end or aim, in the future, with the intention of realizing it" (pp. 235–236). He notes the "highly controversial" nature of this concept for explaining behavior. "Purpose" became a particularly unfashionable term in psychology during the period when behaviorism was most influential. However, some psychologists continued to find it a useful concept. Thus, Woodworth and Marquis (1949), writing during that period stated:

> *Purpose* is goal-directed activity in which the individual has foresight of the end to be accomplished and has definitely commited himself to the action (p. 333).

They noted also that "A purpose can be the most definite of motives and the most powerful" (p. 320). We shall use "purpose" in the same sense but we must emphasize its cognitive aspect as well as its affective side. In order to become flexible readers, students must *know* the purposes of reading and must learn to adjust their skilled acts to different purposes.

Teachers of reading sometimes assume that the purposes of literacy are self-evident. But research has shown that most school beginners have little notion of why people write and read. Vygotsky (1934) found that the young child in Russia "has little motivation to learn writing when we begin to teach it. He feels no need for it and has only a vague idea of its usefulness." Reid (1966) in Scotland and Downing (1970) in England arrived at similar conclusions from their studies of five-year-olds in those countries. The fact that reading is an everyday experience for people like teachers probably leads them to assume that the functions of literacy are self-evident, whereas, in fact, these purposes often have not been consciously thought out. It is helpful in planning strategies for guiding pupils to understand the purposes of literacy to study the various uses of written or printed language that have developed.

A number of authors have discussed these various functions of reading in modern life. Lind (1936) studied adults' reports about their reading in childhood and found four main purposes: (1) for escape, (2) for temporary diversion, (3) for specific use in objective interests, (4) for self-development. Waples (1967) suggests five types of purpose for reading. Some of these are similar to Lind's findings, but others clearly would be at a less self-conscious level: (1) For *instrumental effect*—to achieve some practical goal, for example, to bake a cake; (2) For *prestige effect*—to improve one's own self-image or other people's image of oneself, for example, reading sports magazines to be always up-to-date in conversations with other sports fans; (3) For *reinforcement of an attitude*—to bolster one's political, religious or social beliefs; (4) For *vicarious aesthetic experience*—reading to feel or sense emotions, motives that are not available at firsthand; (5) For *respite*—to escape from troubles, pains, and worries.

In the experiment that we cited briefly in Chapter 3, Postman and Senders gave college students a passage from Chekov to read. There were six groups of students, each group being given different instructions designed to influence their purpose in reading the passage. Group one was told to read it to time how long it took. Group two was told they would be tested for "general comprehension" of the passage. Group three's instruction was to prepare for a memory test of the "specific sequence of events in the story." Groups four, five and six were told they would be tested for certain kinds of "details"—group four, "content"; group five, "wording"; group six, "physical appearance" (this refers to spelling and typing errors deliberately introduced). The college students were all allowed 90 seconds to read the passage, ample time for reading at their own speed. Three minutes later, they had to answer a multiple-choice test of 50 items. Ten items tested general comprehension, ten were on memory for sequence of events, ten on details of content, ten on wording, and ten on "physical" details. Postman and Senders found that the purpose indicated by the different instructions to the different groups influenced their scores on the different parts of the test. The tendency was to remember best the type of information related to the purpose given by the instruction. Furthermore, this was done at the expense of other types of information. However, this loss of other information was not complete. The students did remember some other information beyond what they had been instructed to look for. For example, the students in group one who received no relevant instructions did just as well as group two on the *general* comprehension questions. But this does not contradict the conclusion that purpose gears reading selectively. Rather it indicates that people always have the general motivation to understand and restructure the environment and that this goes on in reading as another motivation alongside the specific goal that readers may set themselves deliberately and consciously.

H. K. Smith (1967) studied senior pupils in the secondary school under two conditions: (1) when told to read for details, (2) when told to read for general impressions. After each type of reading, the pupils were interviewed and questioned about details and general impressions of what they had read. Smith found that good readers varied their techniques according to the purpose they had been set, whereas poor readers made less adjustment in the way they read. When reading for details, the good readers said they made mental summaries and reread facts like names and dates. When reading for general impressions, they paused to evaluate ideas at the end of a paragraph or page, and any rereading done was of whole paragraphs or sentences, not individual words. After reviewing this and other evidence, Gibson and Levin (1975) conclude that "skilled readers are flexible and adaptive in their reading strategies as both the material read and the reader's purpose dictate" (p. 474). Smith (1972) herself, in another article writes that good readers "may use many kinds of comprehension skills and techniques, depending in each case upon their purpose as well as the difficulty and complexity of the content" (p. 90).

In that same article, Smith (1972) makes five suggestions for training children to become purposeful readers: (1) "pupils should be fully aware of the purposes of materials they have been asked to read. They should know what they are expected to obtain from their reading"; (2) "pupils need to learn how to set their own purposes. For some pupils this will be a gradual process. Teachers will need to continue setting purposes for such pupils and guiding them in setting their own goals"; (3) "pupils should be given a wide variety of purposes for reading, both in their reading periods and in their content area subjects"; (4) "the kinds of questions asked should be in harmony with the purposes for which students have been asked to read"; (5) "students should be taught *how* to read for the different purposes" (pp. 92–93).

Research evidence from studies of the effects of questioning children about their reading provides support for the suggestion that pupils should be made aware of its purpose. Hershberger and Terry (1965) compared various typographical techniques for "cuing" learning in either conventional or programmed texts. The different typographical formats did not produce any very interesting results. But in all the formats quiz sheets were inserted at intervals in the programmed texts but not in the conventional ones. The former proved superior with the grade eight pupils in this investigation. Rothkopf (1966) compared three groups of college students who read a long prose passage under three different conditions respectively. Group one had written questions referring to what they were *going to read* interspersed at intervals of three pages in the passage. Group two's interspersed questions at three-page-intervals were about what they *had just been reading,* and group three had *no interspersed questions.* The groups were tested in two ways: what they had learned directly from the use of the questions and whether the effects of questioning spilled over into their general study of the passage. The results showed that both kinds of questioning produced superior performance on the matter directly questioned. But asking questions in advance of the reading produced no bonus in the students' study of other aspects of the passage, whereas asking questions after the reading had been completed did improve the study of material other than that which was the subject of direct questioning. This seems to indicate that getting the questions in advance focuses the reading to a more limited purpose, while just knowing that some questions will be asked but not exactly what they will be leads to a wider selection of facts to remember.

One other experiment should be noted. Farley and Eischens (1971) studied the effect of inserting questions in passages of prose material read by children in grades three, four, five and six. The grade three results were inconclusive, but, for the older children, tests administered immediately after reading and also one week later showed superior performance with inserted questions than without.

Gibson and Levin, reviewing these experiments and others conclude that such questions inserted in the text "can be helpful, with certain reservations. Facilitation by 'test-like events' inserted during the reading process is more likely to result if the tests do not occur too frequently, and if they *follow* rather than precede the relevant material" (p. 437). More important from the practical point of view, Samuels' (1975) experiments show that when readers know beforehand the kinds of questions they will be asked as well as their level of difficulty, they are indeed flexible in their reading rate.

Smith's second suggestion was that readers need to learn to set their own purposes. Bond and Tinker (1973) have stated this principle succinctly: "Prior to reading any unit, the child should be clear as to the purposes for which he is going to read. The most satisfactory purpose is one stated by the pupil himself. When he cannot do this satisfactorily, the teacher's guidance should help provide him with a purpose *acceptable* to him. To be a really good reader, however, the pupil must have learned to set his own purpose" (p. 453).

Carrillo (1973) indicates that this subskill of setting one's own purpose and adjusting one's reading technique accordingly is related to cognitive clarity about function and speed in reading. He writes that, "the reader must realize that he *must slow down* and go through this process in order to continue to comprehend. He must always be *conscious of his level of understanding* of the printed passage.. . . All of this means that instruction in basic comprehension, so that *one knows how much one knows* when reading, is a prerequisite to flexibility" (p. 64). Carrillo also warns teachers "that too much attention in the early stages of reading instruction to phonics, structural analysis, structural linguistics, and/or oral reading, will interfere later with flexibility of rate" (p. 66). Lloyd and Lloyd (1971) believe that many students read always in a word-by-word, inflexible, "bovine" manner, regardless of the type or content of the material because of misleading instruction in reading. To prevent these difficulties of inflexibility in reading, it is essential for teachers to bear in mind the long-term purposes of communication through the written form of language. From the very beginning the teaching of reading should have these long-term goals in view.

Smith's third proposal for developing purposeful reading was that schools should give pupils experience of "a wide variety of purposes for reading." This suggestion, too, is sustained by a recommendation from Bond and Tinker: "It is clear that the child's basic program cannot neglect the content fields right from the start. The basic program should itself reflect the kind of reading he is expected to do in the entire curriculum" (p. 421).

Smith's final suggestion was that students should be taught how to adjust their reading technique to different purposes. Bond and Tinker also suggest methods that can be used for training flexibility in purposeful reading. They point out that, "Opportunities for guidance in adjusting speed of reading to the kind of materials are abundant in teaching units in the content areas. Preparation for every unit should include discussion of the right reading procedures to be employed. . . . Another guidance procedure is to have pupils read the same material several times, each successive time for a different specific purpose such as: (1) to grasp the main idea; (2) to note the important details; (3) to answer specific questions which they are told in advance; (4) to evaluate what is read; etc." (p. 469).

For individuals who have missed this kind of teaching in their earlier schooling, a special program needs to be designed to overcome their rigidity or slowness in reading secondary school or college level books. A number of practical suggestions have been put forward to improve speed and flexibility in reading. Useful articles and books on this practical topic are those by Fry (1963), Karlin (1972), and Miller (1973). During the 1950s there was a strong movement to introduce machines to modify students' reading rates. Most authorities agree now with the conclusion of the study by Traxler and Jungleblut (1960). They found that, "these studies do not indicate that any greater improvement in either speed or comprehension can be obtained through the use of mechanical devices than can be secured with more informal procedures."

Further studies of the effect of purpose on reading behavior are found in the field of reading in the content areas or specialist subjects of the school curriculum. Artley (1948) proposed that there are fundamental differences in the requirements of reading in different school subjects. He pointed out that each subject area has its own special concepts and vocabulary, unique relationships, logic, style, assumptions and basic principles. Russell, wrote: "Different disciplines require varied reading skills because they differ in technical vocabulary, in thought patterns used, and in specialised devices for presenting information such as graphs, symbols, and equations" (pp. 169–170). The special reading styles and techniques which are fitted to specific special subjects is the topic of several books in the field of reading education, for example, Herber's (1970) *Teaching Reading in Content Areas,* and Shepherd's (1960a, 1960b, 1973) three books on reading in social studies, science, and other subjects.

Reinforcement

In Andreas' classification of psychological research on motivation, the third and final motivational concept is "reinforcement." According to Skinner (1953), "reinforcement" is any experienced event that follows a response that increases the future probability of responses in the same class. Skinner states that any stimulus is a "reinforcer" if it increases the probability of a class of response. A "primary" reinforcer is one that satisfies a basic drive such as food for hunger. A "secondary" reinforcer is a stimulus that has become reinforcing after its association with a primary reinforcer. For example, a poker chip can become a secondary reinforcer when it is learned that it can be traded in for food. In reinforcement theory, the analysis of motivation is centered on the relationships, or contingencies, that exist between behaviors and environmental events. In conventional operant conditioning circles, the term "reinforcement" is adhered to and synonyms such as "reward" are shunned because of the extra meanings that have become associated with them in everyday language. For example, Andreas introduces the term "reinforcement" in a paragraph that repeatedly employs the term "reward." But much of the debate in this area of learning theory is about terminology. Skinner himself pointed out that statements employing terms such as "incentive" or "purpose" usually can be reduced to statements about operant conditioning. Thus, most of what we have written heretofor in this chapter could be translated into the language of operant conditioning. Words such as "reinforcement" employed in operant conditioning theory provide one coherent way of analyzing motivation. Reinforcement theory has stimulated much research and produced many changes in teaching methods in the schools such as "behavior modification" systems. Reading instruction is no exception.

Curiously, although behaviorists have prided themselves on their empiricism and objectivity, these virtues are usually applied only in their research methods *after the problem has been defined* and an experiment has been designed. All too often, the definition of the problem has been derived from subjective speculation on the basis of slight, if any, empirical observation of natural phenomena. This is the case with some of the main areas of operant conditioning studies in reading. Staats and his colleagues (Staats, 1968; Staats and Staats, 1962; Staats, Staats, Schutz, and Wolf, 1962) began their work on reinforcement in reading on the basis of the *belief* that motivation in the regular classroom is inadequate. Another founding belief was that tangible reinforcement such as candy or money is especially effective for socially disadvantaged pupils.

Rosen (1956), Terrell, Durkin, and Wiesley (1959), and Zigler and Kanzer (1962) found evidence that intrinsic reinforcement in the form of knowledge of results that one is correct is weaker than tangible reinforcement in facilitating learning in socially disadvantaged children. Ekwall (1973) states that the results obtained by "Hamner (1968) in studying the effectiveness of tangible and social reinforcements are typical of many studies. Hamner used three treatment groups in studying tangible and social reinforcements in culturally-deprived Negro children during instructional periods in individualized reading. His three treatment groups were: tangible reinforcement—a piece of candy, social reinforcement—'that's fine,' and customary group instruction where several chidren were in a group and no planned or deliberate reinforcement was given" (p. 195). The tangible reward treatment produced more correct responses than social reinforcement and the weakest results were from the "customary group instruction" condition.

However, Pikulski's two experiments produced the opposite results. Pikulski (1970) studied the relative effectiveness of (1) material reinforcement (candy); (2) social reinforcement (praise and enthusiasm); (3) knowledge of results; on the word recognition performance of kindergarten boys and girls from lower and middle socioeconomic classes. The results failed to support the hypothesis that children from lower-class backgrounds respond better to tangible rewards. In the second study (Pikulski, 1971), all the subjects were Black first-graders in a low socioeconomic area. They were randomly assigned to three treatment groups in respect of the same three types of reinforcement. Again the hypothesis was not supported. Pikulski concludes: "Thus, the results again suggest that children from low socioeconomic backgrounds do not necessarily need candy or some other form of material reinforcement in order for them to respond in an instructional situation. In fact, girls from such a population seem to find the approval and enthusiasm of the examiner significantly more rewarding. Examiner approval and enthusiasm were about as effective as candy with this population of boys" (p. 246).

Other studies have shown that knowledge of results can be a very effective reinforcer and that it may be as effective as a tangible reinforcer. Raygor, Wark and Warren (1966) used a flashing green light as a secondary reinforcer whenever a subject exceeded his previous rate of reading. The results showed that reading rate accelerated under this treatment—especially when the subject was told the function of the green light. D. E. P. Smith (1969) had children plot on a chart their own progress in word recognition and comprehension. The performance of these pupils who got knowledge of results in this way was equal to that of the group of subjects who received money as reinforcement and superior to the group that received reinforcement in the form of teacher praise and free time.

The other basic assumption of Staats and his colleagues has not been investigated. Bloom (1973) points out that "It is evident that children can learn to read under operant instructional arrangements. Using operant procedures, the reading acquisition progresses slowly at first but then rapidly accelerates as a function of training sessions (Staats, 1968). However, it is not possible to say that operant procedures are either superior or inferior to alternative approaches to reading with respect to such skills as word recognition and comprehension. This, of course, reflects the fact that there have been no direct comparisons between instructional programs which have explicitly incorporated operant strategies and other instructional programs" (p. 156). Hence, Staats' assumption that motivation for learning to read in regular (nonoperant) classrooms is inadequate remains an assumption. Moreover, the experiments of Raygor et al. and of Smith cited above raise considerable doubt about its validity.

A paradigm for operant conditioning in reading instruction is provided by the experiment of Staats, Staats, Schutz and Wolf (1962). Six four-year-olds were placed in a "textual program" in which 26 words were arranged so that they could be combined gradually into sentences and then into sets of sentences. The experimental materials consisted in words typed on cards, pictures of each word that was capable of illustration, and some discrimination cards that contained several typed words that could not be pictured. The program began with picture matching, went on to word matching, then matching word to picture, and so on. When the first five words were known, relevant sentences using them were introduced. The six subjects were divided into two reinforcement treatment groups. One group began with social reinforcement only and tangible reinforcement was introduced when the child wanted to stop. The second group began with tangible reinforcement; then after two days it was discontinued, but reintroduced when the child wanted to stop. The tangible reinforcers were candy or a small toy, or a token which was put on a token board. When the board was filled, the tokens could be exchanged for a "secret surprise."

The children who began with tangible reinforcement and then had it withdrawn all wanted to stop after the fifth or sixth day. Those who received no tangible reinforcement at the start all wanted to stop during the first or second day (each "day" there was one 45-minute session). Staats et al. claim that "This was, perhaps, the primary value of the reinforcers: i.e., they strengthened the behaviors of staying in the situation and working" (p. 39). Another experiment by Holt (1971) likewise showed a high level of productivity in terms of the number of words read by first-grade pupils under reinforcement conditions. At first no reinforcement was given and productivity was low, but when reinforcement was introduced (in the form of five minutes in a chosen activity) productivity rose to very high levels.

An example of the token reinforcement system used with older students is provided by the experiment reported by Martin, Schwyhart, and Wetzel (1973). Their study was conducted in six high-school remedial reading classes with a total of 95 students. Three were experimental classes and three were control. In the experimental classes a chart was posted on the bulletin board when each class met. This chart listed work and behavior and the number of points that could be earned for satisfactory performance. Also on the chart was listed each student's name with a space for each day in which the teacher entered the points earned by the students. Points could be gained readily by students who came to class and worked to the best of their ability. No points were subtracted. The points were tokens in the sense that they were linked to grades and other more tangible reinforcers. For six weeks of grade three or above a letter of commendation was sent to the student's parents and counselor. For six weeks of grade two or above the student was allowed to go on a school-sponsored activity, and for six weeks of grade one or above this was increased to two such activities.

There were significant differences in the students' productivity in the experimental versus control classes. In the experimental classes significantly more work was done, significantly more books and assignments were completed. Also there was significantly less aimlessness, absence and tardiness in the experimental classes. But, there was no significant difference in reading improvement under the two conditions. Thus the increase in "productivity" did not result in profits in terms of reading achievements.

A problem mentioned by several authors concerned with the operant conditioning approach to reading instruction is commented on by Ekwall. He states that "Most researchers have been in agreement that there is a wide variation in the manner in which children are likely to respond to various types of reinforcement" (p. 195). In terms of Skinner's own definition, Martin, Schwyhart, and Wetzel write: "Students vary as to what will function for them as reinforcers" (p. 184). This is reminiscent of the finding of our review of theory and research on children's interests. Planning motivating strategies on the basis of generalizations about children's interests, motives, drives, needs, and so on is inadequate. Teachers who relate reading instruction to the child's *individual* motivations are likely to achieve much better results.

Perhaps the most worrying outcome of operant conditioning studies in reading instruction is the rapid extinction of reading behavior when the extrinsic reinforcers are withdrawn. For example, in Pikulski's (1971) experiment he found that "children quickly forget the words they had learned to criterion in this study and fail to recognize the words when they are surrounded by other words" (p. 246). Reviewing the experiments of Staats and his associates, Bloom (1973) concludes that "The effects of such manipulations on reading behavior have been generally consistent with behavioral outcomes obtained within a laboratory setting. For example, under conditions of withdrawal of tokens after consistent reinforcement, there tends to be a marked reduction in reading activity. This closely parallels the phenomenon of extinction in which behavioral output can be drastically reduced subsequent to the termination of reinforcement" (p. 156).

Even more disturbing is the finding cited earlier in this chapter that children's intrinsic interest in an activity is undermined by relating it to a system of extrinsic incentives. Furthermore, we do not know what may be the side-effects of extrinsic reinforcers on the development of children's concepts of the purposes of reading. They may be learning such false concepts as—reading is for getting candy, points, praise and so on.

Related to the operant conditioning studies reviewed above is the teaching method known as "behavior modification" which has been applied quite extensively in remedial education. This approach was derived from Skinner's analysis of the way in which animals can be trained to perform complex feats simply by reinforcing behavior that was closer to the desired performance. Gradually, step by step, such reinforcement leads up to the specific response that is required. However, it may be questioned whether it is the technique or the terminology of behavior modification that is new. Harris and Sipay remark that "It is evident that reinforcement theory provides one kind of theoretical explanation for the strong emphasis that good remedial teachers were placing on motivation long before the concepts of behavioral modification were developed" (p. 328). Perhaps, it is worth adding that good remedial teachers also have not limited their attention to the provision of rewards for responses that happen to be correct. They often have treated their disabled readers as thinking persons who are capable of reasoning about the tasks and problems to be solved in learning how to read.

Attitudes

To Andreas' three categories of motivational concepts we add this fourth type—*attitudes.* Because this does not seem to fit well with "arousal," "incentives," or "reinforcement," we have given it a special section to end this chapter on the affective bases of the acquisition of reading skill.

Attitude is a concept that has developed chiefly in the field of social psychology. Allport (1966) states: "This concept is probably the most distinctive and indispensable concept in contemporary American social psychology. No term appears more frequently in experimental and theoretical literature" (p. 15). Allport cites his own definition written originally in 1935 but which he considers is still viable:

> An attitude is a mental and neural state of readiness, organized through experience, exerting a directive or dynamic influence upon the individual's response to all objects and situations with which it is related (Allport, 1966, p. 20).

The term "attitude" is used rather loosely in everyday conversation, and is often taken to be synonymous with such terms as "belief," "faith," "value," "opinion" and so on. But, in psychology, "attitude" has the more restricted meaning that is contained in Allport's definition. Its most important feature is its "exerting a directive or dynamic influence upon the individual's response." When psychologists measure attitudes they do not seek merely surface opinions. They may ask subjects their opinions, but they are delving deeper for the underlying attitudes that cause such opinions to be expressed and which influence other actions as well as stating certain opinions. Another definition of attitude is that it is *a tendency to behave in a particular manner toward a certain object or situation.* We are interested here in children's tendencies to behave in a particular manner toward books and reading.

Once again we need to recall that attitude is not a distinctly different type of behavior from that discussed under arousal, incentives and reinforcement. Rather these are alternative ways of discussing affective phenomena. Much of what has been discussed in those earlier sections may well have been included here under the heading of attitudes. But, actually, very little use has been made in the field of reading research of the scientific concept of attitude. This is all the more surprising when one considers how fruitful have been the applications of attitude research in other practical areas such as marketing, industrial psychology, politics and so on.

Summers (1977) recently reviewed the development of research instruments for assessing reading attitudes. He concluded that "The small number of studies dealing with instrument development is indicative of the low activity to date in this area. Although we have shelves of writing proclaiming the desirability of developing positive attitudes towards books and reading and, to somewhat lesser extent, materials to use in attitude change in reading, with some exceptions few adequately standardized tools for measuring change in attitude have been developed" (p. 140). Summers accurately states the chief weaknesses in this area of research when he writes: "Adequate conceptualization and definition of reading attitude constructs is still a major problem in research in the field. More application of attitude theory from social psychology could provide useful guidelines." Also "Few existing scales are based on clear underlying concepts. In fact, many scales are not only concept poor but do not exhibit even the rudimentary elements of attitude definition as set out in previous research" (p. 152).

The unsatisfactory state of research on reading attitudes is all the more disappointing when one reads the many speculative generalizations about the importance of positive attitudes toward books and reading.

An indication of future improvement in this research field may be seen in a number of theoretical articles as well as Summers' review cited above. Mathewson (1976) has proposed an affective theory that he terms the "Acceptance Model." He chooses "attitude as the central construct in a model of affective influence upon reading" (p. 656). Mathewson finds it necessary to make a special provision for motivation *in addition to* attitude "to insure that favorable attitude has a separate, energizing process to accompany it." This seems to us to be in conflict with the widely accepted definition of attitude by Allport that we quoted at the beginning of this section.

Mathewson also argues that "there is probably no general attitude toward reading . . . because there is no person who likes *all* types of reading" (p. 659). We would disagree with this view because it is a common observation that a substantial number of pupils do indeed hate *all* types of reading. Mathewson proposes that the attitude that a child has toward a particular book will be specific to that book and it will depend on "three aspects—content, format, and form." But we would point out that in attitude research in other fields it is generally accepted that there may be a general overall attitude toward a class of objects and at the same time a variety of specific attitudes toward particular objects within that class. For example, in a study of Irish women's attitudes toward butter and magarine, Downing (1960) found distinctive attitudes toward these two foods, but there were also quite different attitudes toward different brands of those products. Similarly, we would hypothesize that if people were asked to compare their preference for watching T.V. versus reading a book most people would be able to express a *general* preference even though there are some individual books and some individual T.V. programs that they like and others that they detest. Ewing (1978) also has criticized Mathewson's model on the grounds that "it may omit the importance of something more general, more fundamental than specific factors" (p. 157). Ewing goes on to propose his own "general affective factor model" that "is based on the assumption that the affective contribution to learning can be explained in terms of a general underlying factor, i.e. positive affect produces effective learning and negative affect produces poor learning" (p. 165). Ewing's model is more in accord with attitude theory in social psychology than is Mathewson's.

Despite the above-mentioned logical problems of detail, Mathewson's Acceptance Model provides a structured way of thinking about the relationship between attitudes and reading. In essence, he is proposing that a favorable attitude toward the attributes of a particular book, plus a motive to fulfill some need through reading it, arouses pupils' attention and triggers off the reading comprehension process.

Three types of causal variables have been studied in connection with children's attitudes toward reading: sex differences, home environment, and school experiences.

Sex Differences

American research has found that girls have more positive attitudes toward reading than do boys. For example, Hansen (1969) found that "Girls in the study showed a significantly higher reading attitude than the boys and read a significantly greater number of books" (p. 23). These were American fourth-grade pupils. Another study, this time at secondary school level found that female students scored significantly higher than male students on a Likert (1970) type reading attitude scale: "Females generally have been recognized by reading experts as being more interested in reading than males, as having a more positive attitude toward reading. According to expectation, the females scored significantly higher on the instrument" (Kennedy and Halinski, 1975, p. 521). However, Morris' (1966) important survey of reading in Kent, England found "no difference between the attitudes to reading of boys and girls" aged ten and eleven years (p. 185). Sex differences in reading behavior are not universal across all cultures.

Home Background

Almost everywhere, attitudes toward reading have been found to be associated with certain experiences of children with their parents at home. Hansen's (1969, 1973) two reports on a study of the home literary environment of 48 fourth-grade pupils focused on this question. Their attitudes toward reading were measured on a scale that was said to be reliable and valid, and the scores were related to the responses on a "home literary environment" questionnaire. Also examined were the students' IQs, fathers' occupations, and fathers' education. A multiple regression analysis revealed that the home literary environment made the only significant contribution to the pupils' reading attitudes. IQ, father's occupation and education were not related to the pupils' reading attitudes. Hansen's second report gave a breakdown of the scores on the individual items in the home literary environment questionnaire. This showed that "the one factor that stands out from all the others is the role of the parent in being involved with his child's reading activities. Working with homework; encouraging, helping select, and discussing his reading; reading to him; assistance in looking things up in dictionaries and encyclopedias; and setting reading goals were more important than the mere provision of materials" (Hansen, 1973, p. 98).

Hansen's (1973) results showed that parental modeling was of low importance: "It appears that it is not necessary for parents to be avid readers for them to rear children who are." It is their active interactions with the child's reading that counts. Hansen warns against making gross socioeconomic generalizations about home environments and notes that one of the highest scorers (on the attitude scale) was a child whose parents could not afford many books but who began systematically using the library from the child's birth on.

School Experiences

Oliver (1976) writes that "Attitudes related to reading are influenced by the experiences that the child has in the name of reading" (p. 13). This was recognized more than two centuries ago when Rousseau (1762) commented on Emile's education in reading:

> I would rather he would never know how to read than to buy his knowledge at the price of all that can make it useful. Of what use would reading be to him after he had been disgusted with it forever?

How this disgust for reading can be caused by inappropriate instructional methods is clearly shown in two investigations.

Kelley (1965) reports a pilot program in trying out the introduction of reading in an American kindergarten at the period when this policy was beginning to become more popular. In her pilot program no child was made to read who did not want to, and no child was excluded from the reading group who wanted to read. The preliminary evaluation of the pilot program showed that the children who had learned to read in kindergarten were, by second grade, not only significantly advanced in reading achievement, but also were more positive in their attitudes toward reading.

These good results encouraged the undertaking of a more rigorously controlled experiment to obtain more dependable scientific data on the effects of teaching reading in kindergarten. For this scientific purpose it was necessary to establish an experimental group of kindergartners who *all* received reading and a control group of kindergartners *none* of whom were allowed to read. Because of this design, some children in the control group who wanted to read were frustrated and some children in the experimental group were pressured to read who just could not learn. At the end of the kindergarten year an attitude inventory revealed that the control group had more favorable attitudes than did the experimental group.

Even more devastating are the results reported by Morris (1966) that were cited earlier in this chapter in the section on the causes of failure-threat anxiety. They need to be recalled here. By age eleven, 87 per cent of good readers but only 37 per cent of poor readers had positive attitudes toward reading. Clearly there is a connection between reading achievement level and attitude toward reading. Nonetheless, one third of Morris' poor readers did have positive attitudes toward reading. Thus the relationship between attitude and achievement is not a simple one. Roettger (1980) reports an interview study of fourth, fifth, and sixth graders who had been categorized into two extreme groups—"low attitude/high performance" and "high attitude/low performance," on the basis of their scores on the *Estes Attitude Scales* (Estes, Roettger, Johnstone and Richards, 1976) and on a reading comprehension test. The interview data indicated that the high attitude/low performance pupils "viewed reading as an important tool for survival" in everyday life situations, whereas for the low attitude/high performance pupils "reading was a means of gaining information to help them get good grades, do their school work . . ." (p. 452). This latter group seem likely to become what are termed "nonreaders" in Japan—people who can read but do not choose to do so (Sakamoto and Makita, 1973, p. 445).

Southgate (1973) clearly expressed the practical implications of such findings when she stated: "In all reading tuition the first aim should be to produce children and adults who want to read and who do read" (p. 372). We have noted earlier in this chapter that certain instructional methods are particularly useful in developing purposeful attitudes toward reading. For example, the language-experience approach to reading is the surest method of making reading functional for the child from the start. It is interesting to note that the language-experience approach is the only teaching method specifically advocated in the 500 page Bullock Report (see p. 103 and p. 107). Another method that has the specific aim of fostering favorable attitudes toward reading books is the one we described earlier as the "lure into reading." Bamberger (1972) claims that, "Reports by many teachers show that even the most reluctant and slow readers can be won over by this method and will in fact read a complete book within a few days" (p. 138). Bamberger (1973) emphasizes that "The aim of this Austrian venture has never been to merely develop effective readers but to help bring about lifelong reading interests and lifelong reading habits as well. This goal cannot be achieved through the training of reading skills alone but only when the child has experienced the real joy of reading" (p. 199).

Beside the general overall positive attitude toward reading and books that may be created by programs such as the language-experience approach and the lure into reading, it has been recognized that specific attributes of books may affect children's attitudes toward them. This possibility led Lowery and Grafft (1968) to test the effect of the paperback format of books on the reading attitudes of fourth-grade pupils. An experimental group had paperback books in the classroom while a control group had clothbound editions of the same books. Clothbound editions of these books were available also in the library which the pupils were encouraged to visit. These children's attitudes toward reading were measured on a projective test before and after the eight-week period of the experiment. The attitudes of children in the experimental group were significantly influenced by the use of the paperbacks. The authors of this study report that "Boys and girls who used the paperbacks showed significant increases in their number of pleasant or positive attitudes and a decrease in their number of negative attitudes. . . . It seems that there is 'something' about the paperback book which has an important and positive effect upon the attitudes of fourth grade students" (p. 623).

We agree with Summers' (1977) conclusion that more research should be conducted in this field. His words serve as an apt summing up for this section:

> Attitude research will add an important dimension to the study of affective functioning. Attitudes constitute a significant source of behavioral variance and could serve to integrate and explain a wide range of behavior (p. 153).

Until this field of research on children's attitudes to reading is as systematically developed as it has been in other fields of applied psychology, we shall continue to be able to give only rather generalized answers to those two questions that we posed at the beginning of this chapter: (1) what conditions produce motivation to learn how to read? (2) what conditions produce motivation to engage in reading activities?

CH

12

The Home Background

The pupil's environmental situation in acquiring the skill of reading is shown in Figure 12–1. The limits of the child's universe are those of the culture. They are somewhat distant boundaries. Closer and more definite are the mores of the subculture, and, within this, the habits of the family. The school environment has overlapping boundaries with the other areas. The school environment usually is concordant with the culture but it may be more or less in harmony with the subculture and the family. For example, children are born into an environment which includes the language of the culture as a whole. But they may learn to speak in a family that is part of a subculture which uses a dialect that has low status in the larger culture. When children go to school they may find it is more or less outside the boundaries of their subculture because the teachers reject their dialect. Thus the school environment may or may not cut across the areas of subculture and family. For some children the school zone lies outside their own territory of subculture and family. Such children are often said to be "disadvantaged" because the language and customs of the school are foreign to them and they have to make adjustments to succeed in this strange environment. In contrast, children whose family and subculture are more in harmony with the school environment do not feel like foreigners when they begin their formal education. These four environmental zones—culture, subculture, family and school—all have important influences on children's development of reading skill.

Figure 12–1. "Map" of environmental situation in reading.

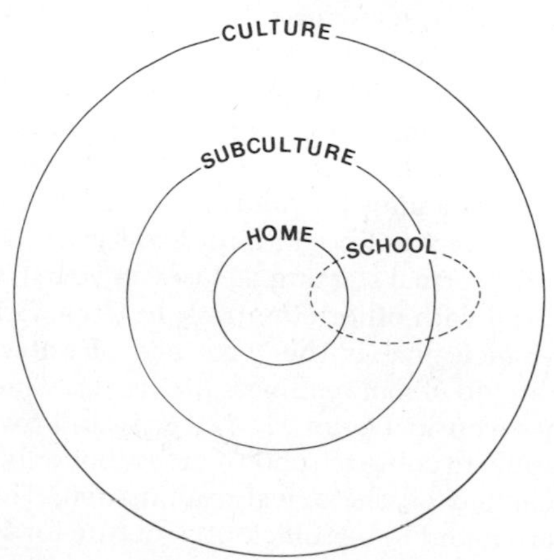

Culture

"Culture" is a technical term from sociology, anthropology, and social psychology that refers to the total way of life that has been developed by a group of human beings and transmitted from generation to generation. It is a neutral descriptive term without value judgment. The vast range of cultural influences is indicated by this definition by Havighurst and Neugarten (1975): "By a *culture* we refer to the patterns and products of learned behavior: the etiquette, language, food habits, religious and moral beliefs, systems of knowledge, attitudes and values; as well as the material things and artifacts produced—the technology—of a group of people" (p. 6). There are innumerable ways in which culture may influence the child's approach to school and literacy acquisition.

Cultural Esteem for Literacy

An overriding cultural influence on the acquisition of literacy is the value that people place on reading and writing abilities. Cultures vary in the position that they assign to literacy learning in their scale of educational priorities. Also some cultures make literacy behavior more appropriate for one part of the population than for another.

It cannot be taken for granted that universal literacy is either expected or even desired in all cultures. For instance, a frequent cause of restriction on literacy has been the preservation of secrecy as in religious or magical books. Goody (1968) concluded that "such restrictive practices tend to arise wherever people have an interest in maintaining a monopoly of the sources of their power" (p. 12). He describes also how literacy is restricted by making the written code too difficult for the majority of people to learn easily or effectively: "The situation of socially restricted literacy is often similar to the technological restrictions imposed by non-phonetic systems of writing, where the sheer difficulties of learning the skill mean that it can be available only to a limited number of people" (p. 19). Goody concludes that China "stands as an extreme example of how, when a virtually non-phonetic system of writing becomes sufficiently developed to express a large number of meanings explicitly, only a small and specially trained professional group in the total society can master it, and partake of the literate culture" (p. 36).

A common problem in raising standards of literacy in the general population is the inertia of written language in comparison with its spoken form and cultural values. Thus, China today does have the national aim of universal literacy, but the Chinese writing system, which previously served well to restrict literacy, is now regarded by many people as a hindrance to cultural aspirations. Mao Tse-tung declared, in 1951, that, "The written language must be reformed; it should follow the common direction of phoneticization which has been taken by the world's languages" (Mills, 1955–1956). Chou En-lai also favored reforming the Chinese writing system (Chou, Wu and Li, 1958).

Certainly it has been recognized that the democratization of literacy may be facilitated by improving the way in which language is coded in the writing system. Diringer (1948) viewed the alphabet as democratic compared with nonalphabetic writing systems, and Goody noted that "the ease of alphabetic reading and writing was probably an important consideration in the development of political democracy in Greece" (p. 55). However, alphabets vary in their degree of alphabeticism. For example, in Finnish the alphabet is a consistent code for the phonemes of that language, whereas English orthography is more complex because it codes other linguistic elements. In addition, the complexity of English orthography is due to a large extent to inertia. When one considers the social history of England and the late development of a national goal of universal literacy there, the hypothesis that twentieth-century aims in the English-speaking countries are hampered by a writing system more suited to the purpose of restricting literacy cannot be dismissed lightly. The lag between the national goals in literacy and the development of the writing system may be a problem that differs only in degree from one culture to another. When the language and writing system are shared by several nations, the lag may have more serious consequences. For instance, the "Right to Read" policy of the United States had to operate with a writing system that was developed in England when this "human right" would have been vigorously denied there.

Citron (1976) argues that restrictive motives continue to apply to literacy in the English-speaking cultures. He theorizes that the complexities of the traditional orthography of English are effective "in keeping the lower classes from encroaching on privileged preserves. Written language was not patented for the poor nor handed down for common folk" (p. 16). Citron's experiments in schools in Detroit showed that spelling "errors" were reduced by about 50 per cent when words were required to be written in a simplified orthography instead of the more complex traditional orthography of English.

The dramatic contrast between cultures that restrict literacy and those that have the aim of universal literacy serves to alert us to the possibility of other less obvious cultural influences on literacy learning. Downing (1973) found evidence that literacy is given differing levels of priority from one culture to another. In Denmark, Norway, and Sweden, for example, great importance is attached to the child's "school readiness" (not "reading" readiness). Children who are not ready for school may not begin until eight years of age. Even the normal starting age (seven years) is late compared with other countries. In Great Britain, for instance, five is the legal age of entry and there are no school readiness provisions. Children under seven in Denmark, Norway, and Sweden may apply to come to school earlier, but only after medical and psychological examination. Then, if they are found to be sufficiently mature for school work, they may be permitted to start school in the year they reach their sixth birthday. In these Scandinavian countries educators emphasize also that school must give the child a relaxed and cautious start in reading. The principle applied at all levels is that the central concern must be the learner, that is, the whole person, not some limited segment of development, such as reading. In other countries, literacy acquisition is given a higher priority. For example, the majority of the world's research, scholarly articles, and theoretical and professional books on reading is sited in the United States. In that country every aspect of the child's educational environment that is influenced by public educational agencies displays the tangible results of the deepest and most extensive national concern for reading ability.

Downing reviewed alternative causes of this greater concern for reading achievements in American culture and concluded that "pressures on the child to learn literacy skills are much greater in some countries than others. There are clear indications that this is based on cultural values. In the scale of values, reading gets a higher priority in some cultures than it does in others. The risk of emotional disturbance due to pressure to learn to read at an early age is considered seriously in some countries but is more or less disregarded in others" (p. 112).

Sex-role Standards

The ways in which literacy is restricted to an elite class have been noted earlier, but sometimes restrictions follow different lines. A high value may be placed on literacy in a culture, but it may be a customary belief that a certain part of the community is less in need of literacy than the rest. The most common form of this discrimination is along sex lines. Historically, in many countries, girls received less literacy training than boys. Today this same trend still persists in some countries. Furthermore, there seem to be other cultural variations in differential attitudes toward boys and girls that may affect their literacy learning behavior.

Nearly all North American investigations, among the more important being those of Samuels (1943), Carroll (1948), Prescott (1955), and Anderson, Hughes and Dixon (1957), show significant differences between boys and girls on reading readiness measures in favor of the girls, though one or two other investigators, for example Potter (1949), and Konski (1955), found no significant differences. Once children are able to read, then North American research also shows quite clearly that on that continent girls have a superiority over boys in the normal classroom situation—for example, Durrell (1940), Alden, Sullivan and Durrell (1941), and Gates (1961). This finding was confirmed by the large-scale research reported by Dykstra and Tinney (1969). They compared 1,659 boys and 1,624 girls from schools in Pennsylvania, Michigan, New York, and New Jersey. Data were collected on reading readiness as well as on reading achievements in grades one and two. The statistical evidence unquestionably showed the superiority of girls both in readiness and in later reading.

In the past, before comparisons began to be made with other countries, it was usually assumed that the female superiority in reading found in the North American studies was a universal human characteristic, and explanations were sought in terms of a differential rate or level of maturation in girls as compared with boys. Thus, Anderson and Dearborn (1952) and Harris and Sipay state that girls tend to reach puberty about one and a half years earlier than boys, and from birth on there are detectable differences in physiological maturity. Similarly, with regard to language development, McCarthy's (1935) finding that, by the twentieth month of life, girls are superior in the production of speech sounds, and also that girls begin to talk somewhat earlier than boys and their childhood vocabularies are larger was widely accepted. Girls' greater maturity in speech had been reported also in a study by Davis (1937). Several studies had found also that speech defects are more common among boys than girls (Lincoln, 1927; Louttit, 1935; Burt, 1937; Missildine and Glasner, 1947).

An unexplained earlier finding was that, when their oral language abilities were equated, Durrell (1940) found that still twice as many boys as girls were reported as poor readers. Furthermore, the earlier maturation of girls has been called in question by more recent studies. For example, Maccoby and Jacklin (1974) conclude that "recent evidence does not clearly indicate that girls undergo more rapid verbal development in the first few years of life" (p. 311).

Anderson and Hughes (1955) related sex differences to their general theoretical position that children who are advanced in general maturity succeed in reading, and those who are retarded physically tend to fail in reading. However, other studies over a long period, for example, those of

Gates (1924), Abernethy (1936), Dearborn and Rothney (1941), and Blommers, Knief and Stroud (1955), have investigated the relationship between mental and physical growth, and found only very low correlations. Stroud (1956), pointed out that rarely did these correlation coefficients exceed .20. He concluded that anatomical and physiological growth are related neither to reading achievement nor to mental development. Thus, there appears to be very little evidence to support the view that general maturity is an important factor in readiness to learn to read. Therefore, it seems unlikely, if girls did mature earlier, it would explain the sex differences that have been found in reading achievements in North American education.

Skepticism of the differential maturation hypothesis is increased when one considers the contrasting patterns of differences between the sexes in their reading achievements from one country to another. In some countries the opposite result to the North American finding has been reported. Boys were found to have superior reading achievements to girls in Nigeria (Abiri, 1969), India (Oommen, 1973), Germany (Preston, 1962), and Finland (Viitaniemi, 1965). In England, which shares some common linguistic and cultural variables with the U.S.A. and Canada, there have been conflicting findings on this question but this conflict of evidence too is different from the general agreement in North American research that girls are at an advantage over boys in beginning reading. Thackray's (1965) first reading readiness survey in England found that the scores of the girls were significantly superior to those of the boys on two of five reading readiness measures. However, Thackray's (1971) second study found no significant differences between boys and girls. With regard to reading achievements in Britain, evidence concerning the relative performance of boys and girls on reading tests also is rather conflicting. Some reading surveys, such as those carried out in the towns of Brighton, Middlesborough and Swansea, found girls superior to boys in reading ability; but the important carefully conducted Ministry of Education reading surveys of 1948, 1952 and 1956, (Ministry of Education, 1950 and 1957) and Morris' (1966) later survey of one English county found no significant difference between the sexes' reading attainments, a trend showing, if anything, that boys were superior to girls. On the other hand, Kellmer Pringle, Butler and Davie (1966) in their study covering Britain as a whole found girls were consistently superior to boys in reading. If one may generalize at all from these conflicting results, the conclusion would appear to be that in Britain there is a rather weak trend for girls to achieve better in reading than boys on average, but that the difference between the sexes is quite unimportant.

Klein (1977) raises a number of questions about the validity of crosscultural comparisons for studying the causation of sex differences in reading achievements. For example, the studies cited thus far have been disparate investigations that were not designed specifically to make crosscultural comparisons. Comparison of their data has to be on a *post hoc* basis.

Unfortunately, planned crosscultural studies thus far have not been very successful. Both of the large-scale crossnational tests of reading conducted by the IEA group (Foshay, Thorndike, Hotyat, Pidgeon, and Walker, 1962; Thorndike, 1973a) ran into such serious methodological problems that no valid conclusions could be drawn regarding sex differences in reading across cultures (Downing, 1973; Downing and Dalrymple-Alford, 1974–1975). However, Johnson's (1973–1974) more modest crosscultural investigation provided comparable statistics from objective testing in four different countries. He administered the same English language reading attainment test in Canada, England, Nigeria and the United States. Only in Canada and the United States was there a clear superiority of the females tested. In Nigeria the males were significantly ahead. In England the boys also had an overall advantage, but the results were more mixed on the various subtests.

It is often asserted that in all countries boys outnumber girls in treatment centers for reading disability. For example, Klein cites Orlow's (1976) contention that many more boys than girls suffer from *Legasthenie* (dyslexia) in Germany. Research statistics confirm a similar trend elsewhere. For example, Schonell (1942) in a survey of 15,000 London school children, found that 5 per cent of boys and 2.5 per cent of girls were retarded in reading development by 1.5 years or more. The Ministry of Education (1950) survey for England found about twice as many boys as girls were in the lowest category of "illiterate."

When one examines the statistics for cases referred to clinics, the consistent difference between the sexes appears even more remarkable. Monroe (1932) and Blanchard (1936) each independently reported that 86 per cent of their reading disability cases were boys. Fernald's (1943) cases were 97 per cent boys, and Young (1938) had 90 per cent boys among 41 reading-disabled cases.

The theory that specific reading disability or dyslexia is a sex-linked hereditary condition is found in almost every text on dyslexia. For example, Miles (1974) writes that "it is more common in boys than in girls . . ." (p. 86). Crosby (1969) states that "dyslexia . . . occurs three to four times as frequently among males as females" (p. 10). Critchley (1970) reviewed the evidence from many clinical surveys and concluded "that about 4 males to 1 female may be accepted as a reasonable figure" (p. 91). There is little doubt that these statistics are accurate. However, Critchley's phrasing raises a very interesting problem about the meaning of such statistics: "Of my own 616 cases referred to me as potential dyslexics, and personally examined, 487 were males and 129 were females" (p. 91). This makes it clear that Critchley's statistics cannot tell us about the *prevalence* of dyslexia in the population. His cases were not a representative sample of the population. His statistics refer only to the *incidence* among boys and girls who were *selected for referral* to his clinic. The same defect is true of all the other statistics on dyslexia of this type. There may be many nonbiological but cultural causes for boys being picked out for special treatment more often than girls. For example, Vernon (1957) has proposed that boys are selected more frequently because their reading failure is more often accompanied by aggressive emotions than it is in the case of girls.

An unusual opportunity to study the prevalence of reading disability among unselected boys and girls in the general population instead of its incidence in those selected for special treatment occurs in the Israeli kibbutz system. The possibility of studying differences between boys' and girls' behavior in the kibbutz system is good because observational and test records are kept routinely on all the children from an early age. Gross (1978) studied a sample of 305 kindergartners, second-graders and fifth-graders randomly selected from a population of 1,871 kibbutz children at these grade levels. She found no significant differences between the sexes in reading performance. Furthermore, "No gender differences were evident in percentage of reading disability cases. Thirteen per cent of both boys and girls were found to be reading disabled (13 out of 102 boys, 12 out of 96 girls)." Even more pertinent was Gross's finding that, "crossed dominance, maturational lag, and 12 addi

of psychopathology were found to

to cases of male reading disability" (p. 153). [illegible] results raise doubts about theories that boys are necessarily at a disadvantage in learning to read because of their biological sex.

One rigorous study of classroom behavior revealed an interesting difference between girls and boys that may provide a bridge to a different kind of explanation of the pattern of achievements of girls' and boys' reading. Samuels and Turnure (1974) used a behavioral observation schedule to investigate sex differences in classroom attentiveness and its relation to reading achievement among a sample of American first-grade boys and girls. They found that the girls were significantly more attentive than boys during the reading period, and that "increasing degrees of attention were related to superior word recognition" (p. 31). Samuels and Turnure relate this finding to that of Cobb and Hops (1973) that overt task-relevant orienting behavior is connected with scholastic achievement. Samuels and Turnure conclude that "the sex difference favoring girls frequently found in reading achievement seems to be mediated by an attentional variable" (p. 31).

Why should these American girls have been more attentive than the American boys in this study by Samuels and Turnure? A probable answer is suggested by what Dwyer (1973) refers to as *"cultural expectations for the male sex role.* Boys' perceptions of school and the reading activity as inappropriate to or in conflict with development of the male sex role may depress boys' achievement" (p. 455). In other words, if reading is not perceived as masculine, it deserves less attention from boys—indeed to pay too much attention to reading may betray femininity.

Dwyer's concept of "cultural expectations" refers to the *source* of students' perceptions of what behavior is appropriate for their sex-roles. The *actual perceptions themselves* are often referred to as "sex-role standards." Thus the *cultural expectations* held by adults and older children influence the development of *sex-role standards* in younger members of the culture. The concept of sex-role standards was proposed originally by Kagan (1964). He found that second- and third-graders considered many school-related objects and activities were feminine. This concept has been developed further by Stein and Smithells (1968, 1969), Stein (1971), and Stein, Pohly, and Mueller (1971). The more popular belief of the American children in the study by Stein and Smithells (1969) was that reading activities are feminine. Tregaskis (1972) found that American boys in first grade already sex-typed reading as feminine. Downing and Thomson (1977) found that the majority of elementary school, high school, and college students as well as a random sample of adults in one Canadian city considered reading a more appropriate activity for young girls than for young boys.

Three studies have found a relationship between reading achievements and either cultural expectations or sex-role standards. Palardy (1969) reported that boy pupils whose first-grade teachers believed that boys are less successful than girls in learning to read, had poorer achievements in reading than a comparable group of boy pupils whose teachers believed that boys are as successful as girls in learning to read. Mazurkiewicz (1960) found that the reading achievement scores of a sample of eleventh-grade boys were higher for those students who considered reading as a masculine activity than for those students who perceived it as feminine. Dwyer's (1974) study of boys and girls in grades two through twelve revealed that sex-role standards contributed significant variance to test scores in reading.

These studies of the relationship between sex-role standards and the reading achievements of boys versus girls referred to above were conducted in either Canada or the United States. A recent study by Downing and an international team of educational researchers (1979) investigated cultural expectations and sex-role standards about reading in Canada, Denmark, England, Finland, Israel, Japan, and U.S.A. A picture test showing various activities and objects including reading and books was administered in each country to six subsamples that approximated to the levels: students in grades one, four, eight, and twelve, college students, and adults. Subjects had to ascribe the activity or object as being appropriate for either a boy or a girl.

The results showed that cultural expectations and sex-role standards were congruent with one another in each country, but that they were different from one country to another. All boys began by accepting reading as a masculine activity. In Canada and the U.S.A. boys quickly learned to allocate reading to the feminine role. But in Denmark and Japan males of all ages continued to regard reading as masculine. In England, Finland and Israel the pattern of development of the male attitudes was more similar to that found in North America, though less exaggerated. An experiment in Berlin, Germany using the same test materials obtained results similar to those reported above from Denmark and Japan. Reading was perceived by males of all ages as appropriate for the masculine role (Valtin, 1979). These findings show that cultural attitudes toward reading as being suited more to one sex-role than the other vary from country to country and that school children quite rapidly adopt these cultural values. However, one must be cautious in generalizing about national characteristics in this way. We need to reflect that there are likely to be many differences between subcultural groups and individuals. Steiner (1981), using the same picture test as Downing et al. found different results in a sample of children in grades one through four in two private Catholic schools in Ohio. The boys in her study did not sex-type reading as feminine. All these results increase our skepticism about theories of biologically determined sex differences in reading performance.

A skeptical view is indicated also by recent medical research on differences between boys and girls in other aspects of their behavior. For example, the extensive research of Money and his colleagues on hermaphrodites and other abnormal sexual developments led Money and Ehrhardt (1972) to conclude that "the brain's primary gender assignment in infancy and early childhood is to code into coherent and separate systems that which constitutes culturally prescribed masculinity versus femininity. This learning assignment is identical for boys and girls. The difference for each sex is the sign, positive or negative, with which each gender system is coded" (p. 244). Green and Money (1969) write that "the child's psychosexual identity is not written, unlearned, in the genetic code, the hormonal system, or the nervous system at birth. The child becomes conditioned to adhere to the positive model which is the one congruous with his rearing and, in the normal course of events, consistent with his anatomy. The opposite or negative valence model becomes a constant reminder of how one should *not* act" (p. 129).

The exact ways in which boys and girls become conditioned to the positive and negative models described by Green and Money has not been ascertained in regard to reading behavior, but Downing and Thackray have hypothesized that cultural institutions in the United States are responsible—for example, parents' differential approval of time being devoted to reading by their sons or daughters (see pp. 20–21). Some investigations have focused on more specific factors within the American cultural bias toward the femininity of reading. Several studies examined the relationship between the sex of the teacher and boys' reading achievements. Preston (1979) reviewed them and concluded that their general consensus is that male teachers are not more successful than female teachers in teaching reading to boys. In the same article, Preston reports his own study conducted in Germany where girls' achievements in reading are not superior to those of boys. He found that the sex of German teachers was not related to the reading achievements of either boys or girls. An effort to modify methods and materials to make them more appealing to American boys in kindergarten was made in an experiment by Stanchfield (1973). By the end of the year boys were equal to girls and their reading achievements remained on an equal level when followed up two years later. But in Tregaskis' (1972) experiment boys in a masculinized first-grade reading program made no better progress than the boys in a control group.

Research on the causes of sex differences in reading has barely begun. As Preston (1979) proposes, "New approaches to the study of factors that affect sex differences in reading achievement are called for. Investigation of adult reading habits in contrasting cultures might provide clues. Also needed is inquiry into the makeup of the elementary school's climate in contrasting cultures" (p. 525).

The Language of the Culture

One important item in the definition of culture given by Havighurst and Neugarten that we quoted earlier in this chapter was "language." In other words, the specific language of a people is an integral part of their culture. Usually, that language in its written form will be the vehicle for reading instruction. We described in Chapter 4 how the task of learning to read differs from one language to another. Hence, those important differences can be said also to be culturally determined. The fundamental importance of these differences is indicated in Luria's (1966a) statement that "the different bases for writing in different languages must entail a different cortical organization" (p. 411). For example, clinical studies in Japan of aphasic patients with and without apraxia of speech by Sasanuma and Fujimura (1971, 1972) seem to indicate that different neural mechanisms are involved in processing Kanji characters (representing morphemes) and Kana characters (representing speech syllables). Leong (1978a) comments that therefore, "The Kana transcription seems to relate to the 'phonological processor' in the brain while the Kanji transcription could bypass such processing" (p. 170). Leong states that, if these Japanese research results are substantiated, it would indicate that the role of the auditory short-term store, so important in learning to read in English, must be diminished in acquiring reading skill in Chinese or the Kanji system of Japanese. The chief point in Leong's article is that fundamental problems of theory and practice in reading instruction cannot be answered without analyzing the nature of the task of learning to read. The specific nature of the task of learning to read depends on the particular written language to be interpreted and this is an integral part of the culture.

Subculture

Wolfson (1976) gives the following definition of "subcultures":

> These are cultures which exist within the framework of a larger culture. In complex and varied societies, e.g. Britain, several sub-cultures, such as black, immigrant, and working class, can be identified. Members of a sub-culture, although adhering to a greater or lesser extent to the values and social norms of the wider culture, also have their own values and norms, and they may differ in social structure and patterns from the main culture of which they form a part. Usually when there are several different sub-cultures one of these becomes dominant, and its particular social patterns and values become the standard ones for the whole culture (p. 121).

Usually the school system of a culture is controlled by the dominant subculture. This is a potentially hazardous situation for all the other subcultures. They may find that the school environment is foreign to their norms and values.

Language Mismatch

Figure 12–2 is a simplified map of the relationship between the language of the child and the language of school instruction. Under unilingual conditions children use their cognitive processes (center circle in Figure 12–2) to make sense of

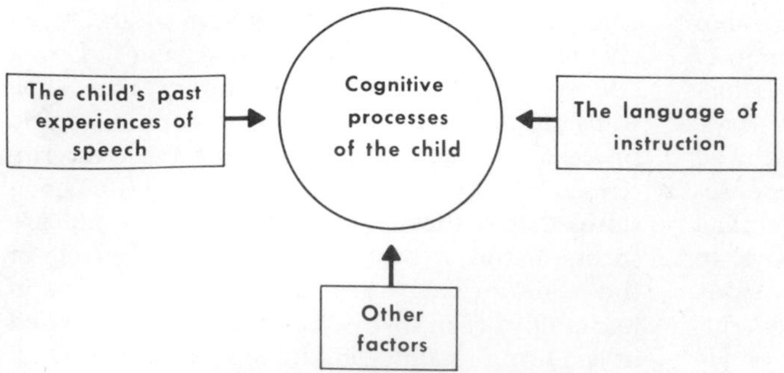

Figure 12–2. "Map" of relationship between the language of the child and the language of school instruction.

"the language of instruction" (right-hand box) on the basis of their "past experiences of speech" (left-hand box). "Other factors" (lower box) may complicate the situation. These may be facilitating or interfering depending on characteristics of individuals and their environments.

Most educators would expect on commonsense grounds that it is harder to comprehend instruction on any subject when it is delivered in a second language (L2) that one does not know at all or does not know well than it is when the instruction is received in the mother tongue. But in the study of language itself there is an additional problem. The teacher's metalinguistic description of language and the language used as the model for literacy may employ linguistic concepts related to L2 that may be meaningless in the child's own experience with L1. In reading instruction, for instance, the teacher may refer to L2 phonemes that do not exist in the child's L1.

In addition to the cognitive difficulty of comprehending instruction given in L2, there is an affective variable that must be taken into account in determining the likely result of being taught to read in L2. In Figure 12–2 it is included in "other factors." For example, if instruction delivered in L2 is perceived as a denigration of the mother tongue, negative emotions may be aroused toward the teacher and the school and the cognitive difficulties may be aggravated. On the other hand, if pupils perceive their own L1 as being unworthy as a medium for education, the possible cognitive facilitation of having instruction delivered in L1 may be diminished or negated by the pupils' negative value judgment of L1 in this role. There are a number of studies that show these cognitive and affective results of a mismatch between the pupil's mother tongue and the language used to deliver instruction in reading.

Garcia de Lorenzo (1975) studied a minority group that lives in Northern Uruguay on the border of Brazil. Their L1 is a dialect of Fronterizo which has a Spanish phonological system but the language is strongly influenced by Portuguese. Thus for children in this area Fronterizo is L1 and Spanish, the official language of school instruction, is L2. It had been noted that the children in this area were repeating grades more frequently than in other parts of the country because of reading problems. The affective variable is clearly present in this example. Garcia de Lorenzo reports that Fronterizo "is discouraged because of its social derogatory connotations" (p. 654). She cites Hensey (1972) whose survey of teachers in this area of Uruguay found that 82 per cent of teachers associated "language problems" with "lower class" social status. The low self-esteem of Fronterizo monolinguals is indicated by the report that they "feel ill-at-ease" in talking with speakers of standard Spanish. Garcia de Lorenzo concludes that the essential learning problem is cognitive: the child "has no bridge [from L1] to the symbols [of L2] introduced to him" (p. 655), but she recognizes that this difficulty is exacerbated by the "guilty" feelings of the children regarding their own L1. She also notes how "nationalism, based on fear, and strong emotional attitudes" has prevented implementation of a bilingual education program. Her conclusion is: "Until such time as it is feasible to introduce bilingual education to the children of the frontier, I see little hope of remedying the problem. Children will be locked into a system which continues to perpetuate the learning problems they face" (p. 657). This Uruguayan case is representative of the extreme difficulty that arises when a mismatch between the L1 of the pupils and the L2 in their instruction causes cognitive confusion that is compounded by negative affect from the perceived social unworthiness of their own L1.

In another study of this problem the cultural attitude toward L2 was less negative. Macnamara (1966), in a study of fifth-grade pupils in Ireland and Britain, compared the English literacy attainments of English speakers (L1) in Ireland whose instruction was delivered in Irish (L2) with the English literacy attainments of English speakers (L1) in Britain whose instruction was delivered in English (L1). He also compared the Irish literacy attainments of two groups in Ireland: children whose L1 was Irish and children whose L1 was English. Macnamara's data showed that, "Native speakers of English in Ireland who have spent 42 per cent of their school time learning Irish do not achieve the same standard in written English as British children who have not learned a second language (estimated difference in standard, 17 months of English age). Neither do they achieve the same standard in written Irish as native speakers of Irish (estimated difference, 16 months of Irish age)" (p. 136). This massive retardation in the development of literacy skills indicates the cognitive effects of this type of language mismatch. For the majority of children and parents in Ireland at that period, the teaching of literacy in an L2 was not their positive choice. It was decreed from a remote government that was in other respects preferable to an alternative one. Most parents probably accepted the bilingual education requirement as unavoidable or with indifference. Most children almost never met a native speaker of Irish. Their instruction must have seemed to them to have been a mysterious ritual. The cognitive confusion caused by the mismatch between the children's L1 and the L2 of instruction was profound. The patriotic ideal of reviving the national language was too remote from reality to provide any positive motivation to overcome the difficulties of learning literacy only in an L2. Thus the affective variable was at best neutral.

In some cases, however, there may be more positive affect toward an L2 when it is used for reading instruction. This seems to have occurred in the "French immersion" programs for English-speaking Canadian children. They usually receive all their instruction, including reading, in L2 (French), but such programs have been for children whose parents volunteer them for it. Indeed, these parents are usually eager to enrol their children in these classes and enthusiastically support them for various reasons.

In the study by Lambert and Tucker (1972), English-speaking children received all of their instruction in French from the time they began school. The achievements of these children in the two experimental classes were compared with control classes of (1) French-speaking children who received all their instruction in French, and (2) English-speaking children who received all their instruction in English. The tests of reading in English administered at the end of grade one showed that the bilingual class had significantly lower scores than the English instruction control classes. The retardation of the bilingual group continued into grade two in one of the experimental classes, but in the other the degree of retardation did not reach statistical significance. But tests of reading in French showed no significant differences between the English-speaking experimental group and their French-speaking controls in grades one and two. In grade three, one of the experimental classes had significantly lower French reading scores than the native French control group, but the research method of comparison was different in the other class and it is difficult to treat the results in the same way. This lack of a significant difference between the experimental bilingual and French-speaking control classes in grades one and two may have been due to the insensitivity of the criterion tests (Downing, 1978). A more recent experiment by Barik and Swain (1976) found that English-speaking Canadian children in their French immersion program at the end of grade one were "not on a par with their French-speaking counterparts in French achievement" (p. 51). Here the difference was significant. Barik and Swain also confirmed that English-speaking children in the French immersion program were at the end of grade one "behind their English-speaking peers attending the regular English program in English language skills which involve reading (word knowledge, word discrimination, and sentence or paragraph reading)" (p. 56).

With regard to the longer-term effect of the French immersion program, in the experiment reported by Barik and Swain, formal instruction in reading and related skills *in English* was introduced for twenty-five minutes per day, beginning halfway through the second year. By the end of the year their English reading achievements seemed to have caught up with those of English-speaking children taught entirely in L1. But the English spelling attainments of the French immersion pupils still showed a "substantial lag." Their French achievement still was "not at par with their native French-speaking peers in French achievement" (p. 57).

One methodological difficulty must be noted in evaluating these French immersion experiments in Canada. It is that the children taking part have not been representative of the population. They have been mostly well above-average in socio-economic class and in intelligence. This has been true also in other Canadian studies of French immersion programs. For example, Lamy (1977), commenting on a similar study by Shapson and Kaufman (1976) remarks that their sampling bias "raises serious questions as to just how successful this technique would be with different social backgrounds" (p. 19).

In another study of this problem, it seems probable that there was positive affect toward both L1 and L2 as media for literacy instruction. This study was conducted in Mexico. In many areas children come to school with an L1 Indian language whereas the national language is Spanish. Two main strategies have developed in this bilingual situation. One group of schools teaches reading only in L2—Spanish, the rationale being that it is better not to waste time on teaching literacy in the vernacular but instead to get straight into Spanish which is the essential language for success in education. The second group of schools begins literacy instruction in L1—the local Indian language—during the first year, and Spanish reading takes over in the second year. Barrera-Vasquez (1953) found that children initially taught in their vernacular read with greater comprehension than those who had been initiated into reading in the L2 Spanish. More recently Modiano (1973) compared thirteen schools of each of the types described above. She used two independent tests of reading comprehension in Spanish and found that initial reading instruction in L1 (Tzeltal or Tzotzil) produced superior reading comprehension in L2 (Spanish) at later stages than did delivery of reading instruction in L2 for the whole period of schooling.

The affective variable in this Mexican bilingual setting is complex. Certainly, however, the attitudes toward Tzeltal and Tzotzil would be positive in both parents and children. On the other hand, many parents are supportive of the view that the school should get on with the teaching of Spanish—the language associated with material success in Mexico. Probably both strategies receive affective support. Modiano's study, therefore, supplies a rather clear example of the cognitive results of matching the language of instruction with the child's past experience of speech in L1.

The fact that learning to read in L1 leads to a positive transfer in later reading in L2 and learning to read in L2 leads to a negative transfer in later reading in L2 has been well known for many years among educators in the former British colonies. For example, Platten's (1953) report to the South Pacific Commission stated that progress in English reading is much quicker when the initial instruction is given in the mother tongue. More recently, Biniakunu (1980) has documented the revival of reading instruction in the mother tongue in Zaire. Biniakunu states that "in 1958, mostly for political reasons, the Belgian colonial authorities imposed French as the only teaching medium. . . . However, by 1966, due to several factors such as low achievement in elementary schools, discontent started growing among parents, teachers and school administrators. . . . As a result, in 1975, when school resumed, the Zairean government decided to shift from French to indigenous languages as the languages of the curriculum" (p. 32).

Another way of handling the mismatch problem is to introduce literacy in L1 but at the same time to begin teaching L2 in spoken form. One example is the project described by Plante (1977). In two Connecticut elementary schools about half of the pupils were Puerto Rican. A random sample of the Spanish-dominant children were selected in each school. In the experimental school these pupils were taught reading in Spanish and they were introduced also to spoken English using an aural-oral approach. Literacy in English was taught to individual pupils as each developed a sufficient English oral vocabulary. The control group pupils in the other school "received a typical English-oriented instruction." Plante claims that the experimental group "achieved a greater growth in Spanish and English reading than did the control group." The greater cognitive clarity produced by reading instruction in the pupils' own mother tongue is indicated by Plante's comment that, "Not only did the experimental group children improve in Spanish reading and language arts, *but they also outachieved the control group pupils in English*" (p. 427, italics added). Plante's study is typical of the many efforts being made to improve reading instruction in bilingual communities in the United States, and the growing concern with this problem in many countries. In America, Ebel (1980) has given an historical account of this movement and indicates some of the practical difficulties it faces. In Britain, Ellis' (1980) research points to the special problem "that L2 readers may resort to different strategies from those deployed by comparable L1 readers" (p. 15).

With reference to American culture, Venezky's (1970c) conclusion sums up this section for us: "For children who do not speak English, it is both foolish and disastrous to attempt to teach reading in standard English. . . . We no longer take seriously the contention that a child (or any other illiterate) can attempt to learn simultaneously to speak and to read a language with other than debilitating results" (p. 335).

Dialect

The importance of the affective variable in reading problems among members of minority subcultures is especially prominent where the subculture has a dialect that is regarded negatively not only by the speakers of the dominant group in the culture but also by the minority dialect speakers themselves. This is well illustrated by contrasting two dialect experiments: Österberg's (1961), in which the subcultural attitudes toward the dialect were positive, and Stewart's (1969, 1975), where the subcultural attitudes were negative.

Österberg conducted an experiment to determine the effects of the mismatch between the subcultural dialect (D1) and the standard dialect of the dominant culture (D2). The research was conducted in the Piteå district of Sweden, which has a "distinctive, archaic and still vital" dialect spoken by some 30,000 people. Observations had indicated that Piteå school children had difficulties in reading and Österberg's hypothesis was that these difficulties "are dialect conditioned and that they spring from the individual's encounter with the standard language" that "begins systematically with school attendance" (p. 133).

To test this hypothesis, Österberg compared an experimental group that was instructed in dialect with a control group that was taught as usual in the standard language. About 350 pupils were allocated randomly to the two groups, and so also were their teachers. Subsequent testing demonstrated that the children in groups D1 and D2 were equivalent in school readiness and intelligence, and in other variables also. Training of the teachers and standardization of their methods were equated, too.

Group D1 began with a ten-week period of reading instruction in the Piteå dialect, while group D2 received parallel instruction except that it was in standard Swedish. A basal reading series was used that was new to all the teachers in both groups. The content was identical in the D1 and D2 readers except for the difference in dialect treatment. After ten weeks, several tests were administered and a further instructional period of twenty-five weeks began in which *both groups* were instructed in D2, except that group D1 was given a gradual transition from D1 to D2 in the first four weeks of this second period.

The tests at the end of the initial ten weeks of instruction found the D1 group to be significantly superior in oral reading, reading rate, and comprehension. These tests were, of course, administered in D1 to the D1 group and in D2 to the D2 group. At the end of the second experimental period, all tests were given *in D2 to both* the D1 and D2 groups. Therefore, at this point the D2 group was being tested in the language in which it had received instruction for thirty-five weeks, whereas the D1 group had been exposed to D2 materials for only twenty-five weeks, or somewhat less if one takes into account the four-week transitional period. Yet in reading D2 material, the D1 group surpassed the D2 group.

Österberg's results provide strong evidence that mismatch between D1 and D2 is an important handicap in learning literacy. Furthermore, his finding that initial D1 instruction is superior in transfer to D2 reading firmly fixes the temporal locus of the trouble. Mismatch has its ill effects in the first initiation phase of learning literacy.

Österberg's results give strong support to Lefevre's (1964) view that "Children should first be taught to read and write the same language that they already speak and understand when they enter school" (p. 6). Lefevre stated that dialect as a "variant of the mother tongue can serve as a basis for language growth and development as nothing else can" (p. 27). The reason he gave is that "Since the child entering school is already experienced at an unconscious level in the basic signals and structures of his language, primary reading and writing instruction should begin with developing his consciousness of them in relation to the graphic system." Furthermore, "If we really want him to learn reading and writing—to become literate—we should not attempt instead to convert him to another dialect, nor to 'purify' his speech" (pp. 43–44). On the contrary, according to McDavid (1969), "A reading program in any language, at any stage in a student's career, is likely to be effective in proportion to its use of the language habits that the student has acquired in speaking" (p. 2).

However, another dialect reading experiment shows that affective variables may outweigh these cognitive considerations. Stewart (1969) cited Österberg's successful experiment in support of a proposal that beginning reading materials in America should be adapted to the Black dialect for children who spoke it. He asserted that "Instead of being ignored or made the target of an eradication program, Negro dialect should actually be used as a basis for teaching oral and written standard English" (p. 184). Stewart produced parallel reading textbooks in D1 (Black dialect) and D2 (standard English) for use in experimental and control classes respectively. The dialect text was based on common language patterns of Black children in Washington, D.C. where it was decided to implement the experimental strategy.

Unfortunately, Stewart's plan was not prepared for the extremely strong negative emotions that interfered with his strategy. Even before the experiment began, Stewart was attacked for introducing "a bad language that shouldn't appear in schools." The experiment itself was wrecked by this self-hate of these people's own dialect. Unlike the proud speakers of Piteå dialect in Sweden, these Black American community leaders despised their own mother tongue and were, according to Stewart (1975), ready to condemn their children to more generations of school failure because of their resistance to the recognition of Black culture in the curriculum of the schools. Wolfram and Fasold (1969) in the same volume that contains Stewart's earlier article warned that "Sociolinguistic research has shown that speakers who use socially stigmatized speech forms sometimes have the same low opinion of such forms as do speakers who do not use them. As a result, even though the Black English materials might be clearer and more natural to some, they may not be acceptable because of the presence of these stigmatized forms" (p. 142). Searle (1972) has given a vivid illustration of this same problem in Tobago.

Giles and Thakerar (1980) warn that "schools in and of themselves cannot bring about a social reformation along the lines of intergroup equalities." This is because "language attitudes do not operate in an intergroup vacuum but often inside a cauldron of intergroup categories and identifications within the classroom" (p. 678).

The contrasting emotional attitudes in the Österberg and Stewart bidialectal experiments demonstrate the importance of the affective variable in situations where there is a potential mismatch between the child's L1 or D1 and the L2 or D2 that may or may not be employed as the medium of instruction. In summary, the evidence from a wide variety of bilingual situations shows that a mismatch between an L1 or D1 of the pupil and an L2 or D2 of reading instruction is a potential source of difficulty in acquiring reading skill. Young school beginners make better progress if their instruction is delivered in their own mother tongue. Of course, often such a strategy is infeasible for a variety of reasons. Even if it is feasible, the cognitive benefits may be negated by negative emotions, as was found in the Black English dialect experiment reviewed above.

Socio-economic Class

Socio-economic classes within a culture also may be regarded as subcultures. Thus, Havighurst and Neugarten state: "Social classes constitute subcultural groups. When people from the same social class meet and converse they soon find they have much in common, even though they may come from different ethnic or religious backgrounds or from different sections of the country. They will find that they live in much the same kinds of neighborhoods, have similar eating habits, dress in much the same ways, have similar tastes in furniture, literature, and recreation, and have about the same amount of education" (p. 6).

Burt (1937) and Schonell (1942) independently established that low achievements in school work were highly correlated with various indices of poverty in their large-scale surveys of schools in London, England. McClaren's (1950) survey of Glasgow, Scotland school children aged five to eight years found a clear relationship between poverty and scores on tests of reading comprehension and word recognition. Fleming (1943) also had found a connection between good reading performance and two indices of economic wealth in Glasgow. Early studies in the United States (Anderson and Kelly, 1931; Ladd, 1933; Bennett, 1938; Gates, 1941) indicated that there was little relationship between reading performance and socio-economic class. However, later

Sheldon and Carrillo (1952) found that retarded readers were more often found in families of lower socio-economic status and where the parents' education was of a low level. Eisenberg (1966a) also reported a relationship between socio-economic class and reading achievement in American city children.

British studies in more recent years have continued to confirm the connection between socio-economic class and reading performance. Thus Kellmer Pringle et al. (1966) in their cohort study of 11,000 seven-year-olds obtained the following percentages of poor readers in the Registrar General's categories of social classes: classes I and II, 7.1; class III, 18.9; classes IV and V, 26.9. Douglas (1964) in a study of more than 5,000 eight-year-olds found significant differences between upper-middle, lower-middle, upper-working and lower-working classes on tests of word recognition and sentence completion. Davie, Butler and Goldstein (1972) have reported data from the National Child Development Study which is a longitudinal investigation of 16,000 children born in one week of March, 1958. Social class emerges as a strong predictor of reading attainment. Wiseman (1964) also found significant correlations between reading achievement and various indices of poor social conditions. Morris (1959) found a correlation of 0.68 between reading comprehension and socio-economic class of the school area. In her later study, Morris (1966) included a special investigation of five schools—three in areas of social classes I and II with high average reading scores, and two in areas of social class V with low average reading scores. From this subsample, 100 poor readers were compared with 100 good readers. Morris found 80 per cent of the poor readers came from the lowest social class whereas 63 per cent of the good readers were from the higher socio-economic classes. She noted also that many of the poor readers in lower class areas had high nonverbal intelligence. Lovell and Woolsey (1964) also found reading retardation was related to low social class independent of intelligence in the 1,800 children aged 14–15 years in their research.

Thus, the general trend of the research evidence in Britain and the United States shows a consistent connection between low socio-economic class and poor achievements in reading. Nor is this trend limited to English-speaking countries. For example, Perelstein de Braslavsky's description of reading in Argentina notes "the correlation between schooling, illiteracy, dropouts and repeaters and economic underdevelopment" (p. 270). All these findings clearly justify Vernon's (1971) conclusion:

> One of the few facts connected with variation in reading achievement on which there is little disagreement is that it is highest in the upper *socio-economic classes,* and decreases steadily as social class declines (p. 95).

But what is the cause? Socio-economic classes are statistical categories that involve many variables. In most studies the children investigated were categorized on the basis of such information as occupation of the father and little, if any, other data on the social class environment was gathered.

Some studies have provided other more definite information. For example, Burt's (1937) London survey reported correlations between backwardness in school work and father's unemployment of 0.676 and overcrowding of 0.890. Wiseman found significant correlations between reading achievement and overcrowding, infant mortality, and illegitimacy for example. However, these probably need to be regarded as indices of general poverty, malnutrition and family disorganization. The causal connection has not been traced. But, obviously, unhealthy living conditions do not support learning. Vernon's (1971) comment should be noted again, "No individual whose mind is dominated by craving for food or by fear of danger, illness or homelessness can take much interest in school activities, or make much effort to work hard" (p. 103).

Intelligence has been a subject of investigation in several of these socio-economic class studies. Sometimes, when IQ's have been matched, the social class differences in reading attainment have almost disappeared (for example, in Morris' (1959) first study in England). But, in view of the fact that the intelligence tests employed usually had a verbal basis, probably the matching on IQ obscured rather than clarified the relationship between social class and reading achievement. Even so, as was noted above, some studies still showed a significant relationship when IQ was controlled.

It has been proposed that the chief factor that may explain the connection between socio-economic class and reading achievement is the language of the class subculture. Several investigations have reported significant differences of various kinds between the speech of lower and higher social class groups. The following examples of such studies are noted: Davis (1937), Deutsch (1965), Lesser, Fifer and Clark (1965),

Newson and Newson (1968). Quite appropriately, Davis (1977) observed that, "until recently, it has been almost axiomatic to identify both oral and written language differences with differences in socio-economic status" (p. 207).

A critical question about these language differences is—why should they cause poorer reading achievements in the lower social classes? The traditional assumption among many educators has been that lower-class language is inferior, deficient, or ineffectual for school learning work. This is the *language deficit hypothesis.*

Although Basil Bernstein may be unhappy about the popular interpretation of his work, Fraser (1976) is accurate in commenting that, "Bernstein's ideas . . . seemed to offer theoretical respectability to the widespread notion that an intrinsic feature of working-class language which was rooted in their way of life, disqualified working-class children educationally and by the same token, justified the notion of the superior educational potential of the middle-class" (p. 3). Bernstein's (1958, 1961, 1971) theory has changed during the twenty years or so of its development, but, basically, he postulates two language codes—the *restricted code* and the *elaborated code.* Both working-class and middle-class children learn adequately the restricted code of ordinary conversation which seems simple grammatically, uses stereotyped expressions, lacks precision for making statements about ideas or emotions, and relies upon gestures, inflection and ancillary explanation to clarify meaning. The elaborated code is characteristically learned in addition only by the middle class. It is more formal, more complex grammatically and permits precise expression and provides more opportunity for organizing experience. Bernstein (1958) claims that the elaborated code is essential for coping with the learning tasks of school. He writes that, for the working-class child, "There is an initial conflict between the need to make and to be sensitive to the mediate responses which formal learning requires and the immediate responsiveness the child has learned from his social structure . . . [that] creates difficulties at many levels" (p. 169).

In his home country, Britain, Bernstein's theory was the stimulus for a considerable amount of research work. A number of studies showed differences in the language of working-class and middle-class subjects that were consistent with Bernstein's theory. But outside of Britain, little support for it has been forthcoming. For example, in Australia a rigorous study by Davis (1977) failed to find the social class differences predicted by Bernstein's theory. Indeed, Davis comments that "the results of this study run almost completely contrary to expectation" (p. 212). Bernstein's own research and that of some of his colleagues has been severely criticized by Stubbs (1976) mainly on the grounds of its paucity of empirical data from *natural* language situations. Fraser too comments that Bernstein's research suffers from the limitation that it is "rarely based on an observation of life as it is lived, much less on participation in it" (p. 6).

Some American authors also have supported the language deficit hypothesis. Jensen (1967), for example, claimed that working-class Black children were inferior in their use of language for conceptual reasoning. Indeed, he found that they were inferior even in the labeling of objects. Adopting Bernstein's terminology, Jensen (1969) concludes that such working-class children fail in school learning because they are lacking in the "flexible, detailed and subtle" language of the "elaborated code" (p. 119). Bereiter and Engelmann (1966) went so far as to develop instructional programs based on the notion that lower-class children are so linguistically deprived that they do not possess the basic concepts for thinking about school learning problems. As they have no language, they must be taught language from scratch.

But is Bernstein's "elaborated code" more effective language for school learning tasks? Labov (1969a), on the contrary, describes it as being often turgid, redundant, bombastic and empty. He notes that, far from being deficient, Black Americans take a great pride in their verbal facility and verbal play is a predominant feature of children's behavior in their subculture. They receive much verbal stimulation, hear well-formed sentences and participate fully in a highly verbal subculture. Unlike Bernstein's work, Labov's conclusions are based on ample empirical research studies conducted in natural situations that are not threatening and repressive as in the formal testing methods of many of the studies that purport to show that lower-class children have a language deficit.

Labov's view is that such subcultural groups have language that is different, not deficient. This is the *language difference hypothesis.* Labov regards the concept of "verbal deprivation" of lower-class children as an illusion. He writes that, "There is no reason to believe that any nonstandard vernacular is in itself an obstacle to learning"

(Labov, 1973, p. 43). He argues that the illusion of language deficit or defect is created by educators' value judgments of nonstandard speech as being imperfect or inferior. A number of other writers are in agreement with Labov's position. For example, Downing and Thackray (1975) review the evidence and conclude that, "The truth is that working-class children are highly competent in *their* language" (p. 40), and they select Goodman's (1969) conclusion to sum up the evidence:

> In every respect the process of language development of the divergent speaker is exactly the same as that of the standard speaker. His language when he enters school is just as systematic, just as grammatical within the norms of his dialect, just as much a part of him as any other child's is (p. 17).

The problem, according to the language difference hypothesis, is that working-class children's norms are *different* from those of their teachers. Labov (1969b) states that "the fundamental situation that we face is one of reciprocal ignorance, where teacher and student are ignorant of each other's system, and therefore of the rules needed to translate from one system to another" (p. 29).

This situation described by Labov is one that is pregnant for increasing children's cognitive confusion about the task of learning how to read. The lower-class speaker is told repeatedly that he is "wrong" when he reads *I have lived here ten years* as "I have live here ten years," but he does not understand why. Similarly he cannot understand why it is "wrong" to write *I don't know nobody.* Thus the language difference, when treated as a defect, causes heightened cognitive confusion in the literacy learner.

The affective variable complicates this situation. When children are told that their natural language is "wrong" or "bad," negative emotions are aroused that create barriers against reading instruction in general. Goodman (1969) observes that, "If the teacher 'corrects' the dialect-based divergent language, this is at cross purposes with the direction of growth of the child. All his past and present language experience contradicts what the teacher tells him. School becomes a place where people talk funny and teachers tell you things about your language that aren't true" (p. 18). Not only are they perceived as not true, but also such "corrections" of children's natural language may be regarded as attacks on their circle of friends and family. Barnitz (1980) observes: "One does not need to reject a child's linguistic heritage as a means of teaching reading in Standard English" (p. 785). But, regretably, such rejection remains an all too common feature of reading instruction in very many countries around the world, although, happily, progressive publications with practical suggestions for coping with nonstandard dialect students are increasingly available (for example, Alexander, 1980).

This discussion of the controversy between the deficit versus difference hypothesis regarding social class dialects would be incomplete without noting Cazden's (1970) thesis that both these hypotheses are inadequate because they neglect patterns of language use that vary with the speaker's situation. She uses the term "communicative competence" to describe how children vary their ways of speaking according to their perception of the situation. Rommetveit (1974) reminds us "how different premises for communication are tacitly and reciprocally endorsed depending upon variant institutional aspects of the interpersonal coordinate of the act of communication. We are writing on the premises of the reader, reading on the premises of the writer, speaking on the premises of the listener, and listening on the premises of the speaker" (p. 63). Houston (1971) has written about the way in which children switch from the school register to the nonschool register according to their perception of the person with whom they are communicating. This aspect of subcultural differences in language seems to be attracting interest among researchers and hopefully our understanding of shifting registers will be greater in the future.

Language is one type of difference between social classes and other subcultures that seems to influence progress in acquiring reading skill. Another type of difference that may be important is experiences of literacy. Several studies have shown a relationship between children's conceptions of literacy and their subcultural background. Downing, Ollila and Oliver (1975) compared 92 non-Indian Canadian children with 72 pupils from two Indian bands in which there was no tradition of literacy and a poverty of experiences of writing and formal concern with language analysis. Their Indian languages are no longer used, except by a few of the oldest men and women in the bands. The Indian children and their parents speak a nonstandard form of English. The non-Indian children, in contrast, came from homes where writing or print was in evidence. Their culture is traditionally literate. All these children were attending kindergarten where they were tested on five reading readiness tests. The Indian children scored significantly lower on all tests. In particular, they were less able to recognize the acts of "reading" and "writing"; they had less mature concepts of the functions of literacy; they knew fewer of the technical terms that are used in reading instruction; and their perception of English phonemes was less well-developed. Downing et al. concluded: "These findings seem to indicate more generally that children's cognitive clarity regarding the functions and task activities of the skills of literacy is influenced by socio-cultural factors" (p. 315).

In a second study, Downing, Ollila and Oliver (1977) investigated concepts of literacy and language in 787 kindergarten children in a large Canadian city. They were divided approximately equally into high, middle, and low socio-economic groups. The pupils from the high group had significantly superior scores to those in the middle and low groups on all three cognitive tests administered in the second month of kindergarten. They concluded that "the child's development of concepts of language is related to experiences of speech or printing at home and in kindergarten. Awareness of the functions or forms of language and consciousness of linguistic categories are fostered in richer home backgrounds . . ." (p. 280).

Clay (1976) compared three subcultural groups in New Zealand: (1) "Pakehas"—the majority white subculture; (2) the native Maori subculture; and (3) Western Samoans, an immigrant subculture. She found that the Samoans made better progress than the Maoris in the initial stages of learning to read. Clay attributed this to the clearer understanding of the purposes of literacy that the Samoan children had derived from frequent experiences of being read to from the Bible and from observing the high value placed on writing and reading letters between their parents and relatives in the home country. The Maori children did not have such experiences.

The third type of subculture in Clay's study—immigrants—has become an increasingly vexing practical problem in many countries of the modern world. In the 1960s, for example, the children of "guest workers" from various countries posed a major difficulty for education systems in Europe. It has been a continuing problem for countries like Australia and Canada that traditionally have received a flow of immigrants from other cultures. The children in these immigrant families often face cognitive difficulties because of the mismatch between the L1 of their old homes and the L2 of their new country. Taschow (1976) has reported a study of 23 boys and girls from families of German origin living in Canada. He found that they were hindered in their acquisition of reading skill because their L1 was German but the school system presented reading only in an L2, English. In England, the influential Bullock Report (1975) noted the "disturbingly low pattern of attainment" among immigrant children. It recommended that:

> No child should be expected to cast off the language and culture of the home as he crosses the school threshold, and the curriculum should reflect those aspects of his life (p. 543).

There are many other ways in which linguistic and behavioral norms differ from one subculture to another, including socio-economic classes. Some of these other differences also may be factors in children's degree of success in becoming literate. We shall study some of these other differences in the next section on *the family* because they are less distinctly related to subcultures. As Downing and Thackray concluded, "We may anticipate that children from lower socio-economic class homes may tend to be ready for reading somewhat later than those from others, but this is due simply to the fact that certain types of experiences are *less likely* to be available to children in poorer homes. Books and other forms of written language are *less likely* to be in evidence. Parental attitudes are *less likely* to be positive toward intellectual activities such as reading. Parents are *less likely* to read to their children. . . . We have emphasised that it is 'less likely' because there is tremendous overlap between the socio-economic classes in all these studies" (p. 37).

The Family

In the final paragraph of the preceding section we noted that the factors in social class differences that probably affect children's reading progress are not absolutely related to class membership. There is overlap between the classes in such factors as, for instance, access to books in the home. Thus, it is not surprising that, when we focus on such specific factors in the family, we find much stronger relationships with school achievements. Wiseman (1968) on the basis of his extensive experience of studies of education and environment concluded:

> Factors in the home environment are overwhelmingly more important than those of the neighbourhood or the school. Of these home influences, factors of maternal care and of parental attitude to education, to school and to books, are of greater significance than social class and occupational level (p. 227).

The research conducted for the British Plowden Commission also stressed the importance of *parents' attitudes:* "The variation in parental attitudes can account for more of the variation in children's school achievement than either the variation in home circumstances [socio-economic class, size of family, parents' education, housing] or the variation in schools" (Department of Education and Science, 1967, p. 181). Parent's attitudes have been shown to be related to children's reading performance in many studies. Fraser (1959) obtained a correlation of 0.66 between twelve-year-olds' school achievement and parental encouragement in Scotland. But the measure of parents' attitudes was only the subjective estimates of the children's teachers who may have been influenced by their knowledge of the children's school work. Douglas (1964) supplemented teachers' assessments of parental encouragement with objective data on such facts as the frequency with which parents had visited their children's school. The children whose parents were most interested in schooling had the highest test scores in reading. Furthermore, the children with most interested parents improved more between the ages of eight and eleven years than children whose parents were least interested. Douglas also had teachers rate the children as hard, average, or poor workers. Only 33 per cent of children with uninterested parents were rated as hard workers, whereas 70 per cent of the children of interested parents were said to be hard workers. Hard working was associated with school achievement and improvement of scores between the ages of eight and eleven years whereas poor working was related to lack of improvement. In a follow-up study, Douglas, Ross and Simpson (1968) found that hard workers with interested parents improved their scores between ages eleven and fifteen years, but hard workers with uninterested parents deteriorated in their test performance. These results show the important effect of parents' attitudes on children's motivation to learn in school.

The significance of motivation in reading development was brought out clearly in a comparison of achievement motivation in good versus disabled readers. Zimmerman and Allebrand (1965) obtained Thematic Apperception Test stories from them and found that the good readers' stories stressed achievement and hard work whereas those of the disabled readers lacked such themes. Vernon's (1971) commentary should be noted here again: "the child is attracted rather than forced by pressure to achieve; and this is reinforced by his identification with his parents and his desire to be like them. Thus, if the parents are themselves well-educated and successful in life, the children are further stimulated to achieve by this identification. Moreover, educated parents tend to show greater encouragement to their children to work well in school than do less educated parents" (p. 107).

The effects of lack of parents' interest in their children's reading was shown clearly in Morris' (1966) research in Kent, England. She found, on the basis of carefully conducted interviews of the children, that only 2 per cent of poor readers received a high level of encouragement from both parents whereas 52 per cent of the good readers had done so. No encouragement at all was received by 46 per cent of poor readers and only 4 per cent of good readers.

The effect of parents' encouragement was found incidentally in a reading readiness training experiment in Denver, Colorado reported by Brzeinski (1964). Experimental group parents were trained in methods of getting their children ready for reading instruction. The children of these parents were found to be better prepared for learning to read than those of parents in the control group who had not received this information on reading readiness activities. But the interesting incidental finding from this experiment was that some of the children in the control group were just as advanced in reading readiness as children in the experimental group. When this phenomenon was further investigated, it was found that these control group children usually came from homes where the parents had made a regular practice of reading to them.

Parents' interest was also shown to be an important factor in a Head Start program in Florida. Willmon (1969) related the extent of parents' participation in this preschool program to their subsequent scores on the Metropolitan test of reading readiness administered in the first week in grade one. The mean group scores of children *whose parents had participated* in the Head Start activities were significantly higher than those of children whose parents had not done so.

More specific ways in which parents may influence children's progress in the acquisition of reading skill have been shown by some authors. Mason's (1980) study of four-year-olds shows that preschoolers begin to understand how features of writing relate to language through parental guidance in the home and elsewhere. Greaney's (1980) research on leisure time reading also suggests a number of ways in which parents influence school children's reading habits. For example, he notes that "much of the leisure reading was carried out . . . when, on account of programming or parental restrictions, television may not have been available to the children" (p. 355).

The possible link between television viewing and reading habits and achievements has been the topic of quite a large number of studies. Neuman (1980) has reviewed several of them. She concludes that, "The relationship between reading and television . . . is far more complex than a simple analysis of the amount of hours viewed and achievement test scores. The context in which children watch (parental control and supervision, discussion of programs) varies widely, as does the type of programs viewed" (p. 805). Neuman nevertheless concludes that it has been demonstrated that television can stimulate students to read. A number of educators have proposed this use of television (for example, Peters' (1980) proposal, "The 1980 Olympics: A Schoolwide TV–Reading Project"). But there is considerable evidence for a link between heavy TV viewing and poor reading achievements or low frequency of reading, as is noted by Moldenhauer and Miller (1980) in their review of several American studies. The strongest evidence that TV viewing inhibits reading behavior comes from the large-scale surveys conducted in Japan. For example, whereas 40 per cent of elementary school children read for 30 to 60 minutes per day in 1960, by 1965 the proportion fell to only 13 per cent. Ownership of television sets increased from 23 to 83 per cent during the same period. Sakamoto and Makita (1973), concluded that in Japan television "has adversely affected the reading activities of children" (p. 445).

It might be assumed that educational television programs deliberately designed to help children learn to read would have a positive influence. Neuman's review and Peters' proposal mentioned above suggest such a conclusion. But the evidence is conflicting. For example Flood (1975) found that educational TV viewing was positively related to reading readiness. But Sawyer and Sawyer (1980) report a negative correlation in these respects that leads them to conclude that "educational television may have a hindering association in the development of the readiness skills necessary for any reading instructional approach" (p. 6).

We cited above Vernon's hypothesis that children's progress in learning to read may be influenced by the model of their parents' behavior. This is supported by results from Morris' (1966) study in Kent, England. She found public library membership in 61 per cent of the mothers and 49 per cent of the fathers of good readers but for the poor readers the corresponding percentages were only 15 and 13. Also the parents of over 40 per cent of good readers had plenty of adult books in the home compared with less than 4 per cent of the homes of the poor readers. As many as 57 per cent of the poor readers came from homes where there were no books at all, whereas this was true of only 7 per cent of the homes of good readers. Sheldon and Carrillo also found that reading disability was associated with homes containing few books.

In this section we have focused on the individual family background and found a close connection between the attitudes and habits of parents as regards literacy and their children's success in acquiring reading skill. It should be noted that there are cultural and subcultural differences too in these attitudes and habits. Several studies referred to earlier in this section found social class differences in the amount of encouragement given to children by their parents. In Douglas' research, encouragement was highest in upper-middle-class parents and it became progressively less toward the lower classes. Also Douglas reported that only 7 per cent of lower-working-class children as compared with 26 per cent of upper-middle-class children were rated as hard workers by their teachers. Kellmer Pringle, Butler and Davie in their study of 11,000 seven-year-olds classified children in terms of whether their parents had "approached" or "not approached" their children's teachers. The proportion in the approached category increased from 46 per cent in social class V to 71 per cent in class I. In the same study 14 per cent of poor readers; 41 per cent of medium readers; and 45 per cent of good readers belonged in the approached category. Himmelweit (1963) found that middle-class parents were more concerned than working-class parents with the school achievement and higher educational and vocational prospects of the 13–

14 year old boys in her study. The middle-class boys had stronger feelings of being able to consult their parents about their activities than did the working-class boys. The latter seemed very much more "on their own" in this respect.

Cultural differences, in comparison with these subcultural variations, are often even more marked. Downing's (1973) comparative reading study in fourteen countries found that in some countries, parents give strong support to the teacher's efforts to help their children become literate. In others, the parents seem more neutral, whereas in still others they may even have a negative influence.

One other factor in the home environment that is thought to be important in several countries is the link between home and school. For example, parental influence in Denmark is believed to be so important as to constitute a specific Danish educational ideology. Nevertheless, parents do not directly influence the content of the curriculum. But the child gains a sense of security through the cooperation of teachers and parents in their educational partnership.

Formal institutions such as Parent-Teacher Associations (PTA) do not necessarily facilitate such cooperation. Often they do work toward that end with some success, but sometimes they become battlegrounds between the opposing beliefs of teachers and parents, and then insecurity is more likely to be felt by many of the children. In the United States, unlike Denmark, PTAs quite often do represent pressure from parents on the curricular content of the school. Many teachers feel such pressure regarding methods of teaching reading. England seems to represent an opposite situation. One English school in the mid 1950s had a white line painted on the school yard and a notice board beside it that declared PARENTS MUST NOT CROSS THIS LINE. But experiments in the East End of London dramatically demonstrated the need for greater cooperation between home and school, and as a result a vigorous movement to improve this situation began. Although on the matter of methods and content of teaching, the professional status of the teacher is strongly maintained and English parents still may not cross the invisible territorial line of professional responsibility. The Bullock Report states firmly: "Parents have an extremely important part to play in preparing the child for the early stages of reading" p. 522).

Sweden also is making increased efforts to relate the child's school environment to that of the home. Swedish teachers previously have been encouraged to make contacts with parents, but the Royal Board of Education has made it mandatory for the individual teacher to make the first contact with the home. The teacher must communicate with the family of each individual in the class before school starts, or early in the term, and then maintain this contact during the school year. Malmquist (1973) avers that a teacher of reading in Sweden "cannot function effectively unless he knows a great deal about some of the most influential individuals and groups in the student's life" (p. 476).

In 1980 a law to strengthen the family–school bond was presented to the Swedish parliament (Documentation Centre for Education in Europe, 1980). In New Zealand, attempts have been made to capitalize on parents' interest in their children's reading instruction at school. A radio series, "On the Way to Reading," with accompanying booklets, has been devised to provide parents with a course designed to inform them about the methods being used in schools (Nicholson, 1980). Criscuolo (1980) points out that parents who are uninformed about the school's reading program easily fall prey to authors of negative publications about the effectiveness of schooling: "Informed and knowledgeable parents can reject the distortions and inaccuracies that often crop up" (p. 166). More positively, Jolly (1980) writes: "Finding ways to help parents be more effective will in the long run make the teachers and schools more effective as well" (p. 995). Jolly reviews some of the ways teachers can help parents. A useful guide to materials for parents is provided in Auten's (1980) article "Parents as Partners in Reading," and a recent book by Cohn (1979) collects many valuable suggestions for parents who want to assist teen-agers to improve their reading and study skills.

Thus in research and practice in a variety of cultures the family is being recognized as a very influential environmental factor in the development of reading skill.

CHAPTER 13

The School Environment

The school is a highly complex environment. We shall classify its many variables into four major categories: (1) physical features of the school; (2) characteristics of the school system; (3) teacher characteristics; (4) other aspects of the school environment.

Physical Features of the School

School Buildings

In his international survey for UNESCO, Gray (1956) found striking differences between countries in the progress made in establishing schools. Although Gray did not provide any empirical evidence, his conclusion that variations in physical amenities are important in literacy learning is indirectly indicated by his suggestions for improving such conditions. Downing's (1973) comparative reading study found the same wide range of differences in such physical facilities provided by different cultures. He noted that several of the national reports in his survey indicated the belief "that old-fashioned or dilapidated school buildings are related to achievements in literacy learning, although direct evidence is not provided in support of this assumption" (p. 122).

That belief was supported by the research of Morris (1959) in England. She developed a measure of the "amenities of the school building" on the basis of "a list of the features of school buildings which, from practical experience, were considered to have the most marked effect on school life" (p. 31). Points for a school building were scored with respect to date of building, head teacher's (principal's) office, staffroom, auditorium and its uses for other school activities (for example, as a dining room), size of classrooms, type of furniture, sinks in classrooms, storage space, type of lighting, sanitation and water supply, cloakroom facilities, playground and field, noise pollution, and general appearance. She found that good reading attainment was associated with superior buildings: "Efficient teachers and a good supply of attractive materials are not the only components of successful reading development. The present study has shown that good buildings are also associated with a high level of attainment . . ." (p. 132).

Morris' (1966) second survey confirmed her original finding that there is a statistically significant relationship between poor school buildings and low reading achievement in the pupils. This was true in her analysis of the data from the whole sample of junior schools (ages seven to eleven) in Kent, England. Moreover, her intensive study of the schools with the best and worst reading results showed that "the children attending schools classed as 'good' on the basis of their reading test results in the survey had much better classroom conditions than the rest of the sample, whereas the converse was true of those in 'bad' schools" (pp. 324–325). Thus, Morris' two important investigations established firmly that the school environment is of fundamental importance in the acquisition of reading skill.

Some more specific physical features of the school have been investigated—its size, location, organization, and supply of teaching materials, for example.

Size and Location of School

It is difficult to separate the variables of size and location of schools. Urban areas generally have larger schools than rural areas. Morris (1959) found a very high correlation between large schools and urban areas. Two of the variables associated with good reading attainment were shown by Morris (1966) to be urban schools and large schools. In her subsample of "good" reading and "bad" reading schools, the "schools which were above average for either attainment or progress were also above average in size" (p. 48).

The causes of the relationship between large schools and superior achievements in reading are complex. Morris (1966) noted that urban areas, large schools, large classes and a high level of nonverbal ability tended to go together as an environmental cluster. She found also that large schools usually have superior buildings. Morris reported that the large size of a school made it easier for the head teacher (principal) to purchase library books. Furthermore, the strong competition for the head teacher's position in such large schools attracted candidates of outstanding qualities. (It should be noted that in England the school principal is more of an educational leader than an administrator). Morris indicated also that it was "easier to recruit suitably-qualified staff" in these large urban schools with superior buildings (pp. 319–320).

Teaching Materials

In Chapter 3 we noted the general principle from psychological research that practice is the foundation of skill acquisition. It follows that the supply of appropriate materials for reading practice should be associated with attainments in reading. Educational research has shown that this is true.

Morris' (1966) survey included an analysis of the quantity and quality of reading materials in the Kentish schools. She found that poor reading was associated with poor provision of books. Morris also evaluated the central library provisions in the schools and found that "not only were the 'poor' readers found to be at a distinct disadvantage with regard to class libraries, but the books generally available to a sizeable proportion were both insufficient in number and unsuitable in content" (p. 326). Downing (1973) found a very wide range of variations in the provision of books in schools in the fourteen countries in his comparative reading investigation. In two countries where reading education was particularly sophisticated, Denmark and Japan, children had especially excellent book environments. The effective cooperation between schools and public library services in Denmark is particularly notable. The development of the public libraries themselves is regarded as a powerful factor in the improvement of children's reading.

The core of the reading program in many countries is the *basal reader* series. Its popularity with teachers probably lies in its structure and grading of difficulty which would appear to allow even the less able children to make progress that can be perceived easily by the teacher. Thus, for many British teachers, the basal reader series "acts both as a reading curriculum and a means of assessing pupils' progress" (p. 376), according to Goodacre (1973). The relative strengths and weaknesses of the rival basal reader series are a common topic of conversation among educators, but choice among them depends on subjective judgment since their publishers rarely, if ever, have any research data on their effectiveness.

The most convincing argument against the general use of a basal reader series is that it is impossible for one beginners' primer, for example, to relate to the backgrounds of all children within a given country. Deutsch (1960), described how reading primers in an inner-city American school were "meaningless" because their contents were quite foreign to the children's life experiences. Whipple (1966) believed that the development of reading skill is hampered when the characters and situations presented in children's readers are foreign to their own home environment. American authors and publishers of basal readers have striven hard to correct this deficiency, so that by the 1980s most major basal readers are multi-cultural. Nevertheless, the fact remains that, in geographically vast countries such as the United States and Canada, it is impossible to relate one set of reading materials to all the varied environments across the nation. For example, there is a great variety of local rural situations that are not met by catering for the multi-cultural inner-city environment. Chesterfield (1978) writes:

> Throughout Latin America, rural primary schools . . . do not generally deal with local problems. . . . Often cultural and language gulfs may exist between teachers and students. When these . . . children arrive at school, they usually encounter a teacher who comes daily from the city to give class, and an urban-oriented curriculum which systematically excludes those things learned at home (pp. 312–313).

Chesterfield's experiment found that providing local reality in the reading materials of first-graders in a rural area of Brazil made an important difference to their progress. The experimental group at the end of the first grade scored significantly higher than a control group on the first grade final examination in reading.

Downing and Thackray (1975) conclude:

> The language-experience approach is the teaching method most likely to insure that the content of children's reading matches their own experience. When children and teachers make up their own books they are much more likely to reflect the real-life activities of the children's own environment and culture as well as their own language than the mass-produced books of any publisher (p. 44).

School System Characteristics

In this section we are concerned with the less tangible variables in the school environment that arise from policy decisions of a school system.

Age of Initiation into Reading

A popular notion is that at a certain age children have a special facility for learning language. This is the *critical period or sensitive period hypothesis.* Its popularity in recent years probably stems from the work of ethologists such as Lorenz (1952) and Tinbergen (1948), who showed that many animals seem to have a strictly limited period for learning some act. For example, it was shown by experiment that chaffinches never learn the song of their species if they hear it only before and after the critical period. However, such a critical period has never been demonstrated in human beings. Their behavior is much more adaptable than that of the lower animals studied by Lorenz and Tinbergen. The human cortex is much better developed for learning.

Nevertheless, some writers have speculated that there is a sensitive period for language learning in children. For example, Chomsky asserts that all children possess an innate linguistic ability which programs them to detect the transformational rules that generate the sentences of their language environment. This view is based on the anecdotal evidence that some children have been seen to exhibit a rather sudden grasp of grammar at an early age. But, as MacCorquodale (1970) notes, "The fact that some, but by *no* means all, children acquire grammatical behavior at a rather early age and rather suddenly (Chomsky finds its rapidity 'fantastic') does not require a previously laid-down inherited grammatical nerve-net nor, even, anything much in the way of a strong prepotency for grammar learning" (p. 93). Chomsky's suggestion is reminiscent of the instinct theories of earlier psychology, whose circularity made them so unproductive. For example: Why do children behave grammatically? Because they have an inborn tendency to behave grammatically. How do you know they have such an inborn tendency? Because children behave grammatically. Thus the label for the behavior becomes its explanation and the behavior the proof of the label.

Current theory and research in the psychology of human behavior indicate that language development can be explained more parsimoniously in terms of *general* learning mechanisms. As MacCorquodale remarks, "That a child learns certain orders, such as adjective–noun, and actor–action sentences, on the basis of a relatively small sampling from the enormous universe of such instances shows simply that a child is able to make complex abstractions and to generalize from them to diverse new instances" (p. 93). The scientific method's principle of parsimony prefers an explanation of language behavior based on a theory of behavior in general rather than a special theory which applies only to language.

Furthermore there is some direct empirical evidence that shows that older people actually are better at most language learning tasks than younger people. For example, Carroll's (1975) research on teaching French as a foreign language in eight different countries concluded that the age for beginning learning was of little importance. The only factor found to be of major significance in Carroll's study was the sheer amount of time spent on the task of learning French. Also, when McLaughlin (1977) reviewed a wide range of publications on foreign language (L2) learning, he found that, "Controlled studies comparing younger children with older children generally indicate that the older children perform better. The results of experimental research comparing young children with adults learning L2 invariably show that the older groups do better." He adds: "Related to the misconception that younger children learn a language more effectively than do older children and adults is the belief that the earlier a child begins to learn an L2, the better (e.g. Andersson, 1969). What evidence there is on this topic points to the opposite conclusion:

Older children do better on almost all aspects of language acquisition than do younger children in comparable circumstances."

The sensitive period for language learning hypothesis was applied directly to reading by Doman. He argued that the sensitive period for language learning occurs nearer to the age of two years than the usual age for entry to school—hence Doman's (1965) book for parents called *Teach Your Baby to Read.* But there is no empirical evidence to support Doman's thesis. Indeed, as McLaughlin's review shows, the general trend of the evidence is to the contrary.

Quite the opposite position has been taken by some educators. For many years, teachers believed that it was harmful to introduce children to reading tasks at too early an age. Several studies were said to have demonstrated that a minimum mental age of six, six and a half, or seven was essential for a successful beginning in learning to read (Morphett and Washburne, 1931; Bigelow, 1934; Witty and Kopel, 1936a, 1936b, 1936c; Dolch and Bloomster, 1937; and Dean, 1939). However, a review of the research methods used in these different studies showed that the minimal mental age found necessary for successful reading depended entirely on the criteria of successful reading—in other words, what the researchers considered to be "reading." Downing and Thackray concluded that "the most that could be claimed for any one of these studies is that they had discovered the minimal mental age required to handle the task of learning *by that particular method of teaching and with those particular books and teaching materials.* Each author made the error of overgeneralising his results from readiness to read the particular materials used in his experiment to readiness to read anything" (p. 53).

This fact was brought out very clearly in a study by Gates (1937). He compared four groups of children in classroom situations which varied as to teacher efficiency, individualization of instruction, and so on. Gates found that the age at which the children were ready to learn to read was specific to the methods and materials that were being used in the different classrooms.

This does not mean that the concept of reading readiness should be abandoned. Rather the concept needs reforming. Reading readiness should be regarded as a question of a gap between the level of development of the child and the level of difficulty of the task. Both can be modified—the child can be prepared for the task and the task can be fitted to the child's level of development—thus closing the readiness gap from both directions. In this context, Vernon (1971) mentions "the child's level of development in conceptual reasoning" (p. 111). Children's cognitive development needs to be considered in deciding what reading instruction tasks should be presented to them. If the task is too difficult, cognitive confusion is likely to be increased, causing affective as well as cognitive damage. Although there is no optimal mental age for all children to begin any kind of reading instruction, the outcome must depend on the particular level of difficulty in conjunction with each individual child's level of cognitive development.

Many educators have recognized intuitively this need to narrow the gap in reading readiness. For example, Downing's (1973) comparative reading study found considerable differences in the age required for beginning reading in different countries—for example, seven in Denmark, six in the United States, and five in Britain. But even a cursory examination of British five-year-olds' basal readers reveals that the initial books are generally simpler than those given to six-year-olds in American schools. This fact was recognized long ago in Gray's (1956) UNESCO survey: "Many pupils who have not acquired a mental age of 6 can learn to read provided the reading materials are very simple and based on interesting, familiar experiences and the methods used are adapted to the specific needs of the learners" (p. 124).

In general, teachers do adapt their instruction to the age level of their pupils. But, even if age is taken into consideration in planning the tasks of reading instruction, the earlier the age of beginning, the greater is the risk of failure. This is because some children lag behind the norm in certain aspects of development that are related to the learning-to-read process, but catch up later. For example, some children have auditory perception and speech problems at age five or six that they grow out of by age seven or eight. In Britain or the United States such children may fail in phonic instruction, whereas in Denmark and Sweden they would not have been placed in danger of failure because of the later age for entry to school.

Time on Task

We noted, in the previous section, Carroll's (1975) research which showed that the age for beginning to learn a foreign language was not as important as the sheer number of hours devoted to that task. Furthermore, in Chapter 3 we saw that Underwood (1964) also concluded that the more time subjects spend in learning the more they learn in laboratory-controlled verbal learning experiments. Hence, it would seem that another important variable in the school environment should be the amount of time that pupils spend on the task of learning to read.

The surveys of Burt (1937) and Schonell (1942) in England both found that irregular attendance was much more frequent among disabled readers than among normal readers. Vernon (1957), however, points out that the chief cause of the reading retardation of the poor attenders may have been their ill health. But in more recent times good health care has become the norm in England. Nevertheless, Morris (1966) found that "over the whole period of their primary schooling [ages 5–11], the good readers had a significantly better record of attendance than the poor readers," but she urged caution in drawing any causal conclusions because the data did not include any direct information on the relation between attendance and reading attainment of individual children. Furthermore, Morris points out that school attendance may be affected by reading failure as well as vice versa. Children who are discouraged by failure find excuses for absence from school, while children who are making progress are eager to go to school. Clay (1972) also has described poor attendance and weakness in reading performance as interactive, each aggravating the situation in turn. A part of this problem, of course, is the lack of practice.

The loss of reading skill through lack of practice has been found also in a number of studies of adult literacy. Balpuri (1958) found that a very serious problem in one of the earlier UNESCO literacy campaigns in India was the students' relapse into illiteracy. Many who had received literacy certificates were functionally illiterate again a year later. Ansari (1961) indicated the need for maintaining practice after the initial instructional period. Gray (1956), in his wider survey, found that "a surprisingly large proportion of adults who have attended literacy classes, and have received certificates based upon 'minimum standards of literacy' sooner or later are unable to engage in even the simplest literacy activities. . . . Their reading skills disintegrate through disuse" (p. 27). Downing (1973) in his comparative reading study reviewed these and other findings from many different countries and concluded that "This category of reading failure should be named exliterates, to distinguish them from those who have never been literate at all" (p. 170). Although the evidence is generally rather indirect and there are potentially confusing interaction variables, it seems reasonable to conclude that time on task is an important aspect of the school environment.

Time under Guidance

The student's "time on task" has been related to the essential need for practicing a skill during its acquisition. But, as was shown in Chapter 3, practice must provide the learner with feedback, and an important element in feedback is the instructor's guidance. Hence, it is essential to consider also the *teacher's* time on task in providing guidance in learning how to read. One way of investigating this interaction is to study the effects of class size, since the time for individual pupil guidance is likely to vary according to the pupil/teacher ratio.

Kemp (1955) found no relationship between class size and level of attainment in a sample of fifty London junior schools (ages 7–11). Another more recent survey in London also found "that little or no differences exist between the reading standards of children in relatively small classes compared with those in larger ones . . ." (Little, Mabey and Russell, 1972, p. 209). Several studies in other locations reached a similar conclusion (Faunce, 1971; Hawkins, 1966; Sartain, 1960). In contrast, Furno and Collins (1967) found in their five-year longitudinal study that pupils in smaller classes (25 or less) made better progress in reading than pupils in larger classes. Frymier (1964) compared six first-grade classes each containing more than 36 pupils to nine classes that each had less than 30 pupils. He concluded that, "In terms of reading achievement . . . first grade students in small classes achieved at a significantly higher level than students in larger classes" (p. 93). Morris' (1959, 1966) two Kent surveys showed that poor reading was associated with smaller classes rather than larger ones. However, in both studies Morris urged caution in interpreting these results because she believed that size of class interacts with other variables.

Downing (1973) found large differences in average class size between different countries, for example, 25 in Sweden, 28 in Denmark, 50 in Paris (France), 38 in Germany (B.R.D.). In several countries, including Sweden, Denmark and the

U.S.A., a system of dividing classes had been introduced; several of the national reports claimed that this had produced better results in reading. The usual procedure for class division is that one half of the class begins and ends the school day earlier than the other half. Thus each group gets a concentrated period of literacy instruction and teacher attention while the other group is absent. Jansen (1973) states that in Denmark, "Division of classes for a few lessons has proved more satisfactory in its results than previous efforts directed at reducing the size of the whole class—for example, from 32 to 28" (p. 292).

This suggests a hypothesis that, in previous studies such as those of Kemp and Morris, class size was too large to make any difference to the children's needs for their teachers' guidance. When the class size is reduced to between 13 and 15, teacher guidance time becomes a more effective variable. Experimental research data on division of classes supports this hypothesis quite strongly. In Balow's (1967) study, classes of 30 were divided to make half-classes of 15. Significant improvement was reported, with first grade emerging as the most important time for this treatment.

Holmes (1962) argued from the results of several previously published studies of reading readiness that, "Other things being equal the earliest age at which a child can be taught to read is a function of the amount of time or help the teacher can give the pupil" (p. 240). On balance, however, Morris' (1966) caution that concomitant circumstances may be important in relation to the size of class seems highly relevant here. What tends to be overlooked are the other environmental variables indicated by Holmes' reservation—"other things being equal." Indeed, other things may be so *unequal* as to produce the opposite effect in some classrooms. *Teaching time is not the same as learning time.* There may be much less learning in a class of twenty-five taught by whole class methods than in a class of fifty following an individualized approach.

The hypothesis that class size interacts with other variables was emphasized in the discussion of the results of a large-scale Canadian study on this problem by Shapson, Wright, Eason and Fitzgerald (1980). They investigated experimentally the effects of four class sizes (16, 23, 30 and 37) in a total of 62 grade four and five classes in Toronto. Teachers' attitudes were influenced favorably by the smaller sized classes, but there was no significant difference in the amount of time teachers spent in talking to individual students and no difference in reading achievements in the different sizes of classes. These authors state:

> It must be pointed out that there was no attempt to experimentally manipulate instructional strategies for the different class sizes. Essentially, this has been a study of "what happens" when class size is changed, but it cannot be considered a study of "what can happen." The results suggest that, in the future, emphasis could be placed on providing teachers with training in specific instructional strategies most appropriate for different class sizes. As well, rather than merely advocating reductions or increases in class size, a more flexible policy could be adopted. For example, class size could be appropriately altered in different situations by redistributing students and time and by changing instructional techniques (p. 151).

Similarly, although the review of what little research on this topic is available led Centra and Potter (1980) to conclude that time on task is significantly related to achievement, nevertheless they accept that "it is not only the quantity but also the quality of time spent in an academic environment which determines a student's progress" (p. 286).

Segmentation of Schooling

The way in which children's schooling is segmented may break the continuity of development in the acquisition of reading skill. Every time there is a change of school or teacher, there are possibilities for inefficient instruction. There may be gaps of information or wasteful repetition of what has been learned already. Most school systems divide schooling into such broad levels as "elementary" and "secondary" and provide separate institutions for each. Within each level, there are segments, usually covering a span of one year, that are called "grades" or "standards." This aspect of the child's school environment may have both positive and negative effects on learning to read. On the positive side, segmentation may provide *special treatment* suited to the developmental level of the child. On the negative side it may create *breaks in the continuity* of skill development that cause the process to be delayed.

Morris' (1959, 1966) two Kent surveys provide some evidence for the positive effects of segmentation. At the time of her research, there were two chief types of segmentation within English elementary education: (1) "infant-only" schools (ages 5–7), followed by "junior-only" (ages 7–11); (2) "junior with infant" schools (ages 5–11). (In recent years many school systems in England have changed to a break at age eight between "first schools" and "middle schools"). In both studies, Morris found that superior reading attainments were associated with segmented schooling. Children who had begun in a separate infant school and then transferred to a junior-only school were better readers on average than those in schools with combined junior and infant levels. Morris (1966) cautions that her results "do not justify the conclusion that this type of organisation in itself is an important factor contributing to satisfactory reading achievement . . ." (p. 321). One must consider what may be the more direct causes of this effect. Downing (1973) noted that in England "a large proportion of children of the younger age group attend entirely separate infant schools under their own administrative head. This head teacher is nearly always a woman, and such positions have created career opportunities for women in the field of the education of the youngest age group. This probably has been an important factor in the improvement of education at this level" (p. 134). Thus, the creation of separate schools for young beginners, aged five to seven, gave their teachers the opportunity to specialize at this level and to provide an efficient environment designed for such very young learners.

On the other hand, there is considerable evidence of the negative effects of segmentation in schooling. Morris' (1959) first Kent survey found that almost 50 per cent of children in the first-year junior classes needed the type of teaching associated with the infant school, whereas most of their teachers were not trained in infant methods and a substantial minority were without any knowledge of how to teach reading. The Bullock Commission in 1975 reacted strongly to these negative findings. They recommended that "reading be regarded as a continuously developing skill and that language be extended to meet increasingly complex demands as the child grows older" (Department of Education and Science, 1975, p. 219). This led them to recommend that "all teachers in training, irrespective of the age range they intend to teach, should complete satisfactorily a substantial course in language and the teaching of reading" (p. 336). The Bullock Report also tackles the problem of lack of continuity in reading instruction caused by the segmentation of children's schooling into arbitrary levels. It suggests the "avoidance of sharp breaks in practice" and a "framework of cooperation" between the different segments (p. 531).

Within the broader levels of schooling the smaller "grade" segments also may cause discontinuity and related damage. Downing (1973) found evidence of the harmful effects of the grade system in several countries in his comparative reading survey. He concluded that the most serious damage caused by the rigid adherance to a grade system is what Oommen (1973) calls "stagnation." Students who fail may have to repeat the year again and again until they improve. The chief cause of this stagnation appears to be failure in reading. Stagnation in turn causes a serious drop-out problem. Perelstein de Braslavsky (1973) reported that 25 per cent of children in first grade in Argentina are repeaters, and Gal (1958) found a similar proportion in France. This policy of repetition of grades leads to a general deterioration of the school. Downing (1973) concludes: "The vicious downward spiral of the effects of such stagnation is predictable from research on the psychology of learning: low levels of aspiration, poor self-image, and so on" (p. 133).

These considerations have led some countries to modify or even abolish the traditional grade system. For example, the Swedish Education Acts of 1962 and 1969 require that the personal resources of the individual child must not only be respected but should be the starting point for the planning of education and teaching. The 1944 Education Act in England contained a dramatic declaration of the move away from the old system of "standards," or "grades." The effective abolition of any official name for "grades" or "standards" and the disappearance of such a concept from teachers' professional discussions is one of the best indications of the reality of individualized education that is to be found in the majority of elementary schools in England today.

Returning to the point of view of the child in the school environment, what we want to emphasize is that the grade system is likely to influence the child's actual experiences in literacy learning via the constraints it places on the teacher's behavior. If getting each child to pass the grade is the official objective, many aspects of the classroom environment are likely to be impoverished from the point of view of the faster learner and to be stressfully overburdening for the slower learner.

It is interesting to reflect that in small rural schools, even though the grade system may be in official use, if the teacher remains in the same position for several years the physical barriers of this arbitrary administrative segmentation are likely to be less noticeable in the child's experience. Some educators have noted that there are psychological advantages in such a situation, and they have advocated its extension deliberately to all primary schools. The most extreme example of this approach is "the classroom teacher tradition" in Denmark, which generally results in the child remaining with the same reading teacher for his or her first seven years in school. Similarly, in Sweden, the child stays with the same teacher for the first three years. A similar effect in enhancing the continuity of the child's experience occurs in schools using multi-age plans such as "vertical grouping" and "family grouping." For example, if three age levels are grouped together and one third moves in and one third moves out each year, the child remains with the same teacher for three years. In addition to the improved continuity and greater possibilities of individualization of instruction in such plans, other facets of the child's experience in literacy learning are likely to be influenced by the longer period of time spent with the same teacher. For example, the personal relationship between child and teacher may be different even in the first year because of the time perspective of the teacher and the pupil.

Teacher Characteristics

> It cannot be emphasized too strongly that the teacher is the biggest single factor for success in learning to read and use language. The school with high standards of reading is the one where the teachers are knowledgeable about it and are united in ascribing to it a very high priority (Department of Education and Science, 1975, p. 212).

Many other authors have made similar assertions. For example, Gray (1956) in his survey for UNESCO stated that "the most important factor in . . . progress in reading is the teacher (p. 130). In more recent times, Dykstra's (1968) discussion of results of the U.S. Office of Education supported first-grade reading studies and their follow-up investigations led him to conclude that the teacher was far more important than the methods and materials in reading instruction. Dykstra's conclusion was based chiefly on his finding that there were larger differences in attainment between classrooms using the same methods and materials for reading instruction than there were between the treatment groups experimentally contrasted on the basis of such methods and materials. However, Dykstra had no direct evidence for a causal connection between qualities of the teachers and their pupils' performance in reading.

Gray (1976) expresses strong doubts as to whether any objective evidence exists to prove that teachers are as important as is so frequently alleged. Although it is not clear exactly how he calculated them, Gray presents correlation coefficients between ratings of teacher competence and reading progress in the only four studies that fitted his criteria for inclusion in his review. These studies were his own unpublished thesis, plus the well-known reports by Morris (1966), Bond and Dykstra (1967), Harris and Serwer (1966), and Harris, Morrison, Serwer and Gold (1968). Gray claims that "The correlations range from 0.03 to 0.30, depending on the study; none of them is statistically significant" (p. 177). Gray concludes that the differences in the effects on children's progress between highly and poorly rated teachers "are small or trivial" (p. 178). In a subsequent article, Gray (1977) again reanalyzed data from Morris' (1966) research to make a similar point. In reply, Morris (1978) argues that Gray was selective in his choice of data for reanalysis and that he ignored the main weight of the evidence from her Kent survey which did, in fact, show "a highly significant *positive* relationship between the teacher variable and children's reading *standards* or attainments" (p. 137).

Morris (1966) in her survey of Kent schools made a rather comprehensive study of the teachers whose pupils' reading was being investigated. She made observations of these teachers when they were teaching reading; she interviewed the teachers and their head teachers; and she studied the teachers' records of their own work. Morris combined the information from these various sources and rated the teachers' contributions to the reading achievement of their pupils . . . on a nine-point scale. When she related her teacher ratings to the reading attainments of their pupils, she found rather high correlations, .47, .52, .54, for the three age levels of the pupils. She concluded that "good readers tend to have better teachers than poor readers during the last three years of their junior course" (p. 147). Morris' words are well chosen because they do not make any claim for a causal connection between these two correlated variables. This is very appropriate, because, as Morris notes, sometimes the best teachers are deliberately allocated to high-achieving pupils. Nevertheless she urges that "this does not minimise the importance of the association found between teachers' grades and the reading achievement of their pupils, since it has shown that the poorer readers were as under-privileged in this respect as they were with regard to the age and ability-range of their classes, their material classroom conditions and reading environment" (p. 148).

This shows the need for deliberate experimentation to obtain evidence on such problems of the causal relationships between variables in the school environment of pupils learning to read. Such experimental data are awaited to provide a more objective judgment on the extent to which progress in reading is influenced by qualities of the teacher. Also one needs answers to the question—*What qualities* of the teacher are significant for the child learning how to read? In pursuing this problem, we must be careful to keep the focus on *characteristics of the teacher.* For example, our first subheading is "teachers' knowledge," not "teacher training."

Teachers' Knowledge

The importance of this characteristic is suggested in the title of Morris' (1973) article, "You Can't Teach What You Don't Know." Morris discusses the kinds of knowledge that a teacher needs to teach reading successfully. Her chief categories are "principal uses of language," "salient characteristics of spoken English," "children's acquisition of speech," "relationships and differences between speech and print," "language processes and pedagogy," and "children's literature." Morris' (1966) research data from her Kent survey showed a relationship between good teachers and good readers, but knowledge was only a part of the system for grading the teachers. However, Morris reported that "high teachers' grades were associated with . . . longer training ($p < 0.05$) [and] . . . longer teaching experience ($p < 0.001$)" (p. 332), both of which might be expected to produce more knowledgeable teachers.

Morris' evidence, slight though it may seem to be, is interesting because, while a great many studies have been reported about the state of teachers' knowledge and how it can be improved, there is a paucity of research on the effects of teachers' knowledge on children's reading attainments. For example, Gagon (1960) found that teachers knew only 68 per cent of the items in one informal test of phonic facts. Schubert (1959) and Ramsey (1962) obtained similar results on other phonics tests. Aaron (1960), on another phonics test, found that education students and experienced teachers could answer on average only 57 per cent of the items. Their scores tended to increase with length of teaching experience. Spache and Baggett (1965) found that only 68 per cent of their subjects knew syllabication rules and therefore comment: "How can they teach pupils a skill which they can do well but do not clearly understand?" (p. 97).

Since the inception of the annual "Summary of Investigations Relating to Reading" in the *Reading Research Quarterly* in the 1960s, each year has seen a growing number of studies on teachers' knowledge and the evaluation of courses designed to improve their knowledge. But the extension of such studies to determine the result on children's reading performance is rarely undertaken. One study that was a move in this direction was reported by Powell (1976). He administered the Artley and Hardin (1971) *Inventory of Teacher Knowledge of Reading* to thirty-six reading resource teachers. He also had these teachers complete a test of "Problems in the Teaching of Reading" which consists of 86 questions about specific problems in the classroom. (Stoll (1971) has shown that this latter test has validity in terms of pupils' progress in learning to read). Powell found a significant relationship between the scores on the two tests, but he considered the correlation (.63) only "moderate." Commenting on this, he suggests that there should be evaluation of what is taught to teachers since "it may have little or no applicability. Another age-old question persists: 'What knowledge is worth knowing?' " (p. 159). The complete October 1980 issue of the *Phi Delta Kappan* was devoted to this topic with reference to teacher education in general. In it, B.O. Smith (1980) calls upon professional organizations to bring about the reform of teacher training which the colleges of pedagogy, he believes, will never face up to themselves.

In connection with Powell's query, Downing's (1973) comparative reading study found large differences in the provisions for training teachers of reading among the fourteen countries investigated. He noted that: "Although countries differ very much in respect to the attention given to reading instruction in teacher training, most of the authors in our team seem to be in agreement that such special training is effective in helping to raise the standards of literacy teaching and learning in the classroom. But it must be frankly admitted that it would be difficult to prove the case for this from any of the data as yet available to us" (p. 132).

Groff (1973) raises another question. In his review of the Artley and Hardin *Inventory of Teacher Knowledge of Reading,* he shows that it has rather low reliability, and argues that this may be due to the fact that there may be professional differences about what constitutes "knowledge" of reading. It is possible that much of the material in this section on teachers' knowledge should be transferred to the next section on *teachers' beliefs,* since the connection between teachers' knowledge and children's progress in learning to read is so tenuous.

Teachers' Beliefs

We have already mentioned in the preceding chapter Palardy's finding that boys' reading achievement was equal to girls in those classes where the teachers believed that boys can learn to read as effectively as girls, whereas in classes where the teachers believed that boys are less able to learn to read than girls, the boys were in fact inferior in their acquisition of reading skill. This result constitutes evidence of the significance of teachers' beliefs. It is reminiscent of the well-known study by Rosenthal and Jacobson (1968)—*Pygmalion in the Classroom.* Pupils whose teachers had been led to believe that the experimenters' tests showed that they would make a spurt in academic achievement in the coming year made more progress than pupils whose teachers had not been so informed. In actual fact, the pupils were equal in academic aptitude.

Rosenthal's experiments have been subjected to academic criticism by a number of authors. Thorndike (1968) and Snow (1969), for example, criticized the methods of collecting test scores and the suitability of the norms that were relied upon. Elashoff and Snow (1971) also found it impossible to replicate the analysis of the data. Furthermore, several attempts to replicate the experiment failed to produce the "Pygmalion effect" (Barber, et al. 1969; Claiborn, 1969; Fleming and Antonnen, 1970). Conversely, a number of other studies have provided support for the phenomenon (Palardy, 1969; Pippert, 1969; Brophy and Good, 1970; Mendoza, Good and Brophy 1971; Rothbart, Dalfen and Barrett, 1971; Rubovits and Maehr, 1971; and Seaver, 1971). It may be noted additionally that neither Thorndike nor Snow denied the possibility that teacher expectation may produce the "Pygmalion effect."

How does this effect operate? Rosenthal's hypothesis was that it stems from teachers' perceptions of their pupils and that the latter mirror these perceptions in their school performance. The way in which teachers' perceptions may be influenced by expectations was shown by the experiment of Foster, Schmidt and Sabatino (1976). They placed 44 teachers in two treatment groups, both of which viewed a videotape of a normal fourth-grade boy carrying out various tasks, including a word recognition test—on which his performance was also normal for his grade level. One treatment group was told that the boy was normal, but the other group was told that he was "learning disabled." The teachers in the latter group rated the boy's behavior as being at a lower grade level than that rated by the group that believed the boy was normal. Also the group given the "learning disabled" misinformation gave significantly more ratings of potential problems of perception, attention, and personality behaviors for the boy than did the other group. Thus the teachers' perceptions of the boy's behavior were significantly influenced by their beliefs about him. Under normal conditions, teachers' perceptions of their pupils may be in some way signaled to the children as feedback about their behavior, progress and so on. In this way pupils may be guided (or misguided) about the effectiveness of their responses in the tasks of reading instruction.

For example, Mendoza et al. found that low achievers received less teacher contact than high achievers. Rubovits and Maehr also found that teacher trainees gave different patterns of reinforcement to students perceived as "gifted" and "nongifted." Brophy and Good concluded that there is a circular process. Teachers provide cues, such as varying amounts of praise; their students respond accordingly; and these responses confirm their teachers' expectations of them. Braun (1973) states the practical implications:

> Teachers need to be keenly aware that their own beliefs regarding socioeconomic level, test information, or sex of the learner too frequently result in structuring a learning situation which produces behaviors commensurate with their beliefs (p. 709).

Another type of belief has to do with the child's language, which we discussed in the preceding chapter in the section on "subculture." There we showed that the notion that speakers of nonstandard dialects are linguistically inferior, incompetent or deprived is a myth. Nevertheless, the myth is a powerful factor in the school environment of the literacy learner. Stubbs stresses the importance of distinguishing "between the characteristics of language itself and the power of people's stereotyped attitudes to language" (p. 16). The persistence of social prejudice among teachers in regard to dialect was brought out clearly in the crosscultural research by Shafer and Shafer (1975). They interviewed teachers in Germany (B.R.D.) and England. Negative attitudes toward nonstandard speech were very prominent. Shafer and Shafer reported that "More than 90 per cent of teachers in this study answered . . . in terms which made it apparent that in their perception the language of children in their school was deficient in one way of another" (p. 255). The persistent power of these negative beliefs about dialect is strikingly illustrated by the finding of Shafer and Shafer that Bernstein's work had been distorted as a defense mechanism for this type of language prejudice. They report that "Time and time again in the course of the study, teachers in both West Germany and England would support their descriptions of the linguistic deficiences of the children they were describing by saying 'As Bernstein has pointed out, these children use a restricted code' " (p. 257).

A third category of teachers' beliefs that may influence the child's school environment during the process of acquiring reading skill are beliefs about instructional methods. Downing (1973) found that the debate about teaching methods had gone on in every country, no matter what the language or orthographic system may be. The essential point of distinction emphasized by the proponents of the alternative methods was whether the *functions* of written language in conveying meaning were emphasized or the *technical features* of the written code were focused upon by the teacher. If functions were to be emphasized, the method required the use of large chunks of language that were immediately meaningful to the child. Downing called all such methods *meaningful chunking* approaches. When the method is aimed at teaching the child how the written code is designed to relate to spoken language, immediate meaningfulness loses priority because it is necessary to focus on the atoms of writing and speech—hence Downing's label *atomistic decoding* for these kinds of methods. Chall (1967) made a similar distinction in her terms "meaning emphasis" versus "code emphasis" methods.

These two alternatives represent a dichotomy of beliefs. Downing (1973) noted the significance of *fashion* in beliefs about teaching methods: "Swings of fashion produce changes in methods of teaching that, more often than not, bear little or no relationship to the findings of educational research. There is no real consensus of research conclusions on the comparative advantages of the various alternative methods described. . . . Usually, research evidence is selected to support the current fashion when its latest method comes into vogue. Then, a new series of researches tends to develop to 'prove' the value of the 'new' trend. The reader will find little help from research quoted in support of current methods from one country to another" (p. 157).

The impact of fashion on teachers' beliefs about reading instruction methods is well illustrated by an article by Cambourne (1980). He describes two types of teachers' attitudes toward "psycholinguistics" in reading education as exemplifed in the work of K. Goodman and of F. Smith. Cambourne points out that both of these viewpoints, which are strongly held by the two groups of teachers, are based on misconceptions of the theory and research of the two authors concerned. In the same article, Cambourne proposes " 'Cambourne's law'—i.e. 'There is an inverse relationship between the degree of complexity experienced by the learner and ease of implementation by the teacher' *or* put another way: 'The less complicated it becomes for learners the more complicating it becomes for teachers, and vice-versa' " (pp. 20–21).

Downing's (1973) comparative reading survey found several other dimensions of teachers' beliefs that may affect the school environment in which the child is learning to read: "child-centered versus curriculum-centered education"; "formal versus informal approaches"; and "individualized versus mass teaching techniques." There is no scientific evidence on the effects of child-centered versus curriculum-centered teaching but there is some research on formal versus informal teaching approaches. Anderson, Byron and Dixon (1956) found that the average age for learning to read was later in an informal school than it was in a formal school, but that after a time, the pupils in the informal school caught up with those taught more formally. In Morris' (1959) first Kent survey she reported a correlation of

0.4 between reading achievement and formal methods, but in her second study Morris (1966) found that this variable was not significant. No significant differences in the reading achievements of formal versus progressive schooling were found either in the studies reported by Gardner (1950), Lovell (1963), and Kellmer Pringle and Reeves (1968). However, although there appears to be no difference in the average reading attainments of children taught by either formal or informal methods, several studies indicate that weaker pupils achieve more under informal conditions than in formal situations. Lovell found a higher proportion of poor readers in the formal schools (14 per cent) than in the informal schools (9.5 per cent). Wiseman (1964) found that special help for the weaker pupils in reading was associated with progressive schools. Gooch (1966) found that the progressive approach was more helpful for less able pupils.

Downing's (1973) other dimension of difference in teachers' attitudes that may affect children's experience in literacy learning is that of "individualized versus mass teaching methods." The teacher's perception of individual differences may be influenced by different methods of school and classroom organization. Austin (1973) proposes that in multi-age classroom plans such as family grouping, in which children are from more than one age group, teachers tend to individualize the instructional program more than they would for a single grade. This is because the spread of ages breaks down the misconception that all children of a particular one-year chronological age group are, for instructional purposes, identical. Teachers' expectations of their pupils' individual differences increase because of the age mix. Thus, the child's individual abilities and style of learning are more likely to be recognized in a multi-aged or family-grouped class than in one that maintains a conventional single grade level. Austin states that even less attention to individual differences is given when special ways of organizing schools on ability tracks or streams are employed, as, for example, in the Joplin Plan.

It is probable that the reader has been questioning our label "teachers' beliefs" for these differences in professional techniques in the classroom. This is a reasonable misgiving. Many of the practices described are imposed on teachers—not chosen by them. It seems likely that teachers' attitudes toward their work will differ very much according to the degree of responsibility that they are given for decisions on methods and materials. But there are likely to be different reactions in different teachers. For example, some teachers will experience greater self-confidence when faith in them is implied by freedom of choice of methods. Others may feel uncertain without more control and regulation by "experts."

That teachers' beliefs are more powerful than supervisors' regulations has been indicated by several studies. Chall and Feldmann (1966) compared teachers' responses to a questionnaire about their declared practices in teaching beginning reading with the results of regular observations of the same teachers at work in their own classrooms. They found no correlation between professed methods and actual methods used and concluded that "teachers using one given method vary in their implementation of that method, that these differences in implementation can be observed reliably, and that the observed practices are not related to those the teachers themselves report" (p. 574). Oommen (1973) recounts some innovations in methods of teaching reading attempted in India, which ran into difficulties. Often the change of method appeared to be *in name only*. Similarly, Perelstein de Braslavsky reported that when the global method was introduced into schools in Argentina, many of the teachers who used it also continued to use the analytic-synthetic system. They believed this combination would forestall failures with the method favored by their supervisors. Feitelson (1952–1953) found that failure in reading was not evenly distributed over the nine matched classes investigated in her research in Israel. Instead a whole class did either well or poorly. It was discovered that the classes of those teachers who had not adhered to the precepts of the officially required method but, in fact, had devoted time to a different approach achieved the better results. Thus, teachers' beliefs may be powerful enough to circumvent official policy on how reading must be taught in a school system.

Several writers indicate that school systems in deciding their policy for reading instruction take into account teachers' reluctance to change their methods (Malmquist, 1973; Dottrens and Margairaz, 1951). Southgate (1965) believes that *teachers' attitudes toward reading* constitute an extremely powerful variable in the child's school environment. She calls it "reading drive"—a sort of perpetual Hawthorne effect providing continuous motivation for reading in the classroom. Southgate and Roberts (1970) relate this to a typology of teachers' beliefs. There is a dichotomy between those who emphasize the mastery of reading skills and those who believe that reading is merely one of children's many interests which should be fostered by incidental learning. This division of teachers' beliefs is between those who believe reading should be *taught* and those who consider that reading is *caught*. Southgate and Roberts recommend that teachers should decide which of these beliefs comes closest to their own particular opinion. Then they should select methods and materials accordingly. This theory emphasizes that teachers teach best when they are teaching by what they believe to be the best method.

Teachers' Personality

Hamachek (1975) made a comprehensive review of research on this issue and concluded that: "Effective teachers appear to be those who are, shall we say, 'human' in the fullest sense of the word. They have a sense of humor, are fair, empathetic, friendly, enthusiastic, more democratic than autocratic, and apparently more able to relate easily and naturally to students on either a one-to-one or group basis. Their classrooms are something akin to miniature enterprise operations in the sense that they are more open, spontaneous, and adaptable to change. Teachers who are less effective apparently lack a sense of humor, grow impatient easily, use cutting, reducing comments in class, are less well integrated, are inclined to be somewhat authoritarian, and are generally less sensitive to the needs of their students" (p. 304).

Samph (1974) used Flanders' (1967) system of studying interaction between pupils and teachers. The pupils were a sample of 155 sixth-graders who were two or more grades retarded in reading achievement. Their attainments were tested before and after a period of seven months with their respective teachers. Samph found that pupils taught by teachers who more frequently displayed behaviors allowing for student freedom of expression, use of pupils' ideas, and praise made better progress than students whose teachers showed these behaviors less frequently.

The need to provide children who are learning how to read with encouraging praise and to appeal to their individual interests is recognized by teachers, according to a questionnaire that Sampson (1969) administered to 675 remedial reading teachers in England. The importance of good social relations between teacher and children was also indicated by this survey. Vernon (1971) states that "The ability to establish sympathetic, friendly and understanding relationships may be one of the most significant factors in teaching skill" (p. 114). Morris (1966) in her second report on reading in Kent, England noted another aspect of this relationship. She found that in classes where the attitude of "respect" for the teacher "was prevalent, it was accompanied by greater application to the task of reading" (p. 140).

In reviewing Mastin's (1963) study of the effects of the enthusiasm of teachers on their pupils' achievements, Hamachek concludes that "teacher enthusiasm may be the most powerful personality characteristic of all when it comes to effective teaching" (p. 303). In this connection, Wilson (1959) asserts that those who teach reading should value reading themselves. Rieck (1977) interviewed thirty-four high-school teachers and selected fourteen who responded that their students failed to read their assignments. Then three hundred of these teachers' students were questioned. The results indicated that these teachers were unconsciously signaling a low opinion of the reading aspect of their courses. Although 52 per cent of these students indicated that they liked to read, 81 per cent admitted that they did not read the assignments set by the teachers concerned in this investigation. Other responses revealed that this neglect to read assignments was caused by these teachers' overt behavior. Rieck concludes: "Teachers who do not read and who do not value reading may pass their limited concept of reading on to their students" (p. 647).

Thus there is evidence that some personality and behavior characteristics of teachers do influence the reading performance of their pupils. However, as Austin (1973) states, we need more research "to bring educators closer to an understanding of the specific forms of teacher behavior that affect the child's learning ability in reading" (p. 533).

An important contribution to this understanding is the recent article by Hale (1980). She addresses the problem of why holistic approaches to reading, such as those proposed by Smith and by Goodman and much earlier by Huey (1908) and Thorndike (1917) "have had so little influence on the teaching of reading in schools. . . ." She suggests that "It is not enough for proposals to make sense theoretically if existing social relationships operate against the adoption of associated practices. . . . The teaching and evaluating of reading abilities are social activities and the social relationships are inevitably built into what is being taught and assessed" (p. 25). Hale relates this problem of reading instruction to the research of Young (1971) on social processes in classrooms. Hale proposes that typically in reading instruction:

> a social relationship based on the teacher's power to direct and control pupils' learning activities can be seen as conducive to an approach to reading as the production of acceptable verbalisation through teacher directed decoding strategies. Furthermore, if the teacher acts as continual evaluator of pupil competence, then a concentration on aspects of reading which can be behaviourally displayed is unavoidable, particularly when it is requisite that measures of competence be quantitatively expressed (p. 27).

She views this as "a particularly strong version of transmission teaching (Barnes, 1976), which involves the teacher acting as specialist, defining what counts as valid knowledge and controlling how it is learnt, pupils being passive receivers of knowledge" (p. 28). Hale proposes that this type of reading instruction is maintained by social constraints which must be taken into account by anyone attempting to introduce innovations.

Other Aspects of the School Environment

There are other characteristics of the school environment besides the physical features of the building, its contents, and teachers. Another factor is the other pupils in the literacy learner's class. These other pupils usually are also the learner's peers in the subcultural environment outside school.

The importance of peer influences on school learning aspirations in general is well established by research (Haller and Butterworth, 1960; Kandel and Lesser, 1969; McDill and Coleman, 1965; Simpson, 1962). However, peer influences are relatively low in importance at the usual age for beginning reading. They become progressively more influential as the pupil grows older. Thus Harris and Sipay (1975) remark, "As children approach the age of 9 or 10, peer influences become increasingly important. If the child belongs to a gang or club, and the group's code is antagonistic to school and derogates school success, it becomes obligatory for a member to neglect learning." On the other hand, Harris and Sipay note that "Within a gang, some learn to read well and others remain nonreaders, and if the gang influence were the only important factor, this would not happen" (p. 299). We would add that a gang has different roles for different members and these may or may not require reading skill or pro-reading or anti-reading attitudes. Reading is influenced by peers in another respect. Lawson (1972) found that fifth-graders' choice of what books they read was significantly influenced by the opinions of their friends and peers whereas choice of television programs and movies was not so affected.

The observation that pupils are importantly influenced by their peers has led some educators to propose that this factor can be harnessed for instructional purposes. This has led to the development of various "peer tutoring" projects in which child teaches child. Allen, Feldman, and Devin-Sheehan (1976) made a comprehensive review of the numerous experiments on peer tutoring. They found very little agreement in their findings and noted many shortcomings in the research designs. One more recent study of a peer tutoring project has been described and evaluated by Boraks and Allen (1977) and Allen and Boraks (1978). In the experimental treatment, the children from grades two through five were taught a series of teaching behaviors which they then applied to each other. Because they alternated tutor and tutee roles, this method was called "Reciprocal Peer Tutoring." This method was compared with direct adult–child tutoring. After twelve weeks it was found that the children in the reciprocal peer tutoring group had made significantly greater improvement in reading as compared with the adult–child tutoring approach. Allen and Boraks suggest that the explanation for their results is that "taking on the role of tutor is beneficial to a child's academic growth. It is necessary to understand a skill or concept personally before trying to explain it to someone else. Being placed in the role of tutor also may have affective consequences for cognitive development" (p. 277).

CHAPTER 14

Reading Disabilities and Difficulties

In different parts of the world there is heightened interest in literacy acquisition and considerable concern for illiteracy. A UNESCO Commission (Faure, Herrera, Kaddoura, Lopes, Petrovsky, Rahnema and Ward, 1973) estimated that by 1980 there would be some 820 million adult illiterates out of a projected world population of 2,825 million people. The estimated world adult illiteracy rate of 29 per cent by this Commission is a matter of deep concern for us all. Illiteracy estimates, especially across national and linguistic boundaries, need to be interpreted with caution. For one reason, the distinction between functional literacy and illiteracy is by no means clear-cut, as discussed in Chapter 1. For another, cross-national comparative studies, both quantitative and qualitative, are fraught with difficulties. In our earlier comparative reading project (Downing, 1973), for example, the claims of low illiteracy rates in Japan, Finland and Germany must be seen in relation to a number of factors, including the validity of evidence presented. Moreover, literacy rates expressed as percentages do not necessarily reflect actual performance levels. Different countries reporting the same illiteracy level may differ in reading performance as they may vary in their concepts of literacy. Even large-scale, cross-national surveys of the IEA type (Thorndike, 1973a) are not immune to methodological and conceptual problems inherent in comparative studies (see Downing and Dalrymple-Alford, 1974–1975).

Concern for illiteracy has led to an awareness in both developed and developing countries that they can no longer content themselves with "perpetually renewing the conditions of their own existence" in the face of rapid social, economic and technological changes. For these reasons, the UNESCO Commission chose a dialectical approach in their report entitled: *Learning to Be: The World of Education Today and Tomorrow.* They emphasized two fundamental goals in the achievement of literacy: lifelong education and the learning society. This stress on learning and renewing implies teaching and learning are inseparable. This philosophy of the learning society was tested in a major project embarked on by UNESCO and UNDP (United Nations Development Program) in 1966. The aim was to overcome the problem of illiteracy by developing a multifaceted literacy program in which instruction in reading, writing and elementary mathematics was cast in a functional, work-related context (Secretariats of UNESCO and UNDP, 1976). One of the findings of the project points to the need for literacy "awareness" as a social norm before the inculcation of literacy skills. Where this consciousness is lacking, reading and writing skills are not necessarily developmental prerequisites. Thus, the report states that "literacy is but one element of a process of lifelong education. It should be allied with knowledge appropriate for improving the individual's condition, always taking into account his or her social environment and natural environment" (p. 191). This long-range view of lifelong education and the learning society applies not only to developing countries but also to developed nations. In the U.S.A. the volume *Toward a Literate Society* (Carroll and Chall, 1975 with its original papers first reported in 1970) represents the program launched in that country in 1970 toward universal literacy. The Right to Read program aimed at achieving by the early 1980s a functional literacy rate of 99 per cent of all Americans under 16 and 90 per cent of all over 16. Across the Atlantic, the Bullock *Report* (Department of Education and Science, 1975) in England emphasized "a language for life."

With this worldwide context of literacy acquisition and illiteracy as the backdrop, we will discuss in this chapter and the next chapter problems and issues of reading disabilities in children in learning the English alphabetic system. These two related chapters logically divide this area into two parts: the first part dealing with reading difficulties or reading backwardness and the second part covering specific reading disability or developmental dyslexia. No dichotomy is implied. Some of the problems in processing print are common to both poor readers and "retarded" readers. But, by and large, the etiology is different. We will need to look at underlying mechanisms accounting for reading failures, with the different groups often subsumed under one umbrella term of children with reading disabilities. Under "reading difficulties" or "reading backwardness" we will discuss such issues as extent of the problem, factors associated with the difficulties, the concept of underachievement and interdependence of decoding and comprehension in these poor readers compared with good readers. Under "specific reading disability" we will examine terms and concepts, brain-behavior relationships, laterality, differential patterns, maturational lag and predictive studies. Underlying our discussion of reading difficulties is the search for processing mechanisms and strategies. The focus is thus on *why* and *how* and *at what point* reading breaks down and on explanations of reading failure. Thus, we are able to learn more about reading processes from studying such breakdowns in information processing as well as from studies of the processes themselves.

Reading Difficulties

There have been many names proposed for the broad group of children with reading problems under discussion. This is not surprising in view of the heterogeneity of these children and the diverse reading problems they exhibit. The vexed issue of different terms and concepts is left to a later section. For our purpose, the overall chapter heading *Reading Disabilities* is used to denote the broad group of children with varying degrees of reading difficulties, whatever the cause. There has been some debate as to whether reading disabilities, and reading difficulties should include children at different intelligence levels (see Hallahan and Cruickshank, 1973). This will entail a different conceptualization of mental retardation or mental subnormality and of the relationship between intellectual deficit and reading disabilities. Rather than get embroiled in this controversy, we will confine our discussion of disabled readers largely to those with average or above-average intelligence. If a cutoff must be selected, then an approximate IQ of 84/85 (one standard deviation below the mean on the Stanford Binet or the Wechsler Intelligence Scale for Children) may be a convenient "demarcation zone." We say this with some trepidation, knowing the standard errors inherent in IQ measures and the difficulties of drawing even a cutoff zone, not to mention a cutoff line. But zone demarcation is needed without necessitating our venturing into the field of mental retardation, which is defined in part on significantly subaverage general intellectual functioning coexisting with other deficits, according to the American Association on Mental Deficiency definition (AAMD) (Grossman, 1977). We are, however, cognizant of the fact that the mentally retarded are also "backward" in reading and in school achievement in general. Space precludes a thorough discussion of the relationship between intellectual retardation and general and specific backwardness. From the survey of the literature and from our perspective we will operationally define reading disabilities in the above terms.

The size of this broad group of nonretarded (in the AAMD sense) children with reading problems whatever the cause is not easy to determine with any precision. This is partly due to the varying meanings of reading and reading proficiency and different methods used in survey studies in different locales or different countries. However, an estimate of some 10 to 12 per cent of school children experiencing reading difficulties may be hazarded as the usual figure reported in English speaking countries. Some researchers may even suggest 12 to 15 per cent as a more realistic figure. Within this estimate of 10 to 12 per cent of school children there is a large number who experience *reading difficulties* for various reasons. Some of the factors contributing to or correlating with reading difficulties are discussed in the preceding chapters on cultural, subcultural, school and home influences and on the affective bases of reading. For practical purposes and in psychometric terms, children with reading difficulties may also be described as those who are at the low end of the reading performance continuum whatever our criteria of reading are. To some extent, this is a statistical artifact, as almost all tests are standardized to conform in their distribution of scores to the ubiquitous normal probability curve. One would therefore expect a certain number of children to score low on an arbitrary cutoff in decoding and/or reading comprehension, just as one would expect a proportional number of high performers on these tasks. Included at the very tail-end of this group of children with reading difficulties and also arising from the distribution, there is a small "hump" of severely disabled readers. This hump cannot be explained on the grounds of just the low end of a normal continuum and similar distributions are also observed in large samples of moderate and severe mental retardation. This smaller subgroup we will call children with *specific reading disability, reading retardation* or *developmental dyslexia.* Again, prevalence rates are difficult to arrive at because of even greater divergence of terms, concepts and etiological factors. A stringent statistic for this subgroup is provided in the comprehensive Leadership Training Institute in Learning Disabilities Report commissioned by the U.S. Office of Education (Bryant and Kass, 1972). These workers estimated that when exclusions are made of visual, hearing, emotional disorders and environmental disadvantages, the prevalence of this hard-to-teach, severely disabled reading subgroup is about one-quarter to one per cent and seldom exceeds four per cent. Gaddes (1976), Spreen (1976), and Yule and Rutter (1976) have discussed at some length problems and social implications associated with epidemiological studies of reading retardation, or, in our context, developmental dyslexia.

Thus, at the outset, we would like to use the term "reading disabilities" to denote the estimated 10 to 12 per cent of nonretarded children with varying degrees of reading problems, whatever the cause. Within this 12 per cent or so of disabled readers there is a large number, possibly as high as 10 per cent, of school children with reading problems. These poor readers are our children with "reading difficulties." Concentrated at the low end of this poor reading continuum is a distinctive distributional "hump" of severely disabled readers. This subgroup we label children with "specific reading disability," "reading retardation" or "developmental dyslexia." Other workers in the field may take issue with this differentiation. We do not wish to give the impression of "what is in a name. . . ." We strive after terms with some exactitude so that they mean something to professionals in the field. Since professionals will probably not agree on exact definitions in the near future, we should heed the admonition of Spreen (1976) that it behooves researchers and practitioners to state clearly what factors were considered in the selection or designation of subjects or children. In the last analysis, rather than expending energy and time on needless debates on one name or another, it is far more important that we move from "label to action" and concentrate on why children fail to read and how we may help them.

Extent of Reading Problems

It was thought at one time that reading difficulties, like poverty, would not always be with us. While abject poverty in developed countries is largely eradicated, reading difficulties seem to be still very much with us. We have mentioned studies conducted in England by Morris (1959, 1966) and Kellmer Pringle, Butler and Davie (1966) in an earlier chapter. Morris found that 14 per cent of a sample of eight-year-old school children were reading not at all or extremely poorly and that half of them remained very poor readers throughout secondary school. Kellmer Pringle, Butler and Davie reported that 18 per cent of 11,000 children entering English junior schools were poor readers and 9.8 per cent were nonreaders. In the U.S.A., the Director of the Right to Read Program estimated that some 18 million adults were functionally illiterate and that some 7 million elementary and secondary school children were reading at least two grades below their "ability" (Holloway, 1971). In Scandinavian countries, Hallgren (1950) estimated 10 per cent of Swedish school children and Hermann (1959) provided a similar figure of 10 per cent of Danish students as having difficulties. In Canada, the Commission on Emotional and Learning Disorders in Children—CELDIC—(1970) estimated between 10 to 16 per cent of Canada's school-age children required diagnostic and remedial help. In Australia, a recent well-conducted survey of literacy and numeracy in Australian schools undertaken by the Australian Council for Educational Research (Keeves, Matthews and Bourke, 1978) shows that close to 20 per cent of the 7,000 ten-year-old students and 15 per cent of the fourteen-year-old students surveyed were thought to need remedial instruction in reading. Keeves, Matthews and Bourke further estimate that 3 per cent of the former group and 0.8 per cent of the latter group of students had not mastered reading skills sufficiently well to comprehend even simple sentences. The researchers point out, however, that there are no marked differences in the level of performance of Australian students compared with their counterparts in Britain and the United States.

It is from these various estimates that the earlier figure of 10 per cent is hazarded as the likely prevalence rate of children with reading difficulties. The extent to which diagnostic and remedial services are available is a function of, among other things, the educational philosophy of the country, the level of awareness of its nationals of literacy problems and the human and material resources available. In recent years, much more has been and is done for these children by different agencies and at different levels: local and national. In Australia, the concern for learning problems and promise for action are reflected in the 1976 Report of the House of Representatives Select Committee on Specific Learning Difficulties (the Cadman Report). Among other recommendations, the Report calls for improved preservice and inservice teacher preparation and emphasizes the need for the identification, prevention and treatment of learning difficulties. In the U.S.A., the Education for All Handicapped Act (Public Law 94–142) provides for the allocation of funds to cater for 12 per cent of handicapped children aged five through seventeen, including 2 per cent of school children with specific learning disabilities for funding purposes. The Act emphasizes meeting individual needs of children. In England, the Bullock Report (Department of Education and Science, 1975) discusses the large number of children who experience considerable difficulty in mastering reading.

For the large number of Johnnys or Marys who cannot read or read poorly, there are many and varied reasons (see our chapters on home, school, and affective bases). There are also many and different Johnnys or Marys. Some are poor decoders, some are poor comprehenders and some are poor in both decoding and comprehension. Some will plod along, reading slowly but accurately, while others read fast but make many errors. Different disabled readers at different age levels and with varying degrees of disabilities also call for different treatment. The third-grade child who is a virtual nonreader may be more amenable to remediation than the sixth-grade retarded reader who may need to be well-motivated to maintain interest in literacy before being taught literacy subskills and skills. The question of *how many* of these children exist is bound up with the question of *who* these children are and *what* they shall be called. In the last analysis, how many of these children we can provide for depends on human and material resources available and how they are deployed, among other factors.

Terms and Concepts

Before proceeding, it is instructive to examine relevant terms and concepts relating to reading difficulties and how they are arrived at. We will sketch the work of Monroe (1932), Burt (1937), Schonell (1942), Robinson (1946), Bond and Tinker (1967, 1973), Clark (1970), and Rutter, Tizard and Whitmore (1970), among others. We will attempt to abstract the commonality underlying them.

In an early study of "children who cannot read" Monroe (1932) carried out detailed analyses of three groups of "reading defects" compared with a control group. She used a "reading index" which was the ratio of "reading grade" over "expectancy grade." The reading grade was the arithmetic average of the six reading measures used for the study and the expectancy grade was the mean of the aggregate of mental age + chronological age + "standard for arithmetic computation". Thus a child with a reading grade mean score of 2.6 and an expectancy grade score of 4.6 would have a reading index of 2.6/4.6 or 0.57. The standard deviations and percentile ranks of reading indices can be derived by referring to a table provided in Monroe's book. This concept of underachievement and the reading index has had considerable effect on the identification of children with reading difficulties even to the present date. A critique of this concept will be attempted in subsequent sections. While it is easy for us, with our current psychometric knowledge, to deride the lack of sophistication of her index, we should not overlook Monroe's pioneering studies of the detailed phenomena in "reading defects." In particular, she observed that there is no hard and fast line between "reader-defect cases" and normal readers and that reading as shown by the reading index does not correlate very highly with intelligence.

Burt (1937), in his classic study of "backwardness" at the time in England, emphasized the plurality of adverse circumstances. He found that in more than 50 per cent of cases of backwardness, there was what he termed "innate mental deficiency" together with correlates of unfavorable physical, home, school, social or temperamental factors. The most conspicuous factor was the lack of proper care by the mother—often the result of her own poverty and ill-health. He also drew attention to the paucity of experiential background in backward children. It must be emphasized that Burt's study reflected the social conditions that existed in England some fifty years ago.

In another English study, Schonell (1942) investigated "backwardness in the basic subjects" of reading, spelling and composition in a school population of 15, 515 children. He differentiated between "retardation" and "backwardness" and, in the latter, between "general backwardness" and "specific backwardness." He defined these terms as follows:

> Retardation or a condition of unrealised intellectual ability . . . characterises bright, normal and dull pupils alike. Retardation may be sufficiently pronounced to be synonymous with general backwardness. Retardation may be regarded as an assessment from an individual standpoint of educational level in relation to intellectual capacity. Backwardness may be regarded as an assessment from a group standpoint of educational level in relation to chronological age capacity. Both retardation and backwardness demand individual and, at times, specially organized methods of treatment (p. 66).

He went on to define specific backwardness (e.g. in reading) as characterizing "children whose ability in a subject (or two allied subjects) was at least 1½ years below their other educational attainments and general intellectual level" (p. 70).

Both Burt and Schonell have contributed substantially to the literature on backwardness, perhaps in slightly different ways. Burt has unravelled the interrelations of complex subcultural, school and home factors and Schonell has provided practical procedures based on scientific conditions. Both scholars have profoundly influenced the thinking of researchers and practitioners in Britain and beyond for many years and this influence has persisted to the present day.

In the U.S.A., Helen Robinson (1946) extended the Monroe study. She investigated over a five-year period 30 cases of "reading disability," with "retardation" varying from 9 months to 75 months, depending on chronological ages which ranged from six years nine months to fifteen years three months. She found that pupils who were seriously retarded in reading exhibited many anomalies—physical, mental, social, and emotional deficiencies and that many of these anomalies bear little or no relation to reading retardation.

Bond and Tinker (1967, 1973) have provided detailed work on diagnosis and remediation of "poor readers." They made a number of observations; the main ones included the following:

1. Reading difficulties may occur at any stage of schooling and can be corrected.
2. Reading difficulties vary from minor to severe ones and a wide range of reading ability is expected.
3. Most disability cases are made rather than born that way. Reading disabilities are sometimes the result of predisposing conditions within the child that are unrecognized, but for the most part, they are brought about by factors in the child's environment at home, at play, and in school (p. 15).

Recognizing the complexity in identifying "reading disability" cases, Bond and Tinker (1973) offered the following definition:

> The disabled reader is, in general, one who has had an opportunity to read, but who is not reading as well as could be expected by his aural verbal ability, his mental capacity, and his success in nonreading learnings. He is, in reality, the child who is at the lower end of the reading distribution when compared with other children of his general capacity (pp. 104–105).

It is of more than passing interest that exactly the same definition was adopted by the authors in the 1973 edition of their 1967 book. The question of aural and reading ability of a child was explained by Bond and Tinker (1967, p. 86) in this way: "A marked discrepancy between his aural verbal and his reading ability is an indication that a child may be a disabled reader." They proceeded to give a formula of IQ times years in school plus 1.0 as equivalent to the child's reading grade. For example, if the child with IQ 70 should have a reading age of 1.7 grades at the end of one year of schooling, a child with an IQ of 100 should read at the grade three level at the end of the second year of schooling, if we accept the Bond and Tinker formula. This concept of expectancy and discrepancy between expected and observed reading performance as a basis of defining reading difficulties is certainly flawed, just as the

Monroe formula is. We may also notice that terms like reading difficulties and reading disabilities seem to be used interchangeably by Bond and Tinker. Their idea of defining reading proficiency in terms of reading and "aural verbal ability" is an interesting one, although they did not pursue this beyond pointing out discrepancies between the two facets of reading by eye and reading by ear. This is part of the larger issue of indexing *reading* comprehension relative to *language* comprehension. The still larger issue of written-oral-cognitive conceptual (W–O–C) comprehension beyond the written-oral (W–O) comprehension has been discussed recently by Carroll (1977).

Clark (1970) carried out a well-planned community study of "specific reading difficulties" in Dunbartonshire, Scotland from 1966 to 1968. Her work was divided into three phases. In phase one the aim was to investigate the reading level and associated characteristics of all children in the community. In all, 1544 children (791 boys and 753 girls) aged 7 + were studied in this phase. Phase two was carried out a year later on all the backward readers in the community. This group consisted of 230 backward readers (138 boys and 92 girls). Still one year later those who continued to be backward readers but who had average intelligence were followed up in detail. An experimental group of 69 children aged nine and a control group of 42 children selected from those who had been at risk at age seven were examined in phase three. The backward reader in Clark's phase two was a child who would fail to "tackle a simple book with which he was not familiar; this was equated with a reading quotient of 85 or less" (Clark, 1970, p. 39). From those children in her phase three, 19 "severely backward readers" were described. Clark estimated the maximum proportion at the severe level of two or more years backward was 1.2 per cent of the population of this age, most of these being boys. The proportion of the "moderately backward" readers (those between one and two years behind the level expected of their peers) was estimated at 5.1 per cent. These percentages included all children with an IQ of 90 or above (on the full, verbal or performance WISC IQ), whatever the cause of their slow progress, provided they were regarded as "at risk" at seven years of age. Some of the main findings from the Clark study were: (1) About 15 per cent of the children were without any independent reading skill (in 1966) after they had been two years at school; (2) Of the 230 backward readers, half still required assistance in the basic skills of reading, even after three years of schooling; (3) Of the severely disabled readers, "It appeared that they would require assistance over a wide range of activities. The striking finding was the *diversity* of disabilities and *not* an underlying pattern common to the group . . ." (p. 128).

The sketch of the above representative works stretching from the 1930s to the early 1970s is of more than historical interest and reveals a number of issues besetting the field of reading disabilities. All the studies are of a descriptive, correlational nature. This is not surprising from an historical point of view. We should bear this in mind when we compare and contrast some of the current empirical studies. We also note a proliferation and lack of agreement of terms and concepts. Terms like reading difficulties, reading backwardness, reading disabilities or even reading defects have been used—all presumably referring to the group we term reading difficulties here. This lack of agreement is not conducive to both research and instruction, as the same term, may refer to different groups of children or different terms may be used for the same children. What merits more careful examination from the research and programming point of view is the implicit or explicit concept of underachievement and the quasi-mathematical formula of achievement quotient/expectancy quotient used for four decades in screening, diagnosing and selecting children for remedial or special education programs. Take as yet one more example of the confused state of definitions from a recent work. In a generally useful volume on diagnosing and correcting "reading disabilities," Spache (1976) offers a "pragmatic" definition of a "retarded" reader as one retarded in a number of major reading subskills and lagging by one or more years if in the primary grades, or by two years or more if older. This reader is also "retarded below that level necessary for full participation in the reading tasks of his age or grade or socioeconomic group," while having had normal opportunities for schooling and despite corrective efforts (p. 6). What Spache calls retarded readers is certainly not the same as what researchers in England would call retarded. His definition is more applicable to our reading difficulties group. The other problem that Spache grapples with, as many other people have done, is to delimit reading difficulties to "a number of major reading skills." He is primarily looking at this from the point of view of teachers. He feels that one area of reading and a small lag (e.g. six months) are manageable by regular classroom teachers. His pragmatic of whether deficiencies in one reading subskill or in a cluster of reading subskills should constitute difficulties is in fact the subject of much contemporary interest. In broad terms, the question is: are poor comprehenders also poor decoders or are comprehending and decoding subskills in poor readers quite separate? In other words, are comprehension and decoding interdependent or are they independent? Cromer (1970) and Perfetti and Hogaboam (1975) have provided different viewpoints, while Golinkoff (1975–1976) has reviewed selected studies bearing on the central question. This will be further explored.

The Concept of Underachievement

It is unfortunate that the notion of learning quotient or achievement quotient derived by dividing various achievement scores by an expectancy score has persisted from Monroe's early days to the present time. While aware of the limitations of this concept, not a few psychologists and administrators still continue to use the reading index or achievement quotient to screen and diagnose children and to prescribe programs for them. The achievement quotient suffers from all the inherent statistical weaknesses of comparing a ratio with another ratio, without taking into account the discrepant errors of measurement in each test and the relationship of one test to another. Crane (1959) and McLeod (1968a, 1968b) have criticized the use of indices so derived.

Related to the use of the achievement or learning quotient is the concept of underachievement. It is believed by many people that children are expected to work up to their "capacity" and that it is well-nigh impossible to achieve over and above their "capacity." Even Burt (1937, p. 35) rather uncharacteristically, asserted that overachievers could only "occur sporadically in a few young bookworms who show an extra zeal or talent in academic work, but less practical shrewdness and common sense. . . ." The unrepentent argument of Burt (1967a) that overachievement is a rare phenomenon is untenable. In actual practice there are as many "overachievers" as there are "underachievers." This is verified in elegant regression studies by Yule, Rutter, Berger and Thompson (1974) in four replications in different populations and different age groups with sample sizes ranging from 1,143 to 2,113. This now discredited dogma that reading achievement should exactly parallel tested intelligence and the empirical finding of as many underachievers as there are overachievers have implications for provisions for disabled readers.

In a monograph on over- and underachievement which deserves to be widely read, Robert Thorndike (1963) indicates clearly that defining and predicting underachievement should take into account: (1) errors of measurement, (2) the heterogeneity of the criterion of achievement, (3) the limited scope of the predictors and (4) the impact of varied experiences on the individual. The basic concept of *regression effect* seems to have eluded most workers using the ratio comparison to derive an achievement score. In essence, regression can be explained as follows. When the correlation between measures is less than unity, the children who are *well above* average on the measure will be less superior on the other, and those *well below* average on the first measure will be less inferior on the second. Thorndike's explanation of the use of predicted scores from a regression equation between aptitude and learning should be heeded. He states that:

> If a simple difference between aptitude and achievement standard scores, or a ratio of achievement to aptitude measure, is computed, the high aptitude group will appear primarily to be "underachievers" and the low aptitude group to be "overachievers." For this reason it is necessary to define "underachievement" as discrepancy of actual achievement from the *predicted* value, predicted upon the basis of the regression equation between aptitude and achievement. A failure to recognize this regression effect has rendered questionable, if not meaningless, much of the research on "underachievement" (p. 13).

Despite this admonition, the achievement quotient continues to be used (see for example, Bond, Clymer, and Hoyt, 1955; Harris, 1970). Decisions were made and continue to be made on the placement of children on the basis of the simple ratio of achievement over expectancy. In an otherwise viable psychoneurological model of learning disorders, Myklebust (1971) invoked the "learning quotient" in very much the same vein as Monroe's reading index. However, there are some workers who have used multiple regression equations to predict reading age from chronological age and IQ (Fransella and Gerver, 1965).

One of the best examples of the practical application of Thorndike's approach to predicting reading disabilities can be found in the detailed Isle of Wight survey undertaken by Rutter, Tizard and Whitmore (1970). They distinguished between reading backwardness and reading retardation. Reading backwardness was defined as an attainment in reading accuracy or comprehension on Neal's (1963) Analysis of Reading Ability test 28 months or more below the chronological age. Reading retardation was defined as an attainment in reading accuracy or comprehension 28 months or more below the level *predicted* on the basis of each child's age and short WISC IQ. The 28 months cutoff was selected to include an estimated five per cent of school children. The intent of Rutter et al. was to overcome statistical objections inherent in the usual achievement quotients and to make adjustments to the WISC IQ through the use of predicted scores. Thus a child with 130 IQ whose reading is only average for the chronological age would be *retarded* in relation to his or her intelligence but not *backward* in absolute terms. In practice, however, such children would also be backward. A few examples will illustrate this. A boy nine years nine months of age with a scaled score of 54 on the WISC short form and scoring eight years ten months on the Neale comprehension test apparently is retarded in reading by eleven months. When adjustment is made to his WISC IQ, his expected reading age is ten years ten months. In other words, he is about two years retarded in his reading comprehension. Another boy aged ten years six months with a short WISC scaled score of 36 (WISC IQ of 83) reading at the same level of eight years ten months shows less discrepancy statistically, as his expected reading age is nine years ten months (Rutter, Tizard and Whitmore, 1970, p. 35). Admittedly, there are flaws with the arbitrary 28 months or below cutoff in the use of the WISC short form and in equating reading accuracy or comprehension solely on the Neale Analysis of Reading Ability test. Overall, the regression approach is generally sound and statistically defensible. Recently, McLeod (1978, 1979) has verified Thorndike's concept. He has derived formulae and provided conversion tables giving the predicted achievement level of children of any IQ level for ages six to fourteen, together with cutoff zones for designating more severely disabled cases. As in the Isle of Wight investigation, the rationale is that from the correlation between the predictor variable (e.g. IQ or mental age) and the criterion variable (e.g. reading accuracy or comprehension score) and the reliability (internal consistency) of the variables, it is possible to calculate the expected reading attainment level for any particular level of the predictor variable. One is thus able to determine if a child's reading performance is on a par with, below or above, this *predicted* value. Also, one can determine the probability of any deviation from the expected value so as to arrive at a decision on placing children for prescriptive programs with reasonable certainty.

Thus, from the elegant formulation of Thorndike (1963), empirical findings of the monumental Isle of Wight investigation (Rutter, Tizard and Whitmore, 1970; Rutter and Yule, 1973; Yule, 1973; Yule and Rutter, 1976; Yule, Rutter, Berger and Thompson, 1974) and the mathematical derivation of McLeod (1978), the discredited achievement or learning quotient should be laid to rest. These researchers have provided a conceptually sound, computationally convenient and hopefully administratively acceptable psychometric method of screening children with reading and other school achievement difficulties. But psychometric screening devices also need to be supplemented by individual diagnosis of children for appropriate educational placement and programming. Parenthetically, we will do well to review some of the proven statistical techniques of scaling of marks and teachers' estimates, perfected for the English eleven-plus examination in the 1940s to the early 1960s, in our consideration of the use of intelligence and achievement scores, teachers' estimates, and age allowances for screening learning difficulties (see for example, McClelland, 1949). The Isle of Wight investigation in particular has shown that there is some validity to the distinction drawn by Schonell (1942) between reading backwardness and reading retardation, just as we have differentiated between reading difficulties and specific reading disability (developmental dyslexia). The Rutter et al. epidemiology study has shown that there are many differences in achievement, in speech and language, in behavioral and overt neurological disorders and in development generally between these two groups of disabled readers.

"Perceptual" Inefficiency

The use of the regression equation for screening children with reading difficulties and the individual diagnosis of more severe cases alert us to the fact that intellectual ability is only one determinant, perhaps an important one, of reading disabilities. Even in the use of intelligence measures, their relationship to reading varies with age and the nature of the sample. Schonell (1942), for example, reported correlation coefficients between intelligence and reading of 0.79 at age eight and 0.44 at age eleven. These figures simply describe the degree of relationship of the two variables and no causation is implied. Intelligence may "cause" reading just as much as "reading" may "cause" measured intelligence. The apparent "shrinkage" of these simple correlation coefficients is due to, among other things, varying reliabilities of intelligence tests at different age levels and, more importantly, to some kind of threshold effect in a large, unselected group. In other words, "intelligence" is more important as a prerequisite at a younger age during reading acquisition; it explains less of the individual variation with older children who are generally fluent readers.

Another important aspect relates to the use of Pearson product-moment correlation coefficients to infer relationship. Thorndike (1963) suggests that the correlation ratio "eta" might be more appropriate, as the intelligence-reading relationship over a wide age range is more likely to be nonlinear rather than linear. More correctly, the *cross-lagged panel correlation* paradigm (see Campbell and Stanley, 1963) should be used. This technique makes use of correlational information relating two variables at two or more points in time. When a given event (Event *X*) consistently precedes the occurrence of another event (Event *Y*) but the opposite does not hold, then we can infer that either: (1) Event *X* is a likely "causc" of Event *Y* or (2) both Events *X* and *Y* are "caused" by some other underlying event. In other words, if the correlation between *P* at time 1 and *Q* at time 2 is larger than the correlation between *Q* at time 1 and *P* at time 2, given reliable measures of *P* and *Q*, then it is likely that *P* "causes" *Q*. The cross-lagged panel correlation technique was used by Crano, Kenny and Campbell (1972) to study the relationship between intelligence and achievement in over 5,000 students. The researchers found that for students of suburban schools the abstract-to-concrete causal sequence predominated, while for inner city school children the opposite held. This finding of intelligence and achievement at grade four and grade six seemingly interacting with socioeconomic class will not be uncovered with the simple correlation technique. More recently, Atkin, Bray, Davison, Herzberger, Humphreys and Selzer (1977) have used the cross-lagged panel technique to analyze 16 cognitive measures in fifth-, seventh-, ninth- and eleventh-grade students and have found aural comprehension as tapping the causal factors involved in intellectual development.

Attention to correct methodology will go a long way toward helping both researchers and practitioners in determining who are the children with reading difficulties. We have seen how the relationship between intelligence and reading achievement will take on a different meaning with the application of regression equations and the use of such techniques as the eta coefficient or the cross-lagged panel analysis. Whatever techniques we use and whatever their merits, we must guard against simplistic notions of a one-to-one relationship and the assumption that simple "causal" factors are necessary and sufficient to explain reading problems. Other factors exist that impinge on reading or not reading—cultural, subcultural, school, home and affect. These aspects have been discussed in some detail in preceding chapters. We will dwell on yet another factor often mentioned as important for reading acquisition, namely, so called perceptual factors. Visual perception and imperception and auditory perception and imperception are often cited as underlying reading difficulties and specific reading disabilities. In our chapters in this volume on neurological substrates and "Seeing and Reading" we have described the main physiological mechanisms of importance to the reading act. We have emphasized the constructive and reconstructive roles of the sense organs and the active participation of readers in the reading process.

Rather than detailing various facets of "perception" and how they may affect reading difficulties, we will just sketch some of the relevant dimensions. Our aim is to show that any perceptual basis we may wish to attribute to reading difficulties operates more at the cognitive level. Readers interested in the role of perception and reading and reading difficulties may want to consult such sources as Barrett (1965), Dykstra (1966), Goins (1958), Robinson (1972a, 1972b), H. Smith (1968), the chapters in visual and auditory perception in Vernon (1957, 1971), and the work of Vellutino (1978, 1979, 1980), among others.

Belief in the efficacy of visual perception and its effect on reading disabilities is derived from several sources. One is the work of developmental psychologists in postulating the dependence of cognitive-linguistic functions on the successful mastery of sensory-motor functions. The other is from clinical psychology where cases of acquired dyslexia and patients with structural brain damage have been found to be deficient and defective in visual-motor tasks. The third source is conventional practice, which from the time of Monroe and Schonell and continuing to the present day, consists of examining "psychographs" or profiles of a child's strengths and weaknesses in order to plan programs. Added to the use of profiles and task analysis, which certainly facilitate teaching, is the erroneous belief of a few members of the optometric profession who unduly overstress the importance of "perception." These and others emphasize such activities as eye-hand coordination, figure-ground position in space, body schema, and sensory integration as being basic to beginning reading proficiency. Their zeal is fanned by commercial programs which purport to develop these "skills" as entities and hence to remediate reading disabilities.

We will examine several empirical studies which bear on the question of "visual perception." What people often think of as perceptual deficiency is best interpreted as perceptual inefficiency and poor information processing. In an early study of prediction for reading failure, de Hirsch, Jansky and Langford (1966) examined 37 variables administered to 53 kindergarten children and found ten of these variables as most predictive in identifying failing readers. In this and subsequent predictive studies (Jansky, 1973), three of the variables have been identified as the best predicting tests—letter naming, word matching and the Bender Gestalt Test (1938, 1946). Of particular interest here is the Bender Gestalt test which has been claimed by some (and erroneously) to measure visual-motor performance. The test is best interpreted as measuring the *integrative* aspect in copying or visual-motor retention (Bender, 1970; Koppitz, 1970). It may be noted that in controlled studies Vellutino, Pruzek, Steger and Meshoulam (1973) and Vellutino, Smith, Steger and Kaman (1975) compared carefully selected reader groups on some common visual motor tasks including the Bender. They found no difference in performing these tasks between poor and normal readers.

In two different studies Katz and Wicklund (1971, 1972) found that good and poor readers at grades five, two and six did not differ in *search time* for an individual letter embedded in a random (nonredundant) string of letters, although the skilled group was faster on a word scanning task. This suggests that some characteristics of words may make them more easily identifiable by skilled rather than less skilled readers. The results also suggest that there are no reader ability differences occurring in the use of direct perceptual information about visual features present on a printed page. The results further suggest a basic retrieval process difference rather than word recognition difference. The main component of word scanning is the retrieval of a name code and good comprehenders have more facility with retrieving name codes.

Steinheiser and Guthrie (1974) compared poor and normal readers matched for age and reading levels on visual search tasks of scrambled word strings and prose materials. They found poor readers took longer search time than age-matched normals in scanning for target words, letters and phonemes. But when compared with younger normal readers matched for reading levels, the poor readers took about the same time to scan for target words, took shorter latencies for letters but significantly longer latencies for phonemes. Steinheiser and Guthrie suggest that poor readers have relatively good ability to detect visual features of letters and words, while they may have difficulties converting graphic symbols to their corresponding sounds.

Mason (1975) raised the possibility that good and poor readers might be different in their abilities to augment visual feature information with redundancy information. The results of her experiments showed that poor readers were equivalent to good readers in identifying individual letters only when low redundant (non-English-like) displays were used. However, good readers were faster than poor readers on both word displays and redundant nonword displays. The issue is whether poor readers read poorly because of a spatial order perception defect that precludes their use of positional redundancy in single letter identification or whether they do not use positional redundancy because they do not read enough to have learned well the positional frequencies of letters in printed English. Mason, Katz and Wicklund (1975) carried out two experiments aimed at testing specifically spatial order memory differences as a function of reading ability with good and poor sixth-grade readers. The researchers found that poor readers have difficulty in encoding, preserving and retrieving spatial relationships in a string of letters. It is possible that a spatial order perception deficit diminishes positional redundancy as a source of information for poor readers.

The above works are selective but representative experimental studies which attempt to explain the role of perception in reading. By eschewing the level-of-performance approach with correlation studies and by appropriate manipulation of experimental variables, we are better able to understand that perceptual factors cannot be the main cause of reading disabilities. Despite strong evidence to the contrary by professionals of such stature as the empirical educationist Gates (1922), the experimental psychologist Vernon (1957, 1971), the neuropsychologist Benton (1962), the ophthalmologist Goldberg (1959) and the neurologist Critchley (1964, 1970), so-called visual perceptual deficiencies are still held up as a causal factor of reading disabilities. Even with nondisabled readers, Robinson (1972b, p. 33) found that ". . . visual perception made no significant contribution to reading with CA [chronological age] and MA [mental age] controlled," and that auditory discrimination had a stronger impact on reading scores. Goldberg (1959) stated in a classic paper that defective vision, muscle imbalance and strabismus (squinting) are not significant factors in reading disability and that convergence insufficiency and weak binocular status may cause fatigue and slow reading, but not retard it. Critchley (1970, pp. 50–64) suggested that even severe reading disability (dyslexia) is independent of error of refraction, muscle imbalance, and imperfect binocular fusion. He added the qualification that subtle ocular examination might uncover certain defects, although these defects could be the product rather than the cause of dyslexia. The American Academy of Pediatrics, the American Academy of Ophthalmology and Otolaryngology and the American Association of Ophthalmology have issued a joint organizational statement (January, 1972) on "the eye and learning disabilities." These organizations state that ". . . there is no peripheral eye defect which produces dyslexia and associated disabilities. Eye defects do not cause reversals of letters, words, or numbers." Deploring the claim of improving the academic skills of disabled readers with treatment based solely on ocular training, these learned societies recognize that remediation is the ultimate responsibility of educational science.

In writing on perceptual inefficiencies of reading disabilities, we have been concentrating on children with reading difficulties variously termed poor readers, backward readers or less skilled readers. There are other perceptual aspects we need to examine such as temporal order perception and cross-modal coding. These functions will be discussed in connection with the chapter on specific reading disability. We would like to emphasize, however, that the literature does not make a sharp differentiation between "backward" and "retarded" or dyslexic children. Thus, at times we are restricted to treating them together rather than as watertight groups.

To come back to perceptual inefficiency in reading disabilities, the practice of prescribing visual perception training exercises as an effective remediation program is still not uncommon. This has led Mann and his associates (Mann, 1970, 1971; Mann and Goodman, 1976) to decry the "fractionating" of educational practices when there is little evidence linking perceptual training and improvement in reading skills. Mann and Goodman point out that perception in so-called perceptual training is an abstraction, is unclear as a concept, represents artificial regression because it forces children to go back to "regressive" activities much less relevant to reading and because it focuses on wrong activities. We concur generally with this view. The only way children can learn to read is by reading, granted we may modify teaching programs and strategies. Unlike the blind or the deaf where modes other than print (e.g. tactile-kinaesthetic) need to be used to acquire literacy, disabled readers must, in the last analysis, come to grips with visible language on a printed page. Mann and Goodman draw on relevant literature to support their argument of the ineffectual use of perceptual training in relation to reading. They suggest the use of criterion-referenced measurement and instructional objectives as alternatives to train children in the skills functional for their living. In a different context, Carver (1972, 1974) has emphasized the need for *edumetric* or criterion-referenced type tests rather than psychometric or norm-referenced tests. The edumetric tests focus attention on ability to read and understand reading materials of increasing difficulty.

"Perception" in Relation to Cognition

To be fair to the protagonists for the role of perception, much of the criticism, such as those raised by Mann and others, is directed against so-called perceptual exercises and their claim of efficacy to remediate reading problems. It is instructive to examine the more current views of two clinical and applied psychologists who have contributed to our understanding of disabled readers. Both Frostig (1975) and Wepman (1975) have recently brought together findings from different fields to explicate their approaches. They have emphasized the *integrative function* of perception, visual and auditory respectively, and have related perception to cognition and development generally. From her long clinical experience, Frostig reminds us that many learning or reading disabled children also experience other disabilities. She sees perception as of central significance and subserving motor functions, language and higher thought processes. The important problem is the integration of perceptual and cognitive abilities so as to further the development of the child. She discusses the psychological, neuro-anatomical and neurophysiological substrates of perception. She relates perception to Piaget's (Piaget and Inhelder, 1969) schema or representation of previous experience and Hebb's (1968) construct of cell assemblies and phase sequences and emphasizes the importance of perceptual activities. Sensory-motor functions and imagery help to control and guide behavior. The integrative functions of perception in these tasks subserve language and thought, which in turn are related to perception. Her chapter is, as yet, the most forceful "manifesto" of Frostig's rationale.

In a similar vein but dealing with audition, Wepman (1975) discusses the role of auditory perception and imperception. The latter term he defines as: "the product of inadequate development or malfunction of the receptive mechanism either at the peripheral end organ or in the nervous system responsible for transmitting sound patterns" (p. 264). Note that auditory imperception may also affect poor readers and more severely disabled readers. Like Frostig, Wepman emphasizes the interrelation of cognition building on perceptual processing development for efficient language formulation and use. In parallel with visual perception, auditory perception can take the form of acuity, discrimination, sequencing, memory and recall of auditory materials. Reading disabilities are seen by Wepman as the interruption in the progression from neural bases to motor, visual, auditory and to cognitive activities converging on formal operation and language. The line of development is necessary, for symbolic behavior and the various functions—visual, auditory, tactile-kinesthetic—are interrelated. Reading comprehension demands a close, integrative working of the perceptual and conceptual processes. Auditory imperception can impair the child at either the perceptual or the conceptual levels and thus delays or impoverishes reading acquisition. Auditory perception, on the other hand, adds materially to language and speech acquisition and in their development to cognitive growth. The three subprocesses at the perceptual level identified as essential to learning are: auditory discrimination, memory and sequential recall. One implication from the clinical program of Frostig and Wepman and their current view is the understanding and acceptance of modality (visual and auditory in the main) differences and preferences in children. This knowledge can then be applied to the identification of such children for early educational processes.

It is appropriate to conclude this section on "Perceptual Inefficiency" by citing a recent experimental analysis of pattern recognition in poor readers. Extending his earlier work (Kolers, 1973b, 1974) of analyzing written symbols into graphemic and other features, Kolers (1975) aimed at assessing good and poor readers in their encoding of the semantic and the graphemic features of sentences. He administered a test of recognition memory for sentences to two groups of school children with a median placement of seventh grade. One group (15 readers) was above-average in reading and this group was matched in age, grade, school and sex with a group of 22 below-average readers. The test enabled separate analyses to be made of graphemic pattern-analyzing subskills required in reading sentences and of a more interpretive subskill. Both skilled and poor readers performed about equally on tests involving language use and grammar, but the poor readers were markedly retarded in their pattern analysis of the texts. Kolers is careful to point out that this graphemic pattern analyzing ability is not the usually defined "visual" problem as such. The difficulty is more associated with cognitive pattern analysis. In this sense, the perceptual basis of reading disabilities operates more at a cognitive level, rather than in the usually understood performance on conventional visual perception tests. The work of Kolers thus lends support to the assertion of Vellutino (1978, 1979, 1980) and Vernon (1957, 1971) that visual or perceptual deficits in reading disabilities will have to be interpreted much more broadly in cognitive terms.

Interdependence of Decoding and Comprehension

Discussions in the preceding section remind us of an early contribution of Calfee in his research program into learning to read. Writing under the chapter heading, "How a child needs to think to learn to read," Calfee, Chapman and Venezky (1972) carefully analyzed the cognitive subskills subserving reading acquisition. For beginning readers, it is clear from the Calfee et al. study that important subskills in the visual and auditory domains have to be mastered (see also Calfee, 1975, 1976, 1977; Calfee and Drum, 1978). In our earlier chapters we have discussed at some length a number of principles in mastering the subskills of reading and in integrating these subskills into an integrative whole. What we want to warn against here is the undue emphasis given in some popular literature to the role of the different modalities and the concomitant perceptual training in these modalities—training not entirely related to reading per se. To the extent that reading is a verbal process, understanding reading disabilities may come by understanding the role of verbal processing as a source of difficulties. Specifically, we are led to the quest for the contribution of decoding to comprehension. From the outset, we must be clear about those concepts and processes in our interpretation of relevant literature. Decoding seems to be the more easily understandable of the two terms. It usually refers to vocalization or identification. Comprehension is the more difficult to define, as we have seen in our chapter on cognitive aspects of reading. At times, comprehension may refer to literal comprehension; at other times, it refers to critical reading; at still other times, it refers to reading for inferences, drawing logical conclusions; and it could refer to all these various interrelated aspects. To some extent, the use of these two terms of decoding and comprehending is constrained by the tests used in quantifying decoding and comprehending subskills. Whatever broad terms we use, the central question is: Are decoding subskills both necessary and sufficient for comprehension? Given the generally accepted notion that comprehension is the goal of reading, there seems to be general accord in the technical and popular literature that decoding is necessary for comprehension. But is it sufficient? Or the question can be turned into the independence vs. interdependence of decoding and comprehension. Specifically, researchers may want to examine the contribution of fast and accurate decoding to the comprehension process and the nature of decoding (e.g. alphabetic and nonalphabetic materials and units of decoding). Recall our discussion of Coding Processes in Chapter 9 where it is explained that reaction times or latencies are used as a closer approximation to the mental operations taking place in reading rather than correlational indices or level-of-performance studies. The concept of fast decoding is in line with the automaticity model of LaBerge and Samuels (1974) that explains how readers can free their attention for comprehension (see also Curtis, 1980).

Given the above background, we will examine some relevant experimental studies on the sources of reading difficulties and specifically the verbal component of difficulties. We will discuss in the main two broad groups of studies in a time sequence to better understand contemporary development. One group pertains to the series of studies by Wiener, Cromer and associates and specifically their difference-deficit model of reading difficulties (Cromer, 1970; Cromer and Wiener, 1966; Oaken, Wiener and Cromer, 1971; Steiner, Wiener and Cromer, 1971; Wiener and Cromer, 1967). The other is the research program on fast and accurate decoding and reading comprehension of skilled and less skilled readers undertaken by Perfetti and associates (Berger and Perfetti, 1977; Goldman, Hogaboam, Bell, and Perfetti, 1980; Hogaboam and Perfetti, 1978; Perfetti, 1977; Perfetti, Finger and Hogaboam, 1978; Perfetti and Goldman, 1976; Perfetti and Hogaboam, 1975). Some of these studies will be sketched below.

Difference-Deficit Models

Wiener and Cromer are among the early workers who attempted to conceptualize reading difficulties in some definable way rather than treat all sufferers of this problem as a broad, undifferentiated group. They distinguished between four kinds or subgroups of reading difficulties: (1) those with a *defect* because of some dysfunction (e.g. sensory impairment), (2) those with a *deficit* because of the absence of some function, (3) those with a *disruption* because of some interference (e.g. hyperactivity) and (4) those with a difference because of a mismatch between an individual's mode of responses and the responses needed for reading. Thus, according to the defect model, the nonfunction or dysfunction must be corrected or some substitute modality or medium must be used. According to the deficit model, the deficiency must be made up in some way, such as through remedial reading. With the disruption model the interference must be removed before adequate instruction can take place. The difference approach emphasizes the need to modify reading materials, or, for that matter, the readers' way of learning, so that the mismatch can be minimized or reduced altogether.

From the above postulate of different kinds of reading difficulties Cromer (1970) studied poor readers (college students) fitting the description of two of the four models and compared the two groups, one with the other, and with good readers. His deficit group lacked vocabulary subskills and possibly decoding subskills, while the difference group seemed to possess vocabulary subskills but failed to read in units larger than single words. As hypothesized, the difference group, but not the deficit group, read as well as the good readers when materials were presented in preorganized phrases. The results suggest that poor readers read word-by-word rather than in meaningful units such as phrases, and that one source of comprehension difficulty may be the way in which poor readers organize reading input.

According to this and the earlier findings, the deficit group was marked by both a vocabulary subskill deficit and a comprehension deficit and the difference group by adequate vocabulary subskills but difficulties in organizing text. Oaken, Wiener and Cromer (1971) tested the hypothesis that the difference group can be helped in their comprehension if reading materials are preorganized into meaningful units. In a study of fifth-grade children they found that in poor readers identification training was not sufficient for improving reading comprehension, as these children do not organize reading materials into appropriate patterns. This was borne out by their other finding that poor readers could comprehend as well as good readers when listening to materials with the words well-defined and well-organized. The rationale was that the high level of organization imposed on the materials helped to guide comprehension. Conversely, when good readers listened to stories with poor auditory input and poor organization, they showed as high a level of comprehension as they did for the good auditory input materials, while the comprehension of the poor readers decreased. Here the good readers must have imposed order on the input. The emphasis of the Oaken et al. study is that word identification is not sufficient for comprehension.

In a later study Steiner, Wiener and Cromer (1971) examined the relationship between comprehension (by providing prior contextual information) and decoding (word identification) in fifth-grade good and poor readers. The children were tested under conditions of paragraph presentation versus single word presentation and comprehension training in the form of story summary with synonyms prior to reading versus no comprehension training. Results showed that poor readers failed to extract syntactic and contextual cues essential for identification even when presented with them. Words were read as if they were unrelated in syntactic or contextual relationship. Thus, this is a failure to identify not just individual lexical items but the whole range of language signaling devices. There are thus implications for teaching in terms of organizing materials into groupings and of utilizing critical contextual cues for both identification and comprehension.

The series of studies of Wiener and Cromer is mentioned as deserving some attention, as they attempted to grapple with the verbal source of reading difficulties. There are definitional problems such as equating decoding with identification and defining comprehension in terms of standardized tests and also methodological flaws (see for example the critique of Calfee, Arnold and Drum, 1976). They have, however, alerted researchers and practitioners to the various sources of reading difficulties and focused attention less on identification and more on contextual devices. Similar experimental work appearing at the time and emphasizing sentence structure in good and poor readers and the inefficiency of poor readers in making use of information inherent in the grammatical structure of a sentence may be cited (e.g. Weinstein and Rabinovitch, 1971). This is of course an integral part of the larger context of syntax and semantics in reading comprehension discussed in Chapter 10. Nearer to our present discussion of reading difficulties may be the analysis of reading errors of six-year-old children who were found to make use of grammatical and meaning cues to recognize words

(Weber, 1970a); the study of errors and response times of third- and sixth-grade children who increasingly used semantic rather than phonetic features (Felzen and Anisfeld, 1970); and above all the successful and unsuccessful use of cues in reading and the approximation of miscues to text in terms of symbol-sound correspondence, syntax and semantics (Goodman, 1968). The research and instructional question boils down to how best children can be helped and guided to use increasingly larger syntactic and semantic cues than the word or other subunits. In terms of models of reading difficulties postulated by Wiener and Cromer in the early 1970s, we will find a parallel development in conceptualizing reading retardation in a paper by Applebee (1971).

Fast, Accurate Decoding in Good and Poor Comprehenders

In a recent review article Golinkoff (1975–1976) discussed the broad components: decoding, accessing the meaning of single words and the text organization process. Sharing the view of Gibson and Levin (1975, p. 5) that reading is "extraction of meaning from text" and taking decoding to mean vocalization or pronouncing the printed word, Golinkoff outlined some of the characteristics of good comprehenders. These requirements include: (1) rapid and accurate word recognition, (2) automatized basic decoding subskills, (3) flexibility and adaptability in using appropriate units as demanded by tasks and (4) awareness of linguistic and cognitive processes. In several studies she examined semantic interference and the relationship of decoding to word comprehension.

Rosinski, Golinkoff and Kukish (1975) found that even grade two children could extract meaning of printed words, though not automatically. Golinkoff and Rosinski (1976) found that with third- and fifth-grade children varying in level of comprehension skill, there was no difference in the extent to which skilled and less skilled comprehenders experienced semantic interference with familiar primer-level words. Both groups could decode these words readily. However, the time it took them to pronounce nonsense CVC trigrams differed considerably. This study suggests that decoding ability and semantic processing may be separable subskills to some extent with familiar first-grade level words. The larger interpretation is that less skilled comprehenders show weak decoding subskills.

Extending their earlier studies, Pace and Golinkoff (1976) reasoned that by manipulating decoding difficulty we should affect retrieval of single-word meaning. More difficult words would likely produce interference for the skilled comprehenders but not for the less skilled group, as semantic interference would not occur for this group of students who could not readily decode the more difficult words. Third- and fifth-grade children comparable to those of the Golinkoff and Rosinski (1976) study were asked to read aloud four lists of words. The easy set was composed of words at the first grade level (e.g. *sock*) and pronounceable CVC trigrams (e.g. *yat*). The difficult series was made up of fifth- and sixth-grade level real words and nonsense words (e.g. *widbolch*). Four conditions of a Stroop type of interference task were imposed: pictures alone, pictures with matching words, pictures with nonmatching words and pictures with nonsense words. Results of analysis of decoding tasks showed that the difficult set of real words was the most difficult for the less skilled third-graders, as hypothesized. These children also experienced the least semantic interference with these words. Thus the complementary findings suggest that facility in decoding and extraction of word meaning are related. Less skilled comprehenders are deficient or inefficient in the utilization of decoding skills. These readers also likely expend an inordinate amount of attention on decoding in the LaBerge and Samuels (1974) sense so that their comprehension suffers.

This brings us to other contemporary studies of decoding and comprehension in skilled and less skilled readers. In their research program Perfetti and associates (Berger and Perfetti, 1977; Goldman, Hogaboam, Bell, and Perfetti, 1980; Hogaboam and Perfetti, 1978; Perfetti, 1977; Perfetti, Finger and Hogaboam, 1978; Perfetti and Goldman, 1976; Perfetti and Hogaboam, 1975; Perfetti and Lesgold, 1977) have examined the interdependence of decoding and comprehension and the nature of fast, accurate decoding in relation to different stimuli. In an earlier study with third- and fifth-grade children, Perfetti and Hogaboam (1975) found that single word vocalization latencies were longer for less skilled comprehenders. There was also an interaction between word type and level of comprehension skill. The groups (skilled and less skilled readers) showed large vocalization latency differences for pseudowords and for low frequency English words but smaller differences for high frequency English words. Knowledge of word meanings may be a less significant factor in vocalization latency for the skilled group than for the less skilled group. Nor can the differential latency be attributed to vocabulary differences, as the word meanings were known to the children and as the greatest difference between the two groups was with the pseudo-words. Perfetti and Hogaboam emphasized that differences in reading comprehension skill are in the main due to differences in the understanding and use of verbal codes, including the extent to which the codes are activated automatically. A corollary of this position is that differences in skilled and less skilled readers will occur for verbal stimuli but likely not for nonalphabetic stimuli such as colors, digits and pictures.

To further evaluate the source of vocalization latency differences in readers of varying skills, Hogaboam and Perfetti (1978) set up three experiments with third- and fourth-graders. In experiment one the reader difference was found to be greater for pseudowords and two-syllable units than for English words and one-syllable units. Less skilled readers were more affected by the number of syllables than the skilled readers. Thus, results support and extend the earlier view of a basic coding process and one not just dependent on whole word requirements. Experiments two and three tested the hypothesis that providing a fixed amount of word experience should benefit skilled readers more than less skilled ones. Or alternatively, that if the quantity of word experience alone is responsible for observed reader differences, then providing comparable degrees of experiences should reduce decoding difficulties. It was found that aural and printed experience with pseudowords led to decreased vocalization latencies for these pseudowords for both reader groups and that there was no effect of meaning on either group. These effects were found to last for some ten weeks. Thus decoding differences are not wholly attributable to prior experience with word units. Processes involving phonetic components may be implicated.

Overall, the three experiments found a large difference in latency between skilled and less skilled readers in the absence of any prior exposure to pseudowords and that equal exposure to word experience did not lead to equal reaction times. The finding of less well developed print-to-sound correspondence in less skilled readers thus supports the early Perfetti and Hogaboam results. These researchers emphasized that the facilitating effect of simple familiarizing experiences only applied to decoding speed, which is taken to reflect internal mental processes, and it is not known if comprehension is actually aided.

In four experiments involving skilled and less skilled third-grade readers Perfetti, Finger and Hogaboam (1978) found that vocalization latencies were a function of set size, number of syllables and stimulus materials. Subjects did not differ in naming colors, digits and pictures. Reader differences were found in words and these increased with number of syllables and letters. Measured reading skill was highly correlated with speed of decoding printed words and less with the nonalphabetic stimuli except for digits. Naming difficulty was ruled out with the less skilled readers. Vocalization tasks in relation to reading could be ordered from nonalphabetic to alphabetic materials according to the demands for retrieval from long-term memory. The ordering was substantiated in a multiple regression analysis. Overall, the findings point to coding problems specific to alphabetic inputs and inefficiency in lexical access among less skilled readers.

From the series of studies carried out by Perfetti and associates, there is evidence for these sources of difficulties with less skilled readers:

1. Less skilled readers show slower lexical access (determining if a word is a word or a nonword). This is not just the case of these readers having a poor lexicon, as the difference is also found with nonwords. It is likely that skilled readers are better able to encode letter strings so that these can be compared with lexical memory without recoding. (Our chapter on coding processes for reading in general has discussed pros and cons for phonological coding and coding strategies).
2. Less skilled readers show longer vocalization latencies to isolated printed words and pseudowords and this applies to alphabetic rather than nonalphabetic materials.
3. Perceptual analysis is possible at several levels in line with interactive models of reading and depth of processing approach (discussed in our chapter on cognitive aspects). Perfetti (1977) indicates the surface and phonological level, the syntactic level and the interpretive or integrative level. His research program has borne out the central role of phonological coding. This does not mean that phonological codes mediate meaning though they are likely to be necessary for meaning.
4. If decoding does not necessarily lead to comprehension, it is more likely due to memory and

language factors. Discourse memory is shown to relate to reading comprehension even when short-term capacity is not. Even if sequential ordering is considered, it is more connected with linguistic structure (Perfetti and Goldman, 1976). Further, less skilled readers show difficulty with general language comprehension and organizing and integrating language units into meaningful relationships are a major source of individual differences in language processing (Berger and Perfetti, 1977; Goldman, Hogaboam, Bell, and Perfetti, 1980; Perfetti, Goldman and Hogaboam, 1979).

In summary, Perfetti and associates have added to our understanding of the verbal source of reading difficulties, especially the role of decoding in comprehension. It may be noted that in their research program they have typically focused on children aged nine to eleven years with IQs greater than 90 and with reading abilities one or two years below grade level or usually below the 30th percentile in standardized achievement tests. A caveat can be entered against the restricted IQ range. This restriction may explain the larger variation of vocalization latencies and the much smaller variation of other sources of individual differences, which may be a partial determinant of IQ under control in the studies (McClelland and Jackson, 1978). This, however, does not weaken the interdependence of decoding and comprehension. In fact, Perfetti is careful to point out that his work refers to less skilled readers only and that decoding latency (rather than decoding per se) is cast within a linguistic context. His work also reveals some qualitative differences between poor or less skilled readers and dyslexics, such as in the area of naming difficulties not found with the former but shown in the latter (Denckla and Rudel, 1976a; Perfetti, Finger and Hogaboam, 1978). That individual differences in memory search rate are due to the encoding of information in working memory, is also supported by the study of Kail and Marshall (1978) with skilled and less skilled third- and fourth-grade readers.

Thus, to return to the earlier question of the independence and interdependence of decoding and comprehension, we have seen the slightly different positions of the Wiener and Cromer group and the Perfetti team. The former group suggests that decoding is not sufficient for comprehension and advocates text organization. The latter group has examined the nature of the interdependence. We are inclined to agree with the latter position. Early in this volume (Chapter 2) we have emphasized reading as a skill—an integrated skill. Subsumed under that is a number of subskills all interrelated. The substrata theory of Holmes (1953, 1970) has provided us with an early model of neurological, psychological and psychometric underpinnings of the complex subsystems related to higher-order systems. This does not mean we favour the holistic view of reading over the subskills approach or the other way round (see also Samuels, 1976b; Samuels and Schachter, 1978). No dichotomy is implied. This is also clear from our discussion of reading as an interactive process involving both "bottom-up" and "top-down" strategies according to learner abilities and task demands (see Chapter 10). There is a switching back and forth from stimulus pattern to meaning and from meaning to the more analytic operations of identification of different units of processing—words, syllables, letters or features. Observations in classrooms and clinical work with disabled readers also convince us that for mature, fluent readers the reading process is more likely an *integrative* one in the sense that they have mastered various subskills to automaticity. They have also mastered the integration to automaticity and can deal flexibly and easily with the subskills. Poor readers, however, are likely to pay more attention to individual subskills such as decoding and in so doing lose track of or cannot cope with the main purpose of reading, which is comprehension. Thus, the breakdown in information processing of poor readers is likely to occur, not at one level, but at a number of levels—graphemic, phonemic, syntactic and semantic. In other words, the various levels of processing in reading are mutually reinforcing and facilitative for skilled readers; they also act singly and in concert to affect poor readers adversely.

Guthrie (1973) has provided support to show that skilled readers are able to integrate subskills into higher-order units, while poor readers still operate at the level of separate subskills and have not integrated these into one holistic process. In this connection, Stennett, Smythe, and Hardy (1975) attempted to elucidate the hierarchical organization of functional interdependence of the main subskills underlying reading. They outlined six possible statistical approaches: step-wise multiple regression, factor analysis, cluster analysis, scaling methods, analysis of variance, and transfer designs (transfer of training). Each approach has its pitfalls and shortcomings, with the transfer design probably having a slight advantage over the others. Using a simplex model of hierarchical analysis, Filp (1975) examined the sequential ordering of a set of six grapheme-morpheme correspondence subskills in a small number of seven and nine year old children reading at the grade two level. She found that in general recognition subskills are less complex (as defined in terms of the invariance of correlation coefficients under any linear transformation) than production subskills with the exception of single letter production. Thus the hierarchy from least complex to most complex subskills is: single letter production, initial letter recognition, consonant-cluster recognition, nonsense word recognition, consonant cluster production and nonsense word production. Despite the small size of the sample, Filp found the observed simplex correlations to be fairly stable. More recently, Leong (1978c, 1980) has found different patterns of antecedent reading subskills in above-average and below-average readers as shown in different models of factor analysis. Poor readers are found to use different strategies in solving cognitive tasks subserving reading.

Componential Analysis of Individual Differences in Reading

In our quest for a better understanding of sources of individual differences in reading we should note at least two further research programs which address themselves to this issue. The work by John Frederiksen (1976, 1977, 1978a, 1978b), the research program by Robert Calfee and associates (Calfee, 1975, 1976, 1977; Calfee, Chapman and Venezky, 1972; Calfee and Drum, 1978; Calfee and Venezky, 1968) and the componential analysis of Robert Sternberg (1977, 1978, 1979) all command attention. The Frederiksen and Calfee programs relate specifically to the question of independence or interdependence of subskills in reading and both programs derive their methodology from the componential analysis of R. Sternberg as well as the independence of stages in information processing models of Saul Sternberg (1969). The chapter on coding processes of lexical access (Chapter 9) has made reference to the additive factor method of S. Sternberg. Because of their contribution to the understanding of processing stages, the studies of Frederiksen, Calfee et al. and R. Sternberg will be discussed below.

The *componential analysis* of R. Sternberg (1977, 1978, 1979) aims at identifying the component internal mental operations in information processing and at examining the relationship of these operations one to the other and to higher-order mental abilities. In essence, the procedure involves the identification of component processes, identification of combination rules for different component processes, identification of combination rules of all these processes, their interrelationship and their relationship to higher-order mental abilities. Reaction times are typically chosen, as they reflect internal mental operations better than other measures, such as test scores as surrogates of some underlying construct. Moreover, reaction time studies typically involve such basic subskills as differentiating words from nonwords or vocalizing or naming words quickly and accurately so that it is difficult for subjects to make errors. Chapter 9 has discussed a number of studies using reaction times and has also outlined some of the methodological problems with this paradigm.

Specifically, the R. Sternberg procedure is basically an application of the subtraction method of reaction times used by F. C. Donders in 1869 as an attempt to isolate processing stages (see Pachella, 1974; Taylor, 1976; Theios, 1973). The assumption is that the time interval between stimulus and response onset consists of a sequence of successive stages, with each one beginning when the preceding one has ended. The difference in mean reaction times for the two tasks is taken as an indication of the duration of the deleted stage and this, in turn, reflects the relative difficulty in processing under the different conditions. With a careful choice or manipulation of different tasks or contrasts among the experimental conditions, it is possible to measure component processing skills. R. Sternberg has used the procedure to investigate processing stages of intelligence in both laboratory and classroom settings. Details of the procedure of componential analysis can be found in Sternberg's (1977) book and a clear exposition is given in a chapter by Sternberg (1978). An example from his investigation of linear syllogisms and analogues will be given as an illustration.

Sternberg (1978) provides the example for syllogistic reasoning of the kind $A:B:C:[D]$ where there are alternatives to $[D]$:

"*Washington* : 1 : : *Lincoln* : (a. *10*, b. *5*)."

A and *B* are encoded from the working memory, Washington being the first president of the U.S. (president (first)). There are other possibilities such as: (portrait on currency (dollar)), (war hero (revolutionary)). The subject has to discover the higher-order relation between *A* and *C* analogy terms through some *mapping* strategy in discovering various attributes that relate Washington and Lincoln together. The analogy is that whereas Washington is the portrait on a one-dollar bill, Lincoln is the portrait on a five-dollar bill. Thus the answer is *5*. From the above example, if subjects are presented with stimuli *A* and *B* and process them (determine the relationship) before the presentation of the *C* and *D* stimuli, then these processing times can be contrasted with those needed if *A, B* and *C* are presented simultaneously. Any difficulty a subject has may be with different components: it could be at the analogy stage or it could be at the encoding stage. This refinement has implications for both research and assessment of instruction. The finer differentiation made possible with the R. Sternberg procedure is not shown in conventional composite test scores, as the subject may simply be regarded as not intelligent. It may be noted, however, that the componential process assumes serial operation and further assumes that total response latencies are the sum of the individual component latencies. While we may debate the pros and cons of this assumption, the componential analysis pinpoints sources of difficulty much more precisely than is possible with aggregate scores.

John Frederiksen (1976, 1977, 1978a, 1978b) has applied the Sternberg componential analysis procedure to the study of individual differences in readers of varying reading abilities. He postulates several phases of reading or levels of processing. These levels are: (1) perceptual encoding including grapheme encoding and encoding multi-letter units; (2) decoding including parsing, phonemic translation and articulatory programming; (3) lexical access including access to the lexicon and retrieval of lexical information; (4) the phrase level including skill in the use of syntactic structure and propositions and (5) interaction among processes occurring at different levels. Frederiksen emphasizes two aspects in his work. First, while the processes are hierarchically arranged, the initiation of higher-order operations does not necessarily depend on the completion of lower-order ones in the hierarchy. Second, there are trade-offs between the use of subskills at one level of processing and the mode of processing and processing efficiency at higher levels. From his maximum likelihood factor analysis of eleven measures dealing specifically with levels (1), (2) and (3) above, Frederiksen found five factors with his high school age readers. These five factors overall were assumed to be uncorrelated with one another from a test of orthogonality, while there were some variations among the correlations. The fact that the factors yielded high multiple correlations with scores on standardized reading tests (vocabulary and comprehension) shows that the multi-letter encoding and the articulatory programming measures were the major predictors. Thus good readers use strategies of phonemic decoding while poor readers recognize words more on the basis of "gestalts." There are also large individual differences in information processing subskills in: the perceptual encoding of sequential letters, the translation of orthographic patterns into "sound" patterns and lexical access. Frederiksen (1977) extended the investigation of effects of sequential redundancy of words to study the influence of textual context on the effective visual field. It was found that effective visual field width was broader when a semantically constrained context was provided. There were significant differences among high and low ability readers in the effect of prior context on visual span. High ability readers showed greater increments in visual span in the presence of contexts than did low ability readers.

The Frederiksen studies taken as a whole lend support to the studies of the Perfetti group. The reasons why readers differing in decoding subskills also differ in their comprehension of written discourse are likely that: (1) subskill deficiencies covary, although the subskills can be functionally independent; and (2) increasing attention paid to decoding by poor readers will impede their comprehension in line with the LaBerge-Samuels (1974) model of automaticity of reading.

In turning from the Frederiksen studies to the work of the Calfee group we will note the same meticulous care for more refined methodology so that we may unravel the complex processes of reading. Calfee and his group tackle the independence or interdependence of component subskills of reading through two broad approaches. One approach is the construction of uncontaminated "clean" tests or tests constructed to measure a selected subskill as precisely as possible (Calfee, 1975, 1977; Calfee, Chapman and Venezky, 1972; Calfee and Venezky, 1968). Another approach is the experimental study of underlying stages of processing in reading (Calfee, 1975, 1976, 1977; Calfee and Drum, 1978).

In the construction of "clean" tests for better

research and assessment of instruction, the basic idea of Calfee is to begin with tasks which make minimal demands on readers so that they make virtually no errors. When this condition of near errorless performance is established, sources of difficulty are systematically introduced so that the reason why a task is difficult to perform under certain conditions might be answered. If under what appears to be reasonable circumstances most children still cannot perform a given task with accuracy, then the task is analyzed and training sessions can be instituted. Calfee's data show that: (1) short, "precise" tests can be effective in identifying competence in a given subskill area and (2) the scores conform to a bimodal distribution rather than to the usual normal distribution. The latter finding calls into question the usual assumptions attendant on tests so standardized. Calfee (1977) explains in some detail how his "all-or-none" tests can be put to practical use in the hands of classroom teachers. He advocates the use of a threshold score by adjusting the cutoff score so that the number of children "misplaced" (false positives and negatives) above and below the cutoff is at a minimum. In this way, teachers can be alerted to deficiencies or inefficiencies in certain subskill areas and can effect appropriate programming. The advocacy of the threshold score is reminiscent of McClelland's (1949) method of adjusting the cutoff zone to reduce "misfits" in connection with secondary school allocation in post world war II in Scotland.

Related to the construction of "precise" tests for identification of skill areas, Calfee (1976, 1977; Calfee and Drum, 1978) has extended the additive factor paradigm of Saul Sternberg (1969) to provide a rigorous test of the model of independence or interdependence of processing components. He has formalized a procedure of variance-covariance analysis of specific linear contrasts and has applied the procedure with some success to the design of reading assessment batteries and to beginning reading. From his ongoing research program on components of reading, Calfee has drawn attention to some central issues relating decoding to reading comprehension. He points out that there is strong evidence that at some stage of reading acquisition a student needs to gain expertise in decoding, but at the same time decoding can be mediated by a process or processes dependent on other components of reading. Under certain circumstances "decoding may operate as a functionally autonomous skill" (Calfee and Drum, 1978, p. 216). This occurs if the curriculum promotes a strong letter-sound translation. But independence should not be equated with prerequisite status.

From his rigorous research program, Calfee has contributed to our understanding of the interrelatedness of processes of reading. He has also provided a theory-based analysis of subprocesses particularly effective for instruction of groups or individual readers.

Some Implications

There are many implications one can draw from the literature on processes of reading in poor readers. Specifically, we will outline three general approaches of relevance to instruction. One relates to conceptualizing programming for poor readers in terms of ordinal interaction. The second relates to decoding and comprehension as related systems rather than separate subskills. The third emphasizes teaching poor readers reading by reading, and the role of practice.

In the conceptualization of instruction for poor readers, an aptitude-by-treatment condition in its extreme form is one of disordinal interaction between programs and reading abilities. This condition is illustrated in Figure 14–1A (see Bracht and Glass, 1968; Campbell and Stanley, 1963). Under this condition of disordinal interaction, neither the hypothetical variable nor treatment has any main effect. In other words, there is no general rule emerging as to whether treatment A or B is the better in respect of the variable. At the point of interaction shown by the dotted line, it would be better to shift from treatment B for those children scoring low on the hypothetical variable to treatment A used for children scoring high on the variable. A more realistic expectation, however, is to exploit ordinal rather than disordinal interactions. This is illustrated in Figure 14–1B. Levin (1972, 1973) has argued for this position. This means that good readers are likely to perform well under all instructional conditions, although less so in some conditions than others. Poor readers will make improvements with some variables (e.g. method B) than with others (e.g. method A). "Retarded" readers remain retarded in reading despite varying conditions. This does not mean this latter group cannot be remediated. What it means is that their prognosis is poor and they do not benefit by the shift in methods under

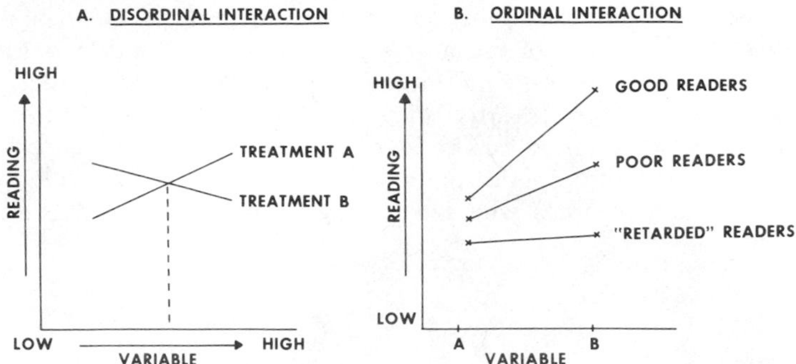

Figure 14–1. Conceptualization of instructional treatment for poor readers.

study. The poor readers, however, do make headway in relation to a different instructional program.

The emphasis on ordinal interactions and the need for flexible programming also highlight another related issue. In the section on "underachievement" we have discussed some of the fallacies of the concept and the attendant statistical pitfalls related to both screening and diagnosis of poor readers. Thorndike (1973b) has clearly explained the impact of reliability, intercorrelation and score difference on the confidence one can place on diagnosis and the resultant dilemma in diagnosis of reading difficulties. One solution is for teachers to continually evaluate their remediation programs and to vary them if they are not effective for the poor readers being remediated. Another solution is to follow the test-teach-test situation, as has been found effective with mentally retarded children (see Leong, 1978b).

Another implication is the need to conceive of and teach decoding and comprehension, not as separate subskills, but as conceptual systems related to each other. Discussion of the interactive model of reading in the chapter on cognitive processes (Chapter 10) has drawn attention to the need to integrate "bottom-up" and "top-down" subskills and the mutually facilitating effects of levels of processing. From the programming point of view there should be a proper integration of graphophonemic, syntactic and semantic information. Teachers should be alert to the way different reading programs make use of certain sources of information and to how individual readers may benefit from specific aspects of particular programs, Pearson (1978) has discussed practical applications of this integrative approach. Commenting on practices in some reading materials of treating vocabulary, decoding, syntax and semantics as separate entities, Calfee and Drum (1978, p. 206) put the point succinctly: "What a student is taught as separate conceptual systems will function as independent processes, and contrariwise, what a student is taught determines in part how he thinks." It cannot be emphasized too strongly that reading is a skill where children need to perform different levels of subskills in an integrated manner.

Another important approach which seems banal in the sense that often facts are banal as they seem self-evident is one not sufficiently emphasized. This is the role of practice to the point of automaticity. With poor readers, or for that matter with "retarded" readers, we believe that they learn to read only by reading. This of course presupposes that different methods may apply and that we must analyze the reading task carefully so that sequential steps can be taken one at a time. There is evidence that poor readers are not practiced in verbal encoding and decoding (e.g. see Perfetti and Lesgold, 1977). The mastery of component subskills of reading to automaticity has been repeatedly emphasized by different workers (Calfee and Drum, 1978; Guthrie, 1978b, LaBerge and Samuels, 1974; Samuels, 1977, 1979). A corollary of the importance of practice to automaticity on the part of learners is the amount of instructional time given them by teachers. Related to the amount of time spent is the way it is spent. These several aspects of practice, of more instructional time and time well spent seem to be sound counsel to be followed by all. Going beyond the empirical studies cited with children learning the alphabetic system, the same principle applies to learning a morphemic system as Chinese, as one of the authors has observed with Chinese children in Hong Kong. Makita's (1968) finding of the "rarity" of reading disability in Japanese children can be attributed to both motivational and practice factors, so often taken for granted in areas where a high premium is placed on literacy acquisition in general and reading acquisition in particular. If this observation is correct, overlearning probably frees readers from attention to certain subskills so that they can attend to other component subskills and this principle applies to different writing systems.

Specific Reading Disability

CHAPTER 15

The whole of this chapter focuses on children with specific reading disability. This usage follows the suggestion of Eisenberg (1966b), Hermann (1959) and Doehring (1968). Eisenberg discussed specific reading disability in terms of failure to learn to read despite proficient instruction, normal intelligence, adequate home environment, intact senses, proper motivation and freedom from gross neurological defects. Hermann (1959) explained specific reading disability this way:

> a defective capacity for acquiring, at the normal time, a proficiency in reading and writing corresponding to average performance; the deficiency is dependent upon constitutional factors (heredity), is often accompanied by difficulties with other symbols (numbers, musical notation, etc.), it exists in the absence of intellectual defect or of defects of the sense organs which might retard the normal accomplishment of these skills, and in the absence of past or present appreciable inhibitory influences in the internal and external environment (pp. 17–18).

The term *specific* in specific reading disability or what Applebee (1971) refers to as "residual disorder" is used in the sense of an "idiopathic condition" or little-known causation according to Eisenberg (1962, p. 4). On the positive side, "specific" could reflect an asymmetry of abilities (Doehring, 1968, p. 130), as children with this disability sometimes show pockets of strengths in areas other than language in its various forms—heard, spoken and written. The term *specific reading disability* operationally defines the small group of children with severe reading difficulties. It is estimated that this small group comprises between one per cent and four per cent of disabled readers and likely forms a small "hump" at the low end of the distribution of reading achievement.

Definitions Further Considered

For the purpose of our discussion the term *specific reading disability* is used interchangeably with *reading retardation* and *developmental dyslexia.* The concept of reading retardation is explained in the previous chapter. If the term *dyslexia* is used sparingly here, it is only because of reservations on the part of some professionals. This ranges from skepticism of individual researchers (e.g. Harris, 1968, 1978–1979; Valtin, 1978–1979) to rejection by official committees (e.g. United Kingdom Department of Education and Science, 1972, 1975). We view the term as an innocuous one in that etymologically dyslexia simply means difficulty with "lexikos" or words—words *seen,* words *heard,* words *spoken,* words *felt* and above all words *internalized.* When qualified, developmental dyslexia as contrasted with acquired dyslexia denotes a form of inefficiency in processing language symbols characteristic of the small group of severely disabled readers who are still in the process of developing language.

It is instructive to note that an authority of the stature of Magdalen Vernon, who eschewed the concept of dyslexia in her 1957 book *Backwardness in Reading* came around to the condition later (Vernon, 1962). In her 1971 book *Reading and its Difficulties,* she regards the problem of "specific developmental dyslexia" as a perennial one requiring further experimental and clinical investigation and devotes close to a third of the book to the subject. From the pioneer work of Rudolf Berlin of Stuttgart in 1887 on dyslexia ("Wortblindheit") the wheel seems to have come full circle. Since that time there have been many clinical studies of the phenomenon. Early studies include "congenital word blindness" by Hinshelwood (1895), Morgan (1896) and the detailed analysis of "strephosymbolia" or "twisted symbols" in children by Orton (1925, 1937). More recent clinical and experimental investigations include those by Johnson and Myklebust (1967), Doehring (1968), Myklebust (1971, 1975, 1978) and Naidoo (1972), among others.

From a neurological perspective Critchley (1964, 1970) discussed developmental dyslexia within the "aphasiological context" with detailed clinical examples. He suggested these premises for the existence of developmental dyslexics who are nosologically apart from the continuum of poor readers:

> persistence into adulthood; the peculiar and specific nature of the errors in reading and writing; the familial incidence of the defect; and the frequent association with other symbol-defects (Critchley, 1964, p. 11).

Benton (1975), on the other hand, has argued from a neuropsychological standpoint that, as dyslexia is essentially a diagnosis by exclusion, the presumption of a neurological basis should not be taken more than as a presumption. This cautious view may be compared and contrasted with Zangwill's (1976) suggestion that dyslexia be approached within the framework of pediatric neurology and that the disorder be taken seriously. "There is no truth in the innuendo that dyslexia is a 'middle class disease,' " he has claimed (p. 310). Whatever the basis, there is evidence from the large-scale Isle of Wight survey (Rutter, Tizard, and Whitmore, 1970) that specific reading disability is sufficiently distinct from general reading backwardness. Rutter and Yule (1973) based their claim on findings of differential sex distribution, neurological correlates and association with speech and language disorders. From results of a five-year follow-up of disabled readers, Yule (1973) showed the generally poor prognosis of *any* reading disability and warned of even poorer prognosis for children with specific reading retardation than for the merely "backward" readers. Drawing together larger studies of five general population groups varying in age and in geographical areas within England, Yule, Rutter, Berger, and Thompson (1974) reaffirmed the qualitative difference between retarded readers and the mainly backward ones in reading.

Acceptance of the psychological, neuropsychological, and clinical realities of this small group of severely disabled readers, and noting them as different from merely backward or poor readers, has not helped much in defining them with precision. Some fourteen years ago, the NINDS monograph *Minimal Brain Dysfunction* (Clements, 1966) attempted to clarify nomenclature for mutual understanding by different professional groups. From an extensive review of the literature to the mid-1960s, the monograph listed 37 extant terms together with their symptomatology. Little wonder this diversity created confusion. The scene is not much clearer to date. The U.S. Education for All Handicapped Children, Act, or Public Law 94–142, referred to in the previous chapter, defines these children as those:

> who have a disorder in one or more of the basic psychological processes involved in understanding or in using language, spoken or written, which disorder may manifest itself in imperfect ability to listen, think, speak, read, write, spell, or do mathematical calculations. Such disorders include such conditions as perceptual handicaps, brain injury, minimal brain dysfunction, dyslexia and developmental aphasia. Such term does not include children who have learning problems which are primarily the result of visual, hearing, or motor handicaps, of mental retardation, of emotional disturbance, or environmental, cultural, or economic disadvantage (U.S. Office of Education, 1976; see also Federal Register, 42(250), 1977, p. 65083).

The Act in many ways is a milestone in the provision for and care of all handicapped children on a national basis. The section quoted above on specific learning disabilities shows the complexity of the problem and the difficulty in coming to grips with a precise, acceptable definition.

It is clear that "what shall the thing be called" has engaged the attention of professions from the 1960s to the present date. Contributors to the 1975 NATO conference on the neuropsychology of learning disorders (Knights and Bakker, 1976) have again drawn attention to the diversity of terms, which may hamper progress in research and programming. Very recently, contributors to the 1976–1977 National Institute of Mental Health (NIMH) conference to appraise current knowledge of dyslexia (Benton and Pearl, 1978) have reiterated their considerable concern for the imprecise definition of what is a heterogeneous group and have attempted their definitions. Panel members of the NIMH group on the nature and prevalence of dyslexia have all registered dissatisfaction with the definition of the condition *by exclusion* as shown in the PL94–142 official definition and other definitions preceding it.

Rutter (1978, p. 12) on the panel comments that the exclusionary definition "suggests that if all the known causes of reading disability can be ruled out, the unknown (in the form of dyslexia) should be invoked. . . ." This to him (and to many others) is a counsel of despair. He emphasizes the *differentiation of syndromes* of dyslexia. The main syndromes suggested are: general backwardness versus specific retardation, differential cognitive patterns, differentiation according to the absence or presence of brain damage, differentiation according to the presence or absence of psychiatric disorders, differentiation according to types of spelling disorders, and differentiation according to genetic background. Differentiations along these main dimensions will in some way accommodate the diverse nature of the group. An empirical method to screen the group is to follow Rutter and his colleagues in their Isle of Wight survey, which defined reading retardation in terms of discrepancy in reading below the child's *predicted* intelligence and chronological age (see earlier section on "Concepts of Underachievement"). Thus Rutter (1978, p. 27) suggests that dyslexia can refer to a "more heterogeneous group of reading disabilities characterized by the fact that reading/spelling attainment is far below that expected on the basis of the child's age or IQ." Another panel member Eisenberg (1978) emphasizes that the categories of exclusion will likely deny services to a large number of children with learning disabilities who also suffer from sociocultural disadvantage and emotional disturbance. His own definition again focuses attention on discrepancy or deviance: "a severe performance deficit (greater than two standard errors of prediction) between the obtained reading level and that expected on the basis of age and intelligence . . ." (p. 41). While he is in agreement generally with his psychiatric colleagues on the panel about the imprecise nature of defining dyslexia in exclusionary terms, Mattis (1978) points out that such observations as "the child not being sensorially deprived, retarded . . ." are often the starting points for clinicians to further diagnose the dyslexic child and offer remediation.

From his neuropsychological perspective, Mattis (1978) offers this definition:

> Dyslexia is a diagnosis of atypical reading development as compared to other children of similar age, intelligence, instructional program, and sociocultural opportunity which, without intervention, is expected to persist and is due to a well-defined defect in any one of several specific higher cortical functions (p. 54).

He also makes the important point that there is a need to differentiate a given disorder observable in dyslexics from that observed in brain-damaged readers. "If it [a given disorder] is also observed in brain-damaged readers, it must logically be considered irrelevant as a factor causal to dyslexia" (p. 56). However, it should be noted that this important qualification is not shared by the PL94–142 definition, nor by Eisenberg, who would like to see a wider coverage of the group. Mattis is careful to note that while the presence of a specific disorder in a critical process implies the presence of dyslexia, the absence of this disorder does not necessarily mean the absence of disordered reading.

Returning to where we started on specific reading disability and reviewing relevant literature, the present authors find the exclusionary definition, though imprecise, offers some basis for diagnostic and remedial work for these children. The emphasis on language disorder is a correct one, as this underlines the developmental nature of dyslexia and as reading is an integral part of the language continuum. We would not, however, concur with the inclusion of "brain injury, minimal brain dysfunction" and some other categories of structural damage. This inclusion confuses rather than clarifies the issue and concept of dyslexia. As it is, not a few reading specialists have identified specific reading disability with organic brain damage (see for example the chapter on dyslexia in an otherwise informative work on reading disabilities by Spache, 1976). A few teachers tend to think of dyslexics in terms of brain damage rather than brain difference or even brain dysfunction. Consequently, there is the danger that they may relegate these children to the "irremediable" group.

Again, terms like minimal brain dysfunction (MBD) should not be confused with dyslexia. MBD denotes a mild, subclinical form of central dysfunction which manifests itself in varying degrees of severity and which subtly affects learning and behavior. Benton (1973) has pointed out that "minimal brain dysfunction" is too vague to be of any specific use, as there is nothing minimal in brain behavior that causes a serious learning disorder. This evaluation is generally shared by many of the contributors to the Knights and Bakker (1976) work on the neuropsychology of learning disorders. Recently, Denckla (1978) discusses the pros and cons of the term MBD. She argues forcefully for consideration of the term as a "place-holding, beginning-to-investigate, 'loose organic line'" concept (p. 228) to allow us to be more aware of *brain variations* in disabled readers. She also presents clinical syndromes subsumed under "minimal brain dysfunctions" and suggests process factors as being important. From another perspective, Cruickshank (1978) argues for the definition of learning disabilities in terms of problems in the acquisition of developmental skills, academic achievement, social adjustment and emotional growth resulting from "perceptual and linguistic processing deficits" (p. 20). He suggests that learning disabilities should be defined irrespective of etiology, of age, of intellectual functioning. Thus this is a far cry from the early days when Kirk (1963) coined the term "learning disabilities" to denote those children with communication (language) disorders, who are relatively free from other disabilities. Cruickshank's proposal underscores the heterogeneous nature of learning disabilities including specific reading disability and the need for multidisciplinary investigation.

It is significant that in January, 1981 the National Joint Committee for Learning Disabilities (NJCLD) representing a number of professional organizations proposed a new definition for learning disabilities (*Perspectives on Dyslexia*, February, 1981). This is a conjoint effort to address problems of assessment and service delivery arising from the current exclusionary definition. The proposed NJCLD definition urges that learning disabilities be recognized as a generic term referring to a heterogeneous group of disorders. These disorders are manifested as significant difficulties in the acquisition and development of one or more of these functions: listening, speaking, reading, writing, reasoning and mathematical abilities. These disorders are intrinsic to the individual and are presumed to be due to central nervous system dysfunction, the evidence for which may or may not be elicited in the course of a neurological examination. In addition, learning disabilities may occur concomitantly with other handicapping conditions or environmental influences. Thus the keynote of the proposed NJCLD definition is on altered processes of acquiring and using information and the need to provide for individual differences and appropriate educational and related services.

Summarizing, we would like to suggest that the definition of specific reading disability in terms of a discrepancy between reading scores and *predicted* intelligence scores and age is conceptually sound and statistically defensible (see discussion on "Underachievement"). The deviance concept also provides a practical means of screening disabled readers. From the psychometric screening and clinical diagnosis, the differentiation into different syndromes or subgroups, as suggested by Rutter (1978) and empirically tested by Mattis (1978), provides more "homogeneous" grouping with sharper focus on characteristics. We are, however, a little more sanguine than Mattis and would like to suggest perceptual-cognitive-linguistic deficits and also differences, rather than defects, as characterizing these severely disabled readers. Thus, one source for understanding specific reading disability is the differential syndromes or patterns of these readers. The other source is their way of processing information, especially linguistic materials. We are thus led back to the understanding of reading processes. Underpinning the concept of differential patterns and processing is the complex brain-behavior relationship (see Rourke, 1975, 1976).

Differential Patterns

Before a discussion of differential syndromes, it is important to remember the heterogeneous nature of any group of disabled readers or subgroups within them. In the classic work *Reading Disability,* Money (1962) brings out succinctly the variability of the reading disabled group in an analogy with psychological medicine:

> It is not at all rare in psychological medicine, nor in other branches of medicine, that a disease should have no unique identifying sign, that uniqueness being in the pattern of signs that appear in contiguity. Out of context, each sign might also be encountered in other diseases, or, in different intensities, in the healthy (p. 16).

He goes on to say that the diagnosis of specific reading disability "will continue not to depend on a single telltale sign, but on the clinical appraisal of the whole configuration of symptoms and test findings" (p. 17). It is this heterogeneity within a broadly homogeneous group that is one of the reasons why some researchers emphasize case studies. Vernon (1957, p. 6), for example, observed that "a great many of the studies of reading backwardness have been made of large, heterogeneous, and ill-defined groups of children" and has advocated in-depth individual studies. These could follow well-defined, large-scale surveys, such as the Isle of Wight study, or the pattern studies to be discussed in this section. The individual studies approach is typified in a work by Koppitz (1971). The need for well-defined sequential diagnosis which is cumulative, relevant, and conducive to appropriate prescriptive programs is also evident.

Empirical and Clinical Studies

Pattern studies of reading difficulties generally deal with two broad groups of children: above- and below-average readers and those with developmental dyslexia. The reference battery has been subtests of the Wechsler Intelligence Scale for Children (WISC), or its downward extension, the Wechsler Pre-School and Primary Scale of Intelligence (WPPSI). Some studies have also added reading-related tasks involving auditory-motor activities (e.g. sound blending, articulation); visual-motor tasks (e.g. visual retention); and decoding skills of matching tasks for letters, letter strings, syllables and words. The research design is usually correlational in nature. The methodology used is mainly the R-technique of factor analysis with a few studies involving cluster analysis. More recently, the Q-technique of factor analysis has been employed.

A good example of pattern studies of above-average and below-average readers is the work of Maxwell (1972a, 1972b). He factor-analyzed the WPPSI subtest scores of above-average and below-average seven-year-old readers. He found the intercorrelations of the subtests for the good readers were consistently and considerably smaller than the corresponding correlation for the poor readers and that the factor structure for this latter group was much less clear-cut. Maxwell, Fenwick, Fenton and Dollimore (1974) further found from the EEG records of two groups of 52 fourteen-year-old good and poor readers that efficient cognitive functioning seemed to require fewer neurons for its elaboration as shown in the mean variance spectra of the EEG. For children retarded in reading, studies include those by Myklebust, Bannochie and Killen (1971) and Wallbrown, Blaha, Wherry and Counts (1974). Myklebust et al. investigated the ability patterns of 116 "moderate learning-disability" children and 112 "severe disability children," each compared with the same number of control children. Wallbrown et al. tested empirically the cognitive structure of 70 disabled readers aged seven to thirteen. In general, differential factor structure on the WISC was found for the disabled readers and their controls.

For clinic samples of children with developmental dyslexia, studies of particular interest were those by Doehring (1968), Naidoo (1972), Mattis (1978), Mattis, French, and Rapin (1975). Doehring compared the pattern of impairment in a group of 39 dyslexic boys aged ten to fourteen with that of two control groups on a total of 109 measures of sensory, motor, perceptual, and verbal abilities. From multivariate analyses, Doehring found that his dyslexics showed an "asymmetry of talents" and lagged in "sequential processing." Naidoo studied the taxonomic structure of performance on perceptual-cognitive tasks in 98 dyslexic boys divided into one group of 56 "reading retardates" and a second group of 42 "spelling retardates," each matched with separate control groups. Mattis et al. examined syndromes in 113 clinic children ranging in age from eight to thirteen years. Eighty-two of these 113 children were diagnosed as dyslexic and of these 82 children, 29 were labeled developmental dyslexic. Mattis et al. found three syndromes which accounted for 90 per cent of the variance in the 82 dyslexic children studied. The syndromes were: (1) language disorder (anomia; disorder of comprehension, imitative speech and speech sound discrimination), this being the most prominent; (2) articulatory and graphomotor dyscoordination, and (3) visuo-constructional difficulties. These syndromes were isolated and empirically refined by disregarding as causal to dyslexia deficiencies in "higher cortical functions" found in a contrast group of brain-damaged readers. Despite the wide age variation and the slight overlap of the syndromes, the Mattis et al. findings shed light on finer differentiation of subgroups of dyslexics.

Recently, Mattis (1978) has reported on preliminary results of a crossvalidation study involving some 400 children with a modal age of eight to ten years. He has confirmed the same three dyslexia syndromes previously found, with 63 per cent of the dyslexic children presenting the language disorder syndrome, 10 per cent the articulatory and graphomotor dyscoordination syndrome, and 5 per cent the visual-perceptual disorder syndrome. There is thus considerable stability in the differential syndromes diagnosed and refined. In a similar vein, a recent Q-technique study by Doehring and Hoshko (1977) of children with "reading problems" differentiated subgroups characterized by: (1) slow oral word reading; (2) slow auditory-visual letter association; and (3) slow auditory-visual association of words and syllables. These subgroups bear a close similarity to the language disorder syndrome of Mattis et al. (1975), the auditory dyslexia of Johnson and Myklebust (1967) and the dysphonetic dyslexia of Boder (1971, 1973).

The question of what constitutes "higher cortical functions" in the generally acceptable definition of Mattis (1978) is not easily answered. What is "higher-up" could be "lower-down" or vice versa, as perceptual-cognitive functions are interrelated. Studies of cognitive patterns of severely disabled readers by one of the present authors (Das, Leong and Williams, 1978; Leong, 1976, 1976–1977, 1980, 1981) have provided an indirect answer. The theoretical postulate is derived from the Russian neuropsychologist Luria's (1966a, 1966b) two basic forms of integrative activity: *simultaneous* (primarily spatial, groups) and *successive* (primarily temporally organized series) syntheses at the perceptual, memory and intellectual levels. For example, simultaneous synthesis at the perceptual level may be manifested in copying of geometric figures, drawing of a map, performance on Koh's Blocks; and at the memory level in "arithmetic difficulties" and "grammatical structure involving arrangement of elements into one simultaneous scheme." In successive synthesis, examples are counting sequences of tapping, digit span and serial learning, such as drawing "0 + + –", while keeping the correct serial order. In Luria's terms simultaneous-successive synthesis can be identified with the functions of specific parts of the cortex, although conscious activity as a complex functional system is the result of concerted working of different brain units. The occipital-parietal area has evolved to be mainly responsible for simultaneous synthesis; the successive is mainly located in the anterior regions, particularly in the fronto-temporal area. The emphasis is again on the working of "complex functional systems" and not on morphological schemes of cerebral localization. The Luria neuropsychological model assumes that the two modes of information processing are available to the individual depending on his/her habitual mode of activities and the demands of the task. The Luria model has been operationalized by Das (see review by Das, Kirby and Jarman, 1975) and the formalism of simultaneous-successive synthesis is provided in a book by the same researchers (Das, Kirby and Jarman, 1979). Using a battery of tasks similar to those exemplified in Luria's work, Leong has found through different factor analyses that severely disabled readers perform significantly poorer than their age- and IQ-control nondisabled readers in both the simultaneous and successive dimensions or factors. There is also some evidence in supplementary qualitative analyses that disabled readers are inefficient in using rules to solve antecedent reading tasks, such as Raven's Progressive Matrices and crossmodal (auditory to visual) coding.

Thus the different pattern studies have shown the efficacy of using empirical methods to refine diagnostic subgroups of severely disabled readers. Early studies tended to emphasize modality preferences (visual/auditory) of these children. Examples are the audiles and visiles of Money (1962) and Wepman (1968), the visual dyslexics and auditory dyslexics of Johnson and Myklebust (1967) and the dysphonetic-dyseidetic dyslexics of Boder (1971, 1973). Current work is directed more toward language-related skills and provides a clearer link to remediation with verbal and linguistic materials. The various studies have also validated the finding of Myklebust, Bannochie and Killen (1971) of different cognitive structures in learning disabled and nondisabled children. They stated that "A learning disability affects the organization of the intellect; hence, cognition itself is modified. The mental abilities of learning-disability children are structured differently. By implication, the processes whereby they learn, whereby they organize experience, also are different" (p. 227). This concept of differential processing offers a workable approach to research and instruction. The emphasis on information processing, though not correlational studies of the differential pattern kind, is also evident in some German studies with "retarded" readers (Scheerer-Neumann, 1978; Valtin, 1978–1979).

Perceptual-Cognitive Deficits or Verbal Deficits?

To some extent comments on "perceptual" inefficiency in the chapter on "Reading Difficulties" also apply to severely disabled readers. But there is this difference. Perceptual differences in "retarded" readers are seen as a *maturational lag* and have been espoused as such by such authors as Bender (1958), Gesell (1945) and Ilg and Ames (1964). The pattern of deficits may be a combination of: impairment in visual-motor tasks, especially figure-copying (Brenner and Gillman, 1966; Brenner, Gillman, Farrell, and Zangwill, 1967), directional confusion (Critchley, 1964; Orton, 1937), calculation deficits (Belmont and Birch, 1966), spontaneous writing and spelling impairment (Zangwill, 1962), and impairment in intermodal associations (Birch and Belmont, 1964; Blank and Bridger, 1966). Each of these deficits has received some support in the literature. The developmental framework postulates that the deficits are related to broader disturbance in higher-integrative functions. Younger disabled readers are more disturbed in sensorimotor integration, whereas older ones are more delayed in language integration skills.

This concept of progressive differentiation is rooted in substantive neurological, linguistic, and neuropsychological formulations. Geschwind (1968) has discussed the relationship between brain maturation and ontogenetic development and points out that the "terminal" zones (left-angular gyri), which have intercortical connections necessary for the mediation of more complex language and crossmodal integration skills, myelinate the latest. Lenneberg (1967) shows that the hemispheric organization of speech evolves from a state of diffuse and bilateral representation in infancy to one of increased lateralization by puberty. Semmes, Weinstein, Ghent, and Teuber (1960) and Semmes (1968) have suggested that the cerebral lateralization of speech stems from lateralization of less complex motor and somatosensory functions which precede the lateralization of speech. Thus the different perspectives of the neurological basis (Geschwind), the biological foundation (Lenneberg), and the neuropsychological substrate (Semmes and associates) all converge to account for a complex function, such as language including reading, as a synthesis of elementary sensorimotor functions whose neural organization already favors specialization in the left hemisphere. Maturation thus refers to the process of successive and overlapping changes in growth in the neurological and psychological aspects of the organism and maturational lag points to a slow or undifferentiated pattern.

The Functional Maturational Lag Postulate

Within the above context Satz and associates (Satz and Sparrow, 1970; Satz and van Nostrand, 1973; Sparrow and Satz, 1970) have proposed the functional maturational lag postulate to explain specific reading disability. Their theory has provided the conceptual and methodological framework for a series of longitudinal studies of some developmental and predictive precursors of dyslexia (Satz and Friel, 1973, 1974; Satz, Friel and Goebel, 1975; Satz, Friel and Rudegeair, 1976; Satz, Taylor, Friel and Fletcher, 1978). In essence, the Satz theory as originally postulated states that specific reading disability relates to a lag in the maturation of the brain, which delays differentially those skills that mature or are in primary ascendency at different chronological ages. Thus, those skills that develop earlier (e.g. perceptual-motor skills) are more likely to be delayed in younger children who lag in functional cerebral development. For older children who are immature, conceptual and linguistic skills are more likely to be delayed.

Over a period of more than six years Satz and his associates carried out a series of *longitudinal predictive studies* based on the Satz maturational lag hypothesis. An original sample of about 500 children on entering kindergarten in a county in Florida were all administered a battery of 16 developmental neuropsychological tests (Satz and Friel, 1973). The same children were again tested at the end of grades one, two, and three from 1972 to 1974 and also at grades four and five in 1975–1976 and the predictors were related to reading proficiency. Multivariate analyses of the follow-up results confirm the high predictive accuracy of the test battery and suggest that specific reading disability is more of a disorder in central processing, which is reflected in perception, memory, cognition and language.

In the three-year predictive follow-up (1970–1973) Satz and his colleagues (Satz and Friel, 1973, 1974; Satz, Friel and Goebel, 1975; Satz, Friel and Rudegeair, 1976) found that eight tests would detect almost all those children at both extreme ends of the reading distribution at the end of grade two. The following three tests consistently ranked the highest: finger localization, alphabet recitation, and recognition-discrimination. In the six-year predictive follow-up (1970–1976) Satz (Satz, Taylor, Friel and Fletcher, 1978) found that the predictive outcomes were almost identical to those of the three-year follow-up. The same predictors as used in 1970 also correctly predicted the extremes (severe and superior) of the reading distribution. The valid positive rate comparing the three-year and six-year follow-ups was 86 per cent for severely disabled readers and also 86 per cent of the superior readers (valid negatives). Again, finger localization ranked the highest and was followed by the Peabody Picture Vocabulary Test (Dunn, 1965), a visual-motor integration test and alphabet recitation. Thus, despite the length of time elapsed and the sources of uncontrollable variables such as growth and increased experience, the predictive outcomes are remarkably stable.

A crossvalidation of the three-year predictive follow-up lends support to the intrinsic validity of the predictors (Satz, Friel and Rudegeair, 1976; Satz, Taylor, Friel and Fletcher, 1978). The Satz et al. 1978 report also includes a separate longitudinal study using the eight abbreviated tests in the battery plus five psycholinguistic measures: vocabulary fluency, ITPA Grammatical Closure (Kirk, McCarthy and Kirk, 1968), Berry-Talbot Comprehension of Grammar Test (Berry, 1969), a syntax test and the Peabody Picture Vocabulary Test. From a step-wise regression analysis Satz et al. found these rankings of the language tests: SES (socio-economic status), ITPA Grammatical Closure, the Peabody, word fluency, Berry-Talbot and the syntax test. They further found from an analysis of the abbreviated battery these rankings: SES, alphabet recitation, and finger localization. There is thus a high stability when the three-year and the six-year follow-ups are compared.

The Satz predictive follow-ups spanning a period close to ten years command attention in our understanding of specific reading disability for a number of reasons. First, the longitudinal studies are theory-based. The maturational lag postulate provides both a conceptual and methodological framework for Satz' prediction of reading disability. Second, the use of multivariate techniques (factor analysis and regression analysis) takes into account the conjoint effect of a number of variables and also the shifting baseline of rapid perceptual, cognitive, linguistic development and brain-maturation in preschool children. The attempt to minimize false-negatives (missing "true" high-risk children) and false-positives (erroneously test-classifying positives) also adds to the efficacy of the Satz work. Third, the stability of results over the lengthy period says much for the sound conception of the theory and the methodological refinement.

In fact, as a theory for the investigation of specific reading disability the cerebral maturational lag postulate is not new. Money (1966, p. 34) drew attention to the need for such kinds of neuro-psychological investigation: "The great majority of reading disability cases will be classifiable not on the basis of brain pathology; but simply as representative of a lag in the functional development of the brain and nervous system that subserves the learning of reading." What is new is that Satz and associates have formalized this assertion and have carried out empirical studies to validate their postulate. The maturational lag hypothesis has the attraction of being consonant with the positions of developmental psychologists (e.g. McV. Hunt, 1961; Piaget, 1926). Severely disabled readers are retarded in their reading acquisition, rather than in the loss of reading ability. As such, they are remediable, if remediation is given in good time, in appropriate measures, and in great intensity. The maturational lag postulate, however, should not be taken to mean that these children will necessarily catch up in the skills in which they are lagging. What it means is that without remediation, they may deteriorate even more than otherwise is the case.

In his summation of the predictive follow-ups, Satz is cautious in his interpretation of the maturational lag postulate. His current position is:

> At present the theory is unclear as to whether the lag in cognitive-linguistic functions which is postulated to develop in older reading-disabled children (ages 11–14) reflects a transitory or more permanent defect in cognitive functioning. It is hypothesized that if the language disorder persists after maturation of the central nervous system is completed, then a permanent defect in function may occur. If true, it would suggest that the lag is associated primarily with earlier stages in development (Satz, Taylor, Friel and Fletcher, 1978, pp. 320–321).

The general question of maturational readiness was tackled earlier by deHirsch, Jansky, and Langford (1966) in a follow-up study of preschoolers. These researchers found that later achievement in reading and writing was predicted significantly better by developmental tests that were maturation-sensitive. In this connection, a recent large-scale verification of the de-Hirsch et al. predictive index of reading failure by Feshback, Adelman, and Fuller (1977) should be mentioned. In a five-year longitudinal study, Feshback et al. followed up two cohorts of 888 and 844 children from a middle-class sample. They aimed at: (1) comparing psychometric versus behavioral kindergarten predictors of reading performance and (2) studying the effect on reading performance of particular classroom and school environments. The use of medical history and demographic data and classroom observation materials have all improved prediction. The follow-up is noteworthy because it emphasizes processes as well as predictors and because it attempts to explain deficits on the part of the child as interaction of both predisposition and situational factors.

To return to the maturational lag postulate, Satz et al. (1978) state that:

> cultural, linguistic, conceptual, and perceptual skills all play an important role in forecasting later reading achievement. In terms of predictive power, however, the contribution of psycholinguistic variables may be secondary to those preconceptual sensory-motor and perceptual skills which have been shown to develop earlier during the ages of five to seven (p. 339).

This position should be taken into account when evaluating such claims as that of verbal deficit conceptualization in dyslexia that Vellutino (1978, 1979, 1980) has recently argued so forcefully. Satz et al. have further invoked the work of White (1965) who has written about the developmental mental shift from preconceptual to conceptual processes in children. The general developmental lag in young children probably manifests itself as conceptual linguistic deficits in older children (see also Vogel, 1974, 1977). There is also support for the central nervous system maturational lag position from Kinsbourne (1973b).

Temporal Order Perception

In his research program Bakker (1967a, 1967b, 1969, 1970, 1972; Bakker and Satz, 1970) has studied the relationship between temporal order perception and reading disability. The investigation is an improvement on the Blank and Bridger paradigm (Blank and Bridger, 1966; Blank, Weider, and Bridger, 1968) and is cast in the epistemological framework of time explication and the neuropsychological dichotic listening model. The concept of temporal order perception is predicated on the fact that the temporal succession of the phonemes in the spoken word correlates to a high degree with the spatial succession of the graphic shapes of the written word. Bakker suggests that the ability to perceive, recognize and reproduce verbal elements (digits, words) in serial order (first, second, third and so on) is an important correlate of reading disability. Bakker found that his controls obtained higher scores on "meaningful" figures than did his poor readers. Also, those children who were "mediators" or who appeared to solve problems by means of verbal mediation achieved better in the temporal ordering of meaningful figures than the nonmediators, while the two groups did not differ with regard to meaningless figures.

Bakker (1970) found that temporal order perception has a differential age effect and suggested that the perception and retention of temporal sequence significantly relate to the age of around seven but not to the age of about ten. Following Fries (1963), he explained that it is during the "transfer stage" of reading that the child learns to transfer from the auditory signals, which he or she has learned, to a set of visual signals in the language system. There is a temporal order perception threshold which functionally interacts with age. Bakker (1970) argues forcefully that:

> It is primarily when the verbal items are presented in a time scheme that disabled readers become differentially impaired. One might therefore conclude that both temporal order perception and verbal mediation represent necessary but not sufficient stimulus conditions by themselves. When both converge as requirements in a learning task, then disabled readers and aphasoid children become differentially impaired (p. 96).

Thus disabled readers do not present verbal labeling problems or sequencing problems as such, but they experience difficulties when time and verbal codes interact.

Bakker has validated experimentally what Benton (1962, p. 86) expressed generally: "Again the question is raised whether one must not think in terms of an interaction of perception and linguistic deficits to account for this form of specific dyslexia." Here the perceptual deficit is temporal order perception and the linguistic deficit is the deficiency in verbal mediation, and both deficits interact. Bakker's investigation is reinforced by the experimental studies of Senf (1969), who examined the memory for visual-auditory stimuli in normal and learning-disabled boys varying in age from about nine to thirteen years. Senf showed that it is the perception and retention of the serial order of digits, rather than the retention of the digits themselves, that discriminate between disabled readers and nondisabled ones.

The reference earlier to aphasoid children brings out the common communication problem between these and dyslexic children. Lowe and Campbell (1965), for example, found that when compared with normal children, aphasoid children were impaired in their ability to indicate which of two rapidly presented tones occured first. They commented that "temporal ordering malfunction of the aphasoid child . . . may be a major factor contributing to his communication problem" (p. 314). This reminds us of the point made by Monsees (1961, p. 83) that "The core of the aphasic disability is a disorder of the temporal sequence, auditory and perhaps visual." Efron (1963) found similar disabilities in adult aphasics with left temporal lobe lesions. His patients might require ten times the normal interval between brief auditory stimuli (pure tones) in order to discriminate their order of succession, or, in some cases, to discriminate successiveness at all. He explained that the relationship between deficits in auditory sequencing and the understanding of spoken language was by no means clear and that "It has not been proved that the defect in temporal order sequencing is the primary *cause* of the inability to understand speech" (Efron, 1967, p. 30). This view is echoed by Rees (1973). She pointed out that there is inadequate support for the notion that the comprehension of heard speech in language-disordered children depends on the fundamental ability to analyze the utterance into a string of phonemes and stressed that such abilities depend on cognitive linguistic functions rather than auditory discrimination as such.

Recently, Tallal (1976, 1980) has shown that both developmental dysphasic children and developmental dyslexic children are not capable of responding correctly to rapidly presented verbal and nonverbal acoustic stimuli, with the dyslexics showing a smaller auditory perceptual deficit. The therapeutic effect of the "stretching" technique of extending the initial formant transitions of, say, stop-consonants (e.g. /ba/) while maintaining the total duration of the consonants is suggested as a possibility. The technique is in fact found to be effective in helping dysphasic and dyslexic children to discriminate previously indiscriminate speech sounds. Thus the Tallal studies provide further refinement of the basic temporal order perception paradigm and succeed in some way in unraveling some of the issues posed by Rees (1973). But there is the larger question of the auditory subskills needed for learning a spoken language and those needed for establishing a system of lexical and phonological representation from printed symbols (see Calfee, Chapman, and Venezky, 1972).

Verbal Processing Deficits

Recently Vellutino and associates (Vellutino, 1977, 1978, 1979, 1980; Vellutino, Harding, Phillips, and Steger, 1975; Vellutino, Pruzek, Steger, and Meshoulam, 1973; Vellutino, Smith, Steger, and Kaman, 1975; Vellutino, Steger, DeSetto, and Phillips, 1975; Vellutino, Steger, Kaman, and DeSetto, 1975; Vellutino, Steger, and Kandel, 1972; Vellutino, Steger, and Pruzek, 1973) have posited a verbal-deficit hypothesis as an alternative conceptualization of specific reading disability. Drawing from his own research program and reviewing a large body of research evidence on visual perception deficiencies, intersensory integration difficulties and auditory dysfunction usually found in severely disabled readers, he systematically teases out conceptual and methodological flaws in individual studies. From his analytic, detective-like work, he builds a case for verbal deficiencies as the main source of difficulties of severely disabled readers. He further suggests that apparent perceptual problems in poor readers at both younger (seven to eight years) and older (nine to fourteen years) age levels are "a secondary manifestation of verbal mediation deficiencies, possibly associated with basic problems" (Vellutino, 1978, p. 107). Some of these language problems include:

1. Rapid, automatic naming deficits related to both accuracy and latency (see Denckla and Rudel, 1976a, 1976b, and our earlier discussion of Perfetti's work in the section on decoding and comprehension in "backward" readers).
2. Difficulties with verbal-association tasks.
3. Deficiencies in understanding syntax (Semel and Wiig, 1975; Vogel, 1974).
4. Deficits in morphology (Vogel, 1977).

Vellutino (1978) points out that his findings of verbal deficits were invariant: "poor readers were consistently differentiated when verbal factors were introduced in the experimental conditions, but did not differ when the effects of verbal encoding were minimized" (p. 107).

Vellutino's studies have alerted us to one source of reading retardation, namely, verbal deficit. Implicit in his reasoning and his own research are these components of difficulties in severely disabled readers:

1. Inefficiency in the acquisition of linguistic rules and linguistic processing.
2. Inefficiency in cognitive-semantic and logical processing.

While Vellutino does not address himself directly to these issues, the books by Wiig and Semel (1976, 1980) have discussed the language, communication, and learning deficits of disabled children and adolescents, and they have provided some remedial suggestions. It should be noted that the findings of Vellutino are at variance with those of researchers who investigated differential cognitive patterns in disabled readers (see section on "Differential Patterns"), as this latter group has emphasized the multi-factorial aspects of dyslexia. The Vellutino view also differs from the maturational lag postulate which emphasizes perceptual-cognitive difficulties at early stages of development.

In evaluating Vellutino's conceptualization it is important to bear in mind the nature of his "dyslexic" subjects. The "probable dyslexic" is diagnosed as a child with "extreme difficulty in identifying single words," with difficulty in recognizing printed words and analyzing their component sounds and above all one with decoding problems quite independent of reading comprehension. Thus "probable dyslexics" comprise the most severely impaired readers in respect of *oral* reading and word analysis subskills, according to the Vellutino (1978) criteria. Thus, we have come full circle to the issue of precise definitions, the issue of diagnostic criteria, and above all the related question of the independence and interdependence of decoding and comprehension as components of reading retardation. Given the complexity of reading as a generalized skill subsuming and integrating a number of subskills and the heterogeneity of retarded readers, or, for that matter, of poor readers, one may wonder if Vellutino's findings are not specific to the rather restricted group defined by his exclusionary criteria.

The critique by the two discussants (Blank, 1978; Doehring, 1978) of the Vellutino work is relevant here. In general, Blank and Doehring would largely concur that "retarded" readers have major difficulties in the language sphere, but the problem still is to determine the precise nature of language and the conditions under which language difficulties occur. Blank emphasizes linguistic awareness or, in our terms, cognitive clarity in readers. She also stresses communication between teacher–child or teacher–child language. This is an area not sufficiently well investigated in reading disability. Her own research into language interactions between teachers and young children deserves attention (Blank, 1973, 1975, 1977). She has devised a coding system as a "beginning tool" to examine the interchanges between teachers and young children. This important question of language in context is a main theme of the Bullock Report and is forcefully argued in a book on language and learning in children by Davies (1977). Blank, Rose, and Berlin (1978a, 1978b) have provided both the conceptualization of "language of learning" and an instrument to assess preschool language interaction.

The view of Doehring (1978) is just as incisive. He takes issue with the single-syndrome paradigm of Vellutino and his processing model of separating perception from short-term memory and long-term memory. To the extent that dyslexia denotes "residual disorder" or that part of reading retardation that we are not fully able to explain (see Applebee, 1971), perceptual, cognitive and linguistic factors must all contribute to the disorder, in varying degrees and at different stages of reading and for children of different age groups. This is the assumption of the multi-factorial approach. Doehring's current work with dyslexics (Doehring and Hoshko, 1977) combined with his previous investigation (Doehring, 1968) has delimited subgroups of disabled readers. His study of rapid processing of print (Doehring, 1976) with children from kindergarten to grade eleven has underlined the importance of levels of processing in reading. He emphasizes that "Advances in our knowledge of dyslexia will probably occur not in the form of dramatic discoveries with a simple paradigm, but through a patient working and reworking of complex sets of experimental variables, with clinical validation wherever possible" (Doehring, 1978, pp. 133–134). He proposes these issues as being relevant for both research and instruction: componential subskills of reading and their relation to reading disability, the role of automaticity in reading problems, syndromes of dyslexia related to failure to achieve automaticity in grapho-phonemic, syntactic, and semantic levels of processing, and intervention strategies directed to these levels. It is thus clear that an understanding of the different forms of reading disabilities presupposes and demands an understanding of different facets of reading processes. This brings us to the issue of neuropsychological research centering on the perennial question of cerebral laterality and reading disability.

Neuropsychological Research—Laterality and Reading Disability

An historical account of laterality-reading relationships shows an early awareness of the subject and what could be considered unsophisticated thinking. Dearborn (1931, 1933) was an early proponent of such a relationship. He found a greater number of his clinic cases showing left dominance, crossed dominance and lack of dominance than among good readers. Monroe (1932) also found more mixed dominance (left hand–right eye and right hand–left eye) in her poor readers. Dearborn noted that reading difficulties were more likely to occur in children who changed over in handedness. Measures of laterality used then included tests of handedness, footedness and eyedness. Usually, handedness related to the hand used to throw a ball, to turn a knob, to trace a pattern, to hammer a nail, to erase the blackboard, to thread a needle, to cut a shape with scissors. Footedness usually referred to the preferred foot in kicking a ball and in jumping. Eyedness was tested with sighting tests. Some of these lateral dominance tests have provided the framework for later, more empirically-based instruments.

The early studies by Dearborn, Monroe and others showed that among clinic cases laterality anomalies had some bearing on reading difficulties. The anomalies of sensory and motoric activities were ascribed to defective or insufficiently developed body image. The interest centered on whether the child should change over to his right hand in what is largely a right-handed world. Laterality was seen as left–right *directional* orientation with reference to the hypothetical vertical mid-line of the body. Deviance was thus linked to left–right confusion. There was little or no reference to the *spatial* coordinate involving the left–right, front–back and above–below cardinal reference axes. In other words, laterality was conceived as a dichotomy and not as a continuum in space. There was, moreover, no reference to the symbolic and language functions involved and consequently the *brainedness* substrate. There was little knowledge of the relationship between the cerebral hemispheres and the favored eye, ear, hand or even foot. The concept of "surface" correlation between sensorimotor preference and reading without regard to functional cerebral specialization lingered even to the 1960s, indeed to the present day, in the form of so-called "neurological organization" of reading. This predilection aside, the early studies by reading specialists alerted us to the underpinning of reading dysfunction, a condition still very much with us today.

Orton's Theory of Cerebral Dominance and Reading Disorders

As Dearborn, Monroe and others were writing in the 1930s, Samuel T. Orton (1925, 1937) investigated the reading, writing and spelling disorders of children from a neuropsychological perspective. He pointed to the clue of frequent occurrence of reversal errors in children with developmental dyslexia. He distinguished between: (1) kinetic reversals, in which the order of letters in a word or the order of the words in a sentence is reversed, and (2) static reversals, involving confusion of a single letter with its mirror image. He explained the pattern of excitation aroused in the cortical hemispheres in visual perception thus:

> The brain contains right and left visual areas which are exactly alike except for their opposite orientation, and we think, therefore, that the existence in the non-dominant hemisphere of engrams of different orientation from those in the dominant hemisphere cannot be lightly dismissed as the probable source of static and kinetic reversals and of the spontaneous ability in mirror reading and mirror writing (Orton, 1937, p. 155).

Thus, according to Orton, a single form arouses two patterns of excitation (engrams) which are mirror-images. The discrimination of a figure from its mirror-image is achieved through the development of lateral dominance which enables one cortical hemisphere to suppress the engrams of the other. When there is incomplete dominance, there is a similarity between the engrams in the two hemispheres and hence reversals occur.

This concept of ambilaterality at the level of the cortex leading to rivalry between the hemispheres and reversal errors and mirror images has not found favor with reading specialists. It is viewed with skepticism by some and condemned as "outdated" by others (e.g. Harris, 1968, p. 164). However, Orton has come to be recognized for his foresight by such neurologists as Masland (1967, 1968). Pribram's hypothesis (1971) that neural activity takes the form of both spatial and temporal codes—the former for representation and the latter for registration of stimuli—reminds one of the engrams about which Orton so presciently wrote nearly fifty years ago. Corballis and Beale (1971, 1976) reviewed laboratory observations on the effects of the essential bilaterality of the nervous systems of animals and humans on left–right responses and mirror-image discrimination among stimuli. They found Orton's account of memory traces plausible and that his hypothesis of reading disability arising from poorly developed lateralization might have been correct, although the details of the theory were untenable.

The heuristic value of Orton's theory also finds some indirect support from studies of split-brain patients (Sperry, 1961, 1964, 1970). Sperry maintains that the corpus callosum has the important function of allowing the two hemispheres to share learning and memory either by transmitting the information at the time the learning takes place or by supplying it on demand later. In the first case, the engrams (or memory traces) of what is learned are laid down both in the directly trained hemisphere and, by way of the corpus callosum, in the other hemisphere as well. In the second case, a set of engrams is established only in the directly trained half, but this information is available to the other hemisphere, when it is required, by way of the corpus callosum. This latter system of single engrams is a sign of lateral dominance. Evidence shows that in most species discrimination of mirror-images proves difficult and that this difficulty is more pronounced at the level of memory, rather than at the purely perceptual level, as Orton postulated.

It may be argued that Orton's concept of learning disorders with a focus on "twisted symbols" is too narrow. For one thing, the paucity of baseline data on the frequency and intensity of so-called reversal errors in the general school population makes it difficult to compare such errors made by poor readers. For another, the proportion of reversal errors compared with consonant and vowel errors is small as shown by Liberman, Shankweiler, Orlando, Harris and Berti (1971). These researchers further stressed that reversals are not just a problem in general form perception, or optical reversibility, but are context-dependent (see also Kolers, 1970). In a later study, Shankweiler and Liberman (1972) found that orientation and sequencing errors were the results of semantic and phonologic confusion, rather than visual-spatial disorder, as had been suggested by Orton. These advances are noteworthy; they also bear out Orton's insight into kinetic errors (reversal of sequence) and static errors (reversal of orientation). Orton's contribution probably lies in his conception of reading disorder as part of speech and language disability and in his attempt to relate this disability to functional organization of the cerebral hemispheres. In an excellent review of neurological aspects of developmental dyslexia, Benton (1975) reminded us of Orton's detailed theoretical formulation and the testable nature of this formulation for scientific evaluation. However, direct, empirical assessment of Orton's postulate awaited the advent in the early 1960s of experimental procedures in audition with the dichotic listening technique and in vision with visual hemifield perception. In what follows, focus will be on dichotic laterality studies for poor readers. Only a brief mention will be made of visual half-field studies.

Dichotic Listening–Overview of Mechanisms

Dichotic listening is the experimental procedure for presenting different messages or stimuli (usually words or syllables) simultaneously to different channels or sense organs (usually the two ears or the dichotic analogue of the ear and the eye). This deceptively simple technique is usually attributed to the experiments on selective attention by Broadbent (1954). Since then and especially with Kimura's (1961a, 1961b) pioneering work relating dichotic listening to pathological brain functions, dichotic studies have been extended to exceptional children. Different groups of these children have been studied within this experimental paradigm: mentally retarded children (Jones and Spreen, 1967), hearing-impaired children (Ling, 1971), high and low achievers (Conners, Kramer, and Guerra, 1969), and disabled readers (Bryden, 1970; Sparrow and Satz, 1970; Leong, 1975b, 1976; Zurif and Carson, 1970).

In general, under free recall conditions with "verbal" materials presented fairly rapidly (see

Studdert-Kennedy and Shankweiler, 1970), most listeners perceive more of the right-ear messages accurately. This right-ear advantage (REA) has been found with dichotic presentation of real words, nonsense syllables, backwards speech and synthetic consonant-vowel (CV) stimuli to right-handed subjects (Kimura, 1961a, 1961b; Kimura and Folb, 1968; Shankweiler and Studdert-Kennedy, 1967). A left-ear advantage is generally found for "nonverbal" materials such as environmental sounds (Knox and Kimura, 1970), musical melodies and pitch contours (Kimura, 1964, 1973; Shankweiler, 1966; Spellacy, 1970). Empirical and clinical studies from the 1960s have further elucidated the meaning of verbal and nonverbal materials and elaborated on the acoustic, linguistic and psychological considerations (see Berlin and McNeil, 1976).

One explanation of the dichotic right-ear advantage is the functional and morphologic asymmetry of the human brain. Under normal conditions, auditory stimuli arriving at the ear travel along contralateral and ipsilateral pathways to bilaterally situated primary auditory receiving areas (Heschl's gyri) in each temporal lobe. The neural connections of the contralateral auditory pathway to the opposite temporal lobe are stronger than the connections of the ipsilateral pathway. Under dichotic conditions, the ipsilateral pathways are suppressed or inhibited (see Sparks and Geschwind, 1968). This evidence comes from dichotic listening experiments using split-brain and hemispherectomized subjects. An alternative explanation is the "transmission loss" of the left-ear signal because of the greater distance it travels. However, right-ear advantage has also been obtained by Bakker (1969, 1970) with monaurally presented verbal stimuli with children. Suppression thus probably contributes to, but is not the basic cause of, the ear difference found in dichotic listening studies.

Overview of Visual Half-Field Laterality Studies

The anatomy of the visual half-fields was described in our Chapter 8 and illustrated in Figure 8–3.

The visual half-field technique is based on the clinical finding of overlapping binocular vision in humans. Images falling on the nasal half of each retina are projected contralaterally to the opposite side of the brain; while images on the temporal hemiretina of each eye project ipsilaterally to the same side of the brain. Thus, it is possible to present visual information to either the left or the right hemisphere. Statements of hemispheric differences are derived from the early studies of Sperry (1968) on commissurotomized subjects and those of Kimura (1961b, 1966) on normal subjects. A basic general finding is the right visual field (left hemisphere) superiority for "verbal" stimuli and the left visual field (right hemisphere) superiority for visuospatial stimuli. However, with word recognition tasks, a directional scanning effect as a result of reading habits cannot be completely ruled out (Scheerer, 1972).

A number of researchers has reviewed or reported on visual half-field laterality studies of children with reading disability: Bakker (1979), McKeever and Huling (1970), Marcel and Rajan (1975), Satz (1976), Witelson (1977), Yeni-Komshian, Isenberg, and Goldberg (1975), among others. They have all noted the inconclusive findings of laterality patterns of "retarded" readers. The not unequivocal results may be attributed in part to these methodological problems: variations in the subjects used (different ages and sex); different nature of the tasks (linguistic such as words, digits or visuospatial such as shapes); variations in the modes of presentation (unilateral or bilateral, horizontal or vertical display, simultaneous or successive presentation); nature of responses (same/different, recognition or recall, manual or vocal).

The more important conceptual interpretation of hemispheric differences in visual half-field inquiries relates to *processing strategies* adopted by children. Bradshaw, Gates and Patterson (1976) have recently reviewed the dichotomies of verbal/visuospatial, serial/parallel and analytic/holistic in visual hemispheric processing differences. From their experiments they have educed evidence to support the hypothesis that the right visual field–left hemisphere and left visual field–right hemisphere difference is more quantitative rather than qualitative. While the analytic/holistic modes of processing may be a more fundamental interpretation of hemispheric differences, the right hemisphere superiority is more apparent in identity matching, while the left hemisphere superiority is more apparent in the analysis of component parts, including visuospatial processing of a gestalt. This explanation of laterality from visual hemifield studies has a bearing on our understanding of reading retardation, as will be further discussed. Other laterality measures include the dichotomous tactual stimulation technique of Witelson (1976) and the lateral gaze and finger-tapping tasks of Kinsbourne (Kinsbourne and Hiscock, 1977).

An Interpretation of Some Dichotic Problems

What emerges from the literature is the lack of clear-cut laterality-reading patterns. In his review on developmental dyslexia, Benton (1975, p. 24) warned that "the vast literature on laterality characteristics and reading skill does not lead to any simple generalizations." He also suggested that "these essentially negative studies . . . do find a weak trend in the direction of a higher frequency of deviant lateral organization in poor readers." Satz (1976) found partial support for his hypothesis of delayed or incomplete hemispheric speech representation in disabled readers. He pointed out the statistical problems of difficulty levels, reliability and the danger of inductive inferences when base rates of hemispheric lateralization are markedly asymmetric in the general population. All these factors contribute to the weak association between behavioral measures and hemispheric specialization, although such a relationship has been shown consistently.

If Benton and Satz are cautious in their formulations and interpretations of the literature, the very recent critique of cerebral lateralization and cognitive development by Kinsbourne and Hiscock (1978) is both direct and thought-provoking. Sharing the view of the nonunitary nature of learning disabilities and the heterogeneity of learning-disabled children, they express their strong doubt on laterality thus: "The literature simply fails to answer the question of whether reading disabilities, or any other kind of learning disabilities, are linked to anomalous lateralization" (p. 174). They base their adverse criticism of laterality studies on methodological and, more importantly, on conceptual grounds. Methodologically, they point out acoustic and statistical problems associated with perceptual studies, especially dichotic listening. Conceptually, they raise some searching and basic issues about cerebral lateralization. They ask and, to some extent, answer important questions pertaining to the meaning of lateralization, the concept of degree of lateralization, of deviation from its prevalent pattern, of cerebral organization and especially the ontogeny or development of lateralization. They also suggest a model for hemispheric specialization from the cumulative work of Kinsbourne (1970, 1973a) on selective attention or expectancy as an important situational variable in hemispheric specialization. Their interpretation of lateralization is fundamentally different from the generally accepted model of Kimura (1961b, 1966). Their questioning of ontogenetic changes in lateralization give a different perspective to such concepts as cerebral maturational lag of disabled readers. For these reasons, a summary of their main arguments on perceptual asymmetry and an interpretation is attempted below.

Methodological Problems—Acoustic and Statistical

The Haskins group (Studdert-Kennedy and Shankweiler, 1970) and the Kresge group (Berlin and Cullen, 1977; Berlin and McNeil, 1976) have critically examined acoustic, phonetic, and linguistic variables in dichotic listening. These researchers have shown that the right-ear advantage is a function of: temporal synchrony of the stimuli, intensity, signal-to-noise ratio and varying frequency bandwidth. They have found that voiceless stop consonants are more intelligible than voiced stop consonants and that dichotic CV and digit tests do not reflect the same neural processes. Failure or insufficient control of some of the above variables often makes interpretation of results difficult.

Statistically, the query of Kinsbourne and Hiscock about the varying scoring methods of within and between ear results and the reliability of dichotic tests is justified. Berlin and Cullen (1977, p. 85) state that as yet transformations of data provide no better measure or more insight into "strength of lateralization of language function." On reliability, there have been more reassuring results recently on dichotic tests with normal adult subjects (Berlin and McNeil, 1976; Fennel, Bowers, and Satz, 1977) and with children (Bakker, van der Vlugt, and Claushuis, 1978). Still, caution has to be exercised in predicting cerebral lateral asymmetries from perceptual scores. This is especially so in any attempt to use dichotic tests for individuals because the studies reported have all dealt with groups. While reliability of perceptual tests is important, it is a necessary but not sufficient condition for validity.

Conceptual Problems—Ontogeny of Lateralization

It is thus relevant to examine the critique of the very concept of laterality and its relevance to reading disability. It is now generally agreed that the term *lateralization* or laterality refers to hemispheric specialization rather than the earlier concept of one hemisphere exercising control over the other (see Benton, 1975; relevant chapters in Knights and Bakker, 1976 and in Segalowitz and Gruber, 1977). There is anatomical, neurological, electrophysiological, cytoarchitetonic and behavioral evidence to show that the principle of early hemispheric equipotentiality, as best articulated in the influential work of Lenneberg (1967), is probably overstated (see Galaburda, LeMay, Kemper, and Geschwind, 1978, Segalowitz and Gruber, 1977). The right hemisphere's capacity to mediate language recovery following early left-hemisphere damage is now interpreted as due to the plasticity of the right hemisphere, rather than hemispheric equipotentiality (Moscovitch, 1977; Rudel, 1978; Witelson, 1977). Conceding that refutation of the equipotentiality hypothesis does not necessarily preclude the degree of hemispheric specialization increases during childhood, Kinsbourne and Hiscock (1978) have queried the uncritical acceptance of progressive lateralization with age, especially as shown in dichotic studies.

The data from various studies are strongly suggestive of an early prepotency of the left hemisphere, but structural asymmetry may not necessarily mean functional asymmetry. Even if functional asymmetry is apparent at an early age, as suggested by studies with preschoolers (Kinsbourne and Hiscock, 1977), it does not necessarily follow that the process of lateralization is complete at an early age. Thus any statement of the all-or-none phenomenon of left lateralization of speech in righthanders, as shown clinically, may need to incorporate the nature of the speech elements and the differential perception of these elements. This approach may reconcile some of the less than conclusive findings on developmental parameters using dichotic CV and digit tasks and dealing with different age groups. Berlin and associates (Berlin, Hughes, Lowe-Bell, and Berlin, 1973; Berlin and McNeil, 1976) explain possible development in right-ear advantage as related to total accuracy of ear scores, phonetic content and nature of errors and the REA as a "biological index of the overloading of a speech processor" (Berlin and McNeil, 1976, p. 355). Porter and Berlin (1975) further emphasize that there are different levels of language processing (as shown by dichotic CV and digit tests) and that each may be lateralized to a different degree or in a different way from the others. Moscovitch (1977) has suggested an extension of this concept to include tests tapping cognition and higher levels of linguistic processing of syntactic and semantic systems over and above the usual phonetic level, as more encompassing in laterality studies.

With structural lateralization accepted at an early age, the question of what is lateralized and if there is progressive lateralization thus evolves round differential lateralization of different language functions. One would therefore have to read Kinsbourne and Hiscock's (1978) statement that "language does not become increasingly lateralized as the child matures" (p. 220) and "the laterality of language representation probably has no relevance to language performance" (p. 221) with their subsequent statement "we are not ruling out the possibility of delayed left-hemisphere maturation in children with language disorders of some kind" (p. 221). Moscovitch (1977, p. 207) seems to be more direct in stating that "experience and maturation affect only the development of language in the left hemisphere, but not the process of lateralization," as a possible explanation of the ontogeny of lateralization. This seems more in accord with the view of language and reading as developmental processes in children. Thus the maturational lag postulate of Satz and studies within the Satz framework can still be accommodated. The important and critical review of Kinsbourne and Hiscock (1978) has alerted us to the danger of overreliance on perceptual measures as an index of cerebral organization and has drawn our attention to the need for proper interpretation of the literature.

While the development of cerebral lateralization may still be an open question, the selective attentional model for hemispheric specialization of Kinsbourne (1970, 1973a) merits consideration. This is one of the "two questions" in dichotic listening discussed by Studdert-Kennedy (1975). In essence, this model states that activation of one hemisphere turns attention towards the opposite side and at the same time would decrease activation of the other hemisphere. Despite some criticism (e.g. Pirozzolo and Rayner, 1977) of its deficiency in explaining visual perceptual asymmetries, on which the original work was elaborated, there is also applicability to auditory phenomenon (see Kinsbourne and Hiscock, 1978). We accept that Kimura's structural model of central occlusion of the ipsilateral signal in dichotic listening explains a number of findings, such as the direct relationship of the right-ear advantage to the degree of verbal encodedness or the degree to which speech sounds undergo context-dependent acoustic variation. But the Kinsbourne model predicting a decrease in the magnitude of the ear advantage with age, as more control over strategies of attending is gained, might better explain some apparently discrepant results in developmental studies. Without denying the role of the structural model, Kinsbourne's work emphasizes situational variables of selectivity, attention, planning and related factors. Thus the nature of the task and hence processing strategies are also important aspects in perceptual asymmetry.

Reading Strategies with Implications for Laterality

This brings us to one intriguing line of research on the *relationship of both the left and right hemispheres and reading* as postulated by Bakker and associates (Bakker, 1973; Bakker, Smink, and Reitsma, 1973). Bakker suggests that the nature of the relation between ear asymmetry and reading ability is dependent on the phase of the learning-to-read process. Proficient early reading, where considerable weight is given to perceptual processes, may go with left or right cerebral laterality. Later stage fluent reading, which depends more on linguistic processes, may go more with left hemisphere laterality. This is supported by data from two further developmental experiments by Bakker, Teunissen, and Bosch (1976). The first one showed that third-grade girls read well with their left or "language" hemisphere, while third-grade boys were equally proficient with either the left or the right ("perceptual") hemispheres. This finding was related to differential stages of reading by the girls and the boys. The second experiment supported the prediction derived from the first experiment that lower-grade girls and higher-grade boys would show laterality-reading patterns similar to those of the third-grade boys and girls respectively. Bakker's postulate of laterality-stages of reading exploits more fully the complementary–different relationships of the two hemispheres (see Krashen, 1976, for an excellent review of this reciprocal relationship) than some of the other laterality-reading models. There is support for the hypothesis in a recent work by Sadick and Ginsburg (1978).

From their concept of differential "lingual" and "perceptual" laterality patterns related to stages of reading, Bakker et al. (1976) also found left- and right-hemisphere advantages going with fast and/or inaccurate reading and with slow and/or accurate reading at the initial stage respectively (see also Bakker, 1979a, 1979b). This is a promising line of research and could generate remediation strategies appropriate for subgroups of poor readers, or for that matter, for individuals. Benton (1975) has stressed the need for *qualitative analysis* of performance characteristics of dyslexic children. Rourke (1978) has summarized ongoing studies in his laboratory on reading, spelling and arithmetic disabilities within a neuropsychological perspective, although no laterality pattern is implied or intended. What is needed is a taxonomy of reading errors within a neuropsychological or neurolinguistic context. There is some substantive literature on children's oral reading errors as elements of grammatical constructions rather than as isolated units (K. Goodman, 1969; Y. Goodman and Burke, 1972; Weber, 1968, 1970a). From the perspective of aphasiology, Marshall and Newcombe (1973) distinguished between these reading disorders: visual dyslexia, "surface" dyslexia and "deep" or phonemic dyslexia (see relevant sections in Chapter 9). The above linguistic and neurolinguistic analyses can with advantage be combined with some of the recent findings of subgroups of "retarded" readers to delineate more clearly the clusters of errors that characterize these children. Doehring and Hoshko (1977), for example, in a Q-technique of factor analysis of children with "reading problems" found three subgroups characterized respectively by: slow oral reading, slow auditory-visual association of words and syllables, and slow auditory-visual letter association. These more specific groupings together with a hierarchical structuring of linguistic errors can be further tested. If it is correct that some poor readers use more of the right-hemisphere strategy, then more of the "perceptual" processes might be exploited. These children can profit more by a more global than an analytic approach in remediation. Alternatively, those disabled readers who show auditory temporal processing difficulties, primarily a left-hemisphere function, could also benefit by this initial approach (see also Tallal, 1976). An extension of this is the question of the relationship between syntactic and semantic aspects of language with laterality.

It is apparent that the relationship of laterality and reading proficiency in children is not a simple one and that it is best explained in terms of processing strategies. The question of "laterality for what" has evolved to focus attention on tasks and on strategies adopted by individuals. Some of the recent dichotic findings of right-ear (left hemisphere) advantage in the detection of musical stimuli by musicians and left-ear (right hemisphere) advantage by nonmusicians (Bever and Chiarello, 1974; Johnson, 1977) can be thus explained. For nonmusicians, perception of music is more at a global level. As a person becomes more musically adept, increasing use is made of a left hemisphere, sequential, analytic mechanism. Gates and Bradshaw (1977) further argue that musical training alone does not invoke a single processing strategy which in turn determines an invariant pattern of cerebral asymmetry. Rather, different strategies are appropriate in different circumstances with music.

A similar explanation applies to visual half-field studies sketched earlier (see Bradshaw, Gates, and Patterson, 1976). This line of process-oriented interpretations of hemispheric difference has been evoked in explaining the significant visual field differences between different typefaces by Bryden and Allard (1976) and in word recognition by Pirozzolo and Rayner (1977). These researchers all stress the recognition of words as a multistage process involving feature analysis by the right hemisphere and decoding and naming by the left hemisphere. Thus the laterality-reading relationship is carried one step further in terms of the right hemisphere specializing for holistic and featural analysis and the left for analytic and naming tasks. Successful performance of word perception, or for that matter early reading, involves a *reciprocal contribution from both the right and left hemispheres,* in varying degrees and for varying individuals at varying stages of reading. This approach seems to lend support to the heuristic value of the innovative ideas of Bakker on laterality patterns related to the learning-to-read process and the corollary of differential error patterns.

In relating processing strategies to hemispheric differences, the traditional verbal and nonverbal distinction has been found to be inadequate. The "serial" and "parallel" processing strategies of Cohen (1973) were found to relate to linguistic materials and could be a concomitant of hemispheric preferences for nominal versus physical analysis. Another promising line might be the simultaneous-successive synthesis of Luria (1966a, 1966b) discussed in the section "Differential Patterns" earlier in this chapter. The Luria paradigm brings to mind Benton's (1975) use of the term "parietal theory" as a possible explanation of dyslexia. This postulate suggests that maldevelopment of the parietotemporo-occipital area, which is concerned with visual, auditory, and somesthetic modalities and their integration, might be a clue for reading retardation. Benton warns that this formulation and the formulation of interhemispheric relations will need substantial empirical support. Kirby and Das (1977) have recently shown that both the simultaneous and successive dimensions are necessary for successful performance in achievement and traditional intelligence tests, though neither dimension, by itself, provides a sufficient condition. There is some evidence that the higher level of language processing (e.g. syllogistic reasoning) is related to the simultaneous dimension. The relationship between simultaneous-successive patterns and reading at various levels needs to be delineated. Bogen (1969) drew attention to this Luria model of simultaneous-successive synthesis and suggested this could be further explored in relation to hemispheric differences.

Implications of Laterality Studies

The foregoing discussion on laterality-reading relationships has dealt with some current concepts and centered on perceptual asymmetry from dichotic studies. Other related aspects such as the important, but vexed, question of handedness have not been considered. The field of the cerebral mechanisms underlying reading disabilities is vast and complex and touches on many disciplines: psychology, neurology, language, and education. Partly because of this complexity and the interrelatedness of the workings of the brain, the findings are less than conclusive. While a poorly established laterality pattern or maldevelopment of the occipital-temporo-parietal lobe by itself does not explain fully reading retardation, this pattern of development in combination with other factors does make the child more vulnerable for learning disorders. It is not the last straw, but a clustering of straws, that breaks the proverbial camel's back. People in related disciplines in the helping professions have to be alert to these "backbreaking straws" so as to help the reading-disabled child in good time and in appropriate measures.

It is significant that very recently, the prestigious National Society for the Study of Education has published its first yearbook in its series of seventy-seven yearbooks on the topic *Education and the Brain* (Chall and Mirsky, 1978). This work with chapters from eminent scientists is a signal recognition of the contribution of the neurosciences to the fields of reading, language, and learning disability. If one message from the book is "remember the brain," the editors aptly add the rejoinder that this should not become "remember *only* the brain." Related disciplines have much to contribute, and learn, from one another. Denckla's (1978) chapter exemplifies this. A strong theme that runs through the book is the importance of cerebral mechanisms for cognition and learning and the interpretation of these mechanisms in terms of information-processing strategies for both learning and teaching (see Wittrock, 1978a). Herein lies the key to our better understanding of reading acquisition and reading disability.

Familial and Mendelian Studies

In the literature there is evidence of the preponderance of dyslexic boys over girls. A ratio of about four boys to one girl is generally suggested (Hallgren, 1950; Orton, 1943; Vernon, 1971). Noting variations from sample to sample of disabled readers, Money (1962, p. 31) is more conservative: "The male incidence is twice that of the female, if not more." In reviewing some 19 studies Critchley (1970) also found a sex predilection with more male than female retarded readers. The general question of sex differences in development is well reviewed by Maccoby and Jacklin (1974) and Wittig and Petersen (1979). In Chapter 12 a review of research on this complex problem revealed the serious sampling difficulty inherent in clinical studies. Nevertheless, the differential distribution as it relates to reading disability is often attributed to sex-influenced inheritance. In this connection, several studies on Mendelian and familial analyses of specific reading disability are relevant and are sketched below.

Early studies included those of Thomas (1905) and Fisher (1905) on multiple cases of dyslexia in individual families. Hallgren (1950) in Sweden is usually credited as among pioneer workers using a statistical and genetic approach to study dyslexia. He investigated "specific dyslexia" in 112 families involving probands of dyslexic children and nearly 400 members of their close relatives (parents and siblings). From his calculation of Mendelian ratios based on those families where one parent was affected, Hallgren noted that dyslexia is attributable to dominance inheritance. Specifically, he suggested that dyslexia is transmitted by an allele (an alternative form of gene) with an autosomal locus (a locus on a chromosome which is not a sex chromosome) and a dominant (as contrasted with recessive) characteristic. This much-quoted Mendelian study is noteworthy as it supports the hypothesis that there is an important familial factor in reading disability. We should, however, note Hallgren's loose definition of dyslexia and the critique of Owen (1978) who cites current biochemical and cytological techniques in analyzing genetic transmission. More recently, Sladen (1970, 1972) has suggested sex-influenced single-gene transmission with lower thresholds for males than females and with dominant expression for the former but recessive characteristic for the latter. Finucci, Guthrie, Childs, Abbey, and Childs (1976) investigated members of the immediate families of twenty disabled readers (15 boys and 5 girls) to determine the prevalence of reading disability within the families. Forty-five per cent of 75 close relatives of the probands were affected—male relatives more so than females. Finucci et al. suggested that reading disability is genetically heterogeneous and cannot be attributed to a single mode of genetic transmission. As well, their technique of using a battery of "tolerance tests" (e.g. transformed passages) to identify adults who might otherwise have compensated for their disability should also be noted.

In a familial study involving 304 elementary and junior-high-school children, Owen, Adams, Forrest, Stolz, and Fisher (1971) sought to identify familial patterns and sibling resemblance in children classified as "educationally handicapped" (EH) on the basis of reading and spelling disability two years below grade expectancy. There were 76 quartets. Each quartet comprised an EH child matched for sex, grade and IQ with an academically successful child and one like-sex sibling of each. One of the main findings is that there are familial patterns of neurological immaturities. This is attributed to multi-factorial genetic predisposition, at least for certain types of reading disabilities. Environmental factors can help when this genetic predisposition is weak. This interaction between genetic predisposition and environmental factors is further emphasized by Owen (1978) and her panel discussant (McClearn, 1978). McClearn emphasizes that it is possible for environmental factors to modify the phenotypic expression of the genotype in multi-factorial inheritance and also likely with Mendelian conditions. As an example of the latter, he cites successful dietary treatment of phenylketonuria (PKU) in mental retardation. He also proposes a multiple-factor model incorporating environmental and genetic conditions with applicability to processes involved in reading.

Recently, Foch, DeFries, McClearn, and Singer (1977) reported on the three-year Colorado Family Reading Study involving 58 reading-disabled children (probands), controls matched on sex, age, grade, school and home background and nuclear families of both probands and controls. The disabled readers with ages from seven to twelve years were selected according to the criteria of IQ greater than 90, reading at one and a half grades below expectancy, with no sensory deficits and living with both biological parents. The study aimed at identifying familial patterns of impairment in cognitive abilities with a battery of tests found to maximally differentiate the probands from their controls. Results of the mean comparisons suggested greater deficits for male relatives of probands than for female relatives on reading, spelling, auditory memory, perceptual speed and verbal reasoning. Mothers and sisters of the probands appeared to be less affected, though there was a significant interaction between sex and family type. Foch et al. speculated on specific genetic mechanisms. Since mothers and sisters of the probands exhibited fewer deficiencies in reading recognition than the male relatives, the simple autosomal dominant hypothesis can be rejected, as otherwise many more female relatives of the probands would show lower scores in the test battery. The data seemed compatible with the model of polygenic transmission with different thresholds for the sexes or a model with a single gene with reduced penetrance in females. The researchers also suggested that it is possible for reading disability to be a heterogeneous disorder with different modes of inheritance and varying environmental precursors.

To sum up this section, it is appropriate to refer to the discussions of McClearn (1978) and Childs, Finucci, and Preston (1978). The several studies sketched have shown evidence of familial distribution of specific reading disability and modes of inheritance. McClearn stresses subtypes of reading disability, each with its own unique etiology and each with its form, locus, and characteristic of genetic transmission. This model will then accommodate the apparently different views of: autosomal dominant inheritance (Hallgren), sex-influenced single-gene transmission (Sladen), genetic heterogeneity (Finucci et al.; Foch et al.) and multi-factorial genetic predisposition interacting with environment (Owen et al.). This view of subtypes is reminiscent of our discussion of subgroups of disabled readers with differential patterns, although these subtypes are not genetically determined. The Foch et al. Colorado findings of manifold deficits in the siblings and parents of their reading disabled probands provide strong evidence for the familial resemblance of reading disability. Such familialness is necessary but not sufficient evidence for genetic variations. Childs, Finucci, and Preston (1978) are cautious in pointing out that it is not possible as yet to state unequivocally whether or not reading disability is genetically determined. Therefore, "the position at the moment is one of designing the appropriate conditions to test these hypotheses" with rigorous tests to differentiate the individuals (p. 309).

Summary

It has been said that there are as many dyslexias as there are dyslexics. This chapter dealing with this severely reading disabled group has discussed a number of issues: subgroups and differential cognitive patterns, maturational lag and predictive follow-ups, temporal order perception, verbal processing and deficits, neuropsychological research focusing on laterality, laterality-related processing strategies, genetic and familial studies. Space and other reasons preclude discussion of other equally important issues. One example is the diagnosis and prescriptive teaching of these children. For those readers who want to pursue further the subject of specific reading disability, there is a number of excellent journals and books dealing with the subject. The early work by Money (1962) has become something of a classic. His later book (Money, 1966) contains different remedial approaches. An in-depth work with theory and practice for teaching is that of Johnson and Myklebust (1967). The latter's several edited volumes on progress in learning disabilities deserve to be read (Myklebust, 1968, 1971, 1975, 1978). Critchley (1964, 1970) has written on the dyslexic child from an aphasiological perspective and has provided clinical cases. Contemporary psychological and neuropsychological works on theory, research, and practice and ones that command attention include Benton and Pearl (1978) and Knights and Bakker (1976, 1979). The list of reference sources is suggestive and by no means exhaustive. It can never be. In an area which is so complex and which requires much multi- and inter-disciplinary research, there will continue to be a need for rigorous, scientific work on various facets of the perplexing problem.

More than a decade ago, Critchley (1968) suggested some seventeen different areas worthy of further exploration in specific reading disability. These areas included: early and efficient diagnosis, delineation of speech and language development, detailed case studies and follow-ups, studies of theory-based programs and remediation, research into brain-behavior mechanisms and information-processing in disabled readers. These areas are still apposite, although some progress has been made in each and all fields. There is yet one more area from the other end of the reading scale, as it were. This is the aspect of *why* and *how* some children learn to read early. The small number of detailed studies of "young fluent readers" from researchers like Clark (1976) in Scotland; Almy (1949), Durkin (1966, 1974–1975) and Steinberg and Steinberg (1975) in the U.S.; King and Friesen (1972) in Canada, and Söderbergh (1971, 1976) in Sweden may yet provide us with some further clues to reading acquisition and reading difficulties. In mentioning these works, we are not suggesting that children should be *taught* to read early. To some extent, early reading is part of the broader question of reading readiness. The theoretical issues and recent conclusions are discussed in the section "Age of Initiation into Reading" in Chapter 13. Suffice it to say that Downing and Thackray's (1975) proposal that readiness should be regarded as a question of a gap between the condition of the child and the demands of the task is a relevant one. Both can be modified—the child can be prepared for the task and the task can be tailored to the child's needs. In his review on when children can learn to read and when they should be taught to read, Coltheart (1979) argued for the importance of extrinsic factors such as curricula and teacher effectiveness rather than intrinsic factors within children as determinants of reading acquisition.

Our interest in early reading relates to the experiences these children have at home and the ways in which they are nurtured to learn to read. Knowledge of this nurturance helps us to provide better guidance to those with reading difficulties. Steinberg and Steinberg (1975) described how they taught their preschool child to read. Steinberg and Yamada (1978–1979) demonstrated that 42 three- and four-year-old Japanese children could learn complicated visual symbols like the Japanese Kanji quickly. The researchers interpreted their experimental findings as emphasizing meaningfulness rather than perceptual complexity in learning written symbols. In her detailed and systematic linguistic experiment in which she taught her daughter Astrid to read between the ages of two years four months and three years five months, Söderbergh (1971) has provided us with a valuable linguistic and psycholinguistic case study of reading acquisition. She has reported further data from ten children between the ages of two and five who learned to read at home in the Stockholm area (Söderbergh, 1976). Of these ten children, five were severely hearing-impaired and two were totally deaf. It is significant to note that the reading of single words, sentences and stories by these children inspired them to "play with" or comment about language. Söderbergh (1976, p. 271) reports on a child's reaction to reading *Srdjan viće* "Srdjan is shouting": "Cay you say: the flower is crying? Yes you can. Can you say: the flower is dancing? Can you say: the flower is pushing the baby carriage? No you can't."

Obviously, the Steinberg and Steinberg, and the Söderbergh intensive case studies are success stories. They show what might be achieved with interested and knowledgeable parents. We would not want to give the impression that parents should set out to teach their four- or five-year-old children to read. In fact, we are skeptical of the facile claims by some overenthusiastic people and commercial enterprises that they can teach young children to read in sixty days! We would like to be convinced by data similar to those detailed by the authors cited. What is emerging from the interesting case studies and the longitudinal studies of the kinds reported by Clark (1976) and Durkin (1966, 1974–1975) is that the attitudes of parents and their willingness to help in response to the child's questions are of paramount importance. Note the interactive aspect of responding to the child's request; the communicative process goes both ways—from child to parent and vice versa. Responses often take the form of the child being read to and the child using language in context. From another route, we are thus led back by case reports, by systematic data, to our various discussions of metalanguage, linguistic awareness, cognitive clarity in reading and the Bullock Report's central theme of "a language for life." That this language can be acquired at an early age sparks some hope for children with reading difficulties, or for that matter, for those with specific reading disability. Both clinical study and experimental investigation are needed to help to unravel the tangled problem of how disabled readers too may "read, mark, learn, and inwardly digest."

References

Aaron, I. E. (1960) "What teachers and prospective teachers know about phonic generalizations," *Journal of Educational Research,* **53,** 323–330.

Abernethy, E. M. (1936) "Relationship between mental and physical growth," *Monographs of the Society for Research in Child Development,* **1,** 7. Washington, D.C.: National Research Council.

Abiri, J. O. O. (1969) *World Initial Teaching Alphabet Versus Traditional Orthography,* unpublished doctoral dissertation, University of Ibadan, Nigeria.

Abrams, J. C., and Smolen, W. O. (1973) "On stress, failure and reading disability," *Journal of Reading,* **16,** 462–466.

Abrams, S. G., and Zuber, B. L. (1972) "Some temporal characteristics of information processing during reading," *Reading Research Quarterly,* **8,** 40–51.

Adams, M. J. (1979) "Models of word recognition," *Cognitive Psychology,* **11,** 133–176.

Adams, M. J., and Collins, A. (1979) "A schema-theoretic view of reading," in Freedle, R. O. (ed.), *New Directions in Discourse Processing, Vol. II.* Norwood, N.J.: Ablex.

Albert, M. L., Yamadori, A., Gardner, H., and Howes, D. (1973) "Comprehension in alexia," *Brain,* **96,** 317–328.

Albrow, K. H. (1972) *The English Writing System: Notes Towards a Description.* London: Longmans.

Alden, C. L., Sullivan, H. B., and Durrell, D. D. (1941) "The frequency of special reading disabilities," *Education* (Boston University) **62,** 32–36.

Alexander, C. F. (1980) "Black English dialect and the classroom teacher," *Reading Teacher,* **33,** 571–577.

Allen, A. R., and Boraks, N. (1978) "Peer tutoring: Putting it to the test," *Reading Teacher,* **32,** 274–278.

Allen, R. V. (1976) *Language Experiences in Communication.* Boston, Mass.: Houghton Mifflin.

Allen, V. L., Feldman, R. S., and Devin-Sheehan, L. (1976) "Research on children tutoring children: A critical review," *Review of Educational Research,* **46,** 355–385.

Allport, D. A. (1977) "On knowing the meaning of words we are unable to report: The effects of visual masking," in Dornič, S. (ed.), *Attention and Performance VI.* Hillsdale, N.J.: Erlbaum.

Allport, D. A. (1979) "Word recognition in reading (tutorial paper)," in Kolers, P. A., Wrolstad, M. E., and Bouma, H. (eds.), *Processing of Visible Language, Vol. 1.* New York: Plenum.

Allport, G. W. (1935) "Attitudes," in Murchison, C. M. (ed.), *Handbook of Social Psychology.* Worcester, Mass.: Clark University Press.

Allport, G. W. (1966) "Attitudes in the history of social psychology," in Jahoda, M., and Warren, N. (eds.), *Attitudes.* Harmondsworth, England: Penguin.

Almy, M. C. (1949) *Children's Experiences Prior to First Grade and Success in Beginning Reading.* New York: Bureau of Publications, Teachers College, Columbia University.

American Academy of Pediatrics (1972) "The eye and learning disabilities." Joint organizational statement prepared by an ad hoc committee of the American Academy of Pediatrics, the American Academy of Ophthalmology and Otolaryngology, and the American Association of Ophthalmology, and approved by the executive committees and councils of these organizations, *Journal of School Health,* **42,** 218.

American Foundation for the Blind (1957) *Itinerant Teaching Service for Blind Children.* New York: American Foundation for the Blind.

Ammons, R. B. (1954) "Knowledge of performance: Survey of literature, some possible applications, and suggested experimentation," *USAF WADC Technical Report No. 54-114.* Wright-Patterson Air Force Base, Ohio.

Ammons, R. B., and Ammons, H. S. (1948) *Ammons Full-Range Picture Vocabulary Test.* Missoula, Montana: Psychology Test Specialists.

Anderson, I. H., Byron, O., and Dixon, W. R. (1956) "The relation between reading achievement and the method of teaching reading," *University of Michigan School of Education Bulletin,* **7,** 104–107.

Anderson, I. H., and Dearborn, W. F. (1952) *The Psychology of Teaching Reading.* New York: Ronald Press.

Anderson, I. H., and Hughes, B. O. (1955) "The relationship between learning to read and growth as a whole," *School of Education Bulletin*, University of Michigan.

Anderson, I. H., Hughes, B. O., and Dixon, W. R. (1957) "The rate of reading development and its relation to age of learning to read, sex, and intelligence," *Journal of Educational Research*, **50**, 481–494.

Anderson, M., and Kelly, M. (1931) "An inquiry into traits associated with reading disability," *Smith College Studies in Social Work*, **2**, 46–63.

Anderson, R. C. (1970) "Control of student mediating processes during verbal learning and instruction," *Review of Educational Research*, **40**, 349–369.

Anderson, R. C. (1972) "How to construct achievement tests to assess comprehension," *Review of Educational Research*, **42**, 145–170.

Anderson, R. C. (1973) "Learning principles from text," *Journal of Educational Psychology*, **64**, 26–30.

Anderson, R. C. (1974) "Substance recall of sentences," *Quarterly Journal of Experimental Psychology*, **26**, 530–541.

Anderson, R. C. (1977) "The notion of schema and the educational enterprise: General discussion of the conference," in Anderson, R. C., Spiro, R. J., and Montague, W. E. (eds.), *Schooling and the Acquisition of Knowledge*. Hillsdale, N.J.: Erlbaum.

Anderson, R. C. (1978) "Schema-directed processes in language comprehension," in Lesgold, A. M., Pellegrino, J. W., Fokkema, S. D., and Glaser, R. (eds.), *Cognitive Psychology and Instruction*. New York: Plenum.

Anderson, R. C., and Kulhavy, R. W. (1972) "Imagery and prose learning," *Journal of Educational Psychology*, **63**, 242–243.

Anderson, R. C., and Ortony, A. (1975) "On putting apples into bottles—a problem of polysemy," *Cognitive Psychology*, **7**, 167–180.

Anderson, R. C., Reynolds, R. E., Schallert, D. L., and Goetz, E. T. (1977) "Frameworks for comprehending discourse," *American Educational Research Journal*, **14**, 367–381.

Anderson, R. C., Spiro, R. J. and Anderson, M. C. (1978) "Schemata as scaffolding for the representation of information in connected discourse," *American Educational Research Journal*, **15**, 433–440.

Anderson, R. C., Spiro, R. J., and Montague, W. E. (eds.), (1977) *Schooling and the Acquisition of Knowledge*. Hillsdale, N.J.: Erlbaum.

Anderson, R. P., Halcomb, C. G., and Doyle, R. B. (1973) "The measurement of attentional defects," *Exceptional Children*, **39**, 534–538.

Andersson, T. (1969) *Foreign Languages in the Elementary School*. Austin, Texas: University of Texas Press.

Andreas, B. G. (1972) *Experimental Psychology* (2nd. ed.). New York: Wiley.

Anisfeld, M. (1969) "Psychological evidence for an intermediate stage in a morphological derivation," *Journal of Verbal Learning and Verbal Behavior*, **8**, 191–195.

Annet, J. (1964) *The Role of Knowledge of Results in Learning: A Survey*. Port Washington, N.Y.: U.S. Naval Training Device Center.

Ansari, N. A. (1961) "Follow-up of literacy," *Indian Journal of Adult Education*, **22**, 19–20.

Applebee, A. N. (1971) "Research in reading retardation: Two critical problems," *Journal of Child Psychology and Psychiatry*, **12**, 91–113.

Arlin, M., Scott, M., and Webster, J. (1978–1979) "The effects of pictures on rate of learning sight words: A critique of the focal attention hypothesis," *Reading Research Quarterly*, **14**, 645–660.

Arnheim, R. (1969) *Visual Thinking*. Berkeley, Calif.: University of California Press.

Artley, A. S. (1948) "General and specific factors in reading comprehension," *Journal of Experimental Education*, **45**, 181–188.

Artley, A. S. (1953) "Oral language growth and reading ability," *Elementary School Journal*, **53**, 321–328.

Artley, A. S. (1980) "Reading: Skills or competencies?" *Language Arts*, **57**, 546–549.

Artley, A. S., and Hardin, V. B. (1971) *Inventory of Teacher Knowledge of Reading*. Columbia, Missouri: Lucas Brothers.

Ashcroft, S. C., (1960) *Errors in Oral Reading of Braille at Elementary Grade Levels*, doctoral dissertation, University of Illinois.

Ashcroft, S. C. (1967) "Blind and partially seeing children," in Dunn, L. M. (ed.), *Exceptional Children in the Schools*. New York: Holt.

Ashton-Warner, S. (1963) *Teacher*. London: Secker and Warburg.

Athey, I. (1977) "Syntax, semantics, and reading," in Guthrie, J. T. (ed.), *Cognition, Curriculum, and Comprehension*. Newark, Del.: IRA.

Atkin, R., Bray, R., Davison, M., Herzberger, S., Humphreys, L., and Selzer, U. (1977) "Cross-lagged panel analysis of sixteen cognitive measures at four grade levels," *Child Development*, **48**, 944–952.

Attneave, F. (1972) "Representation of physical space," in Melton, A. W. and Martin, E. (eds.), *Coding Processes in Human Memory*. New York: Wiley.

Austin, M. (1973) "United States," in Downing, J. (ed.), *Comparative Reading*. New York: Macmillan.

Auten, A. (1980) "Parents as partners in reading," *Reading Teacher*, **34**, 228–230.

Ayers, D., and Downing, J. (1979) "Children's linguistic awareness and reading achievement," Paper presented at the IRA/University of Victoria International Reading Research Seminar on Linguistic Awareness and Learning to Read, June 26–30, 1979, Victoria, B. C., Canada.

Baddeley, A. D. (1979) "Working memory and reading," in Kolers, P. A., Wrolstad, M. E., and Bouma, H. (eds.), *Processing of Visible Language, Vol. 1*. New York: Plenum.

Baker, E. H. (1968) "Motivation for the disadvantaged, special problems," *Grade Teacher*, **85**, 104–107.

Baker, R. G. (1980) "Orthographic awareness," in Frith,

U. (ed.), *Cognitive Processes in Spelling.* New York: Academic Press.

Bakker, D. J. (1967a) "Temporal order, meaningfulness, and reading ability," *Perceptual and Motor Skills,* **24,** 1027–1030.

Bakker, D. J. (1967b) "Left-right differences in auditory perception of verbal and non-verbal material in children," *Quarterly Journal of Experimental Psychology,* **19,** 334–336.

Bakker, D. J. (1969) "Ear asymmetry with monaural stimulation: Task influences," *Cortex,* **5,** 36–42.

Bakker, D. J. (1970) "Temporal order perception and reading retardation," in Bakker, D. J., and Satz, P. (eds.), *Specific Reading Disability: Advances in Theory and Method.* Rotterdam, Netherlands: Rotterdam University Press.

Bakker, D. J. (1972) *Temporal Order in Disturbed Reading.* Lisse, Netherlands: Swets and Zeitlinger.

Bakker, D. J. (1973) "Hemispheric specialization and stages in the learning-to-read process," *Bulletin of the Orton Society,* **23,** 15–27.

Bakker, D. J. (1979a) "Hemispheric differences and reading strategies: Two dyslexias?" *Bulletin of the Orton Society,* **29,** 84–100.

Bakker, D. J. (1979b) "Perceptual asymmetries and reading proficiency," in Bortner, M. (ed.), *Cognitive Growth and Development: Essays in Honor of Herbert G. Birch.* New York: Brunner–Mazel.

Bakker, D. J., and Satz, P. (eds.), (1970) *Specific Reading Disability: Advances in Theory and Method.* Rotterdam, Netherlands: Rotterdam University Press.

Bakker, D. J., Smink, T., and Reitsma, P. (1973) "Ear dominance and reading ability," *Cortex,* **9,** 301–312.

Bakker, D. J., Teunissen, J., and Bosch, J. (1976) "Development of laterality-reading patterns," in Knights, R. M., and Bakker, D. J. (eds.), *The Neuropsychology of Learning Disorders: Theoretical Approaches.* Baltimore: University Park Press.

Bakker, D. J., Van der Vlugt, H., and Claushuis, M. (1978) "The reliability of dichotic ear asymmetry in normal children," *Neuropsychologia,* **16,** 753–757.

Balow, B., Fulton, H., and Peploe, E. (1971) "Reading comprehension skills among hearing impaired adolescents," *Volta Review,* **73,** 113–119.

Balow, I. H. (1967) *A Longitudinal Evaluation of Reading Achievement in Small Classes.* Berkeley, Calif.: University of California.

Balpuri, S. (1958) "Whither adult education in India?" *Fundamental and Adult Education,* **10,** 171–173.

Bamberger, R. (1972) "International activities to promote children's reading and children's literature (with special reference to central Europe)," in Southgate, V. (ed.), *Literacy at All Levels.* London: Ward Lock.

Bamberger, R. (1973) "Leading children to reading: An Austrian venture," in Karlin, R. (ed.), *Reading For All.* Newark, Del.: IRA.

Bamberger, R. (1976) "Literature and development in reading," in Merritt, J. E. (ed.), *New Horizons in Reading.* Newark, Del.: IRA.

Barber, T. X., et al. (1969) "Five attempts to replicate the experimenter bias effect," *Journal of Consulting and Clinical Psychology,* **33,** 1–6.

Barclay, G. L. (1966) "i.t.a. and the emotionally disturbed," in Mazurkiewicz, A. J. (ed.), *The Initial Teaching Alphabet and the World of English.* New York: i.t.a. Foundation.

Barganz, R. A. (1974) "Phonological and orthographic relationships to reading performance," *Visible Language,* **8,** 101–122.

Barik, H., and Swain, M. (1976) "Primary-grade French immersion in a unilingual English-Canadian setting: The Toronto study through grade 2," *Canadian Journal of Education,* **1,** 39–58.

Barnes, D. (1976) *From Communication to Curriculum.* Harmondsworth, England: Penguin.

Barnitz, J. G. (1980) "Black English and other dialects: Sociolinguistic implications for reading instruction," *Reading Teacher,* **33,** 779–786.

Baron, J. (1973) "Phonemic stage not necessary for reading," *Quarterly Journal of Experimental Psychology,* **25,** 241–246.

Baron, J. (1975) "Successive stages in word recognition," in Rabbitt, P. M. A., and Dornič, S. (eds.), *Attention and Performance V.* London: Academic Press.

Baron, J. (1977a) "What we might know about orthographic rules," in Dornič, S. (ed.), *Attention and Performance VI.* Hillsdale, N.J.: Erlbaum.

Baron, J. (1977b) "Mechanisms for pronouncing printed words: Use and acquisition," in LaBerge, D. and Samuels, S. J. (eds.), *Basic Processes in Reading: Perception and Comprehension.* Hillsdale, N.J.: Erlbaum.

Baron, J. (1979) "Orthographic and word-specific mechanisms in children's reading of words," *Child Development,* **50,** 60–72.

Baron, J., and Hodge, J. (1978) "Using spelling–sound correspondences without trying to learn them," *Visible Language,* **12,** 55–70.

Baron, J., and McKillop, B. J. (1975) "Individual differences in speed of phonemic analysis, visual analysis, and reading," *Acta Psychologica,* **39,** 91–96.

Baron, J., and Strawson, C. (1976) "Use of orthographic and word-specific knowledge in reading words aloud," *Journal of Experimental Psychology: Human Perception and Performance,* **2,** 386–393.

Baron, J., and Treiman, R. (1980) "Use of orthography in reading and learning to read," in Kavanagh, J. F., and Venezky, R. L. (eds.), *Orthography, Reading, and Dyslexia.* Baltimore: University Park Press.

Barrera-Vasquez, A. (1953) *The Tarascan Project in Mexico: Use of Vernacular Languages in Education.* Paris: UNESCO.

Barrett, T. C. (1965) "The relationship between measures of pre-reading visual discrimination and first grade reading achievement: A review of the literature," *Reading Research Quarterly,* **1,** 51–76.

Barron, R. W. (1979) "Access to the meanings of printed words: Some implications for reading and for learning to read," in Murray, F. B. (ed.), *The Development of the Reading Process.* Newark, Del.: IRA.

Barron, R. W., and Baron, J. (1977) "How children get meaning from printed words," *Child Development,* **48,** 587–594.

Bartlett, F. C. (1932) *Remembering: A study in Experimental and Social Psychology.* Cambridge, England: Cambridge University Press.

Bartlett, F. C. (1948) "The measurement of human skill," *Occupational Psychology,* **22,** 30–38 and 83–91.

Basser, L. S. (1962) "Hemiplegia of early onset and the faculty of speech with special reference to the effects of hemispherectomy," *Brain,* **85,** 427–460.

Bedwell, C. H. (1972) "The eye, vision, and visual discomfort," *Lighting Research and Technology,* **4,** 151–158.

Bedwell, C. H. (1978) "Binocular vision and near visual performance and fatigue," *Proceedings of Second World Congress on Engophthalmology.* Stockholm: Societas Engophthalmologica Internationalis.

Bedwell, C. H., Grant, R., and McKeown, J. R. (1980) "Visual and ocular control anomalies in relation to reading difficulty," *British Journal of Educational Psychology,* **50,** 61–70.

Beimiller, A. (1970) "The development of the use of graphic and contextual information as children learn to read," *Reading Research Quarterly,* **6,** 75–96.

Belbin, E. (1956) "The effects of propaganda on recall, recognition and behaviour," *British Journal of Psychology,* **47,** 163–174 and 259–270.

Beliakova, G. P. (1973) "The segmentation of speech into words by the oldest preschool children," Paper presented at the Moscow, U.S.S.R. conference on *Fostering Independence and Activity in Children of Preschool Age* (in Russian).

Bellugi, U., and Klima, E. S. (1975) "Aspects of sign language and its structure," in Kavanagh, J. F., and Cutting, J. E. (eds.), *The Role of Speech in Language.* Cambridge, Mass.: MIT Press.

Belmont, L., and Birch, H. G. (1966) "The intellectual profile of retarded readers," *Perceptual Motor Skills,* **22,** 787–816.

Bender, L. (1938) *A Visual Motor Gestalt Test and Its Clinical Use.* New York: American Orthopsychiatric Association.

Bender, L. (1946) *Instructions for the Use of the Visual Motor Gestalt Test.* New York: American Orthopsychiatric Association.

Bender, L. (1958) "Problems in conceptualization and communication in children with developmental alexia," in Hoch, P. H., and Zubin, J. (eds.), *Psychopathology of Communication.* New York: Grune and Stratton.

Bender, L. (1970) "The use of the Visual Motor Gestalt test in the diagnosis of learning disabilities," *Journal of Special Education,* **4,** 29–39.

Bennett, C. (1938) *An Inquiry into the Genesis of Poor Reading* (Contributions to Education, No.755). New York: Teachers College, Columbia University.

Benton, A. L. (1962) "Dyslexia in relation to form perception and directional sense," in Money, J. (ed.), *Reading Disability: Progress and Research Needs in Dyslexia.* Baltimore: Johns Hopkins Press.

Benton, A. L. (1964) "Developmental aphasia and brain damage," *Cortex,* **1,** 40–52.

Benton, A. L. (1966) "Language disorders in children," *Canadian Psychologist,* **7,** 298–312.

Benton, A. L. (1973) "Minimal brain dysfunction from a neuropsychological point of view," *Annals of the New York Academy of Sciences,* **205,** 29–37.

Benton, A. L. (1975) "Developmental dyslexia: Neurological aspects," in Friedlander, W. J. (ed.), *Advances in Neurology, Vol. 7.* New York: Raven Press.

Benton, A. L., and Pearl, D. (eds.), (1978) *Dyslexia: An Appraisal of Current Knowledge.* New York: Oxford University Press.

Bereiter, C., and Engelmann, S. (1966) *Teaching Disadvantaged Children in the Preschool.* Englewood Cliffs, N.J.: Prentice-Hall.

Berger, N. S., and Perfetti, C. A. (1977) "Reading skill and memory for spoken and written discourse," *Journal of Reading Behavior,* **9,** 7–16.

Berlin, C. I., and Cullen, J. K. (1977) "Acoustic problems in dichotic listening tasks," in Segalowitz, S. J., and Gruber, F. A. (eds.), *Language Development and Neurological Theory.* New York: Academic Press.

Berlin, C. I., Hughes, L. F., Lowe-Bell, S. S., and Berlin, H. L. (1973) "Dichotic right ear advantage in children 5 to 13," *Cortex,* **9,** 394–401.

Berlin, C. I., and McNeil, M. R. (1976) "Dichotic listening," in Lass, N. J. (ed.), *Contemporary Issues in Experimental Phonetics.* New York: Academic Press.

Berlyne, D. E. (1957) "Conflict and information-theory variables as determinants of human perceptual curiosity," *Journal of Experimental Psychology,* **53,** 399–404.

Bernstein, B. (1958) "Some sociological determinants of perception: An enquiry into sub-cultural differences," *British Journal of Sociology,* **9,** 159–174.

Bernstein, B. (1961) "Social class and linguistic development: A theory of social learning," in Halsey, A. H., Floud, J., and Anderson, C. A. (eds.), *Education, Economy and Society.* New York: The Free Press.

Bernstein, B. (1971) *Class Codes and Control, Vol. I.* London: Routledge and Kegan Paul.

Bernstein, M. R. (1955) "Relationship between interest and reading comprehension," *Journal of Educational Research,* **49,** 283–288.

Berreta, S. (1970) "Self-concept development in the reading program," *Reading Teacher,* **24,** 232–238.

Berry, M. F. (1969) *Language Disorders of Children: The Basis and Diagnoses.* New York: Appleton.

Beta Upsilon Chapter, Pi Lambda Theta (1974) "Children's reading interests classified by age level," *Reading Teacher,* **27,** 694–700.

Betts, E. A. (1934) "A psychological approach to reading difficulties," *Educational Research Bulletin,* **13,** 135–140, and 163–174.

Betts, E. A. (1935) "Reading disability correlates," *Education,* **56,** 18–24.

Bever, T. G. (1968) "Association to stimulus-response

theories of language," in Dixon, T. R., and Horton, D. L. (eds.), *Verbal Behavior and General Behavior Theory*. Englewood Cliffs, N.J.: Prentice-Hall.

Bever, T. G., and Chiarello, R. J. (1974) "Cerebral dominance in musicians and non-musicians," *Science*, **185**, 137–139.

Bever, T. G., Garrett, M. F. and Hurtig, R. (1973) "The interaction of perceptual processes and ambiguous sentences," *Memory and Cognition*, **1**, 277–286.

Beyard-Tyler, K. C., and Sullivan, H. J. (1980) "Adolescent reading preferences for type of theme and sex of character," *Reading Research Quarterly*, **16**, 104–120.

Bhola, H. S. (1970) "The methods and materials of functional literacy," *Literacy Discussion*, **1**, 31–72.

Biederman, I., and Tsao, Y. C. (1979) "On processing Chinese ideographs and English words: Some implications from Stroop-Test results," *Cognitive Psychology*, **11**, 125–132.

Bierwisch, M. (1970) "Semantics," in Lyons, J. (ed.), *New Horizons in Linguistics*. New York: Penguin.

Bigelow, E. B. (1934) "School progress of under age children," *Elementary School Journal*, **35**, 186–192.

Bilodeau, E. A., and Bilodeau I. McD. (1961) "Motor-skills learning," *Annual Review of Psychology*, **58**, 142–144.

Binet, A. (1969) *The Experimental Psychology of Alfred Binet*, edited by Pollock, R. H., and Brenner, M. W. New York: Springer.

Biniakunu, D. D. (1980) "Learning to read Kikongo: A primer makes a difference," *Reading Teacher*, **34**, 32–36.

Birch, H. G., and Belmont, L. (1964) "Auditory-visual integration in normal and retarded readers," *American Journal of Orthopsychiatry*, **34**, 852–861.

Blakemore, C. (1973) "The language of vision," *New Scientist*, **58**, 674–677.

Blanchard, P. (1936) "Reading disabilities in relation to difficulties of personality and emotional development," *Mental Hygiene*, **20**, 384–413.

Blank, M. (1973) *Teaching Learning in the Preschool: A Dialogue Approach*. Columbus, Ohio: Merrill.

Blank, M. (1975) "Mastering the intangible through language," in Aaronson, D., and Rieber, R. W. (eds.), *Developmental Psycholinguistics and Communication Disorders, Annals of New York Academy of Sciences*, **263**, 44–58.

Blank, M. (1977) "Language, the child, and the teacher: A proposed model," in Robinson, P., and Hom, H. (eds.), *Psychological Perspectives in Early Childhood Education*. New York: Academic Press.

Blank, M. (1978), "Review of *Toward an Understanding of Dyslexia: Psychological Factors in Specific Reading Disability*," in Benton, A. L., and Pearl, D. (eds.), *Dyslexia: An Appraisal of Current Knowledge*. New York: Oxford University Press.

Blank, M., and Bridger, W. H. (1966) "Deficiencies in verbal labelling in retarded readers," *American Journal of Orthopsychiatry*, **36**, 840–847.

Blank, M., Rose, S., and Berlin, L. (1978a) *The Language of Learning: The Preschool Years*. New York: Grune and Stratton.

Blank, M., Rose, S., and Berlin, L. (1978b) *Preschool Language Assessment Instrument (PLAI): The Language of Learning in Practice*. New York: Grune and Stratton.

Blank, M., Weider, S., and Bridger, W. H. (1968) "Verbal deficiencies in abstract thinking in early reading retardation," *American Journal of Orthopsychiatry*, **38**, 823–834.

Bliss, C. K. (1965) *Semantography*. Sydney, Australia: Semantography Publications.

Blommers, P., Knief, L., and Stroud, J. B. (1955) "The organismic age concept," *Journal of Educational Psychology*, **46**, 142–150.

Bloom, R. D. (1971) "Learning to read: An operant perspective," in Davis, F. B. (ed.), *The Literature of Research in Reading with Emphasis on Models*. New Brunswick, N.J.: Rutgers, The State University.

Bloom, R. D. (1973) "Learning to read: An operant perspective," *Reading Research Quarterly*, **8**, 147–166.

Bloomfield, L. (1933) *Language*. New York: Holt.

Bloomfield, L. (1942) "Linguistics and reading," *The Elementary English Review*, **19**, 125–130 and 183–186.

Blumenthal, A. L. (1967) "Prompted recall of sentences," *Journal of Verbal Learning and Verbal Behavior*, **6**, 203–206.

Blumenthal, A. L., and Boakes, R. (1967) "Prompted recall of sentences," *Journal of Verbal Learning and Verbal Behavior*, **6**, 674–675.

Boder, E. (1971) "Developmental dyslexia: Prevailing diagnostic concepts and a new diagnostic approach," in Myklebust, H. (ed.), *Progress in Learning Disabilities, Vol. II*. New York: Grune and Stratton.

Boder, E. (1973) "Developmental dyslexia: A diagnostic approach based on three atypical reading-spelling patterns," *Developmental Medicine and Child Neurology*, **15**, 663–687.

Bogen, J. E., (1969) "The other side of the brain II: An appositional mind," *Bulletin of the Los Angeles Neurological Societies*, **34**, 135–162.

Bolinger, D. L. (1946) "Visual morphemes," *Language*, **22**, 333–340.

Bond, G. L., Clymer, T., and Hoyt, C. J. (1955) *Silent Reading Diagnostic Tests*. Chicago: Lyons and Carnahan.

Bond, G., and Dykstra, R. (1967) "The cooperative research program in first grade reading instruction," *Reading Research Quarterly*, **2**, 5–142.

Bond, G. L. and Tinker, M. A. (1967) *Reading Difficulties: Their Diagnosis and Correction*. New York: Appleton.

Bond, G. L., and Tinker, M. A. (1973) *Reading Difficulties: Their Diagnosis and Correction* (3rd. ed.). New York: Appleton.

Boraks, N., and Allen, A. R. (1977) "A program to enhance peer tutoring," *Reading Teacher*, **30**, 479–484.

Borger, R., and Seaborne, A. E. M. (1966) *The Psychology of Learning*. Harmondsworth, England: Penguin.

Bormuth, J. R. (1970) *On the Theory of Achievement Test Items.* Chicago: University of Chicago Press.

Bormuth, J. R. (1975) "Reading literacy: Its definition and assessment," in Carroll, J. B. and Chall, J. (eds.), *Toward a Literate Society.* New York: McGraw-Hill.

Bormuth, J. R., Manning, J., Carr, J., and Pearson, P. D. (1970) "Children's comprehension of between-and-within-sentence syntactic structures," *Journal of Educational Psychology,* **61,** 349–357.

Bouma, H. (1971) "Visual recognition of isolated lower-case letters," *Vision Research,* **11,** 459–474.

Bourque, M. L. (1980) "Specification and validation of reading skills hierarchies," *Reading Research Quarterly,* **15,** 237–267.

Bower, T. G. R. (1970) "Reading by eye," in Levin, H., and Williams, J. P. (eds.), *Basic Studies on Reading.* New York: Basic Books.

Bracht, G. H., and Glass, G. V. (1968) "The external validity of experiments," *American Educational Research Journal,* **5,** 437–474.

Bradley, R. C. (1969) "Do current reading practices stifle curiosity?" *Reading Teacher,* **22,** 448–452.

Bradshaw, J. L. (1974) "Peripherally presented and unreported words may bias the perceived meaning of a centrally fixed homograph," *Journal of Experimental Psychology,* **103,** 1200–1202.

Bradshaw, J. L. (1975) "Three interrelated problems in reading: A review," *Memory and Cognition,* **3,** 123–134.

Bradshaw, J. L., Gates, A., and Patterson, K. (1976) "Hemispheric differences in processing visual patterns," *Quarterly Journal of Experimental Psychology,* **28,** 667–681.

Bradshaw, J. L., and Nettleton, N. C. (1974) "Articulatory interference and the MOWN-DOWN heterophone effect," *Journal of Experimental Psychology,* **102,** 88–94.

Brain, R. (1961) "The neurology of language," *Brain,* **84,** 145–166.

Bransford, J. D., Barclay, J. R., and Franks, J. J. (1972) "Sentence memory: A constructive versus interpretive approach," *Cognitive Psychology,* **3,** 193–209.

Bransford, J. D., and Franks, J. J. (1971) "The abstraction of linguistic ideas," *Cognitive Psychology,* **2,** 331–350.

Bransford, J. D., and Johnson, M. K. (1972) "Contextual prerequisites for understanding: Some investigations of comprehension and recall," *Journal of Verbal Learning and Verbal Behavior,* **11,** 717–726.

Bransford, J. D., and Johnson, M. K. (1973) "Consideration of some problems of comprehension," in Chase, W. G. (ed.), *Visual Information Processing.* New York: Academic Press.

Bransford, J. D., and McCarrell, N. S. (1974) "A sketch of a cognitive approach to comprehension," in Weimer, W. B. and Palermo, D. S., (ed.), *Cognition and the Symbolic Processes.* Hillsdale, N.J.: Erlbaum.

Braun, C. (1969) "Interest loading and modality effects on textual response acquisition," *Reading Research Quarterly,* **4,** 428–444.

Braun, C. (1973) "Johnny reads the cues: Teacher expectation," *Reading Teacher,* **26,** 704–712.

Brenner, M. W., and Gillman, S. (1966) "Visuomotor ability in school children—a survey," *Developmental Medicine and Child Neurology,* **8,** 686–703.

Brenner, M. W., Gillman, S., Farrell, M., and Zangwill, O. L. (1967) "Visual-motor disability in school children," *British Medical Journal,* **4,** 259–262.

Brewer, W. F. (1972) "Is reading a letter-by-letter process?" in Kavanagh, J. F. and Mattingly, I. G. (eds.), *Language by Ear and by Eye.* Cambridge, Mass.: MIT Press.

Briggs, C., and Elkind, D. (1973) "Cognitive development in early readers," *Developmental Psychology,* **9,** 279–280.

Broadbent D. E., (1954) "The role of auditory localization in attention and memory span," *Journal of Experimental Psychology,* **47,** 191–196.

Broadbent, D. E. (1966) "The well ordered mind," *American Educational Research Journal,* 3, 281–295.

Broadbent, D. E. (1970) "In defence of empirical psychology," *Bulletin of the British Psychological Society,* **23,** 87–96.

Broadbent, D. E. (1975) "Cognitive psychology and education," *British Journal of Educational Psychology,* **45,** 162–176.

Broca, P. (1861) "Remarks on the seat of the faculty of articulate language, followed by an observation of aphemia," in Von Bonin, G. (ed.), *Some Papers on the Cerebral Cortex.* Springfield, Ill.: Thomas, 1960. (Originally "Sur le siège de la faculté de language articulé avec deux observations d'aphéme (perte de parole), Paris, 1861.)

Broca, P. (1888) *Memoires sur le Cervau de l'Homme.* Paris: C. Reinwald.

Brodmann, K. (1909) *Vergleichende Lokalisationslehre der Grosshirnrinde in ihren Prinzipien dargestellt auf Grund des Zellenbaues.* Leipzig, Germany: Barth.

Brooks, G. (1980) "Deaf schoolchildren, reading and sign language," *Journal of Research in Reading,* **3,** 98–105.

Brooks, L. R. (1977) "Visual pattern in fluent word identification," in Reber, A. S., and Scarborough, D. L. (eds.), *Toward a Psychology of Reading.* Hillsdale, N.J.: Erlbaum.

Brooks, L. R. (1978) "Non-analytic correspondences and pattern in word identification," in Requin, J. (ed.), *Attention and Performance, VII.* Hillsdale, N.J.: Erlbaum.

Brooks, L. R., and Miller, A. (1979) "A comparison of explicit and implicit knowledge of an alphabet," in Kolers, P. A., Wrolstad, M. E., and Bouma, H. (eds.), *Processing of Visible Language, Vol. 1.* New York: Plenum.

Brophy, J. E., and Good, T. L. (1970) "Teachers' communication of differential expectations for children's classroom performance: Some behavioral data," *Journal of Educational Psychology,* **61,** 365–374.

Broudy, H. S. (1977) "Types of knowledge and purposes of education," in Anderson, R. C., Spiro, R. J., and Montague, W. E. (eds.), *Schooling and the Acquisition of Knowledge.* Hillsdale, N.J.: Erlbaum.

Brown, A. L. (1975a) "Recognition, reconstruction, and recall of narrative sequences by preoperational children," *Child Development,* **46,** 156–166.

Brown, A. L. (1975b) "Progressive elaboration and memory for order in children," *Journal of Experimental Child Psychology,* **19,** 383–400.

Brown, A. L. (1976) "Semantic integration in children's reconstruction of narrative sequences," *Cognitive Psychology,* **8,** 247–262.

Brown, A. L. (1978) "Knowing when, where, and how to remember: A problem of metacognition," in Glaser, R. (ed.), *Advances in Instructional Psychology.* Hillsdale, N.J.: Erlbaum.

Brown, A. L., and DeLoache, J. S. (1978) "Skills, plans and self-regulation," in Siegler, R. (ed.), *Children's Thinking: What Develops?* Hillsdale, N.J.: Erlbaum.

Brown, A. L., and Murphy, M. D. (1975) "Reconstruction of arbitrary versus logical sequences by preschool children," *Journal of Experimental Child Psychology,* **20,** 307–326.

Brown, A. L., and Smiley, S. S. (1977) "Rating the importance of structural units of prose passages: A problem of metacognitive development," *Child Development,* **48,** 1–8.

Brown, A. L., Smiley, S. S., Day, J. D., Townsend, M. A. R., and Lawton, S. C. (1977) "Intrusion of a thematic idea in children's comprehension and retention of stories," *Child Development,* **48,** 1454–1466.

Brown, R. (1970) "Psychology and reading: Commentary on Chapters 5 to 10," in Levin, H., and Williams, J. P. (eds.), *Basic Studies on Reading.* New York: Basic Books.

Bruner, J. S. (1957a) "On perceptual readiness," *Psychological Review,* **64,** 123–152.

Bruner, J. S. (1957b) "Going beyond the information given," in Gruber, H. E., (ed.), *Contemporary Approaches to Cognition.* Cambridge, Mass.: Harvard University Press.

Bruner, J. S. (1963) *On Knowing: Essays for the Left Hand.* Cambridge, Mass.: Harvard University Press.

Bruner, J. S. (1968) *Toward a Theory of Instruction.* New York: W. W. Norton.

Bruner, J. S. (1970) "The growth and structure of skill," in Connolly, K. (ed.) *Mechanisms of Motor Skill Development.* London: Academic Press.

Bruner, J. S. (1971) *The Relevance of Education.* London: Allen and Unwin.

Bruner, J. S. (1975) "Language as an instrument of thought," in Davies, A. (ed.), *Problems of Language and Learning.* London: Heinemann.

Bruner, J. S. (1978) "The role of dialogue in language acquisition," in Sinclair, A., Jarvella, R. J., and Levelt, W. J. M. (eds.), *The Child's Conception of Language.* New York: Springer.

Bruner, J. S., Goodnow, J., and Austin, G. A. (1956) *A Study of Thinking.* New York: Wiley.

Bryan, W. L., and Harter, N. (1897) "Studies in the physiology and psychology of the telegraphic language," *Psychological Review,* **4,** 27–53.

Bryan, W. L., and Harter, N. (1899) "Studies on the telegraphic language: The acquisition of a hierarchy of habits," *Psychological Review,* **6,** 345–375.

Bryant, N. D., and Kass, C. E. (eds.), (1972) *Leadership Training Institute in Learning Disabilities, Final Report, U.S. Office of Education Project No. 127145.* Washington, D.C.: U.S. Office of Education.

Bryden, M. P. (1970) "Laterality effects in dichotic listening: Relations with handedness and reading ability in children," *Neuropsychologia,* **8,** 443–450.

Bryden, M. P., and Allard, F. (1976) "Visual hemifield differences depend on typeface," *Brain and Language,* **3,** 191–200.

Brzeinski, J. E. (1964) "Beginning reading in Denver," *Reading Teacher,* **18,** 16–21.

Buckingham, B. R. (1940) "Language and reading—a unified program," *Elementary English Review,* **19,** 111–116.

Bühler, K. (1933) *The Mental Development of the Child.* London: Kegan Paul. Trench, Trubner.

Bullock Report—*see* Department of Education and Science (1975).

Burmeister, L. E. (1974) *Reading Strategies for Secondary School Teachers.* Reading, Mass.: Addison–Wesley.

Burt, C. (1937) *The Backward Child.* London: University of London Press.

Burt, C. (1967a) "Capacity and achievement," *Education,* August, 198–201.

Burt, C. (1967b) "Evaluations—Two" in Downing, J. et al., *The i.t.a. Symposium.* Slough, England: National Foundation for Educational Research.

Burt, C. (1968) "Review of J. P. Guilford, *The Nature of Human Intelligence,*" *Contemporary Psychology,* **13,** 546.

Buswell, G. T. (1926) *Diagnostic Studies in Arithmetic, Supplementary Educational Monographs, No. 30.* Chicago: University of Chicago.

Buswell, G. T. (1945) *Non-Oral Reading: A Study of Its Use in the Chicago Public Schools, Supplementary Educational Monographs, No. 60.* Chicago: University of Chicago Press.

Butkowsky, I. S., and Willows, D. M. (1980) "Cognitive-motivational characteristics of children varying in reading ability: Evidence for learned helplessness in poor readers," *Journal of Educational Psychology,* **72,** 408–422.

Cadman, A. G. (1976) *Learning Difficulties in Children and Adults, Report of the House of Representatives Select Committee on Specific Learning Difficulties.* Canberra: Australian Government Publishing Service.

Calfee, R. C. (1975) "Memory and cognitive skills in reading acquisition," in Duane, D., and Rawson, M. (eds.), *Reading, Perception and Language.* Baltimore: York Press.

Calfee, R. C. (1976) "Sources of dependency in cognitive processes," in Klahr, D. (ed.), *Cognition and Instruction.* Hillsdale, N.J.: Erlbaum.

Calfee, R. C. (1977) "Assessment of independent reading skills: Basic research and practical applications," in Reber, A. S., and Scarborough, D. L. (eds.), *Toward a Psychology of Reading.* Hillsdale, N.J.: Erlbaum.

Calfee, R. C., Arnold, R., and Drum, P. (1976) "Review of Gibson and Levin's *The Psychology of Reading,*" *Proceedings of the National Academy of Education,* **3,** 22.

Calfee, R. C., Chapman, R., and Venezky, R., (1972) "How a child needs to think to learn to read," in Gregg, L. W. (ed.), *Cognition in Learning and Memory.* New York: Wiley.

Calfee, R. C., and Drum, P. A. (1978) "Learning to read: Theory, research and practice," *Curriculum Inquiry,* **8,** 183–249.

Calfee, R. C., and Venezky, R. L. (1968) "Component skills in beginning reading," in Goodman, K. S., and Fleming, J. T. (eds.), *Psycholinguistics and the Teaching of Reading.* Newark, Del.: IRA.

Cambourne, B. (1980) "What has 'psycholinguistics' to do with the teaching of reading," *Reading Education,* **5,** 18–21.

Campbell, D. T., and Stanley, J. C. (1963) *Experimental and Quasi-Experimental Designs for Research.* Chicago: Rand McNally.

Campell, N. R. (1957) *The Philosophy of Theory and Experiment.* New York: Dover.

Caramazza, A., and Grober, E., (1976) "Polysemy and the structure of the subjective lexicon," in Rameh, C., (ed.) *Semantics: Theory and Application.* Washington, D.C.: Georgetown University Press.

Carbonell de Grompone, M. (1974) "Children who spell better than they read," *Academic Therapy Quarterly,* **9,** 281–288.

Carnine, D. W. (1976) "Similar sound separation and cumulative introduction in learning letter-sound correspondences," *Journal of Educational Research,* **69,** 368–372.

Carnine, D. W. (1980) "Two letter discrimination sequences: High-confusion-alternatives first versus low-confusion alternatives first," *Journal of Reading Behavior,* **12,** 41–47.

Carpenter, P. A., and Just, M. A., (1975) "Sentence comprehension: A psycholinguistic processing model of verification," *Psychological Review,* **82,** 45–73.

Carpenter, P. A., and Just, M. A. (1977) "Integrative processes in comprehension," in LaBerge, D., and Samuels, S. J. (eds.), *Basic Processes in Reading: Perception and Comprehension.* Hillsdale, N.J.: Erlbaum.

Carrillo, L. W. (1973) "Developing flexibility of reading rate," in Clark, M., and Milne, A. (eds.), *Reading and Related Skills.* London: Ward Lock.

Carroll, J. B. (1968a) "On learning from being told," *Educational Psychologist,* **5,** 4–10.

Carroll, J. B. (1968b) "Review of Holmes and Singer, *Speed and Power of Reading in High School,*" *Research in the Teaching of English,* **2,** 172–184.

Carroll, J. B. (1972) "Defining language comprehension: Some speculations," in Freedle, R. O., and Carroll, J. B. (eds.), *Language Comprehension and the Acquisition of Knowledge.* New York: Wiley.

Carroll, J. B. (1974) "The potentials and limitations of print as a medium of instruction," in Olson, D. R. (ed.), *Media and Symbols: The Forms of Expression, Communication, and Education.* Chicago: University of Chicago Press.

Carroll, J. B. (1975) *The Teaching of French as a Foreign Language in Eight Countries.* Stockholm: Almquist and Wiksell, and New York: Wiley.

Carroll, J. B. (1977) "Developmental parameters of reading comprehension," in Guthrie, J. T. (ed.), *Cognition: Curriculum, and Comprehension.* Newark, Del.: IRA.

Carroll, J. B., and Chall, J. S. (1975) *Toward a Literate Society.* New York: McGraw-Hill.

Carroll, M. W. (1948) "Sex differences in reading readiness at first grade level," *Elementary English,* **25,** 370–375.

Carterette, E. C., and Jones, M. H. (1963) "Redundancy in children's texts," *Science,* **140,** 1309–1311.

Carver, R. P. (1972) "Reading tests in 1970 versus 1980: Psychometric versus edumetric," *Reading Teacher,* **26,** 299–302.

Carver, R. P. (1974) "Two dimensions of tests: Psychometric and edumetric," *American Psychologist,* **29,** 512–518.

Carver, R. P. (1977–1978) "Toward a theory of reading comprehension," *Reading Research Quarterly,* **13,** 8–63.

Cassirer, E. (1944) *An Essay on Man: An Introduction to the Philosophy of Human Culture.* New Haven: Yale University Press.

Cattell, J. M. (1886) "The time it takes to see and name objects," *Mind,* **11,** 63–65.

Cazden, C. B. (1970) "The neglected situation in child language research and education," in Williams, F. (ed.), *Language and Poverty.* Chicago: Markham.

Cazden, C. B. (1972) *Child Language and Education.* New York: Holt.

Cazden, C. B. (1974a) "Two paradoxes in the acquisition of language structure and function," in Bruner, J. S., and Connolly, K. J. (eds.), *The Development of Competence in Early Childhood.* New York: Academic Press.

Cazden, C. B. (1974b) "Metalinguistic awareness: One

dimension of language experience," *The Urban Review,* **7,** 28–39.

CELDIC (1970) *One Million Children, a National study of Canadian Children with Emotional and Learning Disorders.* Toronto: Leonard Crainford.

Centra, J. A., and Potter, D. A. (1980) "School and teacher effects: An interrelational model," *Review of Educational Research,* **50,** 273–291.

Chafe, W. L. (1972) "Discourse structure and human knowledge," in Freedle R. O., and Carroll, J. B. (eds.), *Language Comprehension and the Acquisition of Knowledge.* New York: Wiley.

Chall, J. (1967) *Learning to Read: The Great Debate.* New York: McGraw-Hill.

Chall, J. (1979) "The great debate: Ten years later, with a modest proposal for reading stages," in Resnick, L. B., and Weaver, P. A. (eds.), *Theory and Practice of Early Reading, Vol. 1.* Hillsdale, N.J.: Erlbaum.

Chall, J., and Feldmann, S. (1966) "First grade reading: An analysis of professed methods, teacher implementation and child background," *Reading Teacher,* **19,** 569–575.

Chall, J., and Mirsky, A. F. (eds.), (1978) *Education and the Brain.* Chicago: University of Chicago Press.

Chambers, S. M., and Forster, K. I. (1975) "Evidence for lexical access in a simultaneous matching task," *Memory and Cognition,* **3,** 549–559.

Chao, Y. R. (1968) *Language and Symbolic Systems.* London: Cambridge University Press.

Chapman, L. J., and Hoffman, M. (1977) *Developing Fluent Reading.* Milton Keynes, England: Open University Press.

Chase, R. A. (1972) "Neurological aspects of language disorders in children," in Irwin, J. V., and Marge, M. (eds.), *Principles of Childhood Language Disabilities.* New York: Appleton.

Chasen, B. (1974) "Sex-role stereotyping and prekindergarten teachers," *Elementary School Journal,* **74,** 220–235.

Chesterfield, R. (1978) "Effects of environmentally specific materials on reading in Brazilian rural primary schools," *Reading Teacher,* **32,** 312–315.

Chi, M. T. H., Ingram. A. L., and Danner, F. W. (1977) "Constructive aspects of children's reading comprehension," *Child Development,* **48,** 684–688.

Childs, B., Finucci, J. M., and Preston, M. S., (1978) "A medical genetics approach to the study of reading disability," in Benton, A. L., and Pearl, D. (eds.), *Dyslexia: An Appraisal of Current Knowledge.* New York: Oxford University Press.

Chomsky, C. (1969) *The Acquisition of Syntax in Children from Five to Ten.* Cambridge, Mass.: M.I.T. Press.

Chomsky, C. (1970) "Reading, writing, and phonology," *Harvard Educational Review,* **40,** 287–309.

Chomsky, C. (1978) "When you still can't read in third grade: After decoding, what?" in Samuels, S. J., (ed.), *What Research Has to Say about Reading Instruction.* Newark, Del.: IRA.

Chomsky, N. (1957) *Syntactic Structures.* The Hague, Netherlands: Mouton.

Chomsky, N. (1965) *Aspects of the Theory of Syntax.* The Hague, Netherlands: Mouton.

Chomsky, N. (1968) *Language and Mind.* New York: Harcourt, Brace and World.

Chomsky, N. (1970) "Phonology and reading," in Levin, H., and Williams, J. P., (eds.), *Basic Studies on Reading.* New York: Basic Books.

Chomsky, N. (1972a) *Studies on Semantics in Generative Grammar.* The Hague, Netherlands: Mouton.

Chomsky, N. (1972b) *Language and Mind* (enlarged edition). New York: Harcourt, Brace and World.

Chomsky, N. (1975) *Reflections on Language.* New York: Pantheon.

Chomsky, N. (1976) "On the biological basis of language capacities," in Rieber, R. W. (ed.), *The Neuropsychology of Language.* New York: Plenum.

Chomsky, N. (1977) *Essays on Form and Interpretation.* Amsterdam, Netherlands: North-Holland.

Chomsky, N., and Halle, M. (1968) *The Sound Pattern of English.* New York: Harper and Row.

Chou, En-lai, Wu, Yu-chang, and Li, Chin-hsi (1958) *Reform of the Chinese Written Language.* Peking, China: Foreign Language Press.

Chow, K. L. (1952) "Further studies on selective ablation of associative cortex in relation to visually mediated behavior," *Journal of Comparative and Physiological Psychology,* **45,** 109–118.

Citron, A. F. (1976) "English orthography as conspicuous consumption," *National Directory of Sociology of Education and Educational Sociology,* **1,** 16–23.

Claiborn, W. L. (1969) "Expectancy effects in the classroom: A failure to replicate," *Journal of Educational Psychology,* **60,** 377–383.

Clark, B. (1935) "The effect of binocular imbalance in the behavior of the eye during reading," *Journal of Educational Psychology,* **26,** 530–538.

Clark, B. (1936) "Additional data on binocular imbalance and reading," *Journal of Educational Psychology,* **27,** 471–475.

Clark, C. R., and Woodcock, R. W. (1976) "Graphic systems of communication," in Lloyd, L. L. (ed.), *Communication Assessment and Intervention Strategies.* Baltimore: University Park Press.

Clark, E. V. (1978) "Awareness of language: Some evidence from what children say and do," in Sinclair, A., Jarvella, R. J., and Levelt, W. J. M. (eds.), *The Child's Conception of Language.* New York: Springer.

Clark, H. H. (1973) "The language-as-fixed-effect fallacy: A critique of language statistics in psychological research," *Journal of Verbal Learning and Verbal Behavior,* **12,** 335–359.

Clark, H. H. (1977) "Inferences in comprehension," in LaBerge, D., and Samuels, S. J. (eds.), *Basic Processes in Reading: Perception and Comprehension.* Hillsdale, N.J.: Erlbaum.

Clark, H. H., and Haviland, S. E. (1974) "Psychological

processes as linguistic explanation," in Cohen, D. (ed.), *Explaining Linguistic Phenomenon.* New York: Wiley.

Clark, H. H., and Haviland, S. E. (1977) "Comprehension and the Given-New Contract," in Freedle, R. O. (ed.), *Discourse Production and Comprehension, Vol. 1. Discourse Processes: Advances in Research and Theory.* Norwood, N.J.: Ablex.

Clark, M. M. (1970) *Reading Difficulties in Schools.* Harmondsworth, England: Penguin.

Clark, M. M. (1976) *Young Fluent Readers.* London: Heinemann.

Clay, M. M. (1969) "Reading errors and self-correction behavior," *British Journal of Educational Psychology,* **39,** 47–56.

Clay, M. M. (1972) *Reading: The Patterning of Complex Behaviour.* Auckland, New Zealand: Heinemann.

Clay, M. M. (1974) "Research in brief: Orientation to the spatial characteristics of the open book," *Visible Language,* **8,** 275–282.

Clay, M. M. (1976) "Early childhood and cultural diversity in New Zealand," *Reading Teacher,* **29,** 333–342.

Clements, P. (1979) "The effects of staging on recall from prose," in Freedle, R. O. (ed.), *New Directions in Discourse Processing.* Norwood; N.J.: Ablex.

Clements, S. D. (1966) *Minimal Brain Dysfunction in Children* (NINDB Monograph No. 3). Washington, D.C.: U.S. Dept. of Health, Education, and Welfare.

Cobb, J. A., and Hops, H. (1973) "Effects of academic survival skill training on low achieving first graders," *Journal of Educational Research,* **67,** 108–113.

Cogan, D. G., and Wurster, J. B. (1970) "Normal and abnormal ocular movements," in Young, F. A., and Lindsley, D. B. (eds.), *Early Experience and Visual Information Processing in Perceptual and Reading Disorders.* Washington, D.C.: National Academy of Sciences.

Cohen, G. (1973) "Hemispheric differences in serial versus parallel processing," *Journal of Experimental Psychology,* **97,** 349–356.

Cohn, M. (1979) *Helping Your Teen-age Student: What Parents Can Do to Improve Reading and Study Skills.* New York: E. P. Dutton.

Cole, M. (ed.), (1977) *Soviet Developmental Psychology.* New York: M. E. Sharpe.

Cole, M. F., and Cole, M. (1971) *Pierre Marie's Papers on Speech Disorders.* New York: Hafner.

Collinge, J. (1976) "Teachers and teaching methods," *Elementary School Journal,* **76,** 259–265.

Collins, A. M. and Quillian, M. R. (1972) "Experiments on semantic memory and language comprehension," in Gregg, L. W. (ed.), *Cognition in Learning and Memory.* New York: Wiley.

Coltheart, M. (1979) "When can children learn to read—And when should they be taught?" in Waller, T. G., and Mackinnon, G. E. (eds.), *Reading Research: Advances in Theory and Practice, Volume 1.* New York: Academic Press.

Coltheart, M., Davelaar, E., Jonasson, J. T., and Besner, D. (1977) "Access to the internal lexicon," in Dornič, S. (ed.), *Attention and Performance VI.* Hillsdale, N.J.: Erlbaum.

Conners, C. K., Kramer, K., and Guerra, F. (1969) "Auditory synthesis and dichotic listening in children with learning disabilities," *Journal of Special Education,* **3,** 163–170.

Conrad, R. (1962) "An association between masking errors and errors due to acoustic masking of speech," *Nature,* **193,** 1314–1315.

Conrad, R. (1964) "Acoustic confusion in immediate memory," *British Journal of Psychology,* **55,** 75–84.

Conrad, R. (1972) "Speech and reading," in Kavanagh, J. F., and Mattingly, I. G. (eds.), *Language by Ear and by Eye.* Cambridge, Mass.: M.I.T. Press.

Conrad, R. (1977) "The reading ability of deaf school-leavers," *British Journal of Educational Psychology,* **47,** 138–148.

Cooper, R. M. (1974) "The control of eye fixation on the meaning of spoken language," *Cognitive Psychology,* **6,** 84–107.

Corballis, M. C., and Beale, I. L. (1971) "On telling left from right," *Scientific American,* **224,** 96–104.

Corballis, M. C. and Beale, I. L. (1976) *The Psychology of Left and Right.* Hillsdale, N.J.: Erlbaum.

Corcoran, D. W. J. (1966) "An acoustic factor in letter cancellation," *Nature,* **210,** 658.

Corcoran, D. W. J. (1967) "Acoustic factor in proof reading," *Nature,* **214,** 851–852.

Corcoran, D. W. J. (1977) Personal communication to J. Downing, March 16, 1977.

Coren, S., Porac, C. and Ward, L. M. (1979) *Sensation and Perception.* New York: Academic Press.

Cosky, M. J. (1976) "The role of letter recognition in word recognition," *Memory and Cognition,* **4,** 207–214.

Cowen, E. L., Underburg, R., Verrillo, R. T., and Benham, F. G. (1961) *Adjustment to Visual Disability in Adolescence.* New York: American Foundation for the Blind.

Craik, F. I. M., and Lockhart, R. S. (1972) "Levels of processing: A framework for memory research," *Journal of Verbal Learning and Verbal Behavior,* **11,** 671–684.

Craik, F. I. M., and Tulving, E. (1975) "Depth of processing and the retention of words in episodic memory," *Journal of Experimental Psychology: General,* **104,** 268–294.

Crane, A. R. (1959) "An historical and critical account of the accomplishment quotient," *British Journal of Educational Psychology,* **29,** 252–259.

Crano, W. D., Kenny, D. A., and Campbell, D. T. (1972) "Does intelligence cause achievement? A cross-lagged panel analysis," *Journal of Educational Psychology,* **63,** 258–275.

Criscuolo, N. P. (1980) "Effective ways to communicate with parents about reading," *Reading Teacher,* **34,** 164–166.

Critchley, M. (1964) *Developmental Dyslexia.* London: Heinemann.

Critchley, M. (1968) "Topics worthy of research," in Keeney, A. H., and Keeney, V. T. (eds.), *Dyslexia: Diagnosis and Treatment of Reading Disorder.* St. Louis: C. V. Mosby.

Critchley, M. (1970) *The Dyslexic Child.* London: Heinemann.

Crofts, M. (1971) "Creating a Mundurukú orthography," *Visible Language,* **5,** 49–58.

Cromer, W. (1970) "The difference model: A new explanation for some reading difficulties," *Journal of Educational Psychology,* **61,** 471–483.

Cromer, W., and Wiener, M. (1966) "Idiosyncratic response patterns among good and poor readers," *Journal of Consulting Psychology,* **30,** 1–10.

Cronbach, L. J. (1963) *Educational Psychology* (2nd ed.). New York: Harcourt Brace Jovanovich.

Cronbach, L. J. (1977) *Educational Psychology* (3rd ed.). New York: Harcourt Brace Jovanovich.

Crookes, T. G., and Greene, M. C. L. (1963) "Some characteristics of children with two types of speech disorder," *British Journal of Educational Psychology,* **33,** 31–40.

Crosby, R. M. N. (1969) *Reading and the Dyslexic Child.* London: Souvenir Press.

Cruickshank, W. M. (1978) "When winter comes, can spring. . . ?" *The Exceptional Child,* **25,** 3–25.

Cruickshank, W. M., Bice, H. V., and Wallin, N. E. (1957) *Perception in Cerebral Palsy.* Syracuse, N.Y.: Syracuse University Press.

Curry, R. L. (1967) "Adult literacy—progress and problems," in Schick, G. B., and May, M. M. (eds.), *Junior College and Adult Reading Programs—Expanding Fields.* Milwaukee, Wisc: National Reading Conference.

Curtis, M. E. (1980) "Development of components of reading skill," *Journal of Educational Psychology,* **72,** 656–669.

Das, J. P., Kirby, J. and Jarman, R. F. (1975) "Simultaneous and successive syntheses: An alternative model for cognitive abilities," *Psychological Bulletin,* **82,** 87–103.

Das, J. P., Kirby, J., and Jarman, R. F. (1979) *Simultaneous and Successive Cognitive Processes.* New York: Academic Press.

Das, J. P., Leong, C. K., and Williams, N. (1978) "The relationship between learning disability and simultaneous successive processing," *Journal of Learning Disabilities,* **11,** 618–625.

Davelaar, E., Coltheart, M., Besner, D., and Jonasson, J. T. (1978) "Phonological recoding and lexical access," *Memory and Cognition,* **6,** 391–402.

Davie, R., Butler, N., and Goldstein, H. (1972) *From Birth to Seven: A Report of the National Child Development Study.* London: Longmans.

Davies, A. (ed.), (1977) *Language and Learning in Early Childhood.* London: Heinemann.

Davis, D. F. (1977) "Language and social class: Conflict with established theory," *Research in the Teaching of English,* **11,** 207–217.

Davis, D. R. and Kent, N. (1955) "Intellectual development in schoolchildren, with special reference to family background," *Proceedings of the Royal Society of Medicine,* **48,** 993–995.

Davis, E. A. (1937) *The Development of Learning Skill in Twins, Singletons with Siblings, and Only Children from Age Five to Ten Years* (Institute of Child Welfare Monograph Series, No. 14). Minneapolis, Minn.: University of Minnesota Press.

Davis, F. B. (1968) "Psychometric research on comprehension in reading," *Reading Research Quarterly,* **7,** 628–678.

Davis, F. B. (1971) *The Literature of Research in Reading with Emphasis on Models.* New Brunswick, N.J.: Graduate School of Education, Rutgers, The State University.

Davis, R., and Schmit, V. (1973) "Visual and verbal coding in the interhemispheric transfer of information," *Acta Psychologica,* **37,** 229–240.

Day, H. I., Berlyne, D. E., and Hunt, D. E. (1971) *Intrinsic Motivation: A New Direction in Education.* Minneapolis, Minn.: Winston Press.

Dayton, C. M., and Macready, G. B. (1976) "A probabilistic model for validation of behavioral hierarchies," *Psychometrika,* **41,** 189–204.

De Cecco, J. P., and Crawford, W. R. (1974) *The Psychology of Learning and Instruction.* Englewood Cliffs, N.J.: Prentice Hall.

de Hirsch, K., Jansky, J. J., and Langford, W. S. (1964) "The oral language performance of premature children and controls," *Journal of Speech and Hearing Disorders,* **29,** 60–69.

de Hirsch, K., Jansky, J. J., and Langford, W. S. (1966) *Predicting Reading Failure.* New York: Harper and Row.

Dean, C. D. (1939) "Predicting first grade reading achievement," *Elementary School Journal,* **33,** 609–616.

Dearborn, W. F., (1931), "Ocular and manual dominance in dyslexia," *Psychological Bulletin,* **28,** 704.

Dearborn, W. F. (1933) "Structural factors which condition special disability in reading," *Proceedings of the American Association on Mental Deficiency,* **38,** 266–283.

Dearborn, W. F., and Anderson, I. H. (1938) "Aniseikonia as related to reading disability," *Journal of Experimental Psychology,* **23,** 559–577.

Dearborn, W. F., and Rothney, J. W. M. (1941) *Predicting the Child's Development.* Cambridge, Mass.: Science/Art Publications.

Dechant, E. V., and Smith, H. P. (1977) *Psychology in Teaching Reading* (2nd ed.). Englewood Cliffs, N.J.: Prentice-Hall.

Deese, J. (1958) *The Psychology of Learning.* New York: McGraw-Hill.

Denburg, S. D. (1976–1977) "The interaction of picture

and print in reading instruction," *Reading Research Quarterly,* **12,** 176–189.

Denckla, M. B. (1978) "Minimal brain dysfunction," in Chall, J., and Mirsky, A. F. (eds.), *Education and the Brain.* Chicago: University of Chicago Press.

Denckla, M. B., and Rudel, R. (1976a) "Naming of object drawings by dyslexic and other learning disabled children," *Brain and Language,* **3,** 1–15.

Denckla, M. B., and Rudel R. (1976b) "Rapid automatized naming (RAN): Dyslexia differentiated from other learning disabilities," *Neuropsychologia,* **14,** 471–479.

Dennis, M., and Kohn, B. (1975) "Comprehension of syntax in infantile hemiplegics after cerebral hemidecortication: Left-hemisphere superiority," *Brain and Language,* **2,** 472–482.

Dennis, M., and Whitaker, H. A. (1977) "Hemispheric equipotentiality and language acquisition," in Segalowitz, S. J., and Gruber, F. A., (eds.), *Language Development and Neurological Theory.* New York: Academic Press.

Department of Education and Science (1967) *Children and Their Primary Schools* (the "Plowden Report"). London: Her Majesty's Stationery Office.

Department of Education and Science (1972) *Children with Specific Reading Difficulties* (The Tizard Committee Report). London: Her Majesty's Stationery Office.

Department of Education and Science (1975) *A Language for Life* (the "Bullock Report"). London: Her Majesty's Stationery Office.

DeSoto, C. B. (1961) "The predilection for single orderings," *Journal of Abnormal and Social Psychology,* **62,** 16–23.

Despert, J. L. (1946) "Psychosomatic study of fifty stuttering children. Round table I. Social, physical, and psychiatric findings," *American Journal of Orthopsychiatry,* **16,** 100—113.

DeStefano, J. S. (1972) *Some Parameters of Register in Adult and Child Speech.* Louvain, Belgium: Institute of Applied Linguistics.

DeStefano, J. S. (1980) "Enhancing children's growing ability to communicate," *Language Arts,* **57,** 807–813.

Deutsch, M. (1960) *Minority Group and Class Status as Related to Social and Personality Factors in Scholastic Achievement,* Monograph No. 2, Society for Applied Anthropology.

Deutsch, M. (1965) "The role of social class in language development and cognition," *American Journal of Orthopsychiatry,* **35,** 78–88.

Diener, C. I., and Dweck, C. S. (1978) "An analysis of learned helplessness: Continuous changes in performance, strategy, and achievement cognitions following failure," *Journal of Personality and Social Psychology,* **36,** 451–462.

Dimond, S. J., (1978) *Introducing Neuropsychology: The Study of Brain and Mind.* Springfield, Ill: Thomas.

Diringer, D. (1948) *The Alphabet: A Key to the History of Mankind.* London and New York: Hutchinson.

Ditchburn, R. W., Fender, D. H., and Mayne, S. (1959) "Vision with controlled movements of the retinal image," *Journal of Physiology,* **145,** 98–107.

Documentation Centre for Education in Europe (1980) "Sweden: Home/school relations," *Council of Europe Newsletter,* No. 3, 33–34.

Dodge, R. (1907) "An experimental study of visual fixation," *Psychological Review Monograph Supplements,* **8,** 1–95.

Doehring, D. G. (1968) *Patterns of Impairment in Specific Reading Disability.* Bloomington, Indiana: Indiana University Press.

Doehring, D. G. (1976) "Acquisition of rapid reading responses," *Monographs of the Society for Research in Child Development,* **41,** 2, Serial No. 165.

Doehring, D. G. (1978) "The tangled web of behavioral research on developmental dyslexia," in Benton, A. L., and Pearl, D. (eds.), *Dyslexia: An Appraisal of Current Knowledge.* New York: Oxford University Press.

Doehring, D. G. and Aulls, M. W. (1979) "The interactive nature of reading acquisition," *Journal of Reading Behavior,* **11,** 28–40.

Doehring, D. G., and Hoshko, I. M. (1977) "Classification of reading problems by the Q-technique of factor analysis," *Cortex,* **13,** 281–294.

Dolch, E. W. (1956) "School research in reading," *Elementary English,* **33,** 76–80.

Dolch, E. W., and Bloomster, M. (1937) "Phonic readiness," *Elementary School Journal,* **38,** 201–205.

Doman, G. J. (1965) *Teach Your Baby to Read.* London: Cape.

Donaldson, M. (1978) *Children's Minds.* Glasgow: Fontana/Collins.

Dopstadt, N., Laubscher, F., and Ruperez, R. (1980) *La Représentation de la Phrase Ecrite Chez l'enfant de 6 a 8 Ans.* Masters thesis, Psychology Department, L'Université Toulouse-le-Mirail, France.

Dottrens, R., and Margairaz, E. (1951) *L'Apprentisage de la Lecture par la Méthode Globale.* Paris: Delachaux et Niestle.

Douglas, J. W. B. (1964) *The Home and the School.* London: MacGibbon and Kee.

Douglas, J. W. B., Ross, J. M., and Simpson, H. R. (1968) *All Our Future.* London: Davies.

Downing, J. (1960) "A study of brand images: An experimental approach to attitude measurement," in Market Research Society (eds.), *Attitude Scaling.* London: Market Research Society.

Downing, J. (1963) "Is a 'mental age of six' essential for 'reading' readiness?" *Educational Research,* **6,** 16–28.

Downing, J. (1965) *The Initial Teaching Alphabet Explained and Illustrated.* London: Cassell, and New York: Macmillan.

Downing, J. (1967) *Evaluating the Initial Teaching Alphabet: A Study of the Influence of English Orthog-*

raphy on Learning to Read and Write. London: Cassell.

Downing, J. (1970) "Children's concepts of language in learning to read," *Educational Research,* **12,** 106–112.

Downing, J. (1971–1972) "Children's developing concepts of spoken and written language," *Journal of Reading Behavior,* **4,** 1–19.

Downing, J. (1973) *Comparative Reading.* New York: Macmillan.

Downing, J. (1974) "Bilingualism and learning to read," *Irish Journal of Education,* **8,** 77–88.

Downing, J. (1975a) "The child's concepts of language," in Latham, W. (ed.), *The Road to Effective Reading.* London: Ward Lock.

Downing, J. (1975b) "Language arts in open schools," *Elementary English,* **52,** 23–29.

Downing, J. (1976) *Learning to Read with Understanding.* Wynberg, South Africa: Juta.

Downing, J. (1977a) "The probability of reading failure in i.t.a. and t.o.," *Reading,* **11,** 3–12.

Downing, J. (1977b) "Review: The use of the initial teaching alphabet with emotionally disturbed and socially maladjusted children," *Child: Care, Health and Development,* **3,** 363–372.

Downing, J. (1978) "Strategies of bilingual teaching," *International Review of Education,* **24,** 329–346.

Downing, J. (1979a) *Reading and Reasoning.* Edinburgh: Chambers, and New York: Springer.

Downing, J. (1979b) "Cognitive Clarity and Linguistic Awareness." Paper presented at the Seminar on Linguistic Awareness and Learning to Read, University of Victoria, Canada, June 26–30, 1979.

Downing, J. (1980a) "The reading riddle," *Phi Delta Kappan,* **61,** 592–593.

Downing, J. (1980b) "A reading puzzle," *Reading,* **14,** 17 and 36.

Downing, J. (1981) "Research revisited: Jack Holmes' substrata-factor theory of reading," *Reading Psychology,* **2,** 108–116.

Downing, J., Ayers, D., and Schaefer, B. (1978) "Conceptual and perceptual factors in learning to read," *Educational Research,* **21,** 11–17.

Downing, J., Ayers, D., and Schaefer, B. (1982) *Linguistic Awareness in Reading Readiness (LARR) Test.* Windsor, England: National Foundation for Educational Research-Nelson.

Downing, J., and Dalrymple-Alford, E. C. (1974–1975) "A methodological critique of the 1973 IEA survey of reading comprehension education in fifteen countries," *Reading Research Quarterly,* **10,** 212–227.

Downing, J., Dwyer, C. A., Feitelson, D., Jansen, M., Kemppainen, R., Matihaldi, H., Reggi, D. R., Sakamoto, T., Taylor, H., Thackray, D. V. and Thomson, D. (1979) "A cross-national survey of cultural expectations and sex-role standards in reading," *Journal of Research in Reading,* **2,** 8–23.

Downing, J., and Jones, B. (1966) "Some problems of evaluating i.t.a.: A second experiment," *Educational Research,* **8,** 100–114.

Downing, J., and Oliver, P. (1973–1974) "The child's concept of 'a word,' " *Reading Research Quarterly,* **9,** 568–582.

Downing, J., Ollila, L., and Oliver, P. (1975) "Cultural differences in children's concepts of reading and writing," *British Journal of Educational Psychology,* **45,** 312–316.

Downing, J., Ollila, L., and Oliver, P. (1977) "Concepts of language in children from differing socio-economic backgrounds," *Journal of Educational Research,* **70,** 277–281.

Downing, J., and Thackray, D. (1975) *Reading Readiness.* London: Hodder and Stoughton.

Downing, J., and Thomson, D. (1977) "Sex role stereotypes in learning to read," *Research in the Teaching of English,* **11,** 149–155.

Downing, J., and Timko, H. (1979) Personal communication to C. K. Leong regarding some current experiments on Corcoran's hypothesis.

Downing, J., and Timko, H. (1981) "Acoustic scanning in reading," unpublished paper, University of Victoria.

Downs, R. M., and Stea D. (ed.), (1973) *Image and Environment: Cognitive Mapping and Spatial Behavior.* Chicago: Aldine.

Downs, R. M., and Stea, D. (1977) *Maps in Minds: Reflections on Cognitive Mapping.* New York: Harper and Row.

Dreikurs, R. (1952) "Emotional predispositions to reading difficulties," in Causey, O. S. (ed.), *The Reading Teacher's Reader.* New York: Ronald Press.

Drever, J. (1964) *A Dictionary of Psychology.* Harmondsworth, England: Penguin.

Duncan, C. P. (1951) "The effect of unequal amounts of practice on motor learning before and after practice," *Journal of Experimental Psychology,* **42,** 257–264.

Dunn, L. (1965) *Peabody Picture Vocabulary Test.* Circle Pines, Minn: American Guidance Service.

Dunn-Rankin, P. (1968) "The similarity of lower-case letters of the English alphabet," *Journal of Verbal Learning and Verbal Behavior,* **7,** 990–995.

Dunn-Rankin, P. (1978) "The visual characteristics of words," *Scientific American,* **238,** 122–130.

Durkin, D. (1966) *Children Who Read Early: Two Longitudinal Studies.* New York: Teachers College, Columbia University.

Durkin, D. (1974–1975) "A six year study of children who learned to read in school at the age of four," *Reading Research Quarterly,* **10,** 9–61.

Durrell, D. D. (1940) *Improvement of Basic Reading Abilities.* Yonkers, N.Y.: World Book.

Durrell, D. D., and Brassard, M. B. (1969) *Durrell Listening Reading Series.* New York: Harcourt, Brace and World.

Dwyer, C. A. (1973) "Sex differences in reading," *Review of Educational Research,* **43,** 455–466.

Dwyer, C. A. (1974) "Influences of children's sex role standards on reading and arithmetic achievement," *Journal of Educational Psychology,* **66,** 811–816.

Dykman, R. A., Ackerman, P. T., Clements, S. D., and Peters, J. E. (1971) "Specific learning disabilities: An attentional deficit syndrome," in Myklebust, H. R. (ed.), *Progress in Learning Disabilities, Vol II.* New York: Grune and Stratton.

Dykstra, R. (1966) "Auditory discrimination abilities and beginning reading achievement," *Reading Research Quarterly,* **1,** 5–34.

Dykstra, R. (1968) "Classroom implications of the first grade studies," in Ketcham, C. A. (ed.), *Professional Focus on Reading.* Hattiesburg, Mississippi: College Reading Association.

Dykstra, R., and Tinney, R. (1969) "Sex differences in reading readiness—first-grade achievement and second-grade achievement," in Figurel J. A. (ed.), *Reading and Realism.* Newark, Del: IRA.

Eames, T. H. (1932) "A comparison of the ocular characteristics of unselected and reading disability groups," *Journal of Educational Research,* **25,** 211–215.

Eames, T. H. (1935) "A frequency study of physical handicaps in reading disability and unselected groups," *Journal of Educational Research,* **29,** 1–5.

Eames, T. H. (1948) "Comparison of eye conditions among, 1,000 reading failures, 500 ophthalmic patients and 150 unselected children," *American Journal of Ophthalmology,* **31,** 713–717.

Earp, N. W. (1974) "Challenge to schools: Reading is overemphasized!" *Reading Teacher,* **27,** 562–565.

Ebel, C. W. (1980) "An update: Teaching reading to students of English as a second language," *Reading Teacher,* **33,** 403–407.

Eberl, M. (1953) "Visual training and reading," *Clinical Studies in Reading, II, Supplementary Educational Monographs,* **77,** 141–148.

Eccles, J. C., Ito, M., and Szentágothai, J. (1967) *The Cerebellum as a Neuronal Machine.* New York: Springer.

Edfeldt, A. W. (1960) *Silent Speech and Silent Reading.* Chicago: Chicago University Press.

Edson, W. H., Bond, G. L., and Cook, W. W. (1953) "Relationships between visual characteristics and specific silent reading abilities," *Journal of Educational Research,* **46,** 451–457.

Efron, R. (1963) "Temporal perception, aphasia, and déjà vu," *Brain,* **86,** 403–424.

Efron, R. (1967) "Discussion of paper by Ira J. Hirsh," in Darley, F. L. (ed.), *Brain Mechanisms Underlying Speech and Language.* New York: Grune and Stratton.

Egorov, T. G. (1950) *Essays on the Psychology of Teaching Children Literacy* (in Russian). Moscow: Academy of Education Sciences, R.S.F.S.R.

Egorov, T. G. (1953) *The Psychology of Mastering the Skill of Reading* (in Russian). Moscow: Academy of Education Sciences, R.S.F.S.R.

Ehri, L. C. (1975) "Word consciousness in readers and prereaders," *Journal of Educational Psychology,* **67,** 204–212.

Ehri, L. C. (1976) "Do words really interfere in naming pictures?" *Child Development,* **47,** 502–505.

Ehri, L. C. (1977) "Do adjectives and functors interfere as much as nouns in naming pictures?" *Child Development,* **48,** 697–701.

Eisenberg, L. (1962) "Introduction," in Money, J. (ed.), *Reading Disability: Progress and Research Needs in Dyslexia.* Baltimore: Johns Hopkins Press.

Eisenberg, L. (1966a) "The epidemiology of reading retardation and a program for preventive intervention," in Money, J. (ed.), *The Disabled Reader.* Baltimore: Johns Hopkins Press.

Eisenberg, L. (1966b) "Reading retardation: I. Psychiatric and sociologic aspects," *Pediatrics,* **37,** 352–365.

Eisenberg, L. (1978) "Definitions of dyslexia: Their consequences for research and policy," in Benton, A. L., and Pearl, D. (eds.), *Dyslexia: An Appraisal of Current Knowledge.* New York: Oxford University Press.

Eisenson, J. (1968) "Developmental aphasia: A speculative view with therapeutic implications," *Journal of Speech and Hearing Disorders,* **33,** 3–13.

Eisenson, J. (1972) *Aphasia in Children.* London: Harper and Row.

Ekwall, E. E. (1973) "Motivation and reading—further comments and research," in Ekwall, E. E. (ed.), *Psychological Factors in the Teaching of Reading.* Columbus, Ohio: Merrill.

El Koussy, A. A. H. (1935) "The visual perception of space," *British Journal of Psychology Monograph Supplement,* No. 20.

Elashoff, J. D., and Snow, R. E. (1971) *Pygmalion Reconsidered.* Belmont, Calif.: Wadsworth.

Elkind, D. (1976) *Child Development and Education: A Piagetian Perspective.* New York: Oxford University Press.

Elkonin, D. B. (1963) "The psychology of mastering the elements of reading," in Simon, B., and Simon, J. (eds.), *Educational Psychology in the U.S.S.R.* London: Routledge and Kegan Paul.

Elkonin, D. B. (1971) "Development of speech," in Zaporozhets, A. V., and Elkonin, D. B. (eds.), *The Psychology of Preschool Children.* Cambridge, Mass.: M.I.T. Press.

Elkonin, D. B. (1973a) "U.S.S.R.," in Downing, J. (ed.), *Comparative Reading.* New York: Macmillan.

Elkonin, D. B. (1973b) "Further remarks on the psychological bases of the initial teaching of reading" (in Russian), *Sovetskaia Pedagogika,* pp. 14–23.

Elliott, J., and Connolly, K. (1974) "Hierarchical structure in skill development," in Connolly, K. and Bruner, J. S. (eds.), *The Growth of Competence.* London: Academic Press.

Ellis, A. W. and Marshall, J. C. (1978) "Semantic errors or statistical flukes? A note on Allport's 'On knowing the meaning of words we are unable to report',"

Quarterly Journal of Experimental Psychology, **30,** 569–575.

Ellis, R. (1980) "Learning to read through a second language," *Reading,* **14,** 10–16.

Emery, R. M. (1975), *The Religious Concepts of Pre-School Children in a Christian Community,* unpublished M.A. thesis, University of Victoria, Canada.

Erickson, D., Mattingly, I. G., and Turvey, M. T. (1972) "Phonetic activity in reading: An experiment with Kanji," *Haskins Laboratories Status Report on Speech Research,* SR–33, 137–156.

Estes, T. H., Roettger, D., Johnstone, J., and Richards, H. (1976) *Estes Attitude Scales: Elementary Form.* Charlottesville, Va.: Virginia Research Associates.

Estes, W. K. (1970) *Learning Theory and Mental Development.* New York: Academic Press.

Estes, W. K. (1972) "An associative basis for coding and organization in memory," in Melton, A. W., and Martin, E. (eds.), *Coding Processes in Human Memory.* New York: Wiley.

Estes, W. K. (1975) "Memory, perception, and decision in letter identification," in Solso, R. L. (ed.), *Information Processing and Cognition: The Loyola-Symposium.* Hillsdale, N.J.: Erlbaum.

Evanechko, P., Ollila, L., Downing, J., and Braun, C. (1973) "An investigation of the reading readiness domain," *Research in the Teaching of English,* **7,** 61–78.

Ewing, J. M. (1978) "The place of attitudes in the reading curriculum," in Hunter-Grundin, E., and Grundin, H. U. (eds.), *Reading: Implementing the Bullock Report.* London: Ward Lock.

Fabian, A. A. (1955) "Reading disability: An index of pathology," *American Journal of Orthopsychiatry,* **25,** 319–329.

Fairbanks, G. and Guttman, N. (1958) "Effects of delayed auditory feedback upon articulation," *Journal of Speech and Hearing Research,* **1,** 1–11.

Farley, F. H., and Eischens, R. R. (1971) *Children's Processing of Prose: The Effects of Question Arousal, Text Complexity, and Learner Strata on Short-, Long-Term Retention* (Technical Report No. 201). Madison, Wisc.: Wisconsin Research and Development Center for Cognitive Learning.

Farnham-Diggory, S. (1967) "Symbol and synthesis in experimental reading," *Child Development,* **38,** 221–231.

Farnham-Diggory, S. (ed.), (1972) *Information Processing in Children.* New York: Academic Press.

Farnham-Diggory, S. (1978a) "How to study reading: Some information processing ways," in Murray, F. B., and Pikulski, J. J. (eds.), *The Acquisition of Reading: Cognitive, Linguistic, and Perceptual Prerequisites.* Baltimore: University Park Press.

Farnham-Diggory, S. (1978b) "Precursors of reading: Pattern drawing and picture comprehension," in Lesgold, A. M., Pellegrino, J. W., Fokkema, S. D., and Glaser, R. (eds.), *Cognitive Psychology and Instruction.* New York: Plenum.

Farnham-Diggory, S. and Gregg, L. W. (1975) "Short-term memory function in young readers," *Journal of Experimental Child Psychology,* **19,** 279–298.

Farr, R. (1979) *The Teaching and Learning of Basic Academic Skills in Schools.* New York: Harcourt Brace Jovanovich.

Farrell, G. (1958) "Snellen and the E chart," *Sight Saving Review,* **28,** 96–99.

Farris, L. P. (1936) "Visual defects as factors influencing achievement in reading," *Journal of Experimental Education,* **5,** 58–60.

Faunce, R. W. (1971) *Evaluation of a Reading Program for Severely Retarded Readers.* Minneapolis, Minn.: Minneapolis Public Schools.

Faure, E., Herrera, F., Kaddoura, A. R., Lopes, H., Petrovsky, A. V., Rahnema, M., and Ward, F. C. (1973) *Learning to Be: The World of Education Today and Tomorrow.* Paris: UNESCO.

Federal Register, 42, (250), December, 29, 1977, pp. 65082–65085.

Feitelson, D. (1952–1953) "Causes of scholastic failure among first graders," (in Hebrew), *Megamat (Behavioral Sciences Quarterly),* **4,** 1–84.

Feldman, C. F. (1977) "Two functions of language," *Harvard Educational Review,* **47,** 282–293.

Felzen, E., and Anisfeld, M. (1970) "Semantic and phonetic relations in false recognition of words by third- and sixth-grade children," *Developmental Psychology,* **3,** 163–168.

Fendrick, P. (1935) *Visual Characteristics of Poor Readers* (Contributions to Education No. 656). New York: Teachers College, Columbia University.

Fennel, E. B., Bowers, D., and Satz, P. (1977) "Within-modal and cross-modal reliabilities of two laterality tests," *Brain and Language,* **4,** 63–69.

Fernald, G. M. (1943) *Remedial Techniques in Basic School Subjects.* New York: McGraw-Hill.

Ferreiro, E. (1978) "What is written in a written sentence? A developmental answer," *Journal of Education,* **160,** 25–39.

Feshback, S., Adelman, H., and Fuller W. (1977) "Prediction of reading and related academic problems," *Journal of Educational Psychology,* **69,** 299–308.

Fillmore, C. J. (1968) "The case for case," in Bach, E. and Harms, R. T. (eds.), *Universals in Linguistic Theory.* New York: Holt.

Fillmore, C. J. (1971a) "Types of lexical information," in Steinberg, D. D. and Jakobovitz, L. A. (eds.), *Semantics: An Interdisciplinary Reader in Philosophy, Linguistics, and Psychology.* London: Cambridge University Press.

Fillmore, C. J. (1971b) "Some problems for grammar," in O'Brien, R. J. (ed.), *Report of the Twenty-Second Round Table Meeting of Linguistics and Language Studies.* Washington, D.C.: Georgetown University Press.

Filp, J. (1975) "Relationship among reading subskills: A hierarchical hypothesis," *Journal of Reading Behavior,* **7,** 229–240.

Finucci, J. M., Guthrie, J. J., Childs, A. L., Abbey, H., and Childs, B. (1976) "The genetics of specific reading disability," *Annals of Human Genetics*, **40**, 1–23.

Fior, R. (1972) "Physiological maturation of auditory function between 3 and 13 years of age," *Audiology*, **11**, 317–321.

Firth, J. R. (1958) *Papers in Linguistics, 1934–1951.* London: Oxford University Press.

Fischer, K. M. (1980) "Metalinguistic skills and the competence-performance distinction," in Waterhouse, L. H., Fischer, K. M., and Ryan, E. B. (eds.), *Language Awareness and Reading.* Newark, Del.: IRA.

Fisher, J. (1905) "Case of congenital word-blindness (inability to learn to read)," *Ophthalmic Review*, **24**, 315–318.

Fitts, P. (1951) "Engineering psychology and equipment design," in Stevens, S. S. (ed.), *Handbook of Experimental Psychology.* New York: Wiley.

Fitts, P. (1962) "Factors in complex skill training," in Glaser, R. (ed.), *Training Research and Education.* Pittsburg, Pa.: University of Pittsburgh Press.

Fitts, P. M., and Posner, M. I. (1967) *Human Performance.* Belmont, Calif.: Brooks-Cole.

Flanders, N. (1967) "Teacher influence in the classroom," in Amidon, E. J., and Hough, J. (eds.), *Interaction Analysis: Theory, Research, and Application.* Reading, Mass.: Addison-Wesley.

Flavell, J. H. (1970) "Developmental studies of mediated memory," in Reese, H. W., and Lipsitt, L. P. (eds.), *Advances in Child Development and Behavior, Vol. 5.* New York: Academic Press.

Flavell, J. H. (1976) "Metacognitive aspects of problem solving," in Resnick, L. B. (ed.), *The Nature of Intelligence.* New York: Wiley.

Flavell, J. H. and Wellman, H. M. (1977) "Metamemory," in Kail, R. V., Jr. and Hagen, J. W. (eds.), *Perspectives on the Development of Memory and Cognition.* Hillsdale, N.J.: Erlbaum.

Fleming, C. M. (1943) "Socio-economic level and test performance," *British Journal of Educational Psychology*, **13**, 74–82.

Fleming, E. S., and Antonnen, R. G. (1970) "Teacher Expectancy or My Fair Lady," paper presented at the annual meeting of AERA, Minneapolis, Minnesota, March 1970.

Flexman, R. E., Matheny, W. G., and Brown, E. L. (1950) "Evaluation of the school link and special methods of instruction," *University of Illinois Bulletin*, **47**, No. 80.

Flood, J. (1975) *Predictors of Reading Achievement: An Investigation of Selected Antecedents to Reading,* doctoral dissertation, Stanford University.

Foch, T. T., Defries, J. C., McClearn, G. E., and Singer, S. M. (1977) "Familial patterns of impairment in reading disability," *Journal of Educational Psychology*, **69**, 316–329.

Fodor, J. A., Bever, T. G., and Garrett, M. (1974) *The Psychology of Language.* New York: McGraw-Hill.

Fodor, J. A., Garrett, M., and Bever, T. G. (1968) "Some syntactic determinants of sentential complexity, II: verb structure," *Perception and Psychophysics*, **3**, 453–461.

Fodor, J. D., Fodor, J. A., and Garrett, M. F. (1975) "The psychological unreality of semantic representations," *Linguistic Inquiry*, **6**, 515–531.

Forehand, G. A. (1974) "Knowledge and the educational process," in Gregg, L. W. (ed.), *Knowledge and Cognition.* Hillsdale, N.J.: Erlbaum.

Forster, K. J. (1976) "Accessing the mental lexicon," in Wales, R. J., and Walker, E. (eds.), *New Approaches to Language Mechanisms.* Amsterdam, Netherlands: North Holland.

Forster, K. J., and Chambers, S. M. (1973) "Lexical access and naming time," *Journal of Verbal Learning and Verbal Behavior*, **12**, 627–635.

Foshay, A. W., Thorndike, R. L., Hotyat, F., Pidgeon, D., Walker, D. A., (1962), *Educational Achievements of Thirteen-year-olds in Twelve Countries.* Hamburg, Germany: UNESCO Institute for Education.

Foster, G. G., Schmidt, C. R., and Sabatino, D. (1976) "Teacher expectancies and the label 'learning disabilities' " *Journal of Learning Disabilities*, **9**, 111–114.

Fox, B., and Routh, D. K. (1975) "Analyzing spoken language into words, syllables, and phonemes: A developmental study," *Journal of Psycholinguistic Research.* **4**, 331–342.

Fox, B., and Routh, D. K. (1976) "Phonemic analysis and synthesis as word-attack skills," *Journal of Educational Psychology*, **68**, 70–74.

Fraisse, P. (1963) *The Psychology of Time.* New York: Harper and Row.

Francis, H. (1973) "Children's experience of reading and notions of units in language," *British Journal of Educational Psychology*, **43**, 17–23.

Francis, H. (1977) "Children's strategies in learning to read," *British Journal of Educational Psychology*, **47**, 117–125.

Francis, W. N. (1970) "Linguistics and reading: A commentary on chapters one to three," in Levin, H., and Williams, J. P. (eds.), *Basic Studies on Reading.* New York: Basic Books.

Fransella, F., and Gerver, D. (1965) "Multiple regression equations for predicting reading age from chronological age and WISC verbal IQ," *British Journal of Educational Psychology*, **35**, 86–89.

Franz, S. I. (1930) "The relations of aphasia," *Journal of Genetic Psychology*, **3**, 401–411.

Frase, L. T. (1968) "Effect of question location, pacing, and mode upon retention of prose materials," *Journal of Educational Psychology*, **59**, 244–249.

Frase, L. T. (1969) "A structural analysis of the knowledge that results from thinking about text," *Journal of Educational Psychology*, **60** (Monograph Supp. 6).

Frase, L. T. (1972) "Maintenance and control in the acquisition of knowledge from written materials," in Freedle, R. O., and Carroll, J. B. (eds.), *Language Comprehension and the Acquisition of Knowledge.* New York: Wiley.

Fraser, E. (1959) *Home Environment and the School.* London: University of London Press.

Fraser, G. S. (1976) "Entropy and English: Social Class and Language Development," paper presented at the annual conference of the International Reading Association, Queenstown, New Zealand, August 24–26, 1976.

Frederiksen, C. H. (1975a) "Effects of context-induced processing operations on semantic information acquired from discourse," *Cognitive Psychology,* **7,** 139–166.

Frederiksen, C. H. (1975b) "Acquisition of semantic information from discourse: Effects of repeated exposures," *Journal of Verbal Learning and Verbal Behavior,* **14,** 158–169.

Frederiksen, C. H. (1977) "Semantic processing units in understanding text," in Freedle, R. (ed.), *Discourse Production and Comprehension, Vol. 1.* Norwood, N.J.: Ablex.

Frederiksen, C. H. (1979) "Discourse comprehension and early reading," in Resnick, L. B., and Weaver, P. A. (eds.), *Theory and Practice of Early Reading, Vol. 1.* Hillsdale, N.J.: Erlbaum.

Frederiksen, J. R. (1976) "Decoding Skills and Lexical Retrieval," paper read at the annual meeting of the Psychonomic Society, St. Louis, Missouri, November 13, 1976.

Frederiksen, J. R. (1977) "Text Comprehension and the Effective Visual Field," paper read at the annual meeting of the Psychonomic Society, Washington, D.C., November 12, 1977.

Frederiksen, J. R. (1978a) *A Chronometric Study of Component Skills in Reading* (NR 151–386 ONR Tech. Rep. 2). Cambridge, Mass.: Bolt, Beranek, and Newman.

Frederiksen, J. R. (1978b) "Assessment of perceptual decoding and lexical skills and their relation to reading proficiency," in Lesgold, A. M., Pellegrino, J. W., Fokkema, S., and Glaser, R. (eds.), *Cognitive Psychology and Instruction.* New York: Plenum.

Frederiksen, J. R., and Kroll, J. F. (1976) "Spelling and sound: Approaches to the internal lexicon," *Journal of Experimental Psychology: Human Perception and Performance,* **2,** 361–379.

Freedle, R. O. (ed.), (1979) *New Directions in Discourse Processing.* Norwood, N.J.: Ablex.

Freedle, R. O., and Carroll, J. B. (1972) *Language Comprehension and the Acquisition of Knowledge.* New York: Wiley.

Freeman, F. N. (1920) "Clinical study as a method in experimental education," *Journal of Applied Psychology,* **4,** 126–141.

Freud, S. (1920) *The Psychopathology of Everyday Life.* London: Fisher Unwin.

Frey, H. (1980) "Improving the performance of poor readers through autogenic relaxation training," *Reading Teacher,* **33,** 928–932.

Friend, P. (1980) "Literal and inferential comprehension—separate skills?" *Reading,* **14,** 18–23.

Fries, C. C. (1952) *The Structure of English.* The Hague, Netherlands: Mouton.

Fries, C. C. (1963) *Linguistics and Reading.* New York: Holt.

Frith, U. (1979) "Reading by eye and writing by ear," in Kolers, P. A., Wrolstad, M., and Bouma, H. (eds.), *Processing of Visible Language, I.* New York: Plenum.

Frostig, M. (1975) "The role of perception in the integration of psychological functions," in Cruickshank, W. M., and Hallahan, D. P. (eds.), *Perceptual and Learning Disabilities in Children, Vol. I, Psychoeducational Practices.* Syracuse, N.Y.: Syracuse University Press.

Fry, E. (1963) *Teaching Faster Reading.* London: Cambridge University Press.

Frymier, J. R. (1964) "The effect of class size upon reading achievement in first grade," *Reading Teacher,* **18,** 90–93.

Furno, O. F., and Collins, G. J. (1967) *Class Size and Pupil Learning.* Baltimore: Baltimore Public Schools.

Furth, H. (1970) *Piaget for Teachers.* Englewood Cliffs, N.J.: Prentice-Hall.

Furth, H. (1974) "Language processing and the hearing-impaired child: Discussion by participants," in Stark, R. E. (ed.), *Sensory Capacities of Hearing Impaired Children.* Baltimore: University Park Press.

Furth, H. (1978) "Reading as thinking: A developmental perspective," in Murray, F. B., and Pikulski, J. J. (eds.), *The Acquisition of Reading: Cognitive, Linguistic, and Perceptual Prerequisites.* Baltimore: University Park Press.

Furth, H., and Wachs, H. (1974) *Thinking Goes to School: Piaget's Theory in Practice.* New York: Oxford University Press.

Gaarder, K. R. (1970) "Eye movements and perception," in Young, F. A., and Lindsley, D. B. (eds.), *Early Experience and Visual Information Processing in Perceptual and Reading Disorders.* Washington, D.C.: National Academy of Sciences.

Gaddes, W. (1976) "Prevalence estimates and the need for definition of learning disabilities," in Knights, R. M., and Bakker, D. J., (eds.), *The Neuropsychology of Learning Disorders: Theoretical Approaches.* Baltimore: University Park Press.

Gagon, G. S. (1960) *A Diagnostic Study of the Phonic Abilities of Elementary Teachers in the State of Utah,* doctoral dissertation, Colorado State College.

Gal, R. (1958) *Une Enquête sur les Retards Scolaires.* Paris: L'Institut Pedagogique National.

Galaburda, A. M., LeMay, M., Kemper, T. L., and Geschwind, N. (1978) "Right-left asymmetries in the brain," *Science,* **199,** 852–856.

Gallagher, J. M. (1979) "Problems in applying Piaget

to reading, or letting the bird out of the cage," *Journal of Education* (Boston University), **161**, 72–86.

Garcia de Lorenzo, M. E. (1975) "Frontier dialect: A challenge to education," *Reading Teacher,* **28**, 653–658.

Gardner, D. E. M. (1950) *Long Term Results of Infant School Methods.* London: Methuen.

Gardner, H., Howard, V., and Perkins, D. (1974) "Symbol systems: A philosophical, psychological, and educational investigation," in Olson, D. R. (ed.), *Media and Symbols: The Forms of Expression, Communication, and Education.* Chicago: Chicago University P.

Garner, W. R., Hake, H. W., and Eriksen, C. W. (1956) "Operationism and the concept of perception," *Psychological Review,* **63**, 149–159.

Garnica, O. K. (1973) "The development of phonemic speech perception," in Moore, T. E. (ed.), *Cognitive Development and the Acquisition of Language.* New York: Academic Press.

Garrett, M. F. (1970) "Does ambiguity complicate the perception of sentences?" in Flores d' Arcais, G. B., and Levelt, W. J. M. (eds.), *Advances in Psycholinguistics.* Amsterdam, Netherlands: North-Holland.

Gates, A., and Bradshaw, J. L. (1977) "Music perception and cerebral asymmetries," *Cortex,* **13**, 390–401.

Gates, A. I. (1922) *The Psychology of Reading with Special Reference to Disability* (Contributions to Education No. 129). N.Y.: Teachers College, Columbia U.

Gates, A. I. (1924) "The nature and educational significance of physical status, and of mental, physiological, social and emotional maturity," *Journal of Educational Psychology,* **15**, 329–358.

Gates, A. I. (1936) "Failure in reading and social maladjustment," *Journal of the National Education Association,* **25**, 205–206.

Gates, A. I. (1937) "The necessary mental age for beginning reading," *Elementary School Journal,* **37**, 497–508.

Gates, A. I. (1941) "The role of personality maladjustment in reading disability," *Journal of Genetic Psychology,* **59**, 77–83.

Gates, A. I. (1947) *The Improvement of Reading* (3rd ed.). New York: Macmillan.

Gates, A. I. (1961) "Sex differences in reading ability," *Journal of Educational Research,* **36**, 594–603.

Gates, A. I., and Bond, G. L. (1936) "Failure in reading and social maladjustment," *National Education Association Journal,* **25**, 205–206.

Gates, A. I., and Chase, E. H. (1926) "Methods and theories of learning to spell tested by studies of deaf children," *Journal of Educational Psychology,* **17**, 289–300.

Gazzaniga, M. S. (1970) *The Bisected Brain.* New York: Appleton.

Gazzaniga, M. S. and Hillyard, S. A. (1971) "A language and speech capacity of the right hemisphere," *Neuropsychologia,* 9, 273–280.

Gelb, I. J. (1963) *A Study of Writing.* Chicago: University of Chicago Press.

Gelb, I. J. (1974) "Records, writing, and decipherment," *Visible Language,* **8**, 293–318.

Geschwind, N. (1965) "Disconnexion syndromes in animals and man," *Brain,* **88**, 237–294; 585–644.

Geschwind, N. (1968) "Neurological foundations of language," in Myklebust, H. R. (ed.), *Progress in Learning Disabilities, Vol. I.* New York: Grune and Stratton.

Geschwind, N. (1979) "Asymmetries of the brain—new developments," *Bulletin of the Orton Society,* **29**, 67–73.

Gesell, A. (1945) *The Embryology of Behavior.* New York: Harper and Row.

Gibson, E. J. (1969) *Principles of Perceptual Learning and Development.* New York: Prentice-Hall.

Gibson, E. J. (1972) "Reading for some purpose: Keynote address," in Kavanagh, J. F., and Mattingly, I. G. (eds.), *Language by Ear and by Eye.* Cambridge, Mass.: MIT Press.

Gibson, E. J. (1977) "How perception really develops: A view from outside the network," in LaBerge, D., and Samuels, S. J. (eds.), *Basic Processes in Reading: Perception and Comprehension.* Hillsdale, N.J.: Erlbaum.

Gibson, E. J., and Levin, H. (1975) *The Psychology of Reading.* Cambridge, Mass.: MIT Press.

Gibson, E. J., Osser, H., Schiff, W., and Smith, J. (1963) "An analysis of critical features of letters, tested by a confusion matrix," in *A Basic Research Program on Reading.* Cooperative Research Project No. 639, U.S. Office of Education.

Gibson, E. J., Pick, A., Osser, H., and Hammond, M. (1962) "The role of grapheme-phoneme correspondence in the perception of words," *American Journal of Psychology,* **75**, 554–570.

Gibson, E. J., Shurcliff, A., and Yonas, A. (1970) "Utilization of spelling patterns by deaf and hearing subjects," in Levin, H., and Williams, J. P., (eds.), *Basic Studies on Reading.* New York: Basic Books.

Giles, H., and Thakerar, J. N. (1980) "Language attitudes, speech accommodation and intergroup behavior: Some educational implications," *Language Arts,* **57**, 671–679.

Gleason, H. A. (1965), *Linguistics and English Grammar.* New York: Holt.

Gleitman, L. R., Gleitman, H., and Shipley, E. F., (1972) "The emergence of the child as grammarian," *Cognition,* **1**, 137–164.

Gleitman, L. R., and Rozin, P. (1973) "Teaching by use of a syllabary," *Reading Research Quarterly,* **8**, 447–483.

Gleitman, L. R., and Rozin, P. (1977) "The structure and acquisition of reading I: Relations between orthographies and the structure of language," in Reber, A. S., and Scarborough, D. L. (eds.), *Toward a Psychology of Reading.* Hillsdale, N.J.: Erlbaum.

Glenn, C. G. (1980) "Relationship between story content and structure," *Journal of Educational Psychology,* **72**, 550–560.

Goddard, N. (1974) *Literacy: Language-Experience Approaches.* London: Macmillan.

Goins, J. T. (1958) *Visual Perceptual Abilities and Early*

Reading Progress, Supplementary Educational Monographs No. 87. Chicago: University of Chicago Press.

Goldberg, H. (1959) "The ophthalmologist looks at the reading problem," *American Journal of Ophthalmology,* **47,** 67.

Golden, J. M. (1980) "The writer's side: Writing for a purpose and an audience," *Language Arts,* **57,** 756–762.

Goldman, S. R., Hogaboam, T. W., Bell, L. C., and Perfetti, C. A. (1980) "Short-term retention of discourse during reading," *Journal of Educational Psychology,* **5,** 647–655.

Goldstein, K. (1948) *Language and Language Disturbances.* New York: Grune and Stratton.

Goldstein, K., and Gelb, A. (1918) "Psychologische Analysen hirnpathologischer Fälle auf Grund von Untersuchungen Hirnverletzer. I. Abhandlung zur Psychologie des optischen Wahrnehmungs-und Erkennungsvorganges," *Zeitschrift der Neurologie Psychiatrischen,* **41,** 1–142.

Golinkoff, R. M. (1975–1976) "A comparison of reading comprehension processes in good and poor comprehenders," *Reading Research Quarterly,* **11,** 623–659.

Golinkoff, R. M., and Rosinski, R. R., (1976) "Decoding, semantic processing, and reading comprehension skill," *Child Development,* **47,** 252–258.

Gooch, S. (1966) "Four years on," *New Society,* **193,** 10–12.

Goodacre, E. J. (1970) *School and Home.* Slough, England: National Foundation for Educational Research.

Goodacre, E. J. (1973) "Great Britain," in Downing, J. (ed.), *Comparative Reading.* New York: Macmillan.

Goodman, K. S. (1967) "Reading: A psycholinguistic guessing game," *Journal of the Reading Specialist,* **6,** 126–135.

Goodman, K. S. (1968) "The psycholinguistic nature of the reading process," in Goodman, K. S. (ed.), *The Psycholinguistic Nature of the Reading Process.* Detroit, Mich.: Wayne State University Press.

Goodman, K. S. (1969) "Dialect barriers to reading comprehension," in Baratz, J. C., and Shuy, R. W. (eds.), *Teaching Black Children to Read.* Washington, D. C.: Center for Applied Linguistics.

Goodman, K. S. (1970) "Reading: A psycholinguistic guessing game," in Singer, H., and Ruddell, R. B. (eds.), *Theoretical Models and Processes of Reading.* Newark, Del.: IRA.

Goodman, K. S. (1973) "The 13th easy way to make learning to read difficult: A reaction to Gleitman and Rozin," *Reading Research Quarterly,* **8,** 484–493.

Goodman, K. S. (1976a) "Behind the eye. What happens in reading," Singer, H., and Ruddell, R. B. (eds.), *Theoretical Models and Processes of Reading.* Newark, Del.: IRA.

Goodman, K. S. (1976b) "What we know about reading," in Allen, P. D., and Watson, D. J., *Findings of Research in Miscue Analysis: Classroom Applications.* Urbana, Ill.: NCTE.

Goodman, K. S., Goodman, Y. M., and Burke, C. (1978) "Reading for life: The psycholinguistic base," in Hunter-Grundin, E., and Grundin, H. U. (eds.), *Reading: Implementing the Bullock Report.* London: Ward Lock.

Goodman, N. (1968) *Language of Art: An Approach to a Theory of Symbols.* Indianapolis, Ind.: Bobbs-Merrill.

Goodman, Y. M., and Burke, C. L. (1972) *Reading Miscue Inventory: Procedure for Diagnosis and Evaluation.* New York: Macmillan.

Goodstein, L. D. (1961) "Intellectual impairment in children with cleft palates," *Journal of Speech and Hearing Research,* **4,** 287–294.

Goodstein, L. D., and Lanyon, R. I. (1975) *Adjustment, Behavior, and Personality.* Reading, Mass.: Addison-Wesley.

Goody, J. (1968) *Literacy in Traditional Societies.* London: Cambridge University Press.

Goretsky, V. G., Kiriushkin, V. A., and Shanko, A. F. (1972) "The quest must continue" (in Russian), *Sovetskaia Pedagogika,* **2,** 39–47.

Goto, H. (1968) "Studies on 'inner speech' Part I: Reading and speech movement," *Folia Psychiatrica et Neurologica Japanica,* **22,** 65–77.

Gough, P. B. (1965) "Grammatical transformations and speed of understanding," *Journal of Verbal Learning and Verbal Behavior,* **4,** 107–111.

Gough, P. B. (1966) "The variation of sentences: The effect of delay of evidence and sentence length," *Journal of Verbal Learning and Verbal Behavior,* **5,** 492–496.

Gough, P. B. (1972) "One second of reading," in Kavanagh, J. F., and Mattingly, I. G. (eds.), *Language by Ear and by Eye.* Cambridge, Mass.: MIT Press.

Gough, P. B., and Cosky, M. J., (1977) "One second of reading again," in Castellan, N., Jr., John, P., David, B., and Potts, G. R. (eds.), *Cognitive Theory, Vol. 2.* Hillsdale, N.J.: Erlbaum.

Gould, J. D. (1976) "Looking at pictures," in Monty, R. A., and Senders, J. W. (eds.), *Eye Movements and Psychological Processes.* Hillsdale, N.J.: Erlbaum.

Gray, C. T. (1917) *Types of Reading Ability as Exhibited Through Tests and Laboratory Experiments, Supplementary Educational Monographs, No. 5.* Chicago: University of Chicago.

Gray, J. (1976) " 'Good teaching' and reading progress," in Cashdan, A. (ed.), *The Content of Reading.* London: Ward Lock.

Gray, J. (1977) "Teacher competence in reading tuition," *Educational Research,* **19,** 113–121.

Gray, W. S. (1919) "Principles of method in teaching reading as derived from scientific investigation," in *National Society for the Study of Education, Eighteenth Yearbook, Part II.* Bloomington, Ill.: Public School Publishing Co.

Gray, W. S. (1921) "Diagnostic and remedial steps in reading," *Journal of Educational Research,* **4,** 1–15.

Gray, W. S. (1922) *Remedial Cases in Reading: Their Diagnosis and Treatment, Supplementary Educa-*

tional Monographs, No. 22. Chicago: University of Chicago.

Gray, W. S. (1955) "Current reading problems: A world view," *Education Digest,* **21,** 28–31.

Gray, W. S. (1956) *The Teaching of Reading and Writing.* Paris: UNESCO.

Greaney, V. (1980) "Factors related to amount and type of leisure time reading," *Reading Research Quarterly,* **15,** 337–357.

Green, D. W., and Shallice, T. (1976) "Direct visual access in reading for meaning," *Memory and Cognition,* **4,** 753–758.

Green, R., and Money, J. (1969) *Transsexualism and Sex Reassignment,* Baltimore: Johns Hopkins Press.

Greene, J. M. (1970a) "The semantic function of negatives and passives," *British Journal of Psychology,* **61,** 17–22.

Greene, J. M. (1970b) "Syntactic form and semantic function," *Quarterly Journal of Experimental Psychology,* **22,** 14–27.

Greene, J. M. (1972) *Psycholinguistics: Chomsky and Psychology.* Harmondsworth, England: Penguin.

Greenfield, P. M., and Smith, J. H. (1976) *The Structure of Communication in Early Language Development.* New York: Academic Press.

Greenslade, B. C. (1980) "The basics in reading, from the perspective of the learner," *Reading Teacher,* **34,** 192–195.

Gregory, R. L. (1972) *Eye and Brain.* London: Weidenfield and Nicolson.

Grene, M. (ed.), (1969) *Knowing and Being: Essays by M. Polanyi.* Chicago: University of Chicago Press.

Grimes, J. (1975) *The Thread of Discourse.* The Hague, Netherlands: Mouton.

Groft, P. (1973) "Review: Artley, A. S., and Hardin, V. B., 'Inventory of Teacher Knowledge of Reading'," *Reading World,* **12,** 296–298.

Gross, A. D. (1978) "Sex-role standards and reading achievement: A study of an Israeli kibbutz system," *Reading Teacher,* **32,** 149–156.

Gross, S., Carr, M. L., Dornseif, A., and Rouse, S. M. (1974) "Behavioral objectives in a reading skills program, grades 4–8," *Reading Teacher,* **27,** 782–789.

Grossman, H. J. (ed.), (1977) *Manual on Terminology and Classification in Mental Retardation* (rev. ed.). Washington, D. C.: American Association on Mental Deficiency.

Gruber, E. (1962) "Reading ability, binocular coordination, and the ophthalmograph," *Archives of Ophthalmology,* **67,** 280–288.

Guthrie, J. T. (1973) "Models of reading and reading disability," *Journal of Educational Psychology,* **65,** 9–18.

Guthrie, J. T. (1978a) "Critique: Information processing, model or myth?" in Murray, F. B., and Pikulski, J. J. (eds.), *The Acquisition of Reading: Cognitive, Linguistic, and Perceptual Prerequisites.* Baltimore: University Park Press.

Guthrie, J. T. (1978b) "Principles of instruction: A critique of Johnson's remedial approaches to dyslexia," in Benton, A. L., and Pearl, D. (eds.), *Dyslexia: An Appraisal of Current Knowledge.* New York: Oxford University Press.

Guttman, J., Levin, J. R., and Pressley, M. (1977) "Pictures, partial pictures, and young children's oral prose learning," *Journal of Educational Psychology,* **69,** 473–480.

Guyton, A. C. (1976) *Structure and Function of the Nervous System* (2nd ed.), Philadelphia, Pa: Saunders.

Haber, R. N. (1976) "Control of eye movements during reading," in Monty, R. A., and Senders, J. W. (eds.), *Eye Movements and Psychological Processes.* Hillsdale, N.J.: Erlbaum.

Hagen, M. A. (1974) "Picture perception: Toward a theoretical model," *Psychological Bulletin,* **81,** 471–497.

Hakes, D. T. (1980) *The Development of Metalinguistic Abilities in Children.* New York: Springer.

Hale, A. (1980) "The social relationships implicit in approaches to reading," *Reading,* **14,** 24–30.

Hall, M. (1976) *Teaching Reading as a Language Experience* (2nd ed.). Columbus, Ohio: Merrill.

Hall, M. (1977) *The Language Experience Approach for Teaching Reading* (2nd ed.). Newark, Del: IRA.

Hall, N. A. (1976) "Children's awareness of segmentation in speech and print," *Reading,* **10,** 11–19.

Hall, R. A., Jr. (1961) *Sound and Spelling in English.* Philadelphia, Pa.: Chilton.

Hall, R. A., Jr. (1975) "Review of Vachek, J. (1973), *Written Language,*" *Language,* **51,** 461–465.

Hallahan, D. P., and Cruickshank, W. M. (1973) *Psychoeducational Foundations of Learning Disabilities.* Englewood Cliffs, N.J.: Prentice-Hall.

Halle, M. (1972) "On a parallel between conventions of versification and orthography; and on literacy among the Cherokee," in Kavanagh, J. F., and Mattingly, I. G. (eds.), *Language by Ear and by Eye.* Cambridge, Mass.: MIT Press.

Haller, A. O., and Butterworth, C. E. (1960) "Peer influence on levels of occupation and educational aspiration," *Social Forces,* **38,** 289–295.

Hallgren, B. (1950) "Specific dyslexia (congenital word blindness): A clinical and genetic study," *Acta Psychiatrica et Neurologica,* Supplement, No. 65.

Halliday, M. A. K. (1964) "The linguistic study of literary texts," in Lunt, H. G. (ed.), *Proceedings of the Ninth International Congress of Linguists.* The Hague, Netherlands: Mouton. Reprinted in Chatman, S. and Levin, S. R. (eds.), *Essays on the Language of Literature.* Boston: Houghton Mifflin.

Halliday, M. A. K. (1967) "Notes on transitivity and theme in English, Parts 1 and 2," *Journal of Linguistics,* **3,** 37–81, 199–244.

Halliday, M. A. K. (1973) *Explorations in the Functions of Language.* London: Arnold.

Halliday, M. A. K. (1975) *Learning How to Mean.* London: Arnold.

Halliday, M. A. K., and Hasan, R. (1976) *Cohesion in English.* London: Longmans.

Hamachek, D. E. (1975) *Behavior Dynamics in Teach-*

ing, Learning, and Growth. Boston, Mass.: Allyn and Bacon.

Hamilton, F. M. (1907) "The perceptual factors in reading," *Archives of Psychology,* **1,** 1–56.

Hamner, T. J. H. (1968) *The Relative Effectiveness of Tangible and Social Reinforcement During Individualized Instruction of Beginning Reading,* unpublished doctoral dissertation, University of Alabama.

Hansen, D., and Rodgers, T. S. (1968) "An exploration of psycholinguistic units in initial reading," in Goodman, K. S. (ed.), *The Psycholinguistic Nature of the Reading Process.* Detroit, Mich.: Wayne State University Press.

Hansen, H. S. (1969) "The impact of the home literary environment on reading attitude," *Elementary English,* **46,** 17–24.

Hansen, H. S. (1973) "The home literary environment—a follow-up report," *Elementary English,* **50,** 97–98, and 122.

Hardwick, D. A., McIntyre, C. W., and Pick, H. L., Jr. (1976) "The content and manipulation of cognitive maps in children and adults," *Monographs of the Society for Research in Child Development,* **41,** 3 (Serial No. 166).

Hardyck, C. D., and Petrinovich, L. F. (1970) "Subvocal speech and comprehension level as a function of the difficulty level of reading material," *Journal of Verbal Learning and Verbal Behavior,* **9,** 647–652.

Hardyck, C. D., Petrinovich, L. F., and Ellsworth, D. W. (1966) "Feedback of speech muscle activity during silent reading: Rapid extinction," *Science,* **154,** 1467–1468.

Harlow, H. F., Harlow, M. K., Rueping, R. R., and Mason, W. A. (1950) "A learning motivated by a manipulation drive," *Journal of Experimental Psychology,* **40,** 228–234.

Harman, D. (1970) "Illiteracy: An overview," *Harvard Educational Review,* **40,** 226–244.

Harris, A. J. (1956) *How to Increase Reading Ability* (3rd ed.). New York: Longmans, Green.

Harris, A. J. (1968) "Diagnosis and remedial instruction in reading," in Robinson, H. M. (ed.), *Innovation and Change in Reading Instruction, The Sixty-Seventh Yearbook of NSSE, Pt. II.* Chicago: Chicago University Press.

Harris, A. J. (1970) *How to Increase Reading Ability* (5th ed.). New York: D. McKay.

Harris, A. J. (1978–1979) "A reaction to Valtin's 'Dyslexia: Deficit in reading or deficit in research?' " *Reading Research Quarterly,* **14,** 222–225.

Harris, A. J., Morrison, D., Serwer, B. L., and Gold, L. (1968) *A Continuation of the CRAFT Project: Comparing Reading Approaches with Disadvantaged Urban Negro Children in Primary Grades.* New York: Selected Academic Readings (USOE Project 5-0570-2-12-1).

Harris, A. J., and Serwer, B. L. (1966) *Comparison of Reading Approaches in First Grade Teaching with Disadvantaged Children: The CRAFT Project.* New York: City University of New York (USOE Cooperative Research Project, 2677).

Harris, A. J., and Sipay, E. R. (1975) *How to Increase Reading Ability* (6th ed.). New York: McKay.

Hart, R. A., and Moore, G. T. (1973) "The development of spatial cognition: A review," in Downs, R. M., and Stea, D. (eds.), *Image and Environment.* Chicago: Aldine.

Havighurst, R. J., and Neugarten, B. L. (1975) *Society and Education.* Boston, Mass.: Allyn and Bacon.

Haviland, S. E., and Clark, H. H. (1974) "What's new? Acquiring new information as a process in comprehension," *Journal of Verbal Learning and Verbal Behavior,* **13,** 512–521.

Hawkins, M. L. (1966) "Mobility of students in reading groups," *Reading Teacher,* **20,** 136–140.

Hayes, S. P. (1950) "Measuring the intelligence of the blind," in Zahl, P. A. (ed.), *Blindness.* Princeton, N.J: Princeton University Press.

Head, H. (1926) *Aphasia and Kindred Disorders of Speech.* London: Oxford University Press.

Hebb, D. O. (1955) "Drives and C.N.S. (Conceptual Nervous System)," *Psychological Review,* **62,** 243–254.

Hebb, D. O. (1968) *The Organization of Behavior.* New York: Wiley.

Hécaen, H., and Angelergues, R. (1964) "Localization of symptoms in aphasia," in de Reuck, A. V. S., and O'Connor, M. (eds.), *Ciba Foundation Symposium on Disorders of Language.* London: Churchill.

Helfgott, J. (1976) "Phonemic segmentation and blending skills of kindergarten children: Implications for beginning reading acquisition," *Contemporary Educational Psychology,* **1,** 157–169.

Henry, G. H. (1977) "Receptive field classes of cells in the striate cortex of the cat," *Brain Research,* **133,** 1–28.

Hensey, F. (1972) *The Sociolinguistics of the Brazilian-Uruguayan Border.* Paris: Mouton.

Herber, H. (1970) *Teaching Reading in Content Areas.* Englewood Cliffs, N.J.: Prentice-Hall.

Hermann, K. (1959) *Reading Disability: A Medical Study of Word-Blindness and Related Handicaps.* Springfield, Ill.: Thomas.

Herron, J., Galin, D., Johnstone, J., and Ornstein, R. E. (1979) "Cerebral specialization, writing posture, and motor control of writing in left-handers," *Science,* **205,** 21, 1285–1289.

Hershberger, W. A., and Terry, D. F. (1965) "Typographical cuing in conventional and programmed texts," *Journal of Applied Psychology,* **49,** 55–60.

Hickerson, F. (1970) "The house of last resort," *Journal of Reading,* **13,** 263–268.

Hier, D. B., LeMay, M., Rosenberger, P. B., and Perlo, V. P. (1978) "Developmental dyslexia: Evidence for a subgroup with a reversal of cerebral asymmetry," *Archives of Neurology,* **35,** 90–92.

Himmelweit, H. T. (1963) "Socio-economic background and personality," in Hollander, E. P., and Hunt, R. G. (eds.), *Current Perspectives in Social Psychology.* Oxford: Oxford University Press.

Hincks, E. M. (1926) *Disability in Reading and Its Relation to Personality, Harvard Monographs in Education,* No. 7.

Hinshelwood, J. A. (1895) "Word-blindness and visual memory," *Lancet,* **2,** 1564–1570.

Hirsh, I. J. (1952) *The Measurement of Hearing.* New York: McGraw-Hill.

Hirsh-Pasek, K., Gleitman, L. R., and Gleitman, H. (1978) "What did the brain say to the mind? A study of the detection and report of ambiguity by young children," in Sinclair, A., Jarvella, R. J., and Levelt, W. J. M. (eds.), *The Child's Conception of Language.* New York: Springer.

Hochberg, J. (1970) "Components of literacy: Speculations and exploratory research," in Levin, H., and Williams, J. P. (eds.), *Basic Studies on Reading.* New York: Basic Books.

Hogaboam, T., and Perfetti, C. A. (1978) "Reading skill and the role of verbal experience in decoding," *Journal of Educational Psychology,* **70,** 717–729.

Holden, M. H., and MacGinitie, W. H. (1972) "Children's conceptions of word boundaries in speech and print," *Journal of Educational Psychology,* **63,** 551–557.

Holloway, R. (1971) "Right to read: New director, new approach," *Phi Delta Kappan,* **53,** 221–224.

Holmes, J. A. (1953) *The Substrata-Factor Theory of Reading.* Berkeley, Calif.: California Book Co.

Holmes, J. A. (1962) "When should and could Johnny learn to read," in Figurel, J. A. (ed.), *Challenge and Experiment in Reading.* New York: Scholastic Magazines.

Holmes, J. A. (1970) "The substrata-factor theory of reading: Some experimental evidence," in Singer, H., and Ruddell, R. B. (eds.), *Theoretical Models and Processes of Reading.* Newark, Del.: IRA.

Holt, G. L. (1971) "Effect of reinforcement contingencies in increasing programmed reading and mathematics in first-grade children," *Journal of Experimental Child Psychology,* **12,** 362–369.

Honeck, R. P., Sowry, B. M., and Voegtle, K. (1978) "Proverbial understanding in a pictorial context," *Child Development,* **49,** 327–331.

Hoosain, R. (1973) "The processing of negation," *Journal of Verbal Learning and Verbal Behavior,* **12,** 618–626.

Hoosain, R. (1974) "The processing and remembering of congruent and incongruent sentences," *Journal of Psycholinguistic Research,* **3,** 319–331.

Hoskisson, K. (1975) "Successive approximation and beginning reading," *Elementary School Journal,* **75,** 443–451.

Houston, S. H. (1971) "A re-examination of some assumptions about the language of the disadvantaged child," in Chess, S., and Thomas A. (eds.), *Annual Progress in Child Psychiatry and Child Development.* London: Butterworths.

Hubel, D. H. (1963) "The visual cortex of the brain," *Scientific American,* **209,** 54–63.

Hubel, D. H. and Wiesel, T. N. (1962) "Receptive fields, binocular interaction and functional architecture in the cat's visual cortex," *Journal of Physiology,* **160,** 106–154.

Hubel, D. H., and Wiesel, T. N. (1963) "Shape and arrangement of columns of cat's striate cortex," *Journal of Physiology,* **165,** 559–568.

Hubel, D. H. and Wiesel, T. N. (1965) "Receptive fields and functional architecture of monkey striate cortex," *Journal of Physiology,* **195,** 215–243.

Hubel, D. H. and Wiesel, T. N. (1979) "Brain mechanisms of vision," *Scientific American,* **241,** 150–162.

Huey, E. B. (1908) *The Psychology and Pedagogy of Reading.* New York: Macmillan. (Republished by the MIT Press, Cambridge, Mass., 1968.)

Humphrey, N. (1972) "Seeing and nothingness," *New Scientist,* **53,** 682–684.

Hunt, J. McV. (1961) *Intelligence and Experience.* New York: Ronald Press.

Hunt, L. C., Jr. (1970) "The effect of self-selection, interest and motivation upon independent, instructional and frustrational levels," *Reading Teacher,* **24,** 146–151.

Hunter, C. S. J., and Harman, D. (1979) *Adult Illiteracy in the United States.* New York: McGraw-Hill.

Hunter-Grundin, E. (1979) *Literacy: A Systematic Start.* London: Harper and Row.

Hurtig, R. (1977) "Toward a functional theory of discourse," in Freedle, R. O. (ed.), *Discourse processes: Advances in Research and Theory.* Norwood, N.J.: Ablex.

Hydén, H., and Egyházi, E. (1963) "Glial RNA changes during a learning experiment in rats," *Proceedings of the National Academy of Sciences,* **49,** 618–624. Also reprinted in Landauer, T. K. (ed.), (1967), *Readings in Physiological Psychology.* New York: McGraw-Hill.

Hymes, D. (1972) "Introduction," in Cazden, C. B., John, V. A., and Hymes, D. (eds.), *Functions of Language in the Classroom.* New York: Teachers College, Columbia University Press.

Ilg, F. L., and Ames, L. B. (1964) *School Readiness: Behavior Tests Used at the Gesell Institute.* New York: Harper and Row.

Ingram, T. T. S. (1963) "The association of speech retardation and educational difficulties," *Proceedings of the Royal Society of Medicine,* **56,** 199–203.

Ingram, T. T. S., and Reid, J. F. (1956) "Developmental aphasia observed in a department of child psychiatry," *Archives of Disease in Childhood,* **31,** 161–172.

Inhelder, B., Sinclair, H., and Bovet, M. (1974) *Learning and the Development of Cognition.* Cambridge, Mass.: Harvard University Press.

International Phonetic Association (1949) *The Principles of the International Phonetic Association.* London: International Phonetic Association.

Jackendoff, R. (1972) *Semantic Interpretation in Generative Grammar,* Cambridge, Mass.: MIT Press.

Jackson, J. (1944) "A survey of psychological, social and

environmental differences between advanced and retarded readers," *Journal of Genetic Psychology,* **65,** 113–131.

Jackson, J. H. (1874) "On the duality of the brain," *Medical Press,* 1, 19. Reprinted in Taylor, J. (ed.), (1932) *Selected writings of John Hughlings Jackson, Vol. II.* London: Hodder and Stoughton.

Jackson, P. W. (1968) *Life in Classrooms.* New York: Holt.

Jakobson, R., Fant, C., and Halle, M. (1952) *Preliminaries to Speech Analysis: The Distinctive Features and Their Correlates.* Cambridge, Mass.: MIT Press.

Jakobson, R., and Halle, M. (1956) *Fundamentals of Language.* The Hague, Netherlands: Mouton.

Jansen, M. (1968) "How long will we go on waiting for the great pumpkin?" (in Danish), *Læsepædagogen,* **2,** 6–13. (Also available in English or German from the Danish Institute for Educational Research, Copenhagen, Denmark.)

Jansen, M. (1973) "Denmark," in Downing, J. (ed.), *Comparative Reading.* New York: Macmillan.

Jansky, J. J. (1973) "Early prediction of reading problems," *Bulletin of the Orton Society,* **23,** 78–89.

Jeffrey, W. E., and Samuels, S. J. (1967) "Effect of method of reading training on initial learning and transfer," *Journal of Verbal Learning and Verbal Behavior,* **6,** 354–358.

Jenkins, J. G., and Dallenbach, K. M. (1924) "Oblivescence during sleep and waking," *American Journal of Psychology,* **35,** 605–612.

Jenkinson, M. D. (1967) "Preparing readers for an automated society," in Figurel, J. A. (ed.), *Vistas in Reading.* Newark, Del.; IRA.

Jensen, A. R. (1967) "The culturally disadvantaged: Psychological and educational aspects," *Educational Research,* **10,** 4–20.

Jensen, A. R. (1969) "How much can we boost IQ and scholastic achievement?" *Harvard Educational Review,* **39,** 1–123.

Jensen, H. (1970) *Sign, Symbol, and Script: An Account of Man's Efforts to Write.* London: Allen and Unwin.

John, E. R. (1972) "Switchboard versus statistical theories of learning and memory," *Science,* **177,** 850–864.

Johns, J. L. (1980) "First graders' concepts about print," *Reading Research Quarterly,* **15,** 529–549.

Johnson, D., and Myklebust, H. R. (1967) *Learning Disabilities: Educational Principles and Practices.* New York: Grune and Stratton.

Johnson, D. D. (1973–1974) "Sex differences in reading across cultures," *Reading Research Quarterly,* **9,** 67–86.

Johnson, M. S. (1955) "A study of diagnostic and remedial procedures in a reading clinic laboratory school," *Journal of Educational Research,* **48,** 565–578.

Johnson, P. R. (1977) "Dichotically stimulated ear differences in musicians and nonmusicians," *Cortex,* **13,** 385–389.

Johnson, R. E. (1970) "Recall of prose as a function of the structural importance of the linguistic units," *Journal of Verbal Learning and Verbal Behavior,* **9,** 12–20.

Johnson, R. E. (1973) "Meaningfulness and the recall of textual prose," *American Educational Research Journal,* **10,** 49–58.

Johnson, R. E. (1974) "Abstractive processes in the remembering of prose," *Journal of Educational Psychology,* **66,** 772–779.

Johnson-Laird, S. C. (1968) "The choice of the passive voice in a communicative task," *British Journal of Psychology,* **59,** 7–15.

Jokl, E. (1966) "The acquisition of skills," *Quest,* Monograph 6, 11–28.

Jolly, T. (1980) "Would you like for me to read you a story?" *Reading Teacher,* **33,** 994–997.

Jones, D. and Spreen, O. (1967) "Dichotic listening by retarded children: The effects of ear order and abstractness," *Child Development,* **38,** 101–105.

Jones, J. W. (1961) *Blind Children: Degree of Vision, Mode of Reading.* Washington, D.C.: Government Printing Office.

Judd, C. H., and Buswell, G. (1922) *Silent Reading: A Study of the Various Types, Supplementary Educational Monographs,* No. 23. Chicago: University of Chicago.

Just, M. A., and Carpenter, P. A. (1976) "Verbal comprehension in instructional situations," in Klahr, D. (ed.), *Cognition and Instruction.* Hillsdale, N.J.: Erlbaum.

Kabrisky, M. (1966) *A Proposed Model for Visual Information Processing in the Human Brain.* Urbana, Ill.: University of Illinois Press.

Kagan, J. (1964) "The child's sex role classification of school objects," *Child Development,* **35,** 1051–1056.

Kail, R. V., Jr., and Marshall, C. V. (1978) "Reading skill and memory scanning," *Journal of Educational Psychology,* **70,** 808–814.

Kandel, D. B., and Lesser, G. S. (1969) "Parental and peer influences on educational plans of adolescents," *American Sociological Review,* **34,** 213–223.

Kant, E. (1st ed. 1781, 2nd ed. 1787, trans. Kemp Smith, 1963) *Critique of Pure Reason.* London: Macmillan.

Karlin, R. (1972) *Teaching Reading in the High School* (2nd ed.), Indianapolis, Ind.: Bobbs–Merrill.

Karpova, S. N. (1955) "The preschooler's realization of the lexical structure of speech" (in Russian), *Voprosy Psikhol,* **4,** 43–55.

Katona, G. (1940) *Organizing and Memorizing.* New York: Columbia University Press.

Katz, J. J., and Fodor, J. (1963) "The structure of a semantic theory," *Language,* **39,** 170–210.

Katz, J. J. and Fodor, J. A. (1967) "The structure of a semantic theory," in Jakobovits, L. A. and Miron, M. S. (eds.), *Readings in the Psychology of Language.* Englewood Cliffs, N.J.: Prentice–Hall.

Katz, L., and Wicklund, D. A. (1971) "Word scanning rate for good and poor readers," *Journal of Educational Psychology,* **62,** 138–140.

Katz, L., and Wicklund, D. A. (1972) "Letter scanning

rate for good and poor readers in grades two and six," *Journal of Educational Psychology,* **63**, 363–367.

Kavanagh, J. F. (ed.), (1968) *Communicating by Language: The Reading Process.* Bethesda, Md.: NICHD, U.S. Dept. of Health, Education and Welfare.

Kavanagh, J. F., and Mattingly, I. G. (eds.), (1972) *Language by Ear and by Eye.* Cambridge, Mass.: MIT Press.

Kavanagh, J. F., and Strange, W. (eds.), (1978) *Speech and Language in the Laboratory, School and Clinic.* Cambridge, Mass.: MIT Press.

Kavanagh, J. F., and Venezky, R. L. (eds.), (1980) *Orthography, Reading, and Dyslexia.* Baltimore: University Park Press.

Kavanau, J. L. (1967) "Behavior of captive white-footed mice," *Science,* **155**, 1623–1639.

Kawai, Y. (1966) "Physical complexity of the Chinese letter and learning to read it," *Japanese Journal of Educational Psychology,* **14**, 129–138 and 188.

Kearslake, C., Gardner, M., and Pettican, J. (1966) Personal communication to John Downing.

Keeves, J. P., Matthews, J. K., and Bourke, S. F. (1978) *Education for Literacy and Numeracy in Australian Schools.* Hawthorne, Victoria: Australian Council for Educational Research.

Kellener, T. R. (1973) "Testing, teaching, and retesting syntactic structures in children from five to ten," *Linguistics,* **115**, 15–38.

Kelley, M. L. (1965) "Reading in the kindergarten," in Figurel, J. A. (ed.), *Reading and Inquiry.* Newark, Del.: IRA.

Kellmer Pringle, M. L., Butler, N. R., and Davie, R. (1966) *11,000 Seven-Year-Olds.* London: Longmans.

Kellmer Pringle, M. L., and Reeves, J. K. (1968) "The influence of two junior school regimes upon attainment in reading," *Human Development,* **11**, 25–41.

Kemp, L. C. D. (1955) "Environmental and other characteristics determining attainment in primary schools," *British Journal of Educational Psychology,* **25**, 67–77.

Kennedy, L. D., and Halinski, R. S. (1975) "Measuring attitudes: An extra dimension," *Journal of Reading,* **18**, 518–522.

Kerst, S., Vorwerk, K. E., and Geleta, N. (1977) "The role of phonetic processing in silent reading," *Journal of Reading Behavior,* **9**, 339–352.

Kessel, F. S. (1970) "The role of syntax in children's comprehension from ages six to twelve," *Monographs of the Society for Research in Child Development,* **35**, 6 (Serial No. 139).

Kessen, W. and Kuhlman, C. (1962) "Thought in the young child," *Monographs of the Society for Research in Child Development,* **27**, 2 (Serial No. 83).

Ketcham, W. A. (1951) "Experimental tests of principles of developmental anatomy and neuroanatomy as applied to the pedagogy of reading," *Child Development,* **22**, 186–192.

Kimura, D. (1961a) "Some effects of temporal-lobe damage on auditory perception," *Canadian Journal of Psychology,* **15**, 156–165.

Kimura, D. (1961b) "Cerebral dominance and the perception of verbal stimuli," *Canadian Journal of Psychology,* **15**, 166–171.

Kimura, D. (1964) "Left-right differences in the perception of melodies," *Quarterly Journal of Experimental Psychology,* **16**, 355–358.

Kimura, D. (1966) "Dual functional asymmetry of the brain in visual perception," *Neuropsychologia,* **4**, 275–285.

Kimura, D. (1973) "The asymmetry of the human brain," *Scientific American,* **228**, 70–78.

Kimura, D. and Folb, S. (1968) "Neural processing of backwards-speech sounds," *Science,* **161**, 395–396.

King, E. M., and Friesen, D. T. (1972) "Children who read in kindergarten," *Alberta Journal of Educational Research,* **18**, 147–161.

Kingston, A. J., Weaver, W. W., and Figa, L. E. (1972) "Experiments in children's perception of words and word boundaries," in Greene, F. P. (ed.), *Investigations Relating to Mature Reading.* Milwaukee, Wisc.: National Reading conference.

Kinsbourne, M. (1970) "The cerebral basis of lateral asymmetries in attention," in Sanders, A. F. (ed.), *Attention and Performance, III.* Amsterdam, Netherlands: North Holland.

Kinsbourne, M. (1973a) "The control of attention by interaction between the cerebral hemispheres," in Kornblum, S. (ed.), *Attention and Performance, IV.* New York: Academic Press.

Kinsbourne, M. (1973b) "School problems," *Pediatrics,* **52**, 697–710.

Kinsbourne, M., and Hiscock, M. (1977) "Does cerebral dominance develop?" in Segalowitz, S. J., and Gruber, F. A. (eds.), *Language Development and Neurological Theory.* New York: Academic Press.

Kinsbourne, M., and Hiscock, M. (1978) "Cerebral lateralization and cognitive development," in Chall, J. S., and Mirsky, A. F. (eds.), *Education and the Brain.* Chicago: University of Chicago Press.

Kintsch, W. (1972) "Notes on the structure of semantic memory," in Tulving, E., and Donaldson, W. (eds.), *Organization of Memory,* New York: Academic Press.

Kintsch, W. (1974) *The Representation of Meaning in Memory.* New York: Wiley.

Kintsch, W. (1977) "Reading comprehension as a function of text structure," in Reber, A. S., and Scarborough, D. L. (eds.), *Toward a Psychology of Reading.* Hillsdale, N.J.: Erlbaum.

Kintsch, W. (1978) "Comprehension and memory of text," in Estes, W. K. (ed.), *Handbook of Learning and Cognitive Processes.* Hillsdale, N.J.: Erlbaum.

Kintsch, W., and Kozminsky, E. (1977) "Summarizing stories after reading and listening," *Journal of Educational Psychology,* **69**, 491–499.

Kintsch, W., Kozminsky, E., Streby, W. J., McKoon, G., and Keenan, J. M. (1975) "Comprehension and recall of text as a function of content variables," *Journal of Verbal Learning and Verbal Behavior,* **14,** 196–214.

Kintsch, W., Mandel, T. S., and Kozminsky, E. (1977) "Summarizing scrambled stories," *Memory and Cognition,* **5,** 547–552.

Kintsch, W., and van Dijk, T. A. (1978) "Toward a model of text comprehension and production," *Cognitive Psychology,* **85,** 363–394.

Kirby, J., and Das, J. P. (1977) "Reading achievement, IQ, and simultaneous-successive processing," *Journal of Educational Psychology,* **69,** 564–570.

Kirk, S. A. (1963) "Behavioral diagnosis and remediation of learning disabilities," in *Proceedings of Conference on Exploration into the Problems of the Perceptually Handicapped Child.* Chicago: Perceptually Handicapped Children, Inc.

Kirk, S. A. (1972) *Educating Exceptional Children.* Boston, Mass.: Houghton Mifflin.

Kirk, S. A., McCarthy, J. J., and Kirk, W. (1968) *Examiner's Manual: Illinois Test of Psycholinguistic Abilities* (rev. ed.). Urbana, Ill.: University of Illinois Press.

Kirsch, D. I., Pehrsson, R. S. V., and Robinson, H. A. (1976) "Expressed reading interests of young children: An international study," in Merritt, J. E. (ed.), *New Horizons in Reading.* Newark, Del.: IRA.

Kirsch, I. and Guthrie, J. T. (1977–1978) "The concept and measurement of functional literacy," *Reading Research Quarterly,* **8,** 485–507.

Klahr, D. (1976) *Cognition and Instruction.* Hillsdale, N.J.: Erlbaum.

Klapp, S. T. (1971) "Implicit speech inferred from response latencies in same-different decisions," *Journal of Experimental Psychology,* **91,** 262–267.

Kleiman, G. M. (1975) "Speech recoding in reading," *Journal of Verbal Learning and Verbal Behavior,* **14,** 323–339.

Kleiman, G. M., and Schallert, D. L. (1978) "Some things the reader needs to know that the listener doesn't," in Pearson, D., and Hansen, J. (eds.), *Twenty-Seventh Yearbook of the National Reading Conference.* Clemson, S.C.: National Reading Conference.

Klein, A., and Schickedanz, J. (1980) "Preschoolers write messages and receive their favorite books," *Language Arts,* **57,** 742–749.

Klein, H. A. (1977) "Cross-cultural studies: What do they tell about sex differences in reading?" *Reading Teacher,* **30,** 880–886.

Klima, E. S. (1972) "How alphabets might reflect language," in Kavanagh, J. F., and Mattingly, I. G. (eds.), *Language by Ear and by Eye.* Cambridge, Mass.: M.I.T. Press.

Klima, E. S. and Bellugi U. (1979) *The Signs of Language.* Cambridge, Mass.: Harvard University Press.

Knights, R. M., and Bakker, D. J. (eds.), (1976) *The Neuropsychology of Learning Disorders: Theoretical Approaches.* Baltimore: University Park Press.

Knights, R. M., and Bakker, D. J. (eds.), (1979) *Rehabilitation, Treatment, and Management of Learning Disorders.* Baltimore: University Park Press.

Knox, C., and Kimura, D. (1970) "Cerebral processing of nonverbal sounds in boys and girls," *Neuropsychologia,* **8,** 227–237.

Kolers, P. A. (1966a) "Interlingual facilitation of short-term memory," *Journal of Verbal Learning and Verbal Behavior,* **5,** 314–319.

Kolers, P. A. (1966b) "Reading and talking bilingually," *American Journal of Psychology,* **79,** 357–376.

Kolers, P. A. (1968) "Introduction" to the reissue of Huey, E. B., *The Psychology and Pedagogy of Reading.* Cambridge, Mass.: MIT Press.

Kolers, P. A. (1969) "Reading is only incidentally visual," in Goodman, K. S., and Fleming, J. T. (eds.), *Psycholinguistics and the Teaching of Reading.* Newark, Del.: IRA.

Kolers, P. A. (1970) "Three stages of reading," in Levin, H., and Williams, J. P. (eds.), *Basic Studies on Reading.* New York: Basic Books.

Kolers, P. A. (1973a) "Experiments in reading," *Scientific American,* **227,** 84–91.

Kolers, P. A. (1973b) "Remembering operations," *Memory and Cognition,* **1,** 347–355.

Kolers, P. A. (1973c) "Some modes of representation," in Pliner, P., Krames, L., and Alloway, T. (eds.), *Communication and Affect: Language and Thought.* New York: Academic Press.

Kolers, P. A. (1974) "Two kinds of recognition," *Canadian Journal of Psychology,* **28,** 51–61.

Kolers, P. A. (1975) "Pattern-analyzing disability in poor readers," *Developmental Psychology,* **11,** 282–290.

Kolers, P. A. (1976) "Buswell's discoveries," in Monty, R. A., and Senders, J. W. (eds.), *Eye Movements and Psychological Processes.* Hillsdale, N.J.: Erlbaum.

Kolers, P. A., Wrolstad, M. E., and Bouma, H. (eds.), (1979) *Processing of Visible Language, Volume 1.* New York: Plenum.

Konski, V. (1955) "An investigation into differences between boys and girls in selected reading readiness areas and in reading achievement," *Reading Teacher,* **8,** 235–237.

Koppitz, E. M. (1970) "Brain damage, reading disability and the Bender Gestalt test," *Journal of Learning Disabilities,* **3,** 6–10.

Koppitz, E. M. (1971) *Children with Learning Disabilities: A Five Year Follow-Up Study.* New York: Grune and Stratton.

Kramer, P. E., Koff, E., and Luria, Z. (1972) "The development of competence in an exceptional language structure in older children and young adults," *Child Development,* **43,** 121–130.

Krashen, S. (1973) "Lateralization, language learning, and the critical period: Some new evidence," *Language Learning,* **23,** 63–74.

Krashen, S. D. (1976) "Cerebral asymmetry," in Whitaker, H., and Whitaker, H. A. (eds.), *Studies in Neurolinguistics, Vol. 2.* New York: Academic Press.

Krueger, L. E. (1975) "Familiarity effects in visual information processing," *Psychological Bulletin,* **82,** 949–974.

Krueger, L. E., Keen, R. H., and Rublevich, B. (1974) "Letter search through words and nonwords by adults and fourth-grade children," *Journal of Experimental Psychology,* **102,** 845–849.

Kuffler, S. W., and Nicholls, J. G. (1977) *From Neuron to Brain: A Cellular Approach to the Function of the Nervous System.* Sunderland, Mass.: Sinauer Associates.

Kulhavy, R. W., and Swenson, I. (1975) "Imagery instructions and the comprehension of text," *British Journal of Educational Psychology,* **45,** 47–51.

Kyle, J. G., Conrad, R., McKenzie, M. G., Morris, A. J. M., and Weiskrantz, B. C., (1978) "Language abilities in deaf school-leavers," *Teacher of the Deaf,* **2,** 38–42.

LaBerge, D. (1972) "Beyond auditory coding," in Kavanagh, J. F., and Mattingly, I. G. (eds.), *Language by Ear and by Eye.* Cambridge, Mass.: MIT Press.

LaBerge, D. (1973) "Attention and measurement of perceptual learning," *Memory and Cognition,* **1,** 268–276.

LaBerge, D. (1975) "Acquisition of automatic processing in perceptual and associative learning," in Rabbitt, P. M. A., and Dornič, S. (eds.), *Attention and Performance V.* London: Academic Press.

LaBerge, D., and Samuels, S. J. (1974) "Toward a theory of automatic information processing in reading," *Cognitive Psychology,* **6,** 293–323.

LaBerge, D., and Samuels, S. J. (eds.), (1977) *Basic Processes in Reading: Perception and Comprehension.* Hillsdale, N.J.: Erlbaum.

Labov, W. (1969a) "The logic of nonstandard English," *Georgetown Monographs on Language and Linguistics,* **22,** 1–22, 26, 31.

Labov, W. (1969b) "Some sources of reading problems for Negro speakers of nonstandard English," in Baratz, J. C., and Shuy, R. W. (eds.), *Teaching Black Children to Read.* Washington, D.C.: Center for Applied Lingusitics.

Labov, W. (1973) "The logic of nonstandard English," in DeStefano, J. S. (ed.), *Language, Society, and Education: A Profile of Black English.* Worthington, Ohio: Jones.

Ladd, M. R. (1933) *The Relation of Social Economic and Personal Characteristics to Reading Ability* (Contributions to Education, No. 582). New York: Teachers College, Columbia University.

Lado, R. (1957) *Linguistics Across Cultures.* Ann Arbor, Mich.: University of Michigan Press.

Lakoff, R. (1972) "Language in context," *Language,* **48,** 907–927.

Lambert, W. E., and Tucker, G. R. (1972) *Bilingual Education of Children.* Rowley, Mass.: Newbury House.

Lamendella, J. T. (1977) "The limbic system in human communication," in Whitaker, H., and Whitaker, H. A. (eds.), *Studies in Neurolinguistics, Vol. 3.* New York: Academic Press.

Lamy, P. (1977) "Bilingualism in Canadian education: Issues and research," *Social Sciences in Canada,* **5,** 19–20.

Landau, W. M., Goldstein, R., and Kleffner, F. R. (1960) "Congenital aphasia. A clinicopathologic study," *Neurology,* **10,** 915–921.

Lane, A. (1974) "Severe reading disability and the Initial Teaching Alphabet," *Journal of Learning Disabilities,* **7,** 23–27.

Langer, S. K. (1953) *Feeling and Form.* London: Routledge and Kegan Paul.

Langer, S. K. (1960) *Philosophy in a New Key.* Cambridge, Mass.: Harvard University Press.

Lansdown, R. (1974) *Reading: Teaching and Learning.* London: Pitman.

Lashley, K. S. (1929) *Brain Mechanisms and Intelligence.* Chicago: University of Chicago Press.

Lashley, K. S. (1951) "The problem of serial order in behavior," in Jeffress, L. A. (ed.), *Cerebral Mechanisms in Behavior. The Hixon Symposium.* New York: Wiley.

Lassen, N. A., Ingvar, D. H., and Skinhøj, E. (1978) "Brain function and blood flow," *Scientific American,* **239,** 62–71.

Laurita, R. E. (1971) "Reversals: A response to frustrations?" *Reading Teacher,* **25,** 45–51.

Lawrence, D. (1977) "The effects of counselling on retarded readers," in Reid, J. F., and Donaldson, H. (eds.), *Reading: Problems and Practices* (2nd ed.). London: Ward Lock.

Lawson, C. V. (1972) *Children's Reasons and Motivations for the Selection of Favorite Books,* unpublished doctoral dissertation, University of Arkansas.

Ledbetter, F. G. (1947) "Reading reactions for varied types of subject matter: An analytic study of the eye movements of eleventh grade pupils," *Journal of Educational Research,* **41,** 102–115.

Lefevre, C. A. (1964) *Linguistics and the Teaching of Reading.* New York: McGraw-Hill.

Lenneberg, E. H. (1967) *Biological Foundations of Language.* New York: Wiley.

Leong, C. K. (1970) *An Experimental Study of the Vocabulary of Written Chinese Among Primary III Children in Hong Kong,* paper presented at the Fifteenth Annual Convention, IRA, Anaheim, Calif.

Leong, C. K. (1972) "A study of written Chinese vocabulary," *The Modern Language Journal,* **56,** 230–234.

Leong, C. K. (1973) "Hong Kong," in Downing, J. (ed.), *Comparative Reading.* New York: Macmillan.

Leong, C. K. (1975a) "An efficient method for dichotic tape preparation," *Behavior Research Methods and Instrumentation,* **7,** 447–451.

Leong, C. K. (1975b) "Dichotic listening with related tasks for dyslexics—differential use of strategies," *Bulletin of the Orton Society,* **25,** 111–126.

Leong, C. K. (1976) "Lateralization in severely disabled readers in relation to functional cerebral development and syntheses of information," in Knights, R. M., and Bakker, D. J. (eds.), *The Neuropsychology of Learning Disorders: Theoretical Approaches.* Baltimore: University Park Press.

Leong, C. K. (1976–1977) "Spatial temporal information processing in children with specific reading disability," *Reading Research Quarterly,* **12,** 204–215.

Leong, C. K. (1978a) "Learning to read in English and Chinese: Some psycholinguistic and cognitive considerations," in Feitelson, D. (ed.), *Cross-cultural Perspectives on Reading and Reading Research,* Newark, Del: IRA.

Leong, C. K. (1978b) "Functional diagnosis of mentally retarded children," in Das, J. P., and Baine, D. (eds.), *Mental Retardation for Special Educators.* Springfield, Ill.: Thomas.

Leong, C. K. (1978c) "Understanding reading retardation: Cognitive aspects," in Fink, A. H. (ed.), *International Perspectives on Future Special Education.* Reston, Va.: Council for Exceptional Children.

Leong, C. K. (1980) "Cognitive patterns of 'retarded' and below-average readers," *Contemporary Educational Psychology,* **5,** 101–117.

Leong, C. K. (1981) "Cognitive strategies in relation to reading disability," in Friedman, M. P., Das, J. P., and O'Connor, N. (eds.), *Intelligence and Learning.* New York: Plenum.

Leong, C. K., and Haines, C. F. (1978) "Beginning readers' awareness of words and sentences," *Journal of Reading Behavior,* **10,** 393–407.

Lepper, M. R., Greene, D., and Nisbett, R. E. (1973) "Undermining children's intrinsic interest with extrinsic reward: A test of the 'overjustification' hypothesis," *Journal of Personality and Social Psychology,* **28,** 129–137.

Lerea, L., and Ward, B. (1966) "The social schema of normal and speech-defective children," *Journal of Social Psychology,* **69,** 87–94.

Lesgold, A. M. (1972) "Pronominalization: A device for unifying sentences in memory," *Journal of Verbal Learning and Verbal Behavior,* **11,** 316–323.

Lesgold, A. M. (1974) "Variability in children's comprehension of syntactic structures," *Journal of Educational Psychology,* **66,** 333–338.

Lesgold, A. M., de Good, H., and Levin, J. R. (1977) "Pictures and Young Children's prose learning: A supplementary report," *Journal of Reading Behaviour,* **9,** 353–360.

Lesgold, A. M., Levin, J. R., Shimron, J., and Guttman, J. (1975) "Pictures and young children's learning from oral prose," *Journal of Educational Psychology,* **67,** 636–642.

Lesgold, A. M., McCormick, C., Golinkoff, R. M. (1975) "Imagery training and children's prose learning," *Journal of Educational Psychology,* **67,** 663–667.

Lesgold, A. M., Pellegrino, J. W., Fokkema, S. D., and Glaser, R. (eds.), (1978) *Cognitive Psychology and Instruction.* New York: Plenum.

Lesgold, A. M. and Perfetti, C. A. (1978) "Interactive processes in reading comprehension," *Discourse Processes,* **1,** 323–336.

Lesgold, A. M., Roth, S. F., and Curtis, M. E. (1979) "Foregrounding effects in discourse comprehension," *Journal of Verbal Learning and Verbal Behavior,* **18,** 291–308.

Lesser, G. S., Fifer, G., and Clark, D. H. (1965) "Mental abilities of children from different social class and cultural groups," *Monographs of the Society for Research in Child Development,* **30,** No. 4, Chicago: University of Chicago Press.

Levin, H., and Kaplan, G. J. (1970) "Grammatical structure and reading," in Levin, H., and Williams, J. (eds.), *Basic Studies on Reading.* New York: Basic Books.

Levin, J. R. (1972) "Comprehending what we read: An outsider looks in," *Journal of Reading Behavior,* **4,** 18–28.

Levin, J. R. (1973) "Inducing comprehension in poor readers: A test of a recent model," *Journal of Educational Psychology,* **65,** 19–24.

Levin, J. R. (1976) "What have we learned about maximizing what children learn?" in Levin, J. R., and Allen, V. L. (eds.), *Cognitive Learning in Children: Theories and Strategies.* New York: Academic Press.

Levin, J. R., Bender, B. G., and Lesgold, A. M. (1976) "Pictures, repetition, and young children's oral prose learning," *A V Communication Review,* **24,** 367–380.

Levin, J. R., Davidson, R. E., Wolff, P. and Citron, M. (1973) "A comparison of induced imagery and sentence strategies in children's pair-associate learning," *Journal of Educational Psychology,* **64,** 306–309.

Levin, J. R., and Divine-Hawkins, P. (1974) "Visual imagery as a prose learning process," *Journal of Reading Behavior,* **6,** 23–30.

Levin, J. R., Divine-Hawkins, P., Kerst, S. M., and Guttman, J. (1974) "Individual differences in learning from pictures and words. The development and application of an instrument," *Journal of Educational Psychology,* **66,** 296–303.

Levy, B. A. (1975) "Vocalization and suppression effects in sentence memory," *Journal of Verbal Learning and Verbal Behavior,* **14,** 304–316.

Levy, B. A. (1977) "Reading: Speech and meaning processes," *Journal of Verbal Learning and Verbal Behavior,* **16,** 623–638.

Levy, B. A. (1978a) "Speech analysis during sentence processing: Reading and listening," *Visible Language,* **12,** 81–102.

Levy, B. A. (1978b) "Speech processing during reading," in Lesgold, A. M., Pellegrino, J. W., Fokkema, S. D., and Glaser, R. (eds.), *Cognitive Psychology and Instruction.* New York: Plenum.

Levy, J. (1974) "Psychobiological implications of bilateral asymmetry," in Dimond, S. J. and Beaumont, J. (eds.), *Hemispheric Function in the Human Brain.* London: Elek Science.

Levy-Schoen, A. and O'Regan, K. (1979) "The control of eye movements in reading" (tutorial paper), in Kolers, P. A., Wrolstad, M. E., and Bouma, H. (eds.), *Processing of Visible Language, Vol. 1.* New York: Plenum.

Lewkowicz, N. K. (1980) "Phonemic awareness training: What to teach and how to teach it," *Journal of Educational Psychology,* **72,** 686–700.

Liberman, A. M. (1970) "The grammars of speech and language," *Cognitive Psychology,* **1,** 301–323.

Liberman, A. M., Cooper, F. S., Shankweiler, D. P., and Studdert-Kennedy, M. (1967) "Perception of the speech code," *Psychological Review,* **74,** 431–461.

Liberman, A. M., Delattre, P., and Cooper, F. S. (1952) "The role of selected stimulus variables in the perception of the unvoiced stop consonants," *American Journal of Psychology,* **65,** 497–516.

Liberman, I. Y., Liberman, A. M., Mattingly, I., and Shankweiler, D. (1980) "Orthography and the beginning reader," in Kavanagh, J. F., and Venezky, R. L. (eds.), *Orthography, Reading, and Dyslexia.* Baltimore: University Park Press.

Liberman, I. Y., and Shankweiler, D. (1979) "Speech, the alphabet, and teaching to read," in Resnick, L. B., and Weaver, P. A. (eds.), *Theory and Practice of Early Reading, Vol. 2.* Hillsdale, N.J.: Erlbaum.

Liberman, I., Shankweiler, D., Fischer, W., and Carter, B. (1974) "Explicit syllable and phoneme segmentation in the young child," *Journal of Experimental Child Psychology,* **18,** 201–212.

Liberman, I., Shankweiler, D., Liberman, A. M., Fowler, C., and Fischer, F. W. (1977) "Phonetic segmentation and recoding in the beginning reader," in Reber, A. S., and Scarborough, D. L. (eds.), *Toward a Psychology of Reading.* Hillsdale, N.J.: Erlbaum.

Liberman, I., Shankweiler, D., Orlando, C., Harris, K. S., and Berti, F. B. (1971) "Letter confusions and reversals of sequence in the beginning reader: Implications for Orton's theory of developmental dyslexia," *Cortex,* **7,** 127–142.

Likert, R. (1970) "A technique for the measurement of attitudes," in Summers, G. F. (ed.), *Attitude Measurement.* Chicago: Rand McNally.

Lincoln, E. A. (1927) *Sex Differences in the Growth of American Children.* Baltimore: Warwick and York.

Lind, K. N. (1936) "Social psychology of children's reading," *American Journal of Sociology,* **41,** 454–469.

Lindahl, L. G. (1945) "Movement analysis as an industrial training method," *Journal of Applied Psychology,* **29,** 420–436.

Lindsay, P. and Norman, D. (1972) *Human Information Processing.* New York: Academic Press.

Ling, A. H. (1971) "Dichotic listening in hearing-impaired children," *Journal of Speech and Hearing Research,* **14,** 793–803.

Little, A., Mabey, C., and Russell, J. (1972) "Class size, pupil characteristics and reading attainment," in Southgate, V. (ed.), *Literacy at All Levels.* London: Ward Lock.

Lloyd, B. A., and Lloyd, R. C. (1971) "Paradigms and reading flexibility," *Education,* **92,** 57–65.

Lockhart, R. S., Craik, F. I. M., and Jacoby, L. L. (1975) "Depth of processing in recognition and recall: Some aspects of a general memory system," in Brown, J. (ed.), *Recognition and Recall.* London: Wiley.

Lorenz, K. Z. (1952) *King Solomon's Ring.* London: Methuen.

Lott, D., and Smith, F. (1970) "Knowledge of intra-word redundancy by beginning readers," *Psychonomic Science,* **19,** 343–344.

Lourie, R. S., and Schwarzbeck, C. (1979) "When children feel helpless in the face of stress," *Childhood Education,* **55,** 134–140.

Louttit, C. M. (1935) *Clinical Psychology.* New York: Harper.

Lovell, K. (1963) "Informal vs. formal education and reading attainments in the junior school," *Educational Research,* **6,** 71–76.

Lovell, K., and Woolsey, M. E. (1964) "Reading disability, non-verbal reasoning and social class," *Educational Research,* **6,** 226–229.

Lowe, A., and Campbell, R. (1965) "Temporal discrimination in aphasoid and normal children," *Journal of Speech and Hearing Research,* **8,** 313–314.

Lowery, L. F., and Grafft, W. (1968) "Paperback books and reading attitudes," *Reading Teacher,* **21,** 616–623.

Lukatela, G., Savić, M., Gligorijević, B., Ognjenović, P., and Turvey, M. T. (1978) "Bi-alphabetical lexical decision," *Language and Speech,* **21,** 142–165.

Lukatela, G., Savić, M. D., Ognjenović, P., and Turvey, M. T. (1978) "On the relation between processing the Roman and the Cyrillic alphabets: A preliminary analysis with bi-alphabetical readers," *Language and Speech,* **21,** 113–141.

Lukatela, G., and Turvey, M. T. (1980) "Some experiments on the Roman and Cyrillic alphabets of Serbo-Croatian," in Kavanagh, J. F., and Venezky, R. L. (eds.), *Orthography, Reading, and Dyslexia.* Baltimore: University Park Press.

Lundberg, I., and Tornéus, M. (1978) "Nonreaders' awareness of the basic relationship between spoken and written words," *Journal of Experimental Child Psychology,* **25,** 404–412.

Lunzer, E. A., and Gardner, K. (1979) *The Effective Use of Reading.* London: Heinemann.

Luria, A. R. (1946) "On the pathology of grammatical operations" (in Russian) *Izvestija APN RSFSR,* No. 17.

Luria, A. R. (1947) *Traumatic Aphasia* (in Russian). Moscow: Izd. Akad. Ped. Nauk RSFSR. (English trans. 1970, The Hague, Netherlands: Mouton).

Luria, A. R. (1966a) *Higher Cortical Functions in Man.* New York: Basic Books.

Luria, A. R. (1966b) *Human Brain and Psychological Processes.* New York: Harper and Row.

Luria, A. R. (1973) *The Working Brain: An Introduction to Neuro-psychology.* London: Penguin.

Luria, A. R. (1976) *Basic Problems of Neurolinguistics.* The Hague, Netherlands: Mouton.

Lynch, M. D., and Haase, A. M. (1976) "Self concept in reading instruction programs," in Miller, W. D., and McNinch, G. H. (eds.), *Reflections and Investigations on Reading.* Clemson, S.C.: National Reading Conference.

Lyons, J. (1970) *Chomsky.* Glasgow: Fontana/Collins.

Lyons, J. (1977) *Semantics, Vols. 1 and 2.* London: Cambridge University Press.

Maccoby, E., and Jacklin, C. N. (1974) *The Psychology of Sex Differences.* Stanford, Calif.: Stanford University Press.

MacCorquodale, K. (1970) "On Chomsky's review of Skinner's *Verbal Behavior,*" *Journal of the Experimental Analysis of Behavior,* **13,** 83–99.

MacKay, D. G. (1966) "To end ambiguous sentences," *Perception and Psychophysics,* **1,** 426–436.

MacKay, D. G., and Bever, T. (1967) "In search of ambiguity," *Perception and Psychophysics,* **2,** 193–200.

Mackworth, J. F. (1971) "Some models of the reading process: Learners and skilled readers," in Davis, F. B. (ed.), *The Literature of Research in Reading, with Emphasis on Models.* New Brunswick, N.J.: Graduate School of Education, Rutgers, The State University.

Mackworth, J. F. (1972) "Some models of the reading process," *Reading Research Quarterly,* **7,** 701–733.

Mackworth, N. H. (1977) "The line of sight approach," in Wanat, S. F. (ed.), *Linguistics and Reading, Series 2.* Arlington, Va.: Center for Applied Linguistics.

Macnamara, J. (1966) *Bilingualism and Primary Education.* Edinburgh, Scotland: Edinburgh University Press.

Maier, N. R. F. (1960) "Maier's Law," *American Psychologist,* **15,** 209–212.

Maier, N. R. F. (1961) *Frustration.* Ann Arbor, Mich.: University of Michigan Press.

Makita, K. (1968) "The rarity of reading disability in Japanese children," *American Journal of Orthopsychiatry,* **38,** 599–614.

Malmquist, E. (1958) *Factors Related to Reading Disabilities in the First Grade of the Elementary School.* Stockholm: Almqvist and Wiksell.

Malmquist, E. (1965) "Teaching of reading: A worldwide concern," in Figurel, J. A. (ed.), *Reading and Inquiry.* Newark, Del.: IRA.

Malmquist, E. (1973) "Sweden," in Downing, J. (ed.), *Comparative Reading.* New York: Macmillan.

Mandler, J. M., and Johnson, N. S. (1977) "Remembrance of things parsed: Story structure and recall," *Cognitive Psychology,* **9,** 111–151.

Mann, H. P. (1957) "Some learning hypotheses on perceptual and learning processes with their applications to the process of reading," *Journal of Genetic Psychology,* **90,** 167–202.

Mann, L. (1970) "Perceptual training: Misdirections and redirections," *American Journal of Orthopsychiatry,* **40,** 30–38.

Mann, L. (1971) "Perceptual training revisited: The training of nothing at all," *Rehabilitation Literature,* **32,** 322–335, 337.

Mann, L., and Goodman, L. (1976) "Perceptual training: A critical retrospect," in Schopler, E., and Reichler, R. J. (eds.), *Psychopathology and Child Development: Research and Treatment.* New York: Plenum.

Mann, V. A., Liberman, I. Y., and Shankweiler, D. (1980) "Children's memory for sentences and word strings in relation to reading ability," *Memory and Cognition,* **8,** 329–335.

Marcel, A. J. (1980) "Phonological awareness and phonological representation: Investigation of a specific spelling problem," in Frith, U. (ed.), *Cognitive Processes in Spelling.* New York: Academic Press.

Marcel, A. J., and Patterson, K. E. (1978) "Word recognition and production: Reciprocity in clinical and normal studies," in Requin, J. (ed.), *Attention and Performance, VII,* Hillsdale, N.J.: Erlbaum.

Marcel, T., and Rajan, P. (1975) "Lateral specialization for recognition of words and faces in good and poor readers," *Neuropsychologia,* **13,** 489–497.

Marie, P. (1926) *Travaux et Mémoires.* Paris: Masson.

Marshall, J. C. (1976) "Neuropsychological aspects of orthographic representation," in Wales, R. J., and Walker, E. (eds.), *New Approaches to Language Mechanisms.* Amsterdam, Netherlands: North Holland.

Marshall, J. C., and Morton, J. (1978) "On the mechanics of EMMA," in Sinclair, A., Jarvella, R. J., and Levelt, W. J. M. (eds.), *The Child's Conception of Language.* New York: Springer.

Marshall, J. C., and Newcombe, F. (1966) "Syntactic and semantic errors in paralexia," *Neuropsychologia,* **4,** 169–176.

Marshall, J. C., and Newcombe, F. (1973) "Patterns of paralexia: A psycholinguistic approach," *Journal of Psycholinguistic Research,* **2,** 175–199.

Marshall, J. C., and Newcombe, F. (1977) "Variability and constraint in acquired dyslexia," in Whitaker, H., and Whitaker, H. A. (eds.), *Studies in Neurolinguistics, Vol. 3.* New York: Academic Press.

Marshall, M., Newcombe, F., and Marshall, J. C. (1970) "The microstructure of word-finding difficulties in a dysphasic subject," in Flores D'Arcais, C. B., and Levelt, W. J. M. (eds.), *Advances in Psycholinguistics.* Amsterdam, Netherlands: North Holland.

Marshall, N., and Glock, M. D. (1978–1979) "Comprehension of connected discourse: A study into the relationships between the structure of text and information recalled," *Reading Research Quarterly,* **14,** 10–56.

Martin, C. I. (1955) "Developmental inter-relationships among language variables in children of the first grade," *Elementary English,* **32,** 167–171.

Martin, M., Schwyhart, K., and Wetzel, R. (1973) "Teaching motivation in a high school reading program," in Ekwall, E. E. (ed.), *Psychological Factors in the Teaching of Reading.* Columbus, Ohio: Merrill.

Marwit, S. J., and Stenner, A. J. (1972) "Hyperkinesis: Delineation of two patterns," *Exceptional Children,* **38,** 401–406.

Masland, R. L. (1967) "Lacunae and research approaches to them, III," in Darley, F. L. (ed.), *Brain Mechanisms Underlying Speech and Language.* New York: Grune and Stratton.

Masland, R. L. (1968) "Some neurological processes underlying language," *Annals of Otology, Rhinology, and Laryngology,* **77,** 787–804.

Maslow, A. H. (1943) "A theory of human motivation," *Psychological Review,* **50,** 370–396.

Mason, J. M. (1980) "When do children begin to read: An exploration of four year old children's letter and word reading competencies," *Reading Research Quarterly,* **15,** 203–227.

Mason, J. M., Kniseley, E., and Kendall, J. (1979) "Effects of polysemous words on sentence comprehension," *Reading Research Quarterly,* **15,** 49–65.

Mason, M. (1975) "Reading ability and letter search time: Effects of orthographic structure defined by single-letter positional frequency," *Journal of Experimental Psychology: General,* **104,** 146–166.

Mason, M., Katz, L., and Wicklund, D. A. (1975) "Immediate spatial order memory and item memory in sixth-grade children as a function of reader ability," *Journal of Educational Psychology,* **67,** 610–616.

Massaro, D. W. (ed.), (1975a) *Understanding Language: An Information-Processing Analysis of Speech Perception, Reading, and Psycholinguistics.* New York: Academic Press.

Massaro, D. W. (1975b) "Primary and secondary recognition in reading," in Massaro, D. W. (ed.), *Understanding Language: An Information-Processing Analysis of Speech Perception, Reading, and Psycholinguistics.* New York: Academic Press.

Massaro, D. W. (1978) "A stage model of reading and listening," *Visible Language,* **12,** 3–26.

Mastin, V. E. (1963) "Teacher enthusiasm," *Journal of Educational Research,* **56,** 385–386.

Mathewson, G. C. (1976) "The function of attitude in the reading process," in Singer, H., and Ruddell, R. B. (eds.), *Theoretical Models and Processes of Reading* (2nd. ed.). Newark, Del.: IRA.

Mattingly, I. G. (1972) "Reading, the linguistic process, and linguistic awareness," in Kavanagh, J. F., and Mattingly, I. G. (eds.), *Language by Ear and by Eye.* Cambridge, Mass.: MIT Press.

Mattingly, I. G. (1979) "Reading, Linguistic Awareness and Language Acquisition," Paper written for IRA/ University of Victoria International Reading Research seminar on Linguistic Awareness and Learning to Read, June 26–30, 1979, Victoria, B. C., Canada.

Mattis, S. (1978) "Dyslexia syndromes: A working hypothesis that works," in Benton, A. L., and Pearl, D. (eds.), *Dyslexia: An Appraisal of Current Knowledge.* New York: Oxford University Press.

Mattis, S., French, J. H., and Rapin, I. (1975) "Dyslexia in children and young adults: Three independent neuropsychological syndromes," *Developmental Medicine and Child Neurology,* **17,** 150–163.

Maw, W. H., and Maw, E. W. (1962) "Children's curiosity as an aspect of reading comprehension," *Reading Teacher,* **15,** 236–240.

Maxwell, A. E. (1972a) "Factor analysis: Thomson's sampling theory recalled," *British Journal of Mathematical and Statistical Psychology,* **25,** 1–21.

Maxwell, A. E. (1972b) "The WPPSI: A marked discrepancy in the correlations of the subtests for good and poor readers," *British Journal of Mathematical and Statistical Psychology,* **25,** 283–291.

Maxwell, A. E., Fenwick, P. B. C., Fenton, G. W., and Dollimore, J. (1974) "Reading ability and brain function: A simple statistical model," *Psychological Medicine,* **4,** 274–280.

Mazurkiewicz, A. J. (1960) "Social-cultural influences and reading," *Journal of Developmental Reading,* **3,** 254–263.

McCabe, A. E., Levin, J. R., and Wolff, P. (1974) "The role of overt activity in children's sentence production," *Journal of Experimental Child Psychology,* **17,** 107–114.

McCarthy, D. A. (1935) "Some possible explanations of sex differences in language development and disorders," *Journal of Psychology,* **35,** 155–160.

McClaren, V. M. (1950) "Socioeconomic status and reading ability: A study in infant reading," *Studies in Reading, Vol. 2.* Edinburgh, Scotland: Scottish Council for Research in Education.

McClearn, G. E. (1978) "Review of 'Dyslexia—Genetic aspects'," in Benton, A. L., and Pearl, D. (eds.), *Dyslexia: An Appraisal of Current Knowledge.* New York: Oxford University Press.

McClelland, D. C. (1961) *The Achieving Society.* Princeton, N.J.: Van Nostrand.

McClelland, J. L., and Jackson, M. D. (1978) "Studying individual differences in reading," in Lesgold, A. M., Pellegrino, J. W., Fokkema, S. D., and Glaser, R. (eds.), *Cognitive Psychology and Instruction.* New York: Plenum.

McClelland, W. (1949) *Selection for Secondary Education.* London: University of London Press.

McConkie, G. W., and Rayner, K. (1976a) "Identifying the span of the effective stimulus in reading: Literature review and theories of reading," in Singer, H., and Ruddell, R. B. (eds.), *Theoretical Models and Processes of Reading.* Newark, Del.: IRA.

McConkie, G. W., and Rayner, K. (1976b) "An on-line computer technique for studying reading: Identifying the perceptual span," in Singer, H., and Ruddell, R. B. (eds.), *Theoretical Models and Processes of Reading.* Newark, Del.: IRA.

McCracken, R. A., and McCracken, M. J. (1972) *Reading is Only the Tiger's Tail.* San Rafael, Calif.: Leswing Press.

McCracken, R. A., and McCracken, M. J. (1979) *Reading, Writing, and Language.* Winnipeg, Manitoba: Pegwis.

McDade, J. E. (1937) "A hypothesis for non-oral reading: Argument, experiment, and results," *Journal of Educational Research,* **30,** 489–503.

McDavid, R. I. (1969) "Dialectology and the teaching of reading," in Baratz, J. C., and Shuy, R. W. (eds.), *Teaching Black Children to Read.* Washington, D.C.: Center for Applied Linguistics.

McDill, E. L., and Coleman, J. S. (1965) "Family and peer influence in college plans of high school students," *Sociology of Education*, **38**, 112–116.

McDonald, F. J. (1965) *Educational Psychology*. Belmont, Calif.: Wadsworth.

McGhee, P. E. (1979) *Humor: Its Origin and Development*. San Francisco: W. H. Freeman.

McGinley, P., and McGinley, H. (1970) "Reading groups as psychological groups," *Journal of Experimental Education*, **39**, 36–42.

McGuigan, F. J. (1967) "Feedback of speech muscle activity during silent reading: Two comments," *Science*, **157**, 579–580.

McGuigan, F. J. (1970) "Covert oral behavior during the silent performance of language tasks," *Psychological Bulletin*, **74**, 309–326.

McGuigan, F. J. (1971) "External auditory feedback from covert oral behavior during silent reading," *Psychonomic Science*, **25**, 212–214.

McKeever, W. F., and Huling, M. D. (1970) "Lateral dominance in tachistoscopic word recognition of children at two levels of ability," *Quarterly Journal of Experimental Psychology*, **22**, 600–604.

McKinney, J. D., Mason, J., Perkerson, K., Clifford, M. (1975) "Relationship between classroom behavior and academic achievement," *Journal of Educational Psychology*, **67**, 198–203.

McLaughlin, B. (1977) "Second language learning in children," *Psychological Bulletin*, **84**, 438–459.

McLeod, J. (1968a) "Reading expectancy from disabled readers," *Journal of Learning Disabilities*, **1**, 97–104.

McLeod, J. (ed.), (1968b) *The Slow Learner in the Primary School*. Sydney, Australia: Novak.

McLeod, J. (1975) "Uncertainty reduction in different languages through reading comprehension," *Journal of Psycholinguistic Research*, **4**, 343–355.

McLeod, J. (1978) *Psychometric Identification of Children with Learning Disabilities*. Saskatoon, Sask.: University of Saskatchewan, Institute of Child Guidance and Development.

McLeod, J. (1979) "Educational underachievement: Toward a defensible psychometric definition," *Journal of Learning Disabilities*, **12**, 322–330.

McLeod, J., and Anderson, J. (1970) "An approach to assessment of reading ability through information transmission," *Journal of Reading Behavior*, **2**, 116–143.

McMichael, P. (1977) "Self-esteem, behaviour and early reading skills in infant school children," in Reid, J. F., and Donaldson, H. (eds.), *Reading: Problems and Practices*. London: Ward Lock.

McNeil, J. D. (1974) "False prerequisites in the teaching of reading," *Journal of Reading Behavior*, **6**, 421–427.

McNeill, D. (1966) "Developmental psycholinguistics," in Smith, F., and Miller, G. A. (eds.), *The Genesis of Language: A Psycholinguistic Approach*. Cambridge, Mass.: M.I.T. Press.

McNeill, D. (1968) "On theories of language acquisition," in Dixon, T. R., and Horton, D. L. (eds.), *Verbal Behavior and General Behavior Theory*. Englewood Cliffs, N.J.: Prentice-Hall.

McNeill, D., and Lindig, K. (1973) "The perceptual reality of phonemes, syllables, words and sentences," *Journal of Verbal Learning and Verbal Behavior*, **12**, 419–430.

Mednick, S. A. (1964) *Learning*. Englewood Cliffs, N.J.: Prentice-Hall.

Meltzer, H. S., and Herse, R. (1969) "The boundaries of written words as seen by first graders," *Journal of Reading Behavior*, **1**, 3–14.

Mendoza, S. M., Good, T. L., and Brophy, J. E. (1971) "The Communication of Teacher Expectancies in a Junior High School," paper presented at the annual meeting of AERA, New York.

Merritt, J. E. (1968) "Assessment of reading ability: A new range of diagnostic tests?" *Reading*, **2**, 8–16.

Merritt, J. E. (1970) "The intermediate skills," in Gardner, K. (ed.), *Reading Skills: Theory and Practice*. London: Ward Lock.

Meyer, B. J. F. (1975a) *The Organization of Prose and Its Effects in Memory*. Amsterdam, Netherlands: North-Holland.

Meyer, B. J. F. (1975b) "Identification of the structure of prose and its implications for the study of reading and memory," *Journal of Reading Behavior*, **7**, 7–47.

Meyer, B. J. F. (1977a) "The structure of prose: Effects on learning and memory and implications for educational practice," in Anderson, R. C., Spiro, R. J., and Montague, W. E. (eds.), *Schooling and the Acquisition of Knowledge*. Hillsdale, N.J.: Erlbaum.

Meyer, B. J. F. (1977b) "What is remembered from prose: A function of passage structure," in Freedle, R. O. (eds), *Discourse Production and Comprehension, Vol. 1: Discourse Processes: Advances in Research and Theory*. Norwood, N.J.: Ablex.

Meyer, B. J. F., Brandt, D. M., and Bluth, G. J. (1980) "Use of top-level structure in text: Key for reading comprehension of ninth-grade students," *Reading Research Quarterly*, **16**, 72–103.

Meyer, B. J. F., and McConkie, G. W. (1973) "What is recalled after hearing a passage?" *Journal of Educational Psychology*, **65**, 109–117.

Meyer, D. E., Schvaneveldt, R. W., and Ruddy, M. G. (1974) "Functions of graphemic and phonemic codes in visual word-recognition," *Memory and Cognition*, **2**, 309–321.

Meyer, D. E., Schvaneveldt, R. W., and Ruddy, M. G. (1975) "Loci of contextual effects on visual word-recognition," in Rabbitt, P. M. A., and Dornič, S. (eds.), *Attention and Performance, V*. London: Academic Press.

Midgeley, J. D. (1952) *Report to the Medical Research Council Committee of the Educational Treatment of Deafness*, unpublished.

Miles, T. R. (1974) *The Dyslexic Child*. London: Priory Press.

Miller, G. A. (1951) *Language and Communication.* New York: McGraw-Hill.

Miller, G. A. (1956) "The magical number seven plus or minus two: Some limits on our capacity for processing information," *Psychological Review,* **63,** 81–97.

Miller, G. A. (1965) "Some preliminaries to psycholinguistics," *American Psychologist,* **20,** 15–20.

Miller, G. A. (1972) "Reflections on the conference," in Kavanagh, J. F., and Mattingly, I. G. (eds.), *Language by Ear and by Eye.* Cambridge, Mass.: MIT Press.

Miller, G. A. (1974) "Toward a third metaphor for psycholinguistics," in Weimer, W. B., and Palermo, D. S. (eds.), *Cognition and the Symbolic Processes.* New York: Wiley.

Miller, G. A., Galanter, E., and Pribram, K. H. (1960) *Plans and the Structure of Behavior.* New York: Holt.

Miller, G. A., Heise, G. A., Lichten, W. (1951) "The intelligibility of speech as a function of the context of the test materials," *Journal of Experimental Psychology,* **41,** 329–335.

Miller, G. A., and Isard, S. (1963) "Some perceptual consequences of linguistic rules," *Journal of Verbal Learning and Verbal Behavior,* **2,** 217–228.

Miller, G. A., and Selfridge, J. (1950) "Verbal context and the recall of meaningful material," *American Journal of Psychology,* **63,** 176–185.

Miller, W. H. (1973) *Diagnosis and Correction of Reading Difficulties in Secondary School Students.* New York: Center for Applied Research in Education.

Mills, H. C. (1955–1956) "Language reform in China," *Far Eastern Quarterly,* **15.**

Milner, P. M. (1970) *Physiological Psychology.* New York: Holt.

Ministry of Education, (1950) *Reading Ability: Some Suggestions for Helping the Backward* (Pamphlet No. 18). London: Her Majesty's Stationery Office.

Ministry of Education (1957) *Standards of Reading 1948 to 1956* (Pamphlet No. 32). London: Her Majesty's Stationery Office.

Minsky, M. (1975) "A framework for representing knowledge," in Winston, P. H. (ed.), *The Psychology of Computer Vision.* New York: McGraw-Hill.

Minuchin, P. (1971) "Correlates of curiosity and exploratory behavior in preschool disadvantaged children," *Child Development,* **42,** 939–950.

Missildine, W. H., and Glasner, P. J. (1947) "Stuttering, A reorientation," *Journal of Pediatrics,* **31,** 300–306.

Mittler, P., and Ward, J. (1970) "The use of the Illinois Test of Psycholinguistic Abilities on British four-year-old children," *British Journal of Educational Psychology,* **40,** 43–54.

Modiano, N. (1973) *Indian Education in the Chiapas Highlands.* New York: Holt.

Mohr, J. P. (1976) "Broca's area and Broca's aphasia," in Whitaker, H., and Whitaker, H. A. (eds.), *Studies in Neurolinguistics, Vol. I.* New York: Academic Press.

Moldenhauer, D. L., and Miller, W. H. (1980) "Television and reading achievement," *Journal of Reading,* **23,** 615–619.

Molfese, D. L. (1977) "Infant cerebral asymmetry," in Segalowitz, S. J., and Gruber, F. A. (eds.), *Language Development and Neurological Theory.* New York: Academic Press.

Molfese, D. L., Freeman, R. B., and Palermo, D. S. (1975) "The ontogeny of brain lateralization for speech and nonspeech stimuli," *Brain and Language,* **2,** 356–368.

Money, J. (1962) "Dyslexia: A post conference review," in Money, J. (ed.), *Reading Disability: Progress and Research Needs in Dyslexia.* Baltimore: Johns Hopkins Press.

Money, J. (1966) "On learning and not learning to read," in Money, J. (ed.), *The Disabled Reader: Education of the Dyslexic Child.* Baltimore: Johns Hopkins Press.

Money, J., and Ehrhardt, A. A. (1972) *Man and Woman: Boy and Girl.* Baltimore: Johns Hopkins Press.

Monroe, M. (1932) *Children Who Cannot Read.* Chicago: University of Chicago Press.

Monroe, M., and Backus, B. (1937) *Remedial Reading: A Monograph in Character Education.* Boston, Mass.: Houghton Mifflin.

Monsees, E. (1961) "Aphasia in children," *Journal of Speech and Hearing Disorders,* **26,** 83–86.

Monty, R. A., and Senders, J. W. (eds.), (1976) *Eye Movements and Psychological Processes.* Hillsdale, N.J.: Erlbaum.

Moorhouse, A. C. (1946) *Writing and the Alphabet.* London: Cobbett Press.

Morgan, D. H. (1939) "Twin similarities in photographic measures of eye-movements while reading prose," *Journal of Educational Psychology,* **30,** 572–586.

Morgan, W. P. (1896) "A case of congenital word-blindness," *British Medical Journal,* **2,** 1378.

Morphett, M. V., and Washburne, C. (1931) "When should children begin to read?" *Elementary School Journal,* **31,** 496–503.

Morris, C. (1955) *Signs, Language, and Behavior.* New York: Braziller.

Morris, J. M. (1959) *Reading in the Primary School.* London: Newnes.

Morris, J. M. (1966) *Standards and Progress in Reading.* Slough, England: National Foundation for Educational Research.

Morris, J. M. (1973) "You can't teach what you don't know," in Clark, M., and Milne, A. (eds.), *Reading and Related Skills.* London: Ward Lock.

Morris, J. M. (1978) "Children's reading achievement in relation to their teachers' attributes," in Hunter-Grundin, E., and Grundin, H. U. (eds.), *Reading: Implementing the Bullock Report.* London: Ward Lock.

Morse, W. C. (1951) *A Comparison of the Eye-Movements of Average Fifth- and Seventh-Grade Pupils' Reading Materials of Corresponding Difficulty. Studies in the Psychology of Reading. Monographs in Education, No. 4.* Ann Arbor, Mich.: University of Michigan Press.

Morton, J. (1964) "A model for continuous language behavior," *Language and Speech,* **7,** 40–70.

Morton, J. (1968) "Consideration of grammar and computation in language behavior," in Catford, J. C. (ed.), *Studies in Language and Language Behavior.* Washington, D.C.: U.S. Office of Education.

Morton, J. (1969) "The interaction of information in word recognition," *Psychological Review,* **76,** 165–178.

Morton, J. (1970) "A functional model for memory," in Norman, D. A. (ed.), *Models of Human Memory.* New York: Academic Press.

Morton, J. (1979a) "Word recognition," in Morton, J., and Marshall, J. C. (eds.), *Psycholinguistics, Series II.* London: Elek Scientific Books.

Morton, J. (1979b) "Facilitation in word recognition: Experiments causing change in the logogen model," in Kolers, P. A., Wrolstad, M. E. and Bouma, H. (eds.), *Processing of Visible Language, Vol. 1.* New York: Plenum.

Morton, J. (1980) "The logogen model and orthographic structure," in Frith, U. (ed.), *Cognitive Processes in Spelling.* New York: Academic Press.

Morton, J., and Broadbent, D. E. (1967) "Passive versus active recognition models, or is your homunculus really necessary?" in Wathen-Dunn, W. (ed.), *Models for the Perception of Speech and Visual Form.* Cambridge, Mass.: MIT Press.

Morton, J., and Patterson, K. (1980) "A new attempt at an interpretation or an attempt at a new interpretation," in Coltheart, M., Patterson, K. E., and Marshall, J. C. (eds.), *Deep Dyslexia.* London: Routledge and Kegan Paul.

Mosberg, L. (1978) "Critique: Comments on language by eye and by ear," in Murray, F. B., and Pikulski, J. J. (eds.), *The Acquisition of Reading: Cognitive, Linguistic, and Perceptual Prerequisites.* Baltimore: University Park Press.

Moscovitch, M. (1977) "The development of lateralization of language functions and its relation to cognitive and linguistic development: A review and some theoretical speculations," in Segalowitz, S. J., and Gruber, F. A. (eds.), *Language Development and Neurological Theory.* New York: Academic Press.

Mosenthal, P. (1976–1977) "Psycholinguistic properties of aural and visual comprehension as determined by children's abilities to comprehend syllogisms," *Reading Research Quarterly,* **12,** 55–92.

Mosenthal, P. (1978) "The new and given in children's comprehension of presuppositive negatives in two modes of processing," *Journal of Reading Behavior,* **10,** 267–278.

Mosenthal, P. (1979) "Three types of schemata in children's recall of cohesive and noncohesive text," *Journal of Experimental Child Psychology,* **27,** 129–142.

Moskowitz, A. (1971), *The Acquisition of Phonology,* unpublished doctoral dissertation, University of California at Berkeley.

Mountford, J. (1970) "Some psycholinguistic components of initial standard literacy," *Journal of Typographic Research (Visible Language),* **4,** 295–306.

Murphy, A. T. (1960) "Attitudes of educators toward the visually handicapped," *Sight Saving Review,* **30,** 157–161.

Murray, E. (1932) "Disintegration of breathing and eye movements in stutterers during silent reading and reasoning," *Psychological Monographs,* **43,** 218–275.

Murray, F. B. (1978) "Critique: Development of intellect and reading," in Murray, F. B., and Pikulski, J. J. (eds.), *The Acquisition of Reading: Cognitive, Linguistic, and Perceptual Prerequisites.* Baltimore: University Park Press.

Myklebust, H. R. (ed.), (1968) *Progress in Learning Disabilities, Vol. I.* New York: Grune and Stratton.

Myklebust, H. R. (ed.), (1971) *Progress in Learning Disabilities, Vol. II.* New York: Grune and Stratton.

Myklebust, H. R. (ed.), (1975) *Progress in Learning Disabilities, Vol. III.* New York: Grune and Stratton.

Myklebust, H. R. (ed.), (1978) *Progress in Learning Disabilities, Vol. IV.* New York: Grune and Stratton.

Myklebust, H. R., Bannochie, M., and Killen, J. (1971) "Learning disabilities and cognitive processes," in Myklebust, H. R., (ed.), *Progress in Learning Disabilities, Vol. II.* New York: Grune and Stratton.

Naidoo, S. (1970) "The assessment of dyslexic children," in Franklin, A. W., and Naidoo, S. (eds.), *Assessment and Teaching of Dyslexic Children.* London: Invalid Children's Aid Society.

Naidoo, S. (1972) *Specific Dyslexia.* London: Pitman.

National Society for the Study of Education (1949) *Forty-Eighth Yearbook.* Chicago: University of Chicago.

Naylor, J. C. (1962) "Parameters affecting the efficiency of part and whole training methods: A review of the literature," in *NAVTRADEVCEN Technical Report,* N. 950–1. Port Washington, N.Y.: United States Training Devices Center.

Nebes, R. D. (1977) "Man's so-called minor hemisphere," in Wittrock, M. C., Beatty, J., Bogen, J. E., Gazzaniga, M. S., Jerison, H. J., Krashen, S. D., Nebes, R. D., and Teyler, T. J., *The Human Brain.* Englewood Cliffs, N.J.: Prentice-Hall.

Neisser, U. (1967) *Cognitive Psychology.* New York: Appleton.

Neuman, S. B. (1980) "Television: Its effects on reading and school achievement," *Reading Teacher,* **33,** 801–805.

Neville, M. H., and Pugh, A. K. (1976–1977) "Context in reading and listening: Variations in approach to cloze tasks," *Reading Research Quarterly,* **12,** 13–31.

Newson, J., and Newson, E. (1968) *Four Years Old in an Urban Community.* London: Allen and Unwin.

Nicholson, T. (1980) "Why we need to talk to parents about reading," *Reading Teacher,* **34,** 19–21.

Niles, O. S. (1970) "School programs: The necessary conditions," in Goodman, K. S., and Niles, O. S. (eds.), *Reading: Process and Program.* Urbana, Ill.: NCTE.

Noland, E. C., and Schuldt, W. J. (1971) "Sustained attention and reading retardation," *Journal of Experimental Education,* **40,** 73–76.

Norman, D. A., and Rumelhart, D. E. (1975) "Memory and knowledge," in Norman, D. A., Rumelhart, D. E. and the LNR Research Group (eds.), *Explorations in Cognition.* San Francisco, Calif.: Freeman.

Norvell, G. W. (1946) "Some results of a twelve-year study of children's reading interests," *English Journal,* **35,** 531–536.

Norvell, G. W. (1950) *The Reading Interests of Young People.* Boston, Mass.: Heath.

Norvell, G. W. (1958) *What Boys and Girls Like to Read.* Morristown, N.J.: Silver Burdett.

Nuttin, J. R. (1976) "Motivation and reward in human learning: A cognitive approach," in Estes, W. K. (ed.), *Handbook of Learning and Cognitive Processes, Vol. III.*. New York: Erlbaum and Wiley.

Oaken, R., Wiener, M., and Cromer, W. (1971) "Identification, organization, and reading comprehension for good and poor readers," *Journal of Educational Psychology,* **62,** 71–78.

O'Donnell, H. (1980) "Basic skills in reading—do we know what they are?" *Journal of Reading,* **24,** 166–169.

Office of Education, U.S. (1976) "Assistance to states for education of handicapped children, notice of proposed rulemaking," *Federal Register,* Vol. 41 (No. 230), 52404–52407.

Ogden, C. K. and Richards, I. A. (1923) *The Meaning of Meaning.* New York: Harcourt, Brace and World.

Oldfield, R. C. (1966) "Things, words and the brain," *Quarterly Journal of Experimental Psychology,* **18,** 340–353.

Oliver, M. E. (1976) *Making Readers of Everyone.* Dubuque, Iowa: Kendall/Hunt.

Olshavsky, J. E. (1976–1977) "Reading as problem solving: An investigation of strategies," *Reading Research Quarterly,* **12,** 654–674.

Olson, D. R. (1970) *Cognitive Development: The Child's Acquisition of Diagonality.* New York: Academic Press.

Olson, D. R. (ed.), (1974) *Media and Symbols: The Forms of Expression, Communication, and Education.* Chicago: University of Chicago Press.

Olson, D. R. (1976) "Toward a theory of instructional means," *Educational Psychologist,* **12,** 14–35.

Olson, D. R. (1977a) "From utterance to text: The bias of language in speech and writing," *Harvard Educational Review,* **47,** 257–281.

Olson, D. R. (1977b) "The languages of instruction: On the literate bias of schooling," in Anderson, R. C., Spiro, R. J., and Montague, W. E. (eds.), (1977) *Schooling and the Acquisition of Knowledge.* Hillsdale, N.J.: Erlbaum.

Olson, D. R., and Bruner, J. S. (1974) "Learning through experience and learning through media," in Olson, D. R. (ed.), *Media and Symbols: The Forms of Expression, Communication, and Education.* Chicago: University of Chicago Press.

Oommen, C. (1973) "India," in Downing, J. (ed.), *Comparative Reading.* New York: Macmillan.

Orlow, M. (1976) "Literacy training in West Germany and the United States," *Reading Teacher,* **29,** 460–467.

Ornstein, R. E. (1972) *The Psychology of Consciousness.* San Francisco, Calif.: Freeman.

Orton, S. T. (1925) " 'Word Blindness' in school children," *Archives of Neurology and Psychiatry,* **14,** 581–615.

Orton, S. T. (1937) *Reading, Writing, and Speech Problems in Children.* New York: Norton.

Orton, S. T. (1943) "Visual functions in strephosymbolia," *Archives of Ophthalmology,* **30,** 707–717.

Ortony, A., Reynolds, R. W., and Arter, J. A. (1978) "Metaphor: Theoretical and empirical research," *Psychological Bulletin,* **85,** 919–943.

Osgood, C. E. (1953) *Method and Theory in Experimental Psychology.* New York: Oxford University Press.

Osgood, C. E. (1963) "On understanding and creating sentences," *American Psychologist,* **18,** 735–751.

Osgood, C. E. (1971) "Where do sentences come from?" in Steinberg, D. D., and Jakobovits, L. A. (eds.), *Semantics: An Interdisciplinary Reader in Philosophy, Linguistics and Psychology.* London: Cambridge University Press.

Osgood, C. E., and Richards, M. M. (1973) "From yang and yin to and or but," *Language,* 49, 380–412.

Österberg, T. (1961) *Bilingualism and the First School Language—An Educational Problem Illustrated by Results from a Swedish Dialect Area.* Umeå, Sweden: Västerbottens Tryckeri, AB.

Owen, F. (1978) "Dyslexia—genetic aspects," in Benton, A. L. and Pearl, D. (eds.), *Dyslexia: An Appraisal of Current Knowledge.* New York: Oxford University Press.

Owen, F., Adams, P., Forrest, T., Stolz, L., and Fisher, S. (1971) "Learning disorders in children: Sibling studies," *Monographs of the Society for Research in Child Development,* **36,** 4 (Serial No. 144).

Ozolin, N. G. (1958) "Motor concepts in teaching sports technique," *Theory and Practice of Physical Culture,* **21,** 6.

Pace, J. P., and Golinkoff, R. M. (1976) "Relationship between word difficulty and access of single-word meaning by skilled and less skilled readers," *Journal of Educational Psychology,* **68,** 760–767.

Pachella, R. G. (1974) "The interpretation of reaction time in information processing research," in Kantowitz, B. H. (ed.), *Human Information Processing: Tutorials in Performance and Cognition.* Hillsdale, N.J.: Erlbaum.

Page, W. D. (1980) "Reading comprehension: The purpose of reading instruction or a red herring," *Reading World,* **19,** 223–231.

Paivio, A. (1969) "Mental imagery in associative learning and memory," *Psychological Review,* **76,** 241–263.

Paivio, A. (1971) *Imagery and Verbal Processes.* New York: Holt.

Palardy, J. M. (1969) "What teachers believe—what children achieve," *Elementary School Journal,* **69,** 370–374.

Palermo, D. S., and Molfese, D. L. (1972) "Language acquisition from age five onward," *Psychological Bulletin,* **78,** 409–428.

Papandropoulou, J., and Sinclair, H. (1974) "What is a word? Experimental study of children's ideas on grammar," *Human Development,* **17,** 241–258.

Paris, S. G. (1978) "Memory organization during children's repeated recall," *Developmental Psychology,* **14,** 99–106.

Paris, S. G., and Carter, A. Y. (1973) "Semantic and constructive aspects of sentence memory in children," *Developmental Psychology,* **9,** 109–113.

Paris, S. G., and Lindauer, B. K. (1976) "The role of inference in children's comprehension and memory for sentences," *Cognitive Psychology,* **8,** 217–227.

Paris, S. G., and Mahoney, G. J. (1974) "Cognitive integration in children's memory for sentences and pictures," *Child Development,* **45,** 633–642.

Park, G. E. (1948) "Reading difficulty (dyslexia): From the ophthalmic point of view," *American Journal of Ophthalmology,* **31,** 28–34.

Park, G. E., and Burri, C. (1943a) "The effect of eye abnormalities on reading difficulty," *Journal of Educational Psychology,* **34,** 420–430.

Park, G. E., and Burri, C. (1943b) "Eye maturation and reading difficulties," *Journal of Educational Psychology,* **34,** 535–546.

Parker, D. H. (1970) "Reading rate is multilevel," in Olson, A. V., and Ames, W. S. (eds.), *Teaching Reading Skills in Secondary Schools.* Scranton, Pa.: International Textbook Company.

Patterson, K. E. (1978) "Phonemic dyslexia: Errors of meaning and the meaning of errors," *Quarterly Journal of Experimental Psychology,* **30,** 587–601.

Patterson, K. E. (1979) "What is right with 'deep' dyslexic patients?," *Brain and Language,* **8,** 111–129.

Patterson, K. E., and Marcel, A. J. (1977) "Aphasia, dyslexia and the phonological coding of written words," *Quarterly Journal of Experimental Psychology,* **29,** 307–318.

Pavlov, I. P. (1927) *Conditioned Reflexes.* London: Clarendon Press.

Pavlov, I. P. (1928) *Lecture on Conditioned Reflexes.* New York: International Publishers.

Pearson, P. D. (1974–1975) "The effects of grammatical complexity on children's comprehension, recall, and conception of certain semantic relations," *Reading Research Quarterly,* **10,** 155–192.

Pearson, P. D. (1978) "Some practical applications of psycholinguistic models of reading," in Samuels, S. J. (ed.), *What Research Has to Say About Reading Instruction.* Newark, Del.: IRA.

Pearson, P. D., and Kamil, M. L. (1977–1978) "What hath Carver raud? A reaction to Carver's 'Toward a theory of reading comprehension and rauding,'" *Reading Research Quarterly,* **13,** 92–115.

Pearson, P. D., and Spiro, R. J. (1981) "Toward a theory of reading comprehension instruction," *Topics in Language Disorders,* **1,** 71–88.

Penfield, W., and Rasmussen, T. (1950) *The Cerebral Cortex of Man.* New York: Macmillan.

Penfield, W., and Roberts, L. (1959) *Speech and Brain Mechanisms.* Princeton, N.J.: Princeton University Press.

Perelstein de Braslavsky, B. (1973) "Argentina," in Downing, J. (ed.), *Comparative Reading.* New York: Macmillan.

Perfetti, C. A. (1969) "Lexical density and phrase structure depth as variables in sentence retention," *Journal of Verbal Learning and Verbal Behavior,* **8,** 719–724.

Perfetti, C. A. (1972) "Psychosemantics: Some cognitive aspects of structural meaning," *Psychological Bulletin,* **78,** 241–259.

Perfetti, C. A. (1977) "Language comprehension and fast decoding: Some psycholinguistic prerequisites for skilled reading," in Guthrie, J. (ed.), *Cognition, Curriculum, and Comprehension.* Newark, Del.: IRA.

Perfetti, C. A., Finger, E., and Hogaboam, T. (1978) "Sources of vocalization latency differences between skilled and less skilled young readers," *Journal of Educational Psychology,* **70,** 730–739.

Perfetti, C. A., and Goldman, S. (1976) "Discourse memory and reading comprehension skill," *Journal of Verbal Learning and Verbal Behavior,* **15,** 33–42.

Perfetti, C. A., Goldman, S. R., and Hogaboam, T. W. (1979) "Reading skill and the identification of words in discourse context," *Memory and Cognition,* **7,** 273–282.

Perfetti, C. A., and Hogaboam, T. (1975) "The relationship between single word decoding and reading comprehension skill," *Journal of Educational Psychology,* **67,** 461–469.

Perfetti, C. A., and Lesgold, A. M. (1977) "Discourse comprehension and sources of individual differences," in Carpenter, P., and Just, M. (eds.), *Cognitive Processes in Comprehension.* Hillsdale, N.J.: Erlbaum.

Perspectives on Dyslexia, February 1981, Vol. **6,** No. 1. Towson, Md.: The Orton Society.

Peters, F. J. J. (1980) "The 1980 Olympics: A schoolwide TV-reading project," *Journal of Reading,* **23,** 300–304.

Piaget, J. (1959) *The Language and Thought of the Child.* London: Routledge and Kegan Paul.

Piaget, J. (1969a) *The Mechanisms of Perception.* London: Routledge and Kegan Paul.

Piaget, J. (1969b) *The Child's Conception of Time.* London: Routledge and Kegan Paul.

Piaget, J. (1974a) *La Prise de Conscience.* Paris: Presses Universitaires de France.

Piaget, J. (1974b) *Réussir et comprendre.* Paris: Presses Universitaires de France.

Piaget, J. (1976) *The Grasp of Consciousness: Action and Conception in the Young Child.* Cambridge, Mass.: Harvard University Press.

Piaget, J., and Inhelder, B. (1956) *The Child's Conception of Space.* London: Routledge and Kegan Paul.

Piaget, J., and Inhelder, B. (1969) *The Psychology of the Child.* New York: Basic Books.

Piaget, J., Inhelder, B., and Szeminska, A. (1960) *The Child's Conception of Geometry.* New York: Basic Books.

Pick, A. D., (1978) "Perception in the acquisition of reading," in Murray, F. B., and Pikulski, J. J. (eds.), *The Acquisition of Reading: Cognitive, Linguistic, and Perceptual Prerequisites.* Baltimore: University Park Press.

Pike, K. L. (1947) *Phonemics.* Ann Arbor, Mich.: University of Michigan Press.

Pike, K. L. (1967) *Language in Relation to a United Theory of the Structure of Human Behavior.* The Hague, Netherlands: Mouton.

Pikulski, J. J. (1970) "Effects of reinforcement on word recognition," *Reading Teacher,* **23,** 516–522 and 555.

Pikulski, J. J. (1971) "Candy, word recognition and the 'disadvantaged,'" *Reading Teacher,* **25,** 243–246.

Pintner, R. (1913) "Inner speech during silent reading," *Psychological Review,* **20,** 129–153.

Pintner, R., and Lev, J. (1939) "The intelligence of the hard of hearing school child," *Journal of Genetic Psychology,* **55,** 31–48.

Pippert, R. (1969) *A Study of Creativity and Faith.* Winnipeg, Manitoba: Manitoba Department of Youth and Education.

Pirozzolo, F. J., and Rayner, K. (1977) "Hemispheric specialization in reading and word recognition," *Brain and Language,* **4,** 248–261.

Pitman, I. J. (1961) "Learning to read: An experiment," *Journal of the Royal Society of Arts,* **109,** 149–180.

Plante, A. J. (1977) "The Connecticut 'pairing' model proves effective in bilingual/bicultural education," *Phil Delta Kappan,* **58,** 427.

Platten, G. J. (1953) *The Use of the Vernacular in Teaching in the South Pacific* (Technical Paper No. 44). Sydney, Australia: South Pacific Commission.

Plowden Report—*see* Department of Education and Science (1967).

Polanyi, M. (1964) *Personal Knowledge.* New York: Harper and Row.

Pollard, A. W. (1923–1924) "Elizabethan spelling as a literary and bibliographical clue," *The Library,* fourth series, No. 4.

Porter, R. J., Jr., and Berlin, C. I. (1975) "On interpreting developmental changes in the dichotic right-ear advantage," *Brain and Language,* **2,** 186–200.

Posnansky, C. J., and Rayner, K. (1977) "Visual-feature and response components in a picture-word interference task with beginning and skilled readers," *Journal of Experimental Child Psychology,* **24,** 440–460.

Posner, M. I., Lewis, J. L., and Conrad, C. (1972) "Component processes in reading," in Kavanagh, J. F., and Mattingly, I. G. (eds.), *Language by Ear and by Eye.* Cambridge, Mass.: MIT Press.

Postman, L. (1975) "Verbal learning and memory," *Annual Review of Psychology,* **26,** 291–335.

Postman, L., and Senders, V. (1946) "Incidental learning and generality of set," *Journal of Experimental Psychology,* **36,** 153–165.

Potter, M. (1949) *Perception of Symbol Orientation and Early Reading Success* (Contributions to Education, No. 939). New York: Teachers College, Columbia University.

Poulsen, D., Kintsch, E., Kintsch, W., and Premack, D. (1979) "Children's comprehension and memory for stories," *Journal of Experimental Child Psychology,* **28,** 379–403.

Powell, W. R. (1976) "A study of relationships in teacher proficiency," in Miller, W. D., and McNinch, G. H. (eds.), *Reflections and Investigations on Reading.* Clemson, S.C.: National Reading Conference.

Prescott, C. A. (1955) "Sex difference in Metropolitan readiness test results," *Journal of Educational Research,* **48,** 605–610.

Pressley, G. M. (1976) "Mental imagery helps eight-year-olds remember what they read," *Journal of Educational Psychology,* **68,** 355–359.

Pressley, M. (1977) "Imagery and children's learning: Putting the picture in developmental perspective," *Review of Educational Research,* **47,** 585–622.

Preston, M. I. (1939) "The reaction of parents to reading failure," *Child Development,* **10,** 173–179.

Preston, M. I. (1940) "Reading failure and the child's security," *American Journal of Orthopsychiatry,* **10,** 239–252.

Preston, R. C. (1962) "Reading achievement of German and American children," *School and Society,* **90,** 350–354.

Preston, R. C. (1979) "Reading achievement of German boys and girls related to sex of teacher," *Reading Teacher,* **32,** 521–526.

Pribram, K. H. (1971) *Languages of the Brain.* Englewood Cliffs, N.J.: Prentice-Hall.

Pringle, M. L. Kellmer, Butler, N. R. and Davie, R. (1966) *11,000 Seven-Year-Olds.* London: Longmans.

Pringle, M. L. Kellmer, and Reeves, J. K. (1968) "The influence of two junior school regimes upon attainment in reading," *Human Development,* **11,** 25–41.

Propp, V. (1958) *Morphology of the Folktale* (trans. by Lawrence Scott). Bloomington, Indiana: Research Center in Anthropology, Folklore, and Linguistics (originally published in Russian, 1928).

Pugh, A. K. (1971) "Secondary school reading: Obstacles to profit and delight," *Reading,* **5,** 6–13.

Pugh, A. K. (1975) "The development of silent reading," in Latham, W. (ed.), *The Road to Effective Reading.* London: Ward Lock.

Pugh, A. K. (1980) "Strategies in silent reading," *Reading,* **14,** 27–36.

Pylyshyn, Z. W. (1973) "What the mind's eye tells the mind's brain: A critique of mental imagery," *Psychological Bulletin,* **80,** 1–24.

Ramsey, Z. W. (1962) "Will tomorrow's teachers know and teach phonics?" *Reading Teacher,* **15,** 241–245.

Ravenette, A. T. (1968) *Dimensions of Reading Difficulties.* Oxford: Pergamon.

Ravenette, A. T. (1970) "Reading difficulties—and what

else?" in Gardner, K. (ed.), *Reading Skills: Theory and Practice.* London: Ward Lock.

Raygor, A. L., Wark, D. M., and Warren, A. (1966) "Operant conditioning of reading rate: The effect of a secondary reinforcer," *Journal of Reading,* **9,** 147–156.

Rayner, K. (1977) "Visual attention in reading: Eye movements reflect cognitive processes," *Memory and Cognition,* **4,** 443–448.

Rayner, K. (1978a) "Eye movements in reading, and information processing," *Psychological Bulletin,* **85,** 618–660.

Rayner, K. (1978b) "Foveal and parafoveal cues in reading," in Requin, J. (ed.), *Attention and Performance, VII.* Hillsdale, N.J.: Erlbaum.

Rayner, K., and McConkie, G. W. (1977) "Perceptual processes in reading: The perceptual spans," in Reber, A. S., and Scarborough, D. L. (eds.), *Toward a Psychology of Reading.* Hillsdale, N.J.: Erlbaum.

Rayner, K., and Posnansky, C. (1978) "Stages of processing in word identification," *Journal of Experimental Psychology: General,* **107,** 64–80.

Read, C. (1971) "Pre-school children's knowledge of English phonology," *Harvard Educational Review,* **41,** 1–34.

Read, C. (1975) "Lessons to be learned from the preschool orthographer," in Lenneberg, E. H., and Lenneberg, E. (eds.), *Foundations of Language Development, Vol. 2.* New York: Academic Press.

Read, C. (1978) "Children's awareness of language, with emphasis on sound systems," in Sinclair, A., Jarvella, R. J., and Levelt, W.J.M. (eds.), *The Child's Conception of Language.* New York: Springer.

Reddy, R., and Newell, A. (1974) "Knowledge and its representation in a speech understanding system," in Gregg, L. W. (ed.), *Knowledge and Cognition.* Hillsdale, N.J.: Erlbaum.

Redozubov, S. P. (1947) *The Methodology of Russian Language Instruction in the Primary School* (in Russian). Moscow: Uchpedgiz.

Rees, N. S. (1973) "Auditory processing factors in language disorders: The view from Procrustes' bed," *Journal of Speech and Hearing Disorders,* **38,** 304–315.

Reichurdt, K. W. (1977) "Playing dead or running away—defense reactions during reading," *Journal of Reading,* **20,** 706–711.

Reid, J. F. (1966) "Learning to think about reading," *Educational Research,* **9,** 56–62.

Reid, J. F. (1971) "The most important R" (Part II), *Teachers' World,* 3190 (January 1st.); 18.

Reid, J. F. (1973) "Towards a theory of literacy," in Clark, M., and Milne, A. (eds.), *Reading and Related Skills,* London: Ward Lock.

Resnick, D. P. and Resnick, L. B. (1977) "The nature of literacy: An historical exploration," *Harvard Educational Review,* **47,** 370–386.

Richardson, J. T. E. (1975a) "The effect of word imageability in acquired dyslexia," *Neuropsychologia,* **13,** 281–288.

Richardson, J. T. E. (1975b) "Further evidence on the effect of word imageability in dyslexia," *Quarterly Journal of Experimental Psychology,* **27,** 445–449.

Richek, M. A. (1976) "Effect of sentence complexity on the reading comprehension of syntactic structures," *Journal of Educational Psychology,* **68,** 800–806.

Richek, M. A. (1976–1977) "Reading comprehension of anaphoric forms in varying linguistic contexts," *Reading Research Quarterly,* **12,** 145–165.

Rickards, J. P., and August, G. J. (1975) "Generative underlining strategies in prose recall," *Journal of Educational Psychology,* **67,** 860–865.

Rico, G. L. (1978) "Reading for non-literal meaning," in Eisner, E. W. (ed.), *Reading, the Arts, and the Creation of Meaning.* Reston, Va.: National Art Education Association.

Riding, R. J., and Shore, J. M. (1974) "A comparison of two methods of improving prose comprehension in educationally subnormal children," *British Journal of Educational Psychology,* **44,** 300–303.

Rieck, B. J. (1977) "How content teachers telegraph messages against reading," *Journal of Reading,* **20,** 646–648.

Risberg, J., and Ingvar, D. H. (1973) "Patterns of activation in the grey matter of the dominant hemisphere during memorizing and reasoning," *Brain,* **96,** 737–756.

Rizzo, N. D. (1939) "Studies in visual and auditory memory span with special reference to reading disability," *Journal of Experimental Education,* **8,** 208–244.

Roberts, T. (1980) "Strategies for helping the impulsive reader," *Reading,* **14,** 3–9.

Robertson, J. E. (1968) "Pupil understanding of connectives in reading," *Reading Research Quarterly,* **3,** 387–417.

Robinson, H. M. (1946) *Why Pupils Fail in Reading.* Chicago: University of Chicago Press.

Robinson, H. M. (1953a) "Diagnosis and treatment of poor readers with vision problems," *Clinical Studies in Reading II, Supplementary Educational Monographs* (University of Chicago), **77,** 9–28.

Robinson, H. M. (1953b) "Some poor readers have emotional problems," *Reading Teacher,* **6,** 25–33.

Robinson, H. M. (1968) "Visual efficiency and reading status in the elementary school," in Robinson, H. M., and Smith, H. K. (eds.), *Clinical Studies in Reading III. Supplementary Educational Monographs* (University of Chicago) **97,** 49–65.

Robinson, H. M. (1972a) "Perceptual training—does it result in reading improvement?" in Aukerman, R. C. (ed.), *Some Persistent Questions on Beginning Reading.* Newark, Del.: IRA.

Robinson, H. M. (1972b) "Visual and auditory modalities related to methods for beginning reading," *Reading Research Quarterly,* **8,** 7–39.

Robinson, J. (1967) *The Development of Certain Pronunciation Skills in the Case of Suffixed Words,* unpublished doctoral dissertation, Harvard University.

Roettger, D. (1980) "Elementary students' attitudes toward reading," *Reading Teacher,* **33,** 451–453.

Rommetveit, R. (1974) *On Message Structure.* London: Wiley.

Rosen, B. C. (1956) "The achievement syndrome. A psychocultural dimension of social stratification," *American Sociological Review,* **21,** 205–211.

Rosenbloom, A. A., Jr., (1968) "The relationship between aniseikonia and achievement in reading," in Robinson, H. M., and Smith, H. K. (eds.), *Clinical Studies in Reading III. Supplementary Educational Monographs* (University of Chicago), **97,** 109–116.

Rosenthal, R., and Jacobson, L. (1968) *Pygmalion in the Classroom: Teachers' Expectations and Pupils' Intellectual Development.* New York: Holt, Rinehart and Winston.

Rosinski, R. R. (1977) "Picture-word interference is semantically based," *Child Development,* **48,** 643–647.

Rosinski, R. R., Golinkoff, R. M., and Kukish, K. (1975) "Automatic semantic processing in a picture-word interference task," *Child Development,* **46,** 247–253.

Rothbart, M., Dalfen, S., and Barrett, R. (1971) "Effects of teacher's expectancy on student-teacher interaction," *Journal of Educational Psychology,* **62,** 49–54.

Rothkopf, E. Z. (1965) "Some theoretical and experimental approaches to problems in written instruction," in Krumboltz, J. (ed.), *Learning and the Educational Process.* Chicago: Rand McNally.

Rothkopf, E. Z. (1966) "Learning from written instructive materials: An exploration of the control of inspection behavior by test-like events," *American Educational Research Journal,* **3,** 241–249.

Rourke, B. P. (1975) "Brain-behavior relationships in children with learning disabilities: A research program," *American Psychologist,* **30,** 911–920.

Rourke, B. P. (1976) "Issues in the neuropsychological assessment of children with learning disabilities," *Canadian Psychological Review,* **17,** 89–102.

Rourke, B. P. (1978) "Reading, spelling, and arithmetic disabilities: A neuropsychological perspective," in Myklebust, H. R. (ed.), *Progress in Learning Disabilities, Vol. IV.* New York: Grune and Stratton.

Rousseau, J. J. (1762) Émile (trans. B. Foxley). London: Dent.

Rozhdestvensky, N. S. (ed.), (1961) *S. P. Redozubov. Methods of Teaching Reading and Writing in Primary School: Selected Works* (in Russian). Moscow: Academy of Education Sciences, R.S.F.S.R.

Rozin, P., and Gleitman, L. R. (1977) "The structure and acquisition of reading II: The reading process and the acquisition of the alphabetic principle," in Reber, A. S., and Scarborough, D. L. (eds.), *Toward a Psychology of Reading.* Hillsdale, N.J.: Erlbaum.

Rozin, P., Poritsky, S., and Sotsky, R. (1971) "American children with reading problems can easily learn to read English represented by Chinese characters," *Science,* **171,** 1264–1267.

Rubenstein, H., Lewis, S. S., and Rubenstein, M. A. (1971a) "Homographic entries in the internal lexicon: Effects of systematicity and relative frequency of meaning," *Journal of Verbal Learning and Verbal Behavior,* **10,** 57–62.

Rubenstein, H., Lewis, S. S., and Rubenstein, M. A. (1971b) "Evidence for phonemic recoding in visual word recognition," *Journal of Verbal Learning and Verbal Behavior,* **10,** 645–657.

Rubenstein, H., Richter, M. L., and Kay, E. J. (1975) "Pronounceability and the visual recognition of nonsense words," *Journal of Verbal Learning and Verbal Behavior,* **14,** 651–657.

Rubovits, P. C., and Maehr, M. L. (1971), "Pygmalion Analyzed: Toward an Explanation of the Rosenthal-Jacobson Findings," paper presented at the annual meeting of AERA, New York.

Ruch, M. D., and Levin, J. R. (1977) "Pictorial organization versus verbal repetition of children's prose: Evidence for processing differences," *AV Communication Review,* **25,** 269–280.

Rudel, R. G. (1978) "Neuroplasticity: Implications for development and education," in Chall, J. S., and Mirsky, A. F. (eds.), *Education and the Brain.* Chicago: University of Chicago Press.

Rudner, R. S. (1966) *Philosophy of Social Sciences,* Englewood Cliffs, N.J.: Prentice–Hall.

Rumelhart, D. E. (1975) "Notes on a schema for stories," in Bobrow, D., and Collins, A. (eds.), *Representation and Understanding: Studies in Cognitive Science.* New York: Academic Press.

Rumelhart, D. E. (1977a) "Understanding and summarizing brief stories," in LaBerge, D., and Samuels, S. J. (eds.), *Basic Processes in Reading: Perception and Comprehension.* Hillsdale, N.J.: Erlbaum.

Rumelhart, D. E. (1977b) "Toward an interactive model of reading," in Dornič, S. (ed.), *Attention and Performance VI.* Hillsdale, N.J.: Erlbaum.

Rumelhart, D. E., and Ortony, A. (1977) "The representation of knowledge in memory," in Anderson, R. C., Spiro, R. J. and Montague, W. E. (eds.), *Schooling and the Acquisition of Knowledge.* Hillsdale, N.J.: Erlbaum.

Rupley, W. H., Ashe, M., and Buckland, P. (1979) "The relation between the discrimination of letter-like forms and word recognition," *Reading World,* **19,** 113–123.

Russell, D. H. (1943) "Note on a new theory about visual functioning and reading disabilities," *Journal of Educational Psychology,* **34,** 115–120.

Russell, D. H. (1970) *The Dynamics of Reading.* Waltham, Mass.: Ginn-Blaisdell.

Rutter, M. (1978) "Prevalence and types of dyslexia," in Benton, A. L., and Pearl, D. (eds.), *Dyslexia: An Appraisal of Current Knowledge.* New York: Oxford University Press.

Rutter, M., Tizard, J., and Whitmore, K. (eds.), (1970) *Education, Health and Behaviour.* London: Longmans, and New York: Wiley.

Rutter, M., and Yule, W. (1973) "Specific reading retardation," in Mann, L., and Sabatino, D. (eds.), *The First Review of Special Education.* Philadelphia, Pa.: Buttonwood Farms.

Rutter, M., and Yule, W. (1977) "Reading retardation and antisocial behavior—the nature of the association," in Reid, J. F. (ed.), *Reading: Problems and Practices* (2nd. ed.). London: Ward Lock.

Sachs, J. S. (1967) "Recognition memory for synactic and semantic aspects of connected discourse," *Perception and Psychophysics,* **2,** 437–442.

Sachs, J. S. (1974) "Memory in reading and listening to discourse," *Memory and Cognition,* **2,** 95–100.

Sadick, T. L., and Ginsburg, B. E. (1978) "The development of the lateral functions and reading ability," *Cortex,* **14,** 3–11.

Saffran, E. M., and Marin, O. S. M. (1977) "Reading without phonology: Evidence from aphasia," *Quarterly Journal of Experimental Psychology,* **29,** 515–525.

Sakamoto, T., and Makita, K. (1973) "Japan," in Downing, J. (ed.), *Comparative Reading.* New York: Macmillan.

Saksena, H. P. (1970) "Framework for analysis of functional literacy," *Literacy Discussion,* **1,** 7–30.

Samph, T. (1974) "Teacher behavior and the reading performance of below-average achievers," *Journal of Educational Research,* **67,** 268–270.

Sampson, O. C. (1962) "Reading skill at eight years in relation to speech and other factors," *British Journal of Educational Psychology,* **32,** 12–17.

Sampson, O. C. (1969) "A study of incentives in remedial teaching," *Reading,* **1,** 6–10.

Samuels, F. (1943) "Sex differences in reading achievement," *Journal of Educational Research,* **36,** 594–603.

Samuels, S. J. (1967) "Attentional processes in reading: The effect of pictures on the acquisition of reading responses," *Journal of Educational Psychology,* **58,** 337–342.

Samuels, S. J. (1969) "Cross-national studies in reading: The relationship between the sound-letter correspondence in language and reading achievement," in Figurel, J. A. (ed.), *Reading and Realism.* Newark, Del.: IRA.

Samuels, S. J. (1970) "Effects of pictures on learning to read, comprehension, and attitudes," *Review of Educational Research,* **40,** 397–407.

Samuels, S. J. (1971) "Letter name versus letter sound knowledge in learning to read," *Reading Teacher,* **24,** 604–608.

Samuels, S. J. (1975) "Establishing appropriate purpose for reading and its effect on flexibility of reading rate," *Journal of Educational Psychology,* **67,** 38–43.

Samuels, S. J. (1976a) "Automatic decoding and reading comprehension," *Language Arts,* **53,** 323–325.

Samuels, S. J. (1976b) "Hierarchical subskills in the reading acquisition process," in Guthrie, J. T. (ed.), *Aspects of Reading Acquisition.* Baltimore: Johns Hopkins University Press.

Samuels, S. J. (1977) "Introduction to theoretical models of reading," in Otto, W., Peters, N. A., and Peters, C. W. (eds.), *Reading Problems: A Multidisciplinary Perspective.* Reading, Mass.: Addison-Wesley.

Samuels, S. J. (1979) "The method of repeated readings," *Reading Teacher,* **32,** 403–408.

Samuels, S. J., Begy, G., and Chen, C. C. (1975–1976) "Comparison of word recognition speed and strategies of less skilled and more highly skilled readers," *Reading Research Quarterly,* **11,** 72–86.

Samuels, S. J., Dahl, P., and Archwamety, T. (1974) "Effect of hypothesis/test training on reading skill," *Journal of Educational Psychology,* **66,** 835–844.

Samuels, S. J., Miller, N. L., Eisenberg, P. (1979) "Practice effects on the unit of word recognition," *Journal of Educational Psychology,* **71,** 514–520.

Samuels, S. J., and Schachter, S. W. (1978) "Controversial issues in beginning reading instruction: Meaning versus subskill emphasis," in Pflaum-Connor, S. (ed.), *Aspects of Reading Education.* Berkeley, Calif.: McCutchan.

Samuels, S. J., and Turnure, J. E. (1974) "Attention and reading achievement in first-grade boys and girls," *Journal of Educational Psychology,* **66,** 29–32.

Santrock, J. W., and Ross, M. (1975) "Effects of social comparison on facilitative self-control in young children," *Journal of Educational Psychology,* **67,** 193–197.

Sartain, H. W. (1960) "The Roseville experiment with individualized reading," *Reading Teacher,* **13,** 277–281.

Sasanuma, S. (1975) "Kana and Kanji processing in Japanese aphasics," *Brain and Language,* **2,** 369–383.

Sasanuma, S., and Fujimura, O. (1971) "Selective impairment of phonetic and non-phonetic transcription of words in Japanese aphasic patients: Kana vs. Kanji in visual recognition and writing," *Cortex,* **7,** 1–18.

Sasanuma, S., and Fujimura, O. (1972) "An analysis of writing errors in Japanese aphasic patients: Kanji vs. Kana words," *Cortex,* **8,** 265–282.

Satz, P. (1976) "Cerebral dominance and reading disability: An old problem revisited," in Knights, R. M., and Bakker, D. J. (eds.), *The Neuropsychology of Learning Disorders: Theoretical Approaches.* Baltimore: University Park Press.

Satz, P., and Friel, J. (1973) "Some predictive antecedents of specific reading disability: A preliminary one-year follow-up," in Satz, P., and Ross, J. J. (eds.), *The Disabled Learner: Early Detection and Intervention.* Rotterdam, Netherlands: Rotterdam University Press.

Satz, P., and Friel, J. (1974) "Some predictive antecedents of specific reading disability: A preliminary two-year follow-up," *Journal of Learning Disabilities,* **7,** 437–444.

Satz, P., Friel, J., and Goebel, R. A. (1975) "Some predictive antecedents of specific reading disability: A three-year follow-up," *Bulletin of the Orton Society,* **25,** 91–110.

Satz, P., Friel, J., and Rudegeair, F. (1976) "Some predictive antecedents of specific reading disability: A two-, three-, and four-year follow-up," in Guthrie, J. T. (ed.), *Aspects of Reading Acquisition.* Baltimore: Johns Hopkins University Press.

Satz, P., and Sparrow, S. S. (1970) "Specific developmental dyslexia: A theoretical formulation," in Bakker, D. J., and Satz, P. (eds.), *Specific Reading Disability:*

Advances in Theory and Method. Rotterdam, Netherlands: Rotterdam University Press.

Satz, P., Taylor, G., Friel, J., and Fletcher, J. (1978) "Some developmental and predictive precursors of reading disabilities: A six year follow-up," in Benton, A. L., and Pearl, D. (eds.), *Dyslexia: An Appraisal of Current Knowledge.* New York: Oxford University Press.

Satz, P., and van Nostrand, G. K. (1973) "Developmental dyslexia: An evaluation of a theory," in Satz, P., and Ross, J. (eds.), *The Disabled Learner: Early Detection and Intervention.* Rotterdam, Netherlands: Rotterdam University Press.

Savin, H. B. (1972) "What the child knows about speech when he starts to learn to read," in Kavanagh, J. F., and Mattingly, I. G. (eds.), *Language by Ear and by Eye.* Cambridge, Mass.: MIT Press.

Sawyer, W. E., and Sawyer, J. C. (1980) "Relationships of Preschool Experiences and Reading Readiness Skills: Predicting the Most Efficient Reading Instruction," paper presented at the annual convocation of the Northeastern Educational Research Association, Ellenville, New York.

Schallert, D. L. (1976) "Improving memory for prose: The relationship between depth of processing and context," *Journal of Verbal Learning and Verbal Behavior,* **15,** 621–632.

Schank, R., and Abelson, R. (1977) *Scripts, Plans, Goals, and Understanding.* Hillsdale, N.J.: Erlbaum.

Scheerer, E. (1972) "Order of report and order of scanning in tachistoscopic recognition," *Canadian Journal of Psychology,* **26,** 382–390.

Scheerer-Neumann, G. (1978) "A functional analysis of reading disability: The utilization of intraword redundancy by good and poor readers," in Lesgold, A. M., Pellegrino, J. W., Fokkema, S. D., and Glaser, R. (eds.), *Cognitive Psychology and Instruction.* New York: Plenum.

Schiefelbusch, R. L., and Lloyd, L. L. (eds.), (1974) *Language Perspectives—Acquisition, Retardation, and Intervention.* Baltimore: University Park Press.

Schlesinger, I. M. (1968) *Sentence Structure and the Reading Process.* The Hague, Netherlands: Mouton.

Scholl, D. M., and Ryan, E. B. (1980) "Development of metalinguistic performances in the early school years," *Language and Speech,* **23** (Part 2), 199–211.

Schonell, F. J. (1942) *Backwardness in the Basic Subjects.* Edinburgh, Scotland: Oliver and Boyd.

Schonell, F. J., and Goodacre, E. (1974) *The Psychology and Teaching of Reading* (5th ed.). Edinburgh, Scotland: Oliver and Boyd.

Schrock, R. E., and Grossman, M. (1961) "Pilot study: Motivation in reading," *Reading Teacher,* **15,** 119–121.

Schubert, D. G. (1959) "Teachers and word analysis skills," *Journal of Developmental Reading,* **2,** 62–64.

Schubert, D. G., and Walton, H. N. (1968) "Effects of induced astigmatism," *Reading Teacher,* **21,** 547–551.

Schuell, H. (1950) "Paraphasia and paralexia," *Journal of Speech and Hearing Disorders,* **15,** 291–306.

Scragg, D. G. (1974) *A History of English Spelling.* Manchester, England: Manchester University Press, and New York: Barnes and Noble.

Scriven, M. (1972) "The concept of comprehension: From semantics to software," in Freedle, R. O., and Carroll, J. B. (eds.), *Language Comprehension and the Acquisition of Knowledge.* New York: Wiley.

Searle, C. (1972) *The Forsaken Lover.* London: Routledge and Kegan Paul.

Seaver, W. B. (1971) *Effects of Naturally-Induced Teacher Expectancies on the Academic Performance of Pupils in Primary Grades,* unpublished doctoral dissertation, University of Illinois.

Segalowitz, S. J., and Gruber, F. A. (eds.), (1977) *Language Development and Neurological Theory.* New York: Academic Press.

Selfridge, O. G., and Neisser, U. (1960) "Pattern recognition by machine," *Scientific American,* **203,** 60–68.

Selye, H. (1936) "A syndrome produced by diverse nocuous agents," *Nature,* **138,** 32.

Semel, E. M., and Wiig, E. H. (1975) "Comprehension of syntactic structures and critical verbal elements by children with learning disabilities," *Journal of Learning Disabilities,* **8,** 53–58.

Semmes, J. (1968) "Hemispheric specialization: A possible clue to mechanism," *Neuropsychologia,* **6,** 11–26.

Semmes, J., Weinstein, S., Ghent, L., and Teuber, H. L. (1960) *Somatosensory Changes after Penetrating Brain Wounds in Man.* Cambridge, Mass.: Harvard University Press.

Senf, G. M. (1969) "Development of immediate memory for bisensory stimuli in normal children and children with learning disorders," *Developmental Psychology,* **1,** 1–28.

Serafica, F. C., and Sigel, I. E. (1970) "Styles of categorization and reading disability," *Journal of Reading Behavior,* **2,** 105–115.

Shafer, R. E., and Shafer, S. M. (1975) "Teacher attitudes towards children's language in West Germany and England," in Moyle, D. (ed.), *Reading: What of the Future?* London: Ward Lock.

Shafto, M. (1973) "The space for case," *Journal of Verbal Learning and Verbal Behavior,* **12,** 551–562.

Shallice, T., and Warrington, E. K. (1975) "Word recognition in a phonemic dyslexic patient," *Quarterly Journal of Experimental Psychology,* **27,** 189–199.

Shanahan, T. (1980) "The impact of writing instruction on learning to read," *Reading World,* **19,** 357–368.

Shankweiler, D. (1966) "Effects of temporal lobe damage on perception of dichotically presented melodies," *Journal of Comparative Physiology and Psychology,* **62,** 115–119.

Shankweiler, D., and Liberman, I. Y. (1972) "Misreading: A search for causes," in Kavanagh, J. F., and Mattingly, I. G. (eds.), *Language by Ear and by Eye.* Cambridge, Mass.: MIT Press.

Shankweiler, D., and Liberman, I. Y. (1976) "Exploring the relations between reading and speech," in Knights, R. M., and Bakker, D. J. (eds.), *The Neuropsychology of Learning Disorders: Theoretical Approaches.* Baltimore: University Park Press.

Shankweiler, D., Liberman, I. Y., Mark, L. S., Fowler, C. A., and Fischer, F. W. (1979) "The speech code and learning to read," *Journal of Experimental Psychology: Human Learning and Memory,* **5,** 531–545.

Shankweiler, D., and Studdert-Kennedy, M. (1967) "Identification of consonants and vowels presented to left and right ears," *Quarterly Journal of Experimental Psychology,* **19,** 59–63.

Shannon, C. E. (1951) "Prediction and entropy of printed English," *Bell System Technical Journal,* **30,** 50–64.

Shapson, S., and Kaufman, D. (1976) "French immersion: A Western perspective," in Swain, M. (ed.), *Bilingualism in Canadian Education: Issues and Research (Canadian Society for the Study of Education Yearbook), Vol. 3.* Edmonton, Alberta: Canadian Society for the Study of Education.

Shapson, S., Wright, E. N., Eason, G., and Fitzgerald, J. (1980) "An experimental study of effects of class size," *American Educational Research Journal,* **17,** 141–152.

Shebilske, W. (1975) "Reading eye movements from an information-processing point of view," in Massaro, D. W. (ed.), *Understanding Language.* New York: Academic Press.

Sheldon, W. D., and Carrillo, L. (1952) "Relation of parents, home and certain developmental characteristics to children's reading ability," *Elementary School Journal,* **52,** 262–270.

Shepherd, D. L. (1960a) *Effective Reading in Social Studies.* Evanston, Ill.: Row, Peterson.

Shepherd, D. L. (1960b) *Effective Reading in Science.* Evanston, Ill.: Row, Peterson.

Shepherd, D. L. (1973) *Comprehensive High School Reading Methods.* Columbus, Ohio: Merrill.

Sherman, M. (1968) "Psychiatric insights into reading problems," in Schubert, D. G., and Torgerson, T. L. (eds.), *Readings in Reading: Practice, Theory, Research.* New York: Crowell.

Shnayer, S. W. (1969) "Relationships between reading interest and reading comprehension," in Figurel, J. A. (ed.), *Reading and Realism,* Newark, Del.: IRA.

Shultz, T. R. (1974) "Development of the appreciation of riddles," *Child Development,* **45,** 100–105.

Shultz, T. R. and Pilon, R. (1973) "Development of the ability to detect linguistic ambiguity," *Child Development,* **44,** 728–733.

Shuy, R. W. (1969) "Some language and cultural differences in a theory of reading," in Goodman, K. S., and Fleming, J. T. (eds.), *Psycholinguistics and the Teaching of Reading.* Newark, Del.: IRA.

Sievers, C. H., and Brown, B. D. (1946) *Manual for Improving Your Eye Movements in Reading.* Wichita, Kansas: McGuin.

Sigel, I. E. (1978) "The development of picture comprehension," in Randhawa, B. S., and Coffman, W. E. (eds.), *Visual Learning, Thinking, and Communication.* New York: Academic Press.

Silver, A. A. (1968) "Diagnostic considerations in children with reading disability," in Natchez, G. (ed.), *Children with Reading Problems.* New York: Basic Books.

Silverman, J. S., Fite, M. W., and Mosher, M. M. (1959) "Clinical findings in reading disability children," *American Journal of Orthopsychiatry,* **29,** 298–314.

Simmons, J. (1970) "Towards an evaluation of adult education in a developing country," an unpublished report submitted to UNESCO, cited by Saksena, H. P., "Framework for analysis of functional literacy," *Literacy Discussion,* **1,** 7–30.

Simmons-Martin, A. (1972) "The oral aural procedure: Theoretical basis and rationale," *Volta Review,* **74,** 541–554.

Simon, H. A. (1972) "On the development of the processor," in Farnham-Diggory, S. (ed.), *Information Processing in Children.* New York: Academic Press.

Simons, H. D. (1975) "Transformational phonology and reading acquisition," *Journal of Reading Behavior,* **7,** 49–59.

Simpson, R. L. (1962) "Parental influence, anticipatory socialization, and social mobility," *American Sociological Review,* **27,** 517–522.

Sinatra, R., and Kinsler, K. T. (1976) "Values strategies in the teaching of reading," *Elementary School Journal,* **77,** 159–164.

Sinclair, A., Jarvella, R. J., and Levelt, W. J. M. (eds.), (1978) *The Child's Conception of Language.* New York: Springer.

Sinclair, H. (1978) "Conceptualization and awareness in Piaget's theory and its relevance to the child's conception of language," in Sinclair, A., Jarvella, R. J., and Levelt, W. J. M. (eds.), *The Child's Conception of Language.* New York: Springer.

Singer, H. (1964) "Substrata-factor theory of reading: Grade and sex differences in reading of the elementary school level," in Figurel, J. A. (ed.), *Improvement of Reading Through Classroom Practice.* Newark, Del.: IRA.

Singer, H. (1966) "Conceptualization in learning to read," in Schick, G. B., and May, M. M. (eds.), *New Frontiers in College-Adult Reading.* Milwaukee, Wisc.: National Reading Conference.

Singer, H. (1971) "Theories, models, and strategies for learning to read," in Greene, F. P. (ed.), *Reading: The Right to Participate.* Milwaukee, Wisc.: National Reading Conference.

Singer, H., and Ruddell, R. B. (eds.), (1970) *Theoretical Models and Processes of Reading.* Newark, Del.: IRA.

Singer, H., and Ruddell, R. B. (eds.), (1976) *Theoretical Models and Processes of Reading* (2nd. ed.). Newark, Del.: IRA.

Singer, H., Samuels, S. J. and Spiroff, J. (1973–1974) "The effect of pictures and contextual conditions on learning responses to printed words," *Reading Research Quarterly*, **9**, 555–567.

Skinner, B. F. (1953) *Science and Human Behavior*. New York: Macmillan.

Skinner, B. F. (1957) *Verbal Behavior*. N.Y.: Appleton.

Sladen, B. K. (1970) "Inheritance of dyslexia," *Bulletin of the Orton Society*, **20**, 30–40.

Sladen, B. K. (1972) "Some genetic aspects of dyslexia," *Bulletin of the Orton Society*, **22**, 41–53.

Slobin, D. I. (1966) "Soviet methods of investigating child language," in Smith, F., and Miller, G. A., (eds.), *The Genesis of Language*. Cambridge, Mass.: M.I.T.

Slobin, D. (1966) "Grammatical transformations and sentence comprehension in childhood and adulthood," *Journal of Verbal Learning and Verbal Behavior*, **5**, 219–227.

Smalley, W. A. (1964) "Writing systems and their characteristics," in Smalley, W. A. (ed.), *Orthography Studies*. London: United Bible Societies.

Smith, B. O. (1980) "Pedagogical education: How about reform?" *Phi Delta Kappan*, **62**, 87–91.

Smith, D. E. P. (1969) "Increasing task behavior difficulty in a language-arts program by providing reinforcement," *Journal of Experimental Child Psychology*, **8**, 45–62.

Smith, E. E. (1978) "Theories of semantic memory," in Estes, W. K. (ed.), *Handbook of Learning and Cognitive Processes, Vol. 6: Linguistic Functions in Cognitive Theory*. New York: Wiley.

Smith, E. E., and Spoehr, K. T. (1974) "The perception of printed English: A theoretical perspective," in Kantowitz, B. H. (ed.), *Human Information Processing: Tutorials in Performance and Cognition*. Hillsdale, N.J.: Erlbaum.

Smith, F. (1971) *Understanding Reading: A Psycholinguistic Analysis of Reading and Learning to Read*. New York: Holt.

Smith, F. (1975) "The relation between spoken and written language," in Lenneberg, E. H., and Lenneberg, E. (eds.), *Foundations of Language Development, Vol. 2*. New York: Academic Press.

Smith, F. (1977) "Making sense of reading—and of reading instruction," *Harvard Educational Review*, **47**, 386–395.

Smith, F. (1978) *Understanding Reading: A Psycholinguistic Analysis of Reading and Learning to Read*. (2nd ed.). New York: Holt.

Smith, F. (1980) "The language arts and the learner's mind," in Bray, G., and Pugh, A. K. (eds.), *The Reading Connection*. London: Ward Lock.

Smith, F. and Miller, G. A. (1966) *The Genesis of Language: A Psycholinguistic Approach*. Cambridge, Mass.: M.I.T. Press.

Smith, H. K. (1967) "The responses of good and poor readers when asked to read for different purposes," *Reading Research Quarterly*, **3**, 53–83.

Smith, H. K. (ed.), (1968) *Perception and Reading*. Newark, Del.: IRA.

Smith, H. K. (1972) "Reading for different purposes," in Southgate, V. (ed.), *Literacy at All Levels*. London: Ward Lock.

Smith, H. P., and Dechant, E. V. (1961) *Psychology in Teaching Reading*. Englewood Cliffs, N.J.: Prentice-Hall.

Smith, I. M. (1964) *Spatial Ability: Its Educational and Social Significance*. London: University of London Press.

Smith, P. T. (1980) "Linguistic information in spelling," in Frith, U. (ed.), *Cognitive Processes in Spelling*. New York: Academic Press.

Smith, P. T., and Baker, R. G. (1976) "The influence of English spelling patterns on pronunciation," *Journal of Verbal Learning and Verbal Behavior*, **15**, 267–285.

Smith, P. T., and Groat, A. (1979) "Spelling patterns, letter cancellation and the processing of text," in Kolers, P. A., Wrolstad, M., and Bouma, H. (eds.), *Processing of Visible Language, I*. New York: Plenum.

Snow, R. E. (1969) "Unfinished Pygmalion," *Contemporary Psychology*, **14**, 197–199.

Söderbergh, R. (1971) *Reading in Early Childhood: A Linguistic Study of a Preschool Child's Gradual Acquisition of Reading Ability*. Stockholm: Almqvist and Wiksell. (Reprinted 1977, Washington, D.C.: Georgetown University Press.)

Söderbergh, R. (1976) "Learning to read between two and five: Some observations on normal hearing and deaf children," in Rameh, C. (ed.), *Semantics: Theory and Application*. Washington, D.C.: Georgetown University Press.

Sokhin, F. A. (1974) "Preschoolers awareness of speech and preparation for learning literacy" (in Russian), *Voprosy Psikhologii*, 20, 138–142.

Sokolov, A. N. (1972) *Inner Speech and Thought*. New-York: Plenum.

Southgate, V. (1965) "Approaching i.t.a. results with caution," *Educational Research*, **7**, 83–96.

Southgate, V. (1969) "i.t.a. in practice: Evidence from interviews," in Warburton, F. W., and Southgate V., *i.t.a.: An Independent Evaluation*. London: Murray, and Edinburgh, Scotland: Chambers.

Southgate, V. (1973) "The language arts in informal British primary schools," *Reading Teacher*, **26**, 367–373.

Southgate, V. (1980) "The Books 7 to 9 Year Olds Read and Their Views on Them," paper presented at the annual conference of the United Kingdom Reading Association, Warwick, England, August 1, 1980.

Southgate, V., and Roberts, G. R. (1970) *Reading—Which Approach?* London: University of London Press.

Spache, G. D. (1940) "The role of visual defects in spelling and reading disabilities," *American Journal of Orthopsychiatry*, **10**, 229–239.

Spache, G. D. (1957) "Personality patterns of retarded readers," *Journal of Educational Research*, **50**, 461–469.

Spache, G. D. (1968) "Contributions of allied fields to the teaching of reading," in Robinson, H. M. (ed.), *Innovation and Change in Reading Instruction*, 67th

Yearbook, National Society for the Study of Education, Part II.

Spache, G. D. (1976) *Diagnosing and Correcting Reading Disabilities.* Boston, Mass.: Allyn and Bacon.

Spache, G. D., and Baggett, M. E. (1965) "What do teachers know about phonics and syllabication?" *Reading Teacher,* **19,** 96–99.

Sparks, R., and Geschwind, N. (1968) "Dichotic listening in man after section of neocortical commissures," *Cortex,* **4,** 3–16.

Sparrow, S. S., and Satz, P. (1970) "Dyslexia, laterality and neuropsychological development," in Bakker, D. J., and Satz, P. (eds.), *Specific Reading Disability: Advances in Theory and Method.* Rotterdam, Netherlands: Rotterdam University Press.

Spearritt, D. (1962) *Listening Comprehension—A Factorial Analysis.* Melbourne, Victoria, Australia: Australian Council for Educational Research.

Spearritt, D. (1972) "Identification of subskills of reading comprehension by maximum likelihood factor analysis," *Reading Research Quarterly,* **8,** 92–111.

Spellacy, F. (1970) "Lateral preferences in the identification of patterned stimuli," *Journal of the Acoustical Society of America,* **47,** 574–578.

Sperry, B., Staver, N., Reiner, B. S., and Ulrich, D. (1958) "Renunciation and denial in learning difficulties," *American Journal of Orthopsychiatry,* **28,** 98–111.

Sperry, R. W. (1961) "Cerebral organization and behavior," *Science,* **133,** 1749–1757.

Sperry, R. W. (1964) "The great cerebral commissure," *Scientific American,* **210,** 42–52.

Sperry, R. W. (1968) "Hemispheric disconnection and unity in conscious awareness," *American Psychologist,* **23,** 723–733.

Sperry, R. W. (1970) "Cerebral dominance in perception," in Young, F. A., and Lindsley, D. B. (eds.), *Early Experience and Visual Information Processing in Perceptual and Reading Disorders.* Washington, D.C.: National Academy of Sciences.

Sperry, R. W., and Gazzaniga, M. S. (1967) "Language following surgical disconnection of the hemispheres," in Darley, F. L. (ed.), *Brain Mechanisms Underlying Speech and Language.* New York: Grune and Stratton.

Spielberger, C. D. (1972) "Anxiety as an emotional state," in Spielberger, C. D. (ed.), *Anxiety: Current Trends in Theory and Research.* New York: Academic Press.

Spiro, R. J. (1977) "Remembering information from text: The 'state of schema' approach," in Anderson, R. C., Spiro, R. J., and Montague, W. E. (eds.), *Schooling and the Acquisition of Knowledge,* Hillsdale, N.J.: Erlbaum.

Spiro, R. J., Bruce, B. C., and Brewer, W. F. (eds.), (1980) *Theoretical Issues in Reading Comprehension.* Hillsdale, N.J.: Erlbaum.

Spoehr, K. T., and Smith, E. E. (1973) "The role of syllables in perceptual processing," *Cognitive Psychology,* **5,** 71–89.

Spoehr, K. T., and Smith, E. E. (1975) "The role of orthographic and phonotactic rules in perceiving letter patterns," *Journal of Experimental Psychology: Human Perception and Performance,* **104,** 21–34.

Spreen, O. (1976) "Post-conference summary," in Knights, R. M., and Bakker, D. J. (eds.), *The Neuropsychology of Learning Disorders: Theoretical Approaches.* Baltimore: University Park Press.

Staats, A. W. (1968) *Learning, Language, and Cognition.* New York: Holt.

Staats, A. W. (1974) "Behaviorism and cognitive theory in the study of language: A neopsycholinguistics," in Schiefelbusch, R. L., and Lloyd, L. L. (eds.), *Language Perspectives—Acquisition, Retardation, and Intervention.* Baltimore: University Park Press.

Staats, A. W., and Staats, C. K. (1962) "A comparison of the development of speech and reading behavior with implications for research," *Child Development,* **33,** 831–846.

Staats, A. W., Staats, C. K., Schutz, R. E., and Wolf, M. (1962) "The conditioning of textual responses using 'extrinsic' reinforcers," *Journal of Experimental Analysis of Behavior,* **5,** 33–40.

Stanchfield, J. M. (1973) *Sex Differences in Learning to Read.* Bloomington, Ind.: Phi Delta Kappa.

Stanford Research Institute (1977) *Survey of Basic Skills Programs for Adolescents in Seven States.* Menlo Park, Calif.: Educational Policy Research Centre.

Stanners, R. F., Forbach, G. B., and Headley, D. B. (1971) "Decision and search processes in word-nonword classification," *Journal of Experimental Psychology,* **90,** 45–50.

Stanovich, K. E. (1980) "Toward an interactive-compensatory model of individual differences in the development of reading fluency," *Reading Research Quarterly,* **16,** 32–71.

Starnes, D. R. (1969) "Visual abilities versus reading abilities," *Journal of the American Optometric Association,* **40,** 596–600.

Steffensen, M. S., Joag-Dev, C., and Anderson, R. C. (1979) "A cross-cultural perspective on reading comprehension," *Reading Research Quarterly,* **15,** 10–29.

Stein, A. H. (1971) "The effects of sex-role standards for achievement and sex-role preference on three determinants of achievement motivation," *Developmental Psychology,* **4,** 219–231.

Stein, A. H., Pohly, S. R., and Mueller, E. (1971) "The influence of masculine, feminine, and neutral tasks on children's achievement behavior, expectancies of success, and attainment values," *Child Development,* **42,** 195–207.

Stein, A. H., and Smithells, J. (1968) *The Sex-Role Standards About Achievement Held by Negro and White Children from Father-Present and Father-Absent Homes,* unpublished manuscript, Cornell University, New York.

Stein, A. H., and Smithells, J. (1969) "Age and sex differences in children's sex-role standards about achievement," *Developmental Psychology,* **1,** 252–259.

Stein, N. L., and Glenn, C. G. (1979) "An analysis of

story comprehension in elementary school children," in Freedle, R. O. (ed.), *New Directions in Discourse Processing.* Norwood, N.J.: Ablex.

Steinberg, D. D. (1973) "Phonology, reading, and Chomsky and Halle's optimal orthography," *Journal of Psycholinguistic Research,* **2,** 239–258.

Steinberg, D. D., and Steinberg, M. T. (1975) "Reading before speaking," *Visible Language,* **9,** 197–224.

Steinberg, D. D., and Yamada, J. (1978–1979) "Are whole word Kanji easier to learn than syllable Kana?" *Reading Research Quarterly,* **14,** 88–99.

Steiner, E. E. (1981) *Elementary School Sex-typed Perceptions of Reading and Their Relationship to Reading Achievement,* unpublished doctoral dissertation, University of Akron, Ohio.

Steiner, R., Wiener, M., and Cromer, W. (1971) "Comprehension training and identification for poor readers and good readers," *Journal of Educational Psychology,* **62,** 506–513.

Steinheiser, F., and Guthrie, J. (1974) "Scanning times through prose and word strings for various targets by normal and disabled readers," *Perceptual and Motor Skills,* **39,** 931–938.

Stennett, R. G., Smythe, P. C., and Hardy, M. (1975) "Hierarchical organization of reading subskills: Statistical approaches," *Journal of Reading Behavior,* **7,** 223–228.

Sternberg, R. J. (1977) *Intelligence, Information Processing, and Analogical Reasoning: The Componential Analysis of Human Abilities.* Hillsdale, N.J.: Erlbaum.

Sternberg, R. J. (1978) "Componential investigations of human intelligence," in Lesgold, A. M., Pellegrino, J. W., Fokkema, S. D., and Glaser, R. (eds.), *Cognitive Psychology and Instruction.* New York: Plenum.

Sternberg, R. J. (1979) "The nature of mental abilities," *American Psychologist,* **34,** 214–230.

Sternberg, S. (1969) "The discovery of processing stages: Extensions of Donders' method," *Acta Psychologica,* **30,** 276–315.

Stevens, D. O. (1971) "Reading difficulty and classroom acceptance," *Reading Teacher,* **25,** 52–55.

Stevenson, C. (1966) "i.t.a. with army service populations," in Mazurkiewicz, A. J. (ed.), *The Initial Teaching Aplhabet and the World of English.* New York: i.t.a. Foundation.

Stewart, R. S. (1950) "Personality maladjustment and reading achievement," *American Journal of Orthopsychiatry,* **20,** 410–417.

Stewart, W. A. (1969) "On the use of Negro dialect in the teaching of reading," in Baratz, J. C., and Shuy, R. W. (eds.), *Teaching Black Children to Read.* Washington, D.C.: Center for Applied Linguistics.

Stewart, W. A. (1975) "Teaching Blacks to read against their will," in Luelsdorff, P. A. (ed.), *Linguistic Perspectives on Black English.* Regensburg, Germany: Verlag Hans Carl.

Sticht, T. G. (1972) "Learning by listening," in Freedle, R. O., and Carroll, J. B. (eds.), *Language Comprehension and the Acquisition of Knowledge.* New York: Wiley.

Sticht, T. G. (1978a) "The acquisition of literacy by children and adults," in Murray, F. B., and Pikulski, J. J. (eds.), *The Acquisition of Reading: Cognitive, Linguistic and Perceptual Prerequisites.* Baltimore: University Park Press.

Sticht, T. G. (1978b) "Cognitive research applied to literacy training," in Lesgold, A. M., Pellegrino, J. W., Fokkema, S. D., and Glaser, R. (eds.), *Cognitive Psychology and Instruction.* New York: Plenum.

Sticht, T. G., Beck, L., Hauke, R., Kleiman, G., and James, J. (1974) *Auding and Reading: A Developmental Model.* Alexandria, Va.: Human Resources Research Organization.

Stokoe, W. C., Jr., (1972) *Semiotics and Human Sign Languages.* The Hague, Netherlands: Mouton.

Stokoe, W. C., Jr., Casterline, D. C., and Croneberg, C. G. (1965) *A Dictionary of American Sign Language on Linguistic Principles.* Washington, D.C.: Gallaudet College Press.

Stoll, P. D. (1971) *The Construction and Initial Validation of an Instrument Designed to Assess Problem Solving Proficiency in the Teaching of Reading,* unpublished doctoral dissertation, University of Illinois.

Stotsky, E. A. (1975) "Sentence-combining as a curricular activity: Its effect on written language development and reading comprehension," *Research in the Teaching of English,* 9, 30–71.

Stott, D. H., (1963) *The Social Adjustment of Children: Manual to the Bristol Social Adjustment Guides* (rev. ed.). London: University of London Press.

Stott, D. H. (1977) "Reading and emotional difficulties," in Ridsdale, A. M., Ryan, D., and Horan, J. (eds.), *Literacy for Life.* Adelaide, South Australia: Reading Development Centre.

Stott, D. H., and Sykes, E. G. (1956) *Bristol Social Adjustment Guides.* San Diego, Calif.: Educational and Industrial Testing Service.

Strang, R., and Bracken, D. K. (1957) *Making Better Readers.* Boston, Mass.: Heath.

Strang, R., McCullough, C. M., and Traxler, A. E. (1967) *The Improvement of Reading.* New York: McGraw-Hill.

Strauss, A. A., and Lehtinen, L. E. (1947) *Psychopathology and Education of the Brain-injured Child.* New York: Grune and Stratton.

Stroop, J. R. (1935) "Studies of interference in serial verbal reactions," *Journal of Experimental Psychology,* **18,** 643–662.

Stroud, J. B. (1956) *Psychology in Education.* New York: Longmans, Green.

Stubbs, M. (1976) *Language Schools and Classrooms.* London: Methuen.

Studdert-Kennedy, M. (1975) "Dichotic studies II: Two questions," *Brain and Language,* **2,** 123–130.

Studdert-Kennedy, M., and Shankweiler, D. (1970)

"Hemispheric specialization for speech perception," *Journal of the Acoustical Society of America,* **48,** 579–594.

Sulin, R. A., and Dooling, D. J. (1974) "Intrusion of a thematic idea in retention of prose," *Journal of Experimental Psychology,* **103,** 255–262.

Summers, E. G. (1977) "Instruments for assessing reading attitudes: A review of research and bibliography," *Journal of Reading Behavior,* **9,** 137–166.

Tallal, P. (1976) "Auditory perceptual factors in language and learning disabilities," in Knights, R. M., and Bakker, D. J. (eds.), *The Neuropsychology of Learning Disorders: Theoretical Approaches.* Baltimore: University Park Press.

Tallal, P. (1980) "Auditory temporal perception, phonics, and reading disabilities in children," *Brain and Language,* **9,** 182–198.

Taschow, H. G. (1976) "Reading deficiencies in the German and English languages," in Merritt, J. E. (ed.), *New Horizons in Reading.* Newark, Del.: IRA.

Taylor, D. A. (1976) "Stage analysis of reaction time," *Psychological Bulletin,* **83,** 161–191.

Taylor, E. A. (1937) *Controlled Reading: A Correlation of Diagnostic Teaching and Corrective Techniques.* Chicago: University of Chicago Press.

Taylor, E. A. (1957) "The spans: Perception, apprehension, and recognition," *American Journal of Ophthalmology,* **44,** 501–507.

Taylor, W. L. (1953) "'Cloze procedure': A new tool for measuring readability," *Journalism Quarterly,* **30,** 415–433.

Templeton, S., and Spivey, E. M. (1980) "The concept of word in young children as a function of level of cognitive development," *Research in the Teaching of English,* **14,** 265–278.

Teng, E. L., and Sperry, R. W. (1973) "Interhemispheric interaction during simultaneous bilateral presentation of letters or digits in commissurotomized patients," *Neuropsychologia,* **11,** 131–140.

Terrell, G., Durkin, K., and Wiesley, M. (1959) "Social class and the nature of the incentive in discrimination learning," *Journal of Abnormal and Social Psychology,* **59,** 270–272.

Teyler, T. J. (1975) *A Primer of Psychobiology: Brain and Behavior.* San Francisco, Calif.: Freeman.

Thackray, D. V. (1965) "A study of the relationship between some specific evidence of reading readiness and reading progress in the infant school," *British Journal of Educational Psychology,* **35,** 252–254.

Thackray, D. V. (1971) *Readiness to Read with i.t.a and t.o.* London: Chapman.

Theios, J. (1973) "Reaction time measurements in the study of memory processes: Theory and data," in Bower, G. H. (ed.), *The Psychology of Learning and Motivation, Vol. 7.* New York: Academic Press.

Theios, J., and Muise, J. G. (1977) "The word identification process in reading," in Castellan, N. J., Jr., Pisoni, D. B., and Potts, G. R. (eds.), *Cognitive Theory, Vol. 2.* Hillsdale, N.J.: Erlbaum.

Thomas, C. J. (1905) "Congenital 'word blindness' and its treatment," *Ophthalmoscope,* **3,** 380–385.

Thompson, B. B. (1963) "A longitudinal study of auditory discrimination," *Journal of Educational Research,* **56,** 376–378.

Thompson, M. C., and Massaro, D. W. (1973) "The role of visual information and redundancy in reading," *Journal of Experimental Psychology,* **98,** 49–54.

Thompson, R. A., and Dziuban, C. D. (1973) "Criterion referenced reading tests in perspective," *Reading Teacher,* **27,** 292–294.

Thorndike, E. L. (1917) "Reading as reasoning: A study of mistakes in paragraph reading," *Journal of Educational Psychology,* **8,** 323–332.

Thorndike, E. L. (1930) *Educational Psychology II, The Psychology of Learning.* New York: Teachers College, Columbia University.

Thorndike, R. L. (1941) *Children's Reading Interests.* New York: Teachers College, Columbia University.

Thorndike, R. L. (1963) *The Concepts of Over and Underachievement.* New York: Teachers College, Columbia University.

Thorndike, R. L. (1968) "Review of R. Rosenthal and L. Jacobson, *Pygmalion in the Classroom,"* *American Educational Research Journal,* **5,** 708–711.

Thorndike, R. L. (1971) "Reading as Reasoning," paper presented to Division Fifteen of the American Psychological Association, Washington, D.C., September, 1971.

Thorndike, R. L. (1973a) *Reading Comprehension Education in Fifteen Countries.* Stockholm, Sweden: Almqvist and Wiksell, and New York: Wiley.

Thorndike, R. L. (1973b) "Dilemmas in diagnosis," in MacGinitie, W. H., (ed.), *Assessment Problems in Reading.* Newark, Del.: IRA.

Thorndyke, P. W. (1977) "Cognitive structures in comprehension and memory of narrative discourse," *Cognitive Psychology,* **9,** 77–110.

Tibbetts, S. (1974) "Sex differences in children's reading preferences," *Reading Teacher,* **28,** 279–281.

Tierney, R. J., Bridge, C., and Cera, M. J. (1978–1979) "The discourse processing operations of children," *Reading Research Quarterly,* **14,** 539–573.

Tikofsky, R. S., and McInish, J. R. (1968) "Consonant discrimination by seven-year-olds," *Psychonomic Science,* **10,** 61–62.

Timmons, B. A., and Boudreau, J. P. (1972) "Auditory feedback as a major factor in stuttering," *Journal of Speech and Hearing Disorders,* **37,** 476–484.

Tinbergen, N. (1948) "Social releasers and the experimental method required for their study," *Wilson Bulletin,* **60,** 6–51.

Tinker, M. A. (1951) "Fixation pause duration in reading," *Journal of Educational Research,* **44,** 471–479.

Tinker, M. A. (1958) "Recent studies of eye-movements in reading," *Psychological Bulletin,* **55,** 215–231.

Tinker, M. A. (1965) *Bases for Effective Reading.* Minneapolis, Minn.: University of Minnesota Press.

Tinker, M. A., and McCullough, C. M. (1962) *Teaching Elementary Reading.* New York: Appleton.

Tizard Report—*see* Department of Education and Science (1972).

Tolley, C. W. (1977) "Young people's reading interests—a Gippsland Survey," in Ridsdale, A. M., Ryan, D., and Horan, J. (eds.), *Literacy for Life.* Adelaide, South Australia: Reading Development Centre.

Travers, R. M. W. (1972) *Essentials of Learning.* New York: Macmillan.

Travis, L. E. (1978a) "Neurophysiological dominance," *Journal of Speech and Hearing Disorders,* **43,** 275–277.

Travis, L. E. (1978b) "The cerebral dominance theory of stuttering: 1931–1978," *Journal of Speech and Hearing Disorders,* **43,** 278–281.

Traxler, A. E., and Jungleblut, A. (1960) *Research in Reading During Another Four Years.* New York: Educational Records Bureau.

Tregaskis, G. K. (1972) *The Relationship Between Sex Role Standards of Reading and Reading Achievement of First Grade Boys,* doctoral dissertation, State University of New York.

Treisman, A. M. (1960) "Contextual cues in selective listening," *Quarterly Journal of Experimental Psychology,* **12,** 242–248.

Treisman, A. M. (1961) *Attention and Speech.* Oxford: Oxford University Press.

Tukey, J. W. (1969) "Analyzing data: Sanctification or detective work?" *American Psychologist,* **24,** 83–90.

Turing, A. M. (1950) "Computing machinery and intelligence," *Mind,* **59,** 433–460.

Turvey, M. T. (1973) "On peripheral and central processes in vision: Inferences from an information-processing analysis of masking with patterned stimuli," *Psychological Review,* **80,** 1–52.

Turvey, M. T. (1975) "Perspectives in vision: Conception or perception?" in Duane, D. D., and Rawson, M. B. (eds.), *Reading, Perception, and Language.* Baltimore: York Press.

Tweney, R. D., and Heiman, G. W. (1977) "Psychological processing of sign language: Effects of visual disruption on sign intelligibility," *Journal of Experimental Psychology: General,* **106,** 255–268.

Tzeng, O., and Hung, D. (1980) "Reading in a nonalphabetic writing system: Some experimental studies," in Kavanagh, J. F., and Venezky, R. L. (eds.), *Orthography, Reading, and Dyslexia.* Baltimore: University Park Press.

Tzeng, O. J. L., Hung, D. L., and Wang, W. S. Y. (1977) "Speech recoding in reading Chinese characters," *Journal of Experimental Psychology: Human Learning and Memory,* **3,** 621–630.

Underwood, B. J. (1961) "Ten years of massed practice on distributed practice," *Psychological Review,* **68,** 229–247.

Underwood, B. J. (1964) "Laboratory studies of verbal learning," in Hilgard, E. R. (ed.), *Theories of Learning and Instruction* (Part 1 of the 63rd Yearbook of the National Society for the Study of Education). Chicago: University of Chicago Press.

Underwood, B. J., Ham, M., and Ekstrand, B. (1962) "Cue selection in pair-associate learning," *Journal of Experimental Psychology,* **64,** 405–409.

UNESCO (1965) *Literacy as a Factor in Development.* Paris: UNESCO.

UNESCO and UNDP Secretariat (1976) *The Experimental World Literacy Program: A Critical Assessment.* Paris: UNESCO.

Ushinsky, K. D. (1949) *Collected Works, Vol. 6* (in Russian). Moscow: Academy of Educational Sciences.

Uttal, W. (1972) *Psychobiology of Sensory Coding.* New York: Harper and Row.

Vachek, J. (1973) *Written Language,* The Hague, Netherlands: Mouton.

Valtin, R. (1978–1979) "Dyslexia: Deficit in reading or deficit in research?" *Reading Research Quarterly,* **14,** 201–221.

Valtin, R. (1979) personal communication to J. Downing.

Van Riper, C. (1971) *The Nature of Stuttering.* Englewood Cliffs, N.J.: Prentice-Hall.

Vanderheiden, G. C., and Harris-Vanderheiden, D. (1976) "Communication techniques and aids for the nonvocal severely handicapped," in Lloyd, L. L. (ed.), *Communication Assessment and Intervention Strategies.* Baltimore: University Park Press.

Varley, W. H., Levin, J. R., Severson, R. A., and Wolff, P. (1974) "Training imagery production in young children through motor involvement," *Journal of Educational Psychology,* **66,** 262–266.

Vellutino, F. R. (1977) "Alternative conceptualizations of dyslexia: Evidence in support of a verbal-deficit hypothesis," *Harvard Educational Review,* **47,** 334–354.

Vellutino, F. R. (1978) "Toward an understanding of dyslexia: Psychological factors in specific reading disability," in Benton, A. L., and Pearl, D. (eds.) *Dyslexia: An Appraisal of Current Knowledge.* New York: Oxford University Press.

Vellutino, F. R. (1979) *Dyslexia: Theory and Research.* Cambridge, Mass.: MIT Press.

Vellutino, F. R. (1980) "Dyslexia: Perceptual deficiency or perceptual inefficiency," in Kavanagh, J. F., and Venezky, R. L. (eds.), *Orthography, Reading, and Dyslexia.* Baltimore: University Park Press.

Vellutino, F. R., Harding, C. J., Phillips, F., and Steger, J. A. (1975) "Differential transfer in poor and normal readers," *Journal of Genetic Psychology,* **126,** 3–18.

Vellutino, F. R., Pruzek, R., Steger, J. A., and Meshoulam, U. (1973) "Immediate visual recall in poor and normal readers as a function of orthographic-linguistic familiarity," *Cortex,* **9,** 368–384.

Vellutino, F. R., Smith, H., Steger, J. A., and Kaman, M. (1975) "Reading disability: Age differences and the perceptual-deficit hypothesis," *Child Development,* **46,** 487–493.

Vellutino, F. R., Steger, J. A., DeSetto, L., and Phillips, F. (1975) "Immediate and delayed recognition of visual stimuli in poor and normal readers," *Journal of Experimental Psychology,* **19,** 223–232.

Vellutino, F. R., Steger, J. A., Kaman, M., and DeSetto, L. (1975) "Visual form perception in deficient and normal readers as a function of age and orthographic linguistic familiarity," *Cortex,* **11,** 22–30.

Vellutino, F. R., Steger, J. A., and Kandel, G. (1972) "Reading disability: An investigation of the perceptual-deficit hypothesis," *Cortex,* **8,** 106–118.

Vellutino, F. R., Steger, J. A., and Pruzek, R. (1973) "Inter- vs. intrasensary deficit in paired associate learning in poor and normal readers," *Canadian Journal of Behavioural Science,* **5,** 111–123.

Venezky, R. L. (1967) "English orthography: Its graphical structure and its relation to sound," *Reading Research Quarterly,* **2,** 75–105.

Venezky, R. L. (1970a) *The Structure of English Orthography.* The Hague, Netherlands: Mouton.

Venezky, R. L. (1970b) "Regularity in reading and spelling," in Levin, H., and Williams, J. P. (eds.), *Basic Studies on Reading.* New York: Basic Books.

Venezky, R. L. (1970c) "Non-standard language and reading," *Elementary English,* **47,** 334–345.

Venezky, R. L. (1976) *Theoretical and Experimental Bases for Teaching Reading.* The Hague, Netherlands: Mouton.

Venezky, R. L. (1977) "Research on reading processes: An historical perspective," *American Psychologist,* **32,** 339–345.

Venezky, R. L., Massaro, D. W., and Weber, R. M. (1976) "Modeling the reading process," in Singer, H., and Ruddell, R. B. (eds.), *Theoretical Models and Processes of Reading* (2nd. ed.). Newark, Del.: IRA.

Verbrugge, R. R., and McCarrell, N. S. (1977) "Metaphoric comprehension: Studies in reminding and resembling," *Cognitive Psychology,* **9,** 494–533.

Vernon, M. D. (1957) *Backwardness in Reading.* London: Cambridge University Press.

Vernon, M. D. (1962) "Specific dyslexia," *British Journal of Educational Psychology,* **32,** 143–150.

Vernon, M. D. (1971) *Reading and its Difficulties.* London: Cambridge University Press.

Viitaniemi, E. (1965) "Differences in reading between the sexes," *Kasvatus ja Koulu (Education and School),* **51,** 122–131 and 173–180.

Vince, M. A. (1953) "The part played by intellectual processes in a sensory-motor performance," *Quarterly Journal of Experimental Psychology,* **5,** 75–86.

Vitz, P. C. (1966) "Affect as a function of stimulus variation," *Journal of Experimental Psychology,* **71,** 74–79.

Vogel, S. A. (1974) "Syntactic abilities in normal and dyslexic children," *Journal of Learning Disabilities,* **7,** 103–109.

Vogel, S. A. (1977) "Morphological ability in normal and dyslexic children," *Journal of Learning Disabilities,* **10,** 41–49.

Vorhaus, P. G. (1968) "Rorschach configurations associated with reading disability," in Natchez, G. (ed.), *Children with Reading Problems.* New York: Basic Books.

Vygotsky, L. S. (1934) *Thought and Language* (in Russian) English trans., 1962 by E. Hanfmann and G. Vakar. Cambridge, Mass.: MIT Press.

Wada, J., and Rasmussen, T. (1960) "Intracarotid injection of sodium amytal for the lateralization of cerebral speech dominance: Experimental and clinical observations," *Journal of Neurosurgery,* **17,** 266–282.

Walker, C. H., and Meyer, B. J. F. (1980) "Integrating information from text: An evaluation of current theories," *Review of Educational Research,* **50,** 421–437.

Walker, L. (1975–1976) "The comprehension of speech and writing," *Reading Research Quarterly,* **9,** 144–167.

Walker, L. (1977) "Comprehension of writing and spontaneous speech," *Visible Language,* **11,** 37–51.

Wallbrown, F. H., Blaha, J., Wherry, R. J., Sr., and Counts, D. H. (1974) "An empirical test of Myklebust's cognitive structure hypotheses for seventy reading-disabled children," *Journal of Consulting and Clinical Psychology,* **42,** 211–218.

Waller, T. G. (1977) *Think First, Read Later! Piagetian Prerequisites for Reading.* Newark, Del.: IRA.

Wanat, S. F. (1971) "Linguistic structure in reading: Models from the research of Project Literacy," in Davis, F. B. (ed.), *The Literature of Research in Reading with Emphasis on Models.* New Brunswick, N.J.: Rutgers, the State University.

Wanat, S. F. (1976a) "Language behind the eye: Some findings, speculations, and research strategies," in Monty, R. A., and Senders, J. W. (eds.), *Eye Movements and Psychological Processes.* Hillsdale, N.J.: Erlbaum.

Wanat, S. F. (1976b) "Relations between language and visual processing," in Singer, H., and Ruddell, R. B. (eds.), *Theoretical Models and Processes of Reading.* Newark, Del.: IRA.

Waples, D. (1967) *What Reading Does to People.* Chicago: University of Chicago Press.

Warburton, F. W., and Southgate, V. (1969) *i.t.a.: An Independent Evaluation* (The School's Council Report). London: Murray, and Edinburgh, Scotland: Chambers.

Warren, W. H., Nicholas, D. W., and Trabasso, T. (1979) "Event chains and inferences in understanding narratives," in Freedle, R. O. (ed.), *New Directions in Discourse Processing.* Norwood, N.J.: Ablex.

Wason, P. C. (1965) "The contexts of plausible denial," *Journal of Verbal Learning and Verbal Behavior,* **4,** 7–11.

Wathen-Dunn, W. (ed.), (1967) *Models for the Perception of Speech and Visual Form.* Cambridge, Mass.: MIT Press.

Wattenberg, W. W., and Clifford, C. (1964) "Relation of self-concepts to beginning achievement in reading," *Child Development,* **35,** 461–467.

Webber, B. L. (1980) "Syntax beyond the sentence: Anaphora," in Spiro, R. J., Bruce, B. C., and Brewer, W. F. (eds.), *Theoretical Issues in Reading Comprehension.* Hillsdale, N.J.: Erlbaum.

Weber, R. M. (1968) "The study of oral reading errors: A survey of the literature," *Reading Research Quarterly,* **4,** 96–119.

Weber, R. M. (1970a) "First-graders' use of grammatical context in reading," in Levin, H., and Williams, J. P. (eds.), *Basic Studies on Reading.* New York: Basic Books.

Weber, R. M. (1970b) "A linguistic analysis of first-grade reading errors," *Reading Research Quarterly,* **5,** 427–451.

Webster, R. L., and Lubker, B. B. (1968) "Interrelationships among fluency producing variables in stuttered speech," *Journal of Speech and Hearing Research,* **11,** 754–766.

Webster, R. L., Schumacher, S. J., and Lubker, B. B. (1970) "Changes in stuttering frequency as a function of various intervals of delayed auditory feedback," *Journal of Abnormal Psychology,* **75,** 45–49.

Weinstein, R., and Rabinovitch, M. S. (1971) "Sentence structure and retention in good and poor readers," *Journal of Educational Psychology,* **62,** 25–30.

Welford, A. T. (1968) *Fundamentals of Skill.* London: Methuen.

Wepman, J. M. (1968) "The modality concept," in Smith, H. K. (ed.), *Perception and Reading.* Newark, Del.: IRA.

Wepman, J. M. (1975) "Auditory perception and imperception," in Cruickshank, W. M., and Hallahan, D. P. (eds.), *Perceptual and Learning Disabilities in Children, Vol. 2, Research and Theory.* Syracuse, N.Y.: Syracuse University Press.

Werner, H., and Kaplan, B. (1963) *Symbol Formation.* New York: Wiley.

Wernicke, C. (1874) *Der aphasische Symptomencomplex.* Breslau, Germany: Cohn and Weigert.

Wheat, T. E., and Edmond, R. M. (1975) "The concept of comprehension analysis," *Journal of Reading,* **18,** 523–527.

Whipple, G. (1966) "Inspiring culturally disadvantaged children to read," in Figurel, J. A. (ed.), *Reading and Inquiry.* Newark, Del.: IRA.

Whitaker, H. A., and Selnes, O. A. (1975) "Broca's area: A problem in language brain relationships," *Linguistics,* **154/155,** 91–103.

White, R. T., and Clark, R. M. (1973) "A test of inclusion which allows for errors of measurement," *Psychometrika,* **38,** 77–86.

White, S. H. (1965) "Evidence for a hierarchical arrangement of learning processes," in Lipsitt, L. P., and Spiker, C. C. (eds.), *Advances in Child Development and Behavior, Vol. 2.* New York: Academic Press.

Whiting, H. T. A. (1975) *Concepts in Skill Learning.* London: Lepus.

Whiting, H. T. A., and Brinker, B. D. (1980) "Images of the Act," paper presented at the Conference on Theory and Research in Learning Disability, University of Alberta, Edmonton, Alberta, November 12–14, 1980.

Whorf, B. L. (1941) "The relation of habitual thought and behavior to language," in Spier, L. (ed.), *Language, Culture and Personality.* Menasha, Wisc.: The Sapir Memorial Publication Fund.

Wickelgren, W. A. (1965) "Short-term memory for phonemically similar lists," *American Journal of Psychology,* **78,** 567–574.

Wickelgren, W. A. (1972) "Coding retrieval and dynamics of multitrace," in Gregg, L. W. (ed.), *Cognition in Learning and Memory.* New York: Wiley.

Wiener, M., and Cromer, W. (1967) "Reading and reading difficulty: A conceptual analysis," *Harvard Educational Review,* **37,** 620–643.

Wiener, N. (1948) *Cybernetics.* New York: Wiley.

Wightman, H. J. (1915) "A study of reading appreciation," *American School Board Journal,* **50,** 42.

Wiig, E. H., and Semel, E. M. (1976) *Language Disabilities in Children and Adolescents.* Columbus, Ohio: Merrill.

Wiig, E. H., and Semel, E. M. (1980) *Language Assessment and Intervention for the Learning Disabled.* Columbus, Ohio: Merrill.

Wilkinson, A. M. (1971) *The Foundations of Language: Talking and Reading in Young Children.* London: Oxford University Press.

Wilkinson, A. M., Stratta, L., and Dudley, P. (1974) *The Quality of Listening.* London: Macmillan.

Williams, A. C., and Flexman, R. E. (1949) "Evaluation of the school link as an aid in primary flight instruction," *University of Illinois Bulletin,* **46,** No. 71.

Williams, J. P. (1971) "Learning to read: Six papers in search of a model," in Davis, F. B. (ed.), *The Literature of Research in Reading with Emphasis on Models.* New Brunswick, N.J.: Graduate School of Education, Rutgers, The State University.

Williams, M. (1970) *Brain Damage and the Mind.* Harmondsworth, England: Penguin.

Williams, P. (1976) "Early reading: Some unexplained aspects," in Merritt, J. E. (ed.), *New Horizons in Reading.* Newark, Del.: IRA.

Williams, P., et al. (1971) *Swansea Test of Phonic Skills.* Oxford, England: Blackwell.

Willmon, B. J. (1969) "Reading readiness as influenced by parent participation in Head Start programs," in Figurel, J. A. (ed.), *Reading and Realism.* Newark, Del.: IRA.

Willows, D. M. (1974) "Reading between the lines: A study of selective attention in good and poor readers," *Child Development,* **45,** 408–415.

Willows, D. M. (1978a) "A picture is not always worth a thousand words: Pictures as distractors in reading." *Journal of Educational Psychology,* **70,** 255–262.

Willows, D. M. (1978b) "Individual differences in distraction by pictures in a reading situation," *Journal of Educational Psychology,* **70,** 837–847.

Willows, D. M., and McKinnon, G. E. (1973) "Selective

reading: Attention to the unattended lines," *Canadian Journal of Psychology,* **27,** 292–304.

Wilson, T. M. (1959) "A reader teaches," *Reading Teacher,* **12,** 230–234.

Winograd, T. (1972) "A program for understanding natural language," *Cognitive Psychology,* **3,** 1–191.

Wiseman, D., and Watson, D. (1980) "The good news about becoming a writer," *Language Arts,* **57,** 750–755.

Wiseman, S. (1964) *Education and Environment.* Manchester, England: Manchester University Press.

Wiseman, S. (1968) "Educational deprivation and disadvantage," in Butcher, H. J. (ed.), *Educational Research in Britain, Vol. 1.* London: University of London Press.

Wisher, R. A. (1976) "The effects of syntactic expectations during reading," *Journal of Educational Psychology,* **68,** 597–602.

Witelson, S. F. (1976) "Abnormal right hemisphere specialization in developmental dyslexia," in Knights, R. M., and Bakker, D. J. (eds.), *The Neuropsychology of Learning Disorders: Theoretical Approaches.* Baltimore: University Park Press.

Witelson, S. F. (1977) "Early hemisphere specialization and interhemispheric plasticity: An empirical and theoretical review," in Segalowitz, S. J., and Gruber, F. A. (eds.), *Language Development and Neurological Theory.* New York: Academic Press.

Wittig, M. A., and Petersen, A. C. (eds.), (1979) *Sex-Related Differences in Cognitive Functioning: Developmental Issues,* New York: Academic Press.

Wittrock, M. C. (1978a) "Education and the cognitive processes of the brain," in Chall, J. S., and Mirsky, A. F. (eds.), *Education and the Brain.* Chicago: University of Chicago Press.

Wittrock, M. C. (1978b) "The cognitive movement in instruction," *Educational Psychologist,* **13,** 15–29.

Wittrock, M. C., Beatty, J., Bogen, J. E., Gazzaniga, M. S., Jerison, H. J., Krashen, S. D., Nebes, R. D., and Teyler, T. J. (1977) *The Human Brain.* Englewood Cliffs, N.J.: Prentice-Hall.

Wittrock, M. C., Marks, C., and Doctorow, M. (1975) "Reading as a generative process," *Journal of Educational Psychology,* **67,** 484–489.

Witty, P. (1965) "Studies of children's interests—a brief summary," in Barke, W. B. (ed.), *Teaching Reading: Selected Materials.* New York: Oxford University Press.

Witty, P., and Kopel, D. (1936a) "Heterophoria and reading disability," *Journal of Educational Psychology,* **27,** 222–230.

Witty, P., and Kopel, D. (1936b) "Preventing reading disability: The reading readiness factor," *Educational Administration and Supervision,* **28,** 401–418.

Witty, P., and Kopel, D. (1936c) "Factors associated with the etiology of reading disability," *Journal of Educational Research,* **29,** 449–459.

Wold, R. M., (1969) "The Santa Clara County Optometric Society's perceptual-motor survey," *Optometric Weekly,* **60,** 21–26, 29–31.

Wolf, T. (1977) "Reading reconsidered," *Harvard Educational Review,* **47,** 411–429.

Wolfe, L. S. (1941) "Differential factors in specific reading disability: 1. Laterality of functions," *Journal of Genetic Psychology,* **58,** 45–56.

Wolff, P., and Levin, J. R. (1972) "The role of overt activity in children's imagery production," *Child Development,* **43,** 537–547.

Wolfram, W., and Fasold, R. W. (1969) "Toward reading materials for speakers of Black English: Three linguistically appropriate passages," in Baratz, J. C., and Shuy, R. W. (eds.), Washington, D.C.: Center for Applied Linguistics.

Wolfson, J. (1976) *Cultural Influences on Cognition and Attainment.* Milton Keynes, England: Open University Press.

Wood, C. C., Goff, W. R., and Day, R. S. (1971) "Auditory evoked potentials during speech perception," *Science,* **173,** 4003, 1248–1251.

Woodburne, L. S. (1967) *The Neural Basis of Behavior.* Columbus, Ohio: Merrill.

Woods, B. T., and Teuber, H.-L. (1978) "Changing patterns of childhood aphasia," *Annals of Neurology,* **3,** 273–280.

Woodworth, R. S., and Marquis, D. G. (1949) *Psychology* (20th ed.). London: Methuen.

Wrolstad, M. E. (1976) "A manifesto for visible language," *Visible Language,* **10,** 5–40.

Yarbus, A. L. (1967) *Eye Movements and Vision.* New York: Plenum.

Yedinack, J. G. (1949) "A study of the linguistic functioning of children with articulation and reading disabilities," *Journal of Genetic Psychology,* **74,** 23–59.

Yeni-Komshian, G. H., Isenberg, S., and Goldberg, H. (1975) "Cerebral dominance and reading disability: Left visual field deficit in poor readers," *Neuropsychologia,* **13,** 83–94.

Young, F. A., and Lindsley, D. B. (1970) *Early Experience and Visual Information Processing in Perceptual and Reading Disorders.* Washington, D.C.: National Academy of Sciences.

Young, L. R. (1976) "Physical characteristics of the eye used in eye-movement measurement," in Monty, R. A., and Senders, J. W. (eds.), *Eye Movements and Psychological Processes.* Hillsdale, N.J.: Erlbaum.

Young, L. R., and Sheena, D. (1975) "Survey of eye movement recording methods," *Behavior Research Methods and Instrumentation,* **7,** 397–429.

Young, M. F. D. (1971) *Knowledge and Control.* London: Collier-Macmillan.

Young, R. A. (1938) "Case studies in reading disability," *American Journal of Orthopsychiatry,* **8,** 230–254.

Young, R. O. (1973) "A comparison of reading and listening comprehension with rate of presentation controlled," *AV Communication Review,* **21,** 327–336.

Yule, V. (1978) "Is there evidence for Chomsky's interpretation of English spelling?" *Spelling Progress Bulletin,* **18,** 10–12.

Yule, W. (1973) "Differential prognosis of reading backwardness and specific reading retardation," *British Journal of Educational Psychology,* **43,** 244–248.

Yule, W., and Rutter, M. (1976) "Epidemiology and social implications of specific reading retardation," in Knights, R. M., and Bakker, D. J. (eds.), *The Neuropsychology of Learning Disorders: Theoretical Approaches.* Baltimore: University Park Press.

Yule, W., Rutter, M., Berger, M., and Thompson, J. (1974) "Over- and under-achievement in reading: Distribution in the general population," *British Journal of Educational Psychology,* **44,** 1–12.

Zaidel, E. (1976) "Auditory vocabulary of the right hemisphere following brain bisection or hemidecortication," *Cortex,* **12,** 191–211.

Zangwill, O. L. (1962) "Dyslexia in relation to cerebral dominance," in Money, J. (ed.), *Reading Disability: Progress and Research Needs in Dyslexia.* Baltimore: Johns Hopkins University Press.

Zangwill, O. L. (1972) "Remembering revisited," *Quarterly Journal of Experimental Psychology,* **24,** 123–138.

Zangwill, O. L. (1976) "Thought and the brain," *British Journal of Psychology,* **67,** 301–314.

Zaporozhets, A. V., and Elkonin, D. B. (1971) *The Psychology of Preschool Children.* Cambridge, Mass.: MIT Press.

Zeki, S. M. (1970) "Interhemispheric connections of prestriate cortex in monkeys," *Brain Research,* **19,** 63–71.

Zigler, E., and Kanzer, P. (1962) "The effectiveness of two classes of verbal reinforcers on the performance of middle-class and lower-class children," *Journal of Personality,* **30,** 157–163.

Zimmerman, I. L., and Allebrand, G. N. (1965) "Personality characteristics and attitudes towards achievement of good and poor readers," *Journal of Educational Research,* **59,** 28–32.

Zolkos, H. H. (1958) "What research says about emotional factors in retardation in reading," in Causey, O. S. (ed.), *The Reading Teacher's Reader.* New York: Ronald Press.

Zurif, E. B., and Carson, G. (1970) "Dyslexia in relation to cerebral dominance and temporal analysis," *Neuropsychologia,* **8,** 351–361.

Author Index

C

D

E

F

G

H

I

J

N

O

P

Q

R

S

T

Y

Z

Subject Index

F

G

H

I

L

M

N

O